# Dreaming of what might be

## The Knights of Labor in Ontario, 1880–1900

This study examines the rise and fall of the Knights of Labor in Ontario in the years 1880–1900. As Canada's most industrialized province, Ontario served as the regional center of the Noble and Holy Order of the Knights of Labor, and by 1886 thousands of industrial workers, men and women, enrolled within the ranks of Ontario local and district assemblies. Providing case studies of the Knights of Labor experience in the major cities of Toronto and Hamilton, the book also chronicles the social, political, and cultural impact of the Order across the province. Specific sections of the book detail the development of industrial capitalism and the working class in Ontario to 1890, outline the quantitative dimensions of the Knights of Labor upsurge in the 1880s, and comment on the accomplishments and failures, strengths and weaknesses of this labor-reform body. The major importance of this study lies in the recovery of the late-nineteenth-century working-class vision of an alternative to the developing industrial capitalist society. Dedicated to a more egalitarian social order, the Knights of Labor opposed class privilege, the exploitation of labor, and the many oppressions of an age of acquisitive individualism. Cultivating the bonds of unity among all workers, the Order provided an institutional and cultural rallying point for North American workers, sustaining materially the capacity to resist and to rethink fundamental social and economic questions. Ultimately defeated, the Knights of Labor contributed to the working-class effort to break out of the confines of received wisdoms, and for a number of years instilled within working men and women the capacity to dream of what might be rather than to acquiesce in what was.

# Dreaming of what might be

## The Knights of Labor in Ontario, 1880–1900

Gregory S. Kealey
*Memorial University of Newfoundland*

Bryan D. Palmer
*Simon Fraser University*
*British Columbia*

Cambridge University Press

*Cambridge*
*London New York New Rochelle*
*Melbourne Sydney*

Published by the Press Syndicate of the University of Cambridge
The Pitt Building, Trumpington Street, Cambridge CB2 1RP
32 East 57th Street, New York, NY 10022, USA
296 Beaconsfield Parade, Middle Park, Melbourne 3206, Australia



First published 1982

Printed in the United States of America

*Library of Congress Cataloging in Publication Data*

Keatey, Gregory S., 1948–

Dreaming of what might be.

Bibliography: p.

Includes index.

1. Knights of Labor (Canada) 2. Labor
and laboring classes – Ontario – History.
I. Palmer, Bryan D. II. Title.
HD8109.063K4 331.88'33'09713 81–21615
ISBN 0 521 24430 7 AACR2

## WHAT MIGHT BE

**If the World's Workers were Only Educated and Organized**

## SOCIAL REORGANIZATION

**Universal Democracy and Co-operation—No Wars or Monopolies**

## A BEAUTIFUL IDEAL

**Which can Never be Realized While Labor is Uneducated, Apathetic and Divided**

## AN AIM TO WORK FOR

**By Doing Our Part in Spreading the Light**

It is pretty generally understood by this time among those who are interested in Labor Reform that it is a much wider and more comprehensive question than the mere matter of wages or hours – that it includes everything relating to the mental, moral, and physical advancement of the worker, and implies a war to the death against every influence which tends to depress the condition of Labor. Just let us think for a while what the effect upon government and society would be supposing the great majority of workingmen everywhere were thoroughly educated in the principles of Labor Reform, and determined at any sacrifice to carry them into effect. Let us picture to ourselves the social condition that would result were our ideals realized by the resolute determination of the masses in all civilized lands to use their power for the good of the whole people, instead of letting the selfish few play upon their prejudices and passions, and rule them for the benefit of the upper class.

"Enjolras," *Palladium of Labor*, 26 December 1885

# Contents

# Tables, figures, and maps

## Tables

## Figures



## Maps

# Preface

This book was conceived in 1977 in three-way discussions among the authors and the other surviving member of the Jimuel Briggs Society, Russell G. Hann. A passionate commitment to knowledge, and the orchestrations of Mr. Kealey, convinced us of the necessity of pursuing the Knights of Labor into their eastern and western Ontario lairs, extending our collective work beyond the confines of Toronto and Hamilton. This noble purpose was financially underwritten by a generous research grant from the Social Sciences and Humanities Research Council of Canada, which allowed us to track the equally Noble and Holy Order through small Ontario communities and American industrial cities like Cleveland, Ohio, and Camden, New Jersey, where traces of individuals, Local Assemblies, and a culture of labor reform survived in archives, newspapers, and dilapidated libraries. In the process the collaborators grew closer to their subjects, and their idiosyncracies and personalities (not to mention their delusions) merged with those whom they were studying: Hann, ever depreciated, became A. W. Wright; Kealey, from the Olympian heights of head office, found himself shoved into Powderly's chair; Palmer unassumingly identified with Tom O'Reilly. Those who read these pages will come to understand the implications of such identifications and will no doubt discern the disinterested hand behind these associations.

Although the book that resulted from this trio's efforts has been written entirely by Kealey and Palmer, Hann's input has been vital. Employed as a research associate, he worked extensively in the newspapers and the Powderly Papers. As a friend, colleague, and frequent collaborator on earlier projects, Hann lent the research effort his acute sense of the context of the 1880s, as well as providing a Canadian index to the Powderly Papers that will be consulted at the Public Archives of Canada by future generations of historians. Like many others, then, we owe a considerable debt to Hann, without whom this book could not have been conceived, let alone produced. Old Alec, displaced from the Niagara-on-the Lake of the 1880s and 1890s to Toronto's East End of the 1980s, has our thanks.

We also gratefully acknowledge the assistance of archivists and librarians at various institutions in which we have worked. The enthusiasm and cooperation of both Nancy Stunden and Dan Moore of the Public Archives of

Canada have made our work much easier, as have the information services staff of the Killam Library of Dalhousie University, where Halifax's Powderly has been indulged as Scranton's once was. Like Powderly and O'Reilly of old, we have also benefited from the ranks. Pamela Manley, Debi Wells, Doug Cruikshank, and Jim Frost provided research assistance, while Peter DeLottinville, Jacques Ferland, Allen Seager, and Bruce Tucker shared materials and ideas with us in ways that exemplify a selfless dedication to scholarship. O'Reilly wishes to extend special thanks to Dale Chisamore, who provided the cause with his own materials on Brockville and eastern Ontario. In addition, we would like to thank our typists, Karen Molgaard, Bette Tetreault, and Dallas Strange.

From the beginning of discussions concerning publication of this study we have received nothing but support and encouragement from our editor at Cambridge University Press, Steve Fraser. In addition we would like to thank the Press's readers, Michael Frisch and Alan Dawley, for their critical comments, which helped immensely in revising this book. Far too often the review process is an unsatisfactory one, and as Powderly and O'Reilly we wondered if we might be confronted with a John W. Hayes or a James R. Sovereign. Instead Frisch and Dawley presented us with comments that contained the insights of a DeLeon and the understanding of a Debs. We hope that they and others will see the end product as something more than a *Labor Day Annual*.

G. S. K. (T. V. P.)
B. D. P. (T. O'R.)

Montreal and St. John's

# Abbreviations

| | |
|---|---|
| AFL | American Federation of Labor |
| *AK* | *Adelphon Kruptos* |
| ALU | American Labor Union |
| APA | American Protective Association |
| ARU | American Railway Union |
| CIO | Congress of Industrial Organizations |
| CLU | Central Labor Union (Hamilton) |
| CPR | Canadian Pacific Railway |
| DA | District Assembly |
| DMW | District Master Workman |
| GA | General Assembly |
| GEB | General Executive Board |
| GMW | General Master Workman |
| GST | General Secretary Treasurer |
| GTR | Grand Trunk Railway |
| GWR | Great Western Railway |
| HLPA | Hamilton Labor Political Association |
| HP | Hayes Papers |
| ILP | Independent Labor Party |
| IMIU | Iron Molders' International Union |
| KOL | Knights of Labor |
| LA | Local Assembly |
| MP | Macdonald Papers |
| MW | Master Workman |
| NTA | National Trades Assembly |
| OBU | One Big Union |
| PAC | Public Archives of Canada |
| PP | Powderly Papers |
| TLC | Trades and Labor Congress |
| TSR | Toronto Street Railway |
| TTLC | Toronto Trades and Labor Council |
| TTU | Toronto Typographical Union |
| UBUL | Universal Brotherhood of United Labor |
| WFM | Western Federation of Miners |
| WP | Wright Papers |

# Introduction

> The history of subaltern social groups is necessarily fragmented and episodic. There undoubtedly does exist a tendency to (at least provisional stages of) unification in the historical activity of these groups, but this tendency is continually interrupted by the activity of the ruling groups; it therefore can only be demonstrated when an historical cycle is completed and this cycle culminates in a success. Subaltern groups are always subject to the activity of ruling groups, even when they rebel and rise up: only "permanent" victory breaks their subordination, and that not immediately. In reality, even when they appear triumphant, the subaltern groups are merely anxious to defend themselves . . . Every trace of independent initiative on the part of the subaltern groups should therefore be of incalculable value for the integral historian. Consequently, this kind of history can only be dealt with monographically, and each monograph requires an immense quantity of material which is often hard to collect.
>
> Antonio Gramsci, Italian communist, 1934–5

In the fall of 1886 Wilhelm Liebknecht, Eleanor Marx, and Edward Aveling visited the United States. The distinguished German socialist leader, the brilliant daughter of Karl Marx, and her disreputable lover toured much of the East and Midwest during their fifteen-week stay. Viewing the emerging American working-class movement through the lens of European developments, they found many things that surprised them. Not the least was that "the American people were waiting to hear in their own language what socialism was." The components of the Great Upheaval of 1886 were even more striking: the Knights of Labor, "the first spontaneous expression by the American working people of their consciousness of themselves as a class"; the Central Labor Unions, "more hopeful organisations than even the Knights," because "more avowedly socialistic" and "more avowedly political"; the Socialist Labor Party; and, most important, the United Labor Party in which "the class consciousness of the working people became embodied in a definite political movement of antagonism to the capitalist class." The Avelings concluded on the basis of their observations and discussions with American workers that:

> The example of the American working men will be followed before long on the European side of the Atlantic. An English . . . Labour Party will be formed, foe alike to

> Liberal and Conservative; its ultimate standpoint will be Socialistic, although, like the American Labour Party, it may have to pass through several preliminary stages; and its ultimate fate, like that of its transatlantic prototype, will be the attainment of supreme political, and then of supreme economic power.[1]

A strange notion this – American workers providing English workers with the model for a labor party! Yet such was one view in 1886.[2]

A month after the Avelings returned to England, Friedrich Engels, the old general of international socialism, also reflected on American affairs. 1886 had come as a considerable surprise to him, too; not even he "could foresee that in such a short time the movement would burst out with such irresistible force, would spread with the rapidity of a prairie fire, would shake American society to its very foundations." Recalling the events of May in Chicago (the Haymarket bombing) and of November in New York (the Henry George mayoralty campaign), Engels argued that "the spontaneous, instinctive movements of these vast masses of working people, over a vast extent of country, the simultaneous outburst of their common discontent . . . made them conscious of the fact, that they formed a new and distinct class of American society." This new proletarian class, having recognized its "community of grievances and of interests" and its "solidarity as a class in opposition to all other classes," now sought political representation. Of the contending organizations, Engels commented on three: the Henry George movement; the Knights of Labor; and the Socialist Labor Party. His discerning analysis of the Knights deserves quotation:

> An immense association spread over an immense extent of country . . . held together . . . by the instinctive feeling that the very fact of their clubbing together for their common aspiration makes them a great power in the country; a truly American paradox clothing the most modern tendencies in the most medieval mummeries, and hiding the most democratic and even rebellious spirit behind an apparent, but really powerless despotism.

Beyond this contradictory facade he saw "an immense amount of potential energy evolving slowly but surely into actual force." For, as Engels understood so well:

> The Knights of Labor are the first national organization created by the American working class as a whole; whatever be their origin and history, whatever their shortcomings and little absurdities, whatever their platform and their constitution, here they are, the work of practically the whole class of American wage-earners, the only national bond that holds them together, that makes their strength felt to themselves not less than to their enemies, and that fills them with the proud hope of future victories.

His conclusion, which now seems as odd as the Avelings', was that the Knights represented "the raw material out of which the future of the American working-class movement, and along with it, the future of American society at large, has to be shaped."[3]

The Great Upheaval of 1886 in the United States and the Knights of Labor, its institutional embodiment, thus had a worldwide impact. These events, understandably, impressed themselves on the memories of North American workers. Indeed, historically there has been no moment in the experience of North American labor that weighed so heavily on the collective mind of the working-class movement in the years 1900–30 as that of the Knights of Labor upsurge of the 1880s. Until the resurgence of labor in the 1930s, revealed most dramatically in the rise of the Congress of Industrial Organizations, workers recalled this past and drew upon its many and varied inspirations. When John L. Lewis consciously strove to create an image of himself as part of a long line of "tough people," "fighters," and class militants he recalled (or fabricated) the story of his father's early involvement in the Knights of Labor in Lucas, Iowa, where Tom Lewis helped lead a bitter strike in 1882, an action that supposedly earned him a place on the company's blacklist and exile from the town.[4] Clinton S. Golden, labor intellectual and founder of the United Steel Workers of America, first drank from the fountain of labor solidarity with "Big John" Powderly, brother of the Order's central figure, Terence V. Powderly. "Big John," for whom Clint tended drill at the tender age of twelve, preached the gospel of the Noble and Holy Order long after the Knights had succumbed to employer resistance, the economic crisis of the 1890s, and internal division and trade union opposition. But even in the face of the Knights' ultimate defeat, Powderly's brother remained true to the cause of an all-embracing organization of the American wage earners. He imparted his enthusiasm to his young helper, and Golden recalled of the Knights that: "Their ritualism, the secrecy with which their meetings were conducted, the signs and symbols that gave notice to their members as to when and where meetings were to be held, fired my interest and imagination and in my own mind I resolved that henceforth my lot was cast with that of the wage earners. I began to see class lines and distinctions." Looking back on this experience eighty years later, Golden still described the Knights as "that all-embracing holy order that dared dream of a co-operative commonwealth for industrial America."[5]

Individual statements and recollections were supplemented by a more general remembrance of the place and significance of the Knights of Labor. "Never since the palmiest days of the Knights of Labor," declared Toronto's *Citizen and Country* in the midst of the craft union boom of 1898–1904, "have trade unions taken such a firm hold of the toilers as today."[6] As these turn-of-the-century organizational gains were consolidated, however, some workers could still tar the American Federation of Labor (AFL) with a brush dipped into the resentments of the 1880s and 1890s. In 1903 a Western Federation of Miners (WFM) member from Slocan, British Columbia, wrote to the *Miners' Magazine:* "Now there are thousands of old-line K of Ls in the WFM and the unsavoury acts of the AFL officials have not been altogether forgotten."[7] Twenty years later many radicals and socialists saw this newly arrived, and increasingly conservative, international craft unionism in even more antagonistic terms, characterized in their new name for it – the American Separation of Labor. For their part the AFL pure and simple unionists linked the One Big Union (OBU) with the Knights of Labor, the American Railway Union (ARU) of Eugene Debs, and the American Labor Union (ALU). It was the latest "subtle and pernicious plea again resorted to for the purpose of severing the wage earners from their orderly and practical course of action."[8] By 1929, the radical challenge of the postwar reconstruction years had been at least partially undermined, and in this context of "normalcy" the AFL met in Toronto in October. With southern textile workers urging the organization of their mill towns, observers at the convention reported "a pitch of enthusiasm not seen in labor gatherings since the spring tide of the Knights of Labor."[9]

## Historiography

North American historians, however, have regarded the Noble and Holy Order in a rather different light. Viewed sympathetically in 1886 by Richard T. Ely, the pioneer student of the American working-class movement, the Knights have subsequently more often been either vilified or ignored. Ely, writing in the year of the Great Upheaval, described the Order as "a new phase of the labor movement, established on truly scientific principles, which involved either an intuitive perception of the nature of industrial progress, or a wonderful acquaintance with the laws of economic society." The Order's desire to organize all workers, and especially their work in organizing women and blacks, impressed Ely greatly because it was "in line with the precepts of Christianity," as well as being well suited to the new stage of industrial development.[10] Other contemporary academic accounts, including foreign views, did not share Ely's total enthusiasm, but did treat the Order as a serious labor organization, committed to the organization of the entire working class. One of these observers, Carroll D. Wright, posed the question that was to dominate the literature on the Knights and, in the process, anticipated one common ideological answer:

> [The Order] stands today as an organization representing the opposite of the trades-union, and is bending all its energies to preserve the broad principle of harmonious

interworking of all interests, as against the trades-union idea, which comes closer to human nature, of the preservation of individual interests. Which idea will survive and become the leading fundamental element of the future great labor organizations is the problem.[11]

Wright's question received its answer in the Progressive period, when a significant shift occurred in the historiography of the Knights of Labor. By then, of course, the AFL had emerged as the "future great labor organization"; the Knights were only another discard on history's ash-heap. Perhaps this in itself accounts for the change, but the new view of the Knights appears also to be related to the increasing professionalism of the academic study of labor and in the close identification of scholarship with Progressive reform, especially through the aegis of the National Civic Federation. The career of John R. Commons, for example, provides copious evidence for such an argument.[12] Certainly the new consensus on the Knights differed radically from Ely's approval. In their *A Documentary History of American Industrial Society*, John R. Commons and his associates established in a few brief words what was to become the standard interpretation of the Order. Identifying the Order with the agrarian Patrons of Husbandry by emphasizing its secrecy, ritual, and supposed centralized authority, they introduced it only to dismiss it: "Thousands of headlong recruits brought with them politicians, self-seekers, and camp-followers. Co-operation failed, strikes and boycotts were overdone. The disappointed masses deserted as precipitously as they had enlisted . . . the Knights remained a bushwhacking annoyance on the heels of its successor, the American Federation of Labor."[13] Thus, in one easy passage, they dismissed thirty years of class struggle and an organization to which literally millions of American workers flocked.

University of Chicago labor scholar Robert Hoxie perhaps first formulated this new view with some substance. In his widely read *Trade Unionism in the United States*, published posthumously, he argued that the Knights represented a failed "strain" in American working-class history. This near biological metaphor figured prominently in his analysis: "The Knights of Labor had elements of temporary success but on the whole it was found *unfit*. It is essential to know why."[14] His argument alluded to their supposed high degree of centralization (echoing an earlier study by William Kirk),[15] but the major cause of failure was that: "It was contrary to the reality created by modern industrial forces. Machinery was forcing a materialistic contest. This contest was not between the 'money power' and the people . . . the contest is opposed to industrial peace and goodfellowship ideas; the age of utopianism is past, and the idealistic attitude is not fitted to cope with the workers' problem."[16] Indeed, Hoxie argued, the Order based itself on two false assumptions: "First, it assumed no fundamental disharmony of viewpoint and interest between wageworkers and employers as such . . . secondly, it assumed that the viewpoint and interest of all wageworkers are identical." Hoxie rebutted the first alleged assumption by positing a Marxist understanding of industrial capitalism in which the "two classes are bound to be opposed." For the second rebuttal, however, he claimed only that the assumption was "false for the time, and apparently for the present and discernible future." Following on these arguments: "The Knights of Labor, then, was inevitably doomed to failure, regardless of its political policies, and its disastrous strikes. It was far ahead of its time, altogether utopian." The results were equally clear: "In the success of the American Federation of Labor and the failure of the Knights of Labor have triumphed the principles of weak, federative organizations versus strong, centralized organization, autonomous trade unionism versus labor unionism and industrial unionism, selfish trade interests versus altruistic labor brotherhood, and hard-headed business unionism versus idealistic radicalism."

Hoxie's view of the Order prefigures one major interpretive school of American labor studies. His preoccupation with the Order's failure, his anachronistic penchant for applying hindsight to the 1880s, and the near-determinism of his argument with its references to "failed strain," "unfit," and "inevitably," all can be found in the school that dismisses the Knights as a deviation from the supposed norm of American labor development.[17]

If Hoxie was the first to substantiate this view, undoubtedly its most famous proponent was Selig Perlman who, both in his chapters in Commons' *History of Labour in the United States* and in his immensely influential *A Theory of the Labor Movement*, cemented the Hoxie–Commons argument into orthodoxy. Perlman depicted the Knights of Labor as "the lineal descendent and at the same time the most grandiose culmination of the American labor movement" which "by their wholesale experiment and failure in the eighties permanently discredited the whole idea of producers' co-operation" (and by implication everything else that was bad about the "American" tradition of labor unionism). In addition he railed against "their poorly conducted strikes and the unpsychological 'one big union' principle" which he saw as "products of the 'broad' co-operative and political idealism which scorned trade unionism as opportunistic and narrow." In Perlman's schema only "the socialistic class-consciousness of the immigrant labor movement" saved the American working class from its peculiar fascination with cooperation and antimonopoly politics. Instead the AFL and its "job and wage conscious unionism" came to dominate because "it 'fitted' both the external environment and the American workman's psychology." It "fitted" for three basic reasons: first, "because it recognized the virtually inalterable conservatism of the American community as regards private property and private initiative in economic life"; second, "because it grasped the definite limitations" of the American political system and "used the political weapon only sparingly"; third, "because it was under no delusion as to the true psychology of the American workingman" and "was without illusions with regard to the actual extent of labor solidarity."[18]

Leaving aside Perlman's questionable biological metaphors and his curious "psychological" insights about American workers, let us turn to his historical examination of the Knights to peruse more closely the basis of his grand theory. After an initial grudging acknowledgment that the Knights' structure had distinct advantages for organizing, and while noting that their early work place practice did not differ from that of the trade unions, he nevertheless locates two quite distinct strains of working-class activism, prominent by the late 1870s. One strain, which would become "the modern labour movement of the end of the century" had broken with the past; the Knights, however, had not, and preserved a nonpragmatic, utopian impurity. The evidence for this "impurity" was the presence of a "non-wage earning element" in the Order, consisting of cooperators, currency reformers, land reformers, socialists, and anarchists. There is no attempt to prove that members with those beliefs were not workers, nor is there any attempt to show that similar beliefs were not current among trade unionists in the late 1870s. Having established this false dichotomy between Knights and unionists even before the Order's rise to prominence, Perlman proceeds to the Great Upheaval. Here he certainly is not in any sense guilty of downplaying its importance. Indeed his description invokes the language of class warfare:

> [The Great Upheaval] signalled the appearance on the scene of a new class which had not hitherto found a place in the labour movement – the unskilled. All the peculiar characteristics of the dramatic events of 1886 and 1887, the highly feverish pace at which organizations grew, the nation-wide wave of strikes, particularly sympathetic strikes, the wide use of the boycott, the obliteration, apparently complete, of all lines that divided the labouring class, whether geographic or trade, the violence and turbulence which accompanied the movement – all of these were the signs of a great movement by the class of the unskilled, which had finally risen in rebellion . . . The movement bore in every way the aspect of a social war. A frenzied hatred of labour for capital was shown in every important strike.

This sounds peculiarly unlike an American working class that the AFL's program "fit" perfectly. Why, then, did the Knights of Labor, institutional beneficiaries of the Great Upheaval, fail? The answer Perlman offers depends again more on his assumptions than on historical evidence. He argues that the Order attempted to absorb the unions in 1886 (which is questionable), but it is the Knights' alleged rationale that is at the foundation of his analysis:

> The Knights of Labor endeavoured to annex the skilled men in order that the advantage from their exceptional fighting strength might lift up the unskilled and the semi-skilled. From the viewpoint of a struggle between principles, this was indeed a clash between the principle of solidarity of labour and that of trade separation, but, in reality, each of the principles reflected only the special interest of a certain portion of the working class. Just as the trade unions when they fought for trade autonomy, really refused to consider the unskilled man, so the Knights of Labor were insensible to the fact that their scheme would retard the progress of the skilled trades.

This key argument again rests on assertion. Perlman provided no documentation to establish that the Knights damaged the position of the skilled worker in order to favor the unskilled. As we shall argue throughout, the Order understood the interests of the entire class to be inextricably intertwined, and this attempt to forge solidarity in the face of concerted opposition is at the center of the history of the 1880s. Perlman notes, for instance, that the Knights' decline owed more to the combined assault of capital that it faced after 1886 than to the fights in the labor movement. Perlman details the birth of aggressive employer associations and the increased use of lockouts, iron-clads, blacklists, and Pinkertons, but fails to ask why capital found it necessary to fight the Order so aggressively. The answer, of course, could only undercut his earlier dismissal of the Knights of Labor as something less than a working-class organization.[19]

Perlman's followers are legion. Here we will consider only his two most influential supporters: Lloyd Ulman in the realm of labor economics and Gerald Grob in labor history. Ulman, writing during the heyday of consensus scholarship, dealt with the Knights at length in his study of the emergence of a national labor movement. Here we find an assessment pitting the Commons–Perlman interpretation of the Order against the more positive assessment of Norman Ware, whose work we will discuss later. His lengthy dismissal of Ware's argument (as he renders it) rests on lengthy quotation of trade union attacks on the Order and ultimately on the structural incompatibility of the Order's mixed District Assemblies and its National Trade Assemblies. But, like Perlman, he stresses that the conflict between skilled and unskilled was crucial: "The skilled crafts knew better; they knew that it was best to avoid certain entangling alliances, and it was for this reason that they insisted upon trade autonomy and thus came into conflict with the mixed districts." Indeed, he imputes the same motivations to the Knights of Labor as Perlman: "The dominance of the mixed district meant nothing in fact if it did not imply the subordination of the selfish interests of the crafts to the selfish interests of the unskilled groups." His final *coup de grâce* struck this note, dismissing the Order and Ware's analysis of it:

> The argument that the Knights of Labor was an organization compatible with autonomous national unionism was no more tenable than the assumption upon which it rested – the assumption that the interests of the unskilled were not opposed to those of the skilled union members.

Yet, in his final formulation, Ulman conceded perhaps more than he intended to the possibility raised by the Knights:

> The Knights, relying for their strength upon the solidarity of all trades, were obliged to gamble that the leveling influence of technological change would be great enough to make membership in the Order a matter of self-interest to the unions' members. The trade union, on the other hand, relying for its strength upon the economic isolation of its membership, was obliged to gamble on the permanence of that isolation. The Knights lost this bet.

Although it presented a more intriguing scenario than that of the earlier authors, Ulman's argument nevertheless retreated into technological determinism and relied upon the interpretive force of that old companion of North American economic analysis, "self interest."[20]

In 1961 Gerald Grob published his *Workers and Utopia: A Study of Ideological Conflict in the American Labor Movement 1865–1900.* Without doubt this book has been the single most influential study of the Knights of Labor in recent years. This is somewhat ironic in view of three basic features of the book acknowledged by the author in his preface: first, *Workers and Utopia* is a study of "the development of the *ideology* of organized labor"; second, the book has a deep, consensus-school bias built into its "basic assumptions," namely, that "American unionism is simply a response to the values which American culture emphasizes," itemized as "materialistic, acquisitive, and abundant"; third, the book is almost totally a disciple of the Commons' school. It is odd indeed, then, that this intellectual history of the Order has gained such widespread acceptance. Like his predecessors, Grob's focus is largely on what the Knights' leaders said and wrote, and he places them unambiguously in a late-nineteenth-century utopian reform stream characterized by "a lack of mature class consciousness." This tradition he contrasts with a dichotomous "trade union" position which "implicitly acknowledged the permanence of capitalism and industrial society" and thus "spent most of its time in efforts to devise common programs of immediate economic objectives."

This is, by now, familiar stuff. For Grob, the Knights represent a meandering reform current in which we find a confused swirl of politicians and professional reformers, inept leaders, and archaic thought, all drifting toward the petit bourgeois dream of reestablishing the relationships of an earlier era, "based on the dominance of the small producer." Throughout the 1880s we have the Knights "vainly struggling to hold back the onrushing tide by advocating the restoration and preservation of older values." Meanwhile the trade unions "commenced their rise to power." Because they "accepted the basic framework of the capitalistic system," they succeeded. Echoing Perlman, Grob argues that in "an environment of abundance" and "an acquisitive society that interpreted success largely in terms of material advances," labor leaders had no choice but to build organizations suitable for workers who "thought of themselves as expectant capitalists" and adapted to a society in which "business values had permeated American culture."[21]

There have been few positive analyses of the Knights of Labor to set against these dominant post-1886 historiographical developments. A rare exception is the writing of Norman J. Ware, perhaps the most perceptive student of the Knights of Labor. He saw the Knights of Labor as just that "sort of One Big Union of which Karl Marx would have approved, if – and this is a large 'if' – it could have been transformed into a political organization under socialist leadership." This orientation rested on the argument that the Order was a more thoroughly working-class organization than any other general labor body before or after 1886.[22] In addition, Ware's monograph on the Knights, significantly subtitled "A Study in Democracy," not only argued that "there was nothing inevitable about the failure of the Knights and the success of the Federation" but also asserted that the AFL "was not an advance of the American labor movement, but a strategic retreat of a few craft unions disturbed for their own safety by the remarkable but 'unhealthy' growth of the One Big Union." Ware explicitly rejected the "reform" versus "pure and simple" or "business" unionism model, and argued that all such typologies failed to capture the mix that was the reality of late-nineteenth-century working-class organizations. Moreover, he also warned us against those who "speak too glibly about the failure of the Knights in this or that," for "as propagandists, organizers, and experimenters they had remarkable if ephemeral success," which "put the labor movement on the map." He admitted that their "one major idea or sentiment – the idea of solidarity," was but "a shibboleth, a catchword," but he did not dismiss it. Instead he found it "better than most" and asked who, other than the Knights, had since found a way to succeed in accomplishing that goal. Certainly not the AFL, which he charged with an "exclusiveness" reaching "sterility." Further, unlike the Knights' critics, he pointed out that the AFL had been unable to spread organization to "the great mechanized industries which the Knights once held." Although its posture was unnecessarily defensive, Ware's monograph nevertheless evoked much about the experience of the labor-reform effort:

> The labor movement of the eighties was not a business but a religion, not a doctrinal religion like socialism, but a vague, primitive, embryonic sentiment, a religion in the making . . . meeting places were built co-operatively . . . this sanctuary became the center of the members' lives, their club, union headquarters, school, church, in one. Out of it came most, if not all, of the labor leaders of the future. They came out with some enthusiasm for ideas, a vague humanitarianism, and the conviction that the Knights were "noble and holy." It wore off. A hard-boiled generation now know better . . . But the Knights had no such opportunities. They were serious-minded, highfalutin, sentimental, a little ridiculous, but engaged in a crusade of sorts which seemed to them important. They talked of "honorable toil," of the "sufferings of the masses," of "emancipation from wage slavery," of "justice," and of "rights and wrongs."

Here, then, we have none of the condescension of a winner's history, none of the anachronism that has filled so much of the work of the Knights' critics. Indeed Ware, for all of his difficulties, captured the essential importance of the Knights of Labor:

> The Order tried to teach the American wage-earner that he was a wage-earner first and a bricklayer, carpenter, miner, shoemaker, after; that he was a wage-earner first and a Catholic, Protestant, Jew, white, black, Democrat, Republican, after. This meant that the Order was teaching something that was not so in the hope that sometime it would be.[23]

Despite the tangible strengths of this general approach, Ware's book also has its difficulties. Writing in the late 1920s, Ware had limited documentary materials to work with and those available to him colored his view of the Order detrimentally. The active cooperation of John W. Hayes gave Ware access to a prejudiced view of the Order that only augmented his belief that the decline of the Order owed much to the misleadership of Terence Powderly. In one of his more charitable passages Ware described the General Master Workman (GMW) as "a windbag whose place was on the street corner rousing the rabble to concert pitch and providing emotional compensation for dull lives." This stress on personality and leadership was part of a general tendency on Ware's part to correct for the determinism of the Commons' school's economic interpretation of history. In restoring the "individual ambitions, hatreds, strengths, and weaknesses," however, he overplayed "circumstances and the men," especially with regard to Powderly, Gompers, and New York's fundamentalist-socialist Home Club. Ware's view of the Order's political efforts was also problematic, for, as Leon Fink has argued, it tended to distance the Knights too readily from electoral politics and established institutions. Collapsing the Knights' so-called struggle for democracy into a "popular movement" without necessary and organic connections to the politics of late-nineteenth-century America, Ware came perilously close to anticipating Grob by associating the Order with a broad-based reformism "engrafted upon the movement by the farmers or the radical fringe or socialists and communists of one stripe or another." Ware was at least sensitive to the appeal and potential of such a reform thrust, while Grob is clearly antagonistic and skeptical. But if Ware saw the Order as a working-class movement, he regarded its class content as resting outside the sphere of political engagement, traditionally defined, directed by forces peripheral rather than central to the movement's history and experience. In the Ware framework, then, the Knights rush, leaderless, and without coherence, into the political fray in the highly charged atmosphere of 1886–7, then abdicate totally in 1890–4, as the Order's national leadership suffers paralysis and the agrarian or "western" section takes over, highlighting the populist content of the Knights' world view.[24] Again, it is not that this depiction of the Order lacks value, but that it neglects important realities and compresses too much into a rather small package.

Ware's sympathetic study had some, albeit few, followers in the 1940s and 1950s. There is not sufficient space to discuss them all, but Harry Carman and Henry David provided a more balanced view of the Order in their own work, in their editing of Powderly's autobiographical *The Path I Trod*, and in their aid in helping to find the massive Powderly manuscripts an archival home.[25] Later in the early 1950s came Edward James's empirically rich but relatively unknown Harvard thesis on labor politics in the Gilded Age.[26] Finally, Philip Foner in the first two volumes of his massive history of American labor was favorably disposed to the Knights of Labor attempt to organize the whole American working class, but ultimately fell into a vulgar Marxist parody of the Commons–Perlman view by also finding the Knights irreparably flawed by supposedly middle-class reform interests.[27]

In the 1960s and 1970s a new American working-class history began to be written. Influenced by path-breaking work by Herbert Gutman and David Montgomery, who in turn showed deep debts of gratitude to English Marxist historical writing on the working-class experience, a new generation of historians began to turn to comprehensive community studies and to intensive investigations of the work place to recreate the world of the late-nineteenth-century American working class. As will be evident throughout this book, we identify our work with this group of historians and this book represents an attempt to bring these recently developed insights and modes of investigation to bear on the Knights of Labor in Ontario.[26]

So far we have limited our discussion to American historians. What have their colleagues to the north had to say on the subject? The English-Canadian historiography of the Order is, on the whole, relatively recent. A few pioneering efforts emerged in the 1930s and 1940s, stemming from a combination of the singular social history interests of Fred Landon and from the historical strength of the Order in western Ontario and in Quebec. A University of Western Ontario historian, Landon had studied briefly at Michigan in the early 1920s with Ulrich B. Phillips, one of the collaborators on John R. Commons' massive *Documentary History*. Early in the 1930s Landon began to pursue the Knights as a historical subject and even traveled to Boston to interview the GMW of what remained of the Order. In the process he gained for the University of Western Ontario Library copies of a number of the surviving General Assembly reports of the 1880s which became source material for two M.A. theses completed under Landon's supervision. In 1933 J. I. Cooper wrote a lively and interesting study of the Canadian general election of 1887 calling attention to the considerable political significance of the Order.[29] Four years later Landon himself responded to "the widespread suspicion and fear" that greeted the rise of the Congress of Industrial Organizations (CIO) in North America, and penned a reflective piece assuring his business readers that the CIO was "but a further stage in the long struggle between the craft and the industrial union." To prove his assertion he drew heavily on the Knights of Labor experience.[30] In 1942 Landon availed himself of the opportunity of his Canadian Historical Association presidential address to draw attention once again to the national importance of the Order in the 1880s. Debating Engels's classic view of Canada as "a decaying and retrogressive country . . . ripe for annexation by the United States," he discussed the Order's political impact and especially noted the findings of the Royal Commission on the Relations of Labour and Capital.[31]

In 1945 a second Landon student, Douglas R. Kennedy, completed his study of the Knights in Canada. Published after his premature death as a memorial volume in 1956, the Kennedy thesis became the standard version of the Order's Canadian history. Although as an M.A. thesis this work was promising, it was based on limited sources, almost totally dependent on Norman Ware for its interpretative thrust, and broke little new ground.[32] A less well-known McGill M.A. thesis written for former Landon student J. I. Cooper after World War II was more deserving of a broad readership. Robert W. Cox's insightful and careful study of the Quebec provincial election provided solid, local evidence to support the earlier assertions about the Order's significant political impact.[33]

An even more important work appeared one year later, in 1949, with the completion of Victor Chan's study of the Order. This thesis, also supervised by Cooper, was partially based on the secondary literature, but worked from a much wider reading of the Canadian labor press of the 1880s and added a sharper analysis. Although he overdrew the contrast between the Order in Canada and in the United States (by asserting, for example, that the Canadian Knights were far in advance because of their willingness to engage in political activities), Chan nevertheless developed a novel interpretation of the Order that went beyond Ware and to some degree anticipated the arguments of Gerald Grob:

> The Knights tried to satisfy too many social classes that necessarily conflicted with one another. In this feature lay their decisive weakness: it arose from the economic and social conditions of the time when classes were still fluid, when small-scale industry was still predominant, when even the wage system was still "comparatively new;" when, consequently, social antagonisms were not clear-cut and the interests of the farmer, the small employer and the wage laborer were held to be more or less identical.

His emphasis on the relation of the Order to contemporary social and economic conditions and his notion of the 1880s as a transitional period linking the essentially competitive capitalism of the nineteenth century and its twentieth-century successor, monopoly capitalism, were insightful. In his view, the official leadership of the Knights of Labor trailed behind "the revolutionary activity of the masses – however rudimentary that activity was," but Chan knew that the Order, in spite of its failure, had accomplished much. He quoted prominent Toronto Knight Daniel J. O'Donoghue, who noted that when he spoke in Montreal in 1875, men "came shrinking along in the shadows of the walls so much did they fear lest their employers should come to know where they had been." But eleven years later, with the Order at his and the working class's back, O'Donoghue could declare that "There is no such fear today." Indeed, Chan offered perhaps the most penetrating analysis of the strengths and weaknesses of the Knights of Labor in the Canadian historiography, and closed his thesis with an assessment of the Order's decline that still bears repeating: "Reflecting conditions that were essentially transitory and unsettled, the leaders could have no clear cut policy, no definite objective. Lacking such a policy, the Order consequently failed to present itself as a rallying point for the working class, and became an easy prey to other corroding influences as the opposition of capital and social disinterestedness." Indeed, a major virtue of this unappreciated unpublished study was that there was far less of a predetermined future triumph of business unionism in its pages than in the later influential work of Grob.[34]

Despite these important early studies, the Knights received little attention from mainstream Canadian history and even economist Harold Logan's major institutional study of Canadian labor history awarded them only the most perfunctory notice.[35] The few students who expressed interest in such topics were quickly hurried back into the mainstream of politics and biography. One of those who strayed from that well-beaten path, Frank Watt, did manage, however, to publish an article analyzing the labor-reform ideology of the 1880s for the first time. His discovery of the labor press and especially of "Enjolras" (Phillips Thompson) led him to argue that serious domestic critiques of early industrial-capitalist society existed in Canada – a novel argument for the late 1950s.[36] Finally, in the early 1960s Bernard Ostry considered the relationship of labor to politics in the 1870s and 1880s in a pair of interesting articles. He had carefully researched the political sources, but the perspective was Ottawa- and Toronto-centered. Workers emerged as manipulated victims of the omniscient political managers of the old parties. Moreover, the focus on institutions such as the Trades and Labor Congress (TLC) actually forced the more important local events into the background. The rise of the Knights of Labor, undoubtedly the major event of the 1880s, hardly appears in Ostry's analysis. Instead workers shuffle onstage to deliver a brief political speech in 1886–7 and then hurry back to the wings. There, well before the arrival of Samuel Gompers' AFL, Canadian workers embraced business unionism. While this may appear a useful corrective for those who place all the woes of the Canadian labor movement at the door of American labor imperialism, it is nonetheless an anachronistic view of the 1880s.[37]

The story in Quebec differs little from what has been outlined. A few short research notes on the Knights' experience were published by E. Z. Massicotte in the 1930s. In the mid-1950s, Alfred Charpentier, Catholic labor leader and historian, offered an article on early labor politics in Quebec that noted the Order's pioneering role. Finally one lonely M.A. thesis in the mid-1960s by Jacques Martin surveyed the experience of the Order in Quebec.[38]

The developments in the 1960s and 1970s that we have noted earlier with reference to American working-class historiography have also had their effect in Canada. In the last decade there has been a rapid growth in the general field of labor history and a number of studies have appeared touching on the Knights of Labor experience. In Quebec, for example, Fernand Harvey, both in his study of the Royal Commission on the Relations of Labour and Capital and in a pioneering article, has begun to redirect attention to the Knights.[39] The different experience of the Order in Quebec, where it retained considerable strength into the twentieth century, provided one of the foundations for the emergence of the Catholic confessional unionism that has been studied recently by Jacques Rouillard.[40] Meanwhile, in English Canada a number of community studies have reflected on the Knights' contribution.[41]

## Reinterpretation

The Ontario context of this study is worthy of comment. Given Canada's propinquity to the United States, it was here that the Order had its greatest foreign impact. For the leaders in Philadelphia and Scranton, the 49th Parallel made very little difference to how they ran the Order. Indeed, as we will see later, that occasionally became an issue causing some contention and conflict within the Canadian Order. For the Ontario members, however, we will argue that with the exception of this brief and clouded "Home Rule" episode, nationality exercised little impact. Indeed, the weakness of the Canadian nation state in the 1880s made the natural flow of workers and of labor organization and reform thought not east–west but rather north–south. Thus, Ontario Knights had far more interest in and contact with Knights of Labor headquarters in Philadelphia than they did with their comrades in British Columbia or even in Quebec.

This is not to deny that the distinct national setting had an influence on the history of the Order in Ontario, but rather to suggest that with the obvious exception of a substantially different political system within which the Order vied for social change, it is not clear to us what other factors mattered. For example, if we contend that Ontario was less industrialized than the United States (it was), we immediately come up against not only combined and uneven development in Ontario but the same factor within the vast diversity of the American regional economies of the nineteenth century as well. Thus we present this study of the Knights of Labor as a regional one that needs to be compared and contrasted with similar studies of the Order in Quebec, in the Canadian west, in New York, Pennsylvania, or New England. Until such studies are completed it is difficult to control for considerations of national difference. For our American readers we have provided a long introduction to the economic and social history of late-nineteenth-century Ontario that should allow them to put this study in perspective.

In this book, then, we attempt to investigate the Knights of Labor experience in a new way. By examining the structural situation of the Order, where and when it organized in Ontario, and how many (in rough terms) it drew to its ranks, we believe we can establish its class character and importance. We will argue that the Noble and Holy Order of the Knights of Labor represented a dramatic shift away from past practices within the history of Ontario workers. Although the Knights built on the accumulated experience of the working class, they channeled that experience in new directions. In the words of Raymond Williams, they took a whole series of residual aspects of the class experience, built upon them, and erected a structural and intellectual apparatus that was the beginning of emergent purpose; they moved beyond limited forms of class conflict, always present in industrial capitalist society, to a more thoroughgoing orchestration of class struggle.[42] In short, the Knights of Labor in Ontario created, for the first time, what Lawrence Goodwyn has called a movement culture of alternative, opposition, and potential.[43] In the breadth of their vision, the scope of their organization, and their unique refusal to collapse the cause of workers into this or that reform or amelioration, or restrict entry to the movement to this stratum or that group, the Knights of Labor hinted at the potential and possibility that are at the foundation of the making of a class. Politically, the Order's efforts in the federal, provincial, and municipal fields testified to the movement's willingness and ability to transcend the economic concerns of the work place. At the same time, the Order's important place in the class struggles and confrontations of the last two decades of the nineteenth-century points to problems inherent in viewing the Knights of Labor from the perspective of its leader's antistrike rhetoric. To be sure, both in the political sphere and at the work place, the Knights found themselves caught in many ambiguities and contradictions, among the most important being their political relationship to the established Liberal (Grit) and Conservative (Tory) parties, and their capacity to defend the interests of their membership in the face of fierce employer resistance and a post-1886 trade union opposition. Some, but not all, of these difficulties were of the Order's own making. But as the first expression of the social, cultural, and political emergence of a class, the Knights of Labor understandably groped for answers more than they marched forcefully toward solutions. As we shall argue, the Order was itself inhibited by the context of late-nineteenth-century Ontario, which (aside from its own peculiar "regional" divisions) stood poised between an economy of recently arrived competitive capitalism and the monopoly capitalism that stood literally around the corner with the Laurier boom years of the twentieth century. The Knights, in many ways, straddled each epoch, looking simultaneously forward and backward, longing for the rights they knew to be justly theirs, attacking the monopolists they increasingly saw controlling the business, politics, and culture of their society.

Beyond this general interpretive thrust two additional points need to be made, for they are as much a part of our purpose as any attempt to shift analysis of the Knights of Labor in new directions. First, we have attempted to work through the history of the Knights of Labor in ways that convey as adequately as is possible the human forces behind the doctrines, practices, and campaigns of the 1880s and 1890s. We are in agreement with one principled member of the Order, whose reminiscences are prefaced by this general statement:

When there is so much warmth in the making of labor's history it is strange that there has been so little in the writing of it. As a rule, it has been written by dry-as-dust economists who treat it as if it were the record of the advance of an economic doctrine. As well write the history of the religious movement as if it were the record of the advance of theological doctrine. Labor doctrines have never advanced except as they have been lived and loved by individuals.[44]

Second, we want to insist that the experience of the Knights of Labor be considered, not as some minor episode in labor history, but as an integral part of the late-nineteenth-century Canadian past, in all of its complexities. The rise of the Order was intimately related to the economic and political developments of the period; it was an implicit component of that "manufacturing condition" that came into prominence in the late nineteenth century but that is so often written about with only a cursory view of the laboring class.[45] That historians of politics and business have been willing and able to do this is perhaps understandable, but it does not make for a history premised upon the need to comprehend totality and interrelationship. It is odd, for instance, that much of the political history of these years can be written with only a fleeting glance at the working-class constituency that was so consistently courted by John A. Macdonald, Edward Blake, and others. Phillips Thompson, Toronto Knight of Labor brainworker, claimed in 1885 that, "A determined effort is now being made by the Grit party to capture the Labor vote." Even a source as unimpeachable as the *Journal of Commerce* noted in 1888 that "the future of the artizan fills the whole horizon of politics, and no other class is considered at all."[46] The Tory-inspired *Royal Commission on the Relations of Labour and Capital in Canada* (1889) was probably the impetus behind such a caustic comment, and revealed how seriously the established political structure regarded the pressing question of labor.[47]

Richard J. Kerrigan, a Montreal labor activist who began as a Knight of Labor, joined the Socialist Labor Party, and ended up in the 1920s in the OBU, wrote of "the dynamic year of 1886," in which politics, anti-Knight of Labor pronouncements by the Catholic Church, and a host of other issues flowed together in one inseparable process:

The Knights of Labor grew to alarming proportions in the country, and the Province of Quebec, always the political storm centre of Canada, had to get drastic treatment if it were to be kept safe and sane for law and order. Bishop Tashereau of Quebec launched his famous excommunication decree against the Knights of Labor. . . . Shortly after the political landslide which placed the provincial Liberals in power, the Federal Conservative Government, reeking with financial scandals, and presumably on the principal of the more the merrier, took all the other scandals to its bosom and appealed to the country. So with Home Rule, land thievery, CP Ry scandals, Louis Riel, National Policy, Jesuit machinations, etc., etc., as issues, the electorate would have been hogs for misfortune had they not had some reason to vote for or against the Conservative government. The Labor issue was linked up with the Liberal and the Tory, and had its throat cut accordingly.[48]

This socialist's assessment, with which we might take exception on specific points, nevertheless reveals an understanding of the interconnections of an unfolding history all too rare in academic writing on the period.

It should not be tenable to write a social history of business in the 1880s, for instance, and argue that the early-closing movement was merely one more attempt to flee the evils of competition, to secure order and common practice in the retail trade. There may have been the occasional merchant or association of businessmen that launched some of the first early-closing movements for such reasons.[49] But there was also a push from below, which may well have influenced such farseeing businessmen. Indeed, when one actually looks at specific communities – Chatham, London, Hamilton, Toronto, St. Catharines, St. Thomas, and Ottawa – it is the Knights of Labor that are fighting for early closing and meeting considerable resistance. There was more than one search for order going on as the nineteenth century drew to an end.[50]

To emphasize the point we need only glance at the one event of the 1880s that has captivated historical attention in Canada for almost a century: the Riel uprising of 1885. Here, surely, is an episode of significance far removed from the shadow of the Knights of Labor. Perhaps, and we will not push our argument to the point of absurdity by straining to link the Order and the Métis uprising. Yet it is worth mentioning the case of W. H. Jackson, alias Honoré Joseph Jaxon, Riel's staunchest white ally and in effect his secretary. After the rebellion was crushed, Jackson was brought to trial and acquitted on the grounds of insanity. It took him less than three months to break out of his institutional confinement, and he escaped to the south, where he involved himself in the affairs of a Chicago carpenters' council, conducting its "strike policy." He also gained admittance to the Knights of Labor, and early became associated with the Chicago Labor Press Association, his secretarial skills apparently proving highly marketable. In the summer of 1886, as Powderly and the upper echelons of the Order abdicated all responsibility for the Haymarket martyrs, Jackson campaigned to defend them, urging the publication "of a work now being prepared by the prisoners which will be copyrighted for the benefit of their defence fund and of their families." The anarchist Albert Parsons received his unambiguous endorsement; Jackson praised one of his speeches as a "masterpiece of logical exposition and of sympathetic championship of the cause of the oppressed." Jackson created some dissent in the Order by addressing Knights of Labor audiences in Chicago, Detroit, and other centers on the North West Rebellion, talks that often lasted three-and-one-half hours and that remained loyal to Louis David Riel and the cause of independence. All of this came from one reared in Wingham, Ontario, the small-town milieu that would produce so much support for the Knights of Labor in the 1880s. We are reminded that not all of Ontario was one large cauldron of seething antipapist bigotry.[51]

A quixotic figure like Jackson, who was somewhat removed from the Ontario of the 1880s, can hardly establish the presence of a revolutionary and insurrectionary contingent within the Order. But that is not our point. Rather, we focus on this admittedly atypical element to hint at the possibility that there was an understanding, in certain Knights of Labor circles, that the class and national questions were cut from the same cloth. This understanding was also brought out in the Ontario Order's attempts to overcome the ethnic and religious divisions among workers to promote a wider class solidarity, and in the Knights of Labor defense of Riel, the Métis, and the French Canadians in the pages of the Order's official Canadian journal, the *Palladium of Labor*, or on the public podiums of the day. For his part, Riel himself addressed the Knights of Labor constituency, penning a letter to Patrick Ford's *Irish World*, calling for justice in the Northwest in language that all labor reformers shared and in an argument that alluded to the historical experience of oppression. An advocate of Henry George, living in New York or Toronto, would have responded well to an appeal such as Riel's address to the citizens of the United States:

> Our lands of the North-West Territory, the possession of which had been solemnly guaranteed to us by the government fifteen years ago, have since then been torn from us, and given to land grabbers who have never seen the country; and this after we had cleared the land, torn up the tree trunks, removed the rocks, plowed and sown the earth, and built solid dwellings for ourselves and our children.

One Knight of Labor correspondent, the supposedly demented brother of prominent Ontario Knight and well-known labor activist D. J. O'Donoghue, solicited Powderly's support for an insurrectionary plot to challenge the anti-Riel forces:

> I asked Louis Riel to get up a drive in the Can N.W.T. . . . I am willing to go there and fight to hang if need be allright so long as I am a success at killing a few dozens or hundreds of those Canadian Buggers irrespective of religion or nationality . . . I want to get the Canadian Knights to give me a hand. I would make a fine break in B.C. if I only had the five thousand Knights that are in Victoria with me . . . A

> letter from you by hand to the B.C. Knights would do the thing for me. We could sieze upon the B.C. gov't . . . first. Independence second. Annexation to the U.S. third. And it is necessary to unite Alaska . . . for this would take in B.C. I do not consider England as having any rights at all upon the Am Continent, none that I would respect in any way.

Such tactics and ideas, however atypical, indicate that one cannot divorce the experience of the Ontario Knights of Labor from all that has been considered as central to the history of Canada in these years. Comprehension of the late-nineteenth-century milieu demands a knowledge of the Order, and this in turn sheds new light on the history of economic, social, and political life.[52]

Unlike many of our predecessors, then, we refuse to bury the Knights under an abundance of condescension and hindsight. Instead of analyzing failure and seeking the glorious antecedents of the AFL (or the TLC), we have tried to move beyond the conventional wisdoms. This process has led us into many previously unexplored locales where the Knights flourished and died. In exploring, for the first time, the small-town experience of the Order in eastern and southwestern Ontario we were struck by the forceful presence of the Knights of Labor; in examining the voluminous Canadian, largely Ontario, correspondence to Terence V. Powderly we came to know, perhaps as intimately as is possible, the feelings, values, beliefs, angers, and resentments of men, *and* women, who saw in the Order the way forward to a new, and better, way of life; in reaching into many different contexts we came to realize just how empty many of the old clichés – regarding Knights of Labor–trade union antagonisms or the Order's opposition to strikes – actually were. No Canadian historian has ever effectively countered such views, nor have many seemed aware of the presence of the Knights of Labor and the people who built the movement in Canada; perhaps still fewer care about what it all means.

It is a nuanced appreciation of the Knights that we thus insist upon. That is one reason there are so many words, so many people, so many places, so many events in the pages that follow. This work, like much that we have written, emerges out of an empirical idiom that has deep, impressive, and significant roots in a Marxist tradition of historical inquiry.[53] For details about the Knights of Labor are not the "mere" product of romanticism, nostalgia, or antiquarianism. In challenging the evolution of Canadian industrial-capitalist society in the 1880s, the Knights of Labor raised questions and attacked inequities that are still with us. Their assertion of human values rather than those of "the interests," their vision and their capacity to dream of what might be remind us that the society we ourselves live in is not and was not the product of an uncontested, universally applauded, inevitable progress. The Noble and Holy Order of the Knights of Labor saw a different way forward, glimpsed another kind of social system. They failed to bring it into being and their conception of what might be was certainly flawed, but their critique of the new industrial order prefaced other attacks and helped to establish a tradition of dissent that continues to this day. Without that tradition, without the many challenges it has raised, we might well be in worse shape than we are. To look at the origins of that long history of opposition, then, is to make ourselves aware of important critical insights.[54]

Our stress upon the essentially human context of the emergence of the Knights of Labor in Ontario has drawn us toward the unique accomplishment of the Order; the way in which it forged a movement culture out of the past traditions, strengths, and weaknesses of the working-class experience, and built a conception of alternatives out of the practices of a past firmly embedded in the status quo. Such a process inevitably raised a series of challenges: at the work place; in the political realm; and through changing the intellectual milieu in which the working class operated. These challenges, all aspects of an opposition which placed in heightened relief the class divisions and antagonisms of Canadian society in the late nineteenth century, were often met with stiff rebuke or subtle incorporation. But whatever the response, and whatever the outcome, each challenge was part of a larger process, was cut from a *whole* cloth. The fabric is what we have tried to reconstruct, weaving into the pages of this study the many and varied strands that, individually, count only as so many threads, but when taken together form an impressive bolt of cloth indeed.

We explore that potential in the following pages in different ways and on different levels. Opening our discussion is a general overview of the economic and social context of late-nineteenth-century Ontario. We then proceed to a reconstruction of the structural dimensions of the Order's penetration into Ontario. Then follow detailed examinations of the two most important centers of Knights of Labor activism: in Toronto and Hamilton the Order enrolled impressive numbers of workers, and surviving sources allow a reasonably complete reconstruction of events. Moving beyond these specific communities we then examine general experiences, and try to detail not only the noble and impressive achievements of the Order but its failures and shortcomings as well: the problem of unprincipled parasites and their role in introducing intrigue and discontent; the political activities of the Order in its period of greatest strength (1883–7), and the political wranglings of the years of demise (1887–94); the educational and cultural role of the Order in shifting, if not transforming, the way in which Ontario workers saw the world; and, finally, the rhetoric and reality of class conflict in the 1880s and the Order's place in strikes, lockouts, and other struggles. This kind of approach necessarily leads to some repetition: themes are introduced only to be subsequently trotted out again in a later section; individuals come and go, their actions outlined in one chapter and reexamined in another. We have tried to keep this problem of repetition under control, but there are aspects of the Order's history that overlap; politics and "politicians"; culture and conflict. Issues examined in Toronto and Hamilton inevitably crop up in later chapters. We have taken this approach because it seemed imperative to demonstrate many things, and to convey as thoroughly as possible what happened in the 1880s and 1890s. Toronto and Hamilton, for instance, deserve separate and specific discussions, but part of the purpose of this book is to establish that it was not only in the large (and well-studied) urban centers that the Knights of Labor grew to maturity. Elsewhere, too, in Gananoque, St. Catharines, and Chatham, the Order issued its challenge, even though our knowledge of the working-class presence in these towns is still fragmentary. Thus, we chronicle the wider experience, and take the bad along with the good, in chapters concerned primarily with the Knights of Labor experience outside Ontario's two largest industrial cities. We close with an assessment of accomplishment and failure.

We can end this introduction with a much-quoted passage from Marx's *The Eighteenth Brumaire of Louis Bonaparte*. "Men make their own history, but they do not make it just as they please," wrote Marx in one of his most significant and most ambiguous statements. "They do not make it under circumstances chosen by themselves," he continued, "but under circumstances directly encountered, given and transmitted from the past." These words have been debated for many years, and within the fragmented sections of various Marxist traditions people have been lining up behind the two halves of that introductory statement. But it is the passage immediately following this controversial sentence that most appropriately introduces us to the Knights of Labor and sums up what much of this book is all about:

> The tradition of all the dead generations weighs like a nightmare on the brain of the living. And just when they seem engaged in revolutionising themselves and things, in creating something that has never yet existed, precisely in such periods . . . they anxiously conjure up the spirits of the past to their service and borrow from them names, battle cries and costumes in order to present the new scene of world history in this time-honoured disguise and this borrowed language.[55]

# Part I. Overview

The fact is that the Knights of Labor more fully represented the wage-earners as a whole than any general labor organization either before or after its peak year, 1886.

Norman J. Ware, historian, 1935

All I knew then of the principles of the Knights of Labor was that the motto of the Knights of Labor was, One for All, and All for One.

Abraham Bisno, union pioneer, April 1886

# 1. The working class and industrial capitalist development in Ontario to 1890

In the conclusion to his analysis of capitalist development in Russia, V. I. Lenin succinctly pointed to the twofold historic role of capital: first, to increase the productive forces of social labor; and second, to stimulate the socialization of that labor. Both of these processes, however, manifested themselves in diverse ways in different branches of various national economies. This first chapter seeks briefly to outline aspects of this historic role of capital in Ontario, and set the stage for the following discussion of the Knights of Labor. For across the province the late nineteenth century witnessed the first truly unambiguous stirrings of industrial capital, and these years would serve as the crucible from which Canada as a whole would emerge as an indigenous capitalist economy and society. This momentous shift in the nature of productive relations, as Lenin argued, led "to a change in the mentality of the population," as the spasmodic character of economic development, the rapid transformation of the methods of production, of personal dependence and patriarchalism in social relationships, the mobility of the population, and the influence of the growing industrial centers all culminated in profound alterations in "the very character of the producers." In the Ontario of the 1880s and 1890s the rise and fall of the Knights of Labor was at the heart of this process of change.[1]

To argue the importance of the Canadian industrial revolution of the mid-to-late nineteenth century, as we shall explicitly in this chapter and implicitly throughout the book, is to confront one of the well-established conventional wisdoms of the peculiarities of the Canadians. For the founders of the staples approach to Canadian economic development, an approach that has blossomed into an internationally accepted tradition of political economy, paid little attention to the nineteenth-century origins of Canadian industrial capitalism. The pioneer of this approach, W. A. Mackintosh, held that industrialism awaited the spin-off effects of the turn-of-the-century Laurier wheat boom that would usher in a century destined to be Canada's. For the much-celebrated Harold Innis the country's capitalist experience was to be distorted by the demands of the pervasive American capital that flooded the country. Curiously, both authors shared a focus on the early twentieth century and both ignored, in large part, the earlier industrial revolution that had taken place in central Canada in the period from the 1840s to the 1880s. Recent scholarship in this mainstream of the political economy tradition has begun to pay attention to the process of late-nineteenth-century capitalist industrialization, and the concomitant creation of a Canadian working class. But it remains overwhelmingly concerned with the twentieth-century experience, and gives short shrift to the earlier role of capital and the emergence of factory production in the post-1850 years. In what must stand as one of the classic ironies of supposedly socialist historical investigation, some recent left-nationalist followers of Innis have been influenced by dependency theory and by the writings of Samir Amin on the character of capitalism as a world system, while, at the same time, they are all too willing to dismiss efforts to probe the nature and extent of industrial-capitalist development in Canada and its impact on working-class life as "Metropolitan Marxism."[2]

We stand as part of this Marxist tradition and look, not necessarily toward Mackintosh, Innis, and their current left-nationalist advocates (although all their work forces us to clarify our arguments and provides useful empirical detail), but in the direction of a dissenting scholarship that begins with the populistic muckraker Gustavus Myers and his *History of Canadian Wealth* (1914), consolidates in the 1940s, 1950s, and 1960s with the pioneering efforts of Marxists H. Clare Pentland and Stanley B. Ryerson, and continues with much recent work on the social, cultural, and economic experience of Canadian workers. In all of this work, the late nineteenth century stands as an epoch of capitalist transformation. And this dissident view receives impressive quantitative backing from a number of recent studies by economic historians concerned with the analysis of aggregate data and the extent of real manufacturing output. It would seem that it is no longer possible to deny the indisputable: that the latter half of the nineteenth century saw the creation of a sophisticated transportation network; that these years gave rise to considerable debate leading to the articulation of a strategy of industrial development that pinned the hopes of Canada's rising capitalist class on political consolidation, tariff protection, and settlement; and that a diversified manufacturing sector emerged in central Canada, dominating social life in the young Dominion.[3] Contemporaries knew all this well, for as early as the 1860s the transforming power of capital had become visible in the rise of the steam-powered factory, often reliant upon mechanized production, as in the tailoring or boot and shoe industries. For the *People's Journal* these were the hallmarks of economic vitality, factors which had "set agoing an industrial revolution." In the words of another exuberant authority, writing in 1866, Canadians were "pressing into an altered condition of things . . . THE MANUFACTURING ERA OF OUR HISTORY."[4]

## An industrial revolution

Between 1870 and 1890 the industrial sector tasted the fruits, both bitter and sweet, of this great transformation: establishments capitalized at $50,000 and over increased by about 50 percent; employment in manufacturing rose by 76 percent and output in constant dollar terms by 138 percent; railway mileage increased from 3,000 in 1873 to over 16,000 in 1896; manufacturing's place, in terms of value-added, rose from 19 percent of the Gross National Product in 1870 to 23.5 percent in 1890; the rate of real manufacturing output climbed from 4.4 percent in the decade 1870–80 to 4.8 percent in 1880–90 (although it slipped to 3.2 percent in the 1890s). Thus, the 1880s were an extremely significant moment in the historical rate of growth, surpassed only by the boom years 1900–10 and 1926–9. Indeed, it is the growth of manufacturing facilities in many industries during the cresting fortunes of the National Policy (1880–4) that is most striking. Between 1880 and 1890, for instance, the value of cotton cloth output rose by 125 percent, but even this dramatic increase understated the gains of the decade's first five years: the number of mills, spindles, looms, and capital investment in cotton cloth tripled in that short period.[5]

The creation of the new Canadian nation state in 1867, which we have argued elsewhere was central to the strategies of the Canadian bourgeoisie, led to a boosterism which knew few bounds. H. Beaumont Small, a propagandist of the new order, looked forward in 1868 to the day when "the judicious outlay of capital" would lead to national industrial self-sufficiency and to "a surplus for exportation to the West Indies and central and South America." After a detailed industrial tour of the Canadian heartland, Small predicted that "as our manufactories increase and accumulating capital seeks some means of investment, our future greatness and prosperity must increase also."[6] The optimism paled for a few years at the height of the depression of the 1870s, although even in the stark years of 1874 and 1876 Canadian manufacturers lobbied for access to U.S. export markets. But the 1878 National Policy election with the victory of the Tories' clear commitment to an industrial strategy promised better things for the industrial capitalist in the 1880s. Even a cautionary book, *Sketches of the Late Depression*, after delivering its moral homilies to businessmen "that there is a higher, yet accessible plane of action for the class to reach in their dealings with each other," then went on to chronicle the recent successes of the National Policy tariff in fostering industrial growth.[7]

Ontario stood at the very center of this process of capitalist development. Aggregate data (see Table 1.1) begin to tell the story: capital invested more

Table 1.1. *Aggregate data, Ontario 1871–1911*

| Year | Capital invested ($) | Hands employed | Yearly wages ($) | Value raw material ($) | Value product ($) | Value-added ($) |
|---|---|---|---|---|---|---|
| 1871 | 37,874,010 | 87,281 | 21,415,710 | 65,114,804 | 114,706,799 | 49,591,995 |
| 1881 | 80,950,847 | 118,308 | 30,604,031 | 91,164,156 | 157,989,870 | 66,825,714 |
| 1891 | 175,972,021 | 166,326 | 49,733,359 | 128,142,371 | 239,781,926 | 111,639,555 |
| 1901 | 214,972,275 | 151,081 | 44,656,032 | 138,230,400 | 241,533,486 | 103,303,086 |
| 1911 | 595,394,608 | 216,362 | 95,674,743 | 297,580,125 | 579,810,225 | 282,230,100 |

*Source: Census of Canada*, 1871–1911. Note that the 1901 and 1911 figures are unadjusted in light of the changing criterion employed by the census in enumerating manufacturing establishments. All firms were considered in the 1871–91 period, while only those firms employing five or more hands were considered in 1901 and 1911. The capital invested figures for 1901 and 1911 are computed by adding together the figures for fixed and working capital. There had been no distinction between these realms in the earlier period.

than doubled in each decade between 1870 and 1890, while the number of hands employed increased 90 percent over the twenty-year period. These aggregate data can give us a rough measure of the character of social and productive relations, the setting within which the Knights of Labor operated, and one which they must have influenced.

Table 1.2 illuminates trends within the aggregate data for the years 1871–1911. However crude and unrefined the categories, they reveal important shifts and developments over the course of the period. If, for instance, we take capital invested as a percentage of value-added, we note a steady increase over the years 1871–1901, with the decadal rate of that increase dropping precipitously in the opening years of the twentieth century. Wages, however, exhibit a different trend, and as a percentage of value-added were relatively stable until they fell dramatically in the years 1901–11. When we take capital invested and wages as a percentage of the total product value other trends emerge: capital as a percentage of product value rises steadily over the course of the entire period, while wages as a percentage of value decline only in those years of most pronounced economic growth, the 1880s and 1900s.

At the outset we need to comprehend the severe limitations of the data: trends and developments could be a consequence of many factors – technological innovation, more efficient utilization of capital and/or labor, market factors, price shifts, or the changing character of exploitation – and the lack of consistency in the criteria employed by the census, particularly in the treatment of the small firm, further complicates matters. Nevertheless, such data point, however hesitatingly, to important forces at work in the Ontario economy. First, we can see that wages declined as a percentage of product

Table 1.2. *Trends within the aggregate Ontario data 1871–1911*

| Year | Capital as % of value-added | Wages as % of value-added | Capital as % of product value | Wages as % of product value | Per capita yearly wages ($) | Capital invested yearly per worker ($) | Yearly national growth rates in manufacturing output (%) |
|---|---|---|---|---|---|---|---|
| 1871 | 76 | 43 | 33 | 18 | 245 | 433 | |
| 1881 | 121 | 45 | 51 | 19 | 257 | 684 | 4.4 |
| 1891 | 157 | 44 | 73 | 16 | 287 | 1057 | 4.8 |
| 1902 | 208 | 43 | 89 | 18 | 295 | 1422 | 2.4 |
| 1911 | 210 | 33 | 102 | 16 | 441 | 2751 | 6.0 |

*Source:* Our calculations from census data. Note reservations in source note to Table 1.1. Yearly national growth rates in manufacturing output are taken from Gordon W. Bertram, "Historical Statistics on Growth and Structure of Manufacturing in Canada, 1870–1957," in J. Henripin and A. Asinakoupulos, eds., *C.P.S.A. Conference on Statistics, 1962 and 1963* (Toronto, 1964), pp. 93–146.

value precisely in those years – 1881–91 and 1901–11 – that the growth rates in national manufacturing output soared. This suggests a growing intensification of labor: that these periods, then, saw increasing organization among Ontario workers – first, in the Knights of Labor, and second, in the craft unions during the upheaval of 1898–1904 – should cause no surprise. But to study the character of exploitation we must probe the relationship of wages to value-added, considering the capital input. This leads us to our second speculative hypothesis: it would appear that the social cost of labor was relatively high throughout the course of the late nineteenth century, years which pre-dated Taylorism, broadly conceived. It is not until the turn of the century that wages as a percentage of value-added plunge, even in the face of soaring per capita yearly wages (largely a consequence of inflation, for real wages declined).[8] These turn-of-the-century years also witness a virtual doubling of the capital invested yearly per worker, and, even taking the inflationary context into consideration, leave behind the more modest decadal increases in this relationship characteristic of the years 1871–1901. Yet, despite this mammoth dose of capital in the years associated with the beginnings of Canada's century, capital as a percentage of value-added makes only a marginal, clearly insignificant, gain. Thus, although both the 1880s and the 1900s are years of economic growth and the increasing intensification of labor, it is not until the years 1901–11 that one sees the actual rationalization of productive relations, a shift in the character of exploitation, and the probable degradation of labor. Prior to this date the social costs of labor remained high, a phenomenon confirmed by recent unpublished work by Jacques Ferland.[9] What gains in output did occur in the late-nineteenth-century years were probably more a consequence of capital input than of extraction of surplus from the hide of labor, although these spheres are ultimately impossible to separate analytically.

If this was indeed the trend, then it becomes important to ask what forces kept the social cost of labor high. Lack of a managerial strategy at the work place, "scientifically" conceived, was no doubt one reason, as was the weak technological foundation of production in the 1880s. The mass character of the Knights of Labor, as a movement aimed at uniting all workers, probably played a considerable role in resisting capital's quest to increase output and reduce labor costs through wage reductions or increasing the pace of work. The yearly per capita wage figures confirm this picture. While yearly wages rose only $12 over the course of the 1870s and only $8 throughout the 1890s, the increase for the decade 1881–91 was $30, at least two-and-one-half times as great. To be sure, there are immense problems in such comparisons, for the decade 1871–81 starts near a peak in the economic cycle and ends as the economy is barely coming out of a trough, while the decade 1881–91 exhibits exactly the opposite trend. Nor do these calculations take into account in any sophisticated way earning power, severely reduced by the unemployment, short-time, and layoffs that accompany depression and recession, or speak to the question of the purchasing potential of these per capita figures, in real wage terms. This no doubt renders any systematic attempt to compare per capita yearly wage rates over the course of the late nineteenth century extremely difficult, and the project is rendered even more questionable in light of the impact of the depressions of the 1870s and 1890s. Nevertheless, the increasing employment of women and children throughout the 1880s, at wages much below the male rate, as well as the deflationary context, offset some of the inherent biases in the data.

But even granting all of the ambiguities in this admittedly speculative and tentative argument, much of the data points toward the high social costs of labor in the late-nineteenth-century period; labor seemed relatively better off in these years, in terms of its capacity to extract a larger portion of its product, than it would in later times, when capitalistic appropriation was undoubtedly more refined and effective. The social relations of production, in which worker stood counterposed to employer and in which the nature and extent of organization was of vital importance, must have contributed to this outcome.

Such developments took place, moreover, within the context of a general decline of prices which, using Michell's price index, plummeted from roughly 100 in 1873 to a low of about 75 in 1886. We know little about the social impact of this long-term decline in prices, but if the experience of the United States is at all representative, we might well speculate that although real wages no doubt rose, employers responded to deflation with increased application of technology, intensification of labor, and, most importantly, wage cuts. The latter would have been most prominent in the troughs that a number of economic historians have located around the years 1879–80, 1885, and 1888. Across south-central Canada the strength of the Knights of Labor may have helped to create a situation in which the working class kept wage rates at least partially intact, inhibiting capital's assault and resisting employer efforts to implement wage reductions. If this was the case, then the Order would have played an important role in depressing the rate of profit and curbing the process of capital accumulation; the social cost of labor would have been relatively high, compared to the Laurier boom years of the twentieth century, and the process of appropriation curtailed. Breaking the back of the intransigent Knights would have become a political, social, and economic imperative for an industrial capitalism moving away from the stage of anarchic competition toward monopoly. Monopoly required heightened forms of integration (both in terms of the corporate form and the increasingly

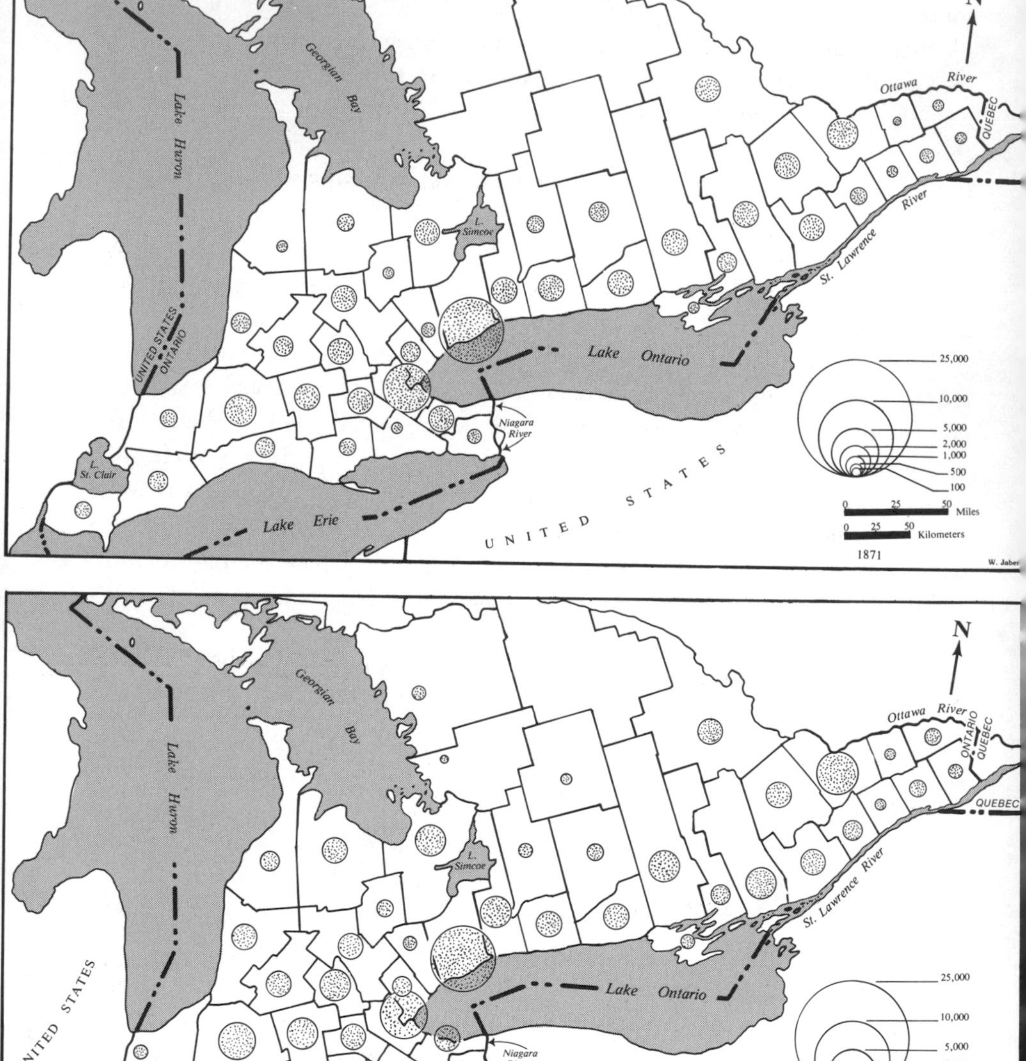


complex relations of finance and industrial capital), an assault on all resistance, passive and active, at the workplace – where rationalization, efficiency, welfare schemes, refined systems of piece/bonus payments, and the open-shop drive were the hallmarks of class relations – *and* the degradation of labor.[10] There is, nevertheless, no mistaking the tremendous expansion in the

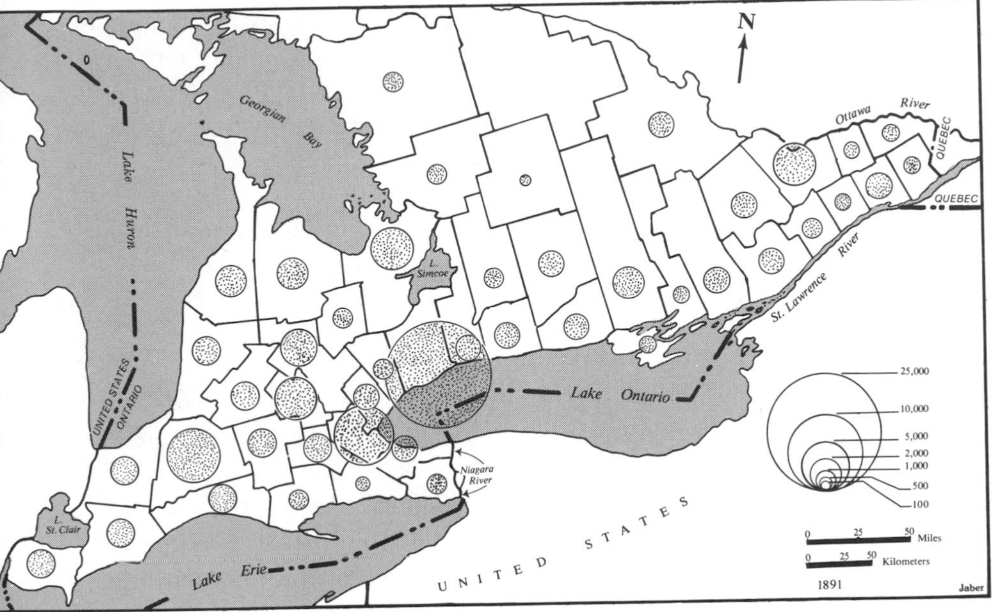


Map 1. Manufacturing employment in Ontario, 1871–91. *Source:* W. G. Dean, ed., *Economic Atlas of Ontario* (Toronto, 1969).

manufacturing sector in this late-nineteenth-century period, a process revealed vividly in the following series of maps (see Map 1). Here we see the impressive quantitative gains in workers employed in manufacturing, plotted by county between 1871 and 1891. As well, we are introduced to the regional context of Ontario's economic history, to the dominance of Toronto–Hamilton, to the underdeveloped but nevertheless significant economic activity along the St. Lawrence and Ottawa rivers, and to the manufacturing importance of various small towns. More than 50 percent of manufacture in the 1880s was located in Canadian communities with populations under 10,000.[11]

The regional economy of Ontario was a far from homogenous entity, however, even as late as the 1880s. The closing years of the nineteenth century were something of a struggle for industrial hegemony, in which the small manufacturing unit servicing a local market gave way to the larger productive concern, often contributing toward the decline of the small town and a shift in the location of industry to the population center of a larger city. Thus, the value-added in all manufacturing activity in York County (Toronto) rose from 27.44 percent in 1870 to 32 percent in 1890. Toronto and Hamilton each accounted for 20 percent of industrial employment in southern Ontario in 1881, although they contained only 6.5 percent of the region's population. Even given this increasing specialization, localization, and gross expansion in the manufacturing sector, however, the 1880s were a decade of contrasts: handicraft forms of production still coexisted with thoroughly mechanized processes; the large factory was still the exception rather than the rule.[12]

In Ontario's iron and steel industry, for instance, a small group of large firms – rolling mills, smelting furnaces, machine shops, and agricultural implements works – were overshadowed numerically by the ubiquitous blacksmith's establishment, of which there were 9,423 in 1890. Even in the fairly advanced sector of agricultural implements production, Ontario possessed 141 factories with an average employment of only 23 workers per plant. There were thus more factories manufacturing agricultural machinery in the province than there were in the entire United States, where the rise of International Harvester in these years revealed the drift toward oligopoly. In general, the size of manufacturing units in Ontario in 1881 remained quite small, with fewer than 5 workers per concern. As Spelt has shown, of 27 of the most important industries on the basis of employment, a mere 8 averaged more than 10 workers per shop. Only cotton mills, with 160 workers per unit, and locomotive works, averaging 135 hands in each establishment, were of factory size. Foundries (brass, iron, lead, and machinery), tobacco works, hosiery mills, printing offices, and agricultural implements shops all employed, on an average, between 14 and 23 workers, although specific firms were certainly far larger.[13]

Moreover, the mixed nature of the economy was revealed in the energy sources utilized by Ontario manufacturers throughout the period. The trend was definitely toward the increasing use of steam power, which by the 1880s was all but dominant in boot and shoe production, and the railway and iron works. Coal, increasingly, was used to supply the heat, rather than wood. Still, as late as 1901 the census stated that steam supplied only 60 percent of total mechanical power used in the province's manufacturing, an indication that in some sectors – especially in textiles, pulp and paper, and flour and grist mills – water power retained some importance. Finally, in the lumbering industry, and in the production of lumber products such as shingles, timber refuse was often used to produce the steam heat, thus avoiding dependence on imported coal. Ontario's 1880s, then, experienced industrial development, but in limited ways: there remained specific barriers to overcome, and significant distances to travel, before a mature industrial capitalism, in its monopoly phase, would consolidate in the province.[14]

## Uneven development

How did this process of advancing but uneven development stamp itself upon the character of specific Ontario locales, where the Knights of Labor would come to prominence in the later years of the nineteenth century? As we have already seen, the industrial cities of Toronto and Hamilton led the way. We have commented on the experience of these major centers in other works and will restrict ourselves here to a mere overview.[15] In the case of Toronto, the local economy was paced by the rapid growth of the clothing industry, which was capturing a growing share of the south-central Canadian market in the years from 1870–90. As the largest single center in the province, Toronto understandably led in the production of shoes, dresses, corsets, men's clothing, and fur goods; in shirt manufacture it ranked second. Dominated by small shops dependent upon local sales, the clothing industry could also give rise to firms like the Crompton Corset Company, which as early as 1881 employed 350 persons and gained a share of the national market. Secondary wood products were also important, as was publishing and printing. In the latter, York County's share of the total Ontario–Quebec output rose from 28.45 percent in 1870 to 41.9 percent in 1890. In a relatively insignificant sector, chemicals, we glimpse the increasingly important role of Toronto as a marketing center: 5.46 percent of the industry was located in York County in 1870; by 1890 this had increased to almost one-quarter. Toronto also housed perhaps the most diverse assortment of iron industries of any Ontario city. Several small shops and factories engaged in specialized, precision-production manufacture, turning out scales, printers' type, and instruments; larger works tended to concentrate on agricultural implements, iron castings and machines, and engines. Massey's, which by 1881 employed 200 men and was served by two private railway sidings connected to the downtown yards, dominated this productive sphere.

Hamilton was perhaps Toronto's most significant rival in this iron and steel sector, and the lack of technological innovation in this sphere in the period allowed the smaller city to retain much of its specialized strength in particular traditional realms of primary iron and steel production and metal fabrication. The Hamilton Rolling Mill Company was southern Ontario's only large producer of primary shapes, and the city also led the province in the production of assorted machinery, iron castings, and sewing machines. As headquarters of the Great Western Railway (GWR), Hamilton in 1881 had attained a unique provincial advantage, and one that greatly stimulated production of locomotives, axles, wheels, and the structural components of railway bridges. The city was also well known as a center of the stove industry, and Hamilton's founders would play a crucial role in uniting their peers across the province in opposition to what they viewed as the pernicious rules and restrictions of output of the Molders' Union. In 1880 iron and steel products accounted for 30.16 percent of all value-added by manufacturing in the county of Wentworth.

Beyond the boundaries of these reasonably well-studied industrial cities lies a virtual no-man's-land, where our knowledge of economic activity is severely restricted. And yet it is clear that in countless Ontario communities capitalist development touched the lives of many workers and employers. Linked closely to this process was the importance of railways, which served as a connecting link, integrating a developing home market. The transportation revolution of the mid-to-late nineteenth century (see Map 2) was perhaps the key element in the shifting location and expansion of manufacturing in these years from 1870–90.[16]

Most of the railways built in southern Ontario after 1881 radiated out from Toronto, further contributing to that city's metropolitan dominance. Eastern Ontario experienced significant railway expansion in the 1880s, a line being constructed from Toronto to Montreal via Peterborough; rail communications were established among Kingston, Belleville, Napanee, and Trenton. Points to the north were also drawn into the connective grid, and Smiths Falls became an eastern divisional point of the Canadian Pacific Railway (CPR) in 1885. But more significant, perhaps, was the rising importance of the old established lines in western Ontario – the Grand Trunk Railway (GTR), Great Western, and Canada Southern – which received great stimulus as the CPR and GTR battled for control of the country's rail lines. In this struggle for hegemony local traffic was actively sought, mileage was expanded, and efforts were made to capture a greater share of the American through traffic. Centers such as St. Thomas and Stratford became links in a chain of economic development, and their wage-earning class was often tied directly to the shops that served the railways or the rail systems themselves. As one Stratford machinist noted in 1890, "the rise and fall of this city depends upon the Grand Trunk," and indeed it did, for the GTR shops employed some 700 workers, many of them highly skilled. In Elgin East (St. Thomas), for instance, there were two car and locomotive works in 1881, employing 158 hands; by 1891 two establishments designated as producers of rolling stock employed 378 male workers. The city had in fact grown rapidly in the 1870s, being transformed from a modest preindustrial service town to a dynamic railway center linked to the major Ontario metropolitan markets. Major shops of the American-owned Canada Southern Railway located there, employing about 700 men by the mid-1880s, and the GWR established a repair shop in the city. By 1885 the New York Central had also commenced similar operations. Because of this rapid growth the city's class boundaries were rigid and geographically specific: the town was divided into quadrants by the various rail lines and the workers lived in the eastern sections.[17]

The railways, through declining freight rates and economies of scale,

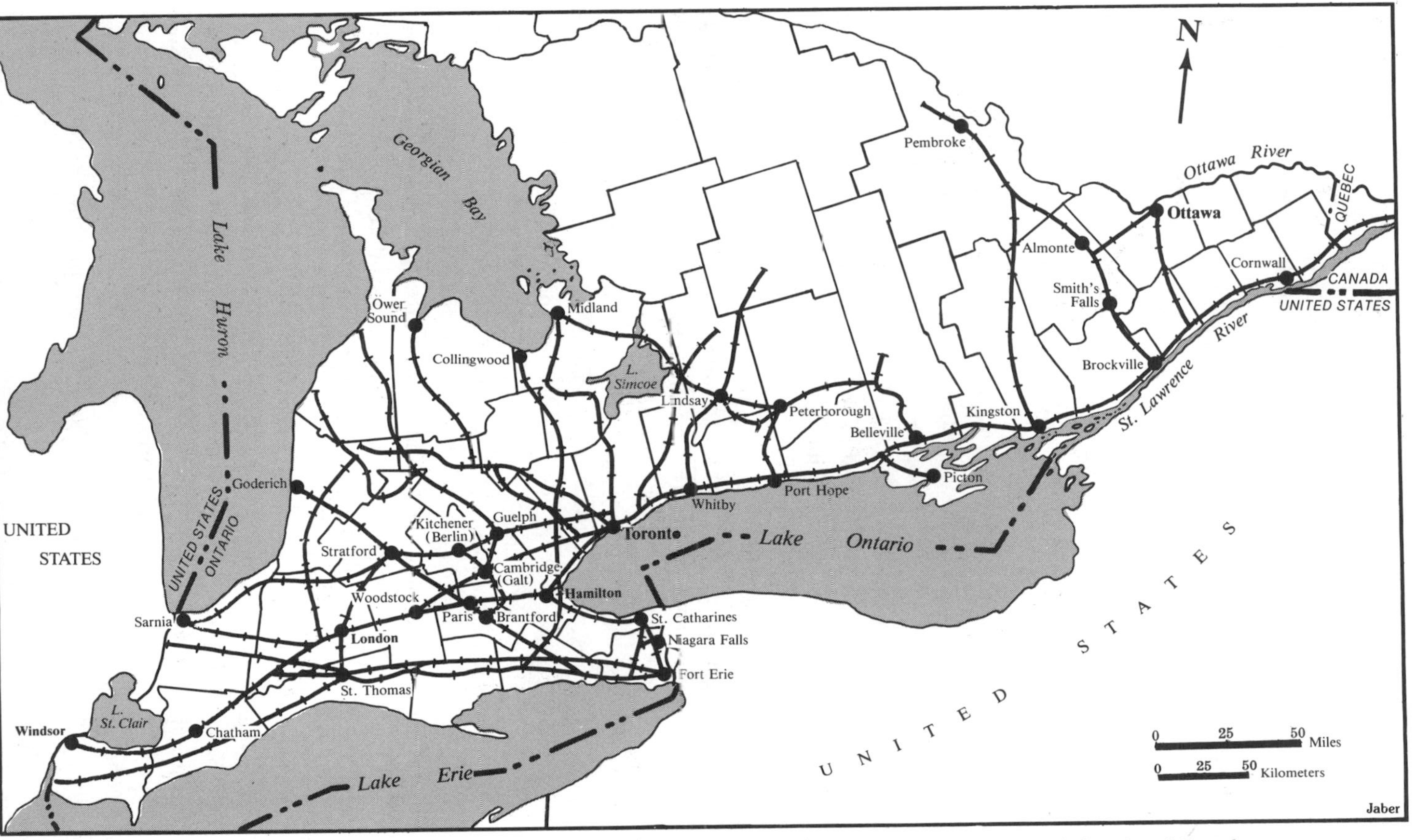


Map 2. Railways in southern Ontario, 1881. *Source:* D. G. G. Kerr, *An Historical Atlas of Canada*.

helped to concentrate economic activity in a number of diversified manufacturing centers, whose growth took place at the expense of the smaller towns where factories were insufficiently developed to capitalize on transport costs compared to their larger, better-situated rivals. London was just such a place. Its strength seemed to reside disproportionately in the food-processing sector, with concentrations of capital in bakeries, breweries, and tobacco-related works. On the eve of the 1880s it had "gained a nationwide reputation as a five-cent cigar manufacturing centre," while Toronto and London, with fourteen of the province's eighty-two breweries, produced well over 50 percent of all the beer by value in southern Ontario. Here the level of production was most decidedly limited by the extent of the market, for brewers had to rely on natural ice to cool their product, which in a prerefrigeration age could not be shipped any great distance. Nevertheless, both Labatt's and Carling's managed to corner an ever-growing share of the Ontario market, which led the latter to expand into the United States in the late 1870s and to Ottawa, Hamilton, and Montreal in the 1880s.[18] Middlesex county produced tobacco goods accounting for 10.07 percent of the total value-added in this sector in Ontario and Quebec in 1880, trailing only Montreal (48.42 percent) and Toronto (17.39 percent). Foods and beverages in the secondary manufacturing sphere, meanwhile, contributed 12.47 percent of the total value-added by manufacturing in the county in 1880, and 12.99 percent in 1890. But the city also gained prominence as a marketing and distributing center for the dairy belt of western Ontario's Middlesex, Oxford, Elgin, Lambton, Perth, and Huron counties. In the textile sphere, the city's garment industry grew on the basis of its proximity to the Niagara Peninsula's cotton mills. Finally, in the wood-processing sector, concerns like the London Furniture Company employed 150 men, while in metal fabricating the city's McClary Manufacturing Company, Ontario Car Works, and E. Leonard & Sons produced stoves, engines, and other goods. These latter firms employed between 80 and 450 hands throughout the decade of the 1880s. Although clearly operating in the shadow of similar businesses in Toronto and Hamilton, such London establishments all benefited from access to trunk railway lines and could penetrate distant markets cheaply.[19]

Other western Ontario towns also exhibited indications of the importance of industrial activity. Brantford's economic place in late-nineteenth-century Ontario was dominated by the Harris (1871), Wisner, and Cockshutt (1877) agricultural implements companies, and a hosiery factory. Harris & Son, taken together with the Massey works of Toronto (and with which it would merge in 1891), accounted for 60 percent of all agricultural implement sales in the Dominion by the mid-1880s. No doubt the presence of this firm explains the impressive place of iron and steel products in Brant county's figures of value-added by manufacturing: 30.89 percent in 1880; 35.29 percent in 1890. Guelph, Galt, Berlin, Hespeler, and even Collingwood to the north all housed similar, if much smaller, manufacturing concerns, producing for local, even regional, markets. Small meat packers and distilleries were among these, as were modestly sized woolen mills, concentrated in Waterloo county, employing an average of thirteen workers each and driven by water power. Small-scale metal fabricating shops, with their origins in blacksmithing, and often devoted to the production of ploughs and other agricultural implements, located readily in the western Ontario region, attracted by the easy access to both the national and local markets. The largest plough manufacturer in the country was, for a time, located in Exeter, north of London, while Ingersoll (1856), Paris (1864), and Sarnia were other such sites. The latter two towns, in particular, were designated "town tariff" points in 1874, and thus received low competitive railway rates that put them in a position of advantage over other locales where standard mileage tariffs prevailed. Foundries dominated the economy of Galt, a town known as "the Manchester of Canada," and three iron-working establishments were functioning as early as 1857. In Guelph a hosiery factory employing over 100 workers, the Raymond Sewing Machine Company (160 employees), the Guelph Sewing Machine Company, and the Crowe Iron Works dominated the industrial landscape. In addition, the Bell Piano and Organ Company employed over 100 hands and shipped its products throughout the British empire. Berlin, a center of German immigrants, was well known for its button, garment, and furniture industries.[20]

In the Niagara Peninsula St. Catharines had taken advantage of the building of the Welland Canal in the 1820s and 1830s to displace Niagara as the major urban center. St. Catharines enjoyed a mixed industrial base with foundries, shipbuilding, axe making, and the production of wheels providing the foundation of local economic life. Other industrial towns also developed along the canal, taking advantage of its water and water power. Chippewa had one of the largest foundries in the country in the years after mid-century, while Beamsville was the location of the important Gibson quarries, which employed larger numbers of skilled stonecutters whose product was shipped throughout Ontario. Thorold and Merritton both contained major cotton mills. The latter town was the site of the Lybster Cotton Company, the oldest mill in Ontario, established in 1860 with Toronto capital.[21] By 1879 it was said to be running at its "fullest capacity in order to supply the demand . . . and to keep up with . . . contracts." With an average of approximately 160 employees per mill, the cotton textile industry was an early

Table 1.3. *Cotton mills in Ontario, 1883–92*

| | | 1883 | | 1892 | |
|---|---|---|---|---|---|
| Name of mill | Location | No. looms | No. spindles | No. looms | No. spindles |
| Canada (1872) | Cornwall | 1000 | 45,000 | 812 | 50,000 |
| Stormont (1879) | Cornwall | 550 | 26,000 | 650 | 27,000 |
| Kingston | Kingston | 300 | 14,000 | 300 | 11,000 |
| Dundas (1862) | Dundas | 450 | 20,500 | 508 | 16,300 |
| Hamilton (1882) | Hamilton | 250 | 12,000 | 65 | 6,000 |
| Ontario (1882) | Hamilton | 250 | 11,500 | 362 | 12,000 |
| Lybster (1860) | Merritton | 300 | 14,000 | 260 | 12,000 |
| Thorold | Thorold | 300 | 14,000 | | |
| Craven (1880) | Brantford | 300 | 14,000 | 270 | 10,000 |
| Merritton (1884) | Merritton | | | 248 | 12,000 |
| Cornwall (1885) | Cornwall | | | n.k. | n.k. |

*Source:* 1883: *Dominion Annual Register and Review*, 1883, p. 346. 1892: *Monetary Times*, 9 September 1892, pp. 277–9. (Our thanks to Peter DeLottinville.)

case of unambiguously large-scale factory production, demanding access to a sufficient supply of labor (see Table 1.3). It was claimed in 1885 that thirteen of the seventeen mills in the province had been started after 1878, that employment had increased 210 percent, and that wages had risen from $202.79 annually to $210.28.[22]

Further to the north and to the east industrial production was less well established, particularly in the area of secondary manufacturing. By the 1880s the Ottawa-Hull and Muskoka regions had secured hegemony over the production of wood products, and a number of mills engaged in the preparation of sawn lumber, shingles, and matches. In 1881 over 800 adults and 64 children worked in Muskoka's seventy-four mills, earning yearly about $775,000. One local historian in the 1930s recorded that in the 1880s "the shantyman was king" and that mills dominated the economy of Owen Sound, Collingwood, Penetanguishene, Parry Sound, Midland, Sturgeon Bay, and Waubashene.[23] Refining and processing the wood products of this region probably spilled over into southern towns like Lindsay and Uxbridge, where a number of sawmills were located. The dominance of lumber was even more pronounced in the Ottawa valley, where the five largest producers in Canada had congregated by 1874. Over 2,500 men were employed in the production of lumber in 1891 in the city of Ottawa alone, and the industry found market outlets in both Britain and the United States. Primary wood products accounted for 30.03 percent of all value-added by manufacturing in

Carleton County in 1880, while secondary wood products contributed a further 3.63 percent.

East of Toronto, along the St. Lawrence River and Lake Ontario, small-scale processing industries and metal fabricating plants attempted to capture a share of a largely local market. Small centers like Trenton and Deseronto clung desperately to their earlier status as major sawmilling and lumber-exporting points, but by the 1880s the heyday of the old timber trade had passed, and with it their prominence. In the larger regional towns, however, there was room for some consolidation. Gananoque ("the Birmingham of Eastern Ontario"),[24] Brockville, Cobourg, Belleville, Smiths Falls, Oshawa, and Kingston all had the ubiquitous foundries, machine shops, and agricultural implements works of the period. G. M. Cossitt & Brothers and Frost & Wood Company established significant agricultural-implements factories in Smiths Falls, the latter company employing over 150 skilled hands, producing goods valued at $150,000 destined for the farms of Canada, Australia, and South Africa. Kingston's large locomotive works employed over 350 workers throughout the early 1880s, and a cotton mill with approximately 200 hands opened in 1882. In the southern section of Ontario County, Oshawa-Cedardale was dominated by the Joseph Hall Works. Concentrating on the production of threshing machines, mowers, and ploughs for the Canadian market, the works employed 250 men as early as 1867. By the 1880s other important shops had long established histories: the McLaughlin carriage works, Masson's seed-drill plant, A. S. Whiting Agricultural Implements, Oshawa Stove Company, W. T. Dingle's Fanning Mills and Seeders, and the Robson & Lauchland Tanneries. The area's six agricultural-implement producers employed 405 hands in 1881, creating products valued at $602,500.[25]

But the most dramatic expression of industrial growth in eastern Ontario was Cornwall's cotton mills. Here was one city where the National Policy tariff of 30–5 percent was never challenged. In 1876 Cornwall's Canada Company Cotton mills were the largest in the nation, the value of the plant hovering near the half million dollar mark, the annual product valued at $400,000. Approximately 350 workers (100 males and 250 females) toiled over 20,000 spindles to earn yearly wages of $75,000. American competition, in the midst of the poor economic conditions of the mid-1870s, was severe, and the company had been forced to implement a series of price cuts. The Americans had many advantages, not the least of which was that, in the words of the mill manager, "they get more work out of their help than we do, and they have more of it. We have to get extra labor in order to control our help and supply the places of those who are sick or who chose to remain away." "I am getting every pound of it that the machinery was calculated to take out of it," he later replied to one inquiry about the possibility of increasing output. Five years later, protected by the newly revised tariff and stimulated by the return to prosperity, Cornwall's three cotton mills – one was a relatively small firm – employed 133 men, 277 women, 186 boys, and 190 girls. Their yearly wages totaled $179,800 and $456,000 worth of material was used to produce cotton goods and cloth valued at $883,000. By the time another half-decade had passed, Cornwall's two major textile producers—the Canada Company and the Stormont – had made impressive expansionary strides. In 1887, for instance, the Canada Company mills had doubled the number of hands employed in 1876, hiring approximately 700 workers, and wages had increased two-and-one-half times, to $208,000 yearly. (Per capita yearly wages had apparently increased significantly: 1876 [$214]; 1883 [$282]; 1884 [$263]; 1885 [$277]; 1886 [$290]; 1887 [298].) At the Stormont mills there were 288 females and 262 males employed, meaning that over 1,200 workers labored in these two large mills in 1887. Small wonder that textile products produced 67.12 percent of the value-added by manufacturing in Stormont county in 1880 and 58.57 percent in 1890. Even the small woolen mills of Cornwall, employing an average of 43 workers, were nine times larger than the provincial average, set by the backwoods mills of Lanark county, where 869 workers eked out a living in the sixty-five water-powered mills under technically backward, capital-starved conditions. Textiles dominated Cornwall more thoroughly, perhaps, than any other industry in any other Ontario town or city, and 47 percent of all cotton mill workers in the province in 1881 worked in the town's mills, creating a product destined for the Montreal garment industry.[26] (For summaries see Tables 1.4 and 1.5.)

## The working class

Across the province, then, in spite of the increasing dominance of Toronto and Hamilton, of underdevelopment, uneven growth, and reliance upon primary production of the old timber staple in some areas, capitalist production was a force to reckon with by the 1880s. It transformed social and productive relations in the large cities as well as in the tiny rural hamlets. In this changed context class came to the fore as a clearly perceived reality; a culture premised upon this historic relationship of antagonism emerged more forcefully than it had in the past, and old distinctions appeared to fade in the face of a common experience and a recognition of the unity of life and work within a generalized system of appropriation. Railroads began the process of integrating a large regional unit, and linked the province to national if not international markets. Town and country increasingly found themselves enmeshed in a setting in which their pronounced differences began to pale before significant similarities. Social costs were many and varied, from the growing impersonalization of the wage relationship to the sooty environment of iron-and-steel-dominated Hamilton to the stark landscape of the milltown. Workers, of course, did not passively accept such developments, which had necessarily been part of a protracted process, and years well before the 1880s witnessed the first stirrings of Ontario's working-class movement. But to appreciate fully the extent to which the Knights of Labor represented a dramatic upsurge of Ontario workers in the 1880s – a confluence of class and culture – it is necessary to comment briefly on the state of labor organization, labor–capital relations, and the character of working-class culture before the coming of the Order.

Prior to the appearance of the Knights, Ontario workers possessed a long history of resistance, challenge, and organization that reached back to the opening decades of the century. As early as 1815 Captain Owen Edward, commodore of the colony's navy, complained to his superiors of the "vile and disorderly conduct" of the shipwrights sent out from England to labor in the Kingston dockyards. Unions were formed in Upper Canada as early as 1827, with Hamilton and York (Toronto) being centers of printers', foundryworkers', and building trades workers' organizations. The Irish led a series of violent and spontaneous strikes and work stoppages on the canals throughout the 1830s and 1840s. Work discipline – in the ports, shops, and fields of the commercially capitalistic but nevertheless largely agrarian society – was persistently opposed, by all range and manner of workingmen and women. A criminal subculture, often linked to the laboring poor through a complex network of family, neighborhood, work place, or prepolitical class grievance/resentment, drew out the more stridently political force of the law, which proved a cornerstone of Tory ideology and practice in these early years. Thus, popular retribution – in the instance of an arsonist's nighttime revenge – and political insurrection during the rebellion of 1837–8 united Tory factions in demonstrations of "the majesty of the law," which required some "terrible examples" to check any instance of plebeian resistance to authority. The restraints upon workers' organizations established in the conspiracy laws, as well as public executions, were proof enough that "justice dare[d] array herself in terrors when it [was] deemed necessary."[27]

All of this, and much, much more, indicates that Ontario workers were not just passive victims in the hands of Upper Canada's Tory rulers. But such diverse, fragmented, and localized reactions to domination also hinted at the limitations of this experience. For, prior to 1850, Ontario's producing

Table 1.4. *Value-added by manufacturing sectors as percentage of total value-added by manufacturing for selected Ontario counties, 1870–90*

| | | York (Toronto) | Wentworth (Hamilton) | Waterloo | Brant | Wellington | Middlesex (London) | Carleton (Ottawa) | Frontenac (Kingston) | Stormont (Cornwall) |
|---|---|---|---|---|---|---|---|---|---|---|
| Food & beverages (primary) | 1870 | 7.81 | 9.80 | 16.66 | 14.80 | 16.22 | 9.11 | 3.06 | 2.57 | 15.71 |
| | 1880 | 6.89 | 4.49 | 15.02 | 6.40 | 10.69 | 4.48 | 5.40 | 3.76 | 5.11 |
| | 1890 | 3.92 | 5.71 | 9.63 | 7.14 | 13.95 | 10.34 | 14.78 | 4.78 | 8.13 |
| Food & beverages (secondary) | 1870 | 19.76 | 3.89 | 14.24 | 8.62 | 7.79 | 5.17 | 5.17 | 9.02 | 1.87 |
| | 1880 | 10.91 | 4.33 | 6.04 | 4.65 | 7.05 | 12.47 | 4.75 | 4.05 | 1.54 |
| | 1890 | 11.36 | 5.38 | 5.90 | 6.34 | 8.74 | 12.99 | 7.40 | 10.37 | 2.15 |
| Tobacco | 1870 | 1.76 | 1.52 | .71 | .54 | .18 | .17 | .00 | .96 | .00 |
| | 1880 | 2.12 | 2.92 | .24 | 1.36 | .31 | 2.79 | .00 | .87 | .00 |
| | 1890 | 1.33 | 1.76 | .61 | 1.12 | .00 | 4.78 | .00 | .00 | 2.86 |
| Leather | 1870 | 10.64 | 6.93 | 7.31 | 11.15 | 12.30 | 11.45 | 9.25 | 19.27 | 10.22 |
| | 1880 | 7.24 | 5.63 | 5.56 | 6.84 | 7.71 | 5.55 | 7.56 | 11.09 | 3.18 |
| | 1890 | 4.37 | 4.67 | 9.64 | 2.76 | 4.92 | 6.75 | 5.34 | 3.50 | 3.14 |
| Textiles | 1870 | 1.11 | 5.04 | 17.47 | .44 | 4.50 | 2.10 | .92 | 1.49 | 30.38 |
| | 1880 | 2.32 | 6.73 | 17.20 | 4.49 | 6.71 | .80 | 2.66 | 2.63 | 67.12 |
| | 1890 | 4.08 | 6.27 | 14.38 | 15.92 | 9.55 | 2.81 | 1.14 | 11.52 | 58.57 |
| Clothing | 1870 | 10.93 | 8.52 | 3.58 | 12.45 | 6.78 | 4.38 | 9.73 | 8.76 | 1.26 |
| | 1880 | 11.58 | 10.62 | 5.51 | 16.26 | 9.37 | 11.42 | 15.67 | 12.48 | 1.90 |
| | 1890 | 17.69 | 16.09 | 9.19 | 6.82 | 9.48 | 14.75 | 19.75 | 18.09 | 1.45 |
| Wood products (primary) | 1870 | 5.04 | 5.79 | 8.18 | 8.31 | 5.95 | 5.03 | 33.06 | 3.29 | 8.14 |
| | 1880 | 5.45 | 4.09 | 4.59 | 6.39 | 7.63 | 5.26 | 30.03 | 3.54 | 5.41 |
| | 1890 | 4.04 | 2.46 | 3.03 | 4.76 | 7.14 | 6.95 | 11.69 | 5.82 | 6.72 |
| Wood products (secondary) | 1870 | 4.71 | 3.01 | 4.81 | 3.67 | 3.34 | 10.23 | 2.95 | 3.02 | 2.23 |
| | 1880 | 4.25 | 2.42 | 7.83 | 2.84 | 5.70 | 5.05 | 3.63 | 2.07 | .84 |
| | 1890 | 5.62 | 3.76 | 11.07 | 2.39 | 8.91 | 7.50 | 8.30 | 2.17 | 2.16 |

| | | | | | | | | | | |
|---|---|---|---|---|---|---|---|---|---|---|
| Paper | 1870 | 2.08 | 1.02 | .00 | .65 | .00 | .00 | .00 | .00 | .96 |
| | 1880 | 1.60 | 1.40 | .00 | .01 | .02 | 3.12 | 12.37 | 4.19 | .00 |
| | 1890 | 1.32 | .87 | .00 | .51 | .02 | .99 | .00 | .00 | 6.77 |
| Printing & publishing | 1870 | 8.46 | 1.62 | 1.16 | 1.68 | 2.31 | 1.36 | 15.96 | 2.07 | 1.02 |
| | 1880 | 9.85 | 3.87 | .42 | 1.87 | 2.37 | 13.60 | 7.92 | 20.37 | 5.20 |
| | 1890 | 10.22 | 7.33 | .91 | 1.65 | 2.26 | 2.80 | 9.93 | 2.82 | .35 |
| Iron & steel | 1870 | 17.01 | 36.63 | 20.00 | 23.70 | 25.28 | 12.79 | 9.96 | 28.27 | 16.89 |
| | 1880 | 23.74 | 30.16 | 24.78 | 30.89 | 23.61 | 9.00 | 4.40 | 6.77 | 5.42 |
| | 1890 | 15.23 | 22.09 | 23.72 | 35.29 | 16.02 | 15.28 | 9.66 | 17.25 | 5.22 |
| Transportation | 1870 | 2.08 | 1.88 | 3.12 | 5.54 | 6.32 | 6.00 | 4.52 | 7.93 | 1.38 |
| | 1880 | 1.47 | 6.86 | 4.25 | 9.42 | 4.35 | 1.28 | 2.82 | 3.05 | .00 |
| | 1890 | 2.56 | 1.79 | 2.59 | 7.97 | 5.79 | 5.01 | 4.32 | 3.47 | 1.06 |
| Nonferrous metal products | 1870 | 1.86 | .41 | .01 | .14 | .06 | .56 | 2.59 | 1.46 | .00 |
| | 1880 | 3.01 | 5.33 | .81 | .03 | 4.83 | 4.24 | 1.24 | 3.40 | 4.28 |
| | 1890 | 3.02 | 10.10 | .11 | .14 | .44 | .76 | 1.16 | .87 | .01 |
| Nonmetallic mineral products | 1870 | 2.31 | 4.05 | 1.67 | 7.08 | 1.92 | 4.15 | 1.81 | 2.00 | 9.36 |
| | 1880 | 3.08 | 6.41 | 1.34 | 4.82 | 3.62 | 4.24 | 1.24 | 3.40 | 4.28 |
| | 1890 | 5.09 | 6.97 | 1.64 | 2.69 | 3.18 | 3.56 | 4.74 | 3.87 | 1.11 |
| Petroleum & coal | 1870 | .21 | 5.10 | .00 | .36 | 1.13 | 24.69 | .00 | .00 | .00 |
| | 1880 | .00 | .16 | .97 | .21 | .44 | 10.09 | .00 | .12 | .00 |
| | 1890 | .02 | .21 | .00 | .00 | .00 | .80 | .00 | .71 | .00 |
| Chemicals | 1870 | 1.10 | 1.12 | .50 | .78 | .71 | 1.72 | .16 | 4.14 | .57 |
| | 1880 | 2.86 | 2.40 | .51 | 1.18 | .54 | .70 | 1.15 | 13.72 | 1.27 |
| | 1890 | 4.02 | 2.05 | 1.89 | 2.95 | .62 | 2.91 | 1.38 | 3.51 | .12 |
| Rubber | 1870 | .06 | .00 | .00 | .00 | .00 | .00 | .00 | .00 | .00 |
| | 1880 | .00 | .00 | .00 | .00 | .00 | .00 | .00 | .00 | .00 |
| | 1890 | .80 | .17 | .00 | .00 | .00 | .01 | .00 | .00 | .00 |
| Miscellaneous | 1870 | 3.06 | 3.66 | .55 | .14 | 5.23 | 1.10 | .72 | 5.74 | .00 |
| | 1880 | 3.64 | 2.18 | 4.91 | 2.33 | 5.04 | 1.00 | .35 | 7.90 | .00 |
| | 1890 | 4.22 | 2.49 | 2.35 | 1.54 | 8.96 | 1.01 | .41 | 11.24 | .14 |

*Source:* Chambers and Bertram, "Urbanization and Manufacturing," pp. 241–55.

Table 1.5. *Manufacturing activity in selected sectors by city/county, 1881 and 1891*

| Industry | Year | Establishments | Hands | Yearly wages ($) | Value of material ($) | Value of product ($) | Value-added ($) | City/county |
|---|---|---|---|---|---|---|---|---|
| Agricultural implements | 1881 | 2 | 113 | 39,969 | 59,078 | 147,500 | 88,422 | Brockville |
| | 1891 | 4 | 159 | 52,750 | 75,900 | 187,500 | 111,600 | |
| | 1881 | 2 | 80 | 27,000 | 80,000 | 135,000 | 50,000 | Brant North |
| | 1891 | 1 | 20 | 7,500 | 48,000 | 50,000 | 10,000 | |
| | 1881 | 2 | 92 | 24,000 | 60,000 | 95,000 | 35,000 | Brant South |
| | 1891 | 6 | 794 | 345,545 | 467,390 | 1,159,785 | 692,395 | |
| | 1881 | 6 | 405 | 149,600 | 175,000 | 602,500 | 427,500 | Ontario South |
| | 1891 | 7 | 155 | 62,000 | 118,793 | 304,150 | 185,357 | |
| | 1881 | 4 | 118 | 39,053 | 86,650 | 147,400 | 60,850 | Waterloo South |
| | 1891 | 5 | 162 | 46,060 | 85,275 | 224,275 | 139,000 | |
| | 1881 | 12 | 129 | 49,150 | 34,950 | 104,950 | 70,000 | Wellington South |
| | 1891 | 8 | 98 | 47,200 | 80,687 | 167,300 | 86,613 | |
| Bakeries & confectioneries | 1881 | 12 | 257 | 79,198 | 436,770 | 564,980 | 128,210 | London |
| | 1891 | 18 | 462 | 109,622 | 485,377 | 710,330 | 224,953 | |
| Boots & shoes | 1881 | 76 | 1232 | 345,343 | 705,600 | 1,290,393 | 584,792 | Toronto |
| | 1891 | 149 | 742 | 316,812 | 575,280 | 1,156,894 | 581,609 | |
| | 1881 | 37 | 345 | 97,959 | 146,110 | 282,130 | 136,020 | Hamilton |
| | 1891 | 71 | 357 | 122,837 | 385,023 | 574,715 | 189,692 | |
| Breweries | 1881 | 10 | 220 | 94,273 | 443,488 | 1,077,500 | 634,012 | Toronto |
| | 1891 | 9 | 400 | 209,400 | 768,300 | 1,395,403 | 626,903 | |
| | 1881 | 5 | 118 | 41,328 | 267,500 | 718,000 | 450,500 | London |
| | 1891 | 3 | 126 | 67,760 | 180,120 | 533,000 | 352,880 | |
| Car & locomotive (or re 1891 classification: rolling stock) | 1881 | 2 | 464 | 217,154 | 70,349 | 287,503 | 217,154 | Hamilton |
| | 1891 | – | – | – | – | – | – | |
| | 1881 | 1 | 200 | 82,402 | 106,446 | 188,848 | 82,402 | Brant |
| | 1891 | – | – | – | – | – | – | |
| | 1881 | 2 | 158 | 25,641 | 172,031 | 253,673 | 81,642 | Elgin East |

| | | | | | | | | |
|---|---|---|---|---|---|---|---|---|
| | 1891 | 2 | 378 | 184,042 | 289,429 | 509,471 | 220,062 | Middlesex East |
| | 1881 | 3 | 495 | 193,663 | 437,000 | 652,478 | 215,478 | |
| | 1891 | 2 | 34 | 16,000 | 19,000 | 52,000 | 33,000 | Cornwall |
| Cotton mills | 1881 | 3 | 736 | 179,800 | 456,000 | 883,000 | 427,000 | |
| | 1891 | 2 | 1191 | 372,172 | 656,000 | 1,310,892 | 654,892 | Lincoln & Niagara |
| | 1881 | 3 | 329 | 56,600 | 200,600 | 376,800 | 176,200 | |
| | 1891 | 2 | 280 | 63,000 | 101,100 | 194,400 | 93,300 | Wentworth |
| | 1881 | 3 | 514 | 144,500 | 339,000 | 613,000 | 274,000 | |
| | 1891 | 2 | 534 | 142,000 | 251,000 | 575,000 | 324,000 | Kingston |
| | 1881 | – | – | – | – | – | – | |
| | 1891 | 1 | 210 | 52,000 | 125,000 | 275,000 | 150,000 | Toronto |
| Dressmaking | 1881 | 72 | 483 | 69,426 | 133,435 | 284,286 | 150,081 | |
| | 1891 | 402 | 1677 | 327,027 | 673,858 | 1,486,952 | 813,094 | Brockville |
| Foundries | 1881 | 3 | 237 | 84,400 | 75,500 | 222,000 | 156,500 | |
| | 1891 | 3 | 241 | 92,200 | 76,000 | 213,000 | 137,000 | Hamilton |
| | 1881 | 28 | 973 | 398,220 | 664,950 | 1,361,540 | 696,590 | |
| | 1891 | 19 | 656 | 303,816 | 492,130 | 965,050 | 472,920 | London |
| | 1881 | 15 | 422 | 168,447 | 217,200 | 567,000 | 249,800 | |
| | 1891 | 13 | 600 | 216,532 | 311,500 | 673,900 | 362,400 | Toronto |
| Printing & | 1881 | 32 | 1233 | 457,984 | 474,303 | 1,223,445 | 759,142 | |
| publishing | 1891 | 74 | 2384 | 1,059,600 | 1,293,607 | 3,094,084 | 1,800,477 | Hamilton |
| Sewing machine | 1881 | 3 | 348 | 129,198 | 107,102 | 301,236 | 194,134 | |
| factories | 1891 | 2 | 201 | 20,400 | 50,030 | 80,500 | 30,470 | Wellington South |
| | 1881 | 2 | 253 | 85,890 | 62,870 | 212,660 | 49,790 | |
| | 1891 | 1 | 162 | 80,000 | 43,538 | 142,550 | 99,012 | Ottawa |
| Shinglesaw mills | 1881 | 5 | 1495 | 389,340 | 1,348,340 | 1,866,315 | 517,830 | |
| | 1891 | 5 | 2676 | 535,000 | 1,981,000 | 2,795,000 | 1,186,000 | Muskoka |
| | 1881 | 74 | 876 | 201,088 | 362,985 | 767,852 | 404,867 | |
| | 1891 | 80 | 1656 | 529,767 | 936,057 | 1,899,960 | 963,903 | Victoria North |
| | 1881 | 31 | 387 | 66,502 | 127,963 | 260,322 | 132,359 | |
| | 1891 | 28 | 245 | 32,007 | 52,703 | 122,628 | 69,925 | Ontario North |
| | 1881 | 40 | 446 | 101,195 | 223,780 | 468,670 | 244,890 | |
| | 1891 | 57 | 528 | 126,981 | 234,085 | 469,000 | 234,915 | |

Table 1.5. (*cont.*)

| Industry | Year | Establishments | Hands | Yearly wages ($) | Value of material ($) | Value of product ($) | Value-added ($) | City/county |
|---|---|---|---|---|---|---|---|---|
| Rolling mills | 1881 | 1 | 225 | 100,000 | 250,000 | 400,000 | 150,000 | Hamilton |
| | 1891 | – | – | – | – | – | – | |
| Tailors & clothiers | 1881 | 61 | 1503 | 349,077 | 849,907 | 1,549,514 | 745,607 | Toronto |
| | 1891 | 216 | 2654 | 839,250 | 1,539,725 | 3,172,355 | 1,632,630 | |
| | 1881 | 31 | 430 | 138,330 | 325,475 | 590,510 | 265,035 | Hamilton |
| | 1891 | 268 | 1145 | 412,772 | 1,194,060 | 2,028,633 | 834,573 | |
| Tobacco | 1881 | 8 | 177 | 38,918 | 53,500 | 195,000 | 141,500 | London |
| | 1891 | 12 | 471 | 123,160 | 169,832 | 466,781 | 276,949 | |
| | 1881 | 8 | 289 | 85,400 | 191,300 | 329,150 | 137,850 | Hamilton |
| | 1891 | 12 | 330 | 77,750 | 175,000 | 312,430 | 137,430 | |

*Source:* Canada, *Census*, 1881 and 1891.

classes had little conception of unity, little awareness of their place in a class society, as a *class*. Rather, they were part of a broad amalgam of useful producers that the ruling elite regarded as a horizontal sort of beast, and a dangerous one at that. Inside that beast, however, among the producers themselves, the animal was carved up into discrete entities: the rough and the respectable; the Irish and the Scots; the printers and the carpenters; the apprentices, journeymen, and masters. Each of these diverse sectoral interests saw themselves as a group apart, not only from the ruling elite, but from each other. Even among specific groups distinctions could be drawn: among the Irish Catholics, Munster and Connaught battled for jobs; shoemakers from York, Kingston, or Toronto identified with their locale rather than their trade. Such specific identifications were a denial of the unifying effect of group culture, and particular strata thus reacted to the more coherent (if also fragmented and division-ridden) rule of the elite in many ways: by mockery, by deference, by evasion, or by violent or reasoned opposition. Much of this is speculative. But what seems reasonably clear is that the producing classes posed a threat (and early forms of class conflict were a part of this) to the ruling elite at the same time that they were essentially impotent.

Such a conception of the early history of Ontario workers raises many interpretive questions, not the least of which are those that revolve around the issues of culture and hegemony. Put simply, we are arguing that the culture of the producing classes, in this period, was a culture that was understandably inhibited in its capacity to resist. If culture can be at all related to the process of opposition, it must be a culture that is embedded within specific productive relations and forms of appropriation that are common, that are perceived as common, and that are, finally, understood as antagonistic, pitting class against class. Because the commercial capitalism of early Ontario had not yet generated this kind of experience, a culture capable of welding early workers together against the dominant class was thus not a possibility. Instead, forms of paternalism mediated class antagonisms, the upwardly mobile artisan defied any notion of a rigidly established class structure, and the rough and the respectable parted company in the kinds of work they did, the character of their family life, and the ways in which they spent their leisure hours. Lower-class behavior, as a whole, seemed dramatically cut off from the established culture of many local elites at the same time that it remained and operated on the turf of those privileged groups. In terms employed recently by Gerald Sider in an analysis of the Newfoundland village fisheries, the producing classes of Upper Canada lacked class consciousness and an alternative hegemony, but they did generate a series of counter-hegemonic cultural forms, an arsenal of symbols, rituals, customs, traditions, and practices that expressed experiences and claims different from those of the elite. The basic limitation of such counter-hegemonic practices lay, not in the use of borrowed symbols and customary behavior, but in the fragmented character of social relations in the political economy of Upper Canada.[28]

This began to change in the 1840s and 1850s, as the increasing sway of capital transformed social, economic, and cultural relations. As we have already noted, the first Canadian railway boom of the early 1850s went far toward producing an integrated home market, the first large-scale mechanized manufactories, and a bourgeois commitment to a strategy of industrial development for the Canadas. Such happenings had noticeable repercussions in the realm of social relations, culminating in the first sustained wave of economistic working-class resistance, what contemporaries referred to as "an insurrection of labor." To be sure, there were many hangovers from an earlier period, in both the form and the content of the class confrontations of the 1850s and in the culture of the working people. No doubt many customary forms of behavior remained, and certainly many of the characteristic divisions retained significance, notably in the distinction between skilled and unskilled. But there were also signs of change. Rather than fragmentation, the 1853–4 upheaval hinted at the beginnings of class consolidation and the possibility of a wider cultural unity among workers. Across the province diverse trade groupings faced similar situations and a common context: they were drawn into a general "wages movement" that saw at least forty strikes involving bricklayers, tailors, shoemakers, printers, bakers, tinsmiths, stonecutters, and masons. Occasionally laborers participated in these battles, although the unskilled waged their job actions in the depressed years after 1855, when navvies led a series of work stoppages on the railways, protesting contractors' failures to meet their payroll obligations. The Irish, once isolated on the margins of working-class life, were now better integrated into this newly developing culture of resistance. We know so little about the cultural realm – leisure activities, pub life, family and kinship, etc. – that it would be foolhardy to speculate recklessly here. Our major point is that an experience that had turned solely on a diverse and often contradictory set of counter-hegemonic cultural forms in the pre-1850 period now encompassed the beginnings, however primitive and incomplete, of what we can readily recognize as a working class pitted against an employing and owning class. While we can speak most emphatically of culture*s* in the years prior to mid-century, the 1850s thus see the initial stages of the breakdown of those pluralities and a movement toward limited forms that hint at the impact of developing social relations of production, in which the common, rather than the fragmented, features of work and everyday life assumed great importance.[29]

Figure 1. The nine-hour men, Hamilton, 1872. *Source: Canadian Illustrated News*, 8 June 1872.

This process continued throughout the 1860s and 1870s and was revealed in the institutional development of the international craft union. Until 1853 most if not all Canadian unions were largely local affairs. Shoemakers' unions were established in Toronto and Hamilton in 1858, but quickly disappeared, and the actual beginning of North American unions in Ontario dates from 1859. Led by the molders, which established Locals in Toronto, Hamilton, London, and Brantford, trade unions expanded quickly throughout the 1860s: railway workers, printers, shoemakers, carpenters and joiners, coopers, machinists and blacksmiths, bricklayers, and cigarmakers also all had Ontario-based trade organizations. The Knights of St. Crispin established at least 19 lodges in the province in the late 1860s and early 1870s. In 1903, when the *Labour Gazette* studied the origins of contemporary trade unions in the province it found that 1 was formed in the 1840s, 3 in the 1850s, 13 in the 1860s, and 18 in the economically depressed years of the 1870s. Moreover, the emergence of such unions was often followed by the establishment of city-based trades assemblies or councils: Hamilton (1863),

Toronto (1871), Ottawa (1872), and St. Catharines (1875) all had such bodies.[30]

Such institutional development reflected the increasing presence of class, testifying to the significance of a defensive posture in the face of employers' persistent efforts to appropriate an increasing share of the product of labor. This led, as well, to the union effort to control production, as firm lines were drawn beyond which capital could not go if it wished to maintain output and reasonably cordial relations with skilled workers possessing a well-developed sense of what was just and fair. Thus the rise of the trade union was more than a mere economistic development, and it contributed to a world-view that set worker against boss, producer against monopolist, and labor against capital.[31]

To see the union, then, through the lens of John R. Commons, as a mere marketplace phenomenon, would be to misinterpret a crucial development. As David Montgomery has noted in another context, a culture does not float on air, and the emergence of the union is a central moment in the historical evolution of the working class and its culture.[32] To divorce the union from such aspects of everyday life as the family and leisure, on the grounds that one is an economistic and institutional development, the other a facet of culture, is folly.

Our contention, then, is that the mid-period of the nineteenth century (1850–80) saw the beginnings of a transformation in the character of class and culture. As industrial capital established the material forces of production along lines that we associate with modern industry, class became a recognizable reality for Ontario workers. This historical development conditioned a cultural consolidation, as the counter-hegemonic forms of the pre-1850 years inched toward a limited, but discernible, alternative hegemony built around more sustained and broadly based moments of resistance and class institutions. This process never ran its course, and was held back by many of the same inhibitions that had divided the producing classes of the earlier period. Divisions between skilled and unskilled, local attachments, links to intermediate strata (small owners, merchants, petty producers), and the astute efforts of segments of the bourgeoisie to accommodate the insurgent working class insured that this class remained a weakened voice of opposition. In the cultural realm, understandably, these are years in which two ways of life are pitted against each other at the same time that they were mediated by nonclass-based alignments. The family may have been one such realm, although we know too little about it to speculate with any degree of assuredness. Associational life, certainly, was part of the process, as fire companies, sporting associations, friendly societies, and institutions of self-help drew workers to their activities. Such nurseries of the industrious classes were often, although not always, dominated by pillars of the community; yet they were also susceptible to being turned to working-class purpose. Domination did not necessarily culminate in the total control of the life of the laborer. And so this period, in terms of class and culture, stands as one of essential ambivalence, in which class is emerging and culture consolidating, but all within the context of limitation. The growth of trade unions in these years was part of this, and by 1880 Canada as a whole possessed fifty-three international unions and a number of purely local or provincial bodies. Ontario had the majority of such organizations.[33]

The strengths as well as the weaknesses of this transition period were revealed starkly in 1872, as Ontario workers mounted an unprecedented struggle to secure the nine-hour day. As a major confrontation that raised to social prominence all the contradictions of the social relations of the time, the events of 1872 indicated how far along the road of antagonism labor and capital had proceeded. Yet, for all the clarity with which such contradictory class relations were posed the struggle for the shorter working day succumbed to the class manipulations of Sir John A. Macdonald and his Tory supporters. In the end, it was Tory hegemony, rather than working-class autonomy, solidarity, and alternative, that emerged the victor. The Nine Hour Leagues, the Canadian Labor Union, the massive involvement of many ranks of skilled workers in a struggle for common betterment all collapsed as the economy dipped into a major depression and workers' interests were subordinated to the political machinations of an elite. By 1879 it appeared that there was little in the way of class opposition to the rising Canadian bourgeoisie, snuggling up to the national interest with its policy of transcontinental railways, industrial development, and settlement of the West. An alternative hegemony, one that had appeared as a possibility in 1872, seemed nowhere to be seen.[34]

But class and cultural forces that have been silenced or are in retreat are not always without meaning, nor are they incapable of being put to use in a new context. The 1880s would witness essential changes, as a working class arrived on the scene, forcefully and unambiguously, for the first time. This class, which had been more than fifty years in the making, and had at its back a culture of ambiguity and diversity, became unmistakably entwined with the rise of the Knights of Labor, a body which took the ambivalence of the past cultural context of working-class life and forced it into a movement culture of opposition. In the expanding economic context of the 1880s Ontario workers made strides toward unifying their lives as productive men and women and their lives as citizens, family members, neighbors, and advocates of change. A whole series of cultural expressions thus linked up with a class content, and the fragmented and sectional concerns gave way to broader demands that encompassed fundamental challenges to the established order of capitalist society. In whatever area one wants to consider – economic, social, political, cultural – the Noble and Holy Order of the Knights of Labor voiced the need to go beyond the existing social relations of production. An alternative hegemony was finally on the agenda, finally in the process of formation.

The significance of the 1880s, as this moment of reaching out, was further confirmed by the gains in organization among workers not necessarily affiliated with the Knights, an expansion in the ranks of organized labor that nevertheless linked up with the Order in many trades and Locals. These years, for instance, saw tremendous growth in unions, and by 1890 Ontario led all of Canada with 146 Locals in 35 centers. Of the 430 unions in the province in 1903, 54 were formed in the 1880s.[35] One of the leading international unions of the decade was the Iron Molders' International Union (IMIU), which built upon the foundations of the 1850s, 1860s, and 1870s to sustain strong Locals in Hamilton (No. 26) and Toronto (No. 28) and, after 1887, an Ontario-wide District organization. The relationship between the IMIU and the Knights cannot be plotted with mathematical certainty, but in Brantford (Standard LA 3811), Hamilton (Library LA 1864), Kingston (Frontenac LA 10539), and Oshawa (Tylors LA 4279) there existed trade assemblies identified as Locals of molders. In addition, we know from scattered sources that Toronto (Maple Leaf LA 2622), Brockville (Franklin LA 2311), Smiths Falls (LA 6722), Lindsay (LA 5402), and Oshawa (Aetna LA 2355 and LA 4428) all contained molders and other metal workers as well. Finally we have considerable reason to suspect that Cobourg (LA 2598), Toronto (LA 5254 and LA 5650), Woodstock (LA 3151 and LA 4992), Galt (LA 6112), and Peterborough (LA 6952) might also have had molder members. The lines between the craft unions and the Knights of Labor were thus never drawn as sharply in reality as they have been by historians subsequently, at least not in the Ontario of the 1880s.[36]

In the history of Canadian labor, then, the 1880s are an extremely important moment, marked by significant expansions in the unionized sector. But this growth, however significant, did not occur in a vacuum, and paled in comparison, quantitatively and qualitatively, to the rise of the Knights of Labor. Chapter 2 will delineate the contours of this remarkable labor upsurge, and plot the Ontario dimensions of what is often referred to in American historiography as the Great Upheaval.[37]

# 2. "Warp, woof, and web": The structure of the Knights of Labor in Ontario

T. V. Powderly issued two warnings to those of us who would write the history of the Knights of Labor:

> To write the history of the Knights of Labor is an impossibility. Its history was the history of the day in which it moved and did its work. I am aware that some young men fresh from college have tried to write the history of the organization but they failed. They applied logic and scientific research; they divided the emotions, the passions, and feelings of the members into groups; they dissected and vivisected the groups; they used logarithms, algebraic formulas, and everything known to the young ambitious graduate of a university.

> It does not do, therefore, to take the historian too seriously; at best he but weaves the warp of fancy into the woof of fact and gives us the web called history.

Powderly, the egotistical and eloquent GMW of the Order, managed to write two histories of the Knights himself, in spite of his own injunction. Having noted Powderly's concern, we will not ignore "the emotions, the passions, and feelings," for without them the Noble and Holy Order would remain incomprehensible. However, in this chapter we will also "dissect and vivisect," beginning not with logarithms or formulas, but with plenty of numbers. After all, that, too, was part of "the history of the day in which it moved and did its work."[1]

The Noble and Holy Order of the Knights of Labor, founded in Philadelphia in 1869, was Canada's most important labor organization before 1900. The Knights' greatest success, predictably, came in Ontario, Canada's industrial heartland. But the Order's success was national in scope with significant concentrations of strength in Quebec, Manitoba, and British Columbia. Although weaker in numbers, the Order also established Local Assemblies (LAs) in Nova Scotia, New Brunswick, and the Northwest Territories (later Alberta). Throughout Canada the Order organized at least 450 LAs and 12 District Assemblies (DAs), making it far and away the largest labor organization in nineteenth-century Canada. Meanwhile, in the United States the Order organized around 15,000 LAs throughout its history, and at its peak strength in 1886–7 almost 7,500 of the LAs existed simultaneously.[2]

Organizationally, the Knights drew workers into their ranks through a relatively simple procedure and institutional apparatus. Individual members

Figure 2. T. V. Powderly in 1879. *Source:* Powderly Papers, Catholic University, Washington, D.C.

joined LAs, either in mixed (diverse occupational affiliations) or trade (adhering more rigidly to specific craft categories) Assemblies. Normally those who were part of a specific trade Assembly followed a particular skilled calling, but occasionally the trade Assembly was merely an organization of all workers employed in the same plant, shop, or factory. For an LA to be organized formally a minimum of 10 members was required and, once established, LAs were known to swell in membership to over 1,000. Initiation fees were set by the Local, but the minimum fee was $1 for men and 50¢ for women. Local dues, again, were controlled by individual Assemblies, but they were to be not less than 10¢ per month. Members were also expected to contribute to the Co-operative fund, the monthly fees being 10¢ for men and 5¢ for women. The cost of organizing such an Assembly was approximately $20, which included a charter, supplies, and a seal, as well as a $10 fee that went to the organizer (in the case of a women's Assembly this fee was $5). If a specific geographical region or trade contained five or more Assemblies a DA could be formed.

DAs were of two types: the National Trade Assembly (NTA), representing the interests of all Assemblies of a specific craft, such as the window-

Table 2.1. *Ontario Knights' Locals by population, 1891 census*

| Population | Total no. Ontario towns | No. with Knights Locals | % | Cumulative % |
|---|---|---|---|---|
| 50,000+ | 1 | 1 | 100.0 | 100 |
| 30,000–49,999 | 2 | 2 | 100.0 | 100 |
| 10,000–29,999 | 6 | 6 | 100.0 | 100 |
| 5,000–9,999 | 15 | 15 | 100.0 | 100 |
| 3,000–4,000 | 24 | 15 | 62.5 | 81 |
| 1,000–2,999 | 89 | 29 | 32.0 | 49 |
| Total | 137 | 68 | 49 | |

glass workers or the telegraph operatives; or the mixed DA, in which diverse interests of many mixed and trade Assemblies were represented. In Canada it was this latter mixed DA that was preeminent, and in Ontario the various DAs were always mixed in form and representative of specific geographical/territorial units. LAs were allowed one delegate in the DA for each 100 members they had enrolled, and one for each additional 100 or fraction thereof. Presiding over all of these bodies were a series of leading elected officials: the Master Workman (MW) of the LA; the District Master Workman (DMW); and many lesser figures. Each DA elected delegates to the annual convention of the Order, the General Assembly, and at this gathering, in turn, were elected the national officers and the General Executive Board. The Order, then, was a highly centralized body, with a well-defined hierarchy and structure; yet it was also egalitarian, and the LAs had a large measure of autonomy, with their own courts to prosecute those who transgressed the disciplines and regulations of knighthood.

## Organization and membership

How many of these LAs were there, where were they, and what type of Assembly prevailed in specific locales? (See Table 2.1.)[3] Although strongest in Ontario's rapidly expanding industrial cities like Toronto and Hamilton, the Knights also penetrated the province's towns, villages, and tiny hamlets. In its approximately thirty-year lifespan (1875–1907), the Order organized Locals in eighty-three towns from Amherstburg in the west to Cornwall in the east, and from Port Colborne in the south to Sudbury in the north. These eighty-three towns contained a total of at least 252 LAs, which in turn formed 10 DAs. Toronto, Hamilton, and Ottawa led the way with 58, 30, and 14 LAs respectively, but the Knights were also active in eight communities of less than 1,000 people, and there were 32 LAs in places with popula-

Map 3. Cities and towns with one or more LAs, 1881–1902.

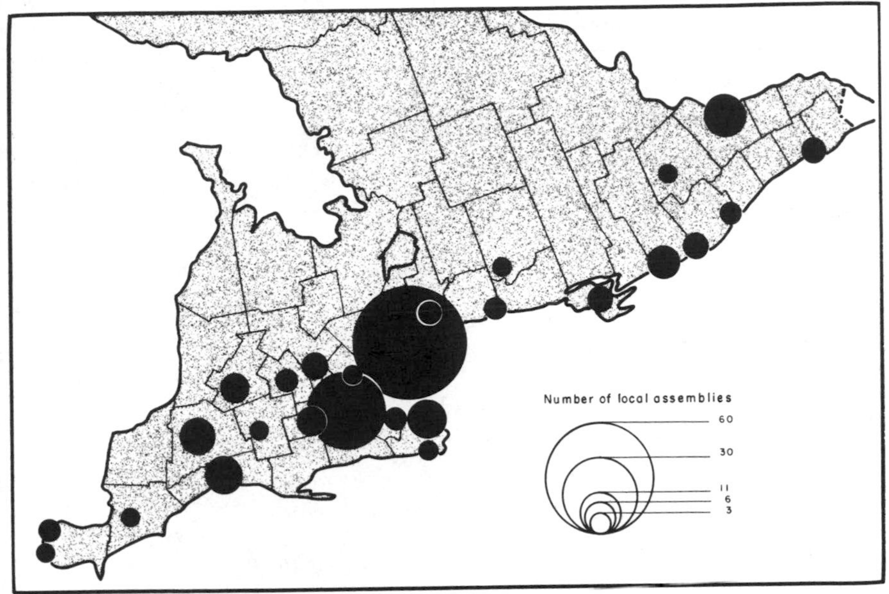


Map 4. Cities and towns with three or more LAs, 1881–1902.

tions of under 3,000. It was this range and dispersal of the Order that was perhaps most significant: of the forty-seven Ontario towns with a population of at least 3,000 in the 1880s, fully thirty-eight, or 81 percent, witnessed the formation of an LA. If we recall the thirty-four railway centers depicted earlier in Map 2, only three did not have an LA. Maps 3 and 4 detail this impressive organization achievement, with Map 3 indicating those centers where the Knights were present and Map 4 portraying graphically the relative strength of the Order in specific locales that contained two or more LAs.

Tables 2.2 and 2.3 provide a further breakdown of the Order's presence in towns and cities across the province. As we have already noted, and as Table 2.2 illustrates forcefully, the Knights of Labor established LAs in all Ontario town with populations exceeding 5,000 in 1881 and/or 1891. The concentrated strength of the Order in the larger industrial cities is revealed dramatically in Table 2.3, where the dominance of Toronto (58 Locals, 23 percent of all Ontario Assemblies) and Hamilton (30 Locals, 12 percent of all Ontario Assemblies) stands out markedly. Considerations of the next three largest cities (Ottawa, London and Kingston) indicate that fully 46 percent of all Knights of Labor LAs were in these centers. These statistics tell us much, yet they can also be deceptive. We know from other types of evidence, and shall see throughout this book, that the Order had a great impact in other,

Table 2.2. *Ontario cities over 5,000, 1881 and 1891*

| | 1881 | | 1891 | | KOL | |
|---|---|---|---|---|---|---|
| | Rank in size of pop. | Population | Rank in size of pop. | Population | No. of Locals | Rank in no. of LAs |
| Toronto | 1 | 86,415 | 1 | 144,023 | 58 | 1 |
| Hamilton | 2 | 35,961 | 2 | 47,245 | 30 | 2 |
| Ottawa | 3 | 27,412 | 3 | 37,269 | 14 | 3 |
| London | 4 | 19,746 | 4 | 22,281 | 7 | 6 |
| Kingston | 5 | 14,091 | 5 | 19,263 | 7 | 6 |
| Guelph | 6 | 9,890 | 7 | 10,537 | 5 | 7 |
| St. Catharines | 7 | 9,631 | 13 | 9,170 | 9 | 4 |
| Brantford | 8 | 9,616 | 6 | 12,753 | 5 | 7 |
| Belleville | 9 | 9,516 | 10 | 9,916 | 4 | 8 |
| St. Thomas | 10 | 8,367 | 8 | 10,366 | 8 | 5 |
| Stratford | 11 | 8,239 | 12 | 9,500 | 5 | 7 |
| Chatham | 12 | 7,873 | 14 | 9,052 | 2 | 10 |
| Brockville | 13 | 7,609 | 15 | 8,791 | 3 | 9 |
| Peterborough | 14 | 6,812 | 11 | 9,717 | 2 | 10 |
| Windsor | 15 | 6,561 | 9 | 10,322 | 3 | 9 |
| Port Hope | 16 | 5,585 | | 5,042 | 3 | 9 |
| Woodstock | 17 | 5,373 | 16 | 8,612 | 2 | 10 |
| Galt | 18 | 5,187 | 17 | 7,535 | 1 | 11 |
| Lindsay | 19 | 5,080 | | 6,081 | 1 | 11 |
| Berlin | | 4,054 | 19 | 7,425 | 5 | 7 |
| Owen Sound | | 4,426 | 18 | 7,497 | 1 | 11 |
| Sarnia | | 3,874 | | 6,692 | 1 | 11 |
| Cornwall | | 5,436 | | 6,805 | 4 | 8 |
| Barrie | | 4,854 | | 5,550 | 1 | 11 |

*Source:* Canada, *Census*, 1881 and 1891.

smaller, Ontario towns. Between November 1886 and October 1889, for instance, thirty-one Ontario Knights received organizers' commissions from Philadelphia headquarters. This number included representatives from all the Ontario DAs, but in addition small-town labor reformers such as Irwin Armstrong of Mt. Forest, James A. Church of Smiths Falls, Richard Stoneham of Clinton, P. J. Ryan of Midland, and Joseph J. Wilson of Owen Sound also became advocates of the Knights of Labor, organizers for the new industrial brotherhood.[4]

How many members were drawn into the ranks of this expanding order? This is a difficult question. At their peak in the United States the Knights were said to have enrolled between 700,000 and 1,000,000 members, but this is a static count taken in the spring months of 1886. The data are question-

Table 2.3. *Ontario Knights' LAs by place*

| Rank | Location | Trade LAs | Mixed LAs | Undesignated LAs | Total | Cumulative total | Cumulative % |
|---|---|---|---|---|---|---|---|
| 1 | Toronto | 35 | 16 | 7 | 58 | 58 | 23 |
| 2 | Hamilton | 19 | 8 | 3 | 30 | 88 | 35 |
| 3 | Ottawa | 7 | 2 | 5 | 14 | 102 | 41 |
| 4 | St. Catharines | 8 | 1 | | 9 | 111 | 44 |
| 5 | St. Thomas | 2 | 6 | | 8 | 119 | 47 |
| 6 | London | 1 | 6 | | 7 | 133 | 53 |
| | Kingston | 5 | 2 | | 7 | | |
| 7 | Guelph | 2 | 3 | | 5 | 153 | 61 |
| | Stratford | 1 | 4 | | 5 | | |
| | Berlin | | 1 | 4 | 5 | | |
| | Brantford | 4 | 1 | | 5 | | |
| 8 | Belleville | 2 | 2 | | 4 | 169 | 67 |
| | Cornwall | 1 | 1 | 2 | 4 | | |
| | Oshawa | 3 | 1 | | 4 | | |
| | Gananoque | | 2 | 2 | 4 | | |
| 9 | Brockville | 3 | | | 3 | 181 | 72 |
| | Port Hope | 2 | 1 | | 3 | | |
| | Thorold | 1 | 2 | | 3 | | |
| | Windsor | 2 | 1 | | 3 | | |
| 10 | 7 Towns | 2 | 7 | 5 | 2 each | 195 | 77 |
| 11 | 57 Towns | 10 | 33 | 14 | 1 each | 252 | 100 |
| Total | 83 | 110 | 100 | 42 | 252 | 252 | |

*Source:* See note 3.

able and tend to underestimate the membership. Moreover, the central problem is the timing of influx into the Order, for the Knights surged to prominence at different moments in different regions. Thus, Jonathan Garlock has estimated that, if one looks beyond peak membership, the American Knights of Labor may well have enrolled over 3,000,000 workers in Assemblies over the course of their history. We are plagued with problems of comparable magnitude in the case of Ontario, for membership data after 1885 are shaky at best, and official estimates seldom reliable. And, as in the United States, the Ontario Knights did not peak until 1886, a year that saw the founding of 99 LAs, and even then the dating of the upsurge varied from region to region within Ontario. Thus, across south-central Ontario the Knights of Labor climbed to their highest membership point in 1886 and then deteriorated, rapidly in some locales, more slowly in others. Towns close to the American border (Brockville and Hamilton, for instance) experienced the Order's impact earliest. But in the Northwest, in the timber country of the Muskoka region, the Order achieved prominence later, as it did in some eastern Ontario towns like Kingston, where the Knights had 1,500 supporters in 1887. In Ottawa the Order's successes came, not in the 1880s, but in the early 1890s. All this is further complicated by the fact that even *within* industrial cities like Toronto and Hamilton, which followed the classic pattern of peaking in 1886, there were some working-class sectors – letter carriers, longshoremen, and laborers–that joined the ranks of the Knights after the Order was in obvious retreat. Thus, any attempt to address the numerical significance of the Order will founder if it is reduced to a count of peak membership at any given point in time.

We can, nevertheless, start with peak official memberships at single points in time for some specific locales. Toronto DA 125's forty-one LAs had 5,000 members in 1886, while Hamilton DA 61's 2,200 workers were organized in thirty LAs. Ottawa DA 6 had 2,000 affiliated in 1892. The London–St. Thomas DA 138 reported a membership of 4,435 in 1886–7, enrolled in thirty-six Assemblies in western Ontario towns like Aylmer, Ingersoll, Listowell, and Wyoming. St. Catharines' DA 207 encompassed some 2,000 advocates in 22 LAs. Other DA peaks were Windsor DA 174's 616, Belleville DA 235's 1548, Uxbridge DA 236's 523, and Berlin DA 241's 348. But perhaps more striking still are some of the individual town reports: Brockville's Franklin LA 2311 with 430 members in November 1883; Gananoque's 700–800 members in 1887; Gravenhurst LA 10669's 300 lumberworkers in June 1888; the 500 cottonworkers in Merritton's Maple Leaf LA 5933 in 1886; Petrolia's Reliable LA 4570 with 500 members in 1886; LA 6722's 200 workers at the Frost and Woods agricultural-implements works in Smiths Falls in August 1887; and the 500 workers of Woodstock's Unity and Concord LAs 3151 and 4922 in 1886. If we recall our earlier discussion of the localized nature of manufacturing activity in various Ontario cities and towns, in fact, we see that the Knights were strong wherever a particular industrial activity predominated: among Cornwall cottonworkers, Hamilton iron- and steelworkers, or St. Thomas railway employees the Order had many advocates.

Available data do not allow us to make any firm calculations on the percentage of the work force organized by the Order, nor would the official membership figures necessarily reveal the true impact: the tendency is always to underrepresent the strength, and the volatility of the rank-and-file further compounds this problem of undercounting. To appreciate fully the numerical significance of the Order we need to understand, not a static cross-sectional profile, but a process and flow, determined, in part, by the movement's vitality and particular events, developments in the economic realm, and social relations. But the figures do not readily allow this, and we are forced to consider the Knights in the context of membership figures that defy all of this, a problem further exacerbated by reliance on census data that correspond only to decadal points and that mask local situations in larger county calculations.

We can begin with the larger picture. If we take the total peak memberships (at specific points in time with no account taken of volatility) across the province and add them together we see that over the course of their history the Knights organized a minimum of 21,800 members. (A figure double this might not overstate the numbers actually enrolled.) This represented 18.4 percent of the hands employed in manufacturing in 1881 and 13.1 percent of those so employed in 1891. If we add to these figures the percentages of workers enrolled in trade unions but not members of the Knights of Labor (and we have no accurate statistics on this phenomenon, although it is estimated that in the United States approximately one-half of the Knights' members were trade unionists) it is apparent that at a very minimum the 1880s saw 20–5 percent of the total manufacturing work force drawn to the ranks of organized labor. This, we need remember, is a higher percentage than any period prior to the post–World War II upsurge, and it is only with the increasing unionization of the public sector in recent decades that we have seen the national figure climb to 35 percent and over. For much of the early twentieth-century period, especially prior to World War I, no more than 10 percent of the nonagricultural work force in Canada was organized.

These aggregate data, of course, distort dramatically, for they include all workers with no regard for region, sex, or age. Some, but not all of this distortion can be eliminated by looking at particular locales, presented in Table 2.4. The limitations of the census impose themselves here, for in attempting to focus on the percentage of the total work force organized we are handcuffed to the 1881 and 1891 figures: the former are problematic because the Knights were not even on the scene at that early date, while the latter are equally flawed because the Order was, by that time, in the throes of decline. Moreover, such data are often available only on a county basis. Locales like St. Thomas get buried in the total county employment figures. Nevertheless, the figures are an indication of the impressive numbers of workers drawn to the Order, and in places like St. Thomas, Kingston, and the Lincoln, Niagara, and Welland regions there is no doubt that the Knights of Labor organized an absolute majority of the people employed in manufacturing.

The census, moreover, did not report on the hands employed in such small towns as Merritton, Chatham, or Gananoque. Yet we know from many sources that the Order was actively engaged in such places. To attempt a crude estimate of the percentage of the work force organized we have taken our figures on membership and compared them to a rough estimate of the

Table 2.4. *Peak Knights of Labor membership as percentage of hands employed in manufacturing in 1881 and 1891*

| City/County | 1881 | 1891 |
|---|---|---|
| Essex (Windsor) | 30.0 | 22.2 |
| London | 29.3 | 22.5 |
| Elgin East (St. Thomas) | 80.0 | 58.6 |
| Hamilton | 33.8 | 22.8 |
| Toronto | 39.3 | 20.4 |
| Brockville | 44.9 | 31.9 |
| Kingston | 101.8 | 56.0 |
| Cornwall | 32.3 | 14.8 |
| Lanark South (Perth, Smiths Falls, Carleton Place) | 21.1 | 18.1 |
| Ottawa | — | 31.7 |
| Lincoln & Niagara & Welland (St. Catharines, Welland, Merritton, Thorold) | — | 50.5 |
| Perth North (Stratford, Listowell) | 36.0 | 30.5 |

*Source:* Canada, *Census*, 1881 and 1891; Knights of Labor, *General Assembly Proceedings;* Ontario Bureau of Industry, *Annual Reports.*

number of hands employed. This latter figure was obtained by taking the total population for 1881. In no case would the work force have been more than 40 percent of the population, and it is unlikely that it would have even reached 20 percent in these years, but we have taken these poles as our gauge. (Note that if we took 20 percent of the populations of Toronto, Hamilton, and Kingston for 1881, we would expect work forces of 17,283, 7,192, and 2,818. The census recorded 1881 industrial work forces of 12,708, 6,473, and 1,473, so in no case have we underrepresented them. Our method, then, can only understate the impact of the Order. And because many of the small towns considered here did not expand greatly in the 1880s, using the 1881 population figures does not pose a great problem.) Table 2.5 reveals how thoroughly the Order penetrated these small Ontario manufacturing towns, organizing an extremely high proportion of the work force.

## Geography

In the rest of this chapter we will sketch an organization profile of the Knights of Labor in Ontario as a preface to our analysis of the meaning of the Knights' phenomenon: perhaps the most dramatic episode in Ontario workers' nineteenth-century history.

The Knights of Labor arrived in Canada surreptitiously some time in 1875 when they organized LA 119 in Hamilton. Of this LA we know nothing. Seven years later, after the Order's emergence from its clandestine existence of the 1870s, Hamilton painters openly formed Alliance LA 1852, for all in-

Table 2.5. *Knights of Labor membership as percentage of work force (estimated at between 20 percent and 40 percent of 1881 population)*

| Town | 20 percent of 1881 population | 40 percent of 1881 population |
|---|---|---|
| Chatham | 25.4 | 12.7 |
| Woodstock | 46.5 | 23.2 |
| Petrolia | 72.0 | 36.0 |
| Merritton | 139.0 | 69.5 |
| St. Catharines | 51.8 | 25.9 |
| Guelph | 17.6 | 8.8 |
| Hespeler | 71.4 | 35.7 |
| Oshawa | 52.0 | 26.0 |
| Gananoque | 87.0 | 43.5 |
| Smiths Falls | 47.9 | 23.9 |

*Source:* See Table 2.4.

tents and purposes the first Canadian LA. Their brothers in Hamilton's booming foundry industry followed quickly with molders' Literary LA 1864. Meanwhile, in St. Catharines, workers from various trades formed the first Canadian mixed LA, 2056.

Why the Order gained its first adherents in Hamilton and St. Catharines remains conjecture, but propinquity to the U.S. border undoubtedly was a factor. This certainly was the case in Brockville, where Franklin LA 2311, initially composed of dockworkers but later a mixed Assembly, was organized by Archer Baker, the MW of the Ogdensburg, New York, Knights of Labor.[5] In late summer and early fall four additional LAs were added in Hamilton (shoemakers, bakers, railroad laborers, mixed), two in Toronto (shoemakers, mixed), and single LAs in Oshawa and Ingersoll (both mixed). The most significant growth of 1882, however, came along Canada's telegraph lines as DA 45, the international organization of telegraph workers, advanced across the continent. Commencing with Morse LA 2163 in Toronto and LA 2218 in Hamilton, DA 45 organized telegraphers in London, Barrie, Brampton, Guelph, Stratford, Ottawa, Brockville, Kingston, Peterborough, Belleville, Port Hope, St. Catharines, Hagersville, Brantford, St. Thomas, and Georgetown in two brief months. In early 1883 they added Simcoe and Preston to this impressive list of Ontario towns. In all but Hamilton, St. Catharines, and Brockville, the telegraphers constituted the Order's first LAs.[6]

As pioneer Canadian Knights the telegraphers played an important role in stimulating the growth of the Order. In Toronto, for example, telegrapher Roger Mullen teamed up with shoemakers William Lane and Michael Der-

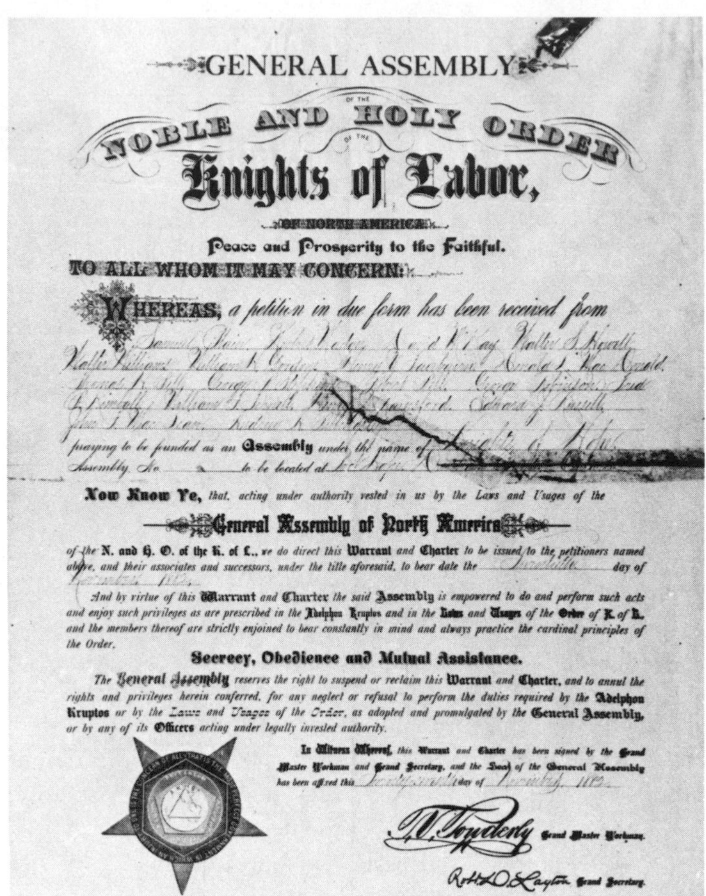

GENERAL ASSEMBLY

OF THE

NOBLE AND HOLY ORDER

OF THE

Knights of Labor,

OF NORTH AMERICA.

Peace and Prosperity to the Faithful.

TO ALL WHOM IT MAY CONCERN:

WHEREAS, *a petition in due form has been received from* [handwritten names]

*praying to be founded as an* Assembly *under the name of* Knights of Hope *Assembly, No.* ___ *to be located at* Port Hope

Now Know Ye, *that, acting under authority vested in us by the Laws and Usages of the*

General Assembly of North America

*of the* N. and H. O. of the K. of L., *we do direct this* Warrant *and* Charter *to be issued to the petitioners named above, and their associates and successors, under the title aforesaid, to bear date the* Twentieth *day of* November 1882.

*And by virtue of this* Warrant *and* Charter *the said* Assembly *is empowered to do and perform such acts and enjoy such privileges as are prescribed in the* Adelphon Kruptos *and in the* Laws *and* Usages *of the* Order *of* K. of L. *and the members thereof are strictly enjoined to bear constantly in mind and always practice the cardinal principles of the Order.*

Secrecy, Obedience and Mutual Assistance.

*The* General Assembly *reserves the right to suspend or reclaim this* Warrant *and* Charter, *and to annul the rights and privileges herein conferred, for any neglect or refusal to perform the duties required by the* Adelphon Kruptos *or by the* Laws *and* Usages *of the* Order, *as adopted and promulgated by the* General Assembly, *or by any of its* Officers *acting under legally invested authority.*

In Witness Whereof, *this* Warrant *and* Charter *has been signed by the* Grand Master Workman *and* Grand Secretary, *and the* Seal *of the* General Assembly *has been affixed this* [handwritten] *day of* November 1882.

T. V. Powderly Grand Master Workman.

Robt. D. Layton Grand Secretary.

Figure 3. Charter of "Knights of Hope" LA 2354, Port Hope, 20 November 1882. *Source:* Public Archives of Canada, MG 28 I 54, photo C 113327.

ham of Pioneer LA 2211 to organize additional Assemblies. DA 45 dominated the Order's Ontario infancy. Representing 60 percent of the initial 30 Locals organized in 1882, it also constituted 55 percent of the membership (see Table 2.6). This overrepresentation, however, disappeared quickly due to the continued expansion of the Order throughout Ontario in 1883 and to the demoralizing impact of DA 45's defeat in the international telegraphers' strike of that summer. As leading Toronto Knight D. J. O'Donoghue noted in 1886, "There is no doubt that the defeat of the telegraphers temporarily checked the growth of the Order not only in Canada but in the United States as well."[7]

Table 2.6. *Knights of Labor, Ontario membership, 1882–3*

| Place | LA name | LA no. | Membership Dec. 1882 | Membership May 1883 |
|---|---|---|---|---|
| Hamilton | Alliance | 1852 | 40 | |
| | Literary | 1864 | | |
| | | 2132 | 25 | |
| | Phoenix | 2156 | | |
| | Hamilton | 2225 | 20 | |
| | Eureka | 2307 | 28 | |
| Toronto | Pioneer | 2211 | 20 | |
| | Excelsior | 2305 | 12 | |
| St. Catharines | Fidelity | 2056 | 23 | |
| Brockville | Franklin | 2311 | 50 | |
| Oshawa | Etna | 2355 | 151 | |
| Ingersoll | Pioneer | 2416 | 20 | |
| (Total) | | | (389) | |
| Telegraphers (Total) | | | (475) | (694) |
| | Toronto Morse | 2163 | 125 | 200 |
| | Hamilton | 2218 | 30 | 34 |
| | London | 2303 | 20 | 45 |
| | Barrie | 2318 | 15 | 31 |
| | Brampton | 2319 | 20 | 15 |
| | Guelph | 2320 | 20 | 29 |
| | Stratford | 2321 | 20 | 15 |
| | Ottawa | 2334 | 25 | 50 |
| | Brockville | 2335 | 30 | 40 |
| | Kingston | 2342 | 20 | 27 |
| | Peterborough | 2343 | 15 | 10 |
| | Belleville | 2351 | 35 | 15 |
| | Port Hope | 2354 | 25 | 30 |
| | St. Catharines | 2358 | 15 | 23 |
| | Hagersville | 2380 | 15 | 28 |
| | Brantford | 2381 | 15 | 30 |
| | St. Thomas | 2402 | 15 | 18 |
| | Georgetown | 2413 | 15 | 26 |
| | Simcoe | 2471 | | 10 |
| | Preston | 2486 | | 18 |

*Sources:* Knights of Labor, General Assembly, *Proceedings;* membership of DA 45 from John Campbell, DMW, to officers and members of LAs of DA 45, Pittsburgh, December 27, 1882 and May 20, 1883, Powderly Papers.

The Order's growth in 1883 (see Table 2.7) was most apparent in Hamilton, where trade Assemblies of cigarmakers, hatters, and plumbers were formed as well as two new mixed Assemblies. In Toronto organization proceeded more slowly, but included the establishment of Maple Leaf LA 2622

Table 2.7. *Knights of Labor, Ontario membership, 1883*

| Place | LA name | LA no. | No. of members |
|---|---|---|---|
| Hamilton | Alliance | 1852 | 129 |
| | Literary | 1864 | 116 |
| | | 2132 | 141 |
| | Phoenix | 2156 | |
| | Hamilton | 2225 | 439 |
| | Eureka | 2307 | 21 |
| | | 2450 | 62 |
| | | 2479 | 28 |
| | | 2481 | 83 |
| | Art | 2569 | 60 |
| | Vulcan | 2586 | 27 |
| | | | (1,106) + 34 telegs. = (1,140) 33% |
| Toronto | Pioneer | 2211 | 191 |
| | Excelsior | 2305 | 55 |
| | Maple Leaf | 2622 | 43 |
| | Queen City | 2782 | 26 |
| | | | (315) + 200 telegs. = (515) 15% |
| St. Catharines | Fidelity | 2056 | 137 |
| | | 2549 | |
| Brockville | Franklin | 2311 | 203 |
| Oshawa | Etna | 2355 | 278 |
| Ingersoll | Pioneer | 2416 | 56 |
| Sarnia | | 2470 | 90 |
| Whitby | | 2510 | 32 |
| Pt. Dalhousie | Harbour | 2513 | 67 |
| Cobourg | | 2598 | 157 |
| Perth | | 2735 | 20 |
| Pt. Hope | | 2786 | 22 |
| Collingwood | | 2812 | 20 |
| Belleville | | 2900 | 31 |
| Silver Brook Mills | | 3012 | 19 |
| Brantford | Pioneer | 2491 | 152 |
| | Maple Leaf | 2817 | 18 |
| | | | (170) |
| Guelph | | 2821 | 11 |
| | | 2980 | 16 |
| | | | (27) |
| | | | 2,750 |
| Other telegraphers | | | 694 |
| Total | | | 3,444 |

*Source:* Knights of Labor, General Assembly, *Proceedings*.

at the Massey agricultural implements factory, and a trade assembly of harness- and saddlemakers. Additional Locals were established at Brantford (mixed), St. Catharines (coopers), Port Hope (mixed), Ottawa, Brantford (woodworkers), Guelph (two LAs – mixed and cigarmakers), and Belleville (wood- and ironworkers). Towns gaining their first LAs included Sarnia (mixed), Preston (telegraph operators), Whitby (mixed), Port Dalhousie (sailors), Cobourg (mixed), Perth (mixed), Collingwood (mixed), and Silver Brook Mills (sawmill operatives). Although membership figures for these years are somewhat unreliable, the Order appears to have had around 3,500 members in Ontario in 1883 (see Table 2.7), of which about 20 percent were telegraphers, about 33 percent resided in Hamilton, and another 15 percent in Toronto.

The following year the Order grew slowly. Hamilton workers organized only two new Assemblies, although significantly the first, Ontario LA 3040 of woolen mill operatives, included women members; some of these women, probably led by Katie McVicar, later in the year organized Excelsior LA 3179, which was composed entirely of women workers – the first women's LA and the first solely women's union in Canada. St. Thomas (Elgin LA 3445) and London (Forest City LA 3305 and Confidence LA 3502) workers expanded the Order beyond telegraphers in those cities for the first time, while workers in Woodstock (Utility LA 3151), Port Colborne (Peninsular LA 3279), and Windsor (Enterprise LA 3281) organized their first Knights of Labor Locals. Toronto, however, witnessed the most significant increase in activity with the founding of Beaver LA 3181 of piano polishers and varnishers, Acme LA 3490 of upholsterers, Unity LA 3491 of trunk- and bagmakers, and Wheatsheaf LA 3499 of bakers.

With the disappearance of DA 45 Locals from the Canadian Order, Ontario membership actually declined in 1884 (see Table 2.8). The approximately 2,600 members were still scattered across the entire province, but with significant concentrations in Hamilton (34 percent) and Toronto (13 percent). Brockville (10 percent) and Guelph (7 percent) were also centers with strong memberships. The slowness of growth in 1884 can best be seen in Table 2.9, which demonstrates not only that 1884 saw the lowest number of new LAs formed but also that the Order experienced a slight decline in the number of Ontario Assemblies in existence.

All of this changed dramatically in 1885. In that year 30 new Locals were organized. As D. J. O'Donoghue later reflected: "During the year 1885 the missionaries of the Order of the Knights of Labor in the Dominion had so aroused the working classes, or at least the very large proportion of them not already organized into trades unions, to the advantages of the new creed that

Table 2.8. *Knights of Labor, Ontario membership, 1884*

| Place | LA name | LA no. | Membership | % |
|---|---|---|---|---|
| Hamilton (DA 61) | Alliance | 1852 | 67 | |
| | Literary | 1864 | 22 | |
| | | 2132 | 82 | |
| | Hamilton | 2225 | 183 | |
| | Eureka | 2307 | 28 | |
| | | 2450 | 34 | |
| | | 2481 | 69 | |
| | Art | 2569 | 52 | |
| | Vulcan | 2586 | 134 | |
| | Ontario | 3040 | 145 | |
| | Excelsior | 3179 | 76 | |
| | | | (892) | 34 |
| Toronto | Pioneer | 2211 | 107 | |
| | Excelsior | 2305 | 25 | |
| | Maple Leaf | 2622 | 90 | |
| | Queen City | 2782 | 26 | |
| | Beaver | 3181 | 52 | |
| | Acme | 3490 | 13 | |
| | Unity | 3491 | 19 | |
| | Wheatsheaf | 3499 | 15 | |
| | | | (347) | 13 |
| Belleville | | 2900 | 127 | |
| Brantford | Pioneer | 2491 | 36 | |
| | Maple Leaf | 2817 | 84 | |
| | | | (120) | |
| Brockville | Franklin | 2311 | 258 | 10 |
| Collingwood | | 2812 | 20 | |
| Guelph | | 2821 | 11 | |
| | | 2980 | 178 | |
| | | | (189) | 7 |
| Ingersoll | Pioneer | 2416 | 113 | |
| London | Forest City | 3305 | 11 | |
| | Confidence | 3502 | 11 | |
| | | | (22) | |
| Oshawa | Etna | 2355 | 16 | |
| Perth | | 2735 | 27 | |
| Port Colborne | Peninsular | 3279 | 17 | |
| Port Dalhousie | Harbour | 2513 | 60 | |
| Port Hope | | 2786 | 109 | |
| St. Catharines | Fidelity | 2056 | 74 | |
| Sarnia | | 2470 | 64 | |
| Silver Brook | | 3012 | 27 | |
| St. Thomas | Elgin | 3449 | 23 | |
| Whitby | | 2510 | 42 | |
| Windsor | Enterprise | 3281 | 12 | |
| Woodstock | Unity | 3151 | 48 | |
| Total | | | (2,607) | |

*Source:* Knights of Labor, General Assembly, *Proceedings*.

Table 2.9. *Ontario LAs by year, 1882–1907*

| Date | New LAs | Existing LAs |
|---|---|---|
| 1882 | 30 | 30 |
| 3 | 24 | 53 |
| 4 | 14 | 49 |
| 5 | 30 | 70 |
| 6 | 99 | 160 |
| 7 | 26 | 144 |
| 8 | 5 | 122 |
| 9 | 5 | 85 |
| 1890 | 4 | 64 |
| 1 | 1 | 55 |
| 2 | 1 | 54 |
| 3 | 4 | 52 |
| 4 | 0 | 16 |
| 5 | 0 | 11 |
| 6 | 0 | 9 |
| 7 | 0 | 4 |
| 8 | 0 | 4 |
| 9 | 2 | 6 |
| 1900 | 0 | 6 |
| 1 | 4 | 9 |
| 2 | 2 | 11 |
| 3 | 1 | 11 |
| 4 | 0 | 8 |
| 5 | 0 | 3 |
| 6 | 0 | 3 |
| 1907 | 0 | 3 |
| Total | (252) | |

*Source:* See Note 1.

'an injury to one should become the concern of all,' that an almost phenomenal rush into the ranks resulted in Ontario in particular."[8] Leading this resurgence were Toronto workers, who formed nine new LAs, St. Thomas workers who followed with four and Brantford, Stratford, and Oshawa mechanics with two each. Older Knights of Labor centers that also added LAs were London, Belleville, Guelph, and Hamilton. Towns gaining their first Local included Amherstburg, International Bridge, Clinton, Tillsonburg, and Carleton Place. Three of these new Locals – Brantford factory and sewing girls LA 3649, Belleville mixed LA 4427, and St. Thomas Grace Darling LA 4650 – were women's Locals. Most of the LAs organized in Toronto were trade assemblies (for example, watchcase makers, barbers, painters, jewellers, silverplaters). Those organized in smaller Ontario centers tended

Table 2.10. *Types of LAs in Ontario*

| Place | Trade | Mixed | Unknown | Total | % mixed | % mixed excl. unknown |
|---|---|---|---|---|---|---|
| LAs in cities over 40,000 | 54 | 24 | 10 | 88 | 27 | 31 |
| LAs in cities 10,000–39,999 | 23 | 21 | 5 | 49 | 43 | 48 |
| LAs in cities 5,000–9,999 | 17 | 20 | 6 | 43 | 47 | 54 |
| LAs in towns under 5,000 | 16 | 36 | 20 | 72 | 50 | 69 |
| All LAs | 110 | 101 | 41 | 252 | 40 | 48 |

*Source:* See note 3.

either to be industrial in form, such as Oshawa agricultural implements workers' LA 4428 or Guelph reed organ builders' LA 4703, or, more often, simply mixed LAs (Pt. Edward, St. Thomas, Stratford, Clinton, Tillsonburg, Carleton Place). It was in small towns, then, that the mixed LA proved most flexible as an organizing device, while the trade Assemblies were more often found in the cities, where a diversified manufacturing base thrived (see Table 2.10). Many of the smaller towns were simply not populous enough to possess sufficiently large groups of tradesmen to form craft unions; the Knights of Labor mixed Assembly thus fit their needs well. As always, there were exceptions to this general pattern. St. Thomas and London, for example, although large and important Knights of Labor centers, possessed few trade Assemblies, but they stand as something of an exception, proving the rule.[9]

Membership data, far from reliable before mid-decade, breaks down completely in 1885. What can be observed, however, is the rapid growth of the Order in Toronto (see Table 2.11), which surpassed Hamilton in membership and established itself as the Knights' major center in Ontario. A host of subsidiary centers, such as Brantford, Stratford, and St. Thomas, also experienced considerable growth. The last two towns were important Ontario railroad centers and workers in that industry represented the base upon which the Order grew.

Organization had picked up in the fall of 1885, and 20 of the 30 new LAs were actually established after 1 October. This impetus continued into 1886 when the organizational stream became a torrential flood. A grand total of 99 Ontario Locals emerged in 1886, despite deliberate efforts by the Knights' leadership to slow down the pace of growth after the mass influx of workers into the Knights of Labor that occurred after striking workers affiliated with

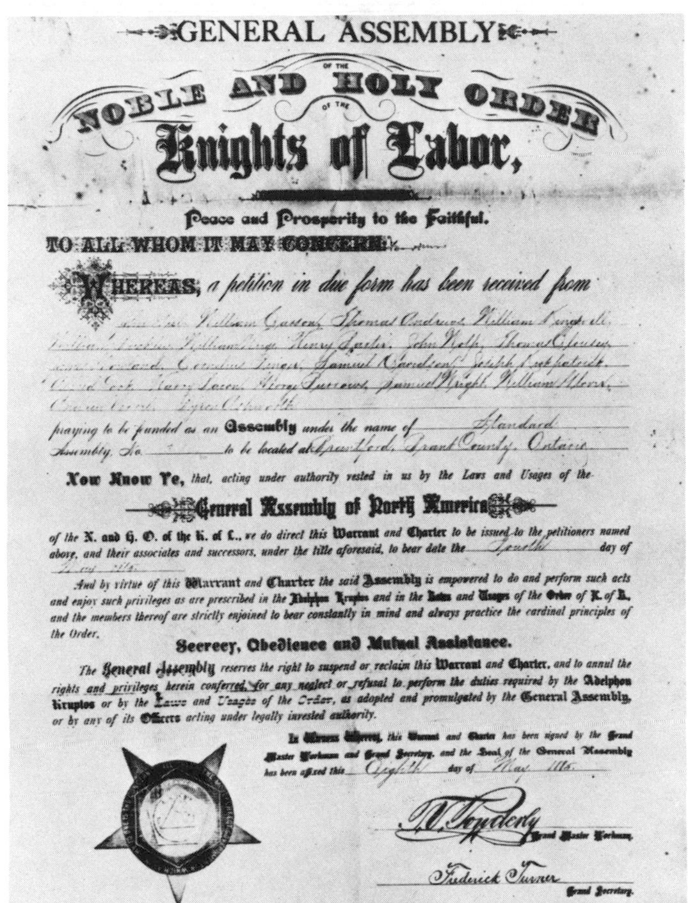

GENERAL ASSEMBLY

OF THE NOBLE AND HOLY ORDER OF THE

Knights of Labor,

Peace and Prosperity to the Faithful.

TO ALL WHOM IT MAY CONCERN:

Whereas, a petition in due form has been received from

praying to be funded as an Assembly under the name of Standard Assembly, No. to be located at Brantford, Brant County, Ontario

Now Know Ye, that, acting under authority vested in us by the Laws and Usages of the

General Assembly of North America

of the N. and H. O. of the K. of L., we do direct this Warrant and Charter to be issued to the petitioners named above, and their associates and successors, under the title aforesaid, to bear date the Fourth day of May 1885.

And by virtue of this Warrant and Charter the said Assembly is empowered to do and perform such acts and enjoy such privileges as are prescribed in the Adelphon Kruptos and in the Laws and Usages of the Order of K. of L. and the members thereof are strictly enjoined to bear constantly in mind and always practice the cardinal principles of the Order.

Secrecy, Obedience and Mutual Assistance.

The General Assembly reserves the right to suspend or reclaim this Warrant and Charter, and to annul the rights and privileges herein conferred, for any neglect or refusal to perform the duties required by the Adelphon Kruptos or by the Laws and Usages of the Order, as adopted and promulgated by the General Assembly, or by any of its Officers acting under legally invested authority.

In Witness Whereof, this Warrant and Charter has been signed by the Grand Master Workman and Grand Secretary, and the Seal of the General Assembly has been affixed this Eighth day of May 1885.

T. V. Powderly
Grand Master Workman.

Frederick Turner
Grand Secretary.

Figure 4. Charter of "Standard" LA 3811, Brantford, 4 May 1885. *Source:* Public Archives of Canada, MG 28 I 54, photo C 113328.

the Order had defeated Jay Gould on the Wabash line of the southwest railway system in the summer of 1885. Within a year of this victory the Order grew from 100,000 to 700,000 and labor's organized ranks – trade unionists as well as Knights – found themselves in the midst of the Great Upheaval. Powderly, and other cautious conservatives in leading positions in the Order, regarded this growth as unhealthy, and grew apprehensive lest the Knights of Labor be regarded as a "striking machine." They threatened to revoke the charters of those Assemblies that engaged in strikes, and in January of 1886 Powderly claimed that the expansion in the ranks was "a mushroom too feverish to be good." Following this statement the General Executive Board issued a March ban on all organizing, effective for forty days, seeking to quell

Table 2.11. *Knights of Labor, Ontario membership, 1885*

| Place | LA name | LA no. | Membership |
|---|---|---|---|
| | | DA 61 | |
| Hamilton DA | Alliance | 1852 | |
| | Literary | 1864 | 36 |
| | | 2132 | 47 |
| | Hamilton | 2225 | 61 |
| | | 2307 | |
| | | 2481 | 58 |
| | Vulcan | 2586 | 72 |
| | Ontario | 3040 | 41 |
| | Excelsior | 3179 | 26 |
| | | 4814 | |
| | | | (341) |
| Toronto | Pioneer | 2211 | 31 |
| | Excelsior | 2305 | 29 |
| | Maple Leaf | 2622 | 56 |
| | Queen City | 2782 | 25 |
| | Beaver | 3181 | 48 |
| | Acme | 3490 | 24 |
| | Unity | 3491 | 39 |
| | Wheatsheaf | 3499 | 55 |
| | Dominion | 3656 | 19 |
| | Covenant | 3684 | 32 |
| | Eureka | 4025 | |
| | Progress | 4298 | |
| | | 4534 | |
| | Annex | 4538 | |
| | Powderly | 4614 | |
| | Alpha | 4679 | |
| | Britannia | 4786 | |
| | | | (358) |
| Amherstburg | Beaver | 4139 | 12 |
| Belleville | | 2900 | 157 |
| | | 4427 | |
| Brantford | Pioneer | 2491 | 52 |
| | Maple Leaf | 2817 | 48 |
| | Olive Branch | 3649 | |
| | Standard | 3811 | 40 |
| | | | (140) |
| Brockville | Franklin | 2311 | 11 |
| Carleton Place | | 4812 | |
| Clinton | | 4673 | |
| Guelph | | 2980 | 237 |
| | | 4703 | |
| Ingersoll | Pioneer | 2416 | 26 |
| Internat'l Bridge | Victoria | 4425 | |
| London | Forest City | 3305 | 65 |
| | Confidence | 3502 | 25 |
| | Beaver | 3558 | 116 |
| | | | (206) |

Table 2.11. (*cont.*)

| Place | LA name | LA no. | Membership |
|---|---|---|---|
| Oshawa | Etna | 2355 | 16 |
| | | 4428 | |
| | Tylors | 4279 | |
| Perth | | 2735 | 22 |
| Pt. Edward | | 4043 | |
| Port Colborne | | 3279 | 48 |
| Port Dalhousie | Harbour | 2513 | 38 |
| Port Hope | | 2786 | 40 |
| St. Catharines | Fidelity | 2056 | 14 |
| Sarnia | | 2470 | 39 |
| Stratford | Green Mtn. | 4378 | |
| | | 4419 | |
| St. Thomas | Elgin | 3449 | 124 |
| | Headlight | 4069 | |
| | Keystone | 4322 | |
| | Star | 4435 | |
| | Grace Darling | 4650 | |
| Tillsonburg | Ivanhoe | 4676 | |
| Windsor | Enterprise | 3281 | 118 |
| Woodstock | Unity | 3151 | 161 |
| Total | | | 2,108+<br>64 LAs<br>10 Hamilton<br>17Toronto |

the rising tide of newly initiated members embarking on strikes, boycotts, and other job actions. But across North America, and in Ontario as well, this attempt to stifle local initiatives produced few concrete results. Toronto led the Canadian expansion with a remarkable 29 new LAs, while Hamilton, although a distant second, still outpaced all other centers with 12. Thorold and London gained 3 each and a number of towns (St. Thomas, Cornwall, Chatham, Berlin, and Windsor) added 2. The 99 LAs organized in 1886 constituted 40 percent of all Locals organized in Ontario in the Order's history.[10]

The rapid growth of the Order in 1886 also led to the establishment of a series of new DAs in Ontario. Hamilton Pioneer DA 61 was joined by Toronto DA 125, St. Thomas DA 138, and Windsor DA 174. Later additions were St. Catharines DA 207, Belleville DA 235, Uxbridge DA 236, Berlin DA 241, and Ottawa DA 6.

In the years after 1886 few such rapid organizational gains were made. But the post-1886 years did not simply reveal the precipitous decline usually described in the historical literature. The Order peaked on a province-wide basis in 1886–1887, to be sure, but in various regions it continued to grow after that date and in other areas the Knights of Labor periodically witnessed renewed efforts. Thus, any consideration of the Knights after 1886 can best be discussed in terms of the various regions of Ontario. This regional focus is conveniently reflected through the Order's DAs themselves. We will not consider Hamilton DA 61 and Toronto DA 125 here, as they are dealt with at length in Chapters 3 and 4. Instead let us turn to the other regional and district strongholds of the Knights.

St. Thomas DA 138, for instance, was founded in July 1886 to service Locals in west-central Ontario. Originally it contained all Locals in Ontario west of the Port Dover and Stratford Railroad. The following year, however, Windsor DA 174 cut Essex County out of its territory. Centered in St. Thomas, a rapidly growing railroad town of about 10,000, DA 138 included a number of other important Knights of Labor centers such as Chatham, London, Stratford, and Woodstock. At the Order's peak in 1886 DA 138 contained well over 5,000 active Knights.

In Stratford, although there had been a telegraphers' Local in 1882–3, organization began solidly in October 1885. Two meetings were held at local hotels; the first with local speakers and the second with J. W. Osborne, a St. Thomas Knight present. Osborne explained the history of the Order, arguing that its purpose was "to elevate the laboring man, to educate him to the ballot." Moreover, he continued, "the time for the labouring man to cringe at the foot of capital has passed, and the mighty power of the labour element would soon make itself so apparent that capital would bow before it." Osborne's fiery message apparently was well received, and after the public meeting was closed, "quite a number were initiated."[11] This new, mixed Green Mountain LA 4378 contained a number of women workers. The major initiative for organizing LAs in the Stratford area came from F. D. Phillips, formerly a Knights' organizer for Wide Awake LA 2069 in St. Louis.[12] Phillips, who worked for U.S. Customs on the Grand Trunk at Stratford, organized Assemblies in other western Ontario centers as well.[13] A second mixed LA 4419 was formed in Stratford in late 1885 and a large public meeting was held, addressed by both Phillips and Toronto's D. J. O'Donoghue.[14] By May 1886 the two LAs had over 600 members and LA 4419 had its own hall. Two additional mixed LAs were added that year (5542 and 8071), the former being a women's Assembly. A correspondent to the Hamilton *Palladium of Labor* attributed the Order's Stratford successes to "a few pushing, energetic men who were connected with a number of other societies."[15] Stratford Knights also opened a Co-operative Cigar Manufacturing

Company which produced the "Little Knight" while employing between twenty and thirty cigarmakers under union rules. The fight between Knights and trade unionists in the cigar industry (see Chapter 4) no doubt affected developments in Stratford detrimentally but the Order nevertheless persisted, reporting 400–500 members in 1887 and 100 in 1888.[16]

St. Thomas enjoyed a similar experience.[17] The Knights organized a telegraphers' Assembly there in 1882 but there appears to have been a year lacuna before the arrival of Elgin mixed LA 3449. It began with 24 members in 1884 but grew rapidly to 124 the following year. In 1885 railroad employees organized Headlight LA 4069 while other Knights organized three mixed LAs (Keystone LA 4322, Star LA 4435, and Grace Darling Women's LA 4640). Two additional Assemblies were added in 1886, Fidelis mixed LA 4929 and Mercantile clerks LA 6707. At its peak in 1886, 1,500 St. Thomas workers belonged to the Order.

There can be no question that in both St. Thomas and Stratford railway workers were central to the Order's success. Headlight LA 4069 clearly led the region and its ranks included as many as 700–800 railroad employees of various descriptions, among them members of the prestigious running trades.[18] Richard Trevellick noted after a St. Thomas lecture that he had organized "37 railroad men one night and received 97 propositions" of which "27 were members of the Brotherhood of Locomotive Engineers."[19] This pattern of dual membership was common throughout the Order but appears to have been especially true of railway workers, who were apparently moving uncertainly toward broader forms of organization.[20]

London was Ontario's fourth largest city in both 1881 and 1891, and grew from around 20,000 to nearly 32,000. The Knights of Labor organized a total of seven LAs there, although the first was a short-lived telegraphers' Local (LA 2303). The Order's peak, here as elsewhere, came in 1886, when it included approximately 1,200 workers. By 1887 this had declined dramatically, but in 1888 a "large increase" was reported and the following year it was again noted that the Order was expanding, especially in the organization of women.[21]

Other strongholds in western Ontario's DA 138 were Chatham with 400 workers in two LAs and a cooperative biscuit factory; Petrolia, an oil producing center; and Woodstock, where there was another cooperative factory, engaged in the production of matches.

Strongest in the years 1884–6, DA 138 declined quickly in the post-1887 years, its precipitous demise paralleling that of another important center, Hamilton's DA 61. From an official peak of 2,275 members in 1886 the DA fell rapidly to a low of 98 in May 1890, a year that saw Joseph T. Marks of London begin efforts to reinvigorate the failing Order.[22] The decline, which had seen the District lose almost one-third of its members in 1887, shattered the Knights of Labor, disrupting many LAs. By July 1888 the DA contained less than 300 affiliates. In March of that year DMW W. J. Shaw had written optimistically of "a slight disposition to revive the work in some of our towns."[23] But by September lecturer A. W. Wright found "The Order in DA 138 in very bad shape."[24] Late that November Shaw explained that in St. Thomas there was but one Local left with only forty-two members: "You know the general story of fever and bad management followed by disgust and of course decay. That is the state of affairs here but the fire still burns in a large number."[25] As late as May 1890 DA 138 remained active. Joseph T. Marks, a leading London Knight, described to Powderly the work underway to reorganize the Order: "I am holding public meetings and visiting locals every week. At our last meeting things were desperate, only six locals and 98 members, however upon taking office I determined to do my best . . . The last quarter showed a slight increase and this one will give a larger one." Marks buttressed these meetings with speeches in Woodstock, Stratford, and St. Thomas.[26]

But, as elsewhere, the Knights of Labor experience did not simply die. Instead it adapted and modified to the changing economic and political climate and reemerged in new forms. In DA 138, for example (see Table 2.12), numbers of former Knights became active in the Patrons of Industry and, following the lead of Marks, they joined the Industrial Brotherhood of Canada, an organization that closely resembled the Order. Obediah Light of Port Burwell explained to John Hayes that the Brotherhood was "taking the place of the K of L in the towns and villages" and thus "the good work is still going on for the emancipation of wage slavery."[27]

In late 1886 Windsor DA 174 was created to cover Essex county (see Table 2.13). Cut out of DA 138's territory, the new District was not greeted with enthusiasm by other western Ontario Knights. The St. Thomas *Canada Labor Courier* objected strenuously, as did Michael J. Kelly, MW of Petrolia's large Reliable LA 4570. Such opposition centered around much more than the small membership officially recorded for the Windsor DA, for the Order probably attracted far more workers than such figures revealed. Many Windsor workers found jobs in Detroit, an important Knights of Labor stronghold, and the St. Thomas-based DA probably had its eye on these members, and felt its jurisdiction threatened. Indeed, DA 138 was something of a stronghold of nationalism, being a hotbed of "Home Rule" (Canadian autonomy) sentiment. Powderly's failure to respond to their objections to the creation of DA 174 must have confirmed them in their suspicions of American domination and a number of Canadian Assemblies in the Windsor area actually affiliated with Detroit DA 50.[28]

In the heart of the Niagara Peninsula, St. Catharines was Ontario's thirteenth largest city in 1881 with a population around 9,000, but it declined rapidly to twenty-fifth by 1891, and fewer people actually lived in the town than before. Although Fidelity mixed LA 2056 was one of Canada's earliest Locals, joined by telegraphers LA 2358 and a short-lived 1883 coopers' LA 2549, St. Catharines' workers nevertheless joined the Order's organizational boom relatively late. Three new LAs were founded in 1886 – mixed LA 2573, Welland Canal sailors LA 7025, and clerks LA 7907. Thus by 1886 about 1,000 St. Catharines' workers had joined the Order, and the following year three additional LAs were established. In May 1887 St. Catharines became the center of Niagara DA 207, which started with just over 2,000 members in the Niagara Peninsula (see Table 2.14). Again, controversy surrounded the creation of the DA, with Hamilton DA 61 registering a protest against losing the territory, which contained the labor stronghold of Thorold. A town of just over 2,000 in the 1880s, like St. Catharines, Thorold was actually declining. Nevertheless, it saw persistent Knights of Labor activity. With only 300 or so industrial workers, its total of three LAs was quite remarkable. Other notable patterns in DA 207 were the various Locals of railroad employees in tiny villages such as Clifton, International Bridge, and York. Also prominent were the stonecutters of the Welland Canal quarries, who had established militant traditions before the arrival of the Knights. Despite this diversified foundation, DA 207 declined in 1888 to about 1,000 members. It continued to be active into the 1890s, however, unlike the western Ontario DAs. By 1893 its fate seemed settled, and the District consisted only of single Locals in Merritton, St. Catharines, and Thorold.[29]

While various DAs were suffering membership losses in 1888, three new DAs emerged in that year. Berlin DA 241 (see Table 2.15), with almost 800 members, was created out of the rapidly declining DA 61. Its organization reflected the rather late start of the Order in this growing section of industrial Ontario. Berlin almost doubled in population between 1881 and 1891, more than doubled its number of industrial workers, and quadrupled its capital invested in industry. Its five LAs, all organized after 1885, give evidence of labor's growth as well. Berlin also possessed the only designated ethnic LA in Ontario: Germania LA 9691. Guelph was the other major center in this DA, which apparently failed in late 1889, "owing to the hostility of the employers towards organized labour and dread of the blacklist." A few of its LAs nevertheless continued.[30]

Table 2.12. *St. Thomas DA 138*

| Place | LA name | LA no. | LA type | Years in existence | Pre-1886 peak | Membership 1886 | 1887 | 1888 | 1889 |
|---|---|---|---|---|---|---|---|---|---|
| Aylmer | | 9694 | | 1887–9 | | | | | |
| Chatham | Royal Oak | 5961 | mixed | 1886–8 | | | 400 | 100 | |
| | | 7150 | mixed | 1886 | | | | | |
| Clinton | | 4673 | mixed | 1885–8 | | | | | |
| Ingersoll | Pioneer | 2416 | mixed | 1882–7 | 113 | | | | |
| Listowell | | 6175 | mixed | 1886 | | 175 | | | |
| London | Forest City | 3305 | mixed | 1884–90 | 65 | | | | |
| | Confidence | 3502 | mixed | 1884–8 | 25 | | | | |
| | Beaver | 3558 | mixed | 1885–90 | 116 | | | | |
| | Harmony | 5099 | mixed | 1886–8 | | 1,200 | 115 | | |
| | London West | 5172 | mixed | 1886–8 | | | | | |
| | Pilot | 7110 | mixed | 1886–8 | | | | | |
| Marthaville | Beehive | 7918 | mixed | 1886 | | | | | |
| Norwich | | 5430 | mixed | 1886–7 | | | | | |
| Oil Springs | Progressive | 6008 | mixed | 1886 | | | | | |
| Petrolia | Reliable | 4570 | mixed | 1885–7 | | 500 | | | |
| Pt. Edward | | 4043 | mixed | 1885–8 | | | | | |
| Pt. Burwell | Equity | 9673 | | 1887–96 | | | | | |
| Ridgetown | | 6704 | mixed | 1886 | | | | | |
| Sarnia | | 2470 | mixed | 1883–6 | 90 | | | | |
| Seaforth | | 7819 | mixed | 1886 | | | | | |

| | | | | | | | | |
|---|---|---|---|---|---|---|---|---|
| Stratford | Green Mountain | 4378 | mixed | 1885–90 | | | | |
| | City | 4419 | mixed | 1885–7 | | 500 | 400–500 | 100 |
| | | 5542 | mixed | 1886 | | | | |
| | | 8071 | mixed | 1886 | | | | |
| St. Thomas | Elgin | 3449 | mixed | 1884–90 | 124 | | | |
| | Headlight | 4069 | r. r. emps. | 1885–7 | 500 | | | |
| | Keystone | 4322 | mixed | 1885–6 | | | | |
| | Star | 4435 | mixed | 1885 | | 1,500 | | |
| | Grace Darling | 4650 | mixed | 1885–6 | | | | |
| | Fidelis | 4929 | mixed | 1886 | | | | |
| | Mercantile | 6707 | mixed | 1886 | | | | |
| Tillsonburg | Ivanhoe | 4676 | mixed | 1885–8 | | 60 | | |
| Woodstock | Unity | 3151 | mixed | 1884–90 | 161 | 500 | | |
| | Concord | 4992 | mixed | 1886 | | | | |
| Wyoming | Home | 5912 | mixed | 1886–8 | | | | |

*Note:* Includes all LAs within the geographic region of the DA, excluding telegraphers' LAs.

Table 2.13. *Windsor DA 174*

| Place | LA name | LA no. | LA type | Years in existence | Membership 1885 | 1886 | 1887 | 1888 |
|---|---|---|---|---|---|---|---|---|
| Amherstburg | Beaver | 4139 | mixed | 1885–8 | 12 | | | |
| | Victoria | 10530 | | 1887–9 | | | | |
| Essex Centre | | 8075 | mixed | 1886 | | 17 | 616 | 373 |
| Windsor | Enterprise | 3281 | mixed | 1884–9 | 118 | | | |
| | | 6922 | r. r. emps. | 1886–8 | | | | |
| | Carpenters | 7912 | carpenters | 1886–90 | | | | |

*Note:* Includes all LAs within the geographic region of the DA, excluding telegraphers' LAs.

The second of the new DAs created in 1888 was Uxbridge DA 236 (see Table 2.16). This District took in Locals situated east of Toronto and west of Belleville reaching north into Ontario's lumber region. Although the DA was centered in Uxbridge, Oshawa – forty miles east of Toronto – was its most important town. A center with a malleable ironworks and agricultural-implements factory, Oshawa had a labor history that stretched back to the 1860s. A strong Iron Molders' International Union Local provided an organizational foothold for the Knights of Labor. Here, as in most places, dual unionism presented no major difficulties. It was in the north, however, that the Order made its most innovative impact, enrolling previously unorganized lumberworkers in its ranks. Gravenhurst LA 10669 led a bitter strike for shorter hours in summer 1888. With about 500 workers in 1888 the DA survived into the 1890s, but experienced difficulties covering such a large area effectively: "The towns where locals are located are many miles apart, from ten to one hundred miles, and the District being young has not had time to accumulate any funds as the membership was small at the beginning and poor at that."[31]

The third new 1888 District was Belleville DA 235 (see Table 2.17), which encompassed the region from Belleville to the Ottawa River. Considerable debate took place over where to situate this DA with a serious but unsuccessful bid coming from the larger center of Kingston, Ontario's fifth largest city with a population between 15,000 and 20,000 over the course of the 1880s. In Kingston, as throughout eastern Ontario in general, the Order developed relatively late. Although a telegraphers' Local had existed in 1882–3, no further Locals appeared until early 1887 when Limestone mixed LA 9452 was formed. Later that year Mayflower LA 10432 of tailoresses and Frontenac LA 10539 of ironworkers entered the Order. In early 1888 longshoremen (probably LA 553) and building trades workers (LA 741) joined the Knights. By late 1887 Kingston claimed 1,500 Knights and the Order "was constantly

Table 2.14. *Niagara DA 207*

| Place | LA name | LA no. | LA type | Years in existence | Pre-1885 peak | Membership 1886 | 1887 | 1888 | 1889 |
|---|---|---|---|---|---|---|---|---|---|
| Beamsville | | 8570 | stonecutters | 1886–96 | | | | | |
| Chippewa | | 5744 | | 1887–8 | | | | | |
| | | 9549 | | 1887 | | | | | |
| Clifton | | 5744 | r. r. emps. | 1886 | | | | | |
| Intn'l Bridge | Victoria | 4425 | r. r. emps. | 1885–6 | | | | | |
| Merritton | Maple Leaf | 5933 | cotton workers | 1886–93 | | 500 | | | |
| Niagara Falls | | 5744 | | 1887 | | | | | |
| Port Colborne | Peninsular | 3279 | mixed | 1884–7 | 48 | | | | |
| Port Dalhousie | Harbour | 2513 | mixed (sailors) | 1883–9 | 67 | | | | |
| Queenston | | 8310 | mixed | 1886–8 | | | | | |
| St. Catharines | Fidelity | 2056 | mixed | 1882–93 | 137 | | 465 | | 140 |
| | | 2543 | coopers | 1883 | | | 42 | | |
| | Advance | 2573 | tailors | 1886–7 | | | 125 | | 100 |
| | Welland Canal | 7025 | sailors | 1886–9 | | 1,000 | 20 | | |
| | | 7907 | clerks | 1886–7 | | | 50 | | 50 |
| | Barry | 9437 | axemakers | 1888–93 | | | 45 | | |
| | Ontario | 618 | wheelmakers | 1887–8 | | | 40 | | |
| | Perseverance | 827 | | 1887–8 | | | | | |
| Thorold | Mountain | 6798 | mixed | 1886–93 | | | | | |
| | Beaver | 7908 | stonecutters | 1886–9 | | | | | |
| | Advance | 8625 | mixed (women) | 1886 | | | | | |
| Welland | Aqueduct | 7902 | mixed (stonecutters) | 1886–8 | | | | | |
| York | | 7623 | r. r. emps. | 1886–7 | | | | | |

*Note:* Includes all LAs within the geographic region of the DA, excluding telegraphers' LAs.

Table 2.15. *Berlin DA 241*

| Place | LA name | LA no. | LA type | Years in existence | Pre-1886 peak | Membership 1886 | 1887 | 1888 | 1889 |
|---|---|---|---|---|---|---|---|---|---|
| Ayr | | 5181 | mixed | 1886 | | | | | 770 (all LAs, bracketed) |
| Berlin | | 7469 | mixed | 1886–8 | | | | | |
| | | 9226 | | 1886–8 | | | | | |
| | | 9690 | | 1887–8 | | | | | |
| | Germania | 9691 | (German) | 1887–8 | | | | | |
| | | 10561 | | 1887–8 | | | | | |
| Brantford | Pioneer | 2491 | mixed | 1883–5 | | | | | |
| | Maple Leaf | 2817 | woodworkers | 1883–7 | | | | | |
| | Olive Branch | 3469 | factory & sewing girls | 1885 | | | | | |
| | Standard | 3811 | molders | 1885–6 | | | | | |
| Galt | | 6112 | mixed | 1886–9 | | | | | |
| Georgetown | | 2413 | mixed | 1882 | | | | | |
| Guelph | | 2821 | mixed | 1883–4 | 11 | | | | |
| | | 2980 | mixed | 1882–92 | 237 | 350 | | | |
| | | 4703 | reed organ bldrs. | 1885–6 | | | | | |
| | | 6275 | mixed | 1886–9 | | | | | |
| Hespeler | | 6058 | mixed | 1886–8 | | 100 | | | |
| New Hamburg | Victoria | 5652 | mixed | 1886 | | | | | |
| Paris | | 4173 | mixed | 1886–8 | | | | | |

*Note:* Includes all LAs within the geographic region of the DA, excluding telegraphers' LAs.

Table 2.16. *Uxbridge DA 236*

| Place | LA name | LA no. | LA type | Years in existence | Pre-1885 peak | Membership 1886 | 1887 | 1888 | 1889 |
|---|---|---|---|---|---|---|---|---|---|
| Cobourg | | 2598 | mixed | 1883–4 | 157 | | | | |
| Collingwood | | 2812 | mixed | 1883–4 | 20 | | | | |
| Gravenhurst | | 10669 | lumberworkers | 1887–9 | | | | 300 | |
| Huntsville | | | | | | | | | |
| Lindsay | | 5402 | mixed | 1886–9 | | | | | |
| Midland | | 6089 | r. r. emps. | 1886–9 | | | | | |
| Norway | | 7623 | | 1887 | | | | | |
| Oshawa | Etna | 2355 | mixed | 1882–9 | 278 | 250 | 80 | | 160 |
| | Tylors | 4279 | iron molders | 1885–9 | | | 44 | | 68 |
| | | 4428 | agric.-impls. workers | 1885–6 | | | | | |
| | Cedar Dale | 9678 | steelworkers | 1887 | | | 50 | | |
| Owen Sound | | 6631 | mixed | 1886–8 | | | | | |
| Peterborough | | 6952 | mixed | 1886–93 | | 80 | 35 | 75 | 45 |
| Port Hope | | 2786 | mixed | 1883–6 | 109 | | | | |
| | | 6727 | sailors | 1886 | | | | | |
| Port Perry | Pride of the North | 5330 | mixed | 1886–90 | | | | | |
| Uxbridge | Maple Leaf | 5331 | mixed | 1886–90 | | | | | |
| Whitby | | 2510 | mixed | 1883–4 | 32 | | | | |

*Note:* Includes all LAs within the geographic region of the DA, excluding telegraphers' LAs.

Table 2.17. *Belleville DA 235*

| Place | LA name | LA no. | LA type | Years in existence | Pre-1886 peak | Membership 1886 | 1887 | 1888 | 1889 |
|---|---|---|---|---|---|---|---|---|---|
| Belleville | | 2900 | wood & iron-workers | 1883–8 | 157 | | | | |
| | | 4427 | mixed (women) | 1885–8 | | | 200 (2900, 4427, 6919 combined) | | |
| | | 6919 | mixed | 1886–8 | | | | | |
| Brockville | Franklin | 2311 | dockworkers | 1882–5 | 258 | | | | |
| | | 6388 | r. r. emps. | 1886 | | | | | |
| Carleton Place | | 4812 | mixed | 1885–9 | | | 40 | 50 | 45 |
| Cornwall | | 6582 | weavers | 1886–9 | | | 180 | | |
| | | 6583 | mixed | 1886–92 | | | | | 166 |
| | | 358 | | 1889 | | | | | |
| | | 696 | | 1890 | | | | | |
| Gananoque | | 7504 | | 1886–7 | | | | | |
| | | 7508 | mixed | 1886–8 | | 200–300 (7504, 7508, ?, 10185 combined) | 500 (7504, 7508, ?, 10185 combined) | 150 | |
| | | ? | | 1886–7 | | | | | |
| | | 10185 | | 1888 | | | | | |
| Kingston | Limestone | 9452 | | 1887–8 | | | | | |
| | | 553 | longshoremen? | 1888 | | | | | |
| | Mayflower | 10432 | tailoresses | 1888 | | | 1,500 (Kingston LAs combined) | 300 | |
| | Frontenac | 10539 | ironworkers | 1887–95 | | | | | |
| | | 741 | bldg. trades | 1888 | | | | | |
| Napanee | Courage | 9216 | | 1886–9 | | | | | 185 |
| Pembroke | | 1226 | | 1889 | | | | | |
| Perth | | 2735 | mixed | 1883–9 | 27 | | | 175 | 50 |
| | | 9487 | | 1888 | | | | | |
| Prescott | Grenville | 696 | | 1888–96 | | | | | |
| Smiths Falls | Unity | 6722 | mixed (agric.-impls. workers) | 1886–8 | | | 200 | | |

*Note:* Includes all LAs within the geographic region of the DA, excluding telegraphers' LAs gaining in numbers and influence."[32] Thus, when DA 235 met for the first time in March 1888 it did so with considerable optimism.[33] The DA had some 1,500 members at its founding. It flourished into the 1890s, although it had serious difficulties in Kingston after 1889.[34] Attempts made in the 1890s to reorganize the DA enjoyed little success.[35]

The pattern of later development and ongoing strength into the 1890s is most apparent, however, in Ottawa. In the nation's capital 100 miles north of Kingston, the Knights enjoyed their last boom in Ontario. Although Ottawa already had a telegraphers' Local, organization really got going in the late 1880s. In 1887 the Ontario Bureau of Industry reported two Assemblies (probably Capital mixed LA 5222 and perhaps clerks LA 2806). In 1888 Frontenac lumberworkers LA 193 was formed and it was joined in 1890 by Chaudière lumberhandlers LA 2966. Ottawa plumbers LA 1034 and Rideau cabinetmakers LA 1619 were organized in 1890. That same year saw a considerable burst of activity with various labor candidacies, an active new Trades and Labor Council, a Knights of Labor Hall at Sparks and O'Connor, and initial discussions about establishing a labor paper. In 1892 a new DA 6 was formed (see Table 2.18), reporting an initial membership of 2,000. Activity continued throughout the 1890s; in June 1893, for example, DA 6 reported ten active LAs with a membership of over 300.[36] In the fall of 1894 there were six LAs still active in DA 6.[37] The Order retained a visible presence in Ottawa into the early 1900s with at least three active Assemblies: letter carriers LA 2422, Capital mixed LA 5222, and Harmonica (musicians?) LA 2588.[38]

Although the Ottawa pattern is not typical, the extremely varied histories of the Knights of Labor in the different regions of Ontario should suggest that considerable care is necessary when generalizing about the causes and timing of the Order's demise. For example, in 1898 John Hayes reported that some thirty new LAs had been organized in Canada outside the jurisdiction of the then functioning DAs (Montreal DA 18, Quebec DA 20 and Glace Bay DA 35).[39] The Order continued to exist even into the twentieth century: federal Department of Labour records indicate single LAs in Ottawa (LA 5222), Kingston (LA 2411), and Hamilton (LA 2455), while in Toronto they note the new DA 180, organized on 6 May 1900, which contained six Locals. Also, in 1901 Ottawa letter carriers organized an additional LA 2422. In 1903 an Assembly emerged in Trenton as well. There were also two closely related organizations: Joseph Marks' Industrial Brotherhood, Directory No. 1 in London, and former St. Catharines' Knights of Labor leader James Carroll's United Wage Earners in Merritton.[40]

In 1902 the Trades and Labor Congress expelled all the Knights' LAs in an

Table 2.18. *Ottawa DA 6*

| Place | LA name | LA no. | LA type | Years in existence | Membership (1889) | 1892 | Jan. 1893 | April 1893 |
|---|---|---|---|---|---|---|---|---|
| Ottawa | Ottawa | 1034 | plumbers | 1890–93 | | | 21 | 21 |
| | Rideau | 1619 | cabinetmakers | 1890–93 | | | | |
| | | 2034 | | 1893 | | | | |
| | | 2422 | letter carriers | 1901–2 | | | | |
| | Commercial | 2806 | clerks | 1883–1904 | | | 30 | 29 |
| | Chaudière | 2966 | lumbermill workers | 1890–4 | 225 | 475 | 50 | 58 |
| | Capital | 5222 | mixed | 1886–1904 | | | 29 | |
| | Letter "O" | 70 | millmen | 1894 | | | | |
| | Progress | 406 | laborers | 1894 | | | | |
| | | 528 | | | | | | |
| | Invincible | 540 | coal carters | 1894 | | | | |
| | | 1017 | | | | | 13 | 13 |
| | | 3744 | | | | | | |
| Hull | | 2676 | | 1891–4 | | | 123 | 161 |
| | | 3724 | | 1893–4 | | | 23 | 26 |

*Note:* Includes all LAs within the geographic region of the DA, excluding telegraphers' LAs.

effort to crush dual unionism, thereby irrevocably separating international unionists and Knights of Labor. This split, coming many years after its equivalent in the United States, was the subject of considerable debate. Even after this so-called Berlin decision, however, many local trades councils refused to act on the orders calling for the banishment of all Knights of Labor.[41] This was true in Toronto, for example, where as late as 1903–4 recently created DA 180 boasted five active Assemblies. Nevertheless, by 1908 the Order in Ontario was dead. In that year even stalwart Excelsior LA 2305 of Toronto failed to report.

Despite this twentieth-century presence, there can be no doubt that the Order's peak strength lay in the 1885–9 period. In those years the Order had organized 66 percent of all LAs and had had between 70 (1885) and 160 (1886) Locals in existence at one time. (See Table 2.9.) What all this means, we would argue, is that the Knights of Labor represented the most important moment in the history of Ontario labor until the coming of the Congress of Industrial Organizations in the late 1930s. More workers were drawn to the cause of the Order in more Ontario communities and in greater numbers than most of us can actually believe. Across the province between 10 and 80 percent of all workers in particular cities and towns – and we stress once more that these are minimum estimates – became Knights of Labor. That structural context was a large part of the warp, woof, and web of the history of the 1880s. We have, against Powderly's advice, divided this out from the emotions, the passions, and feelings of the membership, and it is now time to turn to another aspect of the history of the Order. Chapters 3 and 4 present detailed examinations of the Order in Toronto and Hamilton, the industrial cities in which the Knights of Labor enjoyed their greatest successes, and in which the emotions, the passions, and the feelings of the membership climbed highest.

# Part II. The local setting

Knighthood means justice to every human soul.

Richard Trevellick, Knights of Labor leader, 1885

I have learned to love and honor [the Order] for the instructions it is ever ready to impart; the anxious care it sustains in behalf of justice and individual rights; the desire it expresses not only in words but in deeds to advance the cause of moral and intellectual culture; the hope it cherishes of harmonizing discordant factions; for the determined efforts it has already made to elevate the standard of labor, distribute more equally the profits thereof, and unite the interests of humanity in one common brotherhood.

Lydia Drake, Michigan Knight of Labor, 1883

# 3. Toronto and the organization of all workers

Toronto was the focal point of Knights of Labor activity in Ontario throughout the 1880s. Although it trailed Hamilton and other smaller locales in the initial chartering of LAs, it would grow to maturity as a labor-reform center with more authority and substance. The Order arrived in Toronto in the summer of 1882 and in the following four years the Knights of Labor organized over fifty LAs and, at its peak strength in 1886, it represented almost 5,000 workers. For a brief moment the city's working class stood united together, its unprecedented solidarity engendered by the dramatic street railway strike of 1886. As we will see in Chapter 6, the massive independent labor campaigns of the next winter were but another indication of this solidarity, and challenged the long unquestioned subordination of the working class in the political realm. In these years Toronto's activist contingent of the Knights of Labor rose to national prominence, providing key leaders in the province-wide expansion of the Order. While Phillips Thompson quickly assumed the role of labor theorist and social critic, D. J. O'Donoghue and A. W. Wright established intimate connections and influence with Powderly and the American headquarters of the Knights of Labor as well as with politicians in Toronto and Ottawa. In the highly localized experience of the Knights of Labor in Ontario, Toronto thus stood out as a core of strength and leadership: if eyes on the periphery turned away from the local scene they were likely to be cast in the direction of the metropolitan center, and when pleas were issued for aid and assistance they were often sent to Toronto.

In spite of this obvious significance, however, the Knights of Labor seem to present perhaps the greatest enigma in Toronto working-class life in the late nineteenth century. Conflicting images of old and new are conjured up in the very name of the body. The feudal values of dignity, pride, and self-respect associated with the chivalric appellation "Knights" apparently contrast with the image of solidarity invoked through "Labor," a term, moreover, that roots the Order, not in the romance of the past, but in the realities of industrial-capitalist society. The Order's founder, Uriah S. Stephens, often mixed these themes: "Knighthood must base its claim for labour upon higher grounds than participation in the profits and emoluments and a lessening of the hours of toil and fatigues of labour. These are only physical effects and objects of a grosser nature, and, although imperative, are but stepping stones to a higher cause, a nobler nature."[1] This evocative combination of chivalry and class struggle, of tradition and innovation, occupied a pivotal place in the rhetoric and practice of the Order. What was at issue was not so much an ambiguous tension as a creative if flawed attempt to effect an organizational breakthrough in working-class life.

As the most sophisticated local critics of the new industrial capitalism, the Knights of Labor built upon the lessons of the past to fashion an order they thought capable of forging a new future. They knew well the barriers to be overcome, the defeats that had weakened such efforts in the past, and the difficulties ahead. It was for these reasons that they saw, correctly, the need to cement solidarity with more than mere self-interest, and to cultivate class attachments that extended beyond particular social groupings. If they also took from this past the need to approach strikes cautiously, lest they end in bitter defeats that could only cultivate cynicism, this should not surprise us greatly; if they favored arbitration, rather than outright confrontation, we can see in this not always a collaborationist stance of surrender but an approach to class relations understandable given the limited experience available to late-nineteenth-century labor reformers. In the Ontario of the 1880s, as we have seen, monopoly, for all the cries the Knights raised against it, had not yet got a stranglehold on social and economic life. Working men and women could still conceive of an industrial society in which justice and "fair play" were more than illusory flights of imagination. These were years of economic transition, in which capitalism in Canada was moving toward more concentrated and powerful forms of domination, and labor-reform thought, as articulated by the Knights of Labor, was necessarily rooted in the inhibitions and limitations of that milieu.[2]

In specific settings, however, and particularly in Toronto, it was not such limitations and inhibitions that stamped themselves most notably upon the Knights of Labor experience. Rather, it was the Order's catholic notion of both purpose and organization that seemed essential. As Toronto's *Wage Worker* argued in 1883: "Any and all measures that may tend in the direction of improving the position of the wage-earner, either financial, social, or political comes within the aim of the Order. These ends may and can be best attained by the combined effort of *all* workers irrespective of their trades."[3] Chivalry was thus no mere throwback to an idyllic past: it was conceived by all true Knights of Labor as the bedrock of solidarity upon which a broad reform effort could be sustained. In this sense the Knights of Labor surpassed their more conventional trade union brothers. A detailed discussion of the Order in Toronto indicates the successes and the failures attained and suffered throughout this period of labor upheaval.

## Early development

Toronto's telegraphers organized Morse LA 2163 and joined DA 45, the National Trade Assembly for their craft, thus establishing the Knights of Labor in the city in August 1882.[4] One month later Toronto shoemakers organized Pioneer LA 2211.[5] Undoubtedly the prominence of former Crispins in the Order in the United States, such as Charles Litchman, made the Knights of Labor attractive to shoemakers. Their early prominence alerts us to the important organizational innovation that the Knights represented. Craftsmen who had seen clearly the effects of machinery on their trade, such as coopers and shoemakers, had learned in the 1870s the necessity of reaching out to all workers. Uriah Stephens had argued in 1861 that "as unions now exist" he had "little or no faith in their power to raise the toiler to the position he should occupy" because they were "too narrow and too circumscribed in their field of operations." Instead he envisioned "an organization that will cover the globe" and "include men and women of every craft, creed and color" under the "guiding star mutual assistance."[6] Indeed, this notion was entrenched in the structure of the Order. By constitutional definition:

> The LA is not a mere trade union or beneficial society, it is more and higher. It gathers into one fold all branches of honorable toil, without regard to nationality, sex, creed or color . . . While it retains and fosters all the fraternal characteristics and protections of the single trade union, it also, by the multiplied power of union, protects and assists all.[7]

That craft barriers were often detrimental was perhaps the greatest lesson of the 1870s for some elements of the working-class leadership. When T. V. Powderly, the GMW of the Knights, visited Toronto in 1884, he emphasized the point:

> In the United States fifteen years ago . . . each trade had its own organization, but of concerted action among all branches of trade and labour there was no thought. Then if the question was asked of the mechanic: "Why do you not bring into your union the man who works at your side?" The answer would be, "Why he is only a common labourer."[8]

The Knights, he added, recognized no such distinctions. Two years later the former Scranton machinist connected this insight with his own work place experience:

> With the introduction of labor-saving machinery the trade of machinist was all cut up, so that a man who had served an apprenticeship of five years might be brought in competition with a machine run by a boy, and the boy would do the most and the best. I saw that labor-saving machinery was bringing the machinist down to the level of a day laborer, and soon they would be on a level. My aim was to dignify the laborer.[9]

It is fitting, then, that an 1882 female shoe operatives' strike provided a major impetus for the Knights' introduction to Toronto. In that struggle, the workers likened their movement's character to the mythical attributes of a previous age, claiming that a noticeable feature of the conflict was "the ready assistance" extended to the women workers by their brothers. "The age of chivalry has certainly not passed," claimed the *Trade Union Advocate*, "when we find that men at work at other trades are voluntarily assisting, with money that they can ill spare, the girls that are strong to redress what they consider a grievance." The Toronto labor upheaval of the 1880s thus began with an alliance of resurgent craft unionists and unskilled women, presenting a united front that had not been seen in Toronto since the nine-hour struggle of 1872. Only a few months later the male shoemakers dissolved their union and joined the Order *en masse* in Pioneer LA 2211.[10]

Perhaps the most important event in the early organizational history of the Order in Toronto, however, was the founding of Excelsior LA 2305 in October 1882. This mixed LA also grew out of the shoe operatives' strike. A number of experienced trade unionists, who were later instrumental in the Order's growth throughout Canada, and who had come together earlier in support of the women shoeworkers, created LA 2305. The most important of these, printer and former labor member of the Ontario legislature, Daniel J. O'Donoghue, quickly became Powderly's unofficial Canadian lieutenant and played an integral part in the later delicate negotiations with the Catholic Church. Joining O'Donoghue in LA 2305 were Charles March of the Painters Union, a former president of the Toronto Trades and Labor Council (TTLC) and first chairman and first president of the Canadian Trades and Labor Congress (TLC); Alf Jury, a tailor and pioneer English trade unionist, Free-thinker, and cooperator; John Carter, painter, first president of the Canadian Labor Union (CLU), and president of the Central Co-operative Society; and Phillips Thompson, a prominent journalist and humorist, then becoming Canada's leading labor-reform intellectual.[11] March later explained to Powderly that he "became a member of the Order because its Platform of Principals commended themselves to my reason." This, he added, also applied to "many other friends of mine, who were active and progressive Trade Unionists years before the Order or its Principals were concentrated in a body and platform."[12] O'Donoghue, March, and Jury were almost solely responsible for the central Canadian strategy of the Order until the summer of 1886, when they were displaced by the creation of a Toronto DA, followed by the ascendancy of A. W. Wright in both Canadian labor-reform circles and T. V. Powderly's affections.[13]

O'Donoghue's major contribution to the Canadian Knights lay in thoroughly integrating them into the already established trade union world by obtaining Knights' representation in the Canadian TLC and in the TTLC. O'Donoghue identified this as an essential policy and sought Powderly's aid in 1884.[14] Powderly responded, offering the support that O'Donoghue sought.[15] Despite some initial hostility from TTLC trade unions, the policy succeeded. The major opposition came from the printers, but they were won over in the summer of 1884 when the Order's strong support for their important struggle against the Toronto newspapers consolidated the labor forces.[16] The success of O'Donoghue's strategy laid the basis for the Knights' effective control of both the TTLC and TLC for the next decade, as well as helping to sustain "the boys from 2305" in their informal control of the Toronto Order. Their power rested almost solely on O'Donoghue's special relationship with Powderly, which O'Donoghue cultivated assiduously. The one official position that they held was Charles March's commission as an Organizer, granted in late 1883.[17]

Even after the organization of LAs 2163, 2211, and 2305, the growth of the Knights of Labor in Toronto was slow. The failure of the telegraphers' summer 1883 strike checked expansion for a time. Shoemaker William Lane, Toronto's first organizer, helped charter only two new LAs in 1883 (Maple Leaf LA 2622, a mixed Assembly of workers at the Massey Agricultural Implements Manufacturing Co., and Queen City LA 2782, previously a local union of saddlers and harnessmakers). His successor, Charles March, organized four LAs the following year. Three of these came in the fall of 1884 after the positive publicity the Order received for its support of the printers. As Harry Griffiths had noted, the "sudden turn" of the printers' strike had indeed "set the ball going at full speed."[18]

## "A great awakening"

The great boom in organization began in late 1885 (ten LAs) and continued in the first half of 1886 (thirty-one LAs). The drive that began in October 1885 ended only in the following March, when Powderly froze organizational efforts to give the Order a chance to consolidate. In these eight months thirty-five LAs had been founded. After the lifting of the ban on organizing, four LAs were added in late 1886 and three in early 1887.

The nature of the organizational surge took on many of the trappings of a revival. Young advocates noted that "the demand for K. of L. organizers from almost every section is far in excess of the supply" and termed it "a veritable boom . . . a great awakening amongst those:

Who toil and spin,
Who drink the dregs,
Commit the sin
of being poor."[19]

Another writer carried this metaphor further, explaining that "Sundays are devoted to preaching this second gospel, and spreading the light amongst those whose labor during the week keep them toiling through the evening hours." Moreover, he added, under "the banner of the grand army of workers:

They rest not by day or night, but their march is ever onward, until the cause of humanity shall be triumphant and the she-wolf poverty banished from the earth. Then, and only then, will a true Knight lay aside his lance and shield contented, until then it is the manifest duty of every man and woman to do his or her part or share in spreading what has been aptly called "the gospel of discontent."[20]

Even an old hand like O'Donoghue termed the drive "extraordinary" and claimed further that "'booming' is hardly suggestive enough" to describe the process.[21] In his Ontario Bureau of Industries Report he would lapse into the religious imagery of his fellow enthusiasts when describing the successes of "the missionaries of the Knights of Labor."[22]

The official reports of DA 125 illustrate statistically, if less graphically, this remarkable surge of the Knights. As of 1 July 1885, DA 125 reported ten LAs with a total membership of 358. The next year the Toronto DA counted forty-one LAs and 4,997 members. Membership fell in 1887 and by 1888 DA 125 had declined to 968 members (see Table 3.1).[23]

Table 3.2 provides a complete organizational profile of the Toronto Knights and demonstrates the remarkable range of workers embraced by the Order. From machinists to longshoremen, from carpenters to street railway conductors and drivers, from plumbers to seamstresses, the Knights organized all. The names that the rank and file chose for their LAs are also suggestive. They ranged from the eulogistic – Beethoven, Powderly, Uriah Stephens, Victor Hugo – through the craft oriented – Wheatsheaf, Ironworkers, St. Crispin, George Stephenson – to the local – Queen City, Annex, Dovercourt, Yorkville Star. All, whatever the specific orientation, reverberated with pride, self-respect, and chivalry, and stood as concrete indications of labor's new-found strength.

Table 3.2, while confirming the Order's rapid growth, simultaneously casts some doubt on explanations of its rapid demise. Despite a considerable decline in membership, the number of Locals that persisted into the 1890s reveals that the Knights had a lasting presence in the Toronto labor world, including an early twentieth-century resurgence.

Table 3.1. *Membership in the Knights of Labor in Toronto*

| Date | No. LAs | No. members | Average no. members |
|---|---|---|---|
| July 1882 | 3 | 152 | 52 |
| July 1883 | 5 | 515 | 103 |
| July 1884 | 8 | 347 | 43 |
| July 1885 | 10 | 358 | 36 |
| July 1886 | 41 | 4,997 | 122 |
| July 1887 | 48 | 2,764 | 58 |
| July 1888 | 37 | 968 | 26 |

*Source:* General Assembly, *Proceedings*, 1882–8.

Tables 3.3 and 3.4 draw our attention to an extremely significant factor in the history of the Toronto Knights: their extremely volatile membership. Table 3.3 illustrates this in a static way, showing only the total ebb and flow of members at given points in time. Table 3.4 demonstrates, unfortunately only for the years of extremely slow growth, the vast number of Toronto workers who flowed through the organization. These five LAs suggest that the Order must have directly touched and influenced far more Toronto workers in this decade than the already impressive membership data initially suggest. In addition it explains why O'Donoghue was most impressed not by the "new charters issued" in 1886, but rather by "the very large quota paying up back dues."[24]

Our organizational profile reinforces the notion that the Knights of Labor's clear commitment to organizing all workers regardless of craft, ethnicity, or sex, achieved considerable success in Toronto. Moreover, this success included many skilled workers as well as the previously unorganized unskilled. The immense organizational gains of the Knights in 1885 and 1886 stemmed both from their attempt to organize on an industrial basis across craft lines and from their success in bringing weaker local unions into the Order as whole units. The first technique, for which the Knights are well known, was evident in the unionization of the Massey workers (LA2622), workers in the Toronto musical instrument industry (LA 3181 and LA 3684), Clarke's trunkmakers (LA 3491), the Toronto Street Railway workers (LA 4535), Firstbrooks' boxmakers (LA 5792), and women garment workers (LA 7629). Cases where the Knights replaced former independent unions were the telegraphers (LA 2163), factory shoeworkers (LA 2211), barbers (LA 4538), laborers (LA 5037), bookbinders (LA 5743), handsewed shoemakers (LA 6250), carters (LA 6563), longshoremen (LA 6564), and tailors (LA 8527).

A third method of organization favored the creation of LAs in crafts where

Table 3.2. *Toronto LAs of the Knights of Labor, 1882–1907*

| LA | Month org. | Year org. | Last date known | Occupation | Name of LA |
|---|---|---|---|---|---|
| 2163 | Aug. | 1882 | 1883 | telegraphers | Morse |
| 2211 | Sept. | 1882 | 1893 | shoemakers | Pioneer |
| 2305 | Oct. | 1882 | 1907 | mixed | Excelsior |
| 2622 | Apr. | 1883 | 1896 | mixed (Massey workers)[a] | Maple Leaf |
| 2782 | Aug. | 1883 | 1890 | harnessmakers | Queen City |
| 3181 | May | 1884 | 1893 | piano polishers | Beaver |
| 3490 | Nov. | 1884 | 1890 | upholsterers | Acme |
| 3491 | Nov. | 1884 | 1903 | trunkmakers | Unity |
| 3499 | Nov. | 1884 | 1894 | bakers | Wheatsheaf |
| 3656 | Mar. | 1885 | 1887 | r. r. brakemen | Dominion |
| 3684 | Mar. | 1885 | 1894 | piano woodworkers | Covenant |
| 4025 | July | 1885 | 1893 | watchcase makers | Eureka |
| 4298 | Oct. | 1885 | 1893 | mixed | Progress |
| 4534 | Oct. | 1885 | n.k. | street car employees | |
| 4538 | Oct. | 1885 | 1887 | barbers | Annex |
| 4614 | Dec. | 1885 | 1893 | painters | Powderly |
| 4679 | Dec. | 1885 | 1887 | jewellers | Alpha |
| 4786 | Dec. | 1885 | 1886 | silver-platers | Brittania |
| 4999 | Jan. | 1886 | 1893 | mixed | Dovercourt |
| 5087 | Jan. | 1886 | 1893 | laborers (excavators) | Uriah Stephens |
| 5254 | Feb. | 1886 | 1894 | mixed (ironworkers)[a] | Pride of the West |
| 5399 | Feb. | 1886 | 1886 | cigarmakers | Ontario |
| 5493 | Feb. | 1886 | 1887 | plumbers | Phoenix |
| 5579 | Feb. | 1886 | 1887 | r. r. workers | Headlight |
| 5588 | Feb. | 1886 | n.k. | mixed | Brampton |
| 5625 | Feb. | 1886 | 1893 | teamsters | Royal Oak |
| 5650 | Feb. | 1886 | 1894 | ironworkers | Ironworkers (Parkdale) |
| 5742 | Mar. | 1886 | 1896 | mixed (coopers)[a] | Energy |
| 5743 | Mar. | 1886 | 1894 | bookbinders | Hand in Hand |
| 5792 | Mar. | 1886 | 1894 | mixed (boxmakers)[a] | Star of the East |
| 5845 | Mar. | 1886 | 1893 | tinsmiths | Star of the West |
| 5882 | Mar. | 1886 | 1887 | woodworking machinists | Standard |
| 6250 | Apr. | 1886 | 1893 | handsewn shoemakers | St. Crispin |
| 6290 | Apr. | 1886 | n.k. | mixed | (West Toronto) |
| 6420 | Apr. | 1886 | 1893 | mixed | Onward (Parkdale) |
| 6429 | Apr. | 1886 | 1893 | carpenters | Paragon |
| 6563 | Apr. | 1886 | 1893 | mixed (carters)[a] | Primrose |
| 6564 | Apr. | 1886 | 1907 | longshoremen, coal heavers | Mayflower |
| 6724 | Apr. | 1886 | 1893 | boilermakers | Elite |
| 6953 | May | 1886 | n.k. | mixed (carpenters)[a] | |
| 7210 | May | 1886 | n.k. | mixed (brickmakers)[a] | Yorkville Star |
| 7311 | May | 1886 | 1893 | carriage makers | Hub |
| 7362 | May | 1886 | | mixed (sugar refiners)[a] | Freedom |
| 7629 | May | 1886 | 1893 | mixed | Hope (women) |
| 7661 | May | 1886 | 1893 | brassworkers | Good Intent |
| 7814 | June | 1886 | 1895 | mixed (journalists)[a] | Victor Hugo |
| 8235 | July | 1886 | 1893 | carpenters | Empire |

Table 3.2. (*cont.*)

| LA | Month org. | Year org. | Last date known | Occupation | Name of LA |
|---|---|---|---|---|---|
| 8527 | Sept. | 1886 | 1893 | tailors | Golden Fleece |
| 9005 | Nov. | 1886 | 1893 | machinists | Geo. Stephenson |
| 9344 | Jan. | 1887 | 1893 | brewery workers | Industrial |
| 9433 | Jan. | 1887 | 1894 | musicians | Beethoven |
| 9848 | Mar. | 1887 | 1893 | rattan workers | True |
| 10536 | n.k. | 1887 | n.k. | | Happy Thought |
| 409[b] | | 1889 | 1893 | tailors | Silver Fleece (women) |
| 1960 | n.k. | 1899 | 1904 | r. r. teamsters | Maple Leaf |
| 2099 | n.k. | 1899 | 1900 | | Progress |
| 2138 | n.k. | 1899 | 1904 | letter carriers | Victoria |
| 2454 | n.k. | 1901 | 1904 | coal drivers | Primrose[c] |
| 1537 | n.k. | 1902 | n.k. | | |

[a] Official Knights designation "mixed" but known to be predominantly workers in the bracketed category.
[b] LAs organized after 1888 received the numbers of lapsed Locals.
[c] Probably a reorganization of LA 6563.
*Source:* This table is constructed from: Garlock, "A Structural Analysis"; Forsey, "The Knights of Labor"; Toronto City Directories; TTLC, *Minutes;* TLC, *Proceedings;* Knights of Labor, General Assembly, *Proceedings;* Powderly Papers; and our reading of the Toronto daily press and the Canadian labor press up to 1892.

trade unions already existed and continued to exist, but it was in these areas that trouble occasionally arose between the Order and the unions. In Toronto such disputes affected the bakers (LA 3499), cigarmakers (LA 5399), and carpenters (LA 6429, 6953, and 8253). Conflict also arose in 1886 when a fight in Hamilton between the Cigar Makers International Union 55 and Knights' cigarmakers LA 7955 led to problems in Toronto. This acidic confrontation arose over the chartering of some "scab" cigarmakers into an LA, and is detailed in Chapter 4. It revealed the extent to which rank-and-file Knights of Labor animosity could be engendered by their leaders' often less than forthright attempts to walk the tightrope of trade union–Knights relationships. In the case of the cigarmakers, the Order's public endorsements of the principles of organized labor contrasted with their internal advice to LAs. They paid for such duplicity with the alienation of their cigarmaking supporters, who wasted no time in withdrawing from a body that practiced solidarity only in the breach. Toronto stogiemakers W. B. Varry and W. V. Todd issued their condemnation of the officials of the international Order in uncompromising language: "Resolved that the Knights of Labor under the present Executive Board is a cheat and a fraud to the wage workers and an

Table 3.3. *Membership in individual Toronto LAs, 1882–9*

| LA | 1882 | 1883 | 1884 | 1885 | 1887 | 1888 | 1889 |
|---|---|---|---|---|---|---|---|
| 2163 | 125 | 200 | | | | | |
| 2211 | 20 | 191 | 107 | 31 | 100 | | |
| 2305 | 12 | 55 | 25 | 29 | 45 | 40 | 40 |
| 2622 | | 43 | 90 | 56 | 160 | 81 | 81 |
| 2782 | | 26 | 26 | 25 | | | |
| 3181 | | | 52 | 48 | 30 | | 20 |
| 3490 | | | 13 | 24 | 20 | | |
| 3491 | | | 19 | 39 | 60 | | |
| 3499 | | | 15 | 55 | 100 | 64 | |
| 3656 | | | | 19 | | | |
| 3684 | | | | 32 | 30 | | |
| 4298 | | | | | | | 15 |
| 5845 | | | | | 30 | | |
| 7814 | | | | | 20 | 21 | |
| 8527 | | | | | 261 | 200 | 200 |
| Total | 157 | 515 | 347 | 358[a] | (856)[b] | (406)[b] | (356)[b] |

[a] Only up to 1 July 1885.
[b] Data are not for all Toronto LAs.
*Source:* Data for 1882–5 from Knights of Labor, General Assembly, *Proceedings;* and for 1887–9, Trades and Labor Congress, *Proceedings; Globe,* 3 October 1887.

enemy to all bona fide labor organizations and unworthy of our confidence and support and that this LA show its condemnation . . . by withdrawing in a body from the organization." For LA 5399, which had joined the Order in February 1886 only to take its leave in disgust a brief seven months later, the Knights of Labor proved a deep disappointment.[25]

Such trade union–Knights of Labor disputes, however, were noticeably absent in the pre-1886 years, and the Knights' willingness to organize the entire working class captured the imagination of Toronto and North American workers. Despite some hostility, large numbers of Toronto unionists joined Knights' mixed Assemblies as individuals while retaining their union cards, following the earlier path of "the boys from 2305." Thus the Order in Toronto soon embraced artisans and laborers, Orange and Green, Methodists and Freethinkers, Tories and Grits, men and women, and even black and white. For one critical year, the cultural divisiveness of race, sex, creed, ethnicity, and partisan politics was largely overcome by the sweep of the Knights' organizational efforts and the promise of labor reform. This new unanimity on the part of Toronto workers represented the peak of their first serious challenge to industrial capitalism. Young men recalled this experience vividly for the rest of their lives.[26]

Table 3.4. *Volatility of membership in selected Toronto Locals, 1882–5*

| LA | No. members 1 July 1882 or at first report | Members added 1882–5 | Members deleted 1882–5 | No. of members 1 July 1885 |
|---|---|---|---|---|
| 2211 | 20 | 272 | 261 | 31 |
| 2305 | 12 | 131 | 114 | 29[a] |
| 2622 | 10 | 198 | 152 | 56 |
| 2782 | 26 | 15 | 16 | 25 |
| 3181 | 28 | 50 | 30 | 48 |
| Total | 96 | 666 | 573 | 189 |

[a] In 1886 LA 2305 swelled to 550 members but fell back to 45 within the year. See O'Donoghue to Powderly, 5 April 1886, *PP*.
*Source:* Knights of Labor, General Assembly, *Proceedings*, 1882–5.

In Toronto, for example, Knights organized black workers for the first time. Annex Assembly 4538 (barbers), Primrose 6563 (carters), and Mayflower 6564 (longshoremen and coal heavers), all included black members. This led to racist press jibes, especially with reference to the barbers. A Knights of Labor meeting was described in the *World* by "A Virginian": "The color line was not drawn, and Lord Montgomery of Richmond St., arrayed in purple and fine linen, was as big a toad in the puddle as any of them." A Knight, under the pseudonym "Ethiope," later defended the Order against such racist fulminations: "the colored Knight is as much a representative of the toiling masses on this continent as his white brother, and the spirit which seeks to degrade him and to exclude him . . . is the same arbitrary, tyrannical and aggressive spirit which seeks to rob the white as well as the colored laborer of the fruits of his toil, the enjoyment of life, and the pursuit of happiness." Despite the rather American ring of the vocabulary of this declaration, "Ethiope" went on to point out that the Empire contained many loyal blacks as well as whites.[27]

The clearest indication of the drive to organize all workers came in the Order's concerted effort to organize Toronto women workers. An earlier attempt in Toronto to organize women shoemakers by the Knights of St. Crispin had been wrecked on the shoals of employer intransigence. Even the relative success of the 1882 female shoe operatives' strike had proven to be illusory when the shoe companies later failed to fulfill their commitments to the strikers.[28] Although Toronto unionists had shown interest in the organization of women, it was only after the Knights arrived on the scene that a concerted organizing drive was attempted. In February 1883, for example, "Sewing Machine" criticized the TTLC organizing committee, questioning their "earnestness of purpose."[29] The real effort began in the fall of 1885 and, according to D. J. O'Donoghue, had "the object of improving the conditions generally of young women and girls employed in shops, factories, etc."[30] This effort resulted in the organization of Toronto's first LA composed entirely of women. Hope LA 7629 drew tailoresses and other women workers to its ranks, and received its charter in May 1886.[31] Unlike some women's Assemblies that availed themselves of dispensations to allow men to serve as MW, Hope was completely self-governing.[32] Moreover, unlike their sisters in the Toronto shoe factories earlier in the 1880s, Hope's workers spoke for themselves and allowed their names to appear in print. Women served on the Executive Board of DA 125 from its inception in 1886. A member of the DA Executive Board from 1886, Miss E. Witt, became the District's Director of Women's Work in 1889. K. Lucy Shankland served with her that year on a Committee on the State of the Order.[33]

In 1886 the Order held a series of meetings to try to extend organization among women. In March about seventy tailoresses gathered at Richmond Hall to hear the benefits that joining the Order would offer them.[34] After speeches by Alf Jury and other leading Knights, Mrs. Keefer of the Women's Christian Temperance Union made an impassioned speech in support of the Order. A motion in favor of organization was passed unanimously, and the sisters pledged themselves to meet again the next week and bring their friends. The next meeting, chaired by Mrs. Tomlinson of Hope Assembly, was addressed by Mr. Greerson of Golden Fleece LA 8527 (tailors) and by Miss Ford and Mrs. Greerson.[35] These meetings resulted in a demand by Hope Assembly for a 20 percent wage increase, which was backed by LA 8527.[36]

The Order also brought Leonora Barry, the Knights' General Investigator of Women's Work and Wages, to Toronto in 1888 to help in the organization of women and to investigate the conditions of women workers.[37] In her week-long visit she delivered eight speeches and provided the General Assembly and the DA with a detailed description of women's work and wages in the city.[38] She noted approvingly that there were already "quite a number of women organized." By the time of T. V. Powderly's second visit the following year, an additional mixed women's Assembly, Silver Fleece LA 409, had been established.[39]

An anonymous letter to the *Journal of United Labor*, written by a Toronto woman Knight, chronicled both the ongoing efforts and the difficulties the drive to enroll women encountered:

We are trying to get the working girls of Toronto interested and educated on the subject of labor and the industrial and economic questions which are of vital importance to them. While the conditions of our working girls in Toronto are not as bad as in some of the large cities in the U.S., yet there is much need for reform in many things. One great fault which ought to be overcome among women is their selfishness – working for selfish motives only and overlooking the interests of those who are helpless, thinking it would be unnecessary for them to join our Order unless they received immediate benefits and all the evils which have existed for years to be overcome at once.[40]

The "selfishness" that this writer mentioned undoubtedly stemmed from the fact that for most women industrial workers in Toronto in 1889 work was still generally viewed as an interval between puberty and marriage. The Knights tried to exploit this social reality by organizing socials for men and women workers, thus creating an institutional context that would recognize the particular life-cycle experience of young women workers.[41] One such "At Home" took place in May 1889. Hand-in-Hand LA 5743 sponsored an entertainment in Shaftesbury Hall to which it invited all the women workers in the bookbinding trade. Robert Glockling chaired the meeting, and speeches by Alf Jury and Miss Witt on the values of organization were enhanced by songs and recitals by various men and women of the trade.[42] Another soirée held by Unity LA 3491, the employees in H. E. Clarke's trunk factory, attracted over 250 women.[43] Hope LA 7629, the first Toronto women's Assembly, also sponsored socials. A successful "Fruit Social" in October 1886 featured E. E. Sheppard, *The News*' editor, in the chair, and involved the familiar amalgam of songs, readings, and speeches.[44]

## Ritual and education

This kind of social activity was common among all Knights, not just the women members, and conditioned a solidarity that was reinforced by secrecy and ritual. Although in most late-nineteenth-century fraternal societies secrecy was simply an intriguing adornment, for the Knights it continued to fulfill an important function. In Toronto, for example, Knights were victimized by both the Street Railway Company and by the Heintzman Piano Company. Cases such as these, where jobs depended on the secrecy of the Sanctuary, demonstrated the functional elements of the ritual. At the same time, their solemnity and the values they evoked were a rich celebration of traditional working-class values.[45]

The importance of ritual to the Order was illustrated in many ways. Powderly spent much of his time as GMW adjudicating disputes that arose from divergent readings of the "secret work," the *Adelphon Kruptos*. Some of the earliest correspondence between Powderly and Toronto Knights, for example, concerned the suspected divulgence of the Order's secret work. Roger Mullen, organizer and MW of telegraphers' Morse LA 2163, wrote for advice in the case of the Wynn sisters. One sister, Bella, belonged to the Order, but Laura did not. Laura had aroused his concern by describing a dream: "She dreamt she was in a strange office and shaking hands. Said she shook hands this way (giving our grip) and that one fellow had a wooden fin and could not make it properly." Mullen decided that Bella must have revealed the Order's secret work to her sister, and, consequently, he sought the former's withdrawal card until Laura could be convinced to join. As he had no proof, however, he sought Powderly's approval for his action. Powderly, who by no means answered all his copious mail, not only responded but recommended an ingenious experiment. Instead of requesting her withdrawal Mullen was instructed to give a different grip to those he suspected and, if it was subsequently divulged, he would have proof of their guilt. The results of this complicated procedure are unknown, but this minor episode of intrigue indicates the great importance of ritualistic practice to both local members of the Order and the international leadership.[46] Indeed, secret signs and words were prominent in the early history of the Toronto Order.

When Knights' General Lecturer A. A. Carlton visited Toronto in 1886, admission to his private lecture to the Order was "by password."[47] Finally, Toronto LA 2305 used the secret sign for announcing meetings. The pages of the *Trade Union Advocate* were often graced with symbolic announcements:[48]

| 1 | 26<br>8 |
|---|---|
| | 2305 |

Such numbers and graphics simply noted that Excelsior LA 2305 would meet at 8 o'clock on 26 January.

The same factors that led to the Order's emphasis on ritual also accounted for the importance that Powderly and his lieutenants placed on education. One constant refrain found in their writings and speeches was the necessity of utilizing the Order to educate the working class of the United States and Canada. Labor papers accompanied the Knights' successes throughout Canada, and were a clearly perceived tool in educational efforts. In Toronto the Knights were actively involved with Eugene Donavon's *Trade Union Advocate/Wage Worker*. Donavon's paper commenced publication in 1882, appearing as the organ of the "new era in unionism." Its name changed when it became the voice of the Knights of Labor, its purpose expanding beyond the confinements of trade unionism to the larger aims of the Order. "We feel that our labours ought to embrace the rights, the wrongs, and the material interests of *all* who earn their livelihoods through the sweat of their brow," proclaimed the newly christened *Wage Worker.*[49] This educational effort was carried on by the Hamilton *Labor Union* and *Palladium of Labor* after the demise of Donavon's early venture, and Toronto Knights' intellectuals, such as Phillips Thompson, wrote copiously for the Hamilton journals, which published from 1883–7. In December 1885 the *Palladium* set up a Toronto office as well. The Toronto *Palladium* was purchased in 1886 by A. W. Wright, and transformed into the *Canadian Labor Reformer.* Appearing simultaneously in Toronto was D. J. O'Donoghue's *Labor Record,* which published from 1886 to 1887, when it merged with the *Canadian Labor Reformer.* After this merger and the failure of the Hamilton *Palladium,* the *Labor Reformer* became the official paper of both DA 61 Hamilton and DA 125. It succumbed in 1888 but made a short comeback in late 1889 under the editorial direction of Thompson. Finally, in late 1890 the same editor started the *Labor Advocate* as a copublication of DA 125 and of the TTLC. It lasted until late 1891.[50]

The appearance of the popular daily evening penny paper in this period, a medium aimed at a working-class audience, created yet another outlet for the Knights' propagandistic efforts. In Toronto, *The News,* edited by E. E. Sheppard and Phillips Thompson, ran from 1883 to 1887 as a strongly pro-Knights paper. It was available on a joint subscription with the *Palladium.*[51] The presence of the labor press and of the new popular papers forced the established newspapers to reconsider their attitudes and even their space allocations. Thus John Cameron's *Globe* invited Knights' leader D. J. O'Donoghue to contribute a weekly labor column.[52]

The Order's leaders also made extensive public lecture tours. During these engagements it was customary for the visitor to give at least one large public lecture and later to meet in private with the local Knights. Powderly visited Toronto in 1884, 1889, 1891, and again in 1894; Richard Trevellick did the same in 1883, 1885, and 1886; and other Knights' leaders, including Leonora Barry, A. A. Carlton, T. B. Barry, and Tom McGuire, visited Toronto. Toronto in turn provided speakers for the Ontario hinterland. The labor papers and O'Donoghue's correspondence were filled with descriptions of speaking engagements for O'Donoghue, Alf Jury, Charles March, Phillips Thompson, Sam McNab, and A. W. Wright. These tours of area towns aided immensely in the spread of the Order and often led to the establishment of new LAs. In all of these efforts O'Donoghue and the other Toronto Knights' leaders emphasized education as their major concern. Even at the height of the 1885 organizational boom O'Donoghue wrote: "Organization progresses here at an extraordinary rate . . . I wish to Providence I could say our *education* was increasing in a like ratio but at present I am debarred that privilege. I am very optimistic nevertheless, and do not despair as to a decided improvement in the ultimate result of our efforts."[53] Given these sentiments it was not surprising that O'Donoghue was "delighted" with the General Executive Board's organizing freeze, regretting only that "the time is not longer even" than forty days.[54]

Perhaps of more importance in the educational work than all of this, however, was the very structure of the Order. All LAs had to buy the *Journal of United Labor*, the organ of the Knights, which was filled with educational material about political economy and cooperation and later about the single tax and Bellamyite nationalism.[55] Moreover, every LA meeting had structured into it a discussion of labor in the area, a theoretical consideration of the labor question, and finally the collection of statistics on the local labor situation. In a Toronto speech, Knights' General Lecturer A. A. Carlton described "the local assemblies scattered over the continent" as "the schools of teaching the people to remedy the mistakes of the past."[56] Toronto Assemblies often made arrangements "for the regular reading of essays and delivery of addresses upon the principal questions in which labour is interested."[57] Entrenched in the Knights' constitution was the invocation that "Political Economy should be freely discussed in LAs." "In this way," Section 197 added, "the justice or injustice of members' surroundings is made apparent." From such perceptions of injustice came forth numerous motions and petitions that were forwarded to the Canadian Order's lobbyists in Ottawa and Toronto. Moreover, the collection of data by local Knights was integrated by O'Donoghue into his work compiling labor statistics for the Ontario Bureau of Industry. This job allowed O'Donoghue to appoint Knights' activists as his research allies throughout Ontario and insured the sympathetic collection of material.[58]

All of these educational efforts were an essential part of the Knights' orientation, aimed at the dual transformation of North American workers' consciousness and the society they lived and worked in. One of the major statements of this reform thrust was *The Politics of Labor*, published by Phillips Thompson in 1887.[59] This book distilled the various reform sentiments of the Order, presenting them as a programmatic guide to the membership and the working class at large. Stressed throughout the book was the necessity of education as the key aspect in attaining any long-term change in the social order and political economy. Thompson, both in *The Politics of Labor* and in his editorial writing in the *Palladium*, the *Labor Advocate*, and later in the 1890s in the *Journal of the Knights of Labor*, advanced the notion that workers could not gain by industrial warfare. Strikes, he argued along with other prominent Knights, were outmoded tools that cost the workers far more than they could hope to win. Only through political action, it was maintained, could labor successfully change the society in which it stood confined to inferior status. These views, which were shared by many leaders of the Canadian Order, must be seen as a response to the defeats of the 1860s and 1870s, but they could not find a truly receptive audience among rank-and-file workers, who continually faced the intransigence of employers. While the wider educational thrust gained many adherents, then, the Order's narrow view of the class struggle led it into some ambiguous official positions, which the membership had constantly to grapple with. Arbitration, for instance, was one of the key planks of the Knights' platform, but in an age when most employers denied their workers the rights of collective bargaining, arbitration was all too often unworkable. Blacklisting, yellow dogs, and ironclads were constant companions of these early years of "labor relations," and the strike was a tactic that workers could ill afford to sacrifice or depreciate. It was in this context that the Order attempted to educate its members to regard the strike as a final resort. In Toronto and other Ontario centers, the Knights set up institutional checks to insure that all avenues had been explored before recourse was taken to strike action. But they could never forsake the strike entirely as a weapon, and the Toronto experience is an indication of just how stubbornly the working class clung to this particular mode of confrontation and of how employers forced labor to employ it. Indeed, in Toronto as elsewhere, the choice of whether to strike was often not made by workers, but by employers, who consciously maneuvered their workers into confrontations designed to break all forms of working-class organization and resistance. Education, no matter how thorough, could never overcome this material reality.

## Strikes

The history of Toronto's Knights of Labor is intimately connected with the class conflicts of the 1880s. Their major fights in Toronto, despite their hope for arbitration, were waged over the fundamental right to organize. The Order was associated with at least twenty strikes between 1883 and 1892 (see Table 3.5), although most occurred in the peak years of 1886 and 1887. This represented approximately 23 percent of the total of eighty-eight strikes fought by Toronto workers in this ten-year period, an indication that the Order's efforts to avoid strike situations were not all failures.[60] The first Knights' strike, the 1883 telegraph operatives' struggle, followed the same pattern in Toronto as elsewhere on the continent, and indicated that when

Table 3.5. *Strikes involving the Knights of Labor in Toronto, 1883–92*

| Year | Number | Industries | LA Involved |
|---|---|---|---|
| 1883 | 1 | Telegraph Cos. | 2163 |
| 1886 | 9 | Massey Agricultural Imps. | 2622 |
| | | Cobban Mfrg. Co. | 4786 |
| | | Toronto Street Railway | ? |
| | | Williams Piano Factory | 3181 |
| | | Toronto Street Railway | ? |
| | | Plumbers | 5493 |
| | | C. Boeckh & Sons Brushes | ? |
| | | Labourers | 5087 |
| | | Ewing & Co. Cabinets | 3684 |
| 1887 | 7 | Clarke Trunk Factory | 3491 |
| | | Heintzman Piano Factory | 3181 & 3684 |
| | | Custom Shoemakers | 6250 |
| | | Firstbrook Packing House Factory | 5792 |
| | | Toronto Upholstery Co. | 3490 |
| | | Carpenters | 6429, 6953 & 8235 |
| | | Tailors | 8527 |
| 1889 | 3 | Custom Shoemakers | 6250 |
| | | Bakers | 3499 |
| | | Coopers | 5742 |

the Order was forced to fight the results would be spectacular.[61] Major struggles with the Masseys and with Frank Smith's Toronto Street Railway (TSR) are other examples.

A pattern emerges clearly in the smaller strikes, with issues of workers' control most often being the catalyst.[62] The struggles at Ewing's picture frame factory and Boeckh's brush factory revolved around shop rules and management's impatience with them; at Williams' piano factory it was the standard rate and the boss' refusal to pay it to all LA members.[63] Another example was the successful strike at Cobban's Manufacturing Company where the gilders of LA 4786 struck to limit the number of apprentices and to gain a wage advance. A city-wide strike of plumbers in 1886 concerned not the closed shop, which the Knights had secured, but rather whether there should be more than one rate.[64] The 1887 Crispin LA 6250 strike involved an increase in the city-wide rate previously won by the union, as did the coopers' strike involving Energy LA 5742 in 1889.[65] The last three strikes illustrate well how the Knights often operated precisely as had the predecessor union in their craft. On occasion new Knights' craft Assemblies also were successful in implementing such agreements. In 1886, for example, Acme

LA 3490 (upholsterers) demanded: a standard time rate to replace piece rates; a nine-hour day and a fifty-hour week; a regularized five-year apprenticeship program; and a fixed ratio of one apprentice to three journeymen.[66] The upholsterers won that time, but lost ground again in 1887 when the DA failed to back them in a struggle against the Toronto Upholstery Company.[67]

Knights' Assemblies, especially among previously unorganized workers, fought to establish shop rules equivalent to those enjoyed by skilled workers with long-standing union traditions. How fierce this battle could become at the shop level is illustrated in the following:

> Michael O'Hara, foreman of the workroom of the American Watchcase Company on Adelaide St., was charged at Police court by William Hahn, one of the employees, with assault. The complainant told the Magistrate how O'Hara had on Thursday struck him in the face and threatened to shoot him, at the same time drawing a revolver. He said that the row was caused by his refusal to speak to O'Hara. He had been forbidden to do so by his shop union which O'Hara had refused to join when invited to do so by the other men. Another young man, also a member of the union, told how O'Hara had incurred the body's displeasure by discharging an employee and refusing to ally himself with them.[68]

The convicted foreman responded violently to Eureka LA 4025's attempt to control their work environment; other employers bided their time. Baking, for instance, was one old Toronto craft where the workers had not managed to establish viable craft rules. Wheatsheaf LA 3499 enjoyed significant success in managing to gain reduced hours, a standard rate, and apprenticeship rules in this previously unregulated and viciously competitive industry.[69] Unfortunately, this 1886 agreement broke down quickly and the creation of a dual union of bakers complicated matters considerably.[70] Finally in 1889 unity was restored and a strike won back some of the ground lost after 1886.[71]

Such control struggles, generally waged by skilled workers employed in small craft settings, remind us of how the Order could function very much like the trade union in striving to secure a limited measure of control over the work place lives of its members. In other, larger confrontations, however, it was the right of organization and affiliation with the Knights of Labor that was at issue, a prerequisite to any struggle focused on aspects of workers' control.

One of the Knights' major encounters in Toronto came in February 1886. The Massey agricultural implements manufacturing works had been relocated in Toronto in 1879 after a fire destroyed the company's Newcastle factory. It immediately prospered in Toronto and doubled its size by purchasing its major local competitor in 1881. It employed as many as 700 workers, and quickly became Toronto's largest factory.[72] In over thirty years of production in Newcastle and for the first five years in Toronto, the Masseys knew nothing of organized industrial conflict. The Masseys' Methodist conscience and sound business sense led them to supply their workers with a memorial hall, a library and reading room, a band, a Workmen's Library Association, a Mutual Benefit society, and even an in-house workingman's paper, *The Triphammer.*[73] In contrast, their major American competitor, Cyrus McCormick, was waging an all-out war against his workers in Chicago.[74]

Despite the Masseys' paternalistic schemes, storm clouds appeared at the works as early as 1883. In that year the company reduced wages 12½ percent, dropping the skilled workers from $2 to $1.75 a day and the laborers from $1.25 to $1.10. Although these wage cuts were not actually resisted, "Old Ripsaw" wrote to the *Palladium of Labor* to complain about the reduction.[75] Approximately one year later, blacksmith Sam McNab of LA 2622 corresponded with Powderly about the Masseys' latest cut. The plant had been switched to an eight-hour day from the customary ten and wages reduced accordingly. In McNab's words, "Now the skilled workmen and they are few get $1.50, the labourers and they are many get 88¢." McNab, who had just received his organizer's commission from Powderly, proposed that when the Masseys decided to return to ten hours, the workers should refuse. Instead they should demand eight hours and a wage increase of 10 or 12½ percent to cover the previous reduction. McNab did not expect to win both demands but thought that combining them would at least insure the regaining of the 12½ percent. He advised Powderly that "if we win this shop we can win the town; to lose will make it bad for the Order in this city." The shop was "pretty well organized" and with a demand like this "we could depend on a majority in all the departments." Powderly hurriedly responded that they should not ask ten hours' pay for eight hours' work but rather that they should demand shorter hours and only after that success "go to work on wages." But he cautioned McNab against any precipitous action and advised him to consult the more experienced Toronto Knights' leadership – O'Donoghue, March, and Jury.[76]

The advice of the GMW had its effect, and the Masseys escaped their first strike for another eighteen months.[77] On 18 January 1886 a committee of dissatisfied employees waited on the superintendent of the works and asked that a price list be posted and that they be paid on a fortnightly basis. Superintendent Johnson agreed. Five days later the men sent another committee to ask why this promise had not been carried out. The committee was one man short this time, for Josiah Ablett had been fired. On this occasion Johnson refused to post the price list, claiming that wages were a private matter between each employee and the Masseys and moreover that they did not want visitors to the plant to be able to estimate the company's costs. The men then sought aid from Knights' leaders. A delegation consisting of O'Donoghue, March, Jury, and George Beales interviewed Massey. Massey refused to meet with them and added that he would fire any employee who joined a union. He carried out this threat the following Saturday when five machinists, all prominent LA 2622 members, were dismissed without cause. On Sunday the Knights called an emergency meeting and decided to demand that Johnson rehire the fired men. When he refused the next morning, they struck. Only then did the Masseys learn how extensive was the organization in their factory. Their own estimate was that approximately 400 men went out.[78] An ever-cautious O'Donoghue explained the decision to his leader in Scranton:

> Much as I dread fighting . . . I saw that it was better in this case to risk a contest and all it implied than to desert the men who faced Massey on the strength of their faith in their brothers and the Order in general. Not to have taken the action would have ruined our character. Better far honorable defeat than that it should be said that we had not the pluck to fight for our existence and the rights even of the few.[79]

Daily strike meetings were held at Crocker's Hall near the plant and city Knights and trade unionists rallied to the support of the Massey workers. Order and control typified the workers' actions throughout; the event's tenor was best exemplified in the strikers' parade to city hall on the second day of the strike. The procession protested the massive display of force mounted by Toronto police at the plant. The workers met with W. H. Howland, the recently elected reform mayor, and complained bitterly that the police presence was a gratuitous attack on the Order, unfairly favored management by implying potential violence, and was a misallocation of their taxes. Not only would they guarantee the safety of the Masseys' property, they would personally guard it. As one old striker emphasized in the meeting with Howland, "The act was a direct personal insult to every man who had come out on strike." Howland, whom the Knights had helped elect, promised to investigate their charges and to talk to Massey. The next day, at the mayor's request, the Police Commission ordered the chief of police to remove his guards from the Massey plant. The strikers' cause was also aided immensely on the second day of the strike, when the forty to forty-five molders and their helpers, members of the International Iron Molders' Union, struck in support of the Knights. Even more important than the molders' action was the decision by the highly skilled toolroom workers to support the conflict. This came on the third day of the strike and was probably the critical turning point. Termed by the press "absolutely necessary to the factory," the toolroom workers' support ended any possibility of Massey hiring a scab labor force. It also gave further evidence of the solidarity of all the Massey workers – Knights, unionists, and the unorganized.[80]

Faced with such unity, Massey surrendered on the fifth day of the strike. The intervention of Mayor Howland, the choice of both organized labor and Massey himself in the mayoralty race of the previous month, certainly helped the workers, but it was their unanimity that won the day. The terms of the settlement, according to O'Donoghue, were a complete victory: "We have 'downed' the Massey Manufacturing Company completely. The men who *engineered* the result from behind the scene were Bros. March, Jury, McNab and O'Donoghue, through the intervention of the man *we* elected mayor last January, W. H. Howland."[81]

The five men were reinstated, and Massey agreed to recognize the Knights of Labor in his factory. After the strike, *The Triphammer* spoke of the Masseys' old faith that industrial conflict would never touch them. The strike had arisen "out of a misunderstanding and if the explanations which were made after the strike had been made before there would have been no strike at all."[82] The Masseys learned from their first taste of industrial conflict. On 10 March they announced that they would begin to pay their men fortnightly and would now withhold only five days' pay instead of the previous ten.[83] Later that year they promoted Sam McNab, the DMW of DA 125, to foreman of their blacksmith's shop.[84] They were to have no further labor trouble in the 1880s with the Knights of Labor.

The Knights also learned from this conflict. Faced with a similar situation in the spring of 1886, the Order again proved its willingness to fight. The victory at Masseys', based on class solidarity throughout the plant, extensive public sympathy, and political support from the mayor, undoubtedly prepared the Order for its battle with the TSR.

## The struggle against monopoly

TSR owner, Senator Frank Smith, had for a number of years opposed all attempts by his workers to organize. The intransigence of this Roman Catholic, Tory cabinet minister led to a lockout in March and a strike in May 1886, probably the most bitter labor dispute fought in nineteenth-century Toronto. The story began to unfold during the winter of 1885, when Smith, undoubtedly worried by the labor upsurge, demanded that his men sign an iron-clad agreement that prohibited them from joining a union. As a direct result, the previously unorganized but now insulted employees sought out the Knights of Labor.[85] D. J. O'Donoghue addressed them in secret at the

Knights of Labor Hall in early November. A press leak resulted in a report that the "old hands" had done most of the speaking and urged organization "as the only means by which they could fight the spies and obtain justice from the company."[86] Thirty-one drivers and conductors created LA 4534 that night. Only one week later O'Donoghue reported that a Catholic priest and intimate of Smith was trying to interfere with the new Assembly. O'Donoghue promised to "floor" him and wrote that "we now have a footing on the street railway system and we are determined not to surrender it." O'Donoghue, however, was too optimistic, for the next week it was discovered that "among these 31 there was an informer – a Judas – who told the Superintendent the names of the officers elected as well as the names of all who took the obligation. During the past two weeks these men have been, one by one, discharged." A blanket command from management followed, ordering the remaining Knights to sever their relationship with the Order or be fired. Faced with this ultimatum, O'Donoghue and Jury convinced the men to allow LA 4534 to lapse after only two weeks' existence. The decision was based on a realistic assessment of the available resources: "As old fighters and keeping in view the interests of the men as well as the Order we thought this course best. Cowardice was not the cause for we intend to fight. Without means financially to keep these men idle all winter it would have been cruel and impolitic to have forced them into idleness. Now the Company is keeping them for us. . . . Besides without lapsing they could not rid themselves of the Judas amongst them." Moreover, he added, "We have not lost these men. *They are at work today.*" Finally he issued an even more ominous warning: "Now we are taking steps to fight the Company and Jury and the rest have lost their cunning if this Company has not a hot time of it before we are through with them."[87]

Plans for the coming battle were immediately put into effect. Members from the lapsed LA of street railway employees were taken into O'Donoghue's own mixed Assembly LA 2305; the platform provided by the TTLC, together with the coming mayoralty race, were utilized to attack the street railway for its anti-union labor relations and other practices detrimental to its workers. The street railway franchise was a relatively easy target for O'Donoghue's "whip of scorpions."[88] A chartered monopoly, it dealt with public complaints in an arrogant fashion, infringed its charter with depressing regularity, and was thought by all to have the city council in its pocket. It also oppressed its workers in many blatant ways, paying extremely low wages, demanding excessively long hours, and providing abysmally poor working conditions.[89]

The trouble finally came in March 1886, a far more propitious season for the workers than the previous winter. The Knights began to meet with the street railway workers again that spring and held a large Sunday meeting on 7 March when the workers decided to form a new LA. The men called an emergency meeting at midnight the following Tuesday, after it became evident that Smith and his Superintendent, J. J. Franklin, had employed spies to discover the workers' plans. When the men arrived at work on Wednesday morning, they found the assignment board blank. The company claimed later that it had intended to fire only the men whom it had identified as violating the iron-clad agreement by joining the Knights (some thirty-two). The Knights, however, claimed that the company had in effect locked out its entire work force. The company's intentions mattered little, for the non-Knight street car workers walked out *en masse* with their fellow conductors, drivers, and stable hands. The company attempted to run cars for the duration of the strike using a few loyalists who remained at work (approximately twelve) and a force of strikebreakers hired that week.[90]

Men gathered at the Knights of Labor Hall on Yonge Street on the first morning, and received the Order's full support. O'Donoghue and Jury took the leadership and became spokesmen for the strikers. Crowds gathered daily. The pro-Knights' *News* described the initial confrontation:

> The scene on the streets at various points this morning was a lively one. A large crowd of working men took up a position on the corner of King and George Streets [near the TSR stables] and hooted the drivers and conductors as the cars passed . . . That the men have the sympathy of the great mass of workingmen was shown by the conduct of the drivers of wagons, coal carts, etc., who got in the street tracks and refused to turn out until the cars had been greatly delayed.[91]

By early afternoon the few cars that had managed to leave the stables found themselves surrounded by hostile crowds and blockaded by coal carts, wagons, and drays. The relatively good-natured crowd unhitched the horses but allowed them to be returned to the barns. They then derailed two cars. The company wisely decided to run no more cars that day.

On Thursday the company again tried to run cars, but the crowds, larger than on Wednesday, used the same tactics to prevent normal service. After two cars were derailed by large crowds (estimated in the thousands) the company suspended service for the second time. Mass working-class support for the strikers was again evident in the crowd's actions and also in the city's enthusiastic support of the carters, the heroes of the first two days: "Everywhere the coal carters drove yesterday they were loudly cheered. Had it not been for their hearty co-operation the cars could not have been so easily stopped."[92] The militant support for the strikers from their brothers in other parts of the horse-transport system was no doubt based on family connections and ethnic friendships (there was at this time a considerable interchange of jobs in the general field and a significant concentration of Irish Catholics). Among the "street gamins and apprentices," too, there must have been ties to the streetrailway workers, and this "most clamorous youth" was responsible for much of the mud, stones, and bricks hurled at police and scab drivers.[93] Those whose neighborhood and social links to the strikers were well developed also supported the struggle through the threat of ostracism. One scab driver reported that "a woman with a child in her arms had rushed out of a tavern on King Street West and yelled at him, 'Don't you ever dare come into my place for a drink.'"[94] Throughout the community countless workers rallied to the strikers' cause, consolidating sentiment against the company and its hirelings, joining the roving crowds. Expressions of solidarity also came from Knights much further removed. Montreal's Assemblies intervened actively to convince 200 strikebreakers recruited by Smith not to travel to Toronto.[95]

While the crowd controlled the streets, the street car workers sent a deputation led by Alfred Jury and A. W. Wright to meet Mayor Howland. Again, as in the Massey strike, the Knights regarded the use of police as an "insult." Moreover, they pointed out that the company was violating its City Charter by not maintaining service and emphasized that the striking workers had nothing to do with the crowd and could not be held responsible for its actions. Howland responded in a public letter to Smith.[96] He denounced the Tory senator's actions unhesitatingly, and condemned the street railway's anti-union stand:

> You have by your act produced this trouble, having in its face the knowledge of the result (as your application for police protection in advance of your act proves) deliberately locked out a large body of your men, not on account of any claim for higher wages or shorter hours, but simply for exercising a legal liberty, in joining a lawful body or society. This action of yours having produced the difficulty, and being the cause of the annoyance under which the citizens are labouring, I hold you and your company responsible for it, and hereby demand that you restore to the city the order which existed and to the citizens the convenience they have a right to, as they existed before your action disturbed them.[97]

This unequivocal declaration from the city's chief magistrate contributed considerable legitimacy to the workers' position and, unintentionally, to the crowd's actions.

On the third day the police were given carte blanche for the first time and the crowd, estimated at 7,000, far larger than on the previous day, ceased to be good natured: "The coal carts, express wagons, railway lorries, and vehicles of every conceivable description continued to arrive, and as each obstacle caused the driver to 'down brakes', a wild cheer broke from the crowd, which continually received accessions to its numbers from all the side streets and factories."[98] The crowd forced the first car to return to the stable, but the police won the following encounters. A phalanx of 100 police, aided by the mounted division, fought a running battle with the crowd. After many arrests and a number of serious injuries, the police were successful in breaking a car free of the crowds. The street fighting continued all morning, however, and the most serious battle of the day came at lunch time on Yonge Street, when the mounted police rode briskly through the crowd and involved themselves in individual battles. All papers reported that the police had engaged in indiscriminate clubbing in the afternoon; the police chief, buoyed by his men's success in freeing a few cars, suggested that the militia was not necessary "as yet."[99]

The same afternoon, faced with accelerating violence, a group of aldermen arranged a compromise between Smith and the Knights, which appeared to end the conflict. Smith agreed to take all his workers back, and the Knights greeted the news with enthusiasm and voted overwhelmingly to return to work. The Toronto street cars ran normally on Saturday, 13 March.

The three-day conflict had sparked crowd action on a scale unprecedented in a Toronto labor dispute. Eighteen arrests were made during the strike, most in Friday's vicious battles. Those arrested included Toronto workers from all strata, ranging from laborers to skilled craftsmen. Popular support for victimized workers was not unusual in the annals of Toronto labor disputes, but the virulence of the crowd action was. What transformed the street car lockout into open street warfare between the crowd and the police?

The strike's most perceptive analyst has argued persuasively that the crowd's actions stemmed from a pervasive working-class culture that unanimously condemned the tyrannical behavior of the TSR. Noting the crowd's discipline, David Frank has argued that it was guided by a "moral economy" that scorned scabs and sympathized with the strikers.[100] This analysis can be extended even further, for the street railway was regarded by Toronto workers as a central part of their everyday life. They were totally dependent on it, and included its service in their definition of working-class rights. Attempts by the monopolists to abridge and to exploit these rights had to be dealt with severely. This, then, accounted for Toronto workers' willingness to rush out of their shops and factories to stop the operation of the monopolist's street railway in support of their fellow workers. It was no accident that the Knights of Labor were at the center of this conflict because in many ways their organization embodied this working-class consensus. For example, the carters and other drivers who had supported their fellow transport workers so militantly joined the Knights the next month, and founded Primrose Assembly 6563 after the Knights of Labor came to their aid when they struck against one of the coal companies. Their fellow workers on the docks, the longshoremen and coal heavers, organized simultaneously as Mayflower Assembly 6564.[101]

The consensus that appeared in the streets in March 1886 against the TSR began to break down after the street railway workers returned to their jobs. The Knights claimed victory too early in this struggle. A jubilant O'Donoghue wrote to Powderly on the day after the settlement: "Only a few of the street car employees were or are members of the Order but we would not tell the public. *We have won their battle.* LA 2305 last night had 240 propositions of these men. Jury steered them yesterday to success."[102] The Knight's successes that eventful spring gave the already frenzied organizational drive even more impetus, but further trouble was imminent. Jury's March settlement was ambiguous at best. The workers and their representatives claimed that they had won total victory and that Smith had not only agreed to take the men back but had also accepted their right to organize. Smith, on the other hand, argued that he had only taken the men back on his original terms – no labor organization. This debate ultimately could only be resolved in one way, and in May the conductors and drivers were back on the streets.

It was somewhat surprising that the settlement lasted even two months for, as early as mid-April, the employees reported that Smith was flagrantly violating the agreement.[103] One conductor complained:

> Mr. Franklin tyrannizes over us the same as ever and many have got the sack for no cause whatever; it is one continuous round of petty fault finding for no other reason than to gradually weed all us union men out. But if Senator Smith and Mr. Franklin think they can buck against the Knights of Labor they make a great mistake. The new hands join the union as soon as they come on, and we've got the whole order at our backs.[104]

Only considerable pressure from the Knights' leadership kept the men at work.[105] A few days later the LA sent their secretary, Conductor Donagher, with a list of grievances to Smith. Smith refused even to hear the demands for reinstatement of fired Knights, for a wage increase from $8 and $9 to $10 for all, or for a reduction of hours from twelve to ten for conductors and drivers and eleven for stablemen. The men then sought the intervention of the aldermen who had helped settle the March lockout, but Smith refused to meet them either. In a final attempt at compromise, a TTLC committee visited Smith's partner, George Kiely. He too refused to listen to the demands of the men. Exasperated by further dismissals and having exploited every available means in accordance with Knights' principles, the men struck on Saturday, 8 May.[106]

This time, both sides in the struggle were well prepared. The company did nothing but hire scabs to keep as many cars running as possible and the mayor and aldermen, agitated by the March riots, placed their major emphasis on retaining law and order. Scenes of crowd rule could not be allowed to recur. The mayor's initial statement on this occasion was not an attack on the company, as it had been in March, but instead a proclamation "forbidding gatherings on the street during the strike."[107] Dire warnings of severe punishment were quickly forthcoming: York County Court Judge McDougall, a member of the city Police Commission, warned gratuitously that intimidation would not be permitted; indeed Police Magistrate Denison declared that any defendant found guilty of strike-related violations would face fines and imprisonment on an ascending scale of severity if the incidents multiplied.

The public also responded differently in this second altercation. The mass street actions of March were noticeably absent, no doubt partially owing to the civic authorities' warnings. One also suspects that Frank Smith's fervent denials that he had ever promised in March to withdraw the iron-clad agreement confused some people. Moreover, there had been a significant shift in North American public opinion following the Haymarket bombing, which the sympathetic *News* suggested was at the root of Toronto's less fiery support of the strikers.[108] But the major factor was the strategy of the Knights' leadership. Seemingly embarrassed by the crowd violence of March, they carefully disassociated the Order from those actions. Instead, they called on the general public to boycott the street railway. The predominantly Irish TSR employees were only too familiar with this tactic, imported from their homeland and recently used with great success by the Toronto printers.[109] Thus, from their Sunday meeting at the Irish Catholic Benevolent Union Hall, they "confidently" issued an "appeal to the general public, and to the working classes in particular, to withhold all patronage, even though at some present inconvenience, from this company in its efforts to tyrannically deprive their unfortunate employees of their undoubted right to join or belong to any legal organization they may deem advisable."[110] The boycott's effectiveness, however, depended on the availability of an alternative mode of transport; thus was born the Free Bus Company. On 11 May, the third day of the strike, four buses decorated with union jacks appeared on the Toronto streets. "Pica," the *News*' perspicacious city hall observer, enthused "This is the right way to do business; it not only gives the men work but hits the company in the fountain of monopolistic life – the pocket. Never bother appealing to a capitalist's brain when you can reach his pocket. That is the vital spot."[111] At the start the buses carried an enthusiastic clientele, and contributions were generous. Nevertheless, as each day passed more street cars ran until by 14 May, the *World* reported that the daytime schedule was almost back to normal and one week later the cars even dared to run at night.[112]

Toronto workers did not totally accept the Knights' leadership's strategy. There were a number of incidents of crowd or individual acts of violence against the scab cars.[113] In addition, many individuals acted in various ways to obstruct the street cars. Among those arrested were Edmund Livisky, a planing mill employee; Joseph Donelan, a factory shoemaker; Bernard McGuffin, a Shedden drayman; Chris Conway, a black ice-wagon driver. All were dealt with harshly by Police Magistrate Denison.[114] The one concerted street action occurred on 25 May, when a large crowd gathered to greet the arrival of nine new strikers' buses from Oshawa. Led by the Irish Catholic Benevolent Union Band, the parade of buses and strike supporters proceeded through the Toronto streets. The trouble began when they encountered their first street car, which was cursed, jostled, and stoned. The crowd, estimated by the *News* in thousands, then commenced to attack all the street cars it encountered. Knights' DMW Sam McNab intervened to counsel nonviolence, to order the band to lead the crowd away from the street car routes, and finally to send the crowd home. The next day the Knights again disclaimed any connection with the violence, which they condemned unequivocally. Thus, although there were some supportive crowd actions equivalent to the March strike, they petered out relatively quickly and were never as intense. This lack of violence led "Pica" to comment sardonically on the demonstrative show of civic force: "The police authorities' superhuman efforts to preserve order, when no attempt is being made to break the law is quite touching. . . . I will leave it to the public whether it is not slightly silly to see mounted police capering up and down the streets as though the city were in a state of siege. . . . Perhaps the police authorities are taking excessive precautions through fear that someone will steal them."[115]

The strikers' spirits were high throughout the first few weeks of the strike. In speeches, proclamations, poems and songs they emphatically asserted their demand for the right to organize. One striker invoked this theme in a song inspired by the conflict:

Drive on my lads! No slaves are we,
But sons of Canada the free,
Who prize as life our liberty.
  Drive on, my lads! Drive on!

Drive on! Drive over tyranny!
Drive on for love of Liberty;
Drive on, my lads, to victory!
   Drive on, my lads! Drive on![116]

Another theme often reiterated – the contrast between monopoly's riches and the poverty of the workers – can be seen in the following verse by striker James Downs:

I am a simple labouring man,
   I work upon the car,
To keep those hungry wolves away,
   From the poor street car man's door.

Give us fair play for every day,
It's all we ask of thee.
Our cause is right
We're out on strike,
For a poor man's family.[117]

Other indications of a strong pro-striker response on the part of the working-class community were numerous. Scabs were unable to find boarding houses to reside in; teamsters and carters again did all they could to obstruct the street cars; another ten workers were arrested for various infractions against the franchise; the public, at least initially, overwhelmingly boycotted the cars and donated large sums to the strike when they used the free buses; a city-wide public meeting chaired by Mayor Howland pledged community support to the strikers by passing unanimously motions that were proposed by Knights' leaders O'Donoghue, Jury, and Wright; and, finally, the unions and LAs of Toronto and of all Ontario donated funds and materials to the cause in a forceful and unprecedented expression of solidarity.

Nevertheless, despite the overt sympathies of the Toronto working class and the initial militance and spirit of the strikers, the struggle failed. Ironically, this was partly owing to the success of the leaders' free bus strategy, because the combination of the strikers' buses and the company's street cars provided Toronto with a vastly better transportation system than it had had before and thus the crisis activated by the strike was dissipated. With the transportation problem solved, the conflict settled down into a contest between the rich and long-consolidated street railway monopoly and the new cooperative bus company organized by the strikers and LA 2305 under the leadership of Alfred Jury and John O'Brien, the chairman of the strike committee. What had started simply as a fight against an iron-clad agreement had been transformed into a contest between capital and cooperation. Most Toronto workers recognized that the iron-clad was "a menace against their personal liberty," as one trade union leader told the *World*, and they flocked to the street railway strikers' camp.[118] But when the Knights of Labor leaders began to manifest less of an interest in the strike itself and more concern with the cooperative buses, Toronto workers perhaps thought the main battle had been won.

This general problem of community support was further complicated by a growing dispute between the strikers themselves and the Knights' leadership over the direction of the strike and the creation of the cooperative. The street railway workers were primarily interested in winning the strike and found themselves somewhat unwilling partners in a grand cooperative scheme that left settlement of their strike a side issue. Moreover, the Knights' leadership, as the management of the new cooperative, invested much of the money that was raised in aid of the strike into the buses instead of using it for strike pay. In the first month of the strike, the men complained bitterly that they had only received a little over $20 each. These debates, which began in the third week of the strike, grew ever more bitter. In response, the leaders constantly reminded the workers that they had counseled caution. Unpersuaded, the strikers continued to protest that the leaders were arrogant and made decisions without consultation. The leadership's increasingly insulting answers to public discontent certainly did little to assuage the men's growing bitterness. Unidentified members of the executive committee called the protesters "weak kneed," "snakes in the grass" and dismissed them as "kickers"; D. J. O'Donoghue added fuel to the already smoldering fire by asserting that: "Those who struck to assert a principle are still fighting and have no doubts, only those who expected to have a holiday at the expense of those who were making sacrifices, and were disappointed, were dissatisfied that they did not get a 'haul' before deserting the men whom, in so far as their votes and voices could influence, they encouraged to strike."[119]

This conflict disappeared for a while, after the founding of DA 125 brought renewed support to the strikers, but flared again in mid-June when the *World* astutely noted that the "real trouble is between the superior power of the Knights of Labor, as represented by the management committee of the Co-operative Company, and the street car men's assembly; that the latter are naturally and strenuously opposed to allowing money, which they rightly consider their own, and of which they can get none, going in chunks to sleek outsiders, who are not street-car men, nor even Knights of Labor."[120] The *World* had also earlier hinted at a less overt conflict, but no doubt one that the strikers would find most disconcerting:

As usually happens the Knights and strikers are having their "legs pulled" by the politicians. The head men in the strike are Mr. O'Donoghue (in the employ of the Ontario Government) and Mr. Jury, a prospective labour candidate in the Reform interest for West Toronto. The big thing they are working for is to arouse the workingmen against Sir John, who keeps Frank Smith in his cabinet. It is not to be all that way, however. Aleck Wright has arrived in town, started a labour reform paper and spoke at Wednesday's mass meeting. He has been a faithful organizer and candidate for the Conservatives and men with half an eye are imagining that Aleck is here to checkmate Jury and O'Donoghue. He will have his hands full – the others have got a big start.[121]

The *World*'s cynicism was answered by Wright's assertion the following day that "men may have differences on such outside issues as party politics and yet come together in the cause of labour reform."[122] Nevertheless, additional seeds of doubt had been sown in the strikers' minds by the hint of party politics intervening in the conflict.

By the third week in June it was evident to all that the Knights had lost. Finally, on 24 June the recently organized DA 125 stepped in directly to take over the cooperative. They agreed to investigate charges of financial mismanagement against Jury and O'Donoghue, to assume the bus company's debts, and to liquidate the operation. All this was done under an initial facade of continuing the struggle, but most observers understood this was only to save face. Nevertheless, when fifty-seven strikers petitioned the DA to call off the strike so that they could attempt to regain their jobs, DMW Sam McNab refused. This led to yet another round of public recriminations culminating in striker Charles Gibbons' letter to the *World* appealing for rank-and-file Toronto Knights to consider the position of "men who have worked hard and faithfully since the strike commenced till the last ray of hope had gone."[123]

Thus ended, rather dismally and sordidly, the Knights' fight with Frank Smith. After two strikes, considerable effort, many arrests, a huge outpouring of public support, and untold suffering by the strikers themselves, the Knights were defeated. Smith ran his franchise without organized workers until his charter expired in 1891.[124] In November 1890 a notice was sent from Toronto to the *Journal of United Labor*, addressed "To our Parisian Brothers," warning them that Superintendent Franklin of the TSR was on his way to Paris. After expressing their gratitude that he was leaving Toronto, the workers noted that the Paris brothers should treat him as they would "any other bully or Blackguard."[125] The bitterness of 1886 did not die quickly: before the city refused to renew Smith's lease in 1891, the men again attempted to form a Knights' LA and threatened a strike to shorten their twelve-hour day.[126]

## Factionalism and failure

For the Toronto Assemblies the failure of the street railway strike left both a legacy of bitterness and heavy debts from which the Order never fully recovered. Strife in the Order had begun to surface even before this strike, and opponents were rising to contest the previously unchallenged leadership of "the boys from 2305." The founding of DA 125, which O'Donoghue had bitterly opposed, and the election of Sam McNab as DMW were early manifestations of conflict. Perhaps more significant, however, was the DA's action in ending O'Donoghue's and Jury's ambitious cooperative bus project. The termination of this innovative but costly response to the strike signaled the beginning of open warfare between the O'Donoghue and Wright leadership factions, a complex internal political struggle we will chronicle in detail in Chapter 7. In the limited context of the 1886 strike, however, it was the final blow of defeat.

An analysis of what happened to the street railway LA's executive after the strike makes clear the magnitude of the loss. None of them returned to the employ of the TSR. Six of the nine found related work as teamsters or drivers and the other three gained employment in the building trades as general workers. Meanwhile the strikebreakers retained their new jobs on the street railway.[127] O'Donoghue nevertheless attributed the defeat, in a rather cavalier fashion, to a "want of the requisite confidence in themselves and in their friends."[128]

Only a year later, in the spring of 1887, the Order was again forced to fight for its right to exist, and its weakened state helped to condition an overly cautious reluctance on the part of the Order's Toronto leadership to press class interests consistently in a number of work place contests. The piano-manufacturing firm of Heintzman and Son fired three wood polishers with no explanation. Beaver LA 3181 sent a deputation to Heintzman to demand an explanation. The committee was told it was due to incompetent work. All three men, however, were long-term employees and active Knights and the LA refused to accept this explanation. A DA 125 committee requested permission to inspect the allegedly faulty work. After investigation, the committee ruled that the work was up to standard except for one piece, which they suspected had been placed there to deceive them. On the strength of this report, the DA asked the company to rehire the men. When the company refused, the DA Executive Board suggested arbitration, and even proposed that the arbitrators be chosen from the Toronto Board of Trade. The company twice refused this offer and then fired the LA's MW, again not offering any reason. The LA then met and by a vote of 30 to 1 demanded that he be rehired. When the company once again refused arbitration, the men struck, with DA 125's consent. The other Assembly in the plant, Covenant LA 3684 of piano woodworkers, also took a strike vote and decided by 41 to 1 to support their brother Knights. Seven weeks later, the General Executive Board sent D. R. Gibson of Hamilton to Toronto to try to settle the strike. After various discussions with both sides, he proposed that the firm rehire all their men and submit the original conflict to an arbitration board on which the Knights would be represented by DMW Sam McNab. The company accepted this arrangement, and the men returned to work.[129]

The pattern typified in this strike – of avoiding conflict at almost any cost – became even more evident as 1887 progressed and the DA's embarrassed financial situation worsened. Robert Glockling, District Recording Secretary, traveled to Philadelphia to plead before the General Executive Board for monetary aid to settle the debts incurred through the street railway strike and before the DA's formation. The failure of this mission and an increasing reluctance to strike led to a series of unfortunate incidents that substantially undermined the Order's position in Toronto.[130]

The first of these occurred during the May 1887 strike of LA 5792 against the Firstbrook Packing House Factory. The Knights struck after the dismissal of two LA members, but Firstbrook argued that this was only an attempt to force a closed shop on him. The DA intervened, supported Firstbrook against the men, and ordered the Knights back to work.[131] A second incident came in LA 3490's strike against the Toronto Upholstery Company for a wage increase. The DA again intervened to order their members back to work, and in this case the employers even reported that the DA would aid them in finding replacements if the workers refused. The DA issued an angry rebuttal of the latter charge but did not deny ordering the men back.[132]

A different, but related, problem became evident in the building trades early in 1887 when members of the plasterers and plasterers' laborers unions struck a job because of the presence of non-union lathers. The lathers on the job were, however, members of the Knights of Labor. Rather than representing only a narrow craft unionism, the incident reveals that the trade unionists' objections in this case were based on the Knights' willingness to work at piece rates, a method of pay strongly resisted by skilled building trades workers because of the usually concomitant speed-up. One Knight's response that, "We're Knights of Labor, and that's as good as being in the union, isn't it?" was also to meet with a resounding "No" from Toronto carpenters.[133]

This final and most damaging incident came in August toward the end of a brutal carpenters' strike that lasted almost ten weeks before ending in defeat for the Brotherhood of Carpenters and Joiners and the Amalgamated Society of Carpenters. The third labor organization representing carpenters, the Knights, joined the strike in a half-hearted manner at best, allowing the men to make their own decision, then unilaterally ordering their men back to work early.[134]

A Knights' version of comparable, but unspecified, activity by DA 125 was given by A. W. Wright in a Cornwall speech of 1889. He outlined how a group of Toronto tradesmen in the Order who had won $2.25 for a nine-hour day decided to seek $2.50. When the bosses refused the demand, the LA voted to strike. DA 125, however, would not sanction the strike, on the grounds that it would hurt women and unskilled men in the trade. The "discontented withdrew" and now the workers received the same $2.25 but again worked ten hours. Wright's moral: "The doctrine of each one for his own self would not do."[135] This was an appealing, if abstract, moral, but surely the Order would have done better to fight to raise the wages of all workers in this unspecified craft.

All of this understandably brought to the fore craft union antagonism toward the Order. The DA's sentiments on the strike question were also made clear in 1888 when DA 125 cooperated with Powderly in having T. B. Barry expelled from the Order. The major formal evidence against Barry was the testimony of the DA 125 Executive Board; one of their main charges was that Barry had deprecated education and cooperation and instead counseled strikes and boycotts when he spoke in Toronto.[136] These policies seriously damaged the Order in Toronto. They lost most of their carpenter members after the premature end of the 1887 strike and other groups who left later, such as the factory shoemakers, complained bitterly of the Order's increasing failure to support shop-floor struggles.[137] When the new Boot and Shoe Workers International Union led its first strike in Toronto in 1890, one commentator noted that the strike was "being run by a new society chiefly under the management of young men, who have discarded the old Knights of Labor platform of 'no strike till all other means have failed.'"[138]

Problems arising out of such contentious strikes, however, represented only one of the reasons for the Order's decline. Although less precipitous in Toronto than elsewhere, the "painful decrease in membership in DA 125" was noted as early as September 1887 by Edward Cannon, MW of True LA 3848.[139] Only a week later he wrote again with his explanation: "The Order is growing weak in Canada. Some of the causes are religious ignorance and feelings and political speculators." He added that due to an excessive District tax, LA dues were also too high.[140] These financial tensions had been present from the very birth of DA 125, because large debts had been incurred in the street railway strike. A petition to the General Executive Board (GEB) to forgive the District's back dues had failed in late 1886 and had left the DA with a serious shortage of funds.[141] The unpopular solution had been a DA per capita levy, which caused many complaints.[142] Finally he also suggested that no DA officers receive payment for their services unless they worked full time for the Order.

A similar complaint was received from J. W. Commeford of Yorkville Star LA 7210. He warned Powderly that "the Order in Toronto is run in a very reckless state." Moreover he asked if it was "legal for the District to levy a tax on its members to defray the expenses of a political campaign and forget $1500 of debt they already owe to the citizens for their services during the street railway strike?" Yorkville Star, he asserted, would pay its fair share, "although the expenses is coming so enormous that if they continue levying us it will be sure to swamp us." But what he resented, like Edward Cannon, was "the political dealers and jobbers" who profited from the Order.[143]

The Order had indeed become the target for political speculators, especially after its successful effort to elect W. H. Howland mayor in December 1885. In the following spring A. W. Wright renewed his contact with Toronto workers, after a respite as Secretary of the Canadian Manufacturers Association. Shortly thereafter came plans for a Toronto DA which O'Donoghue did his best to defeat.[144] Later, he complained that "the District 'racket'" was intended to kill the Trades Council and that its major proponents were "local big frogs" who wanted "a little puddle of their own to wallow in."[145] Finally, having lost the battle in Toronto that came at the height of the street railway war, O'Donoghue appealed to Powderly:

> *Do not allow this Charter to be granted.* Some of the locals loudest for the Charter are only in existence some one or two months. Several politicians – municipal and parliamentary – have crept into one or two of the mixed Assemblies and the object is to denigrate the T.L.C. which is obnoxious to one of the political parties – the Tory. Of course a District would soon clash as to jurisdiction and precedence with the Council and then would come trouble with the several International unions represented in the Trades Council.[146]

This desperate request failed and DA 125 was born, over the vocal opposition of "the boys from 2305." The subsequent political intrigues, which saw the rise of A. W. Wright to Lecturer, member of the GEB, editor of the *Journal of United Labor*, and personal confidante of T. V. Powderly, are discussed in detail later in this book. Their effects in Toronto, however, became clear very early. Michael O'Halloran, Master Workman of Maple Leaf LA 2622, wrote to Powderly to complain of Wright's appearance in Ottawa at a Tory banquet: "I cannot see how any officer of this Order can do his duty while

Toadying to any party and particularly as they are the same party who always raise the race and Religion cry at election time and every other time they wish to try and keep the workingmen alienated or divided."[147] O'Donoghue chronicled the Order's decline just as he had described its rise. In the fall of 1889 he commented sarcastically that, "Our DA exists yet, we meet once *every two months*, look at each other, wrangle more or less, hear what the Executive has done (very little, I assure you), approve of the same, and then go home until next meeting."[148] Almost a year later, he wrote more reflectively: "As a result of the reaction of the past two years in the career of the Knights of Labor throughout the continent, and of which this city had its share, DA 125 of Toronto has lost many 'locals.' "[149]

Despite its decline, DA 125, headed by bookbinder Robert Glockling, continued to play an active role well into the 1890s, and the leadership cadre developed by the Order retained the most important positions in the TTLC and even in the national TLC. There was a slight resurgence of interest in the Order in the summer of 1891 which prompted the General Executive Board to meet in Toronto that October.[150] Even O'Donoghue commended these new activities as "praiseworthy efforts to revive an interest in the Order." "Billy," of the International Association of Machinists, noted that upon the formation of the union in Toronto in February 1892, the "Grand Officers show[ed] high respect towards the K of L and its Grand Officers," and that L. H. Gibbons, formerly District Organizer for the Knights in the Toronto region, was active in the machinists' efforts.[151] An Organizing Committee under A. W. Holmes included old Knights stalwarts such as R. L. Simpson, D. A. Carey, Robert Glockling, John W. Davey, George Beales, and John Armstrong. They jointly issued a pamphlet, "The Hope of the Workers," which described the Order as "pledged to work for the abolition of the present inequitable industrial system." Further, they asserted their confidence that the Order afforded "the best form of organization yet devised in the interests of every branch of honorable toil." This appeal was aimed not only at nonmembers but also explicitly at "those who had left our ranks in the past."[152]

There can be little doubt, however, that this tenacity was inflated and manipulated by Knights leaders for a variety of purposes. After the anti-Powderly revolt at the 1893 General Assembly (discussed in Chapter 7), the new General Executive Board sent T. B. McGuire to Toronto to investigate charges that a Powderly–Wright axis had allowed DA 125 to retain its charter only to provide General Assembly credentials to Powderly supporters. McGuire's report confirmed these charges and stripped DA 125 of its District status. McGuire seized the DA books but allowed Glockling to retain the seal, because the latter claimed that there was some hope of reorganizing dormant LAs.[153] There was additional reason for the new leadership to remove DA 125's charter. The Toronto DA and the other remnants of the Order in Canada tended to be strong Powderly loyalists and there was much Canadian criticism of the new Hayes–Sovereign–DeLeon leadership.[154]

The Order did not disappear completely from Toronto and a number of LAs carried on the Knights' name. D. J. O'Donoghue, for example, continued to represent LA 2305 at TLC meetings until the 1902 Berlin decision. The other lasting contribution of the Order was the foundation it laid for the further emergence of international unions in Toronto in the late 1880s and early 1890s. In a number of cases former LAs joined the International as a unit just as independent unions had joined the Knights in the 1880s. The importance of this local continuity of personnel and of trade organization transcended the discontinuities of national or international units.

Although the attempts at reorganization in 1891–2 failed, at least partially owing to the onslaught of the depression, there was to be one last surge. After the economy recovered, three new LAs were organized in 1899: Maple Leaf LA 1960 (railroad teamsters); Progress LA 2099; and Victoria LA 2138 (letter carriers). This success led to the founding of a new Toronto DA 180 in May 1900. DMW Isaac H. Sanderson was a former president of the TTLC (1898–9) and a long-time Knights leader in Mayflower LA 6564 (longshoremen). Sanderson also became Worthy General Foreman on the GEB in 1901 and held that position for a number of years.

The Order's new strength in Toronto lay among unskilled workers. With the exception of Excelsior LA 2305, the Knights represented teamsters, longshoremen, letter carriers, and coal drivers. The Order managed to survive the Berlin decision for a few years, but the economic downturn of 1907-8 tolled its deathknell. Sanderson worked on, but by 1908 his letters painted a dismal picture. In May he explained to John Hayes that "I am still in the land of the living but my companions are few, and I am sorry to say getting fewer each day." He admitted that they had suspended meetings, "although once in awhile we get together a few of us and make a little noise. Rattle those old bones as it were and by that means get into the press."[155] A few months later he described one of those meetings as a "hot one." Apparently the few remaining Knights, all dual members of various international unions, were unwilling to meet a new direct challenge from the AFL. The debate was so long that for Sanderson it recalled "the old days of 125 when we had all the jawsmiths – Wright, Jury, O'Donoghue."[156] The core problem was the AFL's new offensive to exterminate the remnants of the Order in Toronto. By 1908 they were threatening to expel the Longshoremen's Union if the Local did not rid itself of its old leader Sanderson and other Knights.[157] The Order was not heard from in Toronto after 1908.

Ironically enough the very strengths of the Knights of Labor in Toronto contributed to their decline after the defeat of the street railway strike of 1886. As we shall see in later chapters, had it not been for the intensely political flavor of debate within the Toronto Order, heightened and complicated by the increasingly important role of A. W. Wright in the years of decline, the bitter confrontations within DA 125 might have proved less fatal.

But given a strong leadership, deeply committed to the ambivalences of the Knights of Labor program and factionalized by opposing political allegiances, it was only a matter of time before the wall of solidarity erected in the early 1880s began to crack. In the face of defeat and financial ruin, the Order's official reluctance to strike and its vacillating stance in the post-1886 conflicts weakened Toronto's Knights of Labor and forced the struggle with craft unionism upon them. The contest proved too much for the fading Order, for unions of the skilled were strongest precisely where the Knights of Labor were weakest; at the point of production the unions proved more durable, and survived as the Knights foundered. Toronto printers, molders, and other craft unionists in the 1880s and 1890s engaged in militant struggles to maintain old – or to establish new – traditions of control over production. This had once, as many of the minor strikes led by the Order attest to, been a strength of the Order as well, but it was no longer the case by 1887, as the strike record beginning with the Heintzman and Company fiasco establishes. Craft unionists once respectful of the Order learned to regard the Knights of Labor in a new, and dismal, light. A striking paradox resulted: while the Knights' leaders viewed industrial militancy far too skeptically and cautiously, the craft union leadership failed to translate their shop-floor strength into wider political gains for their class. Knights of Labor leaders conceived social transformation grandly but in the end, pushed from many different sources, shied away from struggle; craft unionists fought fiercely but for narrowly defined goals. The price of this strategic parting of the ways was paid for in the solidarity of the class as a whole, which disintegrated in the face of many disputes and much bitterness. The grand vision of labor's late-nineteenth-century chivalry retreated into the limited and particularistic concerns of groups of workers for whom "a higher cause" and a "nobler nature" were, for a time, forgotten.

Eugene Donavon had argued in 1883 that "The Order of the Knights of Labor is not a benevolent society exclusively; nor is it a trade union alone; nor is it a political party – it combines the best element of all of these."[158] This was its greatest strength in Toronto. It spearheaded a social movement that confronted the new industrial-capitalist society in all realms. Although it eventually failed as an organization, the Knights of Labor's influence on future developments should never be underestimated. An entire leadership cadre of both the trade union movement and of the emerging socialist movement came to initial prominence as members of the Order. Deeply touched by the Knights' experience, a generation of workers took part in, for at least a short period, a class movement that for the first time organized all workers without regard for race, sex, or skill level.[159] While the Order itself faded into oblivion, most Knights' Locals reorganized under other banners in the 1890s and early 1900s, and the total experience lived on in the collective memory of Toronto's workers. For, as the Boston *Labor Leader* reflected, one of the Knights of Labor's most important contributions lay "in the fact that the whole life of the community is drawn into it, that people of all kinds are together . . . , and that all get directly the sense of each other's needs."[160] This was indeed an invaluable discovery, and it came to Toronto's working class, albeit briefly, only with the Knights of Labor.

In the rival labor center of Hamilton developments within the Order were not dissimilar, and although the specific contours of events diverged somewhat from the Toronto experience, the end result was not markedly different. There, too, disintegration followed upon impressive gains as many LAs succumbed, "in almost every instance because they could not, as they thoughtlessly imagined on becoming Knights of Labor, revolutionize the world in a year or two."[161]

# 4. Hamilton and the Home Club

If Toronto seemed the very center of the activity of the Canadian Knights of Labor, Hamilton exemplified the universal attraction the Order held for industrial workers in late-nineteenth-century North America. The city produced no leader of national or international prominence comparable to an O'Donoghue, a Thompson, or a Wright, although it cultivated a capable layer of secondary leaders who occasionally occupied important Canadian posts and offices within the larger North American Order. Politics, while important, as we shall see in the next section, was in no way as central to the Knights of Labor experience as it was in the provincial capital to the east. Rather, it was Hamilton's role as a major producer of iron products that marked the city off as an industrial center that was of most significance in the Order's local life. As the larger, more economically diverse Toronto seemed dominated by the complex range of archetypal artisanal trades, it was the metalworkers that were of unquestioned importance in Hamilton, and LA 2225 that bore the city name was the largest and most powerful in DA 61, containing 600 iron and steelworkers at its peak. In this sense Hamilton was less peculiarly Canadian, more thoroughly integrated into the North American political economy, than was Toronto. Underlining this difference were the very names appropriated by the two centers: while Toronto claimed its right to be known as the Queen City, Hamilton, by the turn of the century, was taking pride in its reputation as the Pittsburgh of Canada. The experience of the Knights of Labor in Hamilton would reflect this material context: the Order would enter Canada via Hamilton, would hold its 1885 General Assembly in the city, and would rise and fall in a manner that more closely approximated the classic "American" pattern than any other Canadian center of labor reform.

"I became a member of the Knights of Labor about 60 years ago," recalled John Peebles in 1946, "when I was quite a young chap. I thought its programme would revolutionize the world, not only because of its programme which included Co-operation and State ownership of all public utilities . . . and the purification of Politics and of all law and State Administration which also included the full belief in the honesty and sincerity of all members of the order. In short it was a crusade for purity in life generally."[1]

John Peebles, a jeweller-watchmaker in the 1880s, was no ordinary Knight of Labor. He would play an important role in the Central Labor Union (CLU), representative body of Hamilton's organized working-class movement, where he served as a delegate from his LA, filling the position of Secretary of the CLU. In the midst of the Home Club affair of 1886, when Hamilton Knights argued over the chartering of the Progressive Cigarmakers – bitter antagonists of the Cigar Makers' International Union No. 55 – into a Knights of Labor LA, No. 7955, Peebles would resign from the CLU, prompted by his fellow Knights' opposition to the CLU's staunch endorsement of the International Union. On 23 May 1887 the Order would appoint Peebles the official organizer for Hamilton's DA 61. Before the Royal Commission on the Relations of Labor and Capital in Canada, Peebles would speak on behalf of the Hamilton Land Tax Club, and espouse the doctrines of Henry George.[2] He would later become the city's mayor in the early Depression years 1930–3. Yet, despite the uncommon prominence of John Peebles, he embodied much of the common appeal of the Knights of Labor, an appeal manifested in the growth of the Order. Peebles' recollection of the nature of the Knights of Labor was buttressed from many quarters. In words embraced by large numbers of Hamilton workers, the *Palladium of Labor* declared that "a social revolution [was] better than social degradation."[3] Fervently committed to change, Hamilton's Knights of Labor became a thriving force in the 1880s.

## Early growth and appeal

Hamilton became an early center of Knights of Labor activity, serving as the initial point of the expansion of the Order in Canada (see Table 4.1). As early as 1875 the Knights of Labor had secured a place in the city, establishing LA 119 on a secret basis; this early clandestine body had lapsed by 1880. The first openly active Canadian LA apparently had its beginnings in the city in an unfinished basement of the Canadian Life Assurance Building in the fall of 1881, although the actual chartering of the pioneer Assembly did not occur until 14 March 1882, when approximately forty painters and gilders, probably employees of the Grand Trunk shops, banded together in Alliance LA 1852.[4] From that point on the Order expanded rapidly. Hamilton was the site of Canada's first DA, No. 61, which by 1 July 1883 comprised six LAs with a combined membership of 880.[5] A year later DA 61 included twelve LAs, embracing 1,054 members.[6] In the spring of 1885, according to the *National Labor Tribune*, the Canadian stronghold had nine LAs, one with more than 600 members and the remaining eight Assemblies averaging 200 Knights each. Perhaps this was an exaggeration, but this American estimate of Hamilton's importance testified to the early foothold the Order had attained in the city. The depression of the mid-1880s, coupled with the emergence of factional strife, checked this expansion briefly,[7] and at the 1885 convention of the General Assembly, held in Hamilton in the autumn, DA 61 reported only 362 members in eight LAs.[8] With North American labor's upsurge of 1885, prompted by economic recovery, a significant victory of the Order over Jay Gould in the American southwest, and the agitational spurt arising out of the general struggle for the eight-hour day, the Hamilton DA reexperienced a period of intense growth. At the 1887 General Assembly, Hamilton reported a membership of 2,202, organized in no less than thirty-one LAs.[9] These gains would prove transitory, however, and the Hamilton Order was soon in a state of precipitous decline. The report to the 1888 General Assembly outlined the contours of a mass exodus of the Hamilton membership: 1 July 1887 (2,070); 1 October 1887 (1,648); 1 January 1888 (1,288); 1 April 1888 (532); 10 August 1888 (386).[10] Although some of the city's Knights of Labor LAs would survive into the 1890s, and at least one Assembly would be chartered as late as 1901,[11] the Order's post-1888 presence bore little relationship to its earlier prominence and strength. The essential history of the Hamilton Knights of Labor thus concentrates on the brief, but important, years 1882–7.

At the foundation of the Order's meteoric rise lay the eclectic appeal of the Knights, the promise that had drawn John Peebles to its cause. Incorporating aspects of trade unionism, the forms, ritual, and associational strength of the friendly society, and the evangelical zeal of a religion of brotherhood and social justice, the Knights of Labor produced a synthesis that transcended the fragments comprising its whole, and exercised a powerful attraction that drew many nineteenth-century wage earners to its ranks.[12]

Much of this appeal, especially as it related to the practice of craft unionists, merged with the more general efforts on the part of North American skilled workers to control their work place lives. Molders, glassblowers, cigarmakers, and machinists, for instance, were all well versed in the control mechanisms that thrived in many factories and workshops, and that remained embedded in the trade union rules and regulations of the nineteenth-century "autonomous workman." All of these skilled trades were prominent in Hamilton Assemblies; their loyalties to various forms of workers' control formed an integral part of their enthusiastic participation in the Knights of Labor. Terence V. Powderly's 1887 "Official Circular No. 17," addressed "To the Order Throughout the Dominion of Canada," advised members to "Examine carefully and cautiously into the management of inmates of workshops, mills and factories, and speak out against such things as are wrong."

Table 4.1. *Hamilton LAs of the Knights of Labor, 1875–1901*

| LA | Name of Assembly | Membership at peak period | Date established and/or flourished |
|---|---|---|---|
| 119 | | | 1875 |
| 1852 | Painters/Alliance | 150 painters/gilders | 14 March 1882; lapsed 10 June 1885; reorganized January 1886 |
| 1864 | Library/Literary/Molders | 150 mixed | 9 April 1882; 1882–7 |
| 2132 | Shoemakers | 250 boot and shoemakers | 1882–8 |
| 2156 | Phoenix | 40 bakers | 1882–3; 1886 |
| 2218 | | 34 telegraphers | 1882–4 |
| 2225 | Hamilton/Local | 580 iron and steelworkers | 7 September 1882; 1882–7 |
| 2307 | Eureka | 100 tailors | 19 October 1882; 1882–9 |
| 2450 | Cigarmakers | 60 cigarmakers affiliated with CMIU No. 55 | 1883–6 |
| 2455 | | letter carriers | 4 May 1901 |
| 2479 | | hatters | 1883 |
| 2481 | Blacksmiths & Machinists | 200 blacksmiths/machinists | 1883–7 |
| 2494 (Burlington) | | 25 | 1884 |
| 2569 | Art | 80 woodworkers | 1882–4 |
| 2586 | Vulcan | 134 Grand Trunk Railway machinists & blacksmiths | 1883–7 |
| 2807 | | | 1887 |
| 3040 | Ontario | 145 cotton and shoe operatives; men & women | 1884–6 |
| 3179 | Excelsior | 75 women cotton and shoeworkers | 1885 |
| 4814 | Musicians | musicians | 1886–7 |
| 5329 (Dundas) | | mixed | 1886–7 |
| 6798 (Thorold) | Mountain | stonecutters | 1886–8 |
| 6931 | | glassblowers | 1886–7 |
| 6951 | | | 1889 |
| 7522 | | mixed | 1886 |

| | | | |
|---|---|---|---|
| 7624 | | hatters | 1886 |
| 7822 | Longshoreman's | longshoremen/carters/teamsters longshoremen | 1886–7 |
| 7487 | Barbers | barbers | 1886–7 |
| 7955 (also listed as 7956 & 7966) | | cigarmakers/packers affiliated with Progressive CMU No. 34 | 1886–9 |
| 7993 | | mixed | 1886–7 |
| 8121 | | salesmen/clerks | 1886–8 |
| 8412 | | | 1886–8 |
| 8915 | | tailors | 1886–8 |

*Note:* This compilation compares favorably with Hamilton and district data in Garlock and Builder, *Knights of Labor Data Bank*, consulted 9 June 1978. The most significant difference is in membership estimates, where Garlock and Builder data, no doubt resting on official figures computed on the basis of members with paid-up dues, understate the size of various LAs. Relying upon impressionistic estimates of membership, the above table may reflect actual, rather than official, size of the city's Assemblies. For precise data on yearly members, date of establishment, and date of termination of specific Assemblies consult Garlock and Builder, *Knights of Labor Data Bank*.

The *Palladium of Labor*, for instance, constantly reiterated the basic theme that,

> Monopoly must not control,
> The Labor Market heart and soul.

Instead, it and its predecessor, the *Labor Union*, saw the issue of workers' control as an important aspect of the solution to "the problem of the day," the conflict between capital and labor, and noted that "everywhere the claims of labor to control production are being debated by knots of workmen." Indeed, it is impossible to consider the Knights of Labor in Hamilton outside the general context of the upsurge of skilled labor throughout the 1880s. A quick glance at the trades represented in Hamilton's LAs detailed in Table 4.1 should tell us this much.[13]

In Hamilton the issue of control was obviously central to the experience of the Order. Upon the formation of a Longshoreman's Assembly in 1886, which also embraced carters and teamsters, the *Canadian Labor Reformer* reported that LA 7822 "controls the trade." The Assembly struck the wharves in July 1887 in an effort to consolidate this position of strength, but the employers resisted and introduced black strikebreakers.[14] Phoenix Assembly, composed of bakers, negotiated with their employers in the spring of 1886 on terms that spoke strongly of their adherence to the basic tenets of workers' autonomy. Their demands included strict limitation of the number of apprentices, a set ratio of apprentices to the number of journeymen employed, limitation of the hours of labor, an end to night work, standardized wage rates, weekly wage payment, and the regulation of the peddlers' previously chaotic work routines.[15] When the masters' resisted these encroachments upon their terrain, a "true K. of L." posed the ultimate threat: "Now, if the boss bakers of this city think they have full power to work and pay their men as they deem fit they will find that the journeymen have 8,000 Knights at their back and it would be very easy to raise $4,000 or enough to start a large co-operative bakery. And if once started – which I hope it will – the masters may as well sell their wagons to the peddlers, rent their ovens to the bakers, and get out of business as fast as they know how, because we will boycott them until they cannot sell a loaf." It was a powerful inducement, and the master bakers eventually agreed reluctantly to a compromise.[16]

Closely linked to the issue of control was the struggle for the reduction of the working day. Here, too, craft unionists could feel at ease in the Knights of Labor, for Hamilton Assemblies pursued this goal with staunch determination. Men active in the Hamilton-based Nine Hours League of 1872 must have figured prominently in many LAs. John Bland, formerly an activisit in

Figure 5. Knights of Labor procession, Hamilton, 1885. *Source:* Public Archives of Canada, PA-103086.

the 1872 struggle at Wilson, Bowman and Company's sewing machine works, whose dismissal precipitated the first strike in the Canadian nine-hour movement, represented LA 1852 at the third session of the Canadian TLC, convened in Hamilton in 1887.[17] Another nine-hour man, William Omand, present at the 4 May 1872 founding of the Canadian Labor Protective and Mutual Improvement Association, was active in LA 2225 in 1884, where he led a strike at the Gardner Sewing Machine Company.[18] Finally, William J. Vale, probably one of the most active Canadian workers in the cause of the Knights of Labor, was a Hamilton printer who had served time in the 1872 Toronto strike and conspiracy trials.[19]

Beyond this continuity in the personalities dedicated to reduction of the hours of labor stretched the Order's organizational role in the 1886 struggle for the eight-hour day. Hamilton's *Palladium of Labor* printed the 1885 circular urging every "local trade and union or Assembly of the Knights of Labor" to establish "the eight hour law passed by your representatives . . . [as] a fixed rule of action from May 1, 1886."[20] The city's Knights of Labor willingly embraced this call to action, and the cry of "Eight Hours" rang out in many LAs.[21] One cynic, pointing to the failure of 1872, urged cautionary restraint, but was howled down by less conservative forces: "There was the case some years ago when the nine-hour movement was agitated in Hamilton. The time was not ripe for the innovation then, and the cause of labor received a setback from the failure of that agitation. My principle is, be pretty sure you will succeed in pushing a matter of this kind, and then work for all you are worth. I raised my voice in the Central Labor Union against the eight hour movement, but I was in a hopeless minority."[22] Michael Conway, CLU delegate from the Flint Glass Workers Union No. 13, probably affiliated with the glassblowers' Assembly 6931, was more representative. "Many of us mechanics," said Conway, "don't work eight hours a day now. I don't work more than seven hours a day myself. When the mechanics want their hours of labor shortened they are men enough to strike for it."[23] But the eight-hour day was not to be won in 1886, and three years later the Knights of Labor were still agitating for the reduction of the hours of labor, establishing "Times Leagues" in many Canadian cities.[24]

## "In one great combination"

As conscious supporters of struggles for control and the eight-hour day, then, Hamilton's Order drew many craftsmen to its ranks. For the skilled workingman, the Knights thus served as a further support for the ongoing pursuit of traditional goals. Beyond this, the Order's chief significance lay in its role in bridging the gap between skilled and unskilled, drawing together disparate strata of the working class into a common body that fought for common ends. The pragmatic structure of craft organization had inevitably insulated the skilled mechanic from other working-class elements and, aside from any conscious exclusionary ideology, effectively divided the working-class movement. The Knights of Labor did much to overcome this basic problem of labor unity.[25]

Terence V. Powderly, who came to scorn the exclusionary practices of his own organization, the Machinists' and Blacksmiths' Union, saw the Knights of Labor as a potential liberator of the divisiveness bred of separate craft structures:

Aristocrats of Labor, we
Are up on airs and graces,
We wear clean collars, cuffs and shirts,
Likewise we wash our faces.

There's no one quite as good as we
In all the ranks of labor,
The boilermaker we despise
Although he is our neighbor.

The carpenter and molder too,
The mason and the miner,
Must stand aside as we pass by,
Than we there's nothing finer.

But some day, some how, things will change,
Throughout this glorious nation,
And men of toil will surely meet,
In one great combination.[26]

Powderly may well have exaggerated the exclusionary practices of the crafts, but there is no denying the importance of the Knights of Labor in uniting skilled and unskilled.[27] It was a basic premise of the Knights of Labor that, "The war between capital and labor won't come on till laborers quit fighting among themselves," and one of the Order's most tangible contributions to the history of North American workers was its role in consolidating labor's ranks.[28]

The city was the site of the first women's Assembly in Canada, Excelsior Assembly No. 3179, composed of operatives in the cotton and shoe factories. Behind the successful organization of LA 3179 stood Miss Katie McVicar, a shoeworker.[29] McVicar, daughter of a poor Scots tinsmith and his English-born wife, joined two older sisters in the Hamilton labor force in the early 1870s. She began working, like most female factory operatives, while living at home with her parents. Unlike most women workers, however, she never married, and continued working until her early death at the age of 30, in 1886. Her comparative longevity as a worker helps to explain her prominent place in the history of women's organization. In 1883, writing under the pseudonym "Canadian Girl," McVicar corresponded with the *Palladium of Labor*, outlining the need to organize women in factories and domestic service, chronicling the difficulties involved in such thankless labor. She argued that the techniques used in organizing men – holding mass meetings, mounting platforms, and making speeches – would never work for women. Instead she appealed for a few courageous women to come forward, meet with their fellow Knights, and secure aid.[30] Her public appeal was answered by "A Knight of Labor." He urged that careful, secret discussion among female shopmates be undertaken. When ten women favored forming an LA, he suggested, they should contact him through the pages of the *Palladium of Labor*. A formal organization of an LA could then take place. The Order's secret nature rendered it a particularly valuable vehicle for women, he contended, for it allowed them to avoid public notoriety and protected their modesty – an indication that male workers had not totally overcome the limitations of a Victorian view of women. "On behalf of every lover of justice and friend of Labor," this male Knight wished the women "God speed in their noble endeavors." Not long after this exchange of letters, Hamilton's female textile workers and shoe operatives joined with their male counterparts to form LA 3040 in January 1884. In April of that same year, the women shoeworkers formed their own Excelsior Assembly, No 3179. McVicar was long remembered as a key figure in this organizational breakthrough, "the first directress of the first organized Assembly of Women of the K. of L. of Canada."[31]

Hamilton's women workers were not destined to expand upon the base McVicar had done so much to create. Between 1884 and 1885, female membership in LAs 3040 and 3179 declined from 221 to 67. In 1886 Miss McVicar's untimely death dealt women's organization a further blow. Shoemakers' Assembly 2132 sent elaborate floral offerings to her funeral, a mark of respect for one of the few effective Canadian woman organizers capable of playing a public role. Following her death, LA 3179, obviously highly dependent upon Katie McVicar, petitioned T. V. Powderly to appoint male Knights from other Assemblies to preside over the women of Excelsior Assembly.[32] McVicar's presence would be sorely missed.[33]

The Knights extended their appeal beyond the ability to draw unskilled workers, blacks, and women into the working-class movement, and created an organization that drew on the wage workers' attraction to the associational life of the nineteenth-century fraternal society, where ritualistic practices, solemn oaths, elaborate grips, passwords known only to the initiated, strict secrecy, and symbolic behavior cultivated strong ties and attachments. Hamilton workers, like those in Toronto and elsewhere across the province, found this kind of symbolism and secrecy compelling, and adhered to a series of procedures and rites that conditioned solidarity and shielded them from employer hostility. The Order's profuse use of religious imagery and enthusiasm further reinforced them in their commitment to the cause of collectivity.

## "Labor's faith," "Ah Sin," and sobriety

In Hamilton this sense of religion was strong in the minds of workingmen affiliated with the Knights of Labor. Hamilton Racey, a machinist active for the Knights in the political field in 1886, left Canada to become a missionary in China in 1888.[34] Another political activist, Edward Williams, assured Hamilton's ministry that the workers' disillusionment with the Church implied no abandonment of essential religious beliefs: "Labor's faith is strong in the ultimate success of the glorious principles preached by the lowly carpenter and knight of labor who suffered in Labor's cause over 1800 years ago, and Labor's hope will not be in vain."[35] Thomas Towers, a carpenter prominent in the affairs of DA 61, saw labor's duty posed in religious terms:

> Brethren, when we fulfil
> The Masters just demands;
> When we leave unto our children
> With pure hearts and clean hands,
> The duties he assigned to us
> To raise degraded labor; . . .
> God's blessing from Kind nature's heart
> Will bless the Knights of Labor.[36]

"We must depend upon ourselves," Towers later argued, "not as individuals, but as organized labor, inspired by a sympathy born of the natural religion of the soul, the love of humanity which will strengthen our faith in one another, that we can keep our principles ever before us and act up to them without fear of consequence or hope of reward."[37] Towers was perhaps more vocal than many of his fellow Knights, but he undoubtedly captured much of the general sentiment; religious motivation clearly served as a vital plank in the appeal of the Hamilton Knights.[38]

We have wandered a considerable distance from John Peebles' introductory statement, but not without purpose. The eclecticism of the Knights of Labor, their appeal to craftsmen and the unskilled, women, and blacks, and their attraction to the religiously or ritualistically inclined, should be apparent, and it was this kind of blending of purpose and passion that marked the Knights for success, however brief. These were the components of a "crusade for purity in life," a cause whose parameters knew few boundaries, and which therefore gained widespread popular endorsement. For many Hamilton workingmen the Order would represent exactly what they wanted it to, at least for a few exhilarating years.

As crusaders for justice and true religion, as the guardians of the social rights of the oppressed and the downtrodden, the Knights of Labor placed expansion within a purposeful framework: "I see from the Journal that last month saw in the neighbourhood of 190 Locals founded," commented a correspondent in the *Palladium of Labor*. "What does it mean? It means this much, at the low average of 20 per local, thirty-eight hundred men and women pledge in honor to each other, and to the cause of social progress toward that goal, on which is inscribed, 'Peace on earth and goodwill toward men', when that is won, then and not until then will the 'modern chivalry' cease from the work to which they have been called by man's inhumanity to man."[39]

The cause of modern chivalry was given further stimulation by the increasingly impersonalized foundations of an age of rapid capitalist expansion, a process drawing the ire of all true Knights:

> Oh give us one spark of chivalry,
> To illuminate this sordid land,
> Where grubbers save money and preach out,
> The law of supply and demand.[40]

Frank Foster, well known to Knights across North America, drew a vivid picture of the Knights of Labor's self-conception in a lecture before the Hamilton Assemblies at the Opera House in the autumn of 1885:

> We are now standing where the waves part . . . It is the work of modern chivalry in the persons of the Knights of Labor to save the nations from the fate which threatens it, a fate which, if it comes to pass, will be brought about by the war of irreconcilable elements in society. It is the duty of modern chivalry to champion the oppressed, to wage war against tyranny, and to elevate the type of manhood. It is a nobler chivalry than that of the Knights-extant of old for it knows no race, no color, no creed, and it labors for the cause of humanity everywhere.[41]

For Hamilton's *Palladium of Labor*, the Order's purpose was stated in exhilarating lines of verse:

> Work, brothers mine! Work heart and brain,
> Will win the golden age again!
> And love's millenial worlds shall rise
> In happy hearts and blessed eyes!
> Hurrah! Hurrah! true knights are we,
> In labor's lordly chivalry.[42]

In examining the workings of this modern chivalry in Hamilton we will learn much about its successes and its failure.

As in many other Canadian communities, Hamilton's Knights of Labor first caught the public eye during the telegraphers' strike of 1883.[43] Organized into an LA of the National Trade Assembly No. 45, in October 1882, Hamilton's telegraphers struck work in mid-July 1883, becoming part of a "gigantic movement, the most unanimous ever attempted in this country by any trade organization."[44] Demanding the total abolition of Sunday work, the implementation of the eight-hour day and the seven-hour night, equal pay for both sexes, and an increase of 15 percent on all salaries, the telegraphers' conflict utilized tenets of "modern chivalry" to wage a struggle against the "tyranny and unjust treatment" of a "soulless corporation."[45] It was to be a hard-fought battle, with sabotage, the cutting of wires, and the harassment of working operatives; similar tactics were soon to be employed during many North American street railway strikes.[46] Most important, however, was the bond of strength cultivated by men and women aware of their part in a movement of international importance. Hamilton telegraphers received communications from many American cities, often depreciating the efforts of botch workmen, the "cog-hog" gang, and urging all to remain firm in their stand:

> We're bound to fight,
> Our cause is right,
> Monopoly is sore.
> We have left our keys
> To take our ease,
> Let Jay Gould walk the floor.[47]

Large labor demonstrations in Toronto and Oshawa, to which the Hamilton Knights sent delegations, reinforced the strikers' determination to resist their employers.[48] From London, Ontario, came a word from the MW: "Had a rousing meeting last night and initiated six candidates. We have a committee at every train and are heading off all the 'hams,' initiating and sending them back. We number fifteen men, all of whom are in great spirits and show no signs of weakening. We intend to remain out until we go back to the office victorious. Hold the fort boys."[49]

It was not amidst cheers of victory, however, that Hamilton's telegraphers resumed their places at the keys, but in the throes of defeat. By mid-August 1883 the signs of a lost battle were clear, accentuated by the Order's inability to unite the railway and commercial telegraphers. The latter, almost to a man, were affiliated with the Knights of Labor, and bore the brunt of the hardships of the strike. The poorly organized railway telegraphers apparently stayed on the job, hoping that a victory would allow them easy access to the Order. This kind of division, which allowed messages across the wires, undoubtedly undermined the effectiveness of the strike.[50] Coupled with the powerful resistance of an international trust, this basic cleavage spelled defeat. By 15 August 1883 the telegraphers' solidarity of mid-July was beginning to give way to an impatience with the Order. Although many Hamilton Knights refused to acknowledge defeat, insisting that they would continue the strike until directed otherwise by GMW Campbell of the United States, others drifted back to work.[51] At the 1883 General Assembly of the Knights of Labor, the telegraphers expressed a bitter resentment at what they perceived as the Knights' lack of assistance during the strike. By

October 1883 NTA 45, Brotherhood of Telegraphers of the United States and Canada, had withdrawn from the Knights of Labor; with this departure, most of the Canadian telegraphers' Assemblies disappeared.[52]

This first international conflict would set the stage for the Order's future inability to protect the basic work place interests of its members, an inability conditioned by the hostility of the employers, the eclectic ties of the membership's affiliation, and, in the eyes of some historians, the Knights of Labor's fundamentally ambivalent attitude towards strikes.[53] But in these early days of the organization's growth, other aspects of the strike seemed worthy of recognition:

> Disastrous as the strike has been to a large class of workers whose resources have been exhausted in the unequal fight, we are persuaded that, so far as the cause of labor generally is concerned it is worth all and more than all it has cost . . . The steady adherence of the great majority of operators to their cause in the face of discouragements and difficulties which might well have caused them to swerve, is a bright example to other classes of workingmen and women.[54]

Defeated and blacklisted, the telegraphers found little solace in these words, but in terms of the larger working-class movement, the *Palladium of Labor* had grasped much of the importance of this early conflict.[55]

More successful than the telegraphers' strike, and indicative of the extent to which an appetite for control, usually the prerogative of the skilled, could be demonstrated by other segments of the work force, was an 1884 strike involving women operatives at the John MacPherson boot and shoe factory. The strike was initiated 14 February 1884 by fifty-five female operatives expressing disagreement over "a new system of paying wages."[56] At the root of the difficulty was an attempt by the forewoman, Miss Ellicott, to tamper with a long-established scale of prices. The early years of the decade had seen a rapid rise in the cost of living, coupled with increasing profits and rising output at the MacPherson factory. In consequence of these developments, the firm apparently implemented a 10 percent increase for all hands, and bonuses of from $15 to $60 for all foremen and forewomen. The bonus, however, did not fall equally to all of the women, for mechanized improvements in some departments had enabled some women to increase their output drastically, thus producing large wage differentials, payment being essentially by the piece. This created some discontent, and the firm's response was to attempt to equalize wages by rearranging "the bill in such a manner as to take from those who earn a little and give to them who earn less." Whatever the actual mechanism of wage adjustment, and it appears to have been more complex than the women perceived, the shoe operatives saw the matter in terms of a blunt reduction of 10 percent: "We did not like this method and consequently refused to submit to the reduction, and we do not believe there is any class of workers in this city that would not have done the same."[57]

It was the women's view of the conflict that is central, along with the widening parameters of the dispute. It was seen, essentially, as a struggle against the "under bosses," who had implemented the reduction, it was felt, to curry favor with the employers, thus assuring themselves of large bonuses in the future. Control was regarded as an important feature of the dispute.[58] Three women workers explained that "the forewoman has said that we run the bindery to suit ourselves, and as she has lost confidence in us is going to run it according to her ideas. With regard to the above, the case is the other way about. We have lost confidence, and believe that if another party had the management all parties interested would be better served."[59] MacPherson & Company, however, soon came to the support of their supervisory staff, stating that their foremen and forewomen were acting on the company's orders when they implemented the reduction. As from sixty to sixty-five male operatives were thrown out of work, and as other shoe factories, threatening a united front, raised the question of a general reduction of 10 percent imposed on all boot and shoe workers in the city, the strike came to involve more than the women of the MacPherson concern.[60]

Modern chivalry, indeed, had been present at the outset: "They have received promises of financial assistance from the Knights of Labor, although their union is not affiliated with that organization."[61] On 20 February 1884, the shoemakers of the city, members of LA 2132, issued the following declaration: "We, the shoemakers of this city, having examined into the grievances of the female operatives, find that they are justified in resisting a reduction of wages, and pledge ourselves to render all the aid financially and otherwise in our power in assisting them to gain their object."[62] By the first week in March "what seemed at first to be merely a trifling dispute over wages, [had] widened into a serious breach and become a real difficulty." When 125 of the male workers stood by their resolution, refusing to work until the dispute was settled, the firm discharged them, stating that "they were going to get non-union men."[63]

Solidarity eventually won some concessions, and a Knights of Labor deputation effected a reconciliation between the strikers and the firm. Strikebreakers were given their notice, and the old hands – male and female – rehired. The women, although unable to secure the reinstatement of the old scale, did reach a satisfactory agreement on new prices, which softened the severity of the reduction.[64] It had been a victory for modern chivalry, and undoubtedly contributed significantly to the emergence of Katie McVicar's Excelsior Assembly of Hamilton women operatives.

Struggles like these, of course, drew the support of many organized crafts. Indeed, they had followed closely upon the heels of an 1882–3 strike wave led by molders, cigarmakers, bricklayers, painters, carpenters and joiners, and tailors. The telegraphers' and women shoeworkers' battles thus impressed upon the skilled workingman the existence of a mutual discontent. More than the Knights' involvement in strikes, however, cemented this unity.[65]

Equally forceful, as a factor tending to unite skilled and unskilled, was the movement to exclude Chinese workers, a cause embraced by North American Knights with ardent enthusiasm.[66] "Ah Sin," a pseudonym reflecting the writer's orientation, utilized Hamilton's labor press to chronicle the degradation Canadian workers would experience if oriental labor were established in the Dominion. It was an argument filtered through a not-so-subtle lens of racism, but it struck home: Canadian labor had seen enough of employer exploitation of Chinese railway gangs and mineworkers in the past to realize how its own future would be jeopardized if they became a permanent feature of the labor market.[67] "Who of our community do they benefit?" asked "Ah Sin" rhetorically. "Why, the capitalist, speculator and manufacturer; none other – they are the great factor in the making of rich men richer and poor men poorer, marble palaces and dingy poor houses, Great Britain and Ireland over again, luxurious, licentious, riot and tyranny on the one hand and penury, degradation, starvation, and death on the other."[68] While the *Palladium of Labor*, reiterating an argument made in *The National* a decade before, could urge that the Chinese be treated as people, and that the blame for their exploitation be placed squarely on the shoulders of the capitalist, pragmatists like "Ah Sin," who had spent fourteen years of his life in "daily contact" and "continual competition with Chinese coolies," saw the question in less abstract terms: exclusion of an inferior race was the most expeditious solution.[69]

Widespread opposition to the Chinese culminated in a 1 October 1884 demonstration patronized by "ten assemblies of the Knights of Labor, the brotherhood of carpenters and joiners, boilermakers union, cigarmakers union, stone cutters union, iron molders union, amalgamated engineers, glass blowers union, bricklayers and masons union, . . . and unorganized and other workingmen." Estimates of the size of the demonstration ranged from 1,500 to 5,000, the latter almost surely an exaggeration. There was, however, no mistaking the purpose of the gathering or the importance of the event. Marching under banners proclaiming "Free Labor – No Slaves," "The Chinese Must Go," and "Never Fulfill a Tyrant's Will, Nor Willingly Live a Slave," the workingmen pelted mud at Chinese laundries on their route, and gathered to hear speeches condemning the government's use of Chinese labor on the construction of the CPR. David Gibson and George Collis, leading Hamilton Knights, introduced the key speakers. E. E. Sheppard, popular editor of the Toronto *News*, applauded the Order's stand: "The Knights of Labor have the noblest cause in the land, and the dignity and ability didn't come from the 'Knights', but from the 'labor,' and unless the government helped them to uphold their dignity and keep their self-respect that government is certainly criminally to blame, and it was to blame as long as it imported pauper immigrants and Chinese labor." Fred Walters, of Hamilton's Molders' Union, spoke of the honor of being part of such a large demonstration, indicative of the sympathy all working men and women had for the brethren on the Pacific coast. "An injury to one is the appeal to all," was a noble rallying cry, and he was proud of Hamilton's working class for its endorsement of the principle. John Brown, of London's Knights of Labor, brought the support of that city's workingmen, and Phillips Thompson, impressed by the turnout, dubbed Hamilton "the Banner Labor City of Canada, whose example was eagerly looked to all over the country." A resolution to curb pauper and Chinese immigration, heartily endorsed by all present, ended the talks. E. P. Morgan introduced this resolution, and we shall encounter him again.[70]

The *Hamilton Spectator* was quick to condemn the anti-Chinese cause, claiming that Chinese labor posed no threat to the city's mechanics. This critique, true on its own level, ignored the bonds of solidarity being created among the different strata of Hamilton's working class, and failed to realize the significance of thirty-two labor organizations uniting on a common front.[71] Then, too, the wider implications of Hamilton's support for North American labor escaped the *Spectator*'s critical eye. The anti-Chinese agitation, for instance, furthered the cause of independent working-class political action; the Tories' refusal to prohibit the use of "coolie" labor in the construction of the CPR drove one more wedge between Sir John A. Macdonald and the workingman. The Hamilton correspondent to the *Craftsman* condemned the recommendations of the Dominion Chinese Commission, which urged no restrictions on "coolie" immigration until the completing of the CPR: "Of course they listened only to capitalists, whose wine cellars they sampled to their heart's content and stomach's consternation, and Sir John Macdonald told them what kind of report they must present, before they started on their tour of investigation."[72] While the virulent racism feeding on this anti-Chinese sentiment would later pose serious problems for labor unity, the immediate effects of the movement for Chinese exclusion ironically contributed toward working-class solidarity and autonomy.[73]

As in the case of the anti-Chinese agitation, the Knights' support for the temperance movement won the admiration of both skilled and unskilled.[74] Carrying the temperance message into Hamilton were men of prominence in the hierarchy of the Knights of Labor.[75] Terence V. Powderly, for instance, was one of the nineteenth century's most ardent temperance advocates. Before a gathering at Lynn, Massachusetts, he declaimed: "Had I 10,000,000 tongues and a throat for each tongue, I would say to every man, woman and child here tonight: Throw strong drink aside as you would an ounce of liquid hell."[76] Powderly spoke with similar conviction before Hamilton's Knights of Labor on a number of occasions, arguing at the 1885 General Assembly that, "No great reform can be brought about by drunkards, and even when the use of liquor is not carried to excess it generally occasions an expenditure of means and a loss of time, which severely tax the resources of those who could use both to better advantage."[77] Another temperance advocate, Richard R. Trevellick, harped on the same theme, and seldom missed an opportunity to deprecate drink and its consequences when speaking in Hamilton.[78]

Views like these, reinforced by their reiteration by major Canadian labor spokesmen, gained widespread acceptance.[79] A Hamilton "laborer" condemned intemperance as the gravest danger facing workingmen, a product of "the universal thirst for gain."[80] The *Palladium of Labor* argued that "the working classes do not prohibit drink more than others, but they experience its effects more." Intemperance undermined "independence and self-control," leaving the workingman "at the mercy of his employer who, knowing that he has no savings to go back upon, often takes advantage of his necessities and compels him to accept low wages." As "the cause of the ignominious failure of many a movement on the part of workingmen which otherwise had fair prospects of success," strong drink stood condemned by all true labor reformers.[81] "The man who is not man enough to keep from getting drunk," scolded the *Canadian Labor Reformer*, "has not got manhood enough about him to make a good Knight of Labor."[82]

This kind of opposition to intemperance led to a brief flurry of labor and temperance unity, and Powderly himself was invited to speak before the Hamilton gathering of the Royal Templars in the summer of 1886.[83] A leading temperance advocate suggested that "the majority of Union workmen looked strongly upon the Temperance Reform Movement," and urged unity on the political front to secure their common goals.[84] "Tuscarora" acknowledged that "the sturdiest workers in the cause of temperance to be found in Canada" lived in Hamilton, and he phrased his plea for unity in a unique blend of religious imagery and labor-reform rhetoric: "The Temperance Party and Organized Labor should be a unity, and when their leaders call on the enemy to surrender, the walls of Gherico [sic] will come thundering down never to be rebuilt. If there was a new prophet come to earth again he would cry from the housetops, 'Unite and Organize, oh my people!' and the Jesebel of Rome would thirst for his blood. Unite and Organize, oh my people."[85] During the 1886 campaign of the machinist Hamilton Racey, the labor–temperance alliance experienced a brief few weeks of common struggle.[86] With his defeat, however, the united front dissolved, only to be briefly reconstituted during Allan Studholme's twentieth-century campaigns. Hamilton's workingmen continued to adhere to many basic temperance principles.[87]

## Knights and unionists

Both the temperance and the anti-Chinese movements, as well as the strikes of telegraphers and boot and shoe workers, fit neatly into the Knights' conception of modern chivalry. Manly stands for the Order's conception of moral purity, often directly related to the defense of others' demands or essential rights as workingmen and women, drew the endorsement of many of Hamilton's working people. Moreover, as movements and struggles embraced by the unorganized and the trade unionist, applauded by unskilled and skilled, they helped to cultivate unity in the face of diverse experience. The divisions between Knights and craft unionists, which have preoccupied so much of the discussion of the Order's history, were simply nowhere to be seen on the surface of the history of Hamilton's Knights of Labor, at least prior to 1886. Coexistence was more than a peaceful compromise. It was the essential feature of working-class activity in the city. Responding to a merchant's efforts to downplay the Order's strength, the *Palladium of Labor* exclaimed in May 1885: "The Knights of Labor in Hamilton have nine Assemblies, one of them has a membership of over 600, and the others will average at least 200 members each. This gives a total membership of 2,200, but there are more. Hamilton has at least TWO THOUSAND FIVE HUNDRED tried and true members in that organization, who work in unison with all the trade unions in the city, and the *Palladium* has the honor of being recognized as their official organ."[88]

With the formation of the CLU in 1884, this unity was given an institutional expression, and delegates from various Knights' Assemblies met with representatives from the city's craft unions to discuss labor's common problems and priorities. In the midst of the manufacturers' threats to destroy the Cigarmakers' Union, the *Palladium of Labor* could declare: "The Cigarmakers'

Union or any other trade union in this city – and there is about thirty of them – do not stand alone. They are linked together in one unbroken chain, and 'an inquiry to one is the concern of all'. The Organized Labor of Hamilton represent a total membership of over 3,000 men and women . . . As a result of the recent formation of the Central Labor Union, all our Labor Organizations are combined more solid than ever before."[89]

Relationships between Knights and trade unionists were so close that the official organ of DA 61, the *Palladium of Labor*, was often kept financially afloat by contributions from Hamilton's Iron Molders' International Union No. 26.[90] Trade unionist support for the Knights of Labor celebration of Uriah Stephens' birthdate on 4 August 1883 was firmly established, the city's unionists marching beside LAs. David Healey, addressing the combined labor force, struck the receptive note of working-class unity: "Let us determine to lay aside our prejudices and bury our animosities and present a united front against every invader of our liberties." Next year, in what was coming to be billed as labor's annual holiday, craft unionists and Knights again paraded side by side as seven LAs were joined by twenty-one craft unions.[91] On the basis of this kind of unity, the *Hamilton Spectator* predicted a bright future for the Order: "The organization known as the Knights of Labor is comparatively young, but its childhood is mighty; and if in this case it proves true that 'childhood shows the man as morning shows the day,' the manhood of the organization promises to be in its profound and far reaching power greater than that of any association that has yet existed for the amelioration and advancement of the working classes."[92]

The Hamilton paper's assessment of the future prospects of the Order was unduly optimistic. Within three brief years Hamilton's Knights would be in the throes of decline, its Assemblies irreconcilably factionalized, its leadership vilified by the rank and file, and the trade unionists of the various Assemblies of skilled crafts united in opposition to a clique they would slanderously label the Home Club. By 1888 these developments had taken their obvious toll, and from this time on the Knights of Labor in Hamilton exerted virtually no influence in the city's working-class movement. The surface unity of the years 1882–4 gave way to a crisis of disunity in 1886–7. This history of dissension and deterioration tarnished the impressive record of achievement attained by the Order under the guise of modern chivalry.

Despite the solid front presented by Hamilton's Knights of Labor and craft unionists in the early years of organizational growth, the inner history of the Order revealed strains and tensions that would widen to fissures in later years. As early as 6 January 1883, for instance, R. McDougall, recording secretary of Shoemakers' LA 2132, reported to Powderly that:

A dispute has arisen in our Assembly, as to the power of the Assembly, levying a tax on its members, and then forcing the same to be paid. The difficulty arose on the strike of Shoemakers in Montreal. Though not belonging to our Order, yet, we believe that a cut in their wages is the first step towards a reduction in ours, as the competition is so keen in our business between Montreal, and Toronto, and Hamilton. We therefore in our own personal interests (as the majority expressed it) called a special meeting for the purpose of considering the question. At that special red letter meeting it was Resolved, That we levy a tax of fifty cents per week on each member, to aid the Montreal strike. The resolution was passed with but one dissenting vote, in a meeting of near eighty members. The levy was collected from all, with the exception of four members. And now the legality of the levy is questioned. The Assembly wishes to know if they can have power to levy for such purpose on its own members and if so can we force the same to be paid.[93]

Powderly, as he often did, waffled, declining to make a ruling. He let McDougall know that the Assembly should have made their assessment an appeal, in order not to bind individual members to a contribution to the Montreal strikers. While this was sound advice, offered from the easy chair of distance and hindsight, it did little to heal the rifts in the Shoemakers' Assembly. The principle of solidarity, even at this early date was being tested in the halls of one of Hamilton's major LAs. As opposition to the levy escalated, LA 2132, led by the opinionated shoemaker Robert Coulter, was suspended from the DA.[94]

From another quarter came a plea for the defense of trade union principles. Charles Smith, Recording Secretary of LA 2450, composed of cigarmakers affiliated with the International Union's local branch, No. 55, complained to Powderly about the Lafayette, Indiana, cigar manufacturer August Klingeman, who utilized the Knights of Labor white label to mask his unfair labor practices. Employing "broken down women and incompetent hands," he ridiculed Cigar Makers' Union No. 158, which had originally lent him $50 to start his business. Smith, enclosing a clipping from the *Cigar Makers' Official Journal*, suggested that Powderly take immediate steps to discipline Klingeman, if he was indeed a member of the Order. Otherwise, noted the Hamilton cigarmaker, this case would severely harm efforts to organize cigarmakers not enrolled in LAs, and would demoralize those members of the trade who were Knights of Labor.[95] A similar problem preoccupied Eureka Assembly No. 2307, where Hamilton's tailors discussed the use of the Knights of Labor label in south-central Ontario's hat trade. In Hamilton, where the two hat factories were union shops, the issue posed no immediate problem, but in Toronto the "factories [were] foul and only hire[d] boys." Fred Jones, Recording Secretary, raised this question with Powderly, wanting to know if unfair manufacturers could be granted the Knights' label; he received no reply.[96]

Another contentious realm was touched upon by E. S. Gilbert, Recording Secretary of DA 61, who wrote to Powderly concerning the possibility of a dispute between Knights of Labor printers and the International Typographical Union: "In London members of the Typographical Union who are also Knights of Labor are working in a union shop when other men belonging to the same Local Assembly of the Knights as the first but not to the Typographical Union apply for and obtain employment in the shop. Would the first mentioned brothers be justified in quitting work in accordance with their union rules and if so what becomes of their pledge of honor as Knights?"[97] Powderly, once again, gave no opinion. He did, however, urge that if the Typographical Union rules regrettably stipulated that its members quit work upon the hiring of non-union men, the Knights of Labor be dealt with leniently. He suggested that the Typographical Union recognize the Knights' role in eliminating the small-town or country printer who had often taken the place of striking union typographers; the Knights' printers, he reminded the unionists, crossed no picket lines and boycotted struck papers. His solution hinged on joint action. LAs and the International Union should work together to thwart capitalist attempts to divide the working class. Let the Typographical Union give Knights of Labor printers a reasonable time to connect themselves with the union, and harmony of action would prevail, assured Powderly.[98] It was a sensible suggestion, but for the Typographical Union it perhaps posed more problems than it solved.

These issues would return to haunt Hamilton's Knights of Labor at a later date. In the meantime, however, the dissension introduced into many LAs in 1883–4 would be deflected, crossing paths with a man we have previously encountered, E. P. Morgan. Morgan, and his partner in crime, F. L. Harvey, appeared in Hamilton in 1884 and attempted to milk the Order for whatever pecuniary gain could be had. We will outline their activities in detail in Chapter 5. In 1885 they commenced publishing a small advertising sheet, mistitled *Justice*. In the 18 April 1885 issue they editorialized against a strike of Hamilton cigarmakers. This strike would prove of immense significance in the history of Hamilton's Knights of Labor.

Hamilton's Cigar Makers' International Union had, throughout the 1880s, been a bastion of the craft workers' culture of work place control. They had joined, in 1883, with a host of other skilled trades, in a strike wave articulating some of the basic tenets of the nineteenth-century "autonomous workman's" conception of control. Commencing 13 April 1883, the cigarmakers' strike hinged on the central issue of apprenticeship regulation. The conflict lasted well over one and one-half months, and the manufacturers apparently went outside of the city to secure workmen. Eventually, however, these imported cigarmakers proved unsatisfactory, and the Cigar Manufacturers' Association and the International Union submitted the case to a board of arbitration composed of Edward Williams, William Vale, and George Tuckett. With a board consisting of a liberal manufacturer and two prominent Knights of Labor, it is not surprising that the union was victorious. On 1 June 1883 the strike was terminated, "the men having gained the day in all respects." The manufacturers, undoubtedly harboring deep resentment, would bide their time until economic downturn provided an opportune moment to reassert themselves against the union.[99]

That moment came in April 1885, when many of the cigar factories in the city closed, some shops being overstocked, others unable to secure leaf tobacco. During the layoffs, the Cigar Manufacturers' Association informed the union that "owing to the recent change in the tariff in cigars, and the fact that the manufacturers are unable to realize a sufficient advance on a cigar made of scrap filler, considered by your union as a 'shape' cigar . . . [we] therefore ask you to call a meeting of your union as soon as possible, and give the above matter your careful consideration, and make the bill on scrap shapes the same as on ordinary cigars." The union responded quickly, A. C. Gibb informing the association that, "we take no action in the matter, that our prices are low enough now, and that further correspondence in the matter would be useless. It was also resolved that we instruct your body that we consider ourselves out on strike against a lockout."[100]

The first break in the stalemate occurred in late May 1885, one of the manufacturers, J. S. Lillis, informing the union of his desire to effect a reconciliation. Lillis would eventually break ranks with the Manufacturers' Association, give in to the cigarmakers, and run his shop on union principles. Others, like John Kelly, Blumensteil Brothers, and Z. Pattison, had never made common cause with the larger employers, and continued to hire union men, paying the standard rates and operating within the confines of the union's rules and regulations. The union and the association thus remained locked in battle, each side having a base from which it continued its obstinate stand. As more and more imported cigarmakers drifted into the city, shops manned with non-union hands began to open. This open defiance of the union led to widespread trade union support for the Cigar Makers' Union, and sporadic violence against strikebreaking cigarmakers was not uncommon. This was the way the matter stood, with the community polarized, well into the summer of 1886. By this time, however, the cigarmakers who had taken the places of the strikers had been introduced to the harsh discipline of their masters. They desired to protect their basic interests through organization, and petitioned No. 55 for admission to its ranks, adding that they would be willing to pay such fines as the organization cared to levy. Their petition was rejected, a decision that could not have surprised them a great deal. As a last resort, according to their secretary, they joined the Cigarmakers' Progressive Union of America, forming a Hamilton Local, No. 34.[101]

Meanwhile, the rifts in Hamilton's working-class movement, already apparent in the subtle divisions between Knights of Labor and craft unionists, widened. William H. Rowe, editor of the *Palladium of Labor*, launched a relentless attack on Hamilton's International Typographical Union No. 129. Charging the printers with flagrant violations of their union's rules, Rowe labeled the offices of the *Times* and the *Spectator* "rat shops," in which apprentices outnumbered journeymen four to one. "By the Typographical Union of this city allowing such a state of affairs to exist," raged Rowe, "they are simply bringing disgrace on the whole International Typographical Union, and the sooner they make it known to the Organized Labor of the city that they are incompetent to run their Union, the better."[102] In a later rebuke, Rowe linked the printers' deterioration to their absence in the general struggle for the improvement of the lot of the workingman: "The men who are afraid to ask for justice from their own employers, can not be expected to champion the cause of other down-trodden representatives of humanity."[103] Rowe's charges may have had some foundation, for Hamilton printers were relatively acquiescent in these years, playing no role in labor's upsurge of the 1880s, but the crusade was intemperate and achieved little constructive. Moreover, there is a hint that Rowe's attack was rooted in personal malice and the desire for self-betterment. One "Union Printer" accused Rowe of striking out at the union in order to undermine the established dailies and securing the *Palladium of Labor* a permanent situation in the marketplace. Rowe's critic also thought it suspect that a man with such firm principles would toil "day and night in order to make ends meet, howling constantly during the day for shorter hours, and working half the night to save employing men and paying wages or vice versa."[104] Whatever the reasons behind the dispute, Rowe's assault on the printers could only have alienated the affections of many unionists.

Even more disruptive was Rowe's role in the 1885 municipal campaign, where the renegade manufacturer, J. S. Lillis, was running for alderman. The CLU resolved to support no candidate, there being no workingmen in the field. Rowe, however, saw Lillis' abandonment of the Manufacturers' Association as an indicator of his progressive orientation, and demanded support for the manufacturer. When the CLU refused, Rowe precipitated a split in the ranks of the body.[105] Clearly, one of the Knights of Labor's difficulties, in times of strain, was keeping a rein on overly opinionated men of Rowe's type.

More telling, however, were the implications of a dispute between the Hamilton Order and the Hat Finishers' Association of America in February and March 1886, a conflict prefaced by Eureka Assembly's discussion of the label question in 1884. The problem was posed when some twenty members of the Hatters' Union boycotted hats made by shops employing members of the Knights of Labor but not organized on strict union principles. These shops secured a place for their wares among workingmen through the use of the Order's white label, and the Hatters' Union resented this. "We must and should protect our people," William J. Vale wrote to Powderly. "We have the stamp working in another factory and are we to allow these 20 people to boycott us without resenting the matter." Vale concluded that if the dispute was not immediately settled, "we mean to protect our men first, unions afterwards."[106]

## Home Club

It was in this context that the Home Club affair of 1886 erupted. The coming conflict was prefaced with a note in the *Palladium of Labor*, 5 June 1886: "There reach the *Palladium* from all parts of the States and Canada stirring expressings of opinions, to the effect that the Knights of Labor should not infringe on the rights of trade unions. Considerable feeling was caused in this city by the futile attempts to organize scab cigar-makers into an Assembly of the K. of L." Within three weeks, however, "futile attempts" had been transformed into concrete results, the *Hamilton Spectator* reporting that the Cigarmakers' Progressive Union had been "admitted to the Knights of Labor, which Order has extended its protection by affixing its white label on all their goods."[107]

A mass meeting of the CLU convened on 29 June 1886 to discuss the International Union's charges against the Knights of Labor. On the podium were many prominent Hamilton workingmen, most of whom were jointly affiliated with LAs of the Knights of Labor and their respective craft unions. Adolph Strasser, president of the Cigar Makers' International Union, set the tone for the proceedings, posing the question as one of "Unionism Versus Anarchy." He applauded the long and vital history of Hamilton's Cigar Makers' Union, said to be the oldest labor organization in the city, dating from 6 December 1851. He noted that, as the immense turnout suggested, the vast majority of workingmen, Knights of Labor as well as unionists, supported the cigarmakers in their stand against the Progressive Union, a "scab" organization. Finally, he launched his attack on the pernicious Home Club, a motley crew of "dynamiters, anarchists, and office-seekers," disillusioned with the reasonable policies of GMW Powderly. "This mischievous and dangerous element has prominent members right here in Hamilton," thundered Strasser. "I will name them. They are George Collis, William J. Vale, and David R. Gibson. The principle quarters of the Home Club are Washington, Baltimore, Philadelphia, Richmond, and Hamilton. It is a powerful and growing element, as well as an evil element in the Knights of Labor, and threatens the destruction of that grand organization. The Home Club aims to destroy the trades unions all through the country – that is its one great object at present and it seeks to accomplish it by secret underhand means." Hamilton's Knights accepted this assessment, Edward Williams condemning "the greatest mistake that was ever made in Hamilton in connection with the labor movement." Alderman Thomas Brick, ever the opportunist, slandered Collis, Vale, and Gibson, whose efforts to whitewash "scab cigarmakers by chartering them into LA 7955 of the Knights of Labor was a disgrace to the Order." He attributed their failure to attend the meeting as proof of their cowardice: "All they were good for was looking around for paid situations in Labor organizations." A resolution, condemning "certain unscrupulous individuals temporarily in control of District Assembly 61," and urging support of the Cigar Makers' International Union and their blue label, ended the proceedings.[108]

In the weeks to follow, Collis, Vale, Gibson, and additionally, Thomas Towers, continued to be the focus of a hostile harangue. "The great body of the Knights of Labor in this city don't appreciate backdown sneaks and scab whitewashers," noted the *Palladium of Labor*. M. C. Foley of Stratford contended that Vale had attempted to undermine the Stratford Co-operative Cigar Factory, an enterprise run by the Order employing cigarmakers affiliated with both the Knights of Labor and the International Union.[109] When the radical Michigan Knight of Labor, T. B. Barry, visited Hamilton at the invitation of the Home Clubbers he was quickly taken under the wing of supporters of the Cigar Makers' International Union and informed of the mistaken, destructive practices of Collis, Gibson, and Vale. Rumors circulated that the Home Club of Hamilton had granted the Progressive Union a charter when paid to do so by the Cigar Manufacturers' Association.[110] When the Iron Molders' International Union No. 26 passed a resolution condemning the actions of DA 61, and endorsing No. 55's blue label, the *Palladium of Labor* advised others to "Follow in line, brothers, with the vanguard of unionism in Hamilton – ever watchful I.M.U. No. 26."[111] The feeling continued into September 1886, the CLU eventually boycotting the white label of LA 7955.[112]

As the DA convened in Brantford, a correspondent to the *Palladium of Labor* noted that "the celebrated pleader for poor, suffering, down-trodden humanity – in other words 'scab' cigarmakers – accompanied the Hamilton contingent." "Brant" suggested that in forthcoming elections, LAs take pains to bring forth men "as will not bring disgrace on the Order, as three or four of the present Hamilton District Delegates have done." The outside Locals, he assured the *Palladium's* readers, "can all be depended upon for the election of honest men who have the welfare of the Order at heart." And, indeed, when DA 61 elected its delegates to the 1886 General Assembly it cast its ballots for J. J. Murphy of Brantford and Alexander B. Holmes, of the once-suspended Hamilton Shoemakers' Assembly. It was a vote against the Home Club, and Messrs. Collis, Vale, and Towers were soundly defeated.[113] At the 1886 session of the Canadian Trades and Labor Congress, held in Toronto in September, William Berry (of Shoemakers' Assembly No. 2132) and James Ripley (a delegate from the IMIU to the CLU) deplored the dissension dividing Knights and unionists, attributing it to certain unscrupulous leaders rather than the rank and file.[114]

By October some of this public clamor had dissipated, although much remained; DA 61 was instructed by Powderly to accept delegates from LA 7955.[115] A year later the Progressive Union's Assembly still existed, and not until 1889, when DA 61 finally renounced LA 7955, did the Progressive Cigarmakers withdraw from the Hamilton Knights and affiliate with National Trades Assembly 225 of the Order.[116]

But the Home Club dispute, in the long interval separating the eruption of 1886 and the withdrawal of 1889, continued to flare. Three LAs immediately balked at the general slander of 1886, and remained loyal to Collis, Vale, Gibson, and Towers.[117] John Peebles' Assembly, as we have seen, ordered him to withdraw from the CLU. Collis's own Assembly, LA 2586, also remained loyal to the old leadership, and apparently bore Collis no ill will, presenting him with a complete edition of George Eliot's works and an encyclopedia of practical quotations in 1888.[118] James Dore, secretary *pro tem* of LA 2586, wrote to Powderly expressing the Assembly's anger at the efforts to block a reconciliation of the International Union and the Knights. He further expressed bitterness at the manner in which the Home Club affair had been handled, charging the DA with having committed a serious breach of regulations in its stifling of local autonomy.[119]

George Collis, admittedly not an unbiased observer, outlined the situation in a letter to Powderly. Despite his prejudices, the account testifies to his unwavering allegiance to the Order and serves as witness to the essential purity of his motives:

I am somewhat in doubt what course to pursue under the following circumstances. A short time since the Central Labor Union in this city passed a resolution boycotting the Knights of Labor label. This might have been defeated but for the apathy of the members of the K of L coupled with the direct opposition of the Trades Union Element within the K of L. My opinion is that the Local Assemblies must withdraw from the CLU until the obnoxious boycott is removed. If I am sure that I am right I shall not hesitate one moment. I cannot in a communication like this give you any idea of the trouble which the Kickers are giving us here right now.[120]

In the aftermath of the electoral defeats of Hamilton Knights in the provincial and federal elections of 1886–7, this factionalism was heightened.[121] On 9 March 1887, the *Hamilton Spectator* reprinted one unionist's comments on the Knights of Labor, extracted from the *Providence Journal:* "It is despotism instead of democracy, as we supposed. Each assembly is governed by its handful of officers and the members have no voice or vote on important matters. The affairs of any trade, the existence of which may be destroyed, are entrusted to Knights in other lines of business, who, however able or intelligent they may be, are not fitted to meddle with technicalities they do not understand."[122] To many Hamilton unionists enrolled in the Knights of Labor, this critique struck a chord of sympathy, and many craftsmen must have resigned from the Order. On 1 November 1887 the Home Club affair created its last major fracas, and the walls of the DA hall vibrated with dissenting voices as the issue of a reconciliation of the International Union and the Knights was raised once again. The executive board of DA 61 – composed of men like James Henigan who had won their positions in the midst of the condemnation of the Home Club, replacing Collis, Vale, Gibson, and Towers – apparently thought that the irksome affair had run its course. They raised the possibility of a reconciliation of Knights of Labor and trade union interests, apparently at the instigation of Hamilton's union cigarmakers. The cigarmakers suggested that they would be willing to accept members of the Progressive Union into their ranks upon payment of appropriate fines, levied against those who had broken the strike of 1885–6. By this late date, however, only staunch Knights of Labor remained in the Order, the trade union element having retired from DA 61. The result was that the officers were "subjected to considerable abuse for their action." A small majority carried the day for the cause of the white label, and the officers of DA 61 and its executive board, disgusted with this obstinate refusal to reconcile Knights and unionists, resigned to a man. They probably took what remained of the trade union element with them. Those workers who had attacked Hamilton's Order for violating trade union principles had succeeded too well. In launching an all-out attack on the Knights of Labor and condemning Hamilton's Assemblies they had precipitated much discontent and initiated an exodus of trade union advocates. When the dispute between the International and Progressive cigarmakers was finally capable of resolution, the Order had lost so many of its union members that pro-union sentiment no longer had a voice within the DA. Those prominent Knights who had been so viciously flayed for chartering a scab Assembly were able to slip unobtrusively back into control. Thomas Towers was appointed DMW in place of James Henigan. The Home Club, it seems, had returned to roost.[123]

Even this return to the status quo could not heal the divisions within many LAs. Martin O'Driscoll, DMW, informed Powderly that LA 5329 was torn asunder by a severe factionalism, in which two camps opposed each other resolutely, grasping at every opportunity to defeat the other group in all contests.[124] In Musicians' Assembly 4814, where "one could expect to find everything working harmoniously," J. P. reported "discord and troubles"; the Assembly's open reading room, once crowded, was no longer patronized.[125] Factionalism even took a secessionist turn, DA 61 introducing resolutions at the 1887 General Assembly favoring Canadian autonomy.[126] With the appointment by Powderly in 1888 of Montreal's Redmond, Hamilton's Collis, and Toronto's Jury to the Knights of Labor Legislative Committee for Canada, factional strife began to be reflected back upon the Hamilton Order, Western Ontario's DA 138 (St. Thomas-London) raising a strong voice against Collis's appointment and the despotic control of "Czar Powderly." In Hamilton, despite the prominence of many Knights antagonistic to Collis, the Order remained loyal, but it was of little consequence.[127] When Thomas Towers resumed the position of DMW in the fall of 1887 he inherited an impotent organization. A year later, Hamilton's Knights of Labor had functionally ceased to exist. Was this failure the fault of the Home Clubbers?

There was, in fact, probably no Home Club in Hamilton, if we construe its existence as a conspiratorial plot. The *Palladium of Labor's* declaration that "three or four Home Club appointments" had been made in the city because of its prominence as a center of organized labor was nothing more than slanderous speculation.[128] Men whom Norman Ware has placed at the center of the history of the Home Club – W. H. Mullen of Richmond, Virginia, and Victor Drury of New York – did indeed address Hamilton Assemblies, but their talks did not incur the ire of any trade unionists. Rather, they lectured on the eight-hour day, the history of the Order, and labor's rights.[129] As late as April 1886 – a brief two months before the unmasking of the Home Clubbers – Strasser himself had visited the city, and found things to his liking; no vile conspiracy tainted the Knights at that time.[130]

It would be tempting to link Collis, Vale, Gibson, and Towers to the New York-based "Spread the Light" club that was supposedly organized to instruct master workmen affiliated with the Home Club in their socialistic duties. Hamilton's first recruits to the Order were apparently initiated in 1882 by Brooklyn LA 1562 MW William Horan, and Norman Ware places him in the fundamentalist wing of the Home Club. Perhaps a rare Hamilton Knight was enrolled in Victor Drury's "class," which was said to have spread across North America as its original members went among the Order to form other circles of nine, cultivating radicalism in various corners of the North American labor movement. Certainly Drury and Horan were familiar enough in the Canadian industrial center to have won some supporters. If the point is stretched sufficiently, it is possible to see him as the aged New York Knight who penned the following letter to a younger Hamilton comrade in the fall of 1884:

> I can only hope that you and brothers of your cast and temperament will take up the work in all sincerity so that when the younger generation shall be asking for "Light, more light," you will pass the luminous torch of knowledge to them and hand it down more bright and lustrous than you received it at our hands. As . . . told you, we must soon go, and it remains with you to carry on our work. But it must be done without ostentation and without vanity, for love and not for lucre. Yes! We are yet in our infancy, but we will grow to manhood if we have only the patience to pass courageously through our adolescence.[131]

The language of this letter may well have been the stuff of which Home Clubbers were made, and there is more than a hint of utopianism and fundamentalist attachment to secrecy and ritual that Ware claims characterized the "inner ring." But the letter may merely reveal the passion with which many workers took up the cause of labor reform, and as such is imaginatively, rather than concretely, linked to the existence of the Home Club in Hamilton. Unfortunately there is not a great deal of substantial evidence to establish the Home Club in the city. Those Hamilton Knights supposedly affiliated with it bore little resemblance to the shadowy descriptions of New York's fundamentalist-socialist "ring."

None of the Home Clubbers, for instance, had ever denigrated the accomplishments of trade unionism. Only Collis and Towers are not known to have been members of trade unions. William J. Vale was a staunch member of Hamilton's International Typographical Union No. 129, and no enemy of trade unionism.[132] David R. Gibson, before and after joining the Knights, was a highly esteemed member of Hamilton's Bricklayers' and Masons' Union.[133] And although Towers' and Collis' union affiliation must remain in abeyance, both men had a long history in Hamilton's working-class movement, having played some role, apparently, in the 1872 strikes for the nine-hour day. Towers, for instance, had defended *both* Knights of Labor and trade unionists in mid-September 1885, attacking the "drones and non-producers." The prominent Knight of Labor must have flinched in the midst of the Home Club dispute, painfully recalling his poem, "Outcast," published in the *Palladium of Labor* a year earlier:

> Dark lowering clouds are hanging o'er me,
> And vainly I look for the dawn;
> Gloomy is the prospect before me,
> And Shadowy is the path I tread on.[134]

While Towers and Collis, virtually across the street from one another (they lived at 75 and 76 Markland Street, respectively), must have been on intimate terms, there are indications that their relations with other members of the "ring" were separated by the neighborhood divisions of the nineteenth-century city. "I tried my utmost to see Brother Vale in this matter," wrote Collis to Powderly, "but was unable and sent the letter to him by a trusty bearer but he was not at home."[135] This, surely, is not the stuff of which conspiracies are made.

The crime of these men was their devotion to the Order, an allegiance rooted in years of faithful service. Throughout their years in the Order there is no indication in their correspondence that Collis and his friends were ever anything but Powderly's most able and forthright advocates, hardly dedicated to overturning the authority of the GMW. (In the midst of the Home Club dispute Gibson had wired Powderly to come to the city. "The interest of Order at stake," he noted, "Strasser is working here reply immediately.")[136] It was this attachment that led them to commit the major indiscretion of admitting the Progressive Cigarmakers to the DA. It was a breach of solidarity deserving of stiff rebuttal, but it was bred of no sinister, conspiratorial design. The willingness with which Hamilton's Knights of Labor took up the cudgels against Collis, Vale, Gibson, and Towers, viciously opposing their Home Club affiliations, suggests how deeply embedded their resentments and antagonisms against them must have been. As we shall argue in Chapter 5, the efforts of Messrs. Morgan and Harvey were not unrelated to this process, and did much to poison the once fraternal atmosphere of labor-reform circles. Where unscrupulous adventurers, with an eye only for the easy dollar, had sown, Collis, Vale, Gibson, and Towers – honest workingmen all – would reap. The reintegration of the Home Club "clique" into Hamilton's Order – as early as November 1886 Collis and Gibson were again prominent, the former directing Hamilton Racey's December bid for the Ontario legislature, and in July 1887 serving as DA 61's delegate to the General Assembly – is confirmation of the fraudulent nature of many of the accusations of the summer of 1886.[137]

## Decline

If the Home Club, more of an illusion in Hamilton than a conspiratorial clique, was not responsible for the demise of the local Order, what of the often-cited ambivalence of the Knights of Labor toward strikes? Here, too, the answer must be negative. The record of DA 61 was blemished only by the chartering of the Progressive Cigar Makers' Union into LA 7955 and, while a serious mistake, this occurred almost a year after the cigarmakers' strike had drifted into an impasse from which there was no exit. While undoubtedly a breach of principle, it was hardly an act of conscious strikebreaking. Hamilton's Order, as can be seen in the cases of the telegraphers' 1883 battle, the shoemakers' struggle of 1884, the Gardner strike of 1884, and the bakers' 1886 conflict, broke no craft union conceptions of solidarity. Indeed, Hamilton's Order played a central role in at least nine strikes in the years of activism from 1883–7 (see Table 4.2), and this probably accounted for about half of the conflicts waged in the city by trade unionists, Knights, and unorganized workers in the middle years of the decade. Compared to the poor post-1886 record of Toronto's DA 125, for instance, where a strong and relatively centralized leadership followed official strike policy to its inevitable ambivalent conclusion, Hamilton's Knights were only rarely pressed into confrontations that highlighted the differences between trade unionists and advocates of the Order. The single noteworthy exception, feeding directly into the well-publicized American dispute between the Knights of Labor and the International Cigar Makers' Union, proved disastrous. The more general problematic aspects of strike involvement, however, centered on retaining membership in the midst of conflict and, more emphatically, in the throes of defeat; it was a problem that also faced the craft union, but in the union's case, where allegiance was rooted in adherence to certain key planks – the standard rate, apprenticeship regulation, and set limits on the output of members – and a tradition of union control existed in most shops, it was more easily resolved, and organizational continuity sustained.

The very reason for the Knights' rapid growth – the widespread attraction of modern chivalry, the eclectic and nebulous appeal of the Order – thus stands as the central component of the organization's decline. Where men and women banded in concert on the basis of widely diverging, often individual, principles, those same men and women could discard their unity in times

Table 4.2. *Strikes involving Knights of Labor in Hamilton, 1883–7*

| Year | Number | Workers | LA involved |
|---|---|---|---|
| 1883 | 1 | telegraphers | 2218 |
| 1884 | 2 | sewing machine workers | 2225 |
| | | shoeworkers | 2132 |
| 1885 | 3 | shoeworkers | 2132 |
| | | iron and steelworkers | 2225/DA 61 |
| | | cigarmakers | 2450 |
| 1886 | 1 | bakers | 2156 |
| 1887 | 2 | shoeworkers | 2132 |
| | | longshoremen/coal heavers | 7822 |

of trouble, when their organizational affiliation posed problems of a social, economic, political, or ideological nature. This is the story of much of the development of faction and rift in Hamilton's Order, a process exacerbated by men of intemperate leanings, such as the *Palladium of Labor*'s W. H. Rowe, and men of unprincipled character, such as Falconer L. Harvey and Enoch P. Morgan.[138]

Beyond this purely local context lies a history of employer resistance, the staying power of industrial-capitalist social relationships, and the growing hostility of trade unions to the Order's entanglements in their supposed jurisdictions.[139] All impinged on Hamilton's Knights of Labor in the years 1886–8, taking their toll in a forceful fashion. By 1889 Hamilton's Assemblies had dwindled in number and in membership; in terms of their impact the decline was even greater. Reduced to an adjunct of the budding Trades and Labor Council, DA 61's major contribution was the purchase of an old engine house on Walnut Street, which it planned to renovate and establish as a meeting place for organized labor. When Terence V. Powderly came to Hamilton in October 1889, his audience, barely filling half of Larkin Hall, attested to the declining fortunes of the organization he headed.[140]

By the 1890s Hamilton's once vibrant Knights of Labor had been reduced to a shadow of its former self. Henry McStravick, Recording Secretary of District 61, successfully petitioned Powderly in February 1890 to grant a special dispensation to allow the DA to convene with only four LAs in attendance.[141] The tailors' LA 8915 asked Powderly in 1891 to send a good man to help rebuild the Order in Hamilton.[142] In February 1892, LA 8915 took steps toward reorganizing the Knights of Labor in the city, held a meeting, and reported that "the prospects appeared very favourable." Four months later, however, E. S. Gilbert reported that LA 8915 was officially giving up its charter, and forwarded some remaining property and money to the international officers of the Order.[143] The coffin of the Hamilton affiliates of the Noble and Holy Order of the Knights of Labor was finally nailed shut in 1897, Edward Little, Secretary of Quebec's LA 10061, writing to John W. Hayes that he had just returned from the Trades and Labor Congress meeting in Hamilton, an organized town of 45,000 that could not boast of even one LA. David R. Gibson and some other ex-members were still active in labor circles, and harbored fond memories of the once-powerful Order, but nothing else remained. Little suggested that Gibson be commissioned as an organizer, and argued that the city could again be a credit to the Knights of Labor. But nothing came of this, and Little himself was forced to concede that the tragic rift of 1886 continued to divide Hamilton workers eleven years later. The cigarmakers, he noted, were still hostile to the Knights of Labor. Hamilton's Home Club fiasco continued to exercise its disruptive influence.[144]

Indeed, the eulogy to Hamilton's Order was written in 1892, when E. S. Gilbert outlined the demise of LA 8915:

> Its struggle for some time has of course been no more than a struggle to interest the labourers and a hope that the lapse of time would cause the unfortunate dissensions which were the primary cause of our splitting up to be forgotten. While we have not been entirely disappointed in this last respect we have also seen an indifference to the K of L and in fact to every other reform movement settle down on the working people of this place that is painful to think of and while various bodies of men have within the last few months appeared to be on the point of taking advantage of our organization they could not be got together even to organize and the few who have been the rear guard of what once was a splendid organization here have decided to abandon it until the people come back to their senses.[145]

But to understand this eulogy more fully, both with respect to the particular experience of Hamilton and the Home Club and more generally in terms of the Order across Ontario, we must consider various realms of "the unfortunate dissension" that helped to tear the Knights of Labor asunder, as well as the strengths and accomplishments of the province-wide labor movement of the 1880s.

In leaving behind the specific local contexts of Toronto and Hamilton that have been the concern of this section, we move in Part III toward the wider experience. A seamy underside of the Knights of Labor heightened factional fighting, undermined the faith of the membership in the Order's purpose, tarnished the record of achievement and organization, and induced demoralization and discontent. To comprehend the failure of labor's upsurge of the 1880s we must look, not just at men of passionate commitment like John Peebles, but at less noble historical figures, men who would be described as "unscrupulous rascals and infamous damn liars and tricksters at large." We must take the bad men along with the good. They, too, were part of the Knights of Labor, part of the chivalry of the nineteenth century. Similarly, we must take the bad with the good in the political involvement of the Order, which we have neglected in these case studies of Toronto and Hamilton. For politics was an arena that revealed the Order's influence and power, as well as its weaknesses and limitations. In the impressive electoral campaigns of the 1880s we see the challenge mounted by the Order, one that extended beyond specific locales sufficiently to alarm the established political culture. But that culture proved strong enough to meet the challenge, and in the ultimate political defeat of the Order in the post-1886 years a sorry record of factionalism, opportunism, and intrigue dominates the inner history of the far from Noble and Holy Order of the Knights of Labor. To return, however, to where we think this history should end, we close with detailed examinations of the movement culture of opposition forged in the 1880s and the class conflicts that, however often they ended in defeat, served to convince Ontario's Knights of Labor that tyranny and oppression must be opposed, whatever the cost. In that legacy resides much of the significance of "labor's lordly chivalry."

# Part III. The wider experience: Taking the bad with the good

The year 1886 was prolific in events that stirred the world from end to end and particularly affected the social and political tranquility of the American continent . . . The bosses were generous in more ways than one to anything that would destroy the Knights of Labor, until 1890 when Powderly had made the Knights of Labor as safe and sane as it was possible to make it, although this mass form of organization was always a social danger and could not be controlled by Powderly or anybody else, as every trade panic was liable to build the Knights into formidable numbers with its easy methods of access and small dues.

Richard J. Kerrigan, Canadian revolutionary, 1927

The subjective aspects of events, the "atmosphere" in which they took place, is also a condition of history . . . Indeed, can history be made real if [this aspect] is not resuscitated? Shall we leave the task solely to the novelist?

Pierre Vilar, historian, 1976

# 5. "Unscrupulous Rascals and the most infamous damn liars and tricksters at Large": The underside of the Knights of Labor

## Inside traitors

As all Knights of Labor well knew, the triangle or pyramid was the sign of the Order. In St. Thomas, members often wore a silver triangular pin, engraved "KL." It was a symbol meant to convey a sense of strength, resiliency, and resistance, for "no power from the outside [could] have any effect on it." In the words of the *Palladium of Labor* in July 1886, the pyramid stood "firm, unbending, and shapely as ever," despite atacks upon its structure. But the Order found it far more difficult to deflect enemies who worked against its purposes from inside the ranks of the Knights of Labor; these dangerous elements could topple the pyramid, and the Order would be left in ruins. "Inside traitors are most to be feared," concluded the organ of the Canadian Knights of Labor, "and the quicker they are sat upon when discovered, the less their chances will be of accomplishing evil." David Healey put it more colorfully in 1883, in an address commemorating the birthdate of Uriah Stephens, founder of the Knights of Labor. "A fox may be an excellent specimen of his kind," he said, "but he has no business in a convention of chickens."[1]

By the time of the *Palladium of Labor* article the antagonism of North American employers was well known and had already begun to take its toll. In the years to come the Order would often be reminded that its external enemies were not quite this easily written off.[2] Despite the *Palladium of Labor*'s naiveté, however, it had made a forceful point. Elements within the Knights of Labor did create difficulties, discord, and dissension. In LAs created around an eclectic, and often explicitly moral, program, backsliders were bound to appear, and expulsions necessarily followed. Given the political realities of the day, Tory and Grit "wire pullers" understandably sought to turn the Knights of Labor to their own purpose, which was to ingratiate themselves with the established Canadian parties. Men of differing political perspectives thus regularly did battle in District and General Assemblies, as we shall show in Chapters 6 and 7. All of this made the Order something less than a unified movement, and in some cases may well have cracked the walls of solidarity that enclosed the symbolic pyramid.[3] An examination of this internal turmoil tells us much about the Knights of Labor, revealing dark corners of the Order's experience not usually illuminated in the standard histories of political activity and industrial action. For social movements have their sordid underside as well as their outwardly respectable face. And this underside tells us something about the society and the organization that produced and nourished it.[4]

At the most elementary level expulsions for moral failings and violations of obligations provide an indication of the internal difficulties confronting many LAs. The pages of the *Journal of United Labor* detailed the cases of Canadian Knights of Labor driven from the Order for a variety of sins: a Guelph telegrapher, Alexander Mackenzie, expelled for "violation of obligation," most likely a reference to his refusal to support the Order in its 1883 confrontation with Jay Gould's monopoly; John Thompkins, a tobacco roller of LA 1852, Hamilton, dismissed for a brutal and cowardly assault upon a brother Knight; and a group of eight laborers and railroad workers, thrown out of Brockville's LA 2311 for crimes ranging from child murder and theft to defrauding a fellow Knight.[5] The list could be extended almost indefinitely.[6]

These expulsions were taken seriously, as the Powderly correspondence suggests, and the Knights of Labor developed an elaborate judicial structure of courts at the Local and District levels. Martin Daly, of Clifton, Ontario, wrote to the GMW in December 1887, protesting his expulsion from LA 1233, Baltimore, and how it weighed heavily upon him in his new home. The worker had owed a debt and left Baltimore without paying it. Although the debt was not to the Order, this transgression led to Daly's removal from membership in the Knights of Labor. Protesting that if the Order were to be composed only of "those who owes no man a dollar then I say that we would be in a large majority in a fair way to be all expelled," the ex-member sought Powderly's intervention and asked for an official withdrawal card from LA 1233. Such an action would have allowed him to rejoin the Knights of Labor in Canada, for in this place, Daly argued, "there is no blemish on my character neither man, woman or child can say Mr. Daly drinks or neglects his family."[7]

From Napanee, St. Catharines, Windsor, Amherstburg, and other Ontario towns where the Knights of Labor were strong, Powderly was besieged by members requesting procedural information on whether a specific character deficiency or crime merited expulsion, and how to handle individual cases; in rare situations the GMW was even asked if specific persons should be allowed to join the Order.[8] John Gardner, Recording Secretary of LA 2132, Hamilton, wondered if a former Knight of Labor who had committed a murder and been jailed three times for drunkenness and abusing his wife and family should be scratched from the membership rolls.[9] From Chatham came the question, "Will our laws permit a man who owns a Billiard Hall to become a member of the K of L?"[10] These, and many other queries, indicate the strong sense of moral purpose guiding the organization along the paths of labor reform. But they also hint at the pervasive wrangling that disrupted many gatherings of LAs. For the transgressors, despite their failings, must have had allies, and debate over membership and expulsion could often have bred a destructive factionalism.

Thus, in February 1886, Arthur E. Peters of Woodstock's LA 3151 complained to Powderly:

> I received a letter with your signature signed asking me to return my commission. The letter states that Bro. Turner received a letter from my LA accusing me of intemperance Now Bro P I can assure you between *god* and *man* . . . that i defy any living man to say he saw or heard of men passing any Intoxicants between my lips it is a 'Falsehood' . . . now i want to know what i can do to Bro Grinstead when he writes what is not true about me to Bro Turner.

"Let me know as early as possible," concluded the irate Peters, "as our LA meets on Thursday night."[11] The whole affair, which was probably hotly discussed that Thursday evening, may well have turned on something as commonplace as prestige and finance. Peters' accuser, Grinstead, had applied for a commission as organizer about the same time as his adversary. Both men, then, competed in the close quarters of Woodstock's LA. Peters, for one, desired higher things, unsuccessfully applying for a paid position at the Knights of Labor international headquarters, and Grinstead may have laid the charge against him merely to be rid of a thorn in his side, a man whose very presence necessarily detracted from his own prominence.[12] Inside the pyramid of the Canadian Order men could apparently battle for the same mundane self-interests that often moved them in the larger community.

Occasionally, too, this struggle for self-aggrandizement did the Order great harm. The Knights of Labor were never on secure financial footing and LAs and DAs that fell prey to unscrupulous elements must have suffered considerably. DA 207, for instance, forced the resignation of its DMW, A. J. Carrol, charging him with "financial crookedness."[13] Edward Mann, treasurer of the St. Thomas Trades and Labor Council, and a former treasurer of a local assembly of the Knights of Labor, was expelled for his refusal to give up twenty dollars of the Order's money he claimed was due him for services rendered. In choosing not to arbitrate his grievance, Mann earned the scorn of many local residents. "If Mr. Mann's principles were recognized," claimed George Wrigley, editor of the *Canada Labor Courier*, "The order would very soon go to eternal smash."[14] We must not assume that men like Carrol and Mann functioned only as disruptive, self-seeking opportunists; they could well have contributed materially to the building of the Knights of Labor in Canada. The *Palladium of Labor*, for instance, praised John R. Brown of London in October 1884, drawing attention to his exemplary role in organizing workers in the Forest City. Brown had been active throughout the autumn months of the year, and had been present at the Hamilton demonstration against the importation of Chinese labor, bringing with him the support of London's working class. There was no indication in this flurry of organizational activity in late 1884 that Brown, organizer and member of LA 3305, harbored anything but the purest of motives. He was an ardent worker in labor's cause and played an important role in bringing the message of labor reform to the working men and women of Western Ontario.[15] But one year later Brown, in conjunction with a machinist of LA 3558, Charles Elms, was expelled for embezzlement. The exigencies of working-class life, which thousands of Knights of Labor across Ontario faced without dipping into the Assembly's cash box, had apparently proven too much for Brown, and his about-face must have puzzled many London workers.[16]

Less perplexing was the case of Thomas McGeachie, District Recording Secretary of DA 207, and Secretary of LA 2056, St. Catharines. He appeared to be strictly above suspicion in July 1887, when he asked Powderly to attend a large labor demonstration in St. Catharines the next month. But by the fall of the next year he had run afoul of the Order. After defaulting to the amount of $700 or $800, and refusing to yield the financial books and other Knights of Labor property, McGeachie was prosecuted in Local courts and forced to pay a small claim. Although foiled in his attempt to "smash the district up," McGeachie did abscond much the richer for his troubles. Five years later the Order remained on his heels, John W. Hayes writing to Frank Brown of LA 9437, St. Catharines, that McGeachie was in Cleveland and that he had a large amount of money originally secured from the LAs of DA 207. An investigation was urged, but it did not solve the problem. "I sometimes think there is a premium on crookedness," complained St. Catharines Knights of Labor leader J. T. Carey to Powderly, "but hope to see the time there will not be any of it left in this Order."[17]

Men like McGeachie must have done much to weaken the effectiveness of the Canadian Knights of Labor; if there was a threat from within the walls of the pyramid, it came from men like him. Even a cursory glance at a wide array of sources suggests that financial chicanery – which ran the gamut from persistent efforts to avoid dues payments to sophisticated, and quite substantial, embezzlement schemes – was widespread throughout the Order, and "swindlers" and "mercenaries" abounded. And the Order paid in more than just dollars. Indeed, W. R. James, senior judge of the court of DA 207, recognized as much when he petitioned Powderly in the aftermath of the McGeachie trial:

Would you advise us to take vigorous measures in dealing with our members. What I mean is – where a Brother in a local is looked upon as a leader would it be well to get rid of him if he does not work in harmony. There are some who cannot help sowing discord, whether wilfully or not, and it is through this discord that our District is in the condition it is today. We must have unification of thought if we ever expect unity of action, and I look upon those who are not with us as against us, and it would be better to be rid of them. Let them be against us on the outside if they will.

St. Catharines was not the only locale where internal troubles produced demoralization, discontent, and decline.[18]

In Napanee the Order's demise was attributed, in 1889, to the deficiencies of the past officers. William J. Nickle, MW of LA 3305, complained that in London he had "a hard assembly to rule and I am determined to carry it out to the letter as near as possible they have been let run wild and now I have got to tame them." From other quarters, too, came complaints of "kickers," "growlers," and "unruly members," and the disparaging of "rings" and powerful cliques. An assessment levied against all members of the Order or all Assemblies within a District often produced opposition, and many LAs refused. Strikes, as we have seen already and shall detail more fully in Chapter 9, often led to conflicts of opinion and breaches of solidarity. The whole problem of internal discipline was merely exacerbated by the mobility of the Order's membership. C. Hayward, of Amigari, Welland County, suggested some check on wandering Knights of Labor, tramping the country in search of work:

This I am sure would in a great measure do away with what I call impecunious members going around making it a business to beat there way under a cloak of being members of the K of L. Two of these brothers that I assisted out of my private purse, giving me the usual signs and passwords, I took and looked upon it in a right light, should it fall to my lot to be in the same fix I would like and expect the assistance to be given me, but unfortunately in this case, the money went for drink and the members laying around to the Disgrace of the Order here.[19]

The *Palladium of Labor*, apparently, had not misjudged the situation when it stressed the threat from within.

## Alexander W. Wright

This brief glimpse of the internal difficulties of the Order remains shrouded in the obscurity of the local context. Equally problematic is the situation in the upper echelons, where prominent Canadian labor reformers rubbed shoulders with their American counterparts, often embroiling themselves in the petty schemes and partisan alliances that were so prominent a part of the intimate history of the organization. Perhaps no Knight of Labor exemplified this process better than Alexander W. Wright.

Born in Elmira, Ontario, A. W. Wright dabbled in woolen manufacturing in several southwestern Ontario towns until 1873–4. During this period he actively involved himself in the Orange Lodge, and served as color-sergeant in the Ontario Rifles Company that helped to squash the Riel insurrection of 1870. After his brief engagement as a manufacturer, he turned to journalism, and successively edited the Guelph *Herald*, the Orangeville *Sun*, and the Stratford *Herald*. This journalistic activity, coupled with the political and economic crises of the mid-1870s, moved him into the ranks of partisans of the producer ideology. Championed since the late 1850s by Isaac Buchanan, Hamilton merchant-railwayman-politician, the producer ideology turned upon the mutual interests of wage-paying and wage-receiving sectors of the population. Attacking the drones – merchants, bankers, land monopolists, usurers, and nonproducing middlemen – the producer ideology linked the national interest with the people's employment, stressing the importance of the creation of a home market, providing a strategy, albeit muddled, for industrial development. The twin planks of this reform orientation – currency reform and tariff protection – attracted Wright, and he was a vocal supporter of the National Policy, a Tory whose public commitment was to the mutual interests of employers and employees. These views received endorsement in the *National*, a Toronto paper established in 1874 by H. E. Smallpiece and Phillips Thompson, and later taken over by A. W. Wright. As a link between the producer reform agitation of the 1870s and the more explicit movement toward labor reform of the 1880s, the paper popularized the "new nationalism" of the period, prominent in "Canada First." Moreover, it brought Wright and Thompson together as men destined to play leading roles in the labor upsurge of the 1880s. After the collapse of the *National* in 1880, Wright continued to embrace the producer ideology in the pages of the Toronto-based *Commonwealth*, in the halls of the Ontario Manufacturers' Association, where he served as secretary, and in the Canadian Currency Reform League and National Greenback Labor Party (U.S.).

By the 1880s, however, the producer ideology had been dealt a series of harsh blows. The quickening pace of industrial capitalist development, the consequent strains and tensions, and the resulting class conflict had, since the early 1870s, made the split between employers and workers increasingly obvious, and the producer ideology obsolete. Wright, like most reformers, was pushed toward a more explicit class stance, and gravitated toward the

Knights of Labor, claiming to have joined the Order in 1883. He occupied a number of important posts in DA 125, and was also MW of Victor Hugo Assembly 7814, Toronto's gathering place of Knights of Labor intellectuals, journalists, and "brainworkers." By the late 1880s he was actively engaged in the Order, lecturing across Ontario and publishing the *Canadian Labor Reformer*, the official voice of southern Ontario's DAs 61 and 125 in 1887. He stood as a thorough labor reformer, one acutely conscious that pure and simple unionism was no adequate defense against the incursions of an age of monopoly and labor oppression. He clung tenaciously to the producer ideology, and was pushed toward a comprehensive critique of land monopolists, bankers, and railway moguls, the enemies of both worker and employer. At the 1888 General Assembly Wright was elected to the General Executive Board, and subsequently became Secretary. From 1889 to November 1893, he held the important position of editor of the *Journal of the Knights of Labor*. After the demise of the Order he turned to familiar territory, editing the New York-based *Union Printer and American Craftsman* in 1897 and reingratiating himself with the Canadian Tories. In 1895 he was appointed by the federal government to investigate sweat-shop labor in Canada. Wright finished off his days organizing for the Conservative Party in Ontario (1898–1904), presiding over the Canadian Public Ownership League, editing a Tory labor newspaper, the Toronto *Lance* (1909–1914), and serving as vice-chairman of the Ontario Workmen's Compensation Board. He had had an eventful career.[20]

This sketch, of course, is but the skeleton of a man's life. The flesh we put on these bones, particularly those bones that connect part of the history of the Knights of Labor, do not improve the man's looks. For Wright was a blatant opportunist, compulsive factionalist, and self-seeking schemer. When his pocket could be filled, Wright seldom missed an opportunity to do so; when advantage was to be seized, Wright was always quick to move; where he could maneuver politically in a clandestine manner, throwing integrity aside, Wright was almost certain to do so. It was men of Wright's stamp that caused the more politically independent elements of the Knights of Labor to look back on the Order in disgust. R. J. Kerrigan, a Montreal Knight who would later join the Socialist Labor Party and then the One Big Union (OBU), remembered the dirty environment of "political trading" that dominated the "rotten boroughs" of A. W. Wright's Toronto Assemblies. Hankering after the "political plum," men like Wright exemplified those corrupting politicians "who could take the sting out of the Knights of Labor." In the process political lackeys never "looked a gift horse in the mouth," and aspired to become "the Canadian Tammany Machine of Labor."[21]

There is much of the truth in this kind of assessment, although in the case of Wright one must always question who is using whom (for it is hard to believe that Wright ever got the short end of *any* stick). But we will miss something if we see only the charlatan and opportunist. Wright, like most corrupt but astute men, catered to something beyond his own self-interest. In riding the Knights of Labor to his own sordid success, Wright was pushed to defend working-class interests, to articulate an elementary class stance. By building the organization that he could use to his own advantage, Wright helped to create something more than sustenance for parasites like himself.

In March and April 1889, for instance, Wright stumped the American industrial Northeast and south-central Canada, lecturing on behalf of the Knights of Labor. Oratory was obviously his forte, and for two to three hours he would lead an attack on speculation and usury, advocate radical variants of the Single Tax, urge the workingmen to join the "great social revolution" that the Order was attempting to build, and rail against the competitive wage system and the monopolies that grew rich on its spoils. There was much of the producer ideology in all of this, of course, and Wright continued to deprecate strikes, as he had done in the 1870s and would do again in the 1890s. But the climate of the 1880s allowed no ambivalence on the question of the essential antagonism separating capital and labor. "When a street car horse was sick the company procured a doctor for it," thundered Wright at the Knights of Labor Hall in Kingston, "but when a driver was sick he was docked." Blaming the system, rather than individual capitalists, Wright concluded that, "The competitive wage system is a curse under present conditions, when the workmen are in excess of the demand for work, and when no man can use his working powers without first asking permission from capital, in the person of the employers." At the Music Hall in Cornwall, Wright attacked the individualism of the age, and argued that, "Collectivism, or they could call it Socialism if they would, was the only means that could be relied upon to lift up the world." In two months Wright spoke in dozens of places, including Newark, New Jersey, Danbury, Connecticut, Kingston, Cornwall, Montreal, Guelph, Oshawa, Port Dalhousie, Berlin, and Peterborough. He stressed education, organization, and concerted action, and took the message of labor reform to North American workingmen and women.

The irate editorials that followed in his wake, often condemning the "incendiary, intemperate, ill-informed" platform talks, testified to the hostility with which men of property and standing often greeted Wright. One such attack appeared in the *Kingston News:*

Such men as Wright are probably the most potent instruments that the powers of evil in modern times possess. On a more impressionable audience than that which listened to him on Friday night Wright's influence would have been pernicious. Possessed of a glib tongue, having no idea of proportion or moderation in what he says he inspires an easily moved audience with incendiary notions, he skilfully fans into a flame the workingman's smouldering jealousy of his employer and thus he aggravates rather than betters the present relations of labor and capital. The very worst enemies of the laborer are not the capitalists but just such lopsided theorists as A. W. Wright.

The *News* was overreacting, for Wright was no revolutionary. But the fear with which it recoiled from him indicates just how deeply strained class relations had become by 1889, and how the Knights of Labor were regarded as part and parcel of that class tension.[22]

Moreover, while some condemned Wright, others on the opposite side of the class fence found him attractive. Thomas J. O'Neil, MW and Organizer of Napanee's Courage Assembly 9216, wrote to Powderly just prior to Wright's 1889 speaking tour: "This section of the country is sadly in need of organization but fear of the money kings (the Rathbuns) keep the working class in slavery. I expect some good results when Bro. A. W. Wright gets around this way to lecture. The people will then be more enlightened on the great and grand principles of our Order." Other Assemblies, too, saw Wright's lectures as central to their organizational efforts, a stimulus to the growth of the Knights of Labor. As we will discover in Chapter 7 Wright's stint as a lecturer was not without its darker moments, and D. J. O'Donoghue led an attack against "Old Alec's" mishandling of funds and political machinations. But in the open organizing of the Order the slippery Wright may have won many Canadian workers to the cause of the Knights of Labor. There was more to him, then, than blatant careerism.[23]

Behind the scenes, however, Wright's activities throughout the 1880s were less than exemplary. Since 1879, when he proposed an official laudatory biography of Sir John A. Macdonald, Wright was in contact with the Conservative Party and its leader. Indeed, during his stint as Secretary of the Ontario Manufacturers' and Industrial Association, Wright campaigned openly for the Tories, "booming" the National Policy. On the margins of this political activity were a series of clandestine business deals and schemes, aimed at securing Wright and his cronies some easy cash. In these "purely business" transactions, many of which were less than successful, Macdonald's influence was openly solicited; occasionally the Wright connection appealed directly for funds.[24] All of this, in the days of Tory scandal and CPR boondoggle, was not unusual, but it did preface some interesting developments concerning the Knights of Labor.

Wright had always lived, and would continue to live, close to the world of the newspaper. In the 1870s he had been a small-town editor. From the mid-

1880s to the prewar years of the twentieth century his attachments would be to the labor press. In 1884, the failure of Hamilton's *Palladium of Labor*, official organ of the Knights of Labor, appeared imminent. "My knowledge of the parties conducting it convinces me that the paper would not last," wrote Wright to the prime minister. Wright then suggested a plan to thwart the pernicious conspiracy to draw the working class into the Grit ranks (*his* favorite conspiracy), engineered in the allegedly Liberal-dominated Toronto labor movement. He appealed to Macdonald in terms that revealed fully his concerns and approach. A full pocket and conspiratorial intrigue always seemed uppermost in his mind and in his political practice:

> My plan is to have a paper started which will be made the organ of the Knights of Labor and perhaps of the Trade and Labor Council. My idea is that in order to fully obtain and retain the confidence of the working classes the paper should be conducted editorially on a purely labor platform, even antagonizing the conservative party where it could be done harmlessly, but whenever opportunity offered putting in a word that would do good. To start the paper properly so as to insure success it would require about $4000. Ferguson of Welland has obtained control of the newspaper organ of the Grangers (?) and a plan similar to the above might be adopted to influence the farmers. I have had some conversation with the Doctor on the subject.

Nothing came of this scheme immediately, and a month and one-half later Doctor John Ferguson wrote to Macdonald: "Wright is a very good hand to conceive ideas, but poor at carrying them out." Macdonald, who had financed labor papers before, and had loaned a junta of Tory workingmen the funds to purchase the organ of the nine-hour movement, the *Ontario Workman*, apparently did not rise to this occasion.[25]

Wright, then, was undoubtedly a consistent opportunist, an unprincipled manipulator capable of cultivating his own self-interest at every turn. Moreover, he was deeply embedded within the structure of Tory politics in the Ontario of the 1880s, and he could never be relied on to break free from the party of Macdonald. But he was also an astute observer, and if his audience seemed committed to a class stance, he was willing to educate them in the principles of labor reform. He may have unwittingly pushed some late nineteenth-century workers toward a more acute understanding of the inequalities of the social order, cultivating radicalism as he proceeded cynically from town to town. For some in the Order he was a dangerous element, one of the many internal threats to the symbolic pyramid. J. T. Carey of St. Catharines suggested as much to Powderly when he noted that Wright "was worth watching" and hoped that "he will get no position that we can't keep an eye on him."[26] But to others Wright was a distant figure, one of those impressive phantoms who appeared on podiums and moved them with oratory and the promise of change. In the Noble and Holy Order of the Knights of Labor, as in the world of nineteenth-century North America, things were not always what they seemed.

To be sure, it must again be stressed that Wright was capable of good service in the cause of the Knights of Labor and reform in general. As a high-ranking member of the Order, he involved himself in a number of industrial disputes, and although his judgments did not always seem to flow from the best of motives, he often kept the interests of the membership in mind. Exhausting itineraries and extensive public speaking kept him separated from his wife and his idyllic retreat at Niagara-on-the-Lake, which he dearly loved; and he bore the Order's occasional lackadaisical payment of his expenses with a measure of good humor, particularly, of course, when the fact could be turned to factional purpose.[27] The post-1888 years were difficult ones for the organization, yet Wright remained in contact with his old DA in Toronto and took pains to see that Canadian Knights of Labor were remembered in the larger international setting.[28] Finally, in his "Spokeshave" columns in the *Journal of the Knights of Labor*, Wright continued to address issues and concerns rooted in the old producer ideology, attacking land monopolists, usurers, and the competitive wage system. Although antagonistic to socialism and anarchism, he was always ready to strike a blow for populistic reform, and his critique of North American industrial society in the crisis-ridden years of the 1890s was often quite perceptive.[29]

But behind all of this lay the continual quest for gain, jokingly illuminated in Wright's frank correspondence with Powderly. He wrote to the head of the Order in 1892, commenting on a proposed lecture in Richmond, Virginia:

> Davis [John C.] writes that he is to speak in Richmond Wednesday and that I am to be with him. He says we want to show that it is not a fight between capital and labor but that it is capital and labor against the grinding-grasping-monopolistic-soulless-headless money power otherwise the great red dragon. I suppose one of us will represent Labor and the other Capital. I think I'd like the last role if they would furnish me with the proper accessories.

And, again, a year later, commenting on the organization's unwillingness to keep him on staff in the midst of the 1893 shifting of power:

> Yesterday Hayes informed me that he couldn't let me have any more money until the Board had decided my standing. Now although I've had some experience in my time in getting along without money, I confess I never enjoyed it. I own too that I have never been able to acquire that contempt for money which is supposed to mark the true philosopher.[30]

Between 1891 and 1895 Wright's efforts to acquire "the proper accessories" and his unwillingness to cultivate "a contempt for money" led him into some truly amazing financial dealings. He was certainly not, by his own admission, a mere philosopher.

In the early 1890s, for instance, Wright, in alliance with Powderly, John Devlin (a prominent Knight of Labor formerly a U.S. Consul in Windsor), and an unscrupulous (even by Wright's standards) business agent named Gray, published the *Labor Day Annual.* Prominent reformers and politicians bought favorable accounts of their life histories in the *Annual*'s pages, and advertisements were extensively solicited, with Wright and his partners pocketing the proceeds. In two letters to Powderly in the fall of 1893, Wright estimated that they would have "about $1,000.00 to divide up," adding that "If rightly managed there is a lot of money in the *Annual*, and it wouldn't be a wise man's trick to let anyone have a chance to spoil it." Corresponding with H. G. Gray (a man we will meet again), Wright cautioned, "nothing must be said which would give anyone a chance to say that we are trading upon the organization in trying to push the *Annual.*"[31]

At the same time that they were pursuing riches via the pages of the *Labor Day Annual*, Wright and Powderly also struck up the Accident Claims Association, an insurance scheme they felt destined to become "a great financial success." The whole affair seemed to collapse when prominent Knights and Eugene V. Debs refused to dirty their hands with an endorsement, but not before some LAs voiced their opposition. They smelled something rotten in the scheme, and not without cause. For Wright was peddling stock in the Association to rich employers, implying that a subscription would stabilize a labor organization that moved forcefully to stifle strikes, avoiding violent labor–capital confrontations. "You know these fellows who have stolen their millions have great respect for 'conservative' labour organizations," he wrote to Devlin in 1893, "and forbidding strikes is next to godliness in their estimation. If Alger takes stock tell him you suppose he can get from $1000 to $5000 [in] shares, $100.00 to be paid on subscription and that it is not anticipated that there will be any recalls." A living profit and an acquiescent working class must have been an attractive proposition and Wright probably secured some easy dollars in this early workmen's compensation venture, which he tried to "sell" in Ontario as well as the United States.[32] As if this was not enough, Wright and Powderly also flirted with other "big schemes." One involved a railway official who had been connected with the *Labor Day Annual;* another revolved around stock in a mining company traded for advertising space in the *Journal of the Knights of Labor*, and there were probably many others.[33]

Throughout Wright's marginal years in the Knights of Labor, 1893–4, he continued to pursue the dollar. Well aware of his fall from grace, he grasped at every opportunity. "I had a visit this evening from a man who knows a woman who has an invention that there is more money in than even the serpent of 814 [Hayes] ever dreamed of," he wrote to Powderly on 17 January 1894, "and they want us (you and me) to take hold of it." In the same letter, however, he returned to a more familiar scheme, one that he had long since perfected. He informed Powderly of his plan to begin a labor paper, backed by industrialists who would stand to gain from its protectionist stance, and Republicans, who could turn the support of a reform journal to obvious political purpose. He approached the manufacturer John Lorimer of Philadelphia, stressing the necessity of "an industrial policy for the producers" and raging against the threat posed by "ranters like Jerry Simpson." By the end of January he had involved a U.S. Senator and James M. Swank of the American Steel Association. The whole project was conducted with Wright's characteristic conspiratorial intrigue. "The idea is for obvious reasons not to have too many men in the secret," he wrote Devlin. "If some of our anarchist and socialist friends were put in a position to say that the paper was bonussed by prominent republicans or by employers they would use it against us." Wright also planned to use the paper to strike a blow at the Order, and the current leadership that had ousted Powderly and himself: "I am more than anxious to have the paper started, both because we will make money out of it and because we will have some fun with the serpent and his brood . . . and how we could talk to the order, and tell them some of the things he don't want told." Three months later, after some setbacks, Wright informed Devlin of the progress of his plan: "The Paper scheme – project I mean – after a short rest has taken a fresh start and seems likely to go through this time." In the end it all came to nought, but it was not for want of trying. Not until 1897, when Wright edited the *Union Printer and American Craftsman* did he secure the opportunity to settle old scores with the "serpent," John W. Hayes, attack the Knights of Labor, vindicate himself and Powderly, and reassert basic tenets of the producer ideology.[34]

With the labor newspaper's failure to materialize, Wright quickly sought new sources of compensation. He engaged himself as a business agent for groups of American speculators interested in acquiring timber rights and developing certain Central American land holdings. By this late date, Wright had involved himself in the Patrons of Industry, contributing to their official organ, the *Farmers' Sun*, and speaking for them around the province of Ontario. "There is no money in it unfortunately," he confided to Powderly. But he was able to use this and past connections to sell himself as a man eminently qualified to serve the best interests of his employers. In letters to Messrs. Tuthill and De Saville, he outlined his past accomplishments with labor/farmer organizations, adding, "This has given me a wide acquaintance with both the officials and the rank and file of the working classes and farmers from among whom the settlers for your lands would come." From his home at Niagara-on-the-Lake, Wright bombarded Ontario newspaper editors, requesting their support in the land project, urging them to get involved. He advised placing advertisements and reading notices in the *Farmers' Sun*, where he suggested they would be eagerly discussed by the Patrons.[35] In the end, too, this effort seemed to bear little fruit, although Wright's ties to Tuthill placed him on the ground floor of other get-rich-quick schemes.[36]

None of these financial wheelings and dealings ever paid handsomely for Wright, although he no doubt cleared a few dollars here and there, and lived by his wits for many years. When it was all over, Wright wrote to his ally John Devlin: "I suppose Mrs. D. is well pleased that you are out of it. My wife is, she has some hope that we will have some little home life now. Well for such a home bird as I am it has been five years of something like purgatory."[37] For all the spoils of office, it had apparently been lonely at the top of the pyramid.

Alexander W. Wright had traveled a long way from Elmira, Ontario. He had done much to establish the Noble and Holy Order of the Knights of Labor in Canada, and he had done much to bring the organization to the point where an unholy alliance of careerists, complacent hirelings, and committed socialists could bring him and Powderly to their knees. Writing to a friend in Kansas from his Niagara-on-the-Lake home, he confessed:

> For my part I am utterly sick and disgusted with the way in which our order that promised so much for humanity, is being trailed in the dust by an unscrupulous and designing scoundrel for it is Hayes who is the active serpent of mischief . . . McGuire has no mind of his own and is what someone called a moral agnostic, that is one who has no concept of moral right and wrong. Besides Hayes has boasted more than once that McGuire is in his power. Sovereign seems to be as deficient in conscience as he is in backbone and to be simply the obedient tool of an unscrupulous manipulator. With such a body of General Officers what hope is there for the Order . . . When there may be again men like DeLeon of New York who are working and plotting for the disruption of the Order in the hope of building up the socialist party in its ruins.[38]

These may seem like strange words coming from such a man. But the recipient of this letter probably did not think so. He had not read Wright's intimate correspondence, had not seen him lounge at the Philadelphia office, had not overheard those after-dinner conversations closing a score of illicit transactions. He had seen Wright as a talented speaker, an unwavering advocate of labor reform. Many Canadian workingmen and women must have regarded Wright in the same way. The sordid underside of the Knights of Labor, turned up for all to see in the 1890s, had at least worn a face of respectable purpose during labor's upsurge of the 1880s.

## Morgan and Harvey

If men like Wright had indeed exercised an ambivalent impact, popularizing the cause of labor reform and even honestly adhering to its basic tenets at the same time that they created an institutional vehicle for their own betterment, their successors were less complex. We have hinted at this process earlier in this chapter, and it is time to return to the local setting to observe two men, Enoch P. Morgan and Falconer L. Harvey, and their history in the Knights of Labor. Unlike Wright, they made no positive contribution. Their role in the Order turned on pecuniary advancement; their impact proved to be destructive. North American LAs unfortunate enough to admit them to membership paid dearly for their lack of discrimination.

Enoch P. Morgan and Falconer L. Harvey may have first crossed paths in Toronto in 1872–3, in the midst of one of the central moments of nineteenth-century Canadian working-class history, the printers' strike for the nine-hour day. City directories listed a Falconer Harvey, a clerk employed at the Gerrard Street offices of the Colonial Securities Company, and an Enoch P. Morgan, a reporter residing at 26 Victoria Street. Morgan later claimed, with characteristic immodesty, to "have done important service in the Conservative cause" in that troubled period. His contribution, he wrote to Sir John A. Macdonald, was to have induced James Beaty of the *Leader* to withdraw from George Brown's compact and offer his support to the workingmen. When the Tories legalized trade unions, Morgan boasted, "I was myself the first to see the point for politics." Whatever his actual role in the events of 1872–3, Morgan disappeared from view, swallowed up like so many of his peers in the depression of the 1870s.[39] For the next dozen years Morgan's movements revealed a dimension of the process of mobility seldom chronicled in the pages of current treatments of the subject: the bogus "reformer's" perpetual quest for gain.

In May 1877 he appeared in Cleveland, apparently now as a full-fledged newspaper editor and accomplished reporter. Posing as an English journalist, he lectured on the timely topics of "Hard Times" and "Capital and Labor." A few weeks later he was invited into the Patrons of Industry and a labor Political Society known as the Greenback Club. The next month saw him introduced into a secret assembly of the Knights of Labor, elected and instituted as MW. In the railway strikes of 1877, Morgan, of course, figured prominently in the upheaval, addressing "an immense mass meeting in the public square completely filled . . . [with] ten thousand and upwards working-men well mixed with police detectives and militia." In the aftermath of the conflict he claimed to have helped in the creation of a Labor-Greenback press, until he incurred the wrath of Robert Schilling, president of the Greenback Club and well known in the Knights of Labor. Here, Morgan's self-congratulatory account of his actions in Cleveland, outlined in a letter to T. V. Powderly, terminates; it is substantiated in part by reports in the local press.

From another source we learn of his last Cleveland activities. J. M. Brady, MW of DA 47 in Cleveland, informed William H. Rowe, editor of Hamilton's *Palladium of Labor*, that Morgan had indeed been MW of LA 450, the oldest Assembly in the city. He added that his years of membership had been soiled with "the blackest kind of crookedness." Morgan's crime, which would earn him expulsion from the Knights, had been to publish in the daily press "the aims and objects and secret work of our order." When asked to surrender the secret ritual to the Assembly, he could produce only the tattered covers of the *Adelphon Kruptos*. To protect himself, Morgan had given police authorities the names of several members of the Knights of Labor, telling them that if he should be missed these men ought to be held accountable. Through Morgan's efforts, Brady contended, "the Assembly was nearly disorganized," and much bitterness still prevailed in Cleveland's Order years later. Driven out of the Order and, in all likelihood, the city, Morgan headed for greener pastures, his flight financed by the Cleveland daily that had purchased his Assembly's treasured secret work.[40]

Morgan may well have fled to England, for an advertisement in the *Palladium of Labor* places him there in 1881, teaching shorthand at the Young Men's Christian Association, Exeter Hall, London. He apparently also spent time in Chicago.[41] By 1883–4, however, he had definitely established himself in Camden, New Jersey. There, in conjunction with a Paul W. D. (probably alias Falconer L.) Harvey, Morgan edited and managed the Camden *Mirror*, and established a publishing venture at 21 Federal Street. The two men also shared accommodations in a house at 816 Chestnut Street. The *Mirror*, as Morgan told Powderly, was a weekly advocating "the principles of the anti-monopoly league and the K of L." While ill, Morgan had been introduced to Charles Smith, a destitute worker with a wife and three children. Morgan secured work for Smith and as the *Mirror* merged with another paper to form the daily *Morning Journal*, hired him to work on the new paper, paying him half the profits. The two men eventually quarreled, Morgan claiming that Smith coveted his position. Smith was paid off and discharged. Things seemed to go from bad to worse for the luckless Morgan, however, and as

Smith renounced him from one end of town to the other the *Morning Journal* folded. In January 1884 Morgan, penniless, left Camden with his wife and child. His property was sold to pay his debts, and he left with a clear conscience. At least so Morgan told it.[42]

A. J. Milliette, a Camden Knight, and Joseph Mattack, Camden's chief of police, enlarged upon Morgan's account. Milliette, then involved with a suit brought against him by a Philadelphia merchant, attributed his 1884 legal entanglements to those "damn rascals" Harvey and Morgan. The latter was apparently wanted in Indianapolis for "one of his swindles," and in a town in Ontario for seduction. He was also kicked out of a Camden church for slander. He had left the city when one of his schemes had backfired, his ingenious efforts to secure paper and goods from a Philadelphia firm while posing as a Camden councilman having been discovered for the fraud they were. "If you have any business with Morgan and Harvey," concluded Milliette, "you are dealing with unscrupulous rascals and the most infamous damn liars and tricksters at large. Under any other circumstances than to protect a brother craftsman I would be ashamed to acknowledge that I allowed myself to be swindled by such impecunious scallawags, but as it was they beat me out of nearly five hundred dollars." The police chief concurred: the two men were known in the city as frauds, although Harvey, while undoubtedly a scoundrel, could not compare to Morgan. Both had made a tidy profit on their Camden ventures and "departed for parts *unknown*."[43]

Unfortunately for DA 61, their next move was to Hamilton, Ontario. Morgan arrived in the spring of 1884, where he found the *Palladium of Labor* recently "busted." Harvey may have been with him, or followed soon after. After sizing up the situation the men acted quickly. Drawing upon their talents and experience in newspaper work, they engaged in soliciting advertising for the paper, and helped to reestablish the journal in 1884. Morgan began instructing classes in shorthand at the Hamilton Commercial College, and sold subscriptions to the *Palladium of Labor*. Typically, Morgan found it impossible to work with the paper's managing editor, William H. Rowe, whom he found "very unpopular with the business men." Emboldened, perhaps, by their early success in securing advertising contracts totaling nearly $3,000, Harvey and Morgan schemed to break with Rowe, probably in July 1884. The *Palladium of Labor* editor beat them to it, however, and severed their connection with the journal. As a base of operation, both men secured themselves membership in LA 2225. From there they cultivated ties with key individuals involved in the recently established Knights of Labor Co-operative Grocery Store and began, in September 1884, to attack prominent Knights, discredit the *Palladium of Labor*, and sow the seeds of discord. Morgan, always ready to assume a place of prominence, addressed the city's workingmen at the 1 October 1884 demonstration against Chinese labor.[44] In November 1884 Morgan and Harvey produced a "booster" publication containing sketches and descriptions of Hamilton and its industries. On a minor scale it was comparable to the Powderly–Wright *Labor Day Annual.* Instead of labor reformers and unionists, however, businessmen financed its creation. Morgan's and Harvey's work soliciting advertising revenue for the *Palladium of Labor* had not been wasted.[45]

Had Morgan and Harvey been familiar with recent historical work demonstrating the importance of transiency and geographic mobility in the nineteenth century, they would perhaps have chosen their locale with some discretion, hoping to avoid past enemies and labor reformers who knew of their earlier exploits. One would have thought that they would at least have kept a low profile, although that did not seem to be in their character. But, after all, they had crossed a border, entered another country, and they probably assumed that they were relatively safe. They were badly mistaken. Terence V. Powderly arrived in Hamilton in early October 1884 to speak before a gathering at the Pythian Armoury on "Rights and Knights of Labor." Upon his arrival, he was immediately informed that E. P. Morgan, "a disturbing element," was enrolled in the Order in Hamilton. His informant was none other than Charles Smith, Recording Secretary of LA 2450 (Cigarmakers), and past acquaintance of E. P. Morgan.[46] It was Smith's knowledge of Morgan that had undoubtedly provided W. H. Rowe with information regarding Morgan's past, clues that led Rowe to uncover details about the Morgan–Harvey ventures in the United States. On this basis, Morgan was found guilty of the misappropriation of Knights of Labor funds and, in December 1884, Powderly suspended him from DA 61 until he satisfied all claims against himself.[47]

Prior to his suspension, however, the publishing committee of the Knights of Labor, headed by its chairman, the coppersmith and activist George Collis, had probed deeply into the affairs of Morgan and Harvey. Harvey's crimes were chronicled in the Court Records of LA 2225:

> The publishing committee hereby charge brother F. L. Harvey late advertising agent of the "Palladium of Labor" and a member of LA 2225 with conspiring to injure a brother member and with perjury before the court of LA 2225 by stating that Brother Rowe had referred to members of the District Assembly as sons of bitches and further working against the interests of the Order by using knowledge he had gained of the advertisers stating to them that the paper was in difficulties and by stating in a saloon publicly the paper was in the hands of the Sheriff at a time when there was no truth in the statement. Furthermore, with endeavoring to induce advertisers to withdraw their patronage from the paper after he had been paid a commission on such contracts.

Morgan's transgressions followed, in more detail:

The publishing committee hereby charge brother E. P. Morgan, late advertising agent of "Palladium of Labor" and member of LA 2225, 1st: with entering the order as a new member, whereas he had previously been a member of an assembly in Cleveland, Ohio, and whilst a member had caused to be published in daily papers the secret work of the Order, and when asked to hand in the secret work of the assembly he practically refused handing in only the covers of the A.K. – 2nd: and furthermore that he is at present a fugitive from justice, having jumped his bail from Camden, New Jersey – 3rd: that he defrauded the Detroit Assembly of monies while acting as advertising agent and collecting his commission on face value of contract. Whereas he had agreed by side contract that the said contract should be settled for less sum, and further that he benefitted by the said discount, and failed to report the said side contract which he had made – 4th: that on the public street in the vicinity of Wood and Leggat Hardware store he referred to the Districe Master Workman as a son of a B...h – 5th: that in presence of several witnesses he referred to Brother Rowe, manager of the 'Palladium' as a rogue, thief, liar, accusing him of defrauding the District Assembly – 6th: that he placed the official organ of the District, the 'Palladium of Labor', in a difficult position by leaving its service contrary to agreement at a time when family trouble were on the manager, W. H. Rowe.[48]

Collis concluded that both men had come to Hamilton to obtain work on the *Palladium of Labor* as soliciting agents. That accomplished, and after gaining admission to LA 2225, they showed their "true colors." Attempting to discredit the paper by inducing advertisers with whom they had cultivated a rapport to withdraw their support from the paper, they hoped to precipitate the ruin of the *Palladium of Labor*. Their next object would have been to "work their old game" of starting another labor paper to secure some quick advertising profits from it, abandon the enterprise, and leave "the Order in Hamilton in a lurch." With Morgan's suspension, Collis expressed relief to Powderly. A great burden had been lifted from his shoulders: "This affair had caused quite a number of the members to give me the cold shoulder for they were thinking that I was pursuing this man with too much vigor. I attributed it to prejudice. I trust that his oily tongued career will be cut short in our vicinity." The whole unpleasant affair, Collis seemed certain, was now terminated. Moreover, Harvey's arrest for drunkenness in the late fall, and Morgan's December arrest on "swindling charges" promised to "materially hasten" the pair's exit from Hamilton. So confident was Collis that he did not even push for Harvey's expulsion from LA 2225. The tragedy of Morgan's and Harvey's nefarious doings, Collis confessed, was that "due to their swift tongues and glib talk they have induced quite a number of honest members into their camp." But it was Powderly who provided the most insightful comment, scribbling a note on the bottom of a Hamilton letter: "I have squelched Mr. Morgan . . . caus[ing] his name to be dropped from the rolls of the A. he belongs to . . . I took the bull by the horns I don't know where he will take me."[49]

Normally this kind of affair would provide only a footnote to the history of working-class organizations, a detailed glimpse at the underside of labor-reform movements. Yet, in Hamilton, and quite possibly in other cities prominent in the history of the Knights of Labor, this kind of disruption could easily seep into the fissures created by dissent and factional fighting. In the midst of Morgan's indictment, for instance, his LA, No. 2225, was engaged in a battle with the Gardner sewing-machine factory, a strike initiated when the firm fired six members of the Order in May 1884. "The opinion prevailed in LA 2225," wrote E. S. Gilbert to Powderly, "that their discharge was due to the prominent part they had taken in a previous trouble in the same shop and that although the previous trouble had been settled these six men had been marked for discharge . . . The result was that the DA acting on the belief that the men had been victimized declared war on the Company by calling out of the factory all members of the Order."[50] A number of LA 2225's members, however, balked at this directive, an indication of an important breach of solidarity. This refusal to strike resulted in a rash of expulsions from the Order, and LA 2225 was to be embroiled in factional disputes for much of the fall of 1884.[51] Shoemakers' Assembly 2132, as we have seen in Chapter 4, heightened this kind of division by continuing to refuse payment of the assessment levied in the interests of Montreal strikers, an act which led to their brief suspension from the DA.[52]

Amidst this turmoil, E. P. Morgan and F. L. Harvey stood to gain much by denigrating the leadership of Hamilton's DA and creating divisions that would work in their favor. In a letter to Powderly, outlining the development of these local rifts, George Collis stated the gravity of the situation: "We are going through a very trying ordeal just at present in Hamilton and it will require the wisest councils to pull the order through and the question paramount in my mind is whether we shall come out of it brighter and better for the trial or whether we shall be so crippled as to be useless for ever after." Collis then linked much of the dissent in the Order directly to Morgan's vilifications: "I am at present engaged in a trial with that man Morgan and at the last meeting of the court he flourished a letter in my face purportedly to be from yourself calling me a liar . . . I am convinced that in this man we are dealing with an adventurer of the worst kind. Men who are regular leeches on the society with a fair face and a smooth tongue they carry a large number of our simple members away with them and those who do trouble to investigate their base history and present actions are frowned upon and counted as kickers of the worst sort."[53]

D. B. Skelly, a member of LA 2225, was one Knight of Labor apparently drawn in by Morgan or enticed by the possibility of personal profit. He wrote to Powderly 15 December 1884:

> Two years ago the Knights of Labor was in a flourishing condition in Hamilton. Today we have not got a corporals guard in good standing . . . you have not got to go far to find the cause, a political ring has got hold of it . . . have all the machinery in their hands, they have their local and other Courts and if any man has sufficient independence of character to open his mouth against them he is slapped into a court – this case of Harvey, Morgan, Palladium Committee (I have been acting as clerk) has been on hand now some two months and only some 4 or 5 witnesses examined for the prosecution and I must frankly say it is the most disgusting farce [it] could possibly be.

Skelly continued his diatribe with an assault on the arrogance of George Collis, and then noted the ring's "sharp trick . . . in suspending the shoemakers . . . to keep their delegate out of DA 61 till after the next election." As a representative to the Central Labor Union, Skelly also chronicled that body's demise in the hands of "the ring." Finally, perhaps betraying the essential cause of his bitterness, Skelly condemned the "K. of L. ring's" independent political activity, which only served to undermine the strength of the Tory part and contributed to the victories of the Grits. As a staunch supporter of the National Policy, an ardent follower of Sir John A. Macdonald's Conservative Party, and a man with his hand always open for a patronage handout, Skelly could hardly countenance such political sin.[54]

Skelly was eventually removed from his position as court clerk. His predisposition to Morgan and his obstinate refusals to comply with the court's directions, often punctuated with "uncalled for and coarse language," brought about his discharge. This caused yet another factional dispute, MW Allan Studholme arguing that the Judge Advocate of LA 2225's Court had no authority to remove the clerk. It was at this point, as we have seen, that Powderly eventually took matters into his own hands and suspended Morgan in late December 1884.[55]

Powderly was absolutely right to question where all of this would lead, however, for Morgan's suspension was by no means the end. Rifts in the Hamilton Order would not be easily healed. Morgan, after all, had figured prominently in the Knights of Labor as late as 1 October 1884, when he addressed the anti-Chinese demonstration. When William J. Vale's communication endorsing Powderly's ruling that Morgan be suspended from the Order reached LA 2225, the Assembly was highly incensed. William H. Bews, Recording Secretary, wrote to Powderly outlining the general dissatisfaction prevailing in his "and other assemblies as to interference by Powderly in local affairs." Bews demanded a justification of the action. LA 2225 received a curt response from the GMW, stating that no injustice had been committed and that the suspension had been warranted.[56] Morgan, perhaps feeling the limelight a little too hot, retired into the background, not to be heard from for several months. His presence, however, would continue to be felt, and he would soon reappear, in the company of familiar friends.

One of Morgan's allies in LA 2225, for instance, had been James Ailes.[57] Aged about thirty-five, and described as "rather domineering and very egotistical," Ailes provided a central connective link in the Morgan–Harvey plot. He was in a position, by February 1885, to profit immensely at the expense of the Hamilton Order, for he was in charge of DA 61's Co-operative Store. Mr. Ailes' management of the concern, known as Branch No. 1 of DA 61, established 24 June 1884 (not long after Morgan's appearance), had been the subject of some consternation among Hamilton's Knights of Labor for a number of weeks. David R. Gibson testified that on the afternoon of 18 February 1885 DA 61 resolved to dismiss Ailes, and made application for the store's account books. Ailes refused to surrender the books, locking the store and retaining the key. Gibson then testified that Ailes informed him that the books were at his home. Sent to retrieve these accounts was none other than Charles L. Smith, Morgan's old antagonist. When Ailes again refused to give up the books, the case was brought into the Local courts, DA 61 charging Ailes with withholding from the Knights of Labor the stock-in-trade of the association. Ailes countered with a charge of forcible entry against seven leading members of the Order, among them George Collis, William Vale, Thomas Towers, Allan Studholme, and David Gibson. He also claimed that the Knights of labor owed him $253.93. The magistrate, noting that Ailes was the servant of the DA, and that the board of management of the Co-operative Store had purchased the books and paid for them out of the funds of the business, decided the case in favor of DA 61. It was a decision that rankled among some Knights, among them D. B. Skelly of LA 2225 and Robert Coulter, leader of the suspended Shoemakers' Assembly, who continued their opposition to the Hamilton "ring" by testifying on Ailes's behalf. D. J. O'Donoghue wrote contemptuously to Powderly of the dispute: "The members of the co-operative store quarrelled as to management and came to fisticuffs in fighting for possession of the shop. Several were arrested in *flagrante delicto* and appeared before the police magistrate. Being disgusted I did not follow up the proceedings and know not how the matter ended – if ended it be."[58] The trouble was finally concluded in May 1885, with the expulsion of Ailes from LA 2225, "for causing the arrest of seven brother Knights, taking forcible possession of a store, the property of said store belonging to DA 61, and unlawfully removing, detaining, and falsifying books belonging to the co-operative store (Branch No. 1), unlawfully keeping and refusing to hand over money held by him in trust as treasurer of the Hall Committee of the Assembly."[59]

Although Morgan and Harvey were not explicitly involved in the Co-operative Store dispute, there was no doubt that they lurked behind the scenes. The continuing involvement of Smith, on the one hand, and of Skelly and Coulter, on the other, points to a theme of faction and conspiratorial intrigue. The *Palladium of Labor* suggested just this in its comments on the "late troubles," which it attributed to a few "black sheep," ex-members who had been suspended or expelled.[60] But Morgan had more up his sleeve than the grocery store business; tucked inside his shirtcuff was a card borrowed from A. W. Wright's deck. On 24 February 1885, he wrote to Macdonald, soliciting a "few sheckels aid." Morgan claimed that the Knights of Labor, "a secret and powerful organization permeating the whole Dominion with headquarters in Hamilton," was being "wholly worked in Grit interest, the machinery . . . controlled by a few men with Grit promises and patronage swelling their heads." These were words aimed at captivating Macdonald's attention and, that secured, Morgan moved on to emphasize his own role and plan of action:

> But myself and friends have opposed the little dominant clique and held them in check for nearly a year. Just now matters are coming to a focus and a serious split is threatened in the ranks. The fight has become public through a dispute over possession of the Grocery Store owned by the Order. Just at this time we propose starting a weekly paper professedly independent in politics and it will not be a very difficult task to win over to our way of thinking the mass of the members of the order for two thirds of them hang on our lead.

Confident of his ability to displace the *Palladium of Labor* (he claimed to hold a judgement of $350 – Ailes' court charges – against the offices of the paper), Morgan promised to use his paper to "strike out for a new Canadian order of Knights of Labor." To sweeten the pill, he told Macdonald that he already had 300 men "ready to make the new foundation [that could] be safely relied upon to support Sir John."[61]

Coinciding with the Co-operative Store conflict and Morgan's grandiose plans was a rash of expulsions from LA 1864, of mixed callings, in February 1885. Here again there is no explicit connection between Morgan and Harvey and these expulsions, but the rationale of the purge – all the men were sacked for "violation of obligation and with contempt of court"– makes the supposition enticing, especially given Morgan's statement to Macdonald that matters were coming to a head and that a split was developing. Moreover, of the twenty-five men expelled, the majority were between the ages of 19 and 28, likely recruits, as George Collis had pointed out, to the cause of a man of Morgan's talents and charisma.[62] Two expulsions from LA 2225 in April 1885, however, pose no interpretive dilemma. One of the expelled Knights was Daniel McLaren, a machinist driven from the Order for embezzlement of funds; less than two months earlier he had been a strong advocate of James Ailes at the court proceedings in the Co-operative Store dispute. Also expelled was Morgan's old accomplice, Falconer L. Harvey, described as a journalist possessed of a "very sly kind of jenius."[63]

Morgan's confrère had apparently decided to ride out the storm of August–December 1884 and, with Powderly's intervention, which had labeled Morgan as the key culprit, he was given a brief reprieve. In conjunction with Morgan he attempted a minor swindle of a theatrical company in March 1885, but he was relatively inactive in this period.[64] By April 1885, however, he had obviously violated his obligations as a Knight, and his expulsion was meant to terminate his relationship with the Order. A man of Harvey's demonstrated persistence, however, was not easily put off, and his future months would be dedicated to the destruction of the Knights of Labor in Hamilton.

Obviously guided by Morgan, who remained in the background, he chose a tactic that was perhaps familiar to many bogus labor reformers of the 1880s, the creation of an opposing organization. The birth of Hamilton's Universal Brotherhood of United Labor (UBUL), a "fraudulent labor organization" said to be composed of expelled Knights coincided almost exactly with Harvey's expulsion from LA 2225.[65] Commenting on the formation of other rival bodies, reported in the *Denver Enquirer* and *Bay City Vindicator*, the *Palladium of Labor* noted that, "the most dangerous hotheads we have in Hamilton are those who have been expelled for violation of their obligation or some other crooked trick . . . There are a few soreheads in this community, who, for reasons not very creditable to themselves are opposing the Order. They are misrepresenting it and trying to do it an injury."[66] The UBUL apparently had its most active days in late April and early May 1885, holding its first public entertainment in the bricklayers' hall, and attempting, on two occasions, to gain admission to the CLU, first sending representatives of the UBUL, and then posing as members of a nonexistent Painters' Union.[67] By August 1885 the *Palladium of Labor* was ridiculing the grandiose intentions of the Hamilton dissidents: "The U.B. of U.L. which was recently formed in this city for the avowed purpose of 'bustin' the K. of L. has a herculean task on hand, for during the month of July one hundred and ninety new K. of L. assemblies were organized. There are now 4,500 odd assemblies with a membership (in good standing) of one and a half millions. Very nearly 'busted' ain't they. Moyah!"[68] This was an exaggeration of the Order's potency, but it did correctly point to the folly of the UBUL's purpose. By September 1885 the rival body was on its last leg. After securing a reading room and offering memberships for $1 a year, the UBUL found few takers. Their landlord was eventually "stuck for the rent," and the leaders of the organization took to their heels, one of them leaving behind a local police charge of public drunkenness.[69] By May 1886, "that abortion which started in this city last spring under the high-sounding title of the Universal Brotherhood of United Labor" was nowhere to be seen.[70]

We would know nothing beyond these brief snapshots of the UBUL were it not for the abundance of nerve possessed by its main figures. Into the midst of the CLU's April 1885 meeting marched three men, brandishing an officious document, adorned with the seal of a recently formed organization: "To the Officers and Members of the Hamilton Central Labor Union, 25 March 1885, Gentlemen: I have the pleasure of informing you that at the last meeting of the Universal Brotherhood of United Labor, the following members were elected representatives of Legion No. 1, to the C.L.U., viz: D. B. Skelly, James Ailes, and E. P. Morgan."[71] After more than six months of court cases, expulsions, and growing resentments, these men were willing to seek admittance to a body fully aware of their past activities. It was an act that illustrated well Phillips Thompson's observation that:

> I've known men rise through talent, though such
> exceptions are rare,
> And some by perseverance and industry and care,
> There are some who build fortunes by saving a dollar
> a week,
> But the best thing to make your way in the world is
> to travel upon your cheek.[72]

But sheer gall did not win the day this time, and the trio were unceremoniously removed from the meeting. W. H. Bews, Recording Secretary of the CLU, informed the *Palladium of Labor* of the unanimous decision to eject these bogus reformers, and attacked their underhanded efforts to "work themselves into the C.L.U. as the representatives of a *bona fide* workingmen's association."[73]

Upon hearing of this act, W. H. Rowe applauded the CLU's stand, issuing "A Warning to Unprincipled Adventurers and Dupes." In it he outlined the "exceedingly brief history" of the UBUL, an organization composed of "officers, . . . all of whom, with one exception either expelled or suspended Knights of Labor." E. P. Morgan was hailed as the chief "Much-a-much," and F. L. Harvey, "the celebrated traveller and distinguished journalist," was once again his co-worker. D. B. Skelly had been enlisted in their ranks, as well as a few others, "cranks" and "dupes." Rowe then went on to explore the past history of Enoch P. Morgan, noting that he was a fugitive from justice with an "unenviable record" in the West. His main accomplishment was the ability to establish newspapers; in fact, he had started "more than any other person of his age in America." Each new effort, however, "bore the mark of the cloven hoof." Rowe's assessment of the UBUL was unambiguous: "These men are no use to any community, but quite the reverse, they are a detriment, and when they worm themselves into any society, you can depend on it, it is through no honest impute or intent, but simply with a view to 'self' and 'self' alone, and Labor or any other Unions have no use for such Cattle."[74]

Morgan and Harvey had indeed performed with great consistency, issuing a little "advertising sheet" in Hamilton toward the end of March 1885. Under the banner *Justice*, they proclaimed the paper "the official organ of the Universal Brotherhood of United Labor." The Conservative Party may possibly have underwritten this publishing experiment, and the *Palladium of Labor* saw it as a crass political undertaking: "If anything were wanted to expose the partizan animus of the organ of the U.B. of U.L. and the insidious character of the attempt to divide the ranks of Labor in the interest of the Tory party, it is to be found in the latest issue of that precious sheet in the articles assailing the Ontario Government . . . When an ass takes to wear a lion's skin he should always tie his ears back." Whatever the source of support, it was clear that Morgan's and Harvey's weekly was hostile to working-class organization and pandered to the views of manufacturers. It apparently struck a blow against the international Order and Powderly, urged the necessity of "Home Rule," and demanded "absolute control" of the Canadian Assemblies by Canadian Knights of Labor. A St. Thomas "Knight of the Brush" dismissed the venture as "rot," and promised Morgan and Harvey a "ducking" if they should ever set foot in the western Ontario railroad town. In Hamilton the UBUL was quickly pegged a "scab" organization. But elsewhere doubts must have been fostered. "Can it be possible that Morgan has poisoned the good men of that place [Hamilton]," wrote Powderly to O'Donoghue. "Is 'Justice' really the organ of those who father this movement? Do they want the offices? . . . I will never insert a wedge to drive us apart. Why we never knew each other before. We are only just getting acquainted and I wish to keep it up." Powderly, for all his faults, knew the value of labor solidarity; Morgan and Harvey knew the price to be had for fostering division.[75]

In the issue of 18 April 1885, *Justice* editorialized against the cigarmakers' strike, a clash that we have seen would lead into the Home Club fiasco. Ironically, it was Morgan and Harvey who first introduced Hamilton's Knights of Labor to the forthcoming split in their ranks. To strike now was unwise, declared *Justice*, as the trade was slack, and manufacturers were not in need of workers' skills. The editorial aroused the ire of Cigar Makers' International Union No. 55, which issued a statement advising Morgan and Harvey to "mind their own affairs, and leave the discussion of our questions to ourselves, as we are the proper persons to handle our affairs." What prompted *Justice* to intervene in the cigarmakers' dispute is not known. Perhaps it was to curry favor with manufacturers, men of wealth who could obviously keep such a newspaper afloat with advertising revenue. Or the reason may have turned on a more vindictive purpose. Charles Smith, a member of the Cigarmakers' Assembly of the Knights of Labor, was certainly no friend of Morgan and Harvey, and it may have been their purpose to antagonize him. Whatever the reason, *Justice* won few working-class adherents with such a stand, and the paper soon lapsed. It claimed to have been the victim of harassment, and offered a ten-dollar reward for anyone who could inform the management of the identity of the author of an anonymous threatening letter, adorned with a coffin.[76]

As the spring months of 1885 gave way to summer, the UBUL appeared to be headed in the direction of its official organ. Harvey kept the fires alive for a few weeks, instituting libel proceedings against Rowe for his attacks in the *Palladium of Labor*, but the case dragged on in court and was eventually dropped. D. B. Skelly, by mid-June 1885, was pursuing different avenues of self-enrichment, suing the Key Electric Light Company for $75 he felt was his due for "influencing" the City Council in a recent contract tender. By the end of May 1885 a major figure in the UBUL was little more than a memory: "The secrets of Freemasonry have been well kept through many generations, though the members do put their fingers up to their noses when they recall the memory of another Morgan, who claims to be a relative of the former, and is certainly a worthy representative of the 'previous' traitor." Finding the city a little too warm for their liking, Morgan and Harvey apparently absconded, perhaps resuming their charade in a more receptive setting. Morgan, at least, headed for the refuge of the border, stopping briefly at Niagara Falls in July 1885 where he tried to earn an honest dollar, peddling peanuts and selling coffee for 5¢ a cup.[77]

This episode, aside from its intrinsic importance as a chronicle of the vocation of the nineteenth-century labor-reform huckster, has a larger importance in the history of Hamilton's Knights of Labor. As we have seen, Morgan's and Harvey's presence linked a chain of events occurring over the course of a year, commencing with their trails in LA 2225 in August 1884, and terminating with the demise of the UBUL in the summer of 1885. Between these events stood mass expulsions from LA 2225 and LA 1864, the Co-operative Store dispute, the suspension of LA 2132, protests over the course of action pursued by the leaders of DA 61, the formation of a separate organization, the publication of a journal, legal attack on the *Palladium of Labor*, and, in one instance, a formal statement of dissatisfaction with Powderly's intervention in Local affairs. It was a record of achievement, albeit of a negative sort, that few men could equal. There is no doubt that Morgan and Harvey contributed materially to the drastic decline in Hamilton's Order between 1884 and 1885 (from 1,054 to 363), a process heightened by the economic crisis of the mid-1880s. These membership losses would be quickly recouped in the improved conditions of 1886, as many new Assemblies were chartered and the Order, on a superficial level, flourished as it never had before.

But there was one legacy of the Morgan–Harvey affair that would persist. In the midst of the factional fighting of 1884–5, many Hamilton Knights had been won away from their leaders: William J. Vale, 1883 representative to the General Assembly, coordinator of the Morgan–Harvey prosecutions, and member of the organization's international Co-operative Board; George Collis, 1884 representative to the General Assembly, chairman of the local publishing committee, and prominent in the trials of LA 2225; Thomas Towers, Recording Secretary of DA 61 in 1885, arrested in the Co-operative Store confrontation; and David R. Gibson, delegate to the 1885 General Assembly, and a prominent witness in the grocery store court case.[78] Ill feeling had been directed against these men, and many charges must have been made in the privacy of homes, or the safety of groups. While most Knights seemed to have come to regard Morgan and Harvey with appropriate disdain by the early spring 1885, many remained suspicious of the group at the helm of DA 61. These antagonisms would die hard in future months. When the Hamilton Order was plunged into the Home Club dispute of 1886, cracks first opened by Morgan and Harvey widened to destructive fissures. The walls of the symbolic pyramid came tumbling down and there was no one capable of rebuilding the structure. Morgan and Harvey, long since gone, had succeeded better than they knew. Hamilton's Knights of Labor had succumbed to the threat from within.

## "Dangerous times"

What are we to make of all this? Just what is the "historical relevance" of these sordid, nasty affairs? We could reply, like Richard Cobb, that they happened, and that they are therefore worth probing.[79] There is truth enough in that, but there is something more as well. We could hint at the suggestive connections that may have linked the personalities, patterns, and places of this chapter. Morgan and Wright, for instance, may have known each other, and certainly Morgan's associate D. B. Skelly, in his efforts to slice a piece of the patronage pie of the Tory Party, contacted the very same Doctor Ferguson with whom Wright himself was closely associated.

Indeed, these types who sought to turn the movement to their own financial gain may have been quite common. "Colonel" H. G. Gray, for instance, once associated with Powderly and Wright in the production of the *Labor Day Annual* (and eventually judged too untrustworthy even by them) sought out the Order in Ottawa in 1894. He approached J. G. Kilt, editor of *Capital Siftings*, a labor-reform paper. Kilt seemed enticed by Gray's willingness to take "an interest" in the journal, and was drawn to a plan "by which considerable money may be made." Wisely, however, he solicited Powderly's assessment of the well-traveled Colonel Gray. Powderly left no room for misinterpretation. "Under no considerations have anything to do with H. G. Gray for he is thoroughly dishonest and unscrupulous." The GMW had perhaps been bested by the notorious Gray, for he complained that he "ate up all the profits" of the *Annual* in "travelling, riotous living, swell dinners and a multiplicity of marriages." The whole affair, which ended in lost profits for Powderly and A. W. Wright, concluded with a bigamy trial in Chicago, but Gray was set free by "some hitch in the law." Talents such as these were not to be wasted in the Knights of Labor milieu of the mid-1890s, and Gray apparently attached himself to John Hayes, whose own sexual activities must have endeared him to the colonel. Ironically enough, Gray ended up in Hamilton, soliciting advertisements for the *Journal of the Knights of Labor*. Like Powderly and Wright, he too felt aggrieved, and sought a settlement with the Order. "Remember one thing, Old fellow," he closed one letter to Hayes, "and that is that you have absolute power to do just as you please in the settlement, only do not let them delay the matter. You can carry it to court – do anything only get me what is due."[80]

In Montreal A. W. Wright had a rival in William Keys, once a DMW but expelled from his own LA 2436 in 1899. Keys, in fact, often shared the podium with Wright and lectured in Ontario in the late 1880s. He published a collection of "the views of eminent men of the United States and Canada on the labor question, social reform and other economic subjects" in 1896, and it was reprinted in 1904. Remarkably similar to the Wright–Powderly–Gray *Labor Day Annual*, this Knights-of-Labor-backed venture proclaimed the identity of interests of labor and capital. Such views brought Keys into conflict with the radical critics within Montreal's district, among them Bernard Feeny, Richard J. Kerrigan, and William Darlington. Keys and others "cleaned out [the] socialist shysters" in 1896, expelling Kerrigan and Darlington, and leaving the Order "in good and effective shape." The next few years saw Keys's many schemes uncovered. His expulsion resulted from Feeny's and Kerrigan's exposure of his efforts to sell advertising in the name of the labor movement and run an annual banquet on a fraudulent pretense of Knights of Labor support. With men like these operating in and around the Order, it is no wonder that the Knights of Labor failed to effect the social transformation that their leaders promised and the ranks expected.[81]

But there were many other forces that culminated in declining membership and weakened potency, and the underside of the Knights of Labor, while highly disruptive in specific locales and within the upper echelons of the Order, cannot be held totally responsible for the failures of labor reform. The significance of this discussion, rather, lies in what it tells us about the society of nineteenth-century industrial America, and about the Knights of Labor, the organization that issued a basic challenge to that social order. As we have seen, that society was a relatively small place: ideas and men traveled easily within its boundaries, and seemed unaffected by national borders. The period was one of essential class cleavage. The highly successful elements of the underside of the Knights of Labor – men like A. W. Wright – remained in the Order because they could exploit issues of concern to common workingmen and women. Less successful adventurers – the Harveys, Morgans, McGeachies – may have lived off of those issues for a time, but they eventually fled, or were bounced out by those who finally saw them for what they were. Even A. W. Wright eventually lost his appeal. Arthur Fields, a Kingston Knights of Labor organizer, reported to Hayes in 1896 that in Gananoque, Perth, and Napanee advocates of the cause were "down" on Wright, and that a great many negative feelings were being expressed about "Old Alex."[82]

It was the Knights of Labor's eclectic reform orientation, then, that was *both* the source of great strength and the partial cause of failure. Trade unions consolidated their membership around central, limited, concerns related almost solely to the work place; they held their membership in times of crisis, albeit in a weakened state. With the Noble and Holy Order of the Knights of Labor, whose membership was drawn by a more broadly based and consequently more nebulous appeal, solidarity was less secure and more problematic. Its membership was more volatile, less stable; deviations from principle were more likely and more flagrant. There was, of course, an underside of the AFL: embezzlement, graft, and corruption were undoubtedly present, and may have increased with the sophisticated labor bureaucracies of the twentieth century.[83] But there was little room for an A. W. Wright in a nineteenth-century craft union, and even less place for a Morgan, a Harvey, or a Gray. There was, however, space for them in the Knights of Labor; they could even occasionally do good work in the cause. Eventually they would breed turmoil, dissension, and disorder. The pyramid could not withstand the pressure. Bombarded from without and within, its walls crumbled and the house of labor reform collapsed. It was one of the ironies of history that the very forces and attractions that had once shored it up would also undermine its foundation.

This central irony – of strength culminating in weakness – would be revealed most explicitly, however, in the Order's political struggles. In the electoral campaigns that challenged the rule of the established parties, the Knights mounted an opposition based on class perspective and unity. In the face of this impressive effort to overcome past allegiances, the entrenched forces of Grit and Tory proved formidable foes, a development not unanticipated by those Knights seeking, in Richard Trevellick's words, to overcome the "poverty and slavery to the masses that toil" that partisan politics meant. T. W. Brosnan, DMW of Minnesota's DA 79 noted perceptively that, "As we grow older and stronger the politicians will use their most strenuous efforts to get control of the organization." The Michigan radical, Joseph Labadie, was even more forceful and broad ranging in his warning, issued on the eve of the Knights of Labor political upsurge of 1886–7: "Members of organizations, I charge you, beware of the evil influence that will be thrown about you in the future. You have proven yourselves a power, and you enemies will not rest until they either control you by mercenaries in your ranks or destroy you in the future. You have proven yourselves a power, and your enemies will not rest until they either control you by mercenaries in your ranks or destroy you. These are dangerous times for associations. I charge you Grangers, Knights of Labor, Trade Union men, beware!" As Labadie saw clearly, much of the effort to emasculate the challenge of labor reform would cross paths with the kind of unprincipled "mercenaries" we have encountered in these pages, and indeed A. W. Wright will figure prominently in the next few chapters. But the forces at work undermining attempts to sustain an independent working-class political presence were much more pervasive, and in Ontario the Knights of Labor challenge of 1883 – 7 would give way to the internal conflicts of a movement in decline. Brosnan's injunction to stay "true to the principles of the Order," thereby defying the politicians and their tools, was accepted across the province in the early years of the Knights of Labor's history, but not without considerable debate and uneasy compromise.[84]

# 6. The Order in politics: The challenge of 1883–1887

As the Knights of Labor grew in strength, it became necessary for them to attempt to implement their principles through political action. Yet the shoals and reefs of partyism were familiar to all labor reformers. In the words of Hamilton's *Labor Union:* "Partyism is one of the greatest evils of this country. Everybody admits it. The best men of both parties acknowledge it . . . the whole system is a defective machine, like a telephone, which receives the voice of the people and transmits only the voice of the wirepuller." On both sides of the border Knights and other workers regarded politics as a soiled, impure pursuit – a realm where lawyers, rascals, blatherskites, and heelers engaged in deceit in the interests of monopoly. The political arena was not a place to expose one's Knightly principles, for the dangers and temptations were great. In LAs across the province those who sought to use the Order for Grit or Tory advantage induced much disruption. Belleville's LA 2900, for instance, divided when some members attempted to introduce bylaws prohibiting the nomination of "any Person whose sole object is to gain Political Influence." Yet only through representation could the toilers, the producers, and the wealth creators of the country make their voice heard. Moreover, they were only too aware that if they failed to take up the political challenge directly, they could still not avoid the transgressions of the politicians who, as LA 2900 knew well, would penetrate even the sanctuary of the Assembly.[1]

As Labadie and Brosnan realized, the growth of the Order increased its vulnerability: it attracted manipulators, opportunists, and con-men of various descriptions. Nevertheless, strength not partisan pretense propelled the Order into politics. The movement culture, as David Montgomery has recently described the North American working-class late-nineteenth-century ideological consensus, demanded political action. Thus by the mid-1880s as astute an observer as Sir John A. Macdonald worried that his party was not "in a flourishing state." The "rocks ahead" that threatened the Tory "ship" were "Riel, Home Rule, the Knights of Labor and the Scott Act." The Order, present in Canada for only five years, had already made impressive strides. Lewis Allchin was one of its converts, an Oshawa iron molder who, in 1884, told Powderly that he was "waiting for the as yet unformed Independent party to rise phoenix-like from the ashes of corrupt officialdom and sluggish Whiggery." Until then, however, he would continue to "vote in the interests of the working class be the candidates Reform or Conservative."[2]

## First stirrings

Canadian Knights had commenced political activity soon after the organization of the first LAs. In late 1882 in both Toronto and Hamilton preparations were well underway for independent labor political activity. In Toronto the recently renewed TTLC had begun drafting a labor political platform. Meanwhile in Hamilton labor entered the municipal arena and "elected two workingmen for aldermen," as a happy George Havens reported to Powderly. In the same set of municipal elections Toronto labor campaigned strenuously and successfully in the mayoralty race against J. J. Withrow, a master builder, who had actively opposed the nine-hour movement in 1872 and the carpenters in an 1882 strike.[3]

The major evidence of labor's political ambitions came in the 1883 provincial election. Buoyed by their recent municipal successes, Toronto and Hamilton workers united behind independent labor candidates for the first time. This new political force was immediately perceived by the old parties as a major concern. Alexander Morris, the Tory MPP for Toronto East, wrote to Macdonald in mid-January: "The Trade Labour Union [sic] threaten workingmen candidates here and in Hamilton and it would hurt us and help the Grits. I would like an easier seat as I may break down in fighting East Toronto."[4]

In Hamilton the Knights of Labor contributed to the establishment of a tradition of independent political action that had its roots in James Ryan's 1872 creation of the Canadian Labor Protective and Mutual Improvement Association, and culminated in Allan Studholme's elections to the Ontario Legislative Assembly, under the auspices of the Independent Labor Party in 1906, 1908, 1911, and 1915.[5] Studholme, a prominent member of LA 2225 in the years 1882–6, first tasted political activity in the early 1880s, as a member of Hamilton's Labor Political Association, a Knights of Labor body, founded in October 1883 and headed by the coppersmith, George Collis of Vulcan LA 2586, and Robert Coulter of Shoemakers' LA2132. While discord often divided the Order in cities where Knights ran for political office on Grit or Tory tickets, Hamilton remained a stronghold of independent, autonomous political action.[6] In the midst of one battle, a "Knight of the brush" from St. Thomas defended Hamilton's record: "No matter how many branches fall off, the Order will bear good fruit. Let the wage workers of Hamilton stand by the K. of L. and show these would be Union 'busters' that the ballot will be their dynamite, and that when it explodes, it will blow neither Grit or Tory to the head of the polls, but a wage worker who will take some interest in the welfare of his class."[7] The city's Labor Political Association, meeting weekly in the workingmen's club rooms at King and Catharine streets, epitomized this mood of political independence and cultivated a collectivist response to the questions of the day, "apart altogether from partyism." Discussing its positive contribution, the *Palladium of Labor* queried, "where is the advantage to the labouring class of electing a workingman on a Tory or Grit platform? . . . It would accomplish no good to elect a workingman pledged to a servile acceptance of the policy of the party leaders." Editorializing on the Hamilton Knights the Toronto *News* praised labor's orientation: "The headway made by this movement is a good sign. It shows that the people are beginning to realize the evils and abuses of our system, and are dissatisfied with the mismanagement and corruption of both parties. The Hamilton workingmen see that they have been deceived, and their interests systematically neglected by Grits and Tories alike."[8] The Order first pursued this autonomous political path in the February 1883 provincial campaign of Edward Williams.

The English-born Williams was a locomotive engineer and a member of LA 2307. A recent immigrant, he had left England in 1878 and moved to Hamilton from Allandale in 1880. A total abstainer, he was the perfect representation of a respectable workingman. His respectability, however, had not prevented him from leading the townsmen of Stafford, England, in an open revolt against its lord's attempt to enclose the common. Nor a few years later did it prevent him from nominating and helping to elect Alexander Macdonald as the first English Lib-Lab MP.[9]

Conservative politicians sought to entice Williams into their fold, but he refused to be compromised: "if nominated," the Knight of Labor replied, "it must be as a labor candidate, clear of either political party." At a series of mass meetings of workingmen convened in February 1883 to endorse and support Williams, many prominent labor leaders and active Knights spoke in his favor. Thomas Brick, previously a "good, sound conservative," came forward to embrace Williams. His short speeches testified to the distance he had traveled since the late 1870s, when he had been a militant supporter of the Irish Green, battling Orangemen in the streets of Corktown: "He said that men of all classes, creeds and religions – Catholic and Orangemen – were united in this labor movement, and steadily and surely pulling together to accomplish their object, they would do it." The engineer's campaign was but one indication that many Hamilton workers had rejected "the two thoroughly rotten, corrupt and ring ridden parties calling themselves respectively 'Conservative' and 'Reform'." As a prominent carter, Brick knew that the political gentry cultivated his lowly opinion only when votes were to be had: "Before election time they begin to nod at us. We have about 35 votes on the carters' stand and that's why they nod. They call me *Mr.* Brick these days but *Mr.* Brick won't catch me now." Fred Walters, a molder who had probably backed the first Tory workingman elected to the federal parliament in 1872, H. B. Witton, and had switched in disgust to the "Reform" candidate in 1874, pointed toward the political consciousness gradually taking hold among the city's workers. After fourteen years' residence he said "he had, like many others, taken a great deal of taffy from the politicians of Hamilton." But it was "high time a change was made." Let the workers send a representative to Toronto, he urged, "who would more thoroughly adhere to the wants of the people." Williams followed such speeches with persistent promises to campaign for the workingman, and placed full manhood suffrage at the center of his platform. He also called for a Factory Act, the abolition of convict labor, a Bureau of Labour Statistics, and a Ministry of Labour. Many of these planks echoed points in the Knights of Labor Declaration of Principles.[10]

Despite this successful beginning, and the many ward meetings held during the three weeks before the election, the political inexperience of the workers became apparent. D. R. Gibson, for example, wrote to Powderly to inquire into the process by which Knights were to engage in political activity without transgressing the Order's injunction not to discuss politics during an Assembly meeting. Powderly answered promptly that they should debate the electoral campaign immediately after the LA meeting, a technique designed to preserve the Assemblies from partisan wrangling while allowing the members to participate in important political struggles. It was a tactic that the Order would use throughout its active North American political career.[11]

Such a strategy, however, could not put totally to rest the old attachment to partyism. When Williams mounted the platform to champion the cause of the workers, he was met with tumultuous applause. But frequently he had to explain that, despite his ties to the English Liberal Party, he had never joined the Canadian "Reform" group of Edward Blake. Describing himself as a true reformer, he maintained his independence in the face of much skepticism on the part of ardent party advocates, some of whom were themselves workers sympathetic to Williams' cause. "Carpenter" denounced Williams' endorsement by the city workers in the pages of the *Hamilton Spectator*, claiming that it was the product of a "closed-doors, non representative clique," the Knights of Labor. Moreover, he argued that Williams was the "grittiest of Grits" and suggested that workingmen block for the Tory candidate, announcing in "tones of thunder that Hamilton is safe from adventurers, socialistic sheets, and all enemies of law, order and British fair play." As the *Labor Union* put it, the workingman's candidate thereby caused "considerable shaking among the dry bones of partyism." The old parties' response here was the usual one: they were quick to accuse the labor candidate of merely being a stalking-horse to attract votes away from them. Although such charges were leveled by both politically committed papers in Hamilton, the labor press warned workers against "the feeling of suspicion sedulously encouraged by interested parties."[12]

When the votes were counted, Liberal J. M. Gibson again topped the poll with almost 40 percent of the vote, but Williams had acquitted himself well in the three-way race, winning a respectable 23.4 percent. Moreover, Williams had actually won four polls and finished second in four others. Of these eight polls where Williams ran well, a total of six were in Wards 6 and 7 where the working-class vote was strongly concentrated.[13] As the *Labor Union* predicted after the defeat: "The campaign which we have just passed is a fitting preparation for the era of conflict that is now upon us."[14]

Meanwhile in Toronto the elation which accompanied labor's triumph over Withrow led to renewed discussion in the TTLC about participation in the approaching provincial election. However, after considerable debate Eugene Donavon's *Trade Union Advocate* cautioned against labor nominees.[15] This reversal from the paper's earlier enthusiasm for a labor political platform and for the defeat of Withrow stemmed from Donavon's increasing concern "that Grit and Tory is 'sticking out' too plainly for the council's welfare."[16] Donavon, who at the time had moved close to the Knights and was probably a member of Excelsior LA 2305, shared this fear with many others. Numerous letters appeared in the *Advocate* calling for unanimity in labor's ranks and denouncing partyism.[17]

The Council, however, after considerable wrangling about procedures – an unseemly debate from which even the labor press was barred – finally nominated candidates in East and West Toronto.[18] Carpenter Samuel R. Heakes easily won the East Toronto nomination, defeating bricklayer Andrew McCormack by 35 votes to 8. The West Toronto nomination was much more complicated, with six candidates on the initial ballot. After much rancor and a series of meetings the workingmen finally settled on John Carter, a painter active in LA 2305. Carter's main opponent, carpenter Thomas Moor, and Grit stonecutter Alfred Oakley softened some of the ill will by successfully moving that the nomination be made unanimous. Behind the scenes, however, lurked the evil of partyism. Whether intentional or not, the candidates for the East Toronto nomination were both prominent Tory workingmen, while those for West Toronto were easily identified with the Grits. This became only too apparent when the Reform party nominated a candidate to oppose Heakes but allowed Carter to fight the Tories unopposed in West Toronto.[19]

Nevertheless, both sides of the TTLC did attempt to bury their differences in the campaign. At the mass meeting to ratify the nominees, prominent Grit and Tory labor leaders shared the platform and promised to work for the election of Carter and Heakes. Mass meetings during the campaign frequently heard speakers such as W. Hawthorne admit that although he had "always been a rank Conservative," he had "now buried the political hatchet." Similarly, on another evening Reform tailor and leading Knight Alfred Jury pledged that "no matter what he was outside of Toronto, he would be for workingmen first and Grit afterward in the city."[20]

Heakes and Carter both ran on the TTLC labor platform; Heakes had played a prominent role in formulating it. They both emphasized their independence, argued that workingmen deserved representation of their interests in the legislature, and promised various labor-reform measures, especially extension of the franchise. Both men came from English building-trades backgrounds. Heakes, who had come to Toronto as a child in the late 1840s, had been prominent in carpenters' unionism in Montreal and Toronto and had led the fight against Withrow only two months before. Carter arrived in Toronto in 1871 after being blacklisted in England where he had led various painters' strikes and protests. A prominent cooperator and former president of the Canadian Labor Union, Carter was also a leading figure in Toronto lodge life both as an Oddfellow and as a Son of England. He was also a member of Excelsior LA 2305 and thus in the inner Knights' circle of leading labor reformers.[21]

When the vote was counted, the results gave further evidence of the problem of partyism. Carter, running only against Tory trunk manufacturer H. E. Clarke, won a very respectable 48 percent of the vote; Heakes, opposed by both prominent Tory politico Alexander Morris and Reformer John Leys, received only an embarrassing 7 percent.[22] Given the paucity of Heakes's vote, it was not surprising that he finished a distant third in every poll. Carter, on the other hand, won precisely half of the 66 polls, with his main strength in St. John's Ward (9 of 15) and St. Patrick's (13 of 19), both working-class residential areas.

The post mortems, however, as in Hamilton, tended to be optimistic. Eugene Donavon, for example, looked to the future:

> The attempt to lead the masses of manual and mechanical labour out of the usual rut of party politics in the city of Toronto was a brave one, and although not thoroughly successful, yet a great stride was made in that direction. The defeat is but a momen-

tary check to the efforts of those who fought, and will continue to fight for that recognition on the floor of Parliament to which the working classes are in justice entitled.

Two weeks later, he renamed his paper *The Wage Worker* and renewed his commitment to the Knights of Labor.[23] The immediate response may have been optimistic, but later memories of these campaigns festered, especially in the minds of Conservative workingmen. Again, Tory politicians took note, and Toronto MP John Small described a TTLC delegation to Macdonald the following month as "Grits of the worst kind who worked hard against us in the election."[24]

In Hamilton the Knights and other trade unionists turned their attention to municipal politics and in the summer of 1883 forced proconsumer amendments to the city's bread and coal bylaws. The *Palladium* also launched a fiery attack on Hamilton's police magistrate, accusing him of class bias in his sentencing.[25] In late September labor men began meeting to discuss the upcoming municipal elections. To expunge "the fifth rate aldermanic dummies who represent tyrannical monopoly" became the proclaimed aim of these meetings.[26] "Politicians have used us long enough – hereafter we shall use them," the *Palladium* noted, and championed the organization of the Hamilton Labor Political Association (HLPA) in the fall. Its objectives were modest: to secure direct representation for labor in the legislature and to hold public meetings and lectures "to encourage intelligent discussion on all questions of national or local interest or importance to producers."[27] Editorially, the *Palladium*'s W. H. Rowe enunciated the same aim: "The municipality of Hamilton has of late years been little less than a cauldron of seething corruption. Workmen, be not afraid; do your duty though you be bespattered with dirt from the mendacious mudguns of those who are hired to defame you."[28]

The intricacies of the subsequent municipal election are less important than the extremely active role labor played in them. Although the HLPA's recommended slate did not sweep the aldermanic race, a number of those who received labor's backing emerged victorious. Letters to the *Palladium* from "Wage Earner," "Plebian," "Dodger," and others charging corruption enlivened the race. One successful labor candidate came to office wearing the mantle of "ring exterminator." After the election the consensus that emerged claimed significant political success. Clearly, Hamilton workers – led by the Knights and their organ, the *Palladium of Labor* – were on the march.[29]

Following on these successes the HLPA announced in May that it would again run candidates and asked workers not to be "hasty in pledging their support to either of the political parties."[30] DMW W. J. Vale also informed fellow Knights throughout North America of their political gains in Hamilton.[31] These limited gains, however, did not destroy the political hold of the old parties, whose actions continued to threaten labor. This became a dramatic danger in 1884 owing to the Machiavellian machinations of Morgan, Harvey, and their allies described earlier in Chapter 5. In December one of their collaborators, D. B. Skelly, warned Powderly of the Reform ring that he claimed controlled DA 61:

> You will no doubt remember Ed Williams was put into the field for the provincial legislature, the Conservative party offered to take him on their ticket. The Reform party would not, they wanted their own man. The K of L ring would not allow him to accept the Conservative nomination if he did he would have been elected with the largest majority any member ever had in Hamilton. They made a catspaw of him and dragged the poor fellow on the Knights of Labor platform and held him there til *dead* and this was done in the interests of the Grit party that run the Labour Political [Association] into the ground in the same way they buried it. They have done the same with the Central Labour Union.[32]

This conflict would flare again in the next round of electoral conflict.

In the municipal elections of 1884–5 DA 61 and the *Palladium of Labor* experienced a falling out. The newspaper supported renegade manufacturer J. S. Lillis in the aldermanic race, while organized labor refused to endorse candidates that were not actual workers. The Knights did demand, however, that all aldermanic candidates indicate their stand on two key local issues: union wages on all corporation work and the publication of the city's assessment rolls.[33] In addition they supported a few aldermanic candidates. One of these was Irish carter and Knight Thomas Brick, active in supporting Ed Williams in 1883. Brick, a victor both in 1885 and again the next year, subsequently played an important role in publicizing working-class interests.[34] In those two years a number of labor-related issues came before city council. An unsuccessful attempt to gain the eight-hour day for city workers, a failing bid for a public library, and evidence that the Ontario Cotton Company mills had illegally stolen water from the city, all created considerable controversy and helped keep the Order's attention focused on the political arena.[35]

In Toronto events evolved somewhat differently. In addition to keen interests in municipal politics, the Knights also pursued an ambitious lobbying role for labor in Ottawa and in Toronto. The Macdonald federal government constantly found itself under assault from the vigorous offensive launched by D. J. O'Donoghue and his colleagues on the TTLC Legislative Committee (LC). The storming of the Tory federal fortress, however, was not matched with equal vigor in provincial politics, where Oliver Mowat's Grit government began to pioneer a tactic of incorporating labor leaders into patronage posts. One of the first recipients was O'Donoghue himself, who became a clerk in the Ontario Bureau of Industry, thus assuming the major responsibility of preparing the labor statistics for the annual report.

O'Donoghue and the Knights took conscious control of Toronto labor politics in just three short years following the February 1883 election campaign. (Their tactics are worth analyzing because they set the pattern for the following years.) As we have already described in Chapter 3, O'Donoghue was acutely conscious of the necessity of integrating the Knights into the labor movement. A combination of astute maneuvering, fortuitous circumstance, and practical demonstrations of solidarity had brought the Knights of Labor to the forefront of the Toronto labor movement; O'Donoghue's plans had reached fruition.[36]

The new political potency of the Order was evident in the fall of 1884 when T. V. Powderly visited Toronto. Not only was Shaftesbury Hall filled to overflowing to hear his address but prominent on the platform, in addition to labor leaders, were federal Reform leader Edward Blake and the prominent Grit editor and politician T. W. Anglin. Joining the Reformers at the front were Toronto's Tory Mayor Boswell and prominent Tory ward heeler Alderman Piper. Ontario Premier Oliver Mowat respectfully sent his regrets.[37]

The carefully engineered Tory political machine that had held sway since the 1870s in Toronto was thus weakening under the new stress of the Knights' boom. This became evident in the preparations for the December 1884 mayoralty campaign when the Tories expressed considerable fears about the Knights and the working-class vote.[38] Sir David Macpherson explained the Tory difficulties to Prime Minister Macdonald: "I think we can win the election notwithstanding the three powerful influences of Party, temperance, and Industrial Exhibition – opposed to us but something must be done to secure the workingman's vote. The TLC are opposed to our candidates in consequence of the actions of the *Mail* with members of the Typographical Union." Macpherson then appealed for Macdonald to exert pressure upon the Conservative *Mail* to relax its insistence on binding its printers to iron-clad contracts.[39]

In the end, the Grits' obstinacy in again running J. J. Withrow, who had been opposed in 1882 by labor because of his anti-union record, helped save the Tories, securing a narrow 145-vote victory for the Conservative candidate, Alexander Manning. Even given labor's previous dislike of Withrow, the Typographical Union and some prominent TTLC figures such as President Thomas Moor did support the Reform candidate. The TTLC, however, remained formally neutral. Some Tories learned from this experience, warning that changes had to be made because "the whole Conservative system here is rotten to the core." If they were not to be "cleaned out root and branch," then thorough reorganization was called for. The party would eventually act, but not until the 1884–5 lesson was driven home by electoral defeat.[40]

## Mayor Howland

That lesson came in the subsequent municipal election when opponents of Tory Mayor Manning chose W. H. Howland, a candidate who, unlike Withrow, was acceptable to the whole TTLC. A federal campaign was almost a certainty in 1886, and because municipal patronage would be of central concern to both parties in the subsequent contest, Grit and Troy campaigned vigorously in the mayoralty race. As the Howland forces denied Manning what the *World* called "the customary courtesy of a second term in the civic chair," the battlelines were clearly drawn.[41]

The TTLC had prepared itself well for this election. Its new Municipal Committee had carefully studied municipal affairs all year and had provided the Council with an excellent watchdog at City Hall. In early December committees were appointed in each ward to interview the aldermanic candidates on their attitudes to three key issues: the continuation of the popular election of the mayor, which was under attack; a willingness to force the street railway franchise to conform to its charter; and opposition to the use of prison labor on municipal public works. At a special meeting later that month the ward committees reported on the candidates' stances and TTLC support went to those who endorsed the labor position. Of the two mayoralty candidates only Howland unequivocally committed himself to the labor program.[42]

Meanwhile a mass meeting of the Knights of Labor endorsed Howland's candidacy and promised to oppose candidates who failed to disassociate themselves from the *Mail* iron-clad. The printers also succeeded in getting the TTLC to endorse the same strategy of demanding pledges from the candidates "repudiating over their own signatures the stand of the *Mail* towards organized labour."[43] Thus, Howland ran with the united support of the labor movement, probably the first candidate to do so in Toronto's history. Not only had the TTLC and the Knights endorsed Howland but a total of fifteen union Locals and fourteen of Toronto's sixteen LAs had also passed motions of support.[44] With the help of that support he swept to victory, defeating the incumbent, Alexander Manning, by nearly 2,000 votes. An analysis of the vote suggests that the labor support was crucial. Howland's largest majorities were in St. John's and St. Patrick's, which between them accounted for almost half his total majority. Significantly, both had supported Manning in the previous election and were also the only areas where John Carter had outpolled the Tory's H. E. Clarke in 1883.[45]

The Howland candidacy represented extremely well many of the Knights' interests. Not only did he promise to deal toughly with the Toronto Street Railway – thus probably unwittingly allying himself with O'Donoghue's promise to revenge himself on Frank Smith with "a whip of scorpions" – but he also attracted support for his social activism in charity and temperance causes. The coalition of antidrink and labor causes was a potent political force, and one easily joined by the Knights, whose ideology placed a high premium on respectability and temperance.[46]

The Howland election night celebrations confirmed the importance of the working-class vote. Howland's victory speech thanked the workingmen for their confidence, reasserted his friendship to their cause, and claimed their support gave him his greatest pleasure. *News*' editor E. E. Sheppard, a major Howland supporter, triumphantly acclaimed that "the workingmen's verdict showed that money bags do not run this city." TTLC President Thomas Tracy and carpenter Samuel Heakes accepted the generous accolades on behalf of labor. The former asserted that in the future "no body of men would neglect the interests of united labour in Toronto," while the latter warned Howland that he had better deliver on his promises to labour.[47]

City newspapers echoed similar views of the election. The *News*'s labor correspondent observed that, "Men who a few weeks ago were called demagogues, cranks and agitators are today spoken of as leaders in the cause of labour and in future no calculation of election chances will be complete which does not consider the union workingmen of Toronto." He then looked to the future: "This is but the first step. Monday's victory is chiefly useful as showing what can and will be done in the future." Labor observers also looked forward to future struggles. D. J. O'Donoghue, an architect of the Tory's demise, wrote happily to Powderly: "We had a great victory here on Monday last. Labour combined and defeated the *Mail*'s candidate for Mayor by a majority of 1796 . . . The victory of organized labour in Toronto has created dismay in the ranks of party heelers."[48]

This last point was absolutely correct, and the Tories began to rebuild their smashed alliances. In early February Harry Piper, one of the more famous of the *World*'s "corporation ringsters and party jobbers," delivered his post mortem on the mayoralty race. He wrote to Macdonald to remind him that the *Mail*'s conflict with the TTU had "of late assumed a very serious aspect" and that as a result in the last election "our oldest and best committee men had worked for the enemy." The *Mail*, he argued, had to end its politically suicidal war with the printers. Pressure from Ottawa eventually brought the paper to its knees. Through the offices of former printer J. S. Williams and labor leader John Armstrong, a pact was arranged between the *Mail* and the union. A simple concession was not enough: a ceremonial burning of the iron-clad was arranged to be performed before the printers of the *Mail* office. As Piper explained it "the union was *killing our Party* and the Grits were reaping the benefits." Dramatic action had been necessary and the Tories took it. As the Toronto Typographical Union (TTU) reported to the TTLC: "The document was discarded, the men discharged, and most of the old hands sent for and are now at work in the office."[49]

Not to be bested by their partisan rivals, the *Globe* took similar steps to ingratiate itself with Toronto workers. D. J. O'Donoghue described the extraordinary event for Powderly:

> As I told you the *Mail* "caved" and is now a "square" union office. The *Globe* was never a thoroughly union office – simply an open office. Well through the efforts of Jury and March, and whatever little I could help, it has been "worked" and agreed to arbitrate with the union and named as its arbitrators A F Jury, Charles March, George Beales all of LA 2305.

O'Donoghue, ever disingenuous, continued:

> Oh, I forgot, I am included as one of the arbitrators, although known to the Globe as a radical trades unionist and a member of the Typographical Union . . . Just fancy – 4 trade unionists, and one of them interested, chosen by an employer to arbitrate between himself and a trade union. What are we coming to?[50]

In the first three months of 1886, then, the Knights and labor in general were exercising an unprecedented presence in Toronto affairs. Their mayor, W. H. Howland, had also come to their defense in their first big struggles of 1886: first by arranging to arbitrate with the Masseys in February and then by helping to legitimate their resistance to the Toronto Street Railway Company in March. Predictably, their very success engendered increasing difficulties as political opportunists began to descend upon the Order. It was, for example, at this moment that A. W. Wright, whom we have met in the preceding chapter, became active in the affairs of the Order in Toronto.

## Macdonald and incorporation

The rapid rise to political prominence of the Toronto Knights was not unique to that city. From 1884 faithful Tories from all over Ontario wrote warning letters to Macdonald. An anonymous Woodstock "Knight of Labor" who described himself as a "strong supporter of Macdonald and "a friend of the Liberal-Conservative Party" cautioned the Conservative leader in early 1885: "I am also a Knight of Labor and they are getting very numerous and want that we lay aside all politics and work as one man for the man that does what is in the interest of the workingman and mechanic if he is a Cons. or Ref. that makes no difference to us. We will work for the party that works for us." To avoid being "overthrown by the K of L" he proposed that Macdonald ratify the Knights' constitution and pass laws in accordance with the demands of the Declaration of Principles. If this was done, Macdonald would "have our support in a body." Lest his message be ignored, the Woodstock "Knight" reiterated: "The Knights of Labor have the controlling power already in some places and they are getting numerous everywhere, now if you think it worthwhile you can take word of this and you will never need be afraid to come to the country."[51] As the Knights' drive to organize all workers reached its fever pitch in the winter of 1885–6, more letters descended on Macdonald. St. Thomas brakeman A. B. Ingram, whom we will meet again shortly, wrote to acquaint the Tory leader with his new political importance: "I have been elected by several hundred workingmen to serve as a delegate to what they are pleased to term a trade and labor council. This board has selected me as one of their committee to look after legislation, and whatever the results of my labor may be those several hundred workingmen will be largely governed." As he had "always entertained conservative principles," he thought Macdonald might be interested. "In conclusion," he wrote, "please return or destroy this letter."[52] Clearly, not all St. Thomas workingmen shared his concern to retain Tory influence.

Perhaps the most extraordinary of these letters, however, came from Stratford Knight Samuel Beal. Writing in the context of a labor campaign in which the Knights were running candidates for municipal office, Beal explained that although he had been a member of the executive committee of the Middlesex Liberal Association before emigrating in 1882, he now found "Conservative principles in Canada the reverse of what they are in England, here it means to conserve good laws and repeal the bad ones." A highly skilled carpenter, he worked in Stratford's Grand Trunk shops and had joined the Knights in the spring of 1886 "to prevent a strike." "As an old striker," he knew they could prove "a great curse to working men." Beal, who had left England because of "the roseate hues" of Canadian emigration literature, believed that in the new country he could give "his children a better chance than I had in the old country." In every sense, then, Beal fulfills our image of the cautious, respectable artisan with an eye to social betterment. Yet in December 1886 the purpose of his letter to Macdonald was to enlist the government's support for the Stratford Order's political program, which included a Factory Act, workmen's compensation, arbitration, land reform, the abolition of contract labor, currency reform, women's suffrage, and an end to assisted immigration.[53]

Macdonald, ever the astute politician, took note of these developments, and in the fall of 1886 he unveiled his new strategy to capture the working-class vote. Availing himself of an opportunity to address the Workingmen's Liberal Conservative Association of Ottawa and its French equivalent – Le. Cercle Lafontaine – Macdonald, in conjunction with Ontario Tory opposition leader W. R. Meredith, unveiled a two-part plan to win the workingman back to the party: a Bureau of Labour Statistics and a Royal Commission on the Relations of Capital and Labor "on which the working classes will be fully represented." The importance attached to this speech was evident in the preparations for it. Hints of a new labor policy had been given in a previous speech in London. On the evening of the speech a procession of carriages wound through Ottawa's streets to the Opera House. There Macdonald and Meredith were joined by the entire Tory cabinet and Lady Macdonald. Politically, the prime minister's timing was, as always, impeccable. Both provincial and federal elections were rapidly approaching and the threat of independent labor political activities was evident in Quebec as well as in Ontario. The Knights of Labor Declaration of Principles included a demand for a Bureau of Labor and Premier Oliver Mowat's Ontario Reform government had already set up a Bureau of Industry with a labor component under D. J. O'Donoghue. In addition, only a few days before Macdonald's Ottawa speech, Mowat had also finally proclaimed the Ontario Factory Act, which had been passed in 1884 but not implemented owing to the possibility of federal action in the field.[54]

Macdonald's Labor Commission, however, had been under active consideration at least since midsummer. The scrutinizing of prospective candidates to serve on the commission began well before the formal announcement, and Justice Minister John Thompson also delivered opinions on the terms in which to frame the investigation.[55] We do not have the necessary space here to explore in detail the parameters of this Royal Commission, although both the hearings and the preliminary machinations represent a fascinating episode in Canadian working-class history.[56] Nevertheless, three points should be made. First, the commission illustrated well the particular political conjuncture of 1886. Never before, not even in 1872, had labor stood so prominently at the center of the Canadian political stage. Macdonald, then, was simultaneously buying time and meeting specific demands. He had little choice: both Mowat and Blake actively sought labor support in 1886–7. Second, the composition of the commission was quite extraordinary. Seven of the fifteen commissioners represented labor interests: printers John Armstrong (Toronto) and Hugh McLean (London); carpenters Samuel R. Heakes (Toronto) and Urias Carson (Ottawa); Quebec ship laborer Patrick Kerwin; Ottawa blacksmith W. A. Gibson; and Montreal journalist Jules Helbronner, who was nominated by the Montreal Trades and Labour Council. Armstrong, McLean, Kerwin, and Helbronner were also prominent Knights of Labor. As previous studies have shown, these appointments owed a great deal to previously demonstrated Tory loyalism, but no Royal Commission since has had an even remotely similar class composition.[57] Third, the patronage appointees ultimately performed admirable work and the final reports and the published testimony represented as important a political statement in the 1880s as they are a historical source for the 1980s.

A closer look at the Ontario appointments to the commission provides further insight into the Knights and labor politics in the 1880s. The first appointees considered came from Toronto. The *Mail*'s Christopher Bunting, apparently now in a position to recommend labor representatives, initially suggested Sam McNab, Toronto DA 125's DMW and Samuel R. Heakes, prominent Tory carpenter and former labor candidate.[58] About a week later Conservative MPP H. E. Clarke amended Bunting's suggestion, replacing McNab with printer and Knight John Armstrong. Clarke explained his choices carefully, and added:

> I don't think that too much care can be exercised in the formation of this committee. It will be subject to severe criticism by tories, grits, and workingmen . . . We want the workingmen who are gradually drifting away from us and to get them, and keep them, it will be necessary to give much prominence to the planks they favour . . . Protection is the best plank yet . . . I take it the report would favour the National Policy. It would also most likely recommend some mode of arbitration for trade disputes which would be immensely popular with workingmen everywhere.

Finally, Clarke suggested the abolition of tax exemptions and the termination of "the large expenditure on immigration." Macdonald responded approvingly, indicating affirmation of the general strategy, endorsing Heakes, and inquiring further about Armstrong.[59] Later in October when rumors of the Heakes' appointment were greeted by a hostile comment in the *Canadian Labor Reformer* and considerable antagonism among Toronto workers, prominent Tories rallied to Heakes's defense and urged Macdonald to decide quickly upon the composition of the commission, which could be utilized in the rapidly approaching provincial election. This had become doubly important, because not only were labor candidacies probable but Mowat's clever gerrymander of the Toronto seats pointed to obstacles the Tories had to clear.[60]

Toronto workers, as H. E. Clarke had predicted, watched these appointments, announced on 7 December 1886, with considerable interest. John Armstrong drew only acclaim from the Ontario labor press, but Heakes elicited dramatic and near unanimous opposition. This only increased when he broke ranks with Toronto labor and supported the Clarkes against the workingmen's candidates in the provincial election. Armstrong wisely remained faithful to the labor candidates. Disgust with Heakes in Toronto culminated in the condemnation of the commissioner by DA 125 and in a similar TTLC motion.[61] If the Toronto appointment created considerable political difficulties, the Hamilton Commissioner, A. T. Freed, set off a major storm of protest. As the partisan editor of the Tory *Hamilton Spectator*, Freed had shown no previous sympathy for organized labor, and the Hamilton Central Labor Union demanded that Macdonald withdraw Freed and instead appoint "one in whom the working class have confidence." Their unanimous motion concluded that Freed lacked "sympathy with the cause of labor" and was "prejudiced against the interest of the working class." The Knights' *Palladium of Labor* was considerably less polite, describing Freed as "a thorough-paced party hack, ready to write anything for or against labour, so that it would suit the temporary interests of Toryism." Almost a year later the commission gained a second group of members that included three additional Ontario workers: London Knights DMW Hugh McLean and two members of the Workingmen's Liberal-Conservative Association of Ottawa, carpenter Urias Carson and blacksmith W. A. Gibson. While controversy within party circles for these latter patronage plums was intense, the public took little notice.[62]

The Royal Commission was but the first act of a great political drama in the winter of 1886–7. For in the provincial and federal elections of that winter we observe the labor presence at its peak political strength. What had appeared in 1883 to be limited to the industrial cities of Toronto and Hamilton had now spread across Ontario, just as the Knights of Labor organizers had traveled the length and breadth of the province. That winter provincial labor campaigns were fought in London, St. Thomas, St. Catharines, and Sarnia as well as in Toronto and Hamilton, and in the latter two cities serious federal challenges were also mounted. But in addition to the labor candidacies in key Knights of Labor strongholds, the Order and labor in general made their presence felt throughout Ontario by challenging and questioning candidates. Moreover, in countless centers the Order ran members in municipal elections and enjoyed considerable success. Let us look in turn at the December 1886 provincial election, the February 1887 federal election, and then briefly note some of the smaller centers where the Knights were active in local politics.

## "To Toronto we will send him"

Mowat's Ontario Liberal government, as we noted earlier, had proven unusually responsive to the demands of organized labor. The Ontario Bureau of Industry and the Factory Act (1884) represented its greatest claims to working-class support, but it had also passed a myriad of less important, labor-related laws – including various Mechanics Lien Acts, suffrage extension, a never-used arbitration act (1873) – amended Masters and Servants Acts (1884 and 1886), and workmen's compensation (1886).[63] Despite these efforts the government did not receive the labor movement's wholehearted support in 1886. Instead, in six constituencies labor candidates campaigned against one or both of the old parties.

St. Thomas, a railway town and center of DA 138, elected A. B. Ingram to the Legislature in 1886. Ingram was born in Ontario in 1851 and had migrated west to Manitoba as a young man. After serving as a clerk in the Manitoba legislature he returned to Ontario and settled in St. Thomas.[64] A brakeman on the Grand Trunk, Andy emerged as a leading member of railroad employees' Headlight LA 4069 and president of the St. Thomas Trades and Labour Council. As statistician for LA 4069 and later for DA 138, he compiled *Statistics as Collected by Head-Light Assembly*, an early copy of which he sent to T. V. Powderly. The GMW, impressed by this effort, took the time to offer Ingram congratulations: "My work is piling up around me but I cannot forego the pleasure of thanking you for the work 'Headlight' has done. I wish we had more like you. May your headlight oil never run dry."[65]

The St. Thomas labor movement, based on the various railway Brotherhoods and the vigorous presence of the Order, created a Trades and Labour Council in early 1886, avowedly to scrutinize city council and the school board in the interests of workingmen. They came together "as a body of workingmen, who are fully convinced the 'toilers' have some wrongs that should be set right." In the spring and summer of 1886, St. Thomas workers were active in pushing wage demands, expanding organization, lobbying for legislative changes in railway safety legislation, and aiding the new clerks' Mercantile LA 6707 in its quest for an early closing bylaw. Knights' lecturers A. A. Carleton and Richard Trevellick visited the town that summer and in July local Knights organized a new "Western" DA to cover all of Ontario west of Hamilton DA 61, extending as far as the Port Dover and Stratford railway.[66]

At the height of this flurry of activity in mid-July, West Elgin Tories nominated Andy Ingram as their provincial candidate. Ingram won the nomination in a contested race by 42 votes to 17. He promised "the support of the working classes of the city whom he represented," while his opponent argued against the very idea of class representation. The new Tory-Labor candidate was reelected president of the St. Thomas Trades and Labor Council a week later. Anticipating difficulties, Ingram wrote to Powderly seeking his approval, just as he had earlier courted John A. Macdonald. Claiming that Trevellick had advised him to go ahead, Ingram argued that given the riding's large rural vote a purely independent labor candidate would have no chance of victory. Ingram's request for "aid in any way, shape or form" such "as a few lines from you in a circular addressed to the different LAs in this city" went unanswered. Powderly possessed too much experience to be drawn into the partisan political wrangle that he sensed would develop.[67] He was not wrong: across Ontario Tory and labor newspapers (the latter battling among themselves) exchanged insults over Ingram's candidacy. But the St. Thomas brakeman emerged from all of this unscathed in his own locality, and when DA 138 met to choose its General Assembly delegates for Richmond, Ingram became one of their four representatives.[68]

Ingram ran a popular campaign and, despite the labor criticism from afar, he reversed the usual Reform trend in West Elgin and won by a narrow 35-vote margin. He won the city by 447 votes, barely enough to offset his Grit opponent's 412-vote lead in the agrarian section of the riding. The Grits had not helped their chances by trying to disenfranchise St. Thomas working-class voters in contesting the use of the most recent city voters' lists as the basis for the election. Moreover, with the united support of the Labor Council, the Knights, and George Wrigley's *Labor Courier*, Ingram ran with a strong base. The degree to which he campaigned as a workingman's candidate was evident in his broadly promoted election song, "Only a Brakeman":

He is only a brakeman
  Yet always a man
And true to his duty –
  Deny it who can.
His hand may be horny
  With turning the brake
But his mind is most active;
  He makes his foes quake.

For the Brakeman we will vote
  And for Ingram we will work
To Toronto we will send him
  N'er his duty there to shirk.

For to labor's cause he's true,
And our password now shall be –
"Vote and work for *Andy B.*
And hurrah! Shout victory!"

Ingram also pledged himself to "support every measure introduced to better the condition of the working class regardless of who introduces the bill." The late December campaign also allowed the Ingram candidacy to be joined to the municipal campaign being conducted in St. Thomas where the Trades and Labor Council and the Knights had endorsed mayoralty, aldermanic, and school-trustee candidates. In St. Thomas, then, the particularities of class dynamics and the local strength of the Order allowed the emergence of a victorious Tory-Labor alliance – an electoral victory that reversed decades of voting behavior in Elgin County.[69]

A similar conjuncture of forces worked in St. Catharines where prominent Knight, Orangemen, and temperance advocate William Garson, after gaining a labor nomination, received the endorsment of the Reformers. Running only against a Tory candidate, Fidelity LA 2056's Garson won a narrow 15-vote victory based on strong pluralities in towns where the Knights were prominent: St. Catharines itself (+112), Merritton (+68), and Beamsville (+52). Thus, one Liberal-Labor MPP would join Tory-Labor MPP A. B. Ingram.[70]

Other labor candidates ran unsuccessfully in Lambton West, London, Hamilton, and Toronto. A labor candidate was rumored to be running in Ottawa, but this was not, in fact, the case. In Lambton West A. W. Wright threw his hat into the political ring, and as we would be led to expect by our account of him in the last chapter, it did not prove to be the Knights of Labor's finest hour. Wright stood as the nominee of the West Lambton Conservative Convention, posing as the provincial candidate of the Conservative Party and Knights of Labor. He understandably drew sharp attack across the province as members of the Order questioned "the silver-tongued champion of the Labor cause" and his right to stand as the representative of the Knights against the Liberal MPP, Tom Pardee, an important member of Mowat's cabinet. The MW of the Sarnia Assembly that had orchestrated Wright's nomination at the Petrolia convention was said to have "manipulated things there to the detriment of the Order" and "grave charges against him" were laid. Wright's acceptance speech at the Sarnia Town Hall was greeted with cries of, "no, no, not of the Knights of Labor, we had nothing to do with him." As Wright tried to argue his way out of a tight corner – denying he was a Tory, claiming to be a Radical, consolidating ties with temperance advocates, but all the while endorsing the political program of the Conservative party – a leaflet was circulated announcing Sarnia LA 2470's repudiation of Wright. An unnamed Conservative MP and lawyer attacked Wright's financial indebtedness to the Tories, claiming he had been supported by fully $5,000 in party funds during 1886, when the labor-reform advocate served as a Tory functionary and delegate to industrial exhibitions. The MP laughed at Wright's credentials as a labor man. "You generally find able fellows like Wright among the labor organizations," he noted, "climbing their way into office over the backs of the laboring men, while they remain as they are. Why it was notorious that A. W. Wright was one of the old-time Tory wire-pullers and was always at the service of that party." Defensively, Wright issued a statement appealing to the class sensibilities of his potential supporters: "Although tendered a nomination at the hands of the Liberal-Conservative convention, I have not accepted it, nor do I feel that, as a Labor Reformer and a member of the Knights of Labor, I can honestly or consistently do so . . . I think it only just and right to say to the Conservative electors that, while I will be grateful for their support, I can only accept it on condition that I am left free to advocate the reforms which I believe the interests of labor necessitate." The last word rested with Sarnia workingmen, however, who helped to defeat Wright at the polls, and mocked his downfall in a poem entitled, "How Wright was Left":

There was a Knight
Whose name was Wright
Came rushing here to see
How far he might
Serve Tory spite
Opposing Tom Pardee

No Labor Knight
Desired to Fight
At risk of Order cleft
So Mister Wright
They bade good night
And that's how Wright was left.

There may have been something of a Grit opposition here, but Wright's defeat was also a reflection of the workingman's distrust of the "wirepuller." He suffered a 452-vote trouncing, failing to carry even the towns in the riding where the Knights enjoyed considerable strength – Sarnia, Petrolia, Oil Springs, and Point Edward.[71] Other campaigns would also see the Knights of Labor defeated, but the contests were often more honorably waged and the vote much closer.

In London Samuel Peddle ran for the labor party. As in St. Thomas, the groundwork for Peddle's nomination by the Trades and Labour Council had been laid through three years of active political work in the municipal arena. Led by the Knights, the Council had actively engaged in campaigns for shorter hours for corporation workers, for union labor on all municipal contracts, and against tax exemptions for local businesses. Only a few weeks before nominating Peddle, the Council chose Knight and ex-alderman William Scarrow to run for mayor. These political efforts were capped by Peddle's campaign against Tory opposition leader W. R. Meredith in November-December 1886.[72]

Peddle was an Englishman, short in stature, and known in Knights of Labor circles for his intellectual and thoughtful nature. He was a cabinetmaker at the London Manufacturing (Furniture) Company, where he worked on the second floor as a foreman; he had been employed at the establishment for seven years. Like many other Knights of Labor political activists he was a recent migrant from England, where he had been born on the estate of the Earl of Beaconsfield. His father still lived there. An ardent temperance advocate, he was also one of the first London champions of "the labor cause," and had given his "whole attention and reading to the labor problems of the day." In 1883 he emerged as the outspoken backer of the avowedly nonpartisan Workingman's Association, attacking the self-serving antipolitical remarks made by prominent Grit David Mills and Ontario Tory leader W. R. Meredith. Quoting Henry George, Peddle took exception "to a remark previously made that the Legislature could not do much for the workingman, and claimed that they at least had the power to enact a Factory Act, an Employer's Liability Act, and an act to shorten the hours of labour." His own election statement revealed his loyalties and underlined his role as a significant labor reformer: "I have been placed in the field by the Knights of Labor and trades unions, and I shall contest the election for all I am worth. I am a Knight myself; one of the first of the city. I was the mover of the motion at the Workingmen's Association for application with the Knights of Labor. I am now their candidate for the local Legislature in their interests, and I shall stand, representing the masses of workingmen against professional classes."[73]

The campaign immediately revealed the usual efforts to discredit independent labor politics, and the Grits, in particular, attempted to ease Peddle into their camp. The labor reformer was thus forced to issue statements to the *London Advertiser* clarifying his position. "In justice to myself and the party I represent," he wrote toward the end of November 1886, "I must say that your reporter has misrepresented my views. First, in regard to the N.P. I did not say it had not benefitted the furniture trade. The question was 'What are your views on free trade?' I answered, I believe in universal free trade, but situated as we are must have a protective tariff. I did not say the Mowat government fully satisfied the laboring classes." He closed by noting that he hoped to soon be able to "lay our platform fully before the public." When that platform was revealed in early December it endorsed the usual planks common to many 1886 labor campaigns: temperance, manhood suffrage, shorter hours, land reform, among other things, were all enthusiastically endorsed, while partyism and convict labor were vociferously rejected. Underlying all of these causes, however, was a basic thrust, common to all the Order's political struggles. "A great deal is said about developing the natural resources of the country," argued Peddle, "but the development of the nobler natural resources is neglected. Maybe it is socialistic," he closed, "but I believe in universal education." From Toronto, W. H. Howland extended a hand of support to Peddle, and in Hamilton the *Palladium of Labor* saw the electoral struggle as an indicator of London surging "to the front." In temperance circles, which had long been linked with the city's labor movement, support for Peddle was strong, and the WCTU discussed the workingman's electoral effort. All of this was enough to convince the established Reform party, and the Grits endorsed Peddle, refusing to oppose him with their own candidate.[74]

In this context, London's Knights of Labor led the way with a series of impressive mass meetings. In Ward 5, where the greatest concentration of working people was found, "Peddle for the People" was a popular slogan. J. Gayton mounted one Ward 5 platform to urge the election of the workingman's candidate. "Party lines are a fraud," he thundered, "drop them. Your opponent is simply a tool in the hands of a demagogue. [Applause.] We have been fools in the past, but the scales have fallen from our eyes, and we will be fools no longer." The labor candidate for the mayoralty, William Scarrow, saw Peddle as the only opposition to "professional, political, and boodle interests;" other workers championed Peddle and denied vigorously that he was being financed by the Grits. As the *Palladium of Labor* noted, Peddle was running strongly, "dealing out red-hot shot to the old party hacks." One London worker reported that, "Our boys are in good trim and anxious for the fray." In mid-December, Charles E. Hewit of Forest City LA 3305 wrote to Powderly to invite him to speak in the campaign, and workers across the city – independents, Grits, and Tories – rallied to the cause of the labor candidate. An optimistic Hewit echoed the sentiments of many, predicting that "our chances are very good to elect Bro. Peddle."[75]

The Grit capitulation only strengthened the Tory resolve. Rumors circulated that Peddle was an "infidel" and insufficiently well rooted in the city to serve the needs of the local population if elected. Pushed to the wall by the labor candidate's popularity, the Conservatives sought to appease the working-class electorate, but made a ludicrous spectacle:

> Who represents labor? The altogether desperate efforts of the manipulators of last night's Tory meeting in the City Hall to give the platform a labor complexion proved a . . . farce, and will utterly fail in weaning away any from the real workingmen's meeting to be held on Wednesday night in the same place. Observe the array of horny-handed sons of toil and disinterested patriots who filled the big red chairs, and smiled serenely upon the audience below. First and foremost was our own worthy Mayor of race horse and oil monopoly fame, also hero of the great 35-cent tooth powder scandal, the civic bungler greatly responsible for the loss of the G.T.R. locomotive works, and the closing of several of the best streets in the city to please the C.P.R., not to mention the improperly obtained exhibition grounds' fence which surrounds his palatial residence on Waterloo Street. . . . Space fails to portray all the beauties of the band that adorned the platform. They were patriots and veterans, every one, but the features I have noted must suffice for the present.

Tory supporters apparently infiltrated two LAs (3305 and 5172) to oppose Peddle; they received a stiff rebuke from the Knights' local officials. At various meetings conservative supporters distinguished themselves by physically assaulting workingmen, throwing rotten eggs at the platform, and general "rowdyism." But the most effective Tory ploy was undoubtedly to prevent the voters' list being updated. The Trades and Labor Council complained that this move effectively disenfranchised 600 workers.[76]

Opposition of this sort only served to strengthen the determined efforts of Peddle and the Knights of Labor. Moreover, London's workers were beginning to make important links between Conservative policy and the challenges they were issuing to Macdonald and others in the federal government. At his nomination speech Peddle not only attacked his Tory opponent, Meredith ("He has told you that we workingmen are desirous of going too fast, and that we will create a revolution."), but he raised the level of political critique to a higher plane: "Dodgers and pamphlets have been circulated among the workingmen derogatory to me, but I say to the workingman, look out – they are all election dodges intended to deceive and mislead. They contain references to a Royal Commission elected to enter into an investigation of labor difficulties. But the same old trouble is still in the way." After reiterating his 15-point labor-reform platform, Peddle noted that, win or lose, "One thing this election will do – it will educate the people up to the standard of Labor Reform."[77]

The campaign closed with a "rousing rally" for Peddle, with local and southwestern Ontario Knights of Labor prominent in the speech giving. All workingmen were advised to check out their voting status, and urged to

"Draw a good heavy pencil mark opposite the name of Samuel Peddle (Cabinet Maker), . . . driving a nail into the coffin of the boodlers." When the results were in, it was clear that many London workers had done just that, especially in Ward 5, where Peddle received almost 60 percent of the ballot. But the other wards carried the day for Meredith, and he won by 202 votes. His victory margin in 1879 had been more than double this, however, and in 1883 he had secured the seat easily, by acclamation. The labor reformers thus viewed the failure favorably, claiming that Meredith had been "barely saved by the unrevised voters' list." The turnout of only 41 percent was surprisingly low, and charges of corruption, physical assault, and rowdyism were flung at the Conservative machine. Even in defeat the Order and the workingmen it represented seemed content with their accomplishment. In the aftermath of this setback, for instance, the Conservative *Free Press* depicted the Order in the throes of decline, its membership divided over political differences. "Knights of Labor" and "Demos" wrote to oppose such misrepresentations. "We affirm that the K of L is stronger today than at any time in the past," they asserted, and "though we may be knocked out in the first round, we have not thrown in the sponge and do not intend to." These labor reformers closed with a resolute attack on those who would denigrate their camp: "The crop of prejudiced ignoramuses is not yet exhausted, and as long as it keeps up the party press will live. It has seen its best days, however, and like all deep-rooted evils it dies hard. Monopoly is the overshadowing curse of the land."[78]

In Hamilton, working-class politics were equally well established. After the 1883 Williams' candidacy, political discussion had been continued in the Labor Political Association, in the *Palladium* and at City Hall, where the irascible Thomas Brick kept the spirit of political activism alive. Throughout the summer of 1886 the *Palladium* kept a watchful eye on both Toronto and Ottawa for signs of forthcoming elections. Treating the electoral process with some disdain, the *Palladium* declared: "As letters are flying all over the country continuing the legends 'Come along John, we've got lots of money,' and 'send me another 10,000,' we came to the conclusion that a general election was imminent."[79]

Temperance reformers also started to plan for elections that summer, and Royal Templars' leader W. W. Buchanan broached the possibility of a temperance–labor alliance early in the year. In a letter to Powderly, inviting him to address the city's annual temperance camp, he noted: "We recognize here a very close alliance between temperance and labor reforms and we desire to strengthen that alliance." After Mowat called the provincial election, on 26 November, the Hamilton labor movement held a convention that nominated

Knight and Grand Trunk machinist Hamilton Racey as a workingman's candidate. Racey, born in Dundas in 1856, was a prominent evangelical and temperance advocate, formerly associated with the YMCA. He fulfilled perfectly the role of a labor–temperance candidate. The Central Labor Union and a mass meeting of workingmen ratified the convention's choice on the labor side and temperance advocates such as W. W. Buchanan publicly supported Racey.[80]

The Hamilton Tories, however, had a significant trick up their sleeve. Following the precedent they first set in 1872 when they elected H. B. Witton as a Tory-Labor MP, they nominated molder John Burns to contest the provincial seat.[81] A prominent labor reformer and two-time president of the molders' union, Burns found himself attacked and denounced as a turncoat by his former comrades, including his fellow molders. For as the *Palladium* argued: "We want a great deal more than the election of one or a dozen workingmen as party nominees and owing allegiance to this or that monopoly-ridden combination. We want to elect Labor-Reformers – men thoroughly conversant with the Labor problem, . . . so imbued with our principles that on any question they can be depended on to regard it from our standpoint, and speak and vote accordingly." The Tory's "very stupid blunder" became only too apparent, even to themselves, and A. T. Freed, editor of the *Spectator* and newly appointed Royal Commissioner, appealed to Powderly to intervene. After explaining that Burns was a prominent molder still actively working at his trade, Freed went on to plead his case:

> But there are a number of workingmen who are offended with Mr. Burns because he has taken a Conservative nomination, and they have put in nomination a Mr. *Racey*. This gentleman – also a very respectable man – has not a ghost of a chance of success; and his candidature can only have the effect of aiding Mr. Gibson and drawing off votes for Burns. Under these circumstances I have thought it possible you might feel at liberty to write Burns approving of his acceptance of a party nomination in a case where the workingmen are not strong enough to elect their candidate when they are united.[82]

As in an earlier instance – A. B. Ingram's similar letter about his St. Thomas candidacy – Powderly filed the letter with the ominous stamp "No Answer Required." In addition to the attempt to enlist Powderly's support, Burns also emphatically committed himself to labor: "I will stand by my labour principles through thick and thin. I will not forget the man who works by me. In all questions affecting the interests of the labour party I will stand by that party. Those matters will be my first concern."[83]

While these Tory maneuvers took place, the labor campaign got off to an enthusiastic beginning with a mass meeting at the Central Labor Hall. Chairman and Knights' leader George Collis credited the Mowat government's interest in labor in general and Hamilton Grit MPP J. M. Gibson's efforts in particular to the strong showing of Williams in the previous election. He also proposed a "Committee of 600" to raise funds for the campaign. Rather than appealing for large donations, they would instead find 600 faithful workingmen willing to contribute a dollar each. This appeal met with approval and the audience responded "with a wild shout of exultation, and immediately scores of bills were flying in the air." Racey then spoke and a series of Knights followed him to the platform. The evening culminated with the fiery Corktowner Alderman Thomas Brick offering some down-to-earth advice: "Take all the boodle you can get from both parties but don't forget to cast your votes for Racey. Pretend to work for Burns and Gibson but let your friends understand that they are to vote for Racey." Giving complete credit to the labor vote for his aldermanic victory, Brick then turned to the Tory candidate: "I don't blame Jack Burns for what he did. When a millionaire like Sanford pats a poor workingman on the back it's likely to paralyze him . . . We don't want men who would be turned; we're better off without them."[84]

Only a few nights later 3,000 Hamilton workers filled the Palace Rink to hear Racey and a score of labor speakers. Chaired by Knight and molder Fred Walters, soon to be the federal labor candidate, the meeting greeted with high spirits Racey's newly printed platform, which endorsed full man and woman suffrage; the elimination of all property requirements for elective office; the abolition of municipal bonuses; the ending of contract and convict labor; the termination of assisted immigration; temperance; and land reform. Ed Williams followed Racey with an eloquent speech further defining the platform. To "tumultuous cheers," he closed: "Neglect of politics has left us where we are. There are men in this city, however, who have sworn they will never cease to agitate, until the crack of doom if necessary, until they get those rights for which they are now contending." Again, however, Thomas Brick drove home the labor line:

> The party press is setting class against class, and creed against creed, in hopes that it will divide us, while the Labor party is striving to wipe out the sectarian bigotry, which should have been buried in Ireland years ago, and educate the boys to a true sense of the position they at present occupy. The "bloody shirt" will be flaunted in our faces in Corktown, but that is an old game.[85]

A few days later, recognizing the increasing sectarianism of the frightened partisan press, the HLPA passed a resolution abhorring "the efforts put forth by a certain portion of the Ontario press to set creed against creed by appealing to religious prejudices and bigotry." Playing upon what must have been perceived as working-class cynicism of religious enthusiasm and activity, the *Hamilton Spectator* suggested that Racey had severed his ties with the YMCA merely to attract working-class voters. "It is sad to contemplate that before the campaign is over this excellent young man, whose highest ambition had been to advance the cause of evangelical Christianity, may become little better than one of the wicked politicians," wailed the Tory newspaper. Racey replied appropriately to these crocodile tears, shed so profusely in the midst of a political campaign in which the *Spectator* was far from disinterested. "I cannot close without thanking you for the very kind interest which you display in my spiritual welfare," he wrote to the editor, "and can assure you that the sad end which you have predicted for me at the end of the month is entirely uncalled for, as I have no connection with the Tory party, and do not intend to have any." Allan Studholme, a future political activist, epitomized labor's new mood: "The two political parties are dead. We are the party now." Another large campaign meeting took place approximately a week later. This time Toronto's A. W. Wright, the quasi-labor candidate in Lambton West, joined the now familiar array of Hamilton Knights' leaders. Calling for a new National Policy of "No Poverty," Wright gave a fiery endorsment to Racey, distancing himself from Tory candidate Burns: "A new political party should be formed, with the labour cause as its basis, a good reason for its existence being the fact that each of the old parties gives the other such a bad character. In such a party there would be a new political economy, which would take into consideration a more just and enlightened view of the science of the distribution of wealth." In the context of Hamilton workers' independent stand Wright was capable of moving forcefully to the left and abandoning his well-known attachments to the Conservatives.[86] Racey actually did not run as strongly as Williams had in 1883. He gained only 34 fewer votes but saw his percentage of the total vote fall by over six points. In addition he won no polls and finished second in only 5 of 50.[87] Why had labor not increased its strength commensurate to the extraordinary growth of the Order? Probably for two reasons. First, one suspects that the Tory tactic of running a molder won back a few workingmen and that the prominent role of Gibson (the incumbent Grit) in introducing labor measures in the Ontario legislature improved his standing. Second, as we have seen earlier, the Hamilton Knights, despite their valiant efforts to reunite, had been seriously split by the exploits of Morgan and Harvey and subsequently by the Home Club debate in 1885–6.

The final city in which labor contested the provincial election was Toronto. In Hogtown Mayor Howland remained loyal to his working-class constituents in 1886 and aided them in their struggles with the Masseys and later with the TSR. Howland not only stood by labor in the hard times but on frequent occasions expressed his gratitude to it. For example, while chairing an "entertainment" for Maple Leaf LA 2622 and United LA 3491, Howland proclaimed that he was "glad to be there to thank the Knights of Labor for the support they had given in the election." Moreover, he added, "The late strikes [had] proved that the workingmen of Toronto were law-abiding and honest, upright and honorable citizens. During these strikes [he had been] very much impressed with the dignified manner in which they had conducted themselves."[88] Howland stood as a fine example both of the potential of labor politics and of a labor–temperance alliance.

There were other lessons to be drawn from the political contests of 1886 as well. One of these concerned Frank Smith and the Tory government. Already reeling from its battles with Toronto printers, the party had little need for Senator Smith, a minister without portfolio in Macdonald's government, to take on the city's entire labor movement. This Smith, as president of the TSR, certainly did. Needless to say, the denunciations of Smith that flowed in from Knights of Labor LAs all over Ontario were tied to demands that Macdonald repudiate him. Macdonald did not do so, but relied instead on his Labor Commission strategy. The depth of concern felt by Toronto Tories, however, was evident in a warning letter from A. W. Wright:

> The effect on the Conservative Party not only in Toronto but wherever the Knights of Labor and trades unions are organized will be this. If the fight is kept up the Grit wirepullers will be able to get them pledged to oppose all candidates who support the government of which Mr. Smith is a member . . . If for any reason the men are beaten the feeling will only be intensified. We conservatives who are in the Order are powerless to prevent this as the weapon placed in the hands of the Grits is too strong.[89]

In addition, when the TLC met in Toronto that fall, it reasserted its strong support for labor politics in a resolution moved by two Toronto Knights, J. Roney and Michael O'Halloran:

> The working class of this Dominion will never be properly represented in Parliament or receive justice in the legislation of this country until they are represented by men of their own class and opinions, and the members of this congress pledge themselves to use their utmost endeavours to bring out candidates at the ensuing local and Dominion elections in the constituencies in which they reside.

An interesting debate ensued after this motion on an amendment offered by George Wrigley, editor of the St. Thomas *Canada Labor Courier*, and seconded by Bryan Lynch, a Knight and leading Irish Land Leaguer from Toronto. Their amendment proposed that labor vote as a block for the old party candidate who pledged the most in ridings where there were no labor candidates. A number of speakers, including William Bews, former editor of the Toronto edition of the *Palladium*, opposed this, citing difficulties with former members of that type, specifically Hamilton's H. B. Witton. D. J. O'Donoghue, however, came to Witton's defense. The amendment carried, with many speeches recalling Parnell's success in the use of that tactic to further the cause of Irish Home Rule.

Immediately after the debate the Congress greeted a delegation from the Dominion Alliance, the major Canadian temperance organization. The body included Mayor Howland and Toronto alderman J. McMillan, both endorsed in the previous municipal elections by the Knights. The third Toronto member of the delegation, F. S. Spence, drew applause when he identified their greatest enemy as labor's greatest enemy. One delegate shouted the obvious name – Frank Smith – to the delight of all present. The Alliance appeal for cooperative efforts was later endorsed by the convention. The antagonism to the Tories, the possibility of a united front with temperance forces, and the firm commitment to political action, all prefigured the subsequent events of the fall and winter.[90]

Faced with such formidable opposition, Tory policy continued to nurture plans for the recovery of working-class votes. The serious choice of provincial candidates reflected this process. The strongest incumbent, the aged Alexander Morris, declined to seek reelection for health reasons. He, and others, warned Macdonald of the threat from dissident groups, and of the problems posed for the Conservative party by Mowat's gerrymander:

> The position is one of difficulty – Toronto now is one constituency in addition to the old East, Centre and West, Parkdale, Yorkville, Brockton and St. Matthews Ward – electing three members but each elector casting only two votes. How it will work no one can tell – there will be regular party candidates, perhaps two on each side, and possibly labour and temperance candidates.[91]

At the Tory nomination convention workingman John Hewitt, an important labor leader of the 1870s, played a significant role in securing labor representation on the Tory ticket. The two nominees were H. E. "Saratoga" Clarke, a manufacturer of trunks, and E. F. "Sentinel" Clarke. The latter was chosen to placate labor's Tory advocates, and to ease the fears of Morris and the leading Toronto Macdonald supporters that a movement of independent workingmen would damage the chances of the Conservative Party. "Sentinel" Clarke was a major force in the Toronto Typographical Union, with a considerable following in the labor movement and in the working-class world of fraternal societies, where his newspaper, the *Orange Sentinel*, was read avidly. In choosing the two Clarkes, then, the Tories had settled on representatives that they thought they could push as "Capital and Labour."[92]

Toronto workers moved quickly to nominate labor candidates for the provincial contest. DA 125 appointed a committee to consider the question in late October and the TTLC followed in early November. These committees met together and then reported to a joint TTLC–DA 125 meeting at Temperance Hall on 12 November under the chairmanship of Phillips Thompson. The proposal to hold a nominating convention on the basis of one delegate for the first 100 members and one for each additional 100 was endorsed unanimously.[93]

The *News*, while greeting the decision enthusiastically, immediately began to caution against the transgressions of partyism: "A wire-pulling match between Grit and Tory heelers professing to be Labor Reformers would do infinite harm to the cause. The prime consideration to be kept in view in framing a platform and choosing candidates should be the absolute independence as between parties of the men selected." Partyism became divisive only a few days after this warning. Tory bricklayer Andrew McCormack, a frustrated prospective Royal Commissioner, went well beyond the restraints of polite debate in asserting that "O'Donoghue had been bought again and again" and challenged him "to make an assertion to the contrary." O'Donoghue, his Irish noticeably up, did just that by accusing Tory opposition leader W. R. Meredith of offering him a portfolio in a potential Tory cabinet in return for the withdrawal of his support from the 1874 Mowat government. This charge rebounded through the Ontario press for a week, with Meredith issuing a blanket denial and O'Donoghue publishing a sworn affidavit attesting to the truth of his charges. The veracity of the claim was unimportant, but the atmosphere of partisan wrangling it exemplified was of great significance. For example, McCormack, stung by O'Donoghue's charge, immediately proceeded to wash additional dirty linen in public, claiming that Charles March had extended labor candidate Samuel Heakes the promise of Reform support in the 1883 provincial election if he would guarantee that he would support the Mowat government. This accusation March denied emphatically, but it would resurface later in the campaign. Thus, simultaneously with the attempt to build independent labor-reform momentum, a serious outbreak of partyism emerged to cloud the future.[94]

The labor nomination convention took place on 30 November at Richmond Hall. The mammoth six-hour meeting involved nearly ninety delegates representing over sixty labor organizations and approximately 10,000 workers. All press reports commented on the unanimity and lack of political bickering that accompanied the nominations. For the provincial house the delegates chose John Roney and Charles March, both prominent Knights, after four ballots. For the federal house, after only two ballots, Knights E. E.

Sheppard (West Toronto) and Alf Jury (West Toronto) won the nod. The only other candidates to win any significant numbers of votes were John Carter, one of the candidates in 1883, and J. S. Williams. The Knights' prominence was clear, not only in the nominees, but also throughout the proceedings. Almost forty LAs were present, thirteen of them representing over 200 workers each.[95]

Who were the provincial candidates? John Roney, a charter member of Excelsior LA 2305, had left it to help form Maple Leaf LA 2622. A Toronto delegate to the Richmond General Assembly of the Knights of Labor, and a painter by trade, he now worked as foreman of the upholstery department in the car shops of the Credit Valley Railway. A prominent temperance advocate, he was a leading force in the YMCA's Railway Christian Association, an evangelical workingmen's society. The *World*'s correspondent claimed that he "might readily be mistaken for a Methodist clergyman." "An elderly man," he wore "small 'Galway rushers' on either side of his face." Roney was not actually a Methodist but he was a Deacon and Bible-class teacher at Dovercourt Baptist. He had also served as a Toronto correspondent for the *Labor Union* and the *Palladium*, where a number of items appeared under his pseudonym, "Jairo Ney." The evangelical language of these reports made clear one aspect of Roney's thought:

> Ho! Prophets of Redemption come,
> Speak forth in rolling thunder tones,
> Give burning words unto the dumb:
> Give inspiration brave unto the drones.
>
> Speak out, oh, George and Powderly!
> Ring out through all the land,
> The word of life and liberty;
> Labor's quick release demand.[96]

Charles March or "Charley," as he was known throughout Ontario labor circles, was one of the province's most prominent labor reformers. Also a painter, he was a charter member of Excelsior LA 2305 and a close confidant of D. J. O'Donoghue's. A frequent president of the TTLC and a force on its Legislative Committee, he also served two terms as president of the TLC. "A portly gentleman, with full face and sweeping moustache," when dressed up he looked "like the advance agent of a minstrel show."[97] Although there were ominous signs on the horizon – "Sentinel" Clarke's candidacy, the Tory Labor Commissioner Heakes's accusations about March's Grit maneuvers in 1883, and the McCormack–O'Donoghue squabble of November – after the nominating convention labor appeared to be entering the election more united than ever before. This unanimity was emphasized when the TTLC noted its delight with the candidates at a subsequent meeting, and financial support from unions began pouring in.[98]

Meanwhile Mowat's Reformers had their nominating convention and, although it met with considerable opposition, a motion to nominate only one candidate for the three-seat riding eventually carried. Backed by the party leadership, this strategy meant overt Grit backing for labor candidate Charles March. The single candidate subsequently chosen was John Leys, one of the unsuccessful nominees in the previous provincial election.[99]

The first mass meeting of the campaign was held on 6 December at Temperance Hall, where the ratification of the labor candidates took place. DMW Sam McNab chaired the meeting and it got off to an enthusiastic start when a letter of endorsment from Mayor Howland was read. Shortly after the meeting began a telegram arrived from Hamilton molder Fred Walters, who was chairing a Hamilton meeting in support of Racey on that same evening: "The Hamilton wealth producers send congratulations to their Brethren in the Queen City. We are having a rousing and enthusiastic meeting here tonight. Hope you are having the same." Speeches by the candidates followed, all greeted with considerable enthusiasm by the crowd. As one reporter described it, "A little man with a big voice cried: 'Whoop her up again, boys,' with persistent regularity and his words were always the signal for a whirlwind of cheers and applause." John Roney's speech tried to combat the splitting tactics of the old line parties: "They say I am a Conservative. In the first place I'll say I am not a Conservative and never was. I am not a Reformer – that is, not a Grit – and never was. [Cheers] I am a strong independent and always was, [Cheers] and more than that always intend to be. [Cheers]" March followed with a similar speech pledging himself to the labor platform endorsed by their nominating committee. Speeches followed from federal candidates Sheppard and Jury and labor-reform orators Bryan Lynch, Phillips Thompson, A. W. Wright, and D. J. O'Donoghue. The two latter speakers both cautioned against sectarianism and political wirepullers. Once again labor's ranks appeared to have closed behind its independent nominees.[100]

Nightly meetings held in the wards were usually addressed by the appropriate provincial and federal candidates and by the now familiar list of labor spokesmen. Partyism was not in evidence, despite the Tory efforts to antagonize labor with charges of Grit dominance of the campaign. Heakes and a series of rowdy Conservative meetings continued to allude to the past crimes of Toronto's labor leadership, but their attempts to discredit the candidates bore little fruit. At one of Heakes's appearances in Parkdale E. E. Sheppard, Alf Jury, TTLC President Whitten, and Knights DMW Sam McNab led a contingent of workingmen out of the Tory meeting *en masse*, held their own assemblage in the streets, listened to speeches, and ended by marching through the streets singing, "We'll hang Sam Sneakes on a Sour Apple Tree."[101]

About one week before the election, labor held a huge meeting at Shaftesbury Hall, preceded by a torchlight procession complete with banners, illuminations, and bands. Even before the main procession reached the Hall, marches to the gathering point were held with a contingent coming from the west, headed by 400 Massey workers, and another from the east, led by the Irish Catholic Benevolent Union Band. A crowd estimated in the thousands filled the Hall to standing-room only, while an additional thousand were turned away. The procession was divided into wards with each group headed by bands and banners. Among the slogans were: "No Sectarianism"; "We Work and Win"; "Just Laws"; "Vote for March and Roney"; "Equal Representation"; and "No Exemptions." The boxmakers' LA carried a tombstone inscribed: "In Memory of the Late Liberal-Conservative and Reform Parties. Died December 28th, 1886." They also carried a coffin labeled: "All Party Prejudices securely Closed and Nailed Down in this Box." Various Knights leaders addressed the throng, among them St. Catharines's labor candidate William Garson, a well-known Orangeman, and his fellow labor reformer from the Canal city, J. T. Carey, a Catholic. Carey, speaking for Irish Catholic workers, pledged his support to "Billy" and called on Toronto workers similarly to put sectarian disputes behind them. All the Toronto labor candidates followed, and at the meeting's conclusion a motion was passed: "That this meeting place on record its abhorrence of the efforts put forward by a certain portion of the Ontario press to set creed against creed, by appealing to religious prejudice and bigotry." The final week of the campaign saw more of the same, with Knights of Labor and trade unionists across the province praising Toronto labor's attempts to overcome the divisions of party politics and sectarian bigotry.[102]

Despite the optimism and enthusiasm exhibited in the campaign, election day brought failure. The Clarkes swept into office accompanied by the lone Grit candidate John Leys. March and Roney received 4,055 and 3,408 votes respectively. An analysis of the vote is fraught with problems due to Mowat's unprecedented gerrymander. We do know that 14,916 votes were cast from an eligible electorate of 33,296, which indicates a rather low turnout of 44.8 percent. In addition it seems reasonable to surmise that March garnered more votes than Roney because of Grit support. It also seems likely that "Sentinel" Clarke headed the poll, edging out his running mate "Saratoga," because of Tory-Orange-workingman votes that went to him and Roney. Finally the fact that the actual vote tallies fell some 3,000 votes short of the potential total if all 14,916 voters had selected two candidates suggests that a considerable amount of plumping took place. Moreover the much stronger showing of Leys over March indicates that Grits unhappy with their party's endorsement of a workingman were most likely to have voted in that way.[103]

A closer scrutiny of the polls shows that March carried only one of the city's thirteen wards, St. Mark's, which was the city's smallest. Roney failed to carry any. In St. Andrew's and St. Matthew's March finished third, while in St. Stephen's Roney held that spot. Of the city's total of 189 polls March topped 13 and Roney 8 with March finishing in the top three in 41 others and Roney in 32 others. A microanalysis would seem to indicate that the number of straight labor votes were the major source of March and Roney's support. March ran somewhat more strongly due to some Grit backing, but it is instructive to note that in the only wards where Leys headed the poll (St. James and St. Thomas), March, rather than adding Grit labor to straight labor votes finished dismally behind Leys. The contemporary post mortems tended to support these views. E. E. Sheppard, for example, noted at a labor meeting on election night that the Grit vote had plumped for Leys and that temperance votes had not materialized. All, however, took consolation in the fact that Roney's vote probably represented the base of labor support and this 3,400 votes (23 percent) was a big improvement on Heakes's performance in 1883.[104]

Labor in Toronto had little time for reflection on its defeat, however, as the Knights again supported Mayor Howland. Opposed by David Blain, a former Liberal MP from York West, Howland faced a concerted opposition. The *News* rallied to his support, reminding Toronto workers of his role in the Massey strike and of his letter to Frank Smith during the first street railway strike. A concerted effort by the *World* to disrupt the labor support for Howland failed miserably. On the day before the election DMW Sam NcNab reminded Toronto Knights of the need to vote for Howland, "the man who helped us to fight and win." Further, he added, Howland had supported March and Roney. The following day Howland won a majority of nearly 2,500 votes, more than in the previous election. Even the *World* conceded after the election that the labor vote had gone overwhelmingly to Howland and DMW Sam McNab was on the platform at the Howland victory celebration to take some bows for his fellow workers.[105]

## "From party and from faction"

After this victory labor quickly turned its attention to the forthcoming Dominion election, which Macdonald finally called in mid-January. In Toronto labor was well prepared, having already nominated Jury and Sheppard, and the established political parties were forced to confront this independent stand. There was a slight flurry in late January when A. W. Wright, true to his opportunist ways, tried to gain a Labor-National Policy nomination for Toronto Centre, although the November labor convention had decided not to contest the seat.[106] Among the Tories the chief concern was once more the defection from their ranks of once staunch labor support, and brewer Eugene O'Keefe wrote to Macdonald that, "the labor vote is the one I most dread, as it goes in chunks, and can't be depended on." The Grits put labor, and especially the Knights of Labor, at the center of their campaign. Leader Edward Blake appeared on a Knights of Labor platform, devoted speeches to "those subjects which concerned the working classes particularly," and published a Welland talk under the title, "Knights of Labor." An enthusiastic O'Donoghue assured Powderly that "Blake virtually accepts and adopts the platform of the Order." It was in this context that the Grit leadership in Toronto decided not to oppose the labor candidates Sheppard and Jury, although their capitulation to the workingmen caused discontent among some Reformers who felt uncomfortable in the new camp.[107]

On the labor side, the TTLC reinforced its earlier support of the workingmen's candidates and, although the usual grumblings and accusations were made by the odd Tory delegate such as bricklayer Andrew McCormack, by and large unanimity ruled. Labor leaders of both parties prominently campaigned for the workingmen's candidates. Tory and Labor Commissioner John Armstrong, for example, chaired a number of labor meetings and A. W. Wright also spoke at rallies. At one of these Wright endorsed Jury fully "though he had espoused the errors of the Reform party, while he, the speaker, had endorsed the errors of the Conservative party." Thus laborites again appeared united in this political struggle.[108]

Religion, however, once more became a major issue. This time it was not Catholic against Protestant but rather belief against atheism. Jury was a well-known secularist, very active in Free-thought activities, while the most E. E. Sheppard could claim was a vague Deism. Their Tory opponents jumped on this, accusing Jury of atheism, and the flamboyant Sheppard, whose constant attacks on piety, intense devotion to democracy, and penchant for dressing in cowboy garb made him a figure of some notoriety, of dangerous bohemianism. In addition to his Secular Society memberships, Jury was a leading cooperator and had been one of the city's most active trade union leaders since his arrival from London, England, in the early 1870s. A merchant tailor with a small shop, he also was the most prominent of the Grit workingmen until O'Donoghue's arrival. A close friend of O'Donoghue and March, he was part of the triumvirate that had built the Knights of Labor in

Toronto, and Jury's tailor shop had been their central meeting place for a number of years.[109]

Perhaps because of the personal idiosyncrasies of the labor candidates, the Tory nominees hardly campaigned. John Small, the Toronto East candidate, went so far as to fail to show up at his formal nomination. Both Small and Denison refused challenges from Jury and Sheppard to debate the issues. This pattern figured throughout the campaign. Labor held almost nightly ward meetings and several large rallies. Their opponents bided their time. Workers went to the polls on 22 February with a *News* poem of inspiration, "Brothers Arise!":

> Workingmen! Brothers arise!
> From Party and from Faction:
> Let your huzzahs reach to the skies,
> To cheer your men of action.
> Cast off hopeless lethargy –
> Awake from your slumbers!
> Show with pride and energy,
> The greatness of your numbers.[110]

Inspired or not, workers did not elect Sheppard or Jury. In the two-way race in West Toronto, Sheppard drew a highly respectable 47 percent of the vote. In the three-way race in East Toronto, however, Jury finished a distant second with 35 percent. Sheppard actually ran more strongly in West Toronto than any previous Reformer with the exception of Thomas Moss, whose two victories came in the wake of the Pacific Scandal. Jury, however, garnered the lowest vote ever of a losing Reformer – again the single Grit victory in the riding had come in the 1873 election.

A closer look at West Toronto suggests how strongly Sheppard ran. He won one of the four major wards (St. Andrew's) and 30 of the 76 polls. This was a much better showing then the Reform candidate had managed in the 1882 federal election (only 13 of 51 polls and no wards). It also seems likely that it was Tory workingmen's votes, not Grit ones, that moved to Sheppard, as his strength was not in wards where the Reformer McMurrich had run well in 1882. Meanwhile, in East Toronto, Jury led in no wards and in only 2 of 52 polls. This was a worse showing than the Grit candidate in 1882 who had narrowly carried St. Thomas Ward and had led in 7 of 35 polls overall.[111]

The election analyses in the Toronto press and the contestants' comments confirm this numerical analysis. The *World* felt that Toronto workers viewed themselves as citizens and not simply as workers and thus voted accordingly. The *News* on the other hand felt that the sectarian issue of religion, especially

Jury's atheism, had distorted the campaigns. At the election-night meeting Sheppard and Jury both tried to keep the troops' spirits up, Jury arguing: "They were moving along the right path. Direct representation was the correct one. The other lesson was that they should all work to extend the organization. They should be more careful who they took in. The principles of the Order should be read more carefully by its members. . . . Their ranks should be closed up and they should form themselves with a regular political party." March and Roney also spoke, with the latter endorsing the need for the creation of a permanent third party. A. W. Wright, however, instigated a major fight by contending that in Toronto and Hamilton Grits had failed to rally to the labor case.[112]

In Hamilton labor had nominated well-known molder and Knights of Labor activist Fred Walters to run in the 1887 federal election. Active in trade-union circles since the nine-hour movement of 1872, the English-born Walters was described as a much stronger candidate than the previously endorsed provincial campaigner, Hamilton Racey. He was about forty years of age, and had resided in the city for fifteen or twenty years. But he was doomed to lose, the partisan *Spectator* implied, for his views were too advanced, and he was generally regarded "as an English democratic radical of an extreme type." The Grits apparently thought Walters's chances somewhat better, and nominated only one candidate in the two-member seat, thus leaving Walters opposed only by Tories. This led to a flurry of charges that the HLPA and the Reform party had hopped into bed with one another to defeat the Conservatives. These accusations, predictably flung in the face of the labor reformers by committed Tories, may well have had some substance, for the Grit and independent-labor campaigns were waged as a virtual common front against the Conservative candidates. Prominent unions, such as the Iron Molders, endorsed both labor and Reform candidates, and the two "parties" mutually supported one another. Alderman Thomas Brick appeared for "the first time ever on a Grit platform," and the *Spectator* reveled in its denunciations of the "professional workingmen" who had found their place in the ranks of the once-detested Grits. Many Hamilton workingmen, after the sting of Racey's defeat, had obviously opted for a temporary alliance with Edward Blake's conception of "Reform," thinking that this would secure victory for the labor group and send Fred Walters to the Dominion parliament.[113]

But if that strategy seemed necessary in January 1887, it also produced discontent. Dissatisfaction apparently emerged in the Order itself, some members of the various LAs being angered by the so-called Grit–Labor alliance. In Walters's own Molders' Union a smear campaign was launched against him, a unionist of 23-years' standing claiming that the independent-labor candidate had broken ranks with his craft brethren by working in the Copp Brothers' struck foundry during the depression of the 1870s; at the molders' ball a fight erupted as tempers flared over the charges. The electoral struggle of January-February 1887 was thus marked with much bitterness and, in the end, the working-class candidate was narrowly defeated. The Tories emerged victorious, edging out Walters and the Reform party candidate, Rev. Burns, by a meager 161 votes. Walters received an impressive 48.8 percent of the vote, his total coming to 3,410, 2 votes more than the straight Reform nominee. The Knights of Labor member won 18 of 61 polls, but led only in Ward 5. The turnout in the election was a remarkable 75.4 percent. Enthusiastically proclaiming the Conservative victory, the *Spectator* suggested that the CLU be "relegated to the shelves of the museum for obsolete institutions," and pompously dismissed the Order's political potency. The usually buoyant Thomas Brick expressed the labor reformers' disappointment. Reflecting upon Walters' loss, he thought that "the whole labor party combined couldn't boycott a soup kitchen." But in the LA halls the close race must have both frustrated *and* excited labor's advocates. Victory had certainly escaped them (and some may have turned angrily upon the Grits for failing to bring out votes for Walters, while the workingmen muscled their own reluctant ranks to cast a vote for Rev. Burns), but their showing had been sufficiently strong to induce hope. Thus, when one CLU member proclaimed his disgust "with the members of this organization [who] will not support its principles" and threatened to "abandon any further attempt on their behalf," he was placated by Allan Studholme. The young stove-mounter understood such disillusionment, but he had forceful words of advice: "stick to the Labor Party." The disgruntled reformer sheepishly accepted Studholme's counsel. We do not know where he ended up in his later political life, if indeed he had one, but Studholme is easily placed: he sat as Hamilton's Independent Labor Party MPP between 1906 and his death in 1919. All had not been lost in Walters's defeat.[114]

Thus ended the flurry of labor political activity that accompanied the peak of Knights of Labor prominence in Ontario. In the winter of 1886–7, labor put massive efforts into the provincial and federal candidacies. The efforts ranged from independent labor through Tory-and-Grit endorsed labor candidates, varying with the local political context. While coming close in numerous races, only in Lincoln (St. Catharines) and in West Elgin (St. Thomas) did labor emerge victorious. Andy Ingram and Billy Garson went to the provincial legislature as lonely labor victors and with each already pledged to the causes of one of the major parties. Labor thus now had a voice in Toronto, but it was not the independent workingman's voice dreamed of earlier in the year. O'Donoghue assessed the significance of the upsurge of 1886–7 in a letter to Powderly, his Grit sympathies more than a little evident:

> The session of the legislature closes next week. The Knight members have done well so far – particularly, Brother Garson. He was elected a straight labour candidate. Ingram, *it is alleged,* used the K. of L. until he got a political *party nomination* and then ignored the labor party . . . Be these things as they may, and although *we* of Toronto, Hamilton and London were defeated with *our* candidates, the Labor Party has made its impress in Ontario, as is evidenced by the fact that we have more weight before the House this session than we ever had before – and more legislation respecting wage earners.

"Enjolras" (Phillips Thompson) had written in December of 1886 that, "Labour reform campaigns in several Ontario cities are the germs of a new and better political life."[115] But that still remained only a potential after the votes were counted.

## "Into municipal politics"

The *News* in considering all the campaigns of that winter noted that "the members of labor organizations are not as yet sufficiently educated to throw aside their party associations and prejudices and vote in the interests of their class." Nevertheless, these were not grounds for "despondency or discouragement," because comparisons of the recent votes with those of 1883 showed "the steady progress of their ideas." The question, then, was how "to retain the vantage ground we have secured." The *News* proposed that: "In order to establish a firm basis for parliamentary campaigning the Labor Reform party should begin at the beginning and go systematically into municipal contests. Our adversaries derive their principal strength from the preservation of their political organization intact from year to year by the part they take in civic elections. The machine being so frequently in use does not become rusty."[116]

This advice was taken to heart throughout Ontario, and everywhere that the Knights remained strong saw municipal campaigns (often linked to federal efforts) in the ensuing years. One good example of this was Brantford, a city with an active labor movement including a strong Knights of Labor component. In the civic election of January 1886 they decided to remain neutral, but controversies in the following year plunged them into the center of municipal politics. An April mass meeting of Knights heard lecturer F. D. Phillips argue for an active political role. With too many capitalists in the legislature, he argued, it was not surprising that it "crushes Labour down and lifts capital up." Only a few months later "Drawbar," the Brantford correspondent to the *Palladium of Labor*, issued a clarion call for labor representation in politics. This was followed closely by a heated controversy over shorter hours for corporation laborers. The Knights organized a campaign for the nine-hour day, but the City Council ignored their 400-signature petition. Therefore "Drawbar" and the Knights decided on a more explicitly political stance. The new Brantford Trades and Labor Council, organized in September, made municipal politics its major focus and eventually endorsed three aldermanic candidates in December. These candidates issued a proclamation to Brantford workers:

> For years it has been evident that the working people of Brantford are at a serious disadvantage compared with other classes of the community . . . The working people are unrepresented among the law makers. Where they should be in a position to demand justice, they can only offer a humble appeal for what by some has been deemed favour. All this must be remedied. As a step towards that end candidates for seats at City Council have been brought out.

Two of the three were successful and workingmen had a prominent voice on City Council into the 1890s.[117]

Brantford Knights remained inactive in the provincial campaign but in the February federal contest they supported the Grit reformer Patterson. They credited him with active opposition to assisted immigration and, given that his opponent was prominent local industrialist Cockshutt who had just cut his agricultural-implements workers' wages, the choice was quite popular. Patterson was successful and he won the bulk of his majority in the North ward, which had previously been carried by one of the labor aldermen. Thus even in towns where there were no labor candidates, trade unionists and the Order joined to make a working-class presence felt. Moreover, this process could reveal itself in opposition as well as support. In Welland, for example, workingmen attacked the Tory candidate Dr. Ferguson, an established dispenser of patronage and long-time ally and confidante of A. W. Wright. They issued an eight-point list of why labor should reject the Conservative, claiming that "his vague and partial answers to the K. of L. questions [were] unsatisfactory."[118]

Brantford and Welland, however, represent only two examples. Wherever the Knights were present in significant numbers, they made an impact on local politics. Other western Ontario towns where the Order was active included Galt and Chatham. Terence O'Toole, Galt's Knight of Labor correspondent to the *Palladium of Labor*, promoted labor politics by arguing that the town had a "superfluous amount of stupidity on the Council which wants cleaning up." Disenchanted with petty political reforms, he condemned piecemeal measures as "like stopping – or rather trying to stop – the cough of diseased lungs." In Chatham, workers probably saw such reform efforts as valid, and in the February 1887 Dominion election they helped to elect Archibald Campbell in Kent county, the riding going to the Reformers for the first time since Confederation. Although Chatham itself gave the incumbent Tory, Henry Smyth, a majority of 132, the total vote went to Campbell, who was also victorious in a May 1888 by-election. Campbell won these seats in "desperately contested" battles that saw him court the Knights of Labor, the Order being recognized as "a very active organization" whose support was essential to any political victory. The Chatham Knights' political clout was more impressive in the municipal sphere and they elected five of the six candidates that they had endorsed for the town council. Moreover, four of the five were members of Maple Leaf LA 7150.[119]

In eastern Ontario the Knights also displayed electoral strength at the municipal level, but it developed later in the decade, the years 1887, 1888 and even 1889 being most significant. The Knights made their presence felt in Belleville, Cornwall, Gananoque, Kingston, and Prescott. Thomas Sullivan of Belleville's LA 2900 wrote to Powderly of the "flourishing condition" of the Order in that town on the eve of the 1887 federal election. Although the Bay of Quinte workingmen had no candidate of their own, they inched toward a stand of independence. "I know that I cannot recommend the policy of the present government," Sullivan informed the GMW, "and if the Reform party namely Mr. Blake gets elected god knows what they will do." In Cornwall a Knights-supported mayor opposed a local railway bonus and a council with a majority of its members endorsed by the Knights voted to increase the assessment on the local cotton mill.[120] Gananoque's DMW George Toner of DA 236 won election as a councillor, then deputy-reeve, and, finally, reeve in a series of elections. Gordon Bishop, a local trade union activist in the 1930s, recalled the excitement of these races when compiling his reminiscences.[121] Local Knights of Labor in Kingston lobbied the city council and later created a People's Political Party. A slate of candidates for town council was supported by the Order in Prescott. Later still, in Ottawa, in the early 1890s, the local TLC endorsed a labor political platform and supported local candidates. Its major base of support was the Order's membership. Labor unity broke down in the federal election of March 1891 as the Grit printer J. W. Patterson broke from the Trades and Labor Council–Knights of Labor ranks to run as a "Labour candidate," much to the chagrin of many city workers who saw through this effort to use labor "to veil, as it were, the Liberal weakness." Patterson's defeat, however, did not end working-class involvement in local politics, although it signaled the end of any degree of autonomy, and as late as 1894 the Order remained vitally concerned with political issues. DA 6 endorsed the *Free Lance*, which campaigned for the workingman under the masthead "We demand all the Reform that Justice can ask for, and all the Justice that Reform can give."[122] A second paper associated with the Order, George Kilt's *Capital Siftings*, also appeared in 1894 describing itself as "a strong public arm for the working man to lean on" and indicating its desire "to be the organ of labour organizations." Staking out ground to the left of *Free Lance*, *Capital Siftings* began to carry two new columns in the fall of 1894 – "Socialists' Corner," a potpourri of classic socialist quotations, and "Socialist Labor Party," penned by "Karl Marx, Junior." With this opening to the left, the paper also changed its motto to read "To hammer in the facts and rivet them with criticism." Focusing to a large degree on municipal politics, Kilt's paper existed in a state of creative tension with the Ottawa TLC, which under Patterson's lead became increasingly tied to the Liberal Party.[123]

## "It's Boodle and he's king"

In spite of this longevity, however, the aftermath of the provincial and federal elections of the winter of 1886–7 left the Order in the major centers of Hamilton and Toronto in considerable disarray. As we shall see in Chapter 7, and as J. W. Patterson's 1891 defeat and later events in Ottawa revealed, political conflicts bred of partyism were just around the corner; the Knights of Labor was about to pass from a position of strength to one of weakness, its vulnerabilities soon to become a matter of public record. How, then, do we assess the impact of the Knights of Labor on Ontario politics? The two major previous accounts have dismissed the efforts as either problematic tumbles from the seemingly inevitable path to business unionism or, only slightly more persuasively, as simple steps toward "the transition to capitalist democracy" that incorporated the working class into the political system. The problem with both views is their teleological projections on the working-class experience of the 1880s. In the one view the development of business unionism appears as foreordained and the actual political practice of the Knights throughout Ontario fails even to enter into consideration. No doubt if it had, it would only have been dismissed as a reformist and utopian perversion. In the other view the actual crisis of the system is ignored in favor of an argument that the transition was "smooth" and involved no "ruptures." Historical experience is flattened and the actual struggles of the 1880s quickly glossed over, judged by later, quite different developments.[124]

The Knights made significant political efforts and enjoyed some success. They did not overcome all the tensions in the working-class world but for a moment at least they demonstrated the way forward. Their greatest strength lay in local politics, which was closest to their day-to-day experience and where gains were quite tangible – early closing, union wages and jobs on corporation work, just assessments, responsible public transit. They viewed other political efforts with some skepticism, which was why 1886–7 was simultaneously a great achievement and a great disappointment. Their fears of partyism, corruption, graft, and heelers seemed to find confirmation in the partisan wrangling that emerged within the Order in the wake of electoral failure.

This political skepticism, however, cut in many directions. For ultimately the Knights of Labor was not simply a political movement. As the *Palladium* tried to explain, the Order's "aims and objects are distinctly political," but that was not the major task:

> The distinctive work of the Order is the inculcation of principles. It is an educating force. . . . Thus while Knights of Labor will effect the regeneration of politics they will not act avowedly as Knights of Labor, but will carry out the principles taught in the Assembly in supplementary organizations.

The separation was not simply organizational. As T. V. Powderly once put it:

> One reason why political parties degenerate is because the masses of the common people are not educated. If we were, we could more easily discern the difference between good and bad legislation, and we would not be clamouring so often for the repeal of bad laws. The chief aim of the Knights of Labor is to educate not only men, but parties; educate men first, that they may educate parties and govern them intelligently and honestly.[125]

As we shall see in subsequent chapters, the Knights believed in a process of social change that was far more broadly based then any notion of a seizure of political power through electoral means. Participation in politics was not the ultimate expression of the Order but rather only one of many. Both "spreading the light" and "the people's strike" were equally important. The revolution would come from below with the spread of the Knights of Labor and its movement culture; it would not be imposed from above. From the schooling of the LA, from the cooperative stores and shops, from the reformed intelligence of the mass of workers – from all of these would come significant change. Wage slavery would be conquered when workers became educated "citizens." In the words of "the Khan":

Ah! mark him well, that you may know
His leprous face again;
For he will fall as Caesar fell;
And when the foe is slain,
Mid weeping and mid laughter,
Our hearts with joy will sing;
To think the days are gone for aye
When Boodle was the King.

In the post-1886 years, however, "the Khan's" prophecy of ultimate victory was not to be, and instead the Order plunged into the sordid conflicts of partyism that revealed just how thoroughly the established political culture could emasculate the thrust for independent labor politics. As Knights of Labor leaders across North America knew, partisan politics intruded upon the Order's larger purpose at precisely those moments that labor reform faltered. In Ontario the years 1887–94 would see the Order devastated. "The Khan" had indeed penned the Knights of Labor's future in verse, but it was the penultimate lines assessing the resiliency of partisan politics, rather than the utopian conception of his last words, that rang true:

He has more power than Caesar had,
He's mightier than the Czar,
And in your midst, oh! workingmen,
His emissaries are.
He buys your treacherous brothers –
There lies his deadly sting.
Would'st know the man again, dost think?
It's Boodle, and he's King.[126]

# 7. "Politicians in the Order": The conflicts of decline, 1887–1894

In 1886 D. J. O'Donoghue's *Labor Record* warned the budding Canadian labor movement that care should be taken "not to commit itself to the 'friends' of the workingman, who [were] becoming suspiciously active, even now, suggesting this, that, and the other as just the man to run for parliament at the next election." The post-1886 years would remind the Knights of Labor of the wisdom of these words, and of the price to be paid in internal stability should they be ignored. Ironically enough, however, O'Donoghue himself would play a considerable role in fomenting dissent, his own commitment to the Grit machine of Edward Blake placing him in the center of many a controversy. Across the province minor squabbles and political dealings simply confirmed the problem that Powderly pointed out in a letter to St. Catharines' J. T. Carey: "We have too many politicians in the Order whose aim at all times is self. I don't mind a politician who works politics in the interest of the Order but when the politician works the Order in the interest of politics then it is time to set the seal of disapproval on such." From Napanee came the complaint that the Knights of Labor were losing members due to the politically motivated actions of "certain parties" affiliated with other societies and lodges. In the politically charged atmosphere of the nation's capital, "office seekers" polluted Assembly halls. Carey described Ottawa as "one of the Rottenest Places I have ever been in my life there is not many members of the order here but as few as they are there is quite a few among them who wish to use the order for their own ends rather than to better the condition of the workers at large & as a Rule they climb to the top of the order about the fastest that can be done *fair* or *foul.*"[1]

Indeed, if the politics of the Order presented Canadian statesmen and party heelers with one of their largest problems in the 1880s, then the exploitation of political differences that festered within the LAs and the subtle manipulation of party loyalties provided them with a golden opportunity to respond to the challenge of independent labor politics raised in the 1882–7 years. Although Tory blue and Grit red had deep social and cultural roots in the Canadian working-class community, these traditional ties were not sufficient to retain labor's allegiance, and with the development of the independent campaigns of the mid-to-late 1880s the established political culture

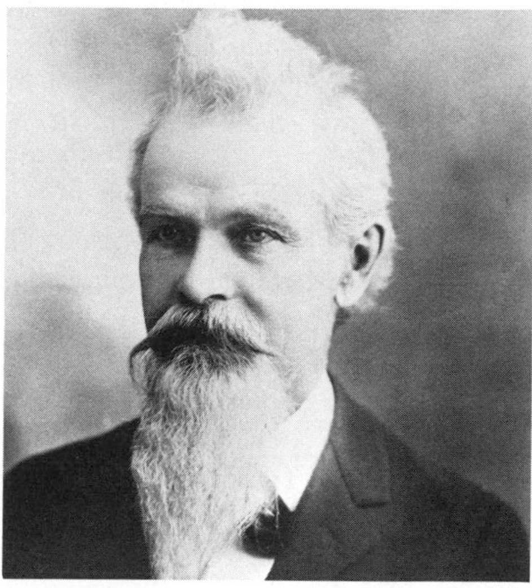

Figure 6. Daniel J. O'Donoghue. *Source:* Public Archives of Canada.

found it necessary to attempt to deflect the threat posed by the Knights of Labor. These intrigues, and the resulting crises that shook the Order to its foundations, are the subject of this chapter.

## O'Donoghue versus Wright

Partisan political argument, as we have already seen, prefaced many of the campaigns of 1886–7, especially in the hotbed of partyism, Toronto. The strength of independent labor politics swept aside much of this debate, at least for the immediate moment. But even alongside the unity of the electoral struggles, factions competed for the control of the Ontario Order. O'Donoghue and "the boys from 2305" built the early Knights of Labor into an effective political apparatus and tied themselves securely to the Grit wagon of Oliver Mowat and Edward Blake. This "Reform" leadership was unopposed, in any meaningful sense, until the spring of 1886, when A. W. Wright returned to the Toronto working-class world and struck the first blow in what would prove a long and divisive contest. Against O'Donoghue's opposition Wright's successful initiative culminated in the creation of a distinct Toronto DA, No. 125, created 17 May 1886 in the midst of the street railway battle. In the process, according to O'Donoghue, he had threatened the carefully constructed balance of Knights of Labor and trade union forces in the local Trades and Labor Council and in the Dominion Trades and Labor Congress, securing for himself a political platform upon which to operate. Wright had thus effected a major coup, terminating O'Donoghue's backroom control of the Toronto Assemblies, previously exercised through the Irish printer's intimate relationship with Powderly. A Tory had taken round one, stealing some of the political thunder of the once all-powerful Grit triumvirate of O'Donoghue, Alf Jury, and Charles March.[2]

In the aftermath of the elections of 1886–7 O'Donoghue and Wright clashed again as a series of acrimonious post mortems led to a rapid revival of political conflict within the upper echelons of the Toronto Knights of Labor leadership. A highly public battle proceeded as each labor advocate questioned the other's role in the campaigns, O'Donoghue utilizing the pages of his *Labor Record* and Wright carrying on the fray in the *Canadian Labor Reformer*. As both men had been far from disinterested in the fortunes of their parties, O'Donoghue being especially vocal in his support for the St. Catharines' "Reform" workingman's candidate William Garson and Wright's fiasco in West Lambton being much publicized, there was a great deal of mud to be slung. The flavor of the exchange was exemplified in O'Donoghue's effort to paint Wright as an unprincipled opportunist: "During all these years I have met, more than once, with the sometimes open and other times covert hostility of a class of transparent frauds – cunning, conniving and unscrupulous fellows – who had floated into the ranks of organized labor for every purpose other than that of doing an honest part in practically improving the general condition of the working classes." The contents of this O'Donoghue–Wright fracas and victory in it, which escaped both, were far less important than the overall impression that it left. Both sides appeared exposed, and in the wake of the 1886–7 defeats workingmen could only wonder if independent labor politics had merely been an illusion manipulated by party hacks. This was a serious problem for, as the Knights began to wane in strength, a retreat into political quiescence and a full-scale surrender to the established party machines was an immediate danger. In Toronto the Tories did all they could to encourage this by running the ever-popular Orange printer, "Sentinel" Clarke in the mayoralty race. With Clarke's smashing victory over the Howland-endorsed candidate, Elias Rogers, politics in Toronto appeared to have returned to normal.[3]

Similar acrimony erupted among St. Thomas Knights of Labor. George Wrigley, editor of the *Canada Labor Courier*, experienced a falling-out with A. B. Ingram, whom he had originally supported. During the federal campaign he had blasted Ingram's open support of the Conservative Party and devoted column after column to accusations that Ingram had repudiated his labor stance. These vicious attacks led the Knights to rally to Ingram's support, and motions attesting to his qualities as a gentleman and a true Knight were adopted; the Tory brakeman had come out ahead. In June 1887 the *Labor Courier* ceased publishing, largely due to DA 138's demand for a public apology from Wrigley stating that he had wronged Ingram and done a great injury to organized labor. Wrigley refused to bend to this ultimatum and, unable to survive what must have been a virtual boycott of his newspaper, found himself and the *Courier* he edited busted. He was also suspended from the Order for six months.[4]

## Home Rule

Into the fissures created by such internecine warfare seeped the national question, as Ontario's Knights of Labor began to question their relationship to the American-based Order and to work their way out of political failure through the provision for a special Canadian Knights of Labor lobbying body that could be heard in Ottawa. Internationalist sentiment has been particularly evident in the history of the Canadian movement. The immigrant origins of the Canadian working class and the binational labor market in which Canadians worked provided a material basis for this ideal.[5] The reform message of the Knights of Labor reflected a similar commitment to the unity of workers of all colors, creeds, sexes, and nations. The Knights actually institutionally implemented this idea to a previously unmatched degree by organizing LAs in England, Scotland, Ireland, Belgium, France, Australia, and New Zealand as well as in Canada.[6] Only the First International itself had extended further.

Canadian workers, however, encountered some difficulties with the international office on occasion.[7] This most often reflected dissatisfaction with various elements of the often inadequate Knights of Labor bureaucracy. Hamilton Knights, for example, wrote numerous letters of complaint to Powderly in late 1882 about Philadelphia's failure to send supplies, charters, commissions, and so on. These complaints were echoed by other Ontario Knights at various times. Discontent first surfaced at the 1884 General Assembly when a Montreal motion for the formation of a Canadian Dominion Assembly was recorded.[8] The following spring Hamilton Knights followed this up. The degree to which this movement was tied to the partisan intrigues of "rascals" such as E. P. Morgan remains unclear, but as early as 1885 there was talk of the creation of a new Order. As we have already noted, Powderly himself wondered aloud, in a letter to O'Donoghue, whether the solid Knights of Hamilton had been poisoned.[9]

Later DMW W. J. Vale of DA 61 warned Powderly that "the time has arrived for the various LAs in Canada to have 'Home Rule.'" The problem as Vale saw it was that a separate Canadian General Assembly "would be a violation of the fundamental principles of the Order, which prescribes for one GA on each of the five continents." Vale's solution was a "Territorial District" for Canada which "should have absolute control over the LAs in the Dominion the same as the present GA."[10] He suggested that a poll of Canadian LAs should decide the issue.

O'Donoghue warned Powderly about this movement in August: "Until reading this you were totally ignorant, doubtless that we in Canada who are of the order, have been and are suffering under foreign tyranny. It was news to me when I read this document." Sparing no angry epithets, he denounced the Hamilton nationalists: "These wiseacre sucklings evidently forgot that they should know no dividing lines either as to nation, creed or colour. There is a class of addle-pated people in this world who are nothing if not big frogs in their own little puddles. These fellows of Hamilton want absolute control!! Well God help the chances of the Order in Canada, should such a thing come to pass." Toronto, he added, was bitterly opposed.[11]

Powderly, too, took the threat seriously. He penned an instant response in the form of a personal note to O'Donoghue and a formal letter to be used as the Toronto Knight saw fit. The letter was an eloquent attack on divisiveness in the Order: "Home rule! These words in the Knights of Labor are saddening, sickening. They indicate that the index on the dial of progress has halted, stopped . . . This will end in confusion for the toiler and joy for the oppressor." Closing with a long Irish parable about a wise priest and the weather, Powderly insisted on international unity.[12] O'Donoghue, after visiting Hamilton, reassured Powderly that "the rank and file" had been "going it blind" and now they had "awakened to the fact that some *schemer* was getting his oar in 'to cover past disappointment.'"[13]

The fall 1885 Hamilton General Assembly solved this particular surge of Canadian nationalism by initiating a Canadian Supply Depot at Hamilton under the control of D. A. Gibson, prominent bricklayers' leader in DA 61. Nationalism, forced into the background by the excitement of 1886, re-emerged in the spring of 1887 and was subsequently used as a political ploy in the skillful hands of A. W. Wright. The movement began in January 1887 when DA 138 meeting in London formed a committee to consider the formation of a Dominion Assembly independent of the General Assembly. Only fraternal relations would remain between the new Dominion Assembly and the General Assembly, they asserted, "as is done in all beneficial societies."[14] O'Donoghue again warned Powderly of the existence of this separatist thrust in a characteristic way, blaming anti-Catholic sentiment, claiming that "the enemies of our Order are again at work trying to get up a severance of our connection with the Order in the U.S."[15] The major impetus behind DA 138's proposal once more concerned the inefficiency of the Philadelphia headquarters. Later that same month O'Donoghue urged Powderly to respond favorably to a DA 125 request for financial aid. This would allow him.

> to be in a position to show that Canada, where deserving, is treated just would [sic] any state of the Union under like circumstances. You know I have no doubts on the matter myself, but I desire to checkmate the "Independent Order in Canada" movement which is being worked vigorously by some although very quietly. I don't know who began it this time, but the circular was issued from Guelph I believe.[16]

O'Donoghue did not gain this particular advantage because the General Executive Board refused DA 125's request.

The national issue regained prominence in the summer of 1887. DA 138 again passed a resolution urging the creation of a Canadian General Assembly.[17] Inadvertently, Powderly furthered their cause when he unthinkingly issued a circular to the Order at large calling on Knights everywhere to celebrate the Fourth of July. Canadian Knights responded with understandable annoyance at this "unconscious neglect of the members situated north of your much favored country," as Hamilton's Albert Cross delicately phrased it. Cross reiterated yet again that "feeling was growing in Canada that the GEB was for the US only and that if members in Canada want their needs attended to they will have to have a Canadian GEB and Canadian Legislative Committee etc." Cross's conclusions were familiar but his rationale was not. He criticized Powderly for transgressing important Knights' principles; by cavalierly slighting Canadian members, argued Cross, "the bonds of unity between the workers of the world" could only be weakened.[18]

A chastened Powderly issued a new circular later that summer to the Canadian Order. In it he claimed to have consulted "several Canadian brothers on what day they would prefer to hold meetings and demonstrations." Their answer, he instructed the Order, was 28 September.[19] As was often the case Powderly appears simply to have been covering his earlier gaffe. A call for 28 September dated on 29 August was not destined to have much effect. Moreover, the date appears to have been chosen simply on the basis that the Hamilton Knights had previously invited Powderly to speak in the Ambitious City on that day. DA 61 certainly kept the pressure on him, although he ultimately canceled his appearance. James Henigan wrote of a "good deal of dissatisfaction of late among the members of the Order in Canada," and then inadvertently added a little to the history of the Home Rule movement: "A few months ago our District received a communication from DA 138 [St. Thomas] stating that a meeting had been called by them of delegates from all the Canadian Districts to take into consideration the propriety of taking some active steps to secure from the GEB that recognition which it is claimed the Canadian members have been deprived."[20]

Meanwhile in Toronto the Home Rule issue also remained at the center of Knights' politics. DA 125 discussed it throughout August, finally deciding in favor.[21] In mid-September the MW of True LA 9848, Edward Cannon, added to Powderly's worries: "There is a program now working in Canada to have a General Assembly for Canada almost independent of the GA of America . . . The principal advocate in DA 125 is the editor of the Canadian Labor Reformer. I hope he is free from selfishness! The question will come up in the next GA. The matter in DA 125 has not been laid before the LAs."[22] Cannon was the first to identify A. W. Wright as a leader of this scheme; having succeeded in his power bid in Toronto through the creation of a DA, "Old Alec" was apparently aiming his sights on bigger prey. About one week later District Recording Secretary W. L. Taylor wrote to Powderly to register DA 125's formal complaint against his August circular, complaining that it was impossible for the Toronto Knights to celebrate on 28 September owing to an earlier DA decision to recognize Labor Day. Moreover, he added, Toronto's General Assembly representatives had been instructed to seek access to Powderly's correspondence "with several Canadian brothers" on the question, as DA 125 had never been consulted.[23] The entire national issue aroused interest throughout Ontario, and a Tillsonburg Knight drew it to the general attention of the Order in a letter to the *Journal of United Labor:*

> The all-absorbing topic of discussion here is, of course, "Home Rule," or the formation of a provincial assembly, partaking of the nature of a state assembly, with a Canadian Executive Board, and for the retention of a certain portion of the funds for legislative purposes, but acting in conjunction with the GEB. The project is meeting with much favour, and the matter will in all possibility come before the GA.[24]

On 30 September Knights from all over Ontario met at a Toronto convention called by DA 125's Sam McNab and A. W. Wright to discuss Home Rule. This resulted in a resolution for the 1887 General Assembly which called for the formation of a "Dominion Assembly." This body would be chartered by the General Assembly and would ultimately be under its direction, but would have "exclusive control over all members within its jurisdiction" and would "collect all moneys, levy all assessments and distribute all supplies in Canada." Moreover "every effort should be made to preserve the cordial relations at present existing between the Order in Canada and the Order in the US."[25] A second successful motion called on the General Assembly to provide Canada with "a Legislative Committee of three members from each Province" who would then "appoint one of their members to attend each session of the Dominion House of Commons" to protect labor interests.[26] This latter thrust, no doubt a recognition that to overcome the political failures of 1886–7 required special attention to the particular Canadian context, seemed more than reasonable, but in the politically charged atmosphere of the post-1886 period it would end up causing more difficulties than it solved.

Powderly had already had considerable warning about Home Rule but received further encouragement from O'Donoghue to resist any such movement. O'Donoghue described the Toronto meeting as "a convention of the discontented (and I am pretty certain of emissaries of our political parties who desire to prevent unity in our ranks at political elections)." If that was not sufficient to discredit the movement, he charged that: "The action of calling a convention was a 'put up job' as the subject was never submitted to all the Local Assemblies in DA 125. All the A's in Toronto who had the subject argued before them *in its true light* declared against this attempt at drawing the *national* line . . . It would take pages to illustrate the *crookedness* under which this scheme has been worked up." As usual, O'Donoghue played on Powderly's Irish Catholic loyalty by at least partially confusing the "national" issue with religious bigotry.[27] In addition Toronto Excelsior LA 2305 and Port Dalhousie Harbour LA 2513 both sent letters to the *Journal of United Labor* opposing the scheme.[28]

Powderly arrived in Minneapolis for the 1887 General Assembly fully cognizant of the threatened Canadian secession. Drawing first blood in his Annual Report, he immediately coopted the Canadian demands. First, he engaged in some careful flattery crediting the Canadian Order with "managing their own affairs" so well that they caused less trouble for the Board "than the smallest state in the Union." Then Powderly launched his counter-proposal, urging the creation of two Provincial Assemblies for Ontario and Quebec and a distinct Canadian Legislative Committee to scrutinize the politicians in Ottawa and lobby for labor legislation. A rhetorical plea for solidarity closed his telling speech:

> In any event there can be but one GA of the Knights of Labor in America. Every artery and nerve of this great organization on this continent must work in harmony. There must be no divisions. No matter if in the States we have allowed too much of our troubles to go to the outside world. The needs of the hour require at our hands an observance of the maxim: We must tolerate each other or else tolerate the common enemy.[29]

Powderly's acumen carried the day. When the Assembly's Committee on Legislation came to report on DA 61's and DA 125's two joint motions regarding a Canadian General Assembly and a Canadian Legislative Committee, the former was simply referred to the General Executive Board where it was tabled and the latter was approved, with the GMW charged to make the appointments.

## The Legislative Committee and the rise of Wright

O'Donoghue subsequently offered his enthusiastic congratulations to Powderly on his victory, and immediately began urging him to proceed to appoint a Canadian Legislative Committee which, he argued, "if composed of the *right* material, can accomplish a great deal more in our interest than can be accomplished in Washington." He also made it clear that Wright would no longer be allowed to control DA 125. O'Donoghue had ended his silence and would now sit as an LA 2305 representative. Wright, "*no friend of Powderly* and the *actual* 'head and snout' of the secession movement," according to O'Donoghue, also recognized that their next major battle would be for control of the Legislative Committee.[30]

O'Donoghue, however, still held the inside track on providing Powderly with Canadian advice. In late November the GMW consulted his trusted Toronto sergeant, asking him for "a key to all these problems so that I may have a little more knowledge of the situation." Before consulting O'Donoghue, Powderly had already recognized the need for a balanced committee respectful of geography and religion. O'Donoghue responded immediately. He ran down Powderly's list of candidates with incisive personal opinions of each. His final recommendations were:

> If the Parliamentary Committee is to be composed of *three* – *one* from the Province of Quebec and two from the Province of Ontario – I advise the appointment of Jury of Toronto, Collis of Hamilton, and Redmond of Montreal – an Agnostic, a Protestant, and a Catholic.
>
> If the Parliamentary Committee is to be composed of *four* – *one* from Quebec and *three* from Ontario, then I advise Little of the city of Quebec, Jury, Collis and March – *two* Protestants, one Catholic and an Agnostic.
>
> If I considered nothing but the best men for this committee and in the interest of the Order pure and simple, I would name Jury, March and Collis.

Powderly accepted O'Donoghue's first suggestion and appointed Jury, Collis, and Redmond, worrying only that "if they kill themselves on religious grounds, they will in all events be separated in death for they will have to go to different planting spots."[31]

O'Donoghue's seeming triumph in personally choosing the Canadian Legislative Committee, however, was destined to be only a Pyrrhic victory.

Powderly, in his original inquiry, had suggested Wright as a possible member, as "being an enemy, I furnish him with work, not on the principle that the devil finds work for idle hands but that I find work for the devil to do." O'Donoghue attacked this idea vigorously:

In justice to Wright I must say that he is not a *personal* enemy of Powderly in direct terms; but he is *anarchistic* in some degree in his editorials in *his paper*, the *Labor Reformer.* He never has a kind word for the General Ex. Board, and of this you are chairman. He is and was one of the strongest connivers at securing a *split* in the Order by advocating and promoting the scheme for an Independent Order of the K. of L. in Canada. Of this we hear but little now however.

No doubt fearing that his antagonism to Wright might appear personal, O'Donoghue then made a fatal error. After imploring Powderly, "*Don't put Wright on this Committee*," he added, "if there is to be a General Lecturer for Canada *let it be* Bro. A. W. Wright." This would be "'making work – and plenty of it – for the *Devil* to do.'" This gratuitous suggestion would haunt O'Donoghue in the near future.[32]

Before those events unfolded, Powderly and O'Donoghue had to weather an unpredicted storm of protest about their arbitrary Legislative Committee appointments. The first complaint came from St. Thomas DA 138 in late January, when it passed a resolution at its annual meeting that before any appointments to the Legislative Committee be made the several Districts in Canada should be polled. Powderly quickly informed them that it was too late and, adopting an apologetic tone, explained that consultation with the various DAs would have taken too long. In future if Ontario would form a Provincial Assembly then he would have an appropriate body to consult. DA 138 eventually backed off, claiming no prior knowledge of Powderly's appointments: "We have no objections to the Brothers whom you appointed and have no sympathy with the politicians' objections that have been raised."[33] That may or may not have been the case, but DA 138's initial resolution definitely detonated a wave of controversy. Toronto DA 125 passed a motion condemning the appointments as arbitrary and demanding that all Canadian Legislative Committee appointments in future be made in consultation "with the duly elected authorities and officers of the several Canadian Districts."[34] Powderly ignored this particular protest, leveled at him by A. W. Wright.

Meanwhile other Canadian Districts rallied to the new Legislative Committee's support. Hamilton DA 61 endorsed the appointment in mid-February. J. T. Carey, an important St. Catharines Knights leader, also endorsed the committee, reassuring Powderly that only the politicians objected. Hamilton's George Collis, one of the Legislative Committee members, made the same accusation, charging that the objections were "actuated by political motives."[35]

Powderly considered polling the Canadian order in order to gain support for his choices but was dissuaded when Collis pointed out that the delay would prevent the Committee from functioning. This, Collis added, was precisely the opposition's aim. He argued that the kickers' actions "showed that they have not laid aside their Political Party leanings" and while charging the Legislative Committee "with being Grits, they are evidently supporters of the present administration." "Supporters," he added, "who have never shown any inclination to introduce any measures of benefit for the toilers."[36]

The new Legislative Committee met in Toronto on 14 January and chose Jury as chairman and Redmond as secretary. They decided to send the former to Ottawa for the parliamentary session and identified a Factory Act, a Workshops Regulation Act, and a Bureau of Labour Statistics as their major lobbying goals. In addition, the committee pledged itself to return as much as possible for the expense, promising to be as economical as possible.[37] Jury apparently fulfilled these committee aims and did an excellent job. St. Catharines' J. T. Carey, for example, reported that:

> We are in a fair way of getting some good legislation for the sailors and railroad men from Parliament this session. I was in Ottawa this spring and think Bro. Jury is the best man that could have been found in the whole Dominion for the position he held no matter what the kickers say.

O'Donoghue, perhaps a less reliable commentator given his closeness to Jury, described the chairman of the Legislative Committee in action:

> The presence in Ottawa of Bro. Jury will be of inestimable value to the labor cause in Canada. He is laying a foundation for good legislation in the future . . . He is the most indefatigable worker I ever knew. From early morning until the House adjourns, let it be at midnight – or in the "sma we hours" of the morning, Jury is to be found either in the Press Gallery or in the Library hunting up materials for his purpose. Since the House met he has had several interviews with John A. Macdonald as well as with several of his colleagues, and all on subjects of vital importance to the wage-earners of Canada . . . No better choice than Jury could have been made.[38]

That O'Donoghue and Jury were well pleased with the results of the session was quite evident in the haste with which the latter produced his Legislative Committee Report. This, with Powderly's permission, was printed in Toronto and circulated "to the Canadian Assemblies (D.A. & L.A.) . . . so that they may realize if possible how badly we require a radical change in the manner of exercising our franchise – realize, if they can, that Labor has few if any *honest* friends or advocates in the present ranks of Political parties in

Canada." Powderly also approved the document heartily.[39] He suggested that it be sent to every MP as well as to all Canadian LAs because "by that means you will give them to understand that someone is taking an interest in them and they will be more likely to take an interest in that somebody hereafter." Powderly also endorsed the report as "a business-like document" which proved the "necessity for the continuation of such a committee." He felt vindicated in his choices for the Legislative Committee, and assessed the lobbying efforts a success.[40]

Having weathered the storm of the Home Rule movement and now in effective control of the Canadian Legislative Committee, "the boys from 2305" appeared to be back on top. But A. W. Wright had not been inactive in this period. In January DA 125 had endorsed him for both a lecturer's position and as examining organizer for Ontario, a post for which O'Donoghue was privately promoting Charles March. In July Wright wrote directly to Powderly in quest of his organizer's commission, which he had still not received. Powderly responded positively and followed up with the more important offer of a position of lecturer under the Educational Fund.[41]

O'Donoghue, undoubtedly, saw the writing on the wall, but throughout 1888 he continued to issue warnings, Cassandralike, to Powderly. His initial reaction was terse and begrudging: "Bro. Wright is a fluent speaker and a shrewd man, and should make his mark as a lecturer – that is, if he is 'in the cause' because of its mission and its principles, and not for A. W. Wright. Time will unravel which and we shall see."[42]

Wright attended the 1888 Indianapolis General Assembly and there completed his coup. Not only did he win election to the General Executive Board but he also managed to win Powderly's trust. In addition, at Wright's suggestion, the Canadian General Assembly representatives named the new Legislative Committee and, significantly, no member of the previous group was reappointed. Instead they named three of their own number, led by a notable Conservative partisan, Uxbridge journalist R. R. Elliot. This decision was not taken openly, and it appears not to have been communicated even to Powderly until early December when A. W. Wright promulgated the act well after the event.[43]

Even before hearing of the Legislative Committee appointments, O'Donoghue had written Powderly a sardonic congratulatory note. After expressing pleasure that the GMW "now had an immediate adviser from Canada," he promised to trouble him "very rarely in the future."[44] Later O'Donoghue and the DA 125 Executive Board registered their discontent with the Legislative Committee appointment and urged Powderly to reconsider. They did not insist on the entire previous committee but did press for Alfred Jury whom they asserted had served the entire Order well "by reason of his long experience in Labor Legislation, his undoubted honesty and fealty to labor's interests, together with the fact that much of his work of last year [remains] only partially done." Powderly ignored this plea and on 30 December notified Hayes to finalize the appointments of Elliot's colleagues, St. Catharines' printer William R. James and Montreal shoemaker Oliver D. Benoit.[45]

Two major battles were brewing in the Order's partisan warfare. The first revolved around the politics of Elliot's Legislative Committee and thus only indirectly touched Wright. The second, however, focused specifically on Wright and his position as lecturer under the Education Fund.

J. T. Carey presaged the first encounter in late spring 1889 after his first exposure to Ottawa as a lobbyist for the TLC. Disgusted with political dealings in the nation's capital, Carey attacked those self-serving Knights whom he encountered there. Although he named only Blackeby, Helbronner, Gibson, and Carson of the Royal Commission on the Relations of Labor and Capital, time would make clear that R. R. Elliot was also high on his list of enemies of the Order. Carey's good friend O'Donoghue complained in May that Elliot's behavior in Ottawa had not converted any of his critics and that labor had "been *robbed* of our right to do certain lawful things." This was an allusion to the complex anticombines law that Clarke Wallace had introduced. This Act, which posed as a populist measure and at first glance appeared to be in the interests of the consumer, actually passed in an amended form that endangered the protection won by labor under the Trade Union Act of 1872 and the various Criminal Law Amendment Acts which followed in the mid-1870s. O'Donoghue pointed out that while this occurred, "Bro. Elliot and Co. . . . were as dumb as oysters" and Wright "whether through a misunderstanding of the case or worse" actually "helped in the work." Later that summer O'Donoghue wrote again on the subject, seeking the Canadian Legislative Committee's Report for the year and simultaneously suggesting that as an economy measure Powderly transform the Knights' lobbying body into a joint committee with the TLC.[46]

O'Donoghue further increased the pressure on Powderly when DA 125 formally opposed the reappointment of Elliot. They accused him of "general neglect" and specified his opposition to the Order's wishes regarding Dickerson's Bill concerning benevolent societies. Moreover they embraced a modified version of O'Donoghue's scheme, proposing that Powderly choose the Knights' Committee from that of the TLC but specifying that Carey chair the body. Quebec's Edward Little registered a similar protest, arguing that Elliot's report was "*a failure* as a labour report, the essence of Conservatism from the first line to the last," and drew Powderly's attention to "how *some of our would-be Labour Reformers* abuse their position by *being Partisan.*"[47]

After the dust had settled in the new year Elliot was back in place in Ottawa, although for a much briefer stay. Again his reinstatement appears to have been accomplished through Wright's influence.[48] There can be little question that by this time Powderly knew the political implications of his alliance with Wright and Elliot. Jury, for example, had protested against Elliot's report as "a partizan document written in the interest of the Tory party the natural enemies of freedom and the workingman." He added that he was "tired of seeing this Order made the tail of the Tory party." Personal commitment to Wright represented at least a partial explanation of Powderly's position. The extent of this commitment became abundantly clear in the other major battle of 1889.[49]

Powderly's Educational Fund developed into one of his greatest debacles. Lecturers sent out into the field in the summer of 1888 turned out to be, on the whole, con men after a fast buck. The two Canadians had a mixed record at best. A. T. Lepine appears to have embezzled the money. Of the $500 he received as a lecturer, he accounted for only about $100. When pushed for more details, he lapsed into embarrassed silence. Privately, Powderly denounced him as a thief: "I want to work in the Lepine *steal* for that fellow had not done anything and all of Quebec denounces him as vigorously now as they recommended him before." Publicly, in his Report to the Order on the Educational Fund, Powderly simply explained that "proceedings are now pending against him for misappropriating this sum."[50] The case of A. W. Wright proved more complicated.

Toronto's Excelsior LA 2305, or more specifically a committee of three from LA 2305 (O'Donoghue, Jury, and Charles Miller) filed a complaint with Powderly and DA 125 against Wright in late October 1887. They found Powderly's accounting to the Order "totally deficient" as far as Wright was concerned and expressed their unqualified disapproval of the lecturer's $1,100 expenditure; they also claimed Wright had canceled many engagements, to the detriment of the Order. In a private letter O'Donoghue posed it all to Powderly slightly more charitably: "To my mind the best that can be said, judging by Canadian experience of the Education scheme is that your idea thereof was a very good one and your honesty of purpose unquestionable. Barefaced cupidity, coupled with laziness, supineness or something akin, thwarted the benefits to be derived from the *idea*, and, in the minds of some, threw a doubt upon the other."[51]

Wright could not avoid such a frontal attack, and with Powderly's complete cooperation he mounted a brutal and crushing defense. Wright first questioned his opponents' tactics, implying that their unwillingness to press formal charges proved the weakness of their case, their moral bankruptcy and, more seriously, deprived him of a formal rebuttal. He then alleged that they were in the Order only "to promote their own petty personal ambitions" and that they resorted to any means "for the purpose of stabbing anyone whom they believed inimical to their schemes." Rising to his polemical best, he described their charges as "venomous," "a mixture of deliberate falsehoods and treacherous insinuations." O'Donoghue and Jury he described as "bitter and unscrupulous enemies of mine" and accused them of controlling and dominating the Local. Miller he dismissed as "a pliant convenient instrument in the hands of the others." The details of their charges he totally ignored.[52]

The "boys from 2305" and Excelsior Assembly itself did not retire from the field so easily. Charles Miller, infuriated by Wright's disdainful dismissal of him, denounced him to John Hayes as a "moral assassin" and accused him of a "deliberate lie." After hurling "this malicious slander back into the teeth of the 'thing' that made it," he expressed his "contempt and loathing for this creature whose baseness is only equalled by his ability to perform the Dr. Jekyll and Mr. Hyde business, for it is not so long ago since this man was arrayed on the side of Capital against Labour." Miller closed his enraged epistle with a demand for a systematic report of Wright's expenditures, again reiterating that the 31 July report was "woefully insufficient."[53]

Early in the new year an investigatory committee of LA 2305, composed of W. B. Prescott, later the International President of the International Typographical Union for many years, Stewart Lyon, a future editor of the Toronto *Globe*, and prominent labor reformer J. H. Gilmour, condemned Wright for "unknightly language." The committee also charged that he had "wilfully and maliciously penned [his response] with the intention of insulting and misrepresenting the Assembly." His actions were those of "one who prefers to belie and defame by innuendo rather than straightforwardly answer those who criticize the actions of an apparently dilatory servant." The report, however, ended simply with an inquiry to Powderly about what should be done next. Predictably, silence prevailed in Scranton.[54]

Almost two months later Gilmour sent Jury's and O'Donoghue's personal response to Powderly. This 35-page typescript reviewed a great deal of history and flailed away mercilessly at Wright. Countering the charge that the members of LA 2305 had initiated the anti-Wright campaign, O'Donoghue and Jury defended their service in labor's cause throughout the 1870s and 1880s and asked rhetorically, "Where was this man Wright all the time? – looking after the loaves and fishes? Part of the time editing a Political Party newspaper, another time a member of a speculative land-grabbing company; again for years the faithful and trusty Secretary of the Ontario Manufacturers' Association, and after the last of these ceased to pay – presto! he blooms as a full-fledged Knight of Labor within the last few years . . . this man has brains." They pointed to Wright's Tory connections, and depreciated his attendance at party banquets when the work of the Order demanded his presence among Ontario's workingmen and women. Finally, they expressed regret at Wright's recent promotion to the General Executive Board. "But one thing is very certain," they concluded, "and that is that if he had not been provided for by the Order he would be doing as he is doing now – living on his wits." In light of all of this, O'Donoghue and Jury wondered, why had Powderly not brought their accusations against Wright before the entire General Executive Board? To this query, Powderly replied indignantly that they had not previously specified this course, but he assured Gilmour that he would now do so. A full four months later Powderly told Gilmour to refrain from writing to him further on the entire matter and instructed him to seek any further information directly from Wright. Nearly one year later Gilmour tried again, writing to Powderly to inform him that Wright had never supplied LA 2305 with the required financial information and to inquire into the final dispositions of A. T. Lepine's case. Powderly did not respond but instead instructed John Hayes to do so. Hayes's answer that Lepine should be charged by his own LA and that Wright had never been investigated brought one final protest from LA 2305.[55]

These depressing details demand our attention because they explain much about the Knights' precipitous decline in Toronto and throughout Ontario. The internecine warfare at the summit of the Order greatly affected the morale of the Knights' rank and file. One small example of this was a resolution from David Carey of Toronto's LA 5792. After noting that labor's interests had been seriously damaged by public partisan involvements of various Knights of Labor leaders, Carey resolved that the DA should cancel the credentials of any delegate who worked in any way for either the Conservative or Reform parties. Furthermore, the MW of the member's LA should enter a charge of conduct unbecoming a Knight and if guilty the member should receive a five-year suspension from the Order. Powderly promised to take this measure to the General Executive Board for discussion. If he did so, it led to no action. Nevertheless, it is indicative of the hostility that partisan intrigue was generating among rank-and-file-Knights.[56] Politically, there can be little doubt that Wright and Elliot did indeed successfully deflect the lobbying activities of the Order away from the virulent critiques of the Macdonald government's inactivity that had informed the first Knights' Legislative Committee report.

The major focus of labor lobbying also had shifted in the process from the

Knights' Legislative Committee to the TLC. Although this initially meant little, as most TLC leaders were also Knights, it would have damaging long-term effects on the Order's position in Canada. In effect, the Knights of Labor had, through Wright's partisan maneuvers, allowed itself to be displaced as labor's major political voice. If this was not totally true by 1890 when Elliot at least put in a token appearance at Ottawa, it certainly became the case thereafter with the disbanding of the Canadian Order's Legislative Committee.

The Canadian General Assembly delegates in 1890 did recommend a Legislative Committee of J. T. Carey, Côté, and an additional member to be nominated by A. W. Wright. This strategy was endorsed by Quebec's LA 10061, although they substituted Patrick Jobin for Côté. It also received O'Donoghue's fervid support. Nevertheless the Committee was not named for 1891, although DA 125 protested vigorously against this inaction. Their protests were joined by those of LA 2305 when Powderly tried to reassure the Toronto Knights by claiming that Wright could attend to such matters for the Order.[57] The "boys from 2305" did win a minor personal victory over Wright's ally Elliot in 1890. At the fall TLC meeting he was elected Secretary for the coming term but, because his credentials had been challenged by his own Uxbridge DA 236, a motion was passed to make his office conditional on an investigation. Wright tried valiantly to enlist Powderly's support in this case but the GMW wisely refused to intervene. Elliot consequently did not hold office.[58]

That fall, despite predictions that they would never dare to visit Toronto, the General Executive Board met in Hogtown. It convened on DA 125's request but it also hoped, as John Hayes put it, "to straighten out some of the stories that have been reported to that DA." Powderly and the Board weathered the storm and retained Toronto's loyalty, although not without facing some difficult meetings. As Powderly explained, "We have been kept well employed since coming here. O'Donoghue, Jury and Gilmour of 2305 have propounded no less than 500 questions. We have held a meeting of the entire Order here and great good was done." This visit to Toronto ended DA 125's role in the Order's infighting, but in securing A. W. Wright in a position of authority it linked the course of Ontario's Knights of Labor with the leadership revolt of 1893–4 in which Powderly was finally displaced as GMW.[59]

## International intrigues

It is difficult to untangle the various strands of the factional alliances emerging in the early 1890s, culminating in the Hayes–Sovereign–DeLeon coup, for no American historian has actually probed carefully the intimate history of the Knights of Labor in these last days of defeat. Here we limit ourselves to Wright's role and to the effects of the Palace revolt on the Order in Ontario. A. W. Wright became the central figure almost by default. It is clear that forces antagonistic to Powderly had been building up strength for a number of years. Factional struggles had figured increasingly in the Order after 1886. Toronto Knights, for example, had earlier taken a prominent role in providing Powderly and the General Executive Board with the rationale for the expulsion of T. B. Barry, one of the GMW's leading opponents. In 1893, however, the alienation of former key ally John Hayes proved too strong for the Powderly forces.[60]

As Wright weathered the storm arising out of Toronto in 1889 he assumed editorial responsibility for the *Journal of the Knights of Labor*, a post that would at once strengthen his hand with Powderly and lay him open to abuse. Even an apparent ally like Tom O'Reilly, once a traveling companion of Wright's and another Powderly loyalist, turned against him. At issue were Alec's slovenly work habits and cavalier handling of the *Journal*. As early as October 1890, the Irishman let it be known that he disapproved of Wright being assigned to any position of importance. "A. W. struts around in borrowed glory and does absolutely nothing," he informed Powderly, adding in another communication that, "He is either indolent or doesn't care a damn as long as he gets his money by doing as little as possible for it." O'Reilly attacked the editor's persistent lies and claimed that Wright was "of no earthly use to anyone." Frustrated, he once commented that "if every man did as little work as A. W. Wright, and all were as well paid for it there would be no industrial question to solve as everyone would be contented and happy." This all began to matter when John W. Hayes also started to take notice.[61]

Hayes's and Powderly's differences dated from 1892 when the GMW began to question his General Secretary-Treasurer's (GST) handling of the Philadelphia headquarters.[62] This led to the limiting of Hayes's power at the General Assembly in St. Louis where supervision of the *Journal* department was taken out of his hands. Subsequently, and perhaps even before, Hayes too began to gather evidence on Wright's activities. Throughout the early months of 1893 he warned Powderly of his Canadian friend's failure to work. Meanwhile Powderly was warning Wright and O'Reilly to watch Hayes carefully for he was "laying schemes to damn everyone of us." As early as December 1892 Powderly was fearful of Hayes's ability to move against him. "He has got us where the hair is short," he wailed to Wright. But Powderly's faithful Canadian advocate replied with confidence, "He thinks he has, no doubt, but then he won't be the first fellow who lived to find out that you're not always sure of your game when you've treed it."

Hayes was indeed scheming. His motives remain somewhat unclear; al-

Figure 7. A. W. Wright, T. V. Powderly, and John Devlin. *Source:* Powderly Papers, Catholic University, Washington, D.C.

though it seems unlikely that they involved concern for the Order. He continually expressed to Powderly worries about the state of the Order's finances for which he, as GST, was responsible. In late February and early March he warned the GMW that the Order was bordering on bankruptcy. Meanwhile he also prepared charges against Powderly, which he filed with Board member T. B. McGuire. McGuire showed these to Powderly, but then the proceedings were inexplicably dropped. Powderly attempted to gain a copy but failed. His own version, however, specified that he had been charged "with being a defaulter, an embezzler, a traitor, a thief, a conspirator and diverse other things." As we shall see, these charges would all resurface later.[63]

Wright, however, became the first target of party infighting. Powderly sent him to Rochester to disentangle a messy boycott declared by National Trades Assembly (NTA) 231 (clothing workers). The GMW suspected that something ugly lay behind the dispute. Wright, after investigating the situation, ordered the boycott lifted, claiming to have consulted with the Tailors' Assembly's Executive Board. This decision led to immediate protests. James

A. Wright complained to Hayes that Wright had not consulted the NTA Executive and Hayes in turn warned Powderly that "there could be a big fight on account of it." There was. The NTA Executive denied A. W. Wright's claim that he had followed the dictates of members of their Board. Instead they pressed charges against him for "abusing the various offices he holds," "entering into secret compacts with the avowed enemies of the Order," "publishing false statements in the Journal of the Knights of Labor," and "treason to the Order." Powderly simultaneously helped Wright to orchestrate his defense, suggesting he get evidence on the NTA's "bleeding of the manufacturers," and appealed to NTA 231 Recording Secretary Jacobson, "in the interest of the Order," to withdraw the charges. This request was understandably refused. A. W. Wright welcomed the charges because they would allow them to expose "the whole conduct of the boycott and the 'soaking' policy of the NTA." Wright exuded confidence that he would win the case; he still had a copy of the letter from an NTA Board member urging "the raising of the Boycott." He also pressed counter-charges against James A. Wright.[64]

After a series of procedural disputes, the case was finally heard on 25 March.[65] The resulting trial transcript was literally filled with legalistic wrangles. Nevertheless, the hearing cleared Wright. It became clear that the boycott had been lifted at the NTA's request and moreover that they appeared to have accepted monetary payments from employers who had been boycotted previously. Again, the details of this case are less important than its role in furthering the disintegration of relationships among the Knights leadership. After the case's resolution Wright took glee in pressing Hayes on his part in the plot:

> I am informed that on the 21st Feby. ult. you received a letter from the National Executive Board of NTA 231, and which enclosed a copy of a letter written by the National MW, in which a request was made that the boycott on the Rochester Clothing Combine be lifted. I think I am entitled to an explanation as to why this letter was not given to me as Secretary of the GEB, and as to why, when you learned that charges had been preferred against me, you did not inform me that you had received such a letter.

Hayes simply claimed that he had never seen the letter. Meanwhile, Powderly assured his trusted Cincinnati lieutenant Hugh Cavanaugh that Hayes had been responsible for the difficult affair. Moreover the NTA pressed an appeal to the GA against the General Executive Board court's ruling. After all this even Powderly began to tire of Wright, complaining to O'Reilly, "Oh, that Wright were . . ."[66]

Throughout this conflict another crisis had been brewing. In early March Hayes had warned Powderly that the Order held insufficient funds to con-

Figure 8. Knights of Labor office staff in the early 1890s; Tom O'Reilly in center. *Source:* Powderly Papers, Catholic University, Washington, D.C.

tinue to meet its various obligations. He noted that although Wright had instructed him to use the various trust funds that he held, he would not do so without specific authorization from Powderly. When Powderly procrastinated, Hayes pressed again for a decision. In April Powderly outlined the position he found himself in: "If I decide that no money shall be appropriated to the uses of the Order it will cripple the whole institution and I cannot do that." Yet for an additional month he dithered; finally in May he acted. In a strong letter to Hayes, Powderly admitted the "Order was in the throes of dissolution." Therefore, extreme actions were necessary: the General Executive Board must forgo some salary money; the *Journal* must be reduced; some staff must be fired; and most important, the various trust funds of the Order, including the Homestead appeal fund, must be liquidated to pay expenses. For the rest of May and into early June the Order appeared to be confronting its financial problems seriously. The tensions inherent in such belt-tightening, however, simply set off another round of acrimonious internecine warfare.[67]

By mid-June tensions reached a new high as Powderly warned Tom O'Reilly and others to "keep a sharp eye on the doings of Hayes." As the situation worsened Powderly grew less and less willing to tolerate Wright's deficiencies. Complaints about Wright's editorial inadequacies received a warmer reception in Scranton, while Wright's schemes, once a source of profit for Powderly, began to be considered in a new light. Both the *Labor Day Annual* and the Accident Claims Association (discussed in Chapter 5) were going from bad to worse and drawing the attention of Hayes and other enemies. Powderly advised Wright to keep the Accident Claims Association under wraps: "Don't allow a single vestige of that paper to be seen around the office." Writing to O'Reilly he moaned of Wright's indiscretions: "Handing the rope to a fellow with the request to tie it round your neck and pull you up is bad enough but to tie the rope, throw it over the limb, place the end in the hands of Hayes and smile out a willing consent to his pulling the rope is just what that ass did." When Wright's allegiance to a radical class stance surfaced in his public congratulation to the pardoned Chicago Haymarket survivors Powderly had had enough:

> I wish you hadn't committed the Journal to the damned fools who were let out of prison by that vote catcher Altgeld. We will have trouble enough of our own to settle without inviting any and I see many ways in which that will come back to us. Let them paddle their own cause, they tried to swamp ours and if the whole brood had been hanged it would have done no harm to the labour movement. I know the cats I am talking about.[68]

All hell broke loose one week later. On 9 July Hayes charged that Wright was not a member of the Order because Toronto's Victor Hugo LA 7814 had lapsed. The LA's history was complicated, but it seemed that Wright and his brother-in-law R. L. Simpson had been keeping the Assembly alive artificially. Wright was therefore "not a member of the Order" and could "not transfer to any other Assembly until his standing is settled." Hayes explained his actions in a separate letter to Powderly listing a series of additional charges against Wright: his personal accounts were unsatisfactory; he had misused the funds of the Order for both the *Labor Day Annual* and the Accident Claims Association; and the *Journal* was a mess: "I want to say frankly, that if any other business were run as our Journal Department has been run during the last year, the man who did the running would be kicked into the street. . . . If Wright is as careless about the Board and the Journal as about his financial account I am not at all surprised." Hayes concluded: "I am tired of being the scapegoat for other people."[69]

Wright's allies did not leap to his defense. Powderly wrote to O'Reilly that "Hayes had Wright this time" and that before rescuing the Canadian he would "let him wriggle in the net awhile." A few days later he did his best to intensify Wright's "wriggling" by warning: "I have a notion to decide that

Hayes is right and Wright is wrong. You leave your pants down for all of them to slap at when a little precaution would prevent it all."

For the next few weeks Wright's fate remained unclear. He returned to Niagara-on-the-Lake for a two-week holiday that only further angered O'Reilly and Powderly. The latter continued to consider extricating himself from the net of conspiracies he and Wright had hatched and claimed to be "disgusted with Wright." O'Reilly harbored similar sentiments and urged Powderly to recoup his losses by suspending *both* Hayes and Wright: "If you take high-handed measures at once I believe thousands will flock back to the Order, and you will regain the personal friendship of such men as Beaumont, Litchman, Campbell, Schilling, Turner, Bailey and scores of others . . . They all loathe and repudiate Hayes and your ill-requited fealty to him has brought down their ill-will on your head." But the habitually indecisive Powderly proved incapable of such a dramatic move; only Hayes's firing of Madge Eiler, the major Powderly loyalist among the secretaries, helped reunite the Powderly forces.[70] In July and August the GMW consolidated his forces as trusted allies across the United States, men supposedly once linked to Powderly in a conspiratorial group within the Order called the "Governor," accumulated damaging evidence on Hayes.[71]

The General Executive Board met in Philadelphia in mid-August and from that point until the November General Assembly each camp grabbed competitively at what remained of the spoils of office; the entire leadership of the Knights was reduced to a virtual cesspool of chicanery and corruption. Hayes hired spies, while Powderly, Wright, and O'Reilly tried to cover their tracks, dissolving the Accident Claims Association, poring over their letterbooks, and struggling desperately to neutralize such troublesome elements as Colonel Gray, the unscrupulous business agent for the *Labor Day Annual* who would eventually find his way into the Hayes camp. Even Powderly thought this fight unbecoming, and wrote to O'Reilly: "You know it makes a decent man smell to be pissed on by a skunk and though he may kill the skunk the smell remains." The affair wound its way toward a conclusion at a stormy mid-September meeting, with Powderly suspending Hayes from office, naming Hugh Cavanaugh GST and John Devlin acting GMW until the difficulties could be settled at the General Assembly.[72]

The results of the historic General Assembly of 1893 are well known, even if the facts behind the final result are shrouded in obscurity: Hayes forged an alliance cemented in the delegates controlled by himself, James Sovereign of Iowa, and the New York socialists Daniel DeLeon and T. B. McGuire. Powderly, who had the constitutional power to present the nominees for election to the General Executive Board refused to endorse men acceptable to this odd conglomeration and as a result he resigned. James Sovereign, head of the so-called western agrarians, assumed the role of GMW. Devlin, Wright, and Powderly were cleared of all the charges of financial malfeasance, but control of the Knights of Labor had eluded them. The unholy alliance of careerist bureaucrats, western radicals, and eastern socialists broke down after the 1894 New Orleans General Assembly as Sovereign reneged on his promise to give the socialists editorial control of the *Journal of the Knights of Labor*. The eastern faction then promptly left the Order to set up a rival Assembly in New York. After fourteen years, then, the long tenure of the GMW had come to an end. No one felt the blow more than A. W. Wright.[73]

Indeed, in the aftermath of the 1893 coup three major defenses of the old Order emerged. Wright penned a "Manifesto" and a "Report to DA 125," while Powderly published a "Statement." Wright's Manifesto was intended as the core document in a general attempt to rebuild the Powderly forces for a power bid at the 1894 General Assembly. The now-familiar tensions resurfaced as Wright procrastinated for weeks. O'Reilly's fury grew, especially as he blamed Wright "for a great deal of what has happened during the past four weeks." Wright's Manifesto was finally completed in late December and mailed to loyal contacts throughout the Order. Arguing that "the official record gives no intelligible idea of what was done" at the Philadelphia General Assembly, the Manifesto then went on to identify Hayes's charges against Devlin, Wright, and Powderly. It contended that after five days of debate the Finance Committee reported "absolutely no foundations for the imputations of dishonesty against the three Brothers named." Moreover, the only detail of Hayes's accusations containing an element of truth concerned the *Labor Day Annual*, which Powderly and Wright had been quite public about. Wright's Manifesto explained further that "so complete was the refutation of the charges of personal dishonesty that the GST was compelled to confess on the floor of the GA . . . that there was absolutely no truth in them." Up to this point Wright had simply reported the proceedings, but here the editorializing began. As Hayes had admitted making false charges, Wright asserted, he should have been expelled. Instead the General Assembly returned him to office. "How?" Wright asked rhetorically, answering: "from the beginning of the session a faction composed of the personal friends and followers of the GST began to hold caucuses." This in turn led to a lengthy filibuster by these "unscrupulous obstructionists." After the pro-Powderly majority had departed deals were made in the caucus that led to Hayes's reelection. Powderly, too, won reelection but the caucus decided to force an unfriendly General Executive Board on him. With a deadlock on this issue Powderly eventually offered his resignation, which was still refused by a majority. But when the stalemate remained, he finally prevailed upon his friends to drop their support and allow the General Assembly to accept his departure from office. The Assembly then chose Sovereign. The Manifesto closed with a general appeal to the Order to consider carefully its delegates to the next Assembly in order to right the wrongs done in 1893. Wright's Report to DA 125 was essentially a longer version of this Manifesto minus the political pitch at the end. The scheme to win control of the 1894 General Assembly received considerable discussion over the following year but, in the end, accomplished little.[74]

Following this unsuccessful effort Joseph Buchanan, an ex-Knight of Labor expelled by Powderly, organized a spring 1894 conference to reunite labor. Members of the AFL, Powderly loyalists, and the Knights of Labor met in late April to work out a program. Again, little came of this effort.[75] The call for the convention, however, was a document of considerable insight. Buchanan argued that the crisis in the labor movement stemmed from a combination of economic depression, the incursions of machinery, and the failure to organize the unskilled. Skilled workers were in serious trouble because "the conditions under which industry is carried on are rapidly changing." The failure of the Knights was thus critical for all. He claimed that decline started after the Richmond convention, not owing to strikes nor to money problems but to:

> The policy of war to the death against all other labour organizations. The thousands of men who had been initiated into the Order and who still retained their membership in the organization of their craft while endeavoring to help the broader movement by working actively with the Knights were told that not only must the unions be wiped out, but that the union men in the Order must give adherence to the program of annihilation or get out.

Buchanan claimed Powderly agreed with this assessment, and joined him in asserting that the key now was to organize all labor: "They must stand or fall with the unskilled workers."[76] Labor unity, however, was not to be achieved.

Powderly's fight with the new Order plummeted to previously unfathomed depths in 1894 when he, Wright, and Devlin sued the Order for back salary. The Order responded in kind and in May expelled Powderly. Initially Powderly hoped to fight this, and gave his support to an opposition movement within the Order led by James Campbell and LA 300, the Assembly of the window glass workers; by August he had given up hope. "The Order is dead," he wrote to O'Reilly, "it has no vitality." Even without his active support the threat was sufficient for the New Orleans General Assembly to refuse to seat fourteen delegates, including LA 300 and the coal miners NTA 135. These groups founded a dissident Order in 1895, but Powderly offered little more than moral encouragement and polite advice. Nevertheless, his counsel is of some interest for it provides insight into what he considered the Knights' major failing:

> Advise the organization of a mixed assembly of the Knights of Labor in every place and have that body when organized assist in the formation into trades unions of such craftsmen as have enough to organize a trade union. Have men of all trades in every Assembly but keep the division of trade, craft, or class matters out of the Assembly. Let it be an open court wherein all matters of interest to labor may be discussed. Men are not permitted to talk politics in the union, let them talk not only politics but everything that may throw light on the affairs of humanity in the Assembly. Reorganize the Knights of Labor on educational lines and knit the Federation of Labor and Knights together as friends everywhere and enemies nowhere.

This new Independent Order, however, also went nowhere; the 1890s would be a decade of fragmentation rather than unity.[77]

Here, once again, the effect of this vicious and vituperative struggle on the remnants of the Order was felt in Canada. From Montreal Bernard Feeny wrote to Powderly to say that the brotherly love he saw in Philadelphia reminded him of Judas Iscariot, but he assured the deposed leader that Montreal's loyalty remained with the old GMW. In Ontario only Toronto DA 125 and Ottawa DA 6 still operated. Both leaned heavily to the Powderly side. Wright reported to Powderly in December 1893 that "the boys over there are disgusted." The Toronto Knights, he added, were "divided in opinion as to whether Hayes or McGuire is the more contemptible." If either went to Toronto they would know before they left "how perfidy, treachery and disloyalty are regarded by men who do not belong to the kind of cannibals who eat their friends."[78] A few months later the Order in Canada considered withdrawing from the international body. Powderly, however, advised them to stay. "Prevent it if you can," he wrote to Wright, "for the snake [Hayes] will show how few in number they are but if they stay in and trouble him he cannot do that." He also wrote to Bernard Feeny in Montreal with a similar message: "Canada should go to the next GA in force and there right a wrong."[79]

Powderly visited Toronto on a temperance tour in April 1894 and availed himself of the opportunity to air his views. Although questioned intensively by O'Donoghue and Gilmour and even virtuously upbraided by the former "for going outside of the AK," he felt that the visit had gone well. His surprising advice, when asked how to rebuild by Rev. Charles Shortt, was: "Organize the Governor: abandon all trade assemblies; initiate members of trade unions into the mixed assemblies; assist in strengthening the trade unions and secure their cooperation to strengthen the mixed assemblies; invite men of all shades of opinion and belief to join the mixed assemblies."[80]

Powderly's success at maintaining Toronto support became evident when

T. B. McGuire of the new General Executive Board visited the city in 1894 to collect the work of the city's LAs. Headquarters alleged that only one Assembly in the metropolitan center be exempt, for all of the others were in bad standing. First visiting Alf Jury, whom he assumed would support Hayes given his antagonism to Wright, McGuire sought out his opinion of the Philadelphia proceedings. Jury responded that:

They had only heard one side as yet. They had Wright's report and had heard Powderly's statement, as these agreed they were disposed to think them true. That so far as they were able to make out what the official report meant it corroborated Wright's report and so they were forced to conclude that Wright had told the truth and if so McGuire and Hayes and the rest of their gang were an inimical pack of scoundrels.

Wright, who took considerable joy in describing these events to Powderly, concluded that "altogether I'm afraid McGuire didn't enjoy his trip." Wright's glee, of course, was uncalled for. His old adversary D. J. O'Donoghue, who had apparently given McGuire "a particularly bad setting out," felt anything but pleased about the state of the Order. When Hayes made the mistake of trying to enlist him in the bitter struggle, O'Donoghue responded eloquently for those who stood far from the Knights' headquarters on Philadelphia's elegant Broad St.:

*Do not use any of my letters for such purpose or in respect of any difference between yourself and Mr. Wright.* I refuse to be in anyway mixed up in your personal quarrels. The situation in my estimation is simply this, in effect, "When rogues fall out honest men may sometimes get their own." I only wish the end would be like that in the fight of the famous Kilkenny cats – when the fight ended there was neither left. Between Mr. Wright and yourself more harm has been done in America to the labour movement than either or both can remedy during the remainder of your lives. Both had splendid opportunities, but with most lamentable results. Wherever or with whomever lies the fault, one thing is beyond doubt, and that is, that between you all – the GMW, the GEB and yourself – the Order has been sadly demoralized, if not totally paralyzed. With each of you apparently it was a battle of "rule or ruin." You appear on top of the heap for the time-being but where is the Order of the past? Not one of the lot appeared ready or offered to stepdown & out of office for the good & welfare of the Order. On the contrary ye gave to the world the sad and disgraceful spectacle of wolves, which, after devouring their prey, turn and destroy each other, regardless of any other consideration. Can we, outside of the "den of thieves" – if what one says of the other is true – be blamed for ordaining "a curse on both your houses."[81]

O'Donoghue's principled response to Hayes's attempt to draw him into the factionalism of decline brings us to the conclusion of our broad discussion of parasites, politics, and politicians within the brief but not insignificant history of the Knights of Labor. These three aspects of the Order's rise and fall were, of course, intimately connected, as we have seen, and our efforts to separate them analytically into distinct chapter discussions has often strained the flow of a narrative and forced some repetition. But this has been necessary, we think, in order to convey adequately the ways in which each of these different, if overlapping, realms contributed to the strengths and weaknesses of the Knights of Labor in Ontario and even to their wider presence across North America. In looking at each area carefully we are reminded, as was O'Donoghue, of the promise and potential that the Order held for many Ontario workers of the 1880s and, equally, of the tragic significance of the failure that was written on every abandoned Assembly wall by the 1890s.

## "Turmoil and misunderstanding"

The alternative hegemony that the Knights of Labor tried to create, and to implement in the realm of independent labor politics, was met with resistance from within and without. The established political culture's resiliency was adequately demonstrated by the persistence of partyism throughout the years of challenge from 1883 to 1887 and by its ascendance in the post-1887 period of collapse. All the while, there were those like Morgan and Harvey for whom labor reform was but another means of self-enrichment, testimony to the difficulties that any movement attempting to replace the crass individualism of the age with a vision of society turning on collective needs and wants would have to confront directly. And, finally, there was the power of the state, and the established political parties that sought to control its purse strings and dispense its power. Mowat, and to a lesser degree Macdonald, interceded in these years to provide Ontario workers with many of the protections and benefits that the Knights of Labor demanded, and consciously sought to siphon discontent and ease organized labor back into the old, familiar fold. Factory Acts, bureaus of labor statistics, arbitration measures, suffrage extension, employers' liability legislation, and improved mechanics' lien Acts were all a part of this process, bred of the fear engendered by the workingman's newly discovered political independence. Through patronage and promise, manipulation and machination, the parties retained their grip, thereby containing much of the oppositional sentiment that flared in the 1880s. In the words of Richard Kerrigan, "The Labor issue was linked up with the Liberal and Tory and had its throat cut accordingly."[82] But the victory was not won easily. If the Canadian political system functioned effectively to stifle dissent, it was not a success that was necessarily inevitable or taken for granted. An alternative hegemony confronted an established hegemony and in the process a contest ensued. Both wrestled for power, and in the resulting twisting of arms the stronger party emerged victorious. But it had been forced into certain crucial concessions and the workingman had established himself as a vital political presence. To be sure, parasites in LAs and politicians within the Order itself had done their bit to insure defeat. They had done irreparable harm to the once powerful Knights of Labor, but we cannot close on this sad note.

No matter how shoddy the closing act – and there can be little doubt that a soiled curtain had fallen on the once Noble and Holy Order – the Knights of Labor had stood for much more. Powderly himself knew this well and said as much in a letter to, of all people, John W. Hayes. In the very midst of their 1893–4 struggle, the GMW penned a defense of the Order in an attempt to explain the failure of the Knights of Labor:

> Whatever may be or may have been the faults or the virtues of the General Officers it is a conviction with me that no act of theirs could avert the impending fate of the Order. Teacher of important and much-needed reforms, she has been obligated to practice differently from her teachings. Advocating arbitration and conciliation as first steps in labor disputes she has been forced to take upon her shoulders the responsibilities of the aggressor first and, when hope of arbitrating and conciliation failed, to beg of the opposing side to do what we should have applied for in the first instance. Advising against strikes we have been in the midst of them. Urging important reforms we have been forced to yield our time and attention to petty disputes until we were placed in a position where we have frequently been misunderstood by the employee as well as the employer. While not a political party we have been forced into the attitude of taking political action.

The GMW no doubt passed over the leadership's deficiencies too easily in this note, but at its conclusion he argued with more strength: "through all the turmoil and misunderstanding the Order has stamped deep its impression for good upon the records of the world and should it collapse to-night those who survive it may point to its splendid achievements in forcing to the front the cause of misunderstood and down-trodden humanity."[83] And indeed the Knights of Labor would be remembered. When the OBU of Canada sought a glorious past to contrast to the dismal realities of AFL-TLC trade unionism in the 1920s, it was the fires of the Knights of Labor it chose to rekindle. "One of the great land-marks in the history of the class struggle," the Knights as "a mass organization, grouped in Geographical units" had prefigured the industrial unionism of the OBU. The Knights had been, above all else, "one big union." How the Order, which had declined to the sorry state outlined in this chapter and then withered away and died, could live on to be celebrated in the birth of revolutionary industrial unionism will be explained in the following chapters.[84]

# 8. "Spread the light!": Forging a culture

## An alternative hegemony

Like all revolutionary movements, the OBU that looked back upon the Knights of Labor experience so favorably knew that to overturn the weight of conventional social relationships the oppositional challenge must extend beyond the political and the economic realms into the sphere of culture. For it was there that the dominance of the ruling class expressed itself in a pervasive and generally unquestioned hegemony. A subordinate class must reach toward an alternative hegemony if it ever hopes to dominate the ethos of society. To realize this alternative hegemony, of course, would be to establish the process whereby power was seized, conventional wisdoms displaced and relationships of authority turned on their heads. As an alternative hegemony passed into hegemony it would assume its place as arbitrator of social, economic, political, and cultural values, expressed through the control of the state apparatus, the educational system, the majesty of the law, and a wide range of formal institutions and informal sanctions. For precisely this reason there is no such historical phenomenon as an alternative hegemony attained. Alternative hegemonies can pass into new hegemonic cultures, although this necessarily involves the rise to power of new classes and the dissolution of old ways of life. The revolutions of 1789 and 1917 were just such epoch-shaking moments of transformation. But even in such periods of upheaval, the problem of consolidating, if not building, a new culture has been immense, often proving a stumbling block with which the revolutionary movement has had to contend.[1] This is not to argue, of course, that a revolution is solely a cultural undertaking, and that the struggles in the more explicitly political and economic spheres are insignificant. But it is to claim that the revolutionary movement postpones this essential aspect of the transformation of society only at great cost, often paying a heavy price in the end. As the initial preparatory stage in any victorious revolutionary struggle, the creation of an alternative hegemony pitted against the reigning hegemony of the dominant class is a development of considerable consequence. Moreover, this process may begin without the active involvement of revolutionaries committed to active intervention in the working-class movement, giving rise to what Edward

Aveling and Eleanor Marx so aptly described as "unconscious socialism."[2] The forging of a culture of solidarity and resistance, of alternative and promise, in which a class is drawn together in opposition to another class, thus stands as a point of departure for the revolutionary movement.

The Knights of Labor drew the respect of Canadian twentieth-century revolutionaries because they were at the center of this kind of activity. We have already noted the challenge they raised in Toronto and Hamilton work places and in the political sphere, and we will continue such discussion in Chapter 9 when we outline the Ontario Order's significant place in the class conflicts of the 1880s. Here we want to lay stress upon the Knights of Labor's role in sustaining this series of challenges through its attempt to forge a culture in which workers saw themselves as a class, and in which members of that class could see past the mystifications of bourgeois domination to the promise and potential of a better world. In the Ontario of the 1880s, we will argue, there was an alternative hegemony in formation. It was caught up in the ambivalences of an economic context not yet fully consolidated, for the 1880s were a decade of transition to a mature industrial capitalism in its monopoly stage; it was led, not by revolutionaries, but by men and women committed to reform. In the end, this alternative hegemony did not win the day, although it raised a series of challenges and oppositions that remain with us yet. If its life span was short, the issues it addressed seem timeless. We refer to this creative moment as a movement culture, a recognition that the Knights of Labor built upon a culture of class experience that had little direction and unity to consolidate a class effort that sought to transform the very nature of the society in which workers of the 1880s found themselves.[3]

To argue this way, however, demands a specific view of culture. First, culture poses tremendous interpretive problems because it is marked by contradictory thrusts: at once totalizing and all-inclusive, it is also capable of highlighting social differences that reflect a wide range of experience. To move beyond this totalizing aspect of culture, in which all members of a particular society appear to stand apart from all members of another society, rooted in a different time and place, culture must be scrutinized materially thereby revealing marked divergences in styles of life, modes of thought, value systems, and ways of making a living. The totalizing facade of culture then disappears to reveal profound differences, not the least of which is associated with class: a concept of culture is displaced by a recognition of cultures. Second, culture is perhaps too eclectic and imprecise a term to capture sufficiently rigorously its particular components. In this chapter, for instance, we will outline the Knights of Labor contribution to the creation of a movement culture through an examination of a range of cultural forms and accomplishments: ritual, procession, and rhetoric; the "high culture" of reform thought at the ideological pinnacle of resistance and the "low culture" of doggerel that everywhere followed in the wake of and reflected the stance of class awareness; the unique nineteenth-century fusion of the woman and class questions and the creative link between ethnicity and class that emerged out of the convergence of the Irish Land League and the Order. In all of this we are seeing specific activities and personalities, but it is not the events and the individuals that are paramount. Taken together they suggest a cultural undertaking of opposition that marked the 1880s off from previous decades of class experience. The Knights of Labor, in short, built upon a class culture to create a movement culture, taking the differences in ways of life that had existed for so long and channeling them toward the demand for change. This achievement, however shortlived, places the Knights of Labor at the center of an understanding of the North American working class.

Even here, however, we must recognize significant analytical difficulties. The class culture that predated the rise of the Knights of Labor, for instance, reflected many continuities with older, established modes of behavior, rooted in practices that extended back to the early nineteenth century. We can recognize, for theoretical purposes, the distinction between this residual class culture, marking off worker from employer, directing us toward two very different ways of life, and the emergent, movement culture, represented by the Knights of Labor, that embraced a new organizational form, uniting previously divided segments of the working class, proclaiming the potential of a new social order. But it is problematic, if not impossible, to isolate these two strands, separating here a residual aspect, there an emergent development, for surviving evidence is almost entirely colored by the movement's presence, by its ideology, leadership, and by the challenge it presented to bourgeois stability. In fact, the Order's effectiveness stemmed from the dialectical relationship of residual *and* emergent, class *and* movement. On the one hand, the Knights of Labor developed out of the class culture while, on the other hand, they pushed that culture forward, posing alternatives, striking a posture of opposition. In this sense mundane aspects of everyday life, which conditioned a sense of class place, were, in Henri Lefebvre's words, "but a field and a half way house, a halting place and a springboard, a moment made of moments (desires, labors, pleasures – products and achievements – passivity and creativity – means and ends – etc.), the dialectical interaction that is the inevitable starting point for the realization of the possible."[4] Gramsci put the case more bluntly, and less metaphorically, in 1919 when he argued that "The associative and solidaristic principle becomes essential for the labouring class, changes the psychology and the behaviour (customs) of workers and peasants."[5] But as Raymond Williams has argued, the emergent culture, in the absence of any revolutionary transformation that would install it as the dominant culture, exists historically as a pressing, rather than realized phenomenon. Always struggling, it is best understood in terms of preemergence, constantly running headlong into the dominant culture's forms of hegemony.[6] To view the cultural context of the Ontario worker in this way is to capture much of the significance of the Knights of Labor in the closing decades of the nineteenth century, and to root the men and women of the movement in the particular milieu in which the "labor question" first came to prominence in Canada.

## Symbols of solidarity

Brockville's Samuel F. Miller was one of these men of the movement. A molder by trade, active in his union, he had been born in 1856 and identified himself as a Protestant. On the night of 16 November 1883, Miller probably was present in a "large room blazing with light, tastefully decorated with flags, bunting, and pictures, and thronged with merry citizens, their wives, daughters and sweethearts." He was a member of Franklin LA 2311, Knights of Labor, composed primarily of dock workers, but including on its membership list representatives of nearly every trade. Franklin Assembly had been organized by Mr. Archer Baker of Ogdensburg, New York, on 2 December 1882, with a charter membership of 20. Less than a year later it was said to embrace 430 able-bodied men, and supported a Mutual Benefit Association, entitling married and unmarried members to $5–7 a week during sickness. The expansion in the ranks of LA 2311 had prompted the Order to search for larger rooms, and in mid-November 1883 the town's Knights of Labor celebrated the successful acquisition of a new meeting place.[7]

On the evening of 16 November the Brockville Knights of Labor hall was the scene of much public merriment, revelry, and dancing, interrupted only by a midnight supper at the Central Hotel. Other nights, however, were more solemn, and entrance to the rooms of Franklin Assembly was restricted to those committed to deeply held convictions:

> To-night we meet within the mystic halls
> Of these our brothers, whose emblazoned shields
> Glow forth in golden splendor on our walls,
> Greeting with joy the sword our Order wields,
> Fraternal greetings give we back again
> To Damien and to Pythias, Knights of old,
> Who counted friendship better than all gain
> Of worldly praise or ill-begotten gold,

Like them we succor give, uplift the low,
Hold out the helping hand to all who need,
And buckle on the armor 'gainst the foe
Whose impious hands are stained with blood and greed.
Of old, encased within their mail of steel,
Their shields reflecting back the sun's bright ray,
Their hearts made strong with love's inspiring zeal,
The knights went forth the victors of the day.
Their deeds are told in legend and in song;
But while we dream of the chivalry of yore
And wish for knighthood to redress all wrong,
We know our time has braver deeds in store.[8]

Like the English socialist poet William Morris, Samuel Miller and his fellow Knights of Labor were immersed in a tradition of romantic rebellion, an effort to overcome the actualities of "the age of shoddy," dominated by the "monopolists" and "upper tendom," with aspirations that linked all that was truly noble in the past with all that would be promising in the future. The eclectic, deeply moralistic, reform effort of the Knights of Labor that we have seen in Toronto and Hamilton sought, in effect, "to make the past part of the present." In the symbolism and richly suggestive ritual of the Noble and Holy Order of the Knights of Labor, both the strengths of the past, and the purposes of the present were revealed, introducing us, as well, to the class culture upon which the Knights constructed their alternative vision.[9]

The symbolism of the Knights of Labor, which commonly manifested itself in a chalked mark on the sidewalk outside the door of a detested businessman,[10] or in a sign placed dramatically at the end of a Canadian letter to Terence V. Powderly,[11] came to the membership with the LA's charter. The Knights of Hope Assembly in Port Hope was chartered 20 December 1882:

empowered to do and perform such acts and enjoy such privileges as are prescribed in the Adelphon Kruptos and in the Laws and Usages of the Order of the K. of L., and the members therefore are strictly enjoined to bear constantly in mind and always practice the cardinal principles of the Order,

Secrecy, Obedience, and Mutual Assistance

These cardinal virtues (S.O.M.A.) formed the corners of the ubiquitous triangle, which we have already noted served as the sign of the Order, and symbolized the program, aspirations, achievements, collective existence, and emotional power of the Knights of Labor.[12]

The three lines of the triangle, which was always an equilateral construction, conjured up a series of meanings. First, these lines represented creation, existence, and dissolution, and when combined they signified humanity.

Second, the lines of the triangle indicated "the three elements . . . essential to man's existence and happiness: land, labor, and love." Finally, linking these practical and humanistic concerns was a third reading of the lines, and one expressive of the Order's interest in work and social values:

> These three lines are also emblematic of production, exchange, and consumption. To make production profitable such articles as are produced must be passed into the hands of the consumer. To give the products of one's toil without a fair equivalent would not be in harmony with the principles of equity, therefore they must be exchanged for values; whether these values consist of money or the produce of another's toil is not material, so long as producer and consumer are satisfied.

These lines, then, which joined together to form "the great seal of Knighthood," meant much to the membership. And there were other symbolic meanings expressed visually in the signs of the Order. The triangle, for instance, was always encased within the circle, or globe. Representative of society in general, the circle also indicated that "the bond of unity by which the membership is bound together should be without end" and that if "a solid, undivided front toward the enemy" was maintained, "attack from the outside" would in no way injure the "Circle of Universal Brotherhood" surrounding each individual Knight of Labor. Other lines, too, expressed beliefs, values, and commitments, and radiated out from the circle or triangle: Justice, Wisdom, Truth, and Industry, were but four such values symbolized. Indeed, the signs, seals, and symbols of the Order were easily turned to purposes both general and specific.[13]

The *Palladium of Labor*, for instance, adapted the symbolic triangle to a crude version of the labor theory of value. Depicting a triangle with a line drawn diagonally through the middle, it argued that, "The full pyramid, represents what labor earns. The heavy black line across, represents the unholy part taken by the fiend's hired men, the usurers, the bloodsuckers who don't work – who live by the sweat of other men's brows."[14] An early version of the Order's ritual, the *Adelphon Kruptos* (*AK*), stipulated the symbols of "opening service," the allegorical journey that had to be traveled before the LA's business could be conducted: "A Globe being placed on the outside of the Outer Veil; a copy of the Sacred Scriptures closed; and a box or basket, containing blank cards on a triangular Alter, red in color, in the centre of the vestibule; a Lance on the outside of the Inner Veil, or entrance to the Sanctuary, over the wicket; that the initiated may know that an Assembly of the ********* are in session." Secrecy, certainly (the Globe was placed *outside* the Sanctuary), and perhaps even combativeness (the Lance signified defense), were enshrined in this service, as was the solemnity of membership (blank cards resting on a triangular, red altar). The MW's station was designated by a column, three feet high, the shaft of which resembled a "bundle of sticks." As Powderly once explained, this tightly bound group of rods indicated strength: "One attempt to break a bundle of sticks is sufficient to prevent a second effort in that direction. If all branches of trade are bound together in one Order, the difficulty experienced in overcoming their combined forces is so much greater than that which would be felt in a struggle against one alone . . . [proving] that 'in union there is strength.'"[15] An entire world of symbolism thus rooted the membership in the movement, and specific symbolic pieces reinforced working-class traditions of collectivity in an age of hostile, individualistic pieties.

## Rituals of mutuality

Beyond symbolism, the initiation rites and practical rituals – the secret signs, words, handclasps – of the Order also united forms with content, or purpose. But to appreciate the significance of this process, we must do more than merely describe; the importance of elaborate ritual must be recovered, located in a wider world where class experience, feelings, and values lent force and meaning to the expressions and signs of the Knights of Labor "secret work."[16] To regard this ritual and symbolism as "misplaced ingenuity," as a simple adornment of "emotional furniture," leads us away from the essential point.[17] Gordon Bishop of Gananoque noted that the ritualistic passwords and secrets of the Order insured large attendances at ordinary meetings, and riveted the workers to a cause. Members, he recalled, "did not forget their obligation easily." In the case of the Noble and Holy Order of the Knights of Labor, ritual and symbolism were deeply embedded in the realities of working-class life, and in decoding these phenomena we enter the cultural context of the expectations of the Order's advocates, expectations that posed alternatives and challenges to an entrenched industrial capitalism and its perceived inequalities.[18]

Indeed, the extensive organizational successes of the Knights of Labor owed much to the carefully constructed ritual developed by the Order's founder, Uriah Stephens. His *AK* has often been regarded as a product of religious beliefs and training, but it actually resembled the secret work of other labor and fraternal societies far more than any Christian ceremony, and echoed a tradition of radical secular thought.[19] More elaborate than many labor rituals, the *AK* shared with them the complicated rites of the fraternal society, a common masonic heritage.[20] But this heritage was adapted radically. The hierarchical system of degrees, for instance, was abandoned, and the *AK* proudly disclaimed the need for expensive regalia: "The only jewels

Figure 9. U.S. Stephens, founder of the Knights of Labor. *Source:* Powderly Papers, Catholic University, Washington, D.C.

worn by the Order are those of the heart – honour and fraternity. The only regalia is that of neat, tidy dress. The only conduct, cordial, harmonious, and fraternal." This innovation underscored the Order's commitment to overcome divisions among working people, emphasizing the nobility of all labor and the need for solidarity. "All members, whether they hold positions or not, occupy the same level," noted Powderly. "This is to indicate that there are no degrees of rank, no upper or lower class – all men are admitted on an equal footing . . . all branches of honorable toil are regarded in the same light by the Order of the Knights of Labor."[21] The initiation rites, pass-words, secret signs, and procedural rules reiterated these core beliefs and values.

Every Knight of Labor experienced initiation, a ritualistic procedure that saw him or her pledge eternal secrecy, strict obedience, and scrupulous charity toward new brothers and sisters, the triangular principles of S.O.M.A.

Each new initiate vowed to defend the interest and reputation of all true members of the Order, employed or unemployed, fortunate or distressed, and was instructed that:

> By labor is brought forth the kindly fruits of the earth in rich abundance for our sustenance and comfort; by labor (not exhaustion) is promoted health of body and strength of mind; and labor garners the priceless stores of wisdom and knowledge. It is the "Philosopher's Stone," everything it touches turns to gold. "Labor is noble and holy." To defend it from degradation, to divest it of the evils to body, mind, and estate, which ignorance and greed have imposed; to rescue the toiler from the grasp of the selfish is a work worthy of the noblest and best of our race.

Upon admittance to the Order, the recently christened Knight was informed that "open and public associations have failed, after a struggle of centuries, to protect or advance the interest of labor," and that the Knights of Labor merely imitated "the example of capital," endeavoring "to secure the just rewards of our toil." "In all the multifarious branches of trade," the convert was told, "capital has its combinations, and whether intended or not, it crushes the manly hopes of labor and tramples poor humanity in the dust." To counteract this distressing tendency of the modern age, the Order asserted:

> We mean to uphold the dignity of labor, to affirm the nobility of all who earn their bread by the sweat of their brow . . . We shall, with all our strength, support laws made to harmonize the interests of capital and labor, for labor alone gives life and value to capital, and also those laws which tend to lighten the exhaustiveness of toil. We shall use every lawful and honorable means to procure and retain employ for one another, coupled with just and fair remuneration, and should accident or misfortune befal one of our number, render such aid as lies within our power to give, without inquiring his country or his creed; and without approving of general strikes among artisans, yet should it become justly necessary to enjoin our oppressor, we will protect and aid any of our number who thereby may suffer loss.[22]

In these ritualized incantations, which resounded in LA halls across North America, lie much of the ambiguity and ambivalence, as well as the promise and potential of the Knights of Labor. Coincident with the initiate's pledge to approach relationships between contending classes cautiously, for instance, was the primary commitment to the defense of working-class interests and the willingness to confront the oppressor and thwart the general process of the degradation of labor.

Once initiated, the individual Knight's attachment to collective principles was consolidated through the rituals of periodic meeting. The *AK* established a collection of signs, passwords, grips, and challenges that governed entrance to the LA's meetings, and provided means by which members could, in strange company, ascertain if there were Knights present. Both the signs and the language of communication were rooted in a conception of the basic dignity of all labor, and the essential role of work, as a vital human activity, in all social relationships. When admitted to an Assembly, the Knight first made the sign of obliteration, a complex act involving the palms, the central feature being the motion of wiping the left hand with the right. The language of the sign – "to erase, obliterate, wipe out" – was related to purging unnecessary thoughts, "as the draughtsman erases useless lines." The same procedure was undertaken upon leaving an Assembly, signifying, once again, obliteration, this time symbolic of the pledge "to keep profoundly secret everything seen, heard, or done by yourself or others." The sign of obliteration was answered by the sign of decoration, offered by the Venerable Sage, who reminded all that "Labor is noble and holy." Outside the Assembly the Knight could determine the presence of other Knights by declaring "I am a worker." A fellow Knight would reply "I too earn my bread with the sweat of my brow," drawing his right hand across the forehead from left to right, with the back of the hand to the front. In situations of distress a Knight could utter, "I am a *stranger.*" If he heard the response, "a stranger should be assisted," he knew he was among friends. Upon seeing any Knight cheated or imposed upon, or upon hearing a member of the Order thoughtlessly divulge something of a secret nature, a member would form the sign of caution, a movement of certain fingers across portions of the face.[23]

Working people were drawn to this elaborate ritual for many reasons. On grounds of form alone it must have been thoroughly familiar, for many nineteenth-century Canadian workingmen belonged to fraternal societies. Within the Order it was common for members to patronize a multitude of lodges and associations, testimony to the rich social network of late-nineteenth-century working-class life.[24] George Goodwin, statistician of Courage Assembly 9216, Napanee, informed Powderly in 1888 that, "We in Canada are made up of men of whom are members of several associations such as Masons, Oddfellows, Workmen, Orangemen, Foresters and others."[25] "A Member of Three Secret Societies" defended Freemasonry, Oddfellowship, and "that excellent society the Knights of Labor" in the pages of the *Palladium of Labor*, arguing that in living up to the tenets of these fraternal orders, a man would be a good Christian and a worthy member of society. From Stratford came the report that, "two good large Assemblies with a total membership of over six hundred are working, and a charter for a third is daily expected. That of the first Assembly appears to have been granted to a few pushing, energetic men, who were connected with a number of other societies, and to this fact is generally conceded the rapid growth and present deep-rooted state of the principles of the Order." Many of these pioneers were, as well as members of the fraternal lodges of numerous societies, also ardent "workers" in the cause of trade unionism, as O'Donoghue pointed out to Powderly in the fall of 1883.[26] London's R. H. Yeo, a merchant tailor affiliated with LA 3558, "boomed" the Knights of Labor in April 1886. He claimed that every worker in the city's Ward 5 was cemented by his membership in the Foresters, the Shepherds, the Masons, and the Knights of Sherwood Forest. The Recording Secretary of DA 138, W. J. Shaw, advised Powderly of the benefits of "Home Rule" in 1888, drawing upon his experience as a member of the Independent Order of Odd Fellows.[27] Government bills aimed at the regulation of secret societies thus understandably angered Canadian Knights, and they expressed their concern to the GMW. Ritual and secrecy, then, seemed part of the very fabric of the cultural life of late nineteenth-century workers; as Mason, Orangeman, Unionist, or Knight, the workingman found nothing strange or awkward in solemn oaths, rich symbolism, intricate handclasps, suggestive signs, and complex initiation procedures. But the singular class basis of the Order was not forgotten. In Welland someone asked "if the Knights of Pythias are a branch of the Knights of Labor." Not exactly, replied the local paper, "They are mostly Knights who don't labor."[28]

Aside from the formal assimilation of ritual, the secrecy that stood by its side had a pragmatic value. Workers who had experimented with organization in the nineteenth century often faced employer hostility, and many were victimized, hounded from one work place to another, driven from their jobs and their homes. Secrecy, in this context, made profound sense, and in many Canadian towns in the 1880s and 1890s ritualistic admission procedures, secret meetings, and signs of recognition and obliteration were guarded and defended with jealousy, recognized as essential measures, protection against informers and antagonists.[29] So important was the "secret work" to the Knights of Labor that trusted lecturers like Richard R. Trevellick were often dispatched to Ontario to address LAs on the subject. When A. E. Fields attempted to reorganize the Order in Kingston in 1895, his first move was to request the *AK*. Without this important document, he thought, demoralization and eventual disintegration of the town's LAs were inevitable.[30] Secrecy, symbolism, and ritual thus united forms with content, presenting a package easily understood and valued by late-nineteenth-century workers.

But the ultimate attraction and strength of the symbolism and ritual of the Knights of Labor did not rest on a process of unconscious adaptation, defensiveness, or mere self-interest, although all of these undoubtedly played a role in consolidating membership around the principles of secrecy, obedience, and mutual assistance. Reverberating throughout the *AK* was the centrality of class pride, the awareness of the worth of the workingman and woman. It was this, above all else, that served as a magnet and drew adherents to the cause. By the late 1880s North American workers and employers stood divided, as years of experience had produced divergent ways of life, opposing values, and conflicting perspectives. The symbolism and ritual of the Knights of Labor revolved around this essential development, infusing old forms with new purpose and passion. A. J. H. Duganne captured something of this process, sharpest in the 1880s, in a poem "The Knights of Labor":

> Under "three great lights,"
> With "companion knights,"
> He had knelt at Masonic altars;
>
> Every evening he met,
> With "companions" to get
> "More light" on his way as a workman,
>
> But never a light,
> On his way as a Knight
> In his battle for wages of labor.
>
> So the man to his heart,
> Like a man, spake apart,
> Till his heart answered many reflections:
> "What prevents you?" it said –
> "Heart to heart – head to head –
> From imparting Masonic direction?"
>
> And in manhood's name,
> Make known your claim,
> To be honored as Knights of Labor.[31]

Richard Mullen, representative of DA 84, Richmond, Virginia, also revealed something of this emerging sense of class purpose, couched in symbolism and the romance of history.[32] In October 1885, at the Hamilton meeting of the General Assembly, he presented Powderly with a gavel composed of wood taken from three monuments to the struggle for American liberty: St. John's Church, where Patrick Henry first uttered the words, "Give me liberty or give me death"; a grapevine near Yorktown, where Cornwallis surrendered to Washington; and Libby Prison, which gained notoriety during the Civil War, when "men went forth to battle to free a race of people from the bonds of slavery." To Mullen, these three locales symbolized the first and second American revolutions, prefacing the third:

> I take pleasure, sir, in placing this plain memento of past history in your hands as the representative head of the army that is to work a third revolution, and liberate not merely a race of people, but a whole world of people from the galling chains of slavery. I know, sir, that I utter the sentiments of my brethren who have commissioned

me to present this token, when I say, God grant that this gavel may live to sound the call at which the representatives of a world of freeman shall gather together in bonds of S.O.M.A.[33]

The cheers with which Canadian workers greeted Mullen's speech, so heavily dependent upon the historic struggles of Americans, emphasized the internationalist thrust of the Order, and the token gavel represented causes that Ontario workers found no difficulty in embracing. That gavel, and all that it conjured up in the mind of a Knight of Labor, linked past and present. Symbol and ritual, in short, spoke to the accumulated context of years of daily life.

## Residual and emergent

By 1875, when the Knights of Labor first entered Canada on a secret basis, Ontario's workers had approximately fifty years of experience behind them. In these years class divisions had emerged, overcome certain forces mediating or obscuring social cleavages, and bred antagonism and struggle. A distinct working-class way of life had gradually come into being, conditioned by an associational network within the community, trade organizations, work place customs, deeply held values, and cherished beliefs. Workers like Ottawa's Daniel O'Donoghue, elected as the first workingman's representative to the Ontario Legislature in 1874, and a figure destined to be centrally involved in the Knights of Labor, had been socialized into this culture, reared on the cultural matrix of fire companies, sporting clubs, and institutions of self-help so prominent in many central Canadian towns and cities.[34] Major moments of confrontation – first, during what was hailed as an "insurrection of labour" in 1853–4, and second, in the nine-hour struggles of 1872 – had done much to bring into being an independent working class. But the blurring of class lines (most notable in the absence of an uncompromising class perspective) still persisted, and many workers consciously identified with paternalistic superiors, benevolent employees, or pillars of the community. Skilled and unskilled remained distinct social strata, as the absence of laborers in the 1872 movement for the shorter working day suggests; the Jubilee Riot that erupted in Toronto in 1875 as the city's Protestant Irish reacted to a Catholic procession was proof enough that Orange and Green occupied different, and mutually exclusive, worlds. But all of this was on the brink of transformation. In the 1880s, ushered in by the termination of the depression of the 1870s, the 1879 National Policy, and capitalist consolidation, we can glimpse a class culture at work. This culture was, to be sure, residual, as it grew out of past ways of life, and offered, at best, only a weak and muffled challenge to the bourgeois order, but as the symbolism and ritual of the Knights of Labor implied, it was inching toward a recognition of essential class differences, and it knew well the place of collectivity and solidarity in the world of the worker.

The historian bumps into this culture in every corner of the 1880s and early 1890s, in dusty archival folders, in the torn pages of the daily press, in testimonies before Royal Commissions, and in the political sphere. It is particularly audible in the rhetoric of labor reform, emanating from the many working-class newspapers of the period. In the pages of well-known Hamilton-Toronto journals, such as the *Labor Union*, *Palladium of Labor*, *Wage Worker*, *Trade Union Advocate*, *Canadian Labor Reformer*, and *Labor Advocate*, the culture was at its most vibrant and visible. The existence of other organs, from the voice of O'Donoghue, the *Labor Record*, to the St. Thomas *Canada Labor Courier*, edited by George Wrigley, a future farmers' advocate and socialist, through labor papers barely known to have existed – Ottawa's *Free Lance* and *Capital Siftings*, London's *Evening News* (issued by printers in the midst of an 1884 strike), Brockville's *Equalizer* – demonstrated the scope and strength of the working-class presence in these years.[35] As a living, breathing reality, this presence, and the culture it conditioned, was pervasive, and it is surprising how little attention has been paid to it.[36]

A tradition of collectivity was the bedrock upon which this culture consolidated, and labor unity, mutual aid, and solidarity were visible manifestations. Festivals, dinners, and workingmen's balls lent it force, "cementing together the bonds of unity," as the *Ontario Workman* early commented.[37] Picnics and dinners, too, came to assume an importance beyond mere recreation:

> Such outings do far more good than is generally supposed – they bring together members of a craft and make strangers into fast friends, and any person of common discernment can see the benefit of common mechanics knowing each other. It is of the greatest benefit for them to do so, either in fair weather when clouds are gathering, or when they burst. For that reason we hope that tradesmen will never fail to have their annual outings in the summer season and social gatherings in winter, as it all tends to make them more united and competent to fight the Monster (Capital) when occasion requires.[38]

Similarly, in the case of parades:

> There's something in such gatherings,
> That should fill us all with glee,
> And may we live for many years
> Reunions grand to see
> For well we know if sons of toil

Will all go hand in hand
There's none can us asunder break
If all united stand.[39]

In an earlier epoch such collective undertakings had often softened class antagonisms and blunted social polarization, as master and man marched side by side, lounged together at a printers' "wayzgoose" at a lakeside park, or toasted their mutual concerns over cabbage and goose. Cultural festivities could still function in this way, of course, and throughout the 1880s many factors continued to mediate class differences. But by this late date the unmistakable tendency was for such events to recognize the fifty years of class formation and confrontation that had colored social life in a society increasingly under the sway of industrial capital. A union ball could be a stark reminder of class relationships, as in 1883, when a contingent of iron molders sarcastically offered thanks to their employers for a recent wage reduction with a printed program entitled, "To Our Generous Employers."[40] The independence of the culture was thus presenting its face, marking it off from the accommodationist stance of earlier years. Self-proclaimed working-class holidays, known as labor festivals, celebrated this development. When the Canadian government officially sanctioned such events and proclaimed Labor Day in 1894, the engineer Edward Williams, once prominent in the Knights of Labor, thought the act "a tardy recognition of those noble beings who in the past, through vituperation and calumny, suffered persecution for defending rights and liberties of men, and who claimed that the Trades Union was destined to develop the highest type of manhood in the march of civilization, and as feudalism followed barbarism, so education and enlightenment would tend slowly but successfully to bring about the freedom of thought and action which asserts the equality of rights before the law."[41]

There was nothing all that new in most of this, although the increasing consciousness of class reflected in the culture of the post-1879 years was a departure from past ambiguities. But, as *forms*, parades, festivals, dinners, and other collective endeavors were *residual*, and had been part of a working-class way of life since early in the century. Stylized, even ritualized, means of protest remained common. Hamilton weavers charivaried women strikebreakers in 1890; workers in London mocked class enemies in the aftermath of a riotous street railway strike, parading streets with a coffin labeled "For a Small-man," a denigration of T. C. Smallman, resident director of that classic monopoly the Street Railway Company; and, during the Knights-of-Labor-led Chaudière strike in Hull, Quebec (1891), unskilled workers blackened their faces and marched in imitation of the militia who had been summoned to preserve order.[42]

Working-class culture, as we have suggested in other published work and in earlier chapters of this book, thus had a long and vital history in the major industrial cities of late-nineteenth-century Ontario.[43] What is most striking in the 1880s, however, is the penetration of this culture – in both its residual and emergent, class and movement, forms – into the industrial villages, towns, and cities of eastern, central, and western Ontario. Across the province, the Knights of Labor built upon the traditions of associational life, collectivity, and mutuality to forge a culture of solidarity. Intimately connected with this process was the emergence of a network of organic intellectuals, workingmen (and even a few women) who articulated the hopes and vision of the new movement that sought to establish the cooperative commonwealth. Strongest in the metropolitan centers of Hamilton and Toronto, the push for labor reform also surfaced in literally hundreds of Ontario communities, towns, and cities ranging in size from London to Amherstburg. The base of this cultural process rested firmly on a series of seemingly minor events. These commonplace happenings revealed how easily the Order assumed leadership in orchestrating the multifarious aspects of the residual dimensions of a class culture, turning them toward emergent purpose.

## Festivities and funerals

In Thorold, for instance, where women and stonecutters predominated in the LAs, Knights of Labor hops, dances, and balls seemed to set the pace of the town's social life in the heady days of organizational upsurge of 1886–7. Mountain Assembly (6798), Beaver Assembly (7908), and the women's Advance Assembly (8625) all organized such festivities at the local rollerskating rink, drawing large crowds from St. Catharines, Merritton, Welland, and Niagara Falls, often conveyed in special Knights of Labor streetcars. These entertainments helped establish Mountain Assembly "as one of the strongest organizations in town" and, in the case of one January 1887 "grand hop," reinforced notions of working-class self-help and mutual assistance, the proceeds going to a disabled worker.[44] Similar dances, musicals, assemblies, entertainments, and festive presentations, honoring a respected workmate, were organized by LAs in Ottawa, Belleville, Windsor, Ingersoll, and Gananoque – to name but five hubs of activity.[45] Sarnia's Knights of Labor raised over $300 for their cause in late 1884 by engaging Wren's Comedy Company at the Town Hall.[46] Sixty miles to the east, LAs of the Order in London utilized dances and musicals to consolidate ties with the city's iron molders' union, and to introduce organizers and lecturers to the membership.[47] Women workers in Brantford and Hamilton seemed particularly successful in their "entertainments," and were much encouraged by Knights of Labor activists.[48] These occasions were no doubt moments of recreation that diverted people from the everyday concerns of the next day's work, the next week's groceries, and the next month's rent – the range of insecurities the next year could bring. But they were also exhilarating reminders of self-worth. New York's Victor Drury, an articulate and radical Knight of Labor associated with the socialist faction of New York's Home Club, argued before a musical given by Hamilton's DA 61:

> I have heard from the lips of those who are here that this meeting is called by an organization known as the Knights of Labor. It is claimed by some that the working classes are ignorant, that they are brutes and imbeciles, and are, in fact, the dregs of society. And yet what do I find? I believe that I see before me an audience of working men and women, and the first thing I heard when I came in this hall was the excellent piano playing of two ladies . . . honest people who earn their bread by the sweat of [their] brow and rob not any man.[49]

These were words that reinforced a sense of class place and class pride, words which must have echoed in many a Knights of Labor hall in the midst of similar musicals, entertainments, and dances.

Working toward the same purpose, and even more forceful in demonstrating the presence of the movement, were the many "monster" picnics, holiday celebrations, demonstrations, excursions, and local parades arranged by Knights of Labor committees. These outings, which began with the Order's effective entrance into Ontario in 1883, appeared to peak at the crest of organizational activity in 1886, and slowly tapered off, became less prominent in the early 1890s and confined to the frontiers of Knights of Labor penetration, such as the Ottawa lumber valley, where the idea of the cooperative commonwealth arrived late, and survived longer. As indicators of growth and strength, such social undertakings played a significant role in the forging of a culture.

As Canadian Knights of Labor battled Jay Gould's telegraph monopoly in August 1883, for instance, the Order in Hamilton celebrated the birthdate of Uriah Stephens (4 August), while Oshawa's Knights of Labor used the local civic holiday "as a suitable excuse for a grand demonstration and parade," the proceeds going to the striking operatives. At Hamilton 2,000–3,000 skilled and unskilled workers marched under British, Canadian, and American flags, "emblematic of the international solidarity of labour." Knight of Labor joined craft unionist in a display of working-class unity. David Healey of Rochester, New York, addressed the demonstrators, providing them with a number of dishes in a general "intellectual feast." The meal consisted of the typical labor-reform message, stressing the need to educate the people to attack the enemy:

> They can eventually wipe out despotism and monopoly, abolish wars and armies, and proclaim emancipation to all mankind. Were we once united no power on earth could stay the world's freedom. Monopoly of the soil, monopoly of labor, monopoly of suffrage, monopoly of nature's treasures. This many-headed dragon would be destroyed. Monopoly is today the greatest enemy of mankind, monopoly is the invention of Satan to make his empire powerful in every land. Monopoly is the heartless, cruel slave-driver that holds in needless servitude a thousand millions of mankind. Monopoly is the magic wand of power which enables the Rothschilds of Europe to dictate the terms on which kings shall go to war. Monopoly is the philosopher's stone in the hands of the oppressor, converting into gold the sweat of labor and the tears of poverty. With the monopolist, with the individual, with the man, I have no quarrel; but thrice cursed of heaven be the system. 'Twas born of avarice and suckled at the breast of tyranny. With justice, with liberty, with God upon our side, victory is certain as the onward march of civilization. This is my dream.

As Healey urged "a united front against every invader of our liberties," the city's printers, proclaiming "the press as the defence of Labor and the medium of intellectual elevation of the masses," distributed a sheet entitled, "The elevation of Labor is the advancement of the State." The impact of all this was not lost on the daily press, the *Hamilton Spectator* concluding that "Union is strength. This old adage was never more forcibly illustrated in Hamilton than yesterday afternoon, when the monster procession of the city's artisans filed its way through the street . . . the present occasion will long be remembered, marking as it does a memorable epoch in the history of trades unionism." Healey took his dream and his message to Toronto and Oshawa during the following weeks, lecturing in support of the striking telegraphers, and speaking before Oshawa's civic holiday demonstration. Organized by Etna Assembly (2355), the Oshawa event featured a mile-long procession, many speeches, and an afternoon of sports. It drew unionists and Knights of Labor from Toronto, Bowmanville, Cobourg, Whitby, and Hamilton. Molders from the Joseph Hall Works struck a commemorative medallion in the midst of the parade. The entire event was judged to be "the most brilliant sight seen in Oshawa for many years."[50]

Belleville's civic holiday was similarly celebrated on 18 August 1884, as the Order led a large group of molders, unorganized workers, volunteer firemen, and interested citizens to Bleecker's Grove, where "the triangle, an emblem of the Knights of Labor, was prominent in the arrangement of fixtures." Bringing the word of labor reform to the city's workers was a quartet of prominent Toronto Knights of Labor, Phillips Thompson, Charles March, Alfred Jury, and D. J. O'Donoghue. A Mr. Wallbridge, representing Belleville's Knights of Labor, introduced the speakers "saying he was proud to stand before an audience with the colors of the Knights of Labor upon his breast, that he was proud of all honest laborers, and should always be proud of being one of them." O'Donoghue stressed the benefits of organization for women workers, and perhaps struck a responsive chord in one young woman's mind. Marie Joussaye, later active in the organization of the Toronto Working Woman's Protective Association (also known as the Working Girls' Union) first surfaced after this demonstration, dedicating some lines of verse "To The Knights of Labor" in the pages of a local newspaper. Joussaye first questioned:

> The praises sung of wealthy men,
> Of prince, and duke, and peer,

and closed with a memorial to more humble men:

> You will find no monarch who can show
> A record half so grand.
> God bless great Labor's true born Knight,
> The honest laboring man.

Two years later, the "Belleville sister's" poetry appeared, not in the *Belleville Intelligencer*, but in the *Journal of United Labor*, official international organ of the Knights of Labor, and in O'Donoghue's Toronto *Labor Record*. "Labor?" asked one stanza. "Why yes my friend I do," was the prompt reply. The last lines spoke of Joussaye's recently acquired commitment:

> Oh workingmen and women,
> Who toil for daily bread,
> Cheer up, don't be discouraged,
> There's better times ahead.
> Be faithful to our Order
> Obey and keep its laws,
> And never fail when you've a chance
> To advocate our cause.
> And so we'll stand together
> United heart and hand
> And make our cause victorious
> All over every land.

Won over to the Knights of Labor in the early years of organizing in Belleville, Marie Joussaye would continue to struggle for labor's cause in the difficult years of decline in the 1890s.[51]

Converts like Joussaye were no doubt quite rare, but the parades, demonstrations, and civic holiday celebrations that had prompted her fraternal poem to the Knights of Labor were not. In border towns like Sarnia, Windsor, and Gananoque LAs of the Knights of Labor often joined their American counterparts in demonstrations of international labor solidarity. A Port

Huron demonstration in September 1886 drew a number of western Ontario Knights to hear Powderly and Trevellick speak, while the Order's Dominion Day festivities in Hamilton in 1884 attracted American workers from Buffalo and other upstate New York towns. When 3,000 Detroit workingmen marched under banners proclaiming "The Coming Knights of Labor," and "We Want Reciprocity," picturing Tom Barry, Henry George, Powderly, and Trevellick, they were joined by a Windsor delegation, headed by a large broom bearing the inscription, "K. of L. clear the way."[52] Internationalism, a basic premise of the movement culture, won strong adherents on marches like these.[53]

The value of such events, of course, lay in stimulating working people to a more vigorous support of the labor-reform platform. In surmounting a host of unmentioned difficulties, local Knights across the province must have consolidated their attachments to the Order's program of reform. But the problems involved in orchestrating such awesome demonstrations of labor's strength often restricted the zeal of the committed, or induced restraint. Thus, Thomas J. O'Neil of Napanee wrote to Powderly in the fall of 1887:

> We consider the getting up of a Labor Demonstration and making a success of it a very important factor for the success of the Labor Cause in this locality. There is a big work to be done here and requires patience to insure success. We propose to have a monster demonstration here on the 24th of May next and shall commence in January. What we will require for the occasion will be an able exponent of all the Labor question – if you could recommend one to us we shall be pleased – as the farmers in this section having been hit by Co-operative business look with disfavor on any organization tending to co-operation.[54]

Ingersoll's Alex J. Johnson, Recording Secretary of LA 2416, also saw a labor demonstration as a large step forward, tending "greatly to the increase of [the] order in this vicinity."[55] In manufacturing-distributing centers like these, surrounded by agricultural lands, farmer–labor unity must have been an important consequence of successful rallies. When the Dundas Knights of Labor held their first demonstration in August 1886 they noted explicitly that it was their purpose "to endeavor to awaken an interest in Labor Reform among the farming community," and they invited a large body of neighboring "agriculturalists."[56]

The success of such efforts can be measured by the sheer magnitude and diversity of labor demonstrations during the summer months of 1886–7, a period of extensive Knights of Labor organizing. In Toronto, the membership gains of past months were visible in "a gigantic labour procession" in early September 1886, inaugurating, according to the *Canadian Labor Reformer*, a labor holiday throughout the Dominion. Reports claimed that nearly 8,000 unionists and Knights of Labor had taken part in the demonstration, led by such prominent labor leaders as Richard F. Trevellick, DA 125's MW, Sam McNab, J. T. Carey of St. Catharines, J. R. Brown of Oshawa, and long-time labor advocate John Armstrong.[57] Such an impressive showing surprised few in a stronghold of organized labor like Toronto, but equally forceful processions had occurred elsewhere as well.

As the Iron Molders' International Union convened in London in early July 1886, labor's ranks seemed to expand noticeably and the city's LAs and molders' union led 4,000 workingmen and women through the streets. The *London Advertiser* captured the meaning of the unbroken line of craftsmen, women workers, and unskilled laborers, many of them – barbers, typographers, and metalworkers – mounted on vehicles displaying work techniques, when it entitled coverage of the parade, "In Their Might."[58]

London's demonstration was followed by similar processions in Chatham, St. Catharines, Stratford, Woodstock, and Lindsay (judged a rare failure due to the town's inability to attract workers from surrounding villages, towns, and cities). These small Ontario towns seemed transformed, their populations swollen by incoming Knights from Aylmer, Tillsonburg, Norwich, Ingersoll, Welland, Thorold, St. Thomas, and London, their streets shadowed with banners proclaiming, "Labor is Noble and Holy," "The Injury to One is the Concern of All," and "Welcome to All Honest Toilers," their buildings decorated with flags and bunting. Wildly dressed "calithumpians" cavorted along the routes of the parades, as workers rode the ubiquitous wagons demonstrating the "arts and mysteries" of honest labor. In Woodstock, 80–100 cars representing almost every branch of industry formed the core of the procession of 1,000–2,000 people. Many of these vehicles were two stories high drawn by four horses. They contained bakers making bread, tinsmiths fashioning dishes, furniture men at work, barbers cutting hair, coopers finishing a barrel, sewing machines in motion, paperhangers decorating a model house, printers setting type, caneworkers strapping chairs, and countless other groups of workers. Niagara Peninsula Knights of Labor celebrated the civic holiday in St. Catharines on 15 August 1887. Three thousand strong, they marched through the town with banners proclaiming, "Labor Rise and Defend Your Dignity," "The Land for the People," and "Long Hours Must Go," and surprised "many of the spectators, who had no idea that the workingmen were so well organized." As imposing spectacles of class pride, dignity, and self-worth, these processions prepared working people for the inevitable speeches that always followed such parades. And here, too, the message was unmistakable. Alderman McCall of St. Thomas told those gathered in Woodstock of the odiousness of class distinctions. "As the poor man walked the streets," he related, "he had to raise his hat to the rich, but did anyone ever see a rich man raise his hat to a poor one?" He hoped that if *he* ever raised his hat to a rich man, "his arm would break and that no doctor in the country would set it." Richard Trevellick assured those massed at Chatham that one day soon the monopolists would have to work or die of starvation. That day, he promised, would be ushered into being by the Knights of Labor, and would grant the common worker the independence that had been the sole property of the monopolist.[59]

One year later, on 1 July 1887, Ingersoll's Order celebrated Dominion Day. The crowd was estimated at 5,000, swelled by Knights of Labor supporters from Woodstock, London, and St. Thomas. Labor's East Elgin representative, A. B. Ingram, addressed the throng, as did St. Thomas's Alderman Hess and Ingersoll's mayor. A lacrosse match, a play, a garden social, and miscellaneous sporting contests provided the entertainment, but a local Knight, Joseph Brady, may well have appealed to the largest group present when he denounced "the controlling power that capital had over labor." While hoping that all had enjoyed themselves during the day, he reminded them of the ultimate purpose: "A fair day's work for a fair day's pay."[60] It was in the context of happenings such as these that the Order spread "like wildfire throughout Canada," and that western Ontario manufacturing, distribution, and railroad centers like Brantford, Ingersoll, Woodstock, London, and St. Thomas made "rapid strides toward perfection in organization." As the "good work" continued, a culture was on the march.[61]

Labor demonstrations of this stature seemed rare in eastern Ontario, although the Ottawa-Hull region witnessed significant processions in the early 1890s, and the Order there retained its potency longer than in south-central Canada.[62] But smaller affairs seemed more characteristic, as in Gananoque in the fall of 1887, when 300 Knights of Labor accompanied F. M. Fogg from his hotel to the Dufferin Hall, where he addressed a public meeting on the labor question.[63] In the place of the "gigantic labour procession," however, eastern Ontario Knights substituted the "monster" picnic and excursion, the islands of the St. Lawrence being particularly conducive to this kind of activity. Picnics and excursions, of course, were also utilized by the Order in south-central and southwestern Ontario,[64] and had often followed closely upon the heels of a dramatic procession, but in the eastern Ontario towns of Brockville, Kingston, and Gananoque they appeared in sharper relief, perhaps because of labor's relatively subdued presence, or smaller numbers.[65] August civic holidays in Gananoque were traditionally celebrated with a mammoth Knights of Labor picnic on Hay Island or at Lindsay's Grove. Drawing 2,000–3,000 people, these outings also consolidated ties with the

Order in nearby Kingston. After the 1887 picnic, which featured a wide array of sports, including a tug-of-war between rival Assemblies, the local paper commented: "Probably no gathering anywhere near the size ever took place here, where there was such good order and so little disturbance through drink. Altogether we think the Knights of Labor have reason to congratulate themselves . . . They have shown that they are a power in the community, able to command respect."[66]

Also commanding respect, both in the general community and among the membership, was the Order's strict attendance at funerals of deceased brothers and sisters. Upon the death of a member, the LA mourned its loss with a special Memorial Assembly, appointing an historian, knight of the unbroken vow, poet, and eulogist.[67] Funerals became a moment of appreciation of the accomplishments of ordinary men and women, a chance to commemorate the ties that had meant so much over the course of a lifetime, the very touchstone of solidarity. "Men who fail to show respect to the dead," argued the *Palladium of Labor*, "seldom or ever respect anything outside of their own precious selves."[68] Attendance at funerals, then, became a collective as opposed to individual choice, a matter of principle and pride. Across the province Knights of Labor rallied to the sides of those who had recently passed out of their midst; "in a body" was the manner in which they paid their last respects.[69] Death often drew out the generosity built into a long-standing culture of collectivity and mutual aid. LA 3040, in Hamilton, helped a struggling Mrs. George Mills after her husband's death with a cash donation.[70]

But perhaps the most dramatic statement on the importance of funerals in the culture of Ontario workers in the 1880s was made in Brockville, in mid-June 1883. One of the town's young sons, William Hutcheson, was a 28-year-old union molder, and a member of the Knights of Labor, a man who, had he lived, would not have been unlike LA 2311's Samuel F. Miller. Like many other late-nineteenth-century "sand artists," Hutcheson had tramped a good deal in his time: he had worked in Oshawa, and had only been in Troy, New York, three short weeks, working at the Cooperative Stove Foundry, before his untimely death. Hutcheson had arrived in Troy at an inauspicious moment. For months a strike had raged at the Troy Malleable Iron Company. Part-owner and manager of the concern, William Sleicher, Jr., hired and armed nonunion men, and confrontations were common. William Hutcheson had been the tragic victim of one such street battle between unionists and non-unionists. Six members of Troy's Lodge No. 2 of the Iron Molders' International Union accompanied his body to his old home, among them two other "old Brockville boys." The resulting funeral was described as "an imposing spectacle," followed by "one of the largest corteges ever seen in . . . town." Friends and spectators crowded outside the house where the service was held, and the procession to the grave was headed by the Knights of Labor, the Molders' Union, the Battalion Band, and deputations from various labor societies and unions. The Troy molders expressed open indignation at Hutcheson's foul murder, attacking the employer responsible; they referred to the dead molder as a "comrade." All of this for a man less than 30 years old who had left Brockville some time before, an unmarried transient with few apparent roots. There was a class stance operative in this Brockville funeral, a culture at work.[71]

In all of this, from the pounding footsteps of thousands of workers marching in Toronto, through a day of sports in Ingersoll, to, finally, a tearful funeral in Brockville, a labor "hop" in Thorold, or a joyous day of picnics, speeches, and frolicking on an idyllic island in the St. Lawrence River, we catch glimpses of a self-generating culture of collectivity, mutuality, and solidarity. An understanding of class place and pride stood at the core of this culture, as well as individual longing for a better world. Forging a multitude of diverse, often contradictory, individual longings into a collective assertion was the movement itself. As an exhilaratingly creative but flawed effort, the Knights of Labor was the very embodiment of human striving that evolved out of residual components of a class culture, nudged toward new, or emergent, purpose by those who embraced the cause of labor's rights – men and women who, by advocating reform, did much to create a culture of "democratic promise." Their aim was the realization of a community of wage earners gathered together in the sacred bonds of S.O.M.A. The difficulty we ourselves experience in comprehending their vision and their striving is a measure of significant failures – theirs *and* ours.[72]

But in the 1880s that failure was not a settled fact, etched in historical concrete; the sharp clarity of defeat was not yet there for all to see. Thousands of Ontario workers took Richard Trevellick's words to heart when he promised that the Knights of Labor would "make Labour respectable by having men and women respect themselves, and while courteous and kind, refuse to bow and cringe to others because they possess wealth and social position."[73] Certainly Thomas J. O'Neil, of Napanee's Courage LA 9216, regarded such proclamations with appropriate seriousness, and wrote to Powderly that "This section of the country is sadly in need of organization, but fear of the money kings (the Rathbuns) keep the working class in slavery."[74] Railroad men, organized in Headlight LA 4069 of St. Thomas, acted upon Trevellick's words in 1885. They conducted their own statistical survey of their town of 11,000 with the intention of using "all lawful means of obtaining their rights, also to educate those of our members who heretofore have permitted others to do their thinking, thereby allowing themselves to be used as mere machines in the hands of unscrupulous men."[75] The *Labor Union* proclaimed its mission in mid-January 1883: "to Spread the Light; to expose the inequalities of distribution by which the few are enriched at the expense of the many. To call things by their right names, and to point out to workingmen how these inequities could be redressed and the workingman secure the full reward of his toil."[76] Employers found much to dislike in the words of Trevellick, O'Neil, LA 4069, and the *Labor Union*. Their actions throughout the 1880s spoke loudly of their fears and antagonisms. They regarded the increasing consciousness of class, and threat of active opposition, as a dangerous development. By 1891 the business community was convinced that "the spirit of trades unionism is strangling honest endeavour, and the hard-working, fearless thorough artisan of ten years ago is degenerating into the shiftless, lazy, half-hearted fellow who, with unconscious irony, styles himself a knight of labor."[77] The culture had, as well as advocates, staunch opponents.

## Labor's intellectuals

It was in the midst of a virtual war between these contending forces (in which battles were both intellectual and practical) that the labor-reform cause gained hard-won adherents. And it was in this context that the "educational" thrust so prominent in the Order's own priorities consolidated. LAs became, in the parlance of the 1880s, "schools of instruction" in which the lessons learned turned on the principles of labor reform and reached a mass audience in literally hundreds of reading rooms, Knights of Labor libraries, and Assembly halls. An early history of American coal miners claimed that the Order was "the best educational institution for workingmen ever devised," and described the LAs as schools frequently owned by the members and run "on the co-operative plan." From this milieu came many future leaders and able rank-and-file speakers of the United Mine Workers of America. In the words of Richard Trevellick, it was in the "schoolroom" of the LA where members first learned "their duties and their rights."[78]

A handful of committed publishers/editors/journalists provided much of the text of instruction. Often practical printers themselves, these men struggled through the 1880s and 1890s, working into the early morning hours to put out their weekly journals, devoted, as in the case of the *Palladium of Labor*, "To the Interests of Workingmen and Workingwomen." Always balanced delicately on the brink of financial ruin, such newspapers kept afloat during these years only by dint of extraordinary effort, personal perseverance, and occasional support from a long-established trade union. Smothered by their dependence on advertising revenue, limited by their subscribers' inability to contribute financially, with circulation often hovering around the 1,000 mark, seldom over 5,000, these papers occupied an unenviable position in the often gloomy world of the nineteenth-century press. Small wonder that the men who kept them going were occasionally ill tempered, and indiscriminatingly combative, as with Hamilton's William H. Rowe (perhaps, even St. Thomas's George Wrigley, who faced considerable opposition in his stand against labor's Tory representative, A. B. Ingram), or constantly maneuvering to attain economic ends, like the notorious but resourceful A. W. Wright.[79] But whatever their personal idiosyncrasies these men attempted to move the class beyond economism, striving "to take a broader and more comprehensive view of the entire subject of Labor Reform than is embodied in mere unionism, and to grasp and apply those great underlying principles of equity and justice between men which alone can permanently and satisfactorily solve the issues between Labor and Capital."[80] This was an important component of what Frank Watt has referred to as the "freely germinating" radicalism of the 1880s, a phenomenon spawned by the presence of the Knights of Labor.[81] As the turn-of-the-century social gospel fiction writers well knew, that radicalism owed much to the individuals who started, staffed, and sustained the labor press; men who stirred others to want more than what was parsimoniously handed to them.[82]

In their strivings to challenge people to want different things, and to envision a more egalitarian order, the reform editors may well have been aided, as well as undermined, by popular evening dailies like the *Toronto News*. Even established Grit organs like the *London Advertiser* and the Toronto *Globe* courted a working-class readership, running columns like "The Knights of Labor Corner" that provided a haven for bohemian journalists and dissident writers. Men like these took their stand against what they referred to as "intellectual prostitution" and attacked their peers who failed to sympathize with labor's plight.[83] It was in this milieu that Canada's most significant late-nineteenth-century labor reformer eventually came of age as a radical social critic. Phillips Thompson started the intellectual odyssey that would take him from the humor columns of the daily press through the Knights of Labor to the post-1900 Socialist Party in the early 1860s while working for the *St. Catharines Post*. He penned an attack on those denigrating the mechanic and the farmer, "the bone and sinew of the country." Rejecting the rampant Toryism characteristic of political discourse in the Canadas, he struck an early blow for the developing producer ideology, advocating union of the Canadian provinces along republican lines, "a United British American Independent Republic."[84] By the early 1870s, as Jimuel Briggs, Thompson was

Figure 10. Phillips Thompson. *Source:* Public Archives of Canada.

engaged in a perpetual satirical attack upon the foundations of the Canadian social and political order; in the closing years of the decade, after rejecting the elite nationalists of the Canada First movement, and after assimilating a healthy dose of American radical social thought while working in the United States, he moved directly toward an explicit attack and joined the Knights of Labor.[85]

In all his writings, Thompson consistently sought to elevate people's conception of their own sense of self, striking at deeply rooted feelings of inadequacy; such inner insecurities, he knew, were part of the range of forces working against active opposition to the inequities of the age. "There is far too much, even in our ranks of the worship of so-called 'eminent' and leading men," he once noted. To combat this problem he directed some of his most innovative work toward the cultural realm, arguing again and again for an end to class distinctions: "Every relic of class distinction, every social movement based upon the permanent inferiority of one section of the community to another should be fought by all means in our power. Snobbery in its various manifestations is the great bulwark of capitalistic injustice." For Thompson, as for so many labor reformers of the 1880s, the task was to "Spread the Light," upholding the power of thought, educating the people to see the world in new, liberating ways. The industrial struggle was waged not just in the factories, mines, and shops but in the realm of ideas. It was this important insight that led Thompson into a critique of bourgeois culture, its literature, art, and music. "So much of the lore of the past is misleading by establishing wrong ideals for our admiration, perverting facts and subtly inculcating the doctrine of superior rights to the ruling and privileged classes and humility and subserviency as the correct attitude for the toiling masses," he argued in 1885. Political economy and history needed to be rewritten, to reveal the "monstrous character of the wrongs long maintained in the names of patriotism and loyalty." Citing Henry George, H. S. Hyndman, Karl Marx, and Edward Kellogg, Thompson noted that this process was well underway. In literature he saw the works of Dickens, Hugo, and George Eliot as worthy of emulation, while the poets Whitman and Swinburne drew his praise. "The literature of the future will be the powerful ally of democracy and reform," he contended, "instead of the prop and buttress of every form of legalized wrong and injustice." In writings like these Thompson enriched the labor-reform critique of conventional life.[86]

Representing the "high" side of the movement culture, Thompson's work was a sustained critique of all facets of Canadian industrial-capitalist society in the 1880s. In the limited, parochial context in which it emerged, as Russell Hann has argued, lay the origins of Canadian socialism. Throughout the 1880s, however, Thompson's significance was of a more elementary character: always suitable for mass consumption, his message was nevertheless unique in refusing to sacrifice intellectual integrity, even artistic worth. Its presence in the reform journals and on Knights of Labor platforms across Ontario insured that working people who flocked to the Order would gain an understanding of their oppression that was more than mere crude condemnation. For Thompson – in his editorial and journalistic endeavors in the established and labor-reform newspapers of the late nineteenth century, in his book *The Politics of Labor*, and in his many speeches and debates – provided an evaluation of contemporary life that was as formidable as anything that the genteel intellectual figures of the time could marshal in defense of the rule of monopoly and the "uppertendom." This confluence of a sophisticated and radical scrutiny of life in the Ontario of the 1880s had its echoes in many spheres and was voiced by an active contingent of Knights of Labor speakers and organizers; it was quietly assimilated, if not loudly endorsed, by local, home-grown labor reformers who appeared in virtually every Canadian manufacturing town in the 1880s; and it crept into the "low" realms of the movement culture, appearing in anonymous lines of verse or social criticism. It was, in short, at the center of the recruiting drive that brought the Knights of

Labor to prominence. As an exemplary "brainworker" in labor's cause, Thompson was but the most able of many labor-reform advocates.

Those cities in which Thompson figured centrally – Toronto and Hamilton – proved to be the home base of an important group of labor spokesmen, whose impact would be felt across the province. D. J. O'Donoghue, A. W. Wright, Alfred Jury, Charles March, George Collis, William Vale, and Edward Williams emerged as central figures in the Knights of Labor in these years. Such men, aside from their considerable presence in the metropolitan centers, often took their views to neighboring cities and towns, their talents as speakers appreciated by the many new recruits they drew to the reform cause. O'Donoghue and Jury regularly spoke in the civic halls of small-town Ontario, instructing audiences in the need for organization. When Dundas workers first discussed the possibility of a Knights of Labor demonstration in their town they decided on the "able, eloquent, fearless and strictly honorable and honest exponent of labor's cause," Ed Williams, as their guest lecturer.[87] On 15 May 1885 George Collis (traveling under the alias "Sandy the Tinker") lectured in London, laying before the workers of that city "the declaration of principles of the Knights of Labor as a remedy, if not the cure, for the evils from which humanity is suffering." The next evening he addressed "a private meeting of the Order." An Oshawa Knight offered his thanks to men like Collis, writing to the *Palladium of Labor* that, "The Knights of Hamilton are to be congratulated for the missionaries they have sent throughout the country." These well-known Ontario proponents were joined by such Knights of Labor notables and advocates as Powderly, Trevellick, Henry George, Tom Barry, Leonora Barry, Frank Foster, and F. M. Fogg, and in this way the ideology of labor reform spread across the province.[88]

The seeds of labor-reform thought planted by these itinerant spokesmen bloomed in places that seem strange to those who know Ontario and its labor movement today – small towns like Ingersoll, Picton, and Petrolia – the converts to labor's ranks coming from all walks of life, bringing diverse and rich talents to bear on the developing critique of Canada's industrial-capitalist society. One of the more striking cases was that of Galt's J. L. Blain, a well-educated "rat from the sinking ship of aristocracy." Blain had involved himself in a manufacturing concern only to see "a large sum of money disappear in the pockets of Sheriffs lawyers and others through the competition of gigantic manufacturing corporations which run the smaller fry off the track." This experience turned the Galt resident around, and he became a lecturer, addressing the subject of "Capital and Labor," proposing remedies for the "present unjust state of society in which 50% of the products are absorbed by non-producers."[89]

The closing decades of the nineteenth century also nurtured men like Walter A. Ratcliffe, the blind and deaf socialist poet of Listowel (home of LA 6175). His works turned "with a bond of deep sympathy to the sufferings of mankind;" agonized as the people bore "the fetters of ceaseless toil" while the wealthy revelled "in vastly disproportionate luxury;" and condemned "the poverty made hopeless by great monopolies of land." He sang of a coming era when mankind would be free, and he promised men and women that the new order would shatter the limitations of the past:

> What mists would melt, what illusions flee,
> If from enslaving self man might be free.

As one of the "outposts of misfortune," Ratcliffe illuminated how bravely misfortune could be borne, and how it could be overcome:

> Perish Briton, perish Gaul!
> Sons of Canada, be all!
> From your limbs your fetters shake;
> Sons of Canada, awake![90]

Hamilton's Thomas Towers, carpenter poet and Knights of Labor activist, wrote similarly throughout the 1880s, but his words often stressed the organizational solution raised by the Order:

> Why do ye bow in cringing fear
> Unto thy fellow kind,
> When on this earth thou art the power,
> The master hand and mind.
>
> Wouldst thou be free, then hasten,
> Join freedom's gathering host,
> And let thy life, an action be,
> And not an empty boast.

In "To The Toilers," Towers urged the downtrodden to:

> Come into the fold of the righteous,
> You'll find there a crown and a throne;
> For the earth belongs to the people,
> And the wealth of a world is your own.

The embittered "Vincent" was less optimistic than either Ratcliffe or Towers, and concentrated on attacking the "Mammon Worshippers":

> Let all faith be turned to falsehood,
> And all love be turned to hate,
> Let life be a brutal struggle
> Every man against his mate.

But, ironically enough, as "Vincent" railed against the dominant culture, depicting life under capitalism as a "hopeless slavery, the only release from which is death and the only result of which is to prepare a few more lives for a fate possibly similar," he served notice of the strength, resiliency, and potential of the movement culture of which he was a part.[91]

The poet's vision was thus an important stimulus to labor reform in the years of most intense Knights of Labor activity. As part of an oral culture now essentially lost, surviving only as fragments of verse adorning the pages of the labor press, popular poetry in an age of working-class upheaval built upon the class and movement cultures to deepen working people's appreciation of the need for change. As Toronto's bookbinders, organized in LA 5743, reported: "In the Order of the Knights of Labor there is an Order of Business which calls for readings, poems, etc., and by this means members are educated."[92] Poetry helped, in short, to create a sympathetic audience for the many labor spokesmen who emerged as advocates of the Knights of Labor:

And hosts of artisans are fired
In their industrial hives,
With the same spirit that inspired
The "Farmer of St. Ives";
Which has brought forth a giant power,
Without the gun and sabre,
Before which tyrannies shall cower.
Hail to the Knights of Labor.[93]

Most of these worker–Knight of Labor intellectuals of the 1880s, if they did not reside in Toronto or Hamilton, have left only the most indistinct record on the past, although we know many of them through their pseudonyms: St. Thomas's "Knight of the Brush" and "True Reformer;"[94] Brantford's "Drawbar," an employee of the GTR workshops;[95] or "Pete Rolea," from the oil-producing community of western Ontario.[96] An Everett, Simcoe County sawmill worker, signing himself simply "A Workman," wrote to the *Palladium of Labor* of work and its discontents in the lumber industry and the consequent formation of an LA of Knights of Labor. "There is but one remedy," he argued, "and that is let every workman become a Knight of Labor and assert his rights."[97] "Portsmouth," a humorist from the Kingston area, urged upon workers another solution to their problems, stressing the benefits of literacy. In a regular *Labor Union* feature, "Our Spelling Reform Column," this "felo-worker" issued his satirical plea: "The strongest opozition we have iz the 'upperten' or *bon on* who say that if this iz akomplisht the wurkingman kan spel as well as us. That'z the skeleton in the kupboard!"[98] "J. B." proposed a toast to the "Valiant Knights" from the small town of Jordan, Ontario:

> Press on, ye valiant Knights, press on;
> Your cause is just, prevail it must,
> The world awaits the dawn.
> The pulse of time must cease to beat,
> When Knights of Labor own defeat,
> We urge you then, press on.[99]

"Lignum Vitae" reported to the *Journal of United Labor* on the progress of Guelph LAs 2980 and 4703: "The masses are beginning to believe us when we tell them this endless toil for a miserable existence was never intended by an all-wise creator. I wish I had only more time that I could go out to these people and invite them into an Order whose object is the complete emancipation of all mankind, and lift from off their necks the yoke of subjection, and often tyranny of a few."[100] From virtually every corner of the province, then, anonymous correspondents informed labor newspapers of the local state of reform agitation.

In their own communities these men more often had real names. J. W. Osborne of St. Thomas stumped western Ontario in the interests of the Order, addressing Knights of Labor meetings, calling for an end to working-class subserviency, proclaiming that "the mighty power of the labor element would soon make itself so apparent that capital would bow before it."[101] In Galt and Hespeler, Terence O'Toole, as comfortable with a quote from Burns as he was in a discussion of Irish Home Rule (which he would travel to Toronto to take part in), boomed the reform cause.[102] Grimsby's W. T. Church took his stand against "interested politicians, scheming wire-pullers, and even so-called ministers of the gospel, urged on by pampered and bloated aristocrats, . . . doing all in their power to widen the gap between Capital and Labor, and establish a claim of superiority for the former." He praised the "hundreds of brave and fearless men and women . . . standing up boldly in defense of human rights, human equality, eternal justice, and universal brotherhood, establishing papers devoted to Labor and Labor reform in every section of the country, thus educating a sentiment that will e'er long bring joy and comfort to the hearts and homes of millions of toilers the world over." Out of such efforts, he felt sure, "The whole earth shall be lighted, As Eden was of old."[103] Henry Schuhl of Hamilton, an ordained minister, enlightened German workers on the principles and objects of the Knights of Labor, traveling to Berlin to address Germania LA 9691.[104]

Perhaps one of the most important of these home-grown reformers was London's Joseph Marks. Marks was a tinsmith in the Grand Trunk Railway shops and his long-standing involvement with labor stretched into the 1920s. As one of the leading figures in the Ontario Independent Labor Party (ILP), and editor of the militant, influential London- (later Toronto-) based *Industrial Banner*, Marks joined Hamilton's ILP representative (1906–19), Allan Studholme, in a group of early-twentieth-century workingmen's advocates who had first cut their activist teeth on Knights of Labor struggles in the 1880s.[105] A young man when the Order first established itself in western Ontario, Marks apparently played little part in the early organizational efforts in London, which were dominated by LA 3305's John R. Brown. By 1888, however, the Grand Trunk worker had emerged as Recording Secretary of LA 7110. He informed the *Journal of United Labor* that "a number of our brothers are clubbing together to buy a hall in conjunction with the United Labor Co-operative Association, to be used as a permanent headquarters and Assembly Room, with reading room and library attached." Engaged in the thankless task of "hunting up delinquents," Marks predicted "a gratifying increase in membership." January, he noted, had been "a month of grand work and we have gained considerable ground." These winter efforts paid few dividends, and western Ontario's Knights of Labor declined noticeably in the next two years: DA 138 (St. Thomas-London) suffered a severe membership loss in the first six months of 1888, declining from 609 to 283.[106] In May 1890 Marks was at it again, this time as DMW of DA 138, doing his utmost to rebuild the Order. "I am holding public meetings and visiting locals every week," he wrote to Powderly. He had addressed audiences of 300 in St. Thomas, Woodstock, and Stratford in March and April, lecturing on Edward Bellamy's conception of nationalism, and hoped to increase DA 138's membership by 900 in the remaining months of the year. "True men in the order had fought on in the face of many disappointments," he noted, "and today were beginning to see the fruits of their labor." All of this Marks did at his own expense, in spite of being ill for six weeks. "We mean business," was the determined note upon which he ended his letter to Powderly.[107]

Good intentions and hard work produced few tangible gains, however. By the early 1890s, the Order in western Ontario had definitely succumbed. But even this did not dampen the spirits of the indefatigable Marks. He was probably instrumental in establishing an educational experiment, the "Open Forum," later renamed the Radical Club, in London, and may have been involved in the publication of the *Searchlight*, a short-lived journal of an obscure organization, the Canadian Co-operative Commonwealth, a movement obviously battling to revive certain Knights of Labor principles.[108] Whatever their minor successes, these ventures quickly passed into oblivion. Replacing them was the Industrial Brotherhood, organized in the spring of 1891 at

Woodstock – the creation, almost single-handed, of Joseph T. Marks. Following in the footsteps of the People's Party of the United States, the Brotherhood sought to organize "a new and comprehensive movement to include all classes of workers, with the object of advancing needed social reforms." Very much like the now defunct Knights of Labor, the Industrial Brotherhood campaigned under the motto, "The equality of all, irrespective of race, creed, or condition, and the right of one citizen to the same advantages as those enjoyed by an other." Its central organizing principle was "Mutual Aid."[109] Marks was able to secure the Brotherhood representation in the TLC in 1894, although this involvement did not last long, as the established trade union movement expressed little interest in independent working-class politics. Nevertheless, Marks continued to beat the drum of the new organization, addressing audiences throughout western and central Ontario, popularizing the cause in the pages of the Industrial Brotherhood's official organ, the *Industrial Banner* and, in the opening years of the twentieth century, establishing the Labor Educational Association. In all of this, of course, he was merely resurrecting those causes he had championed as a Knight of Labor: education, social reform, and the organization of the whole class. As Marks's involvement in labor reform shifted in the first decade of the twentieth century toward the emerging Independent Labor Party, the institutions he had created out of his late-nineteenth-century experience also moved accordingly. A new generation of labor reformers embraced new causes in a new context, building the present, as had the Knights of Labor, out of the accomplishments of the past.[110] Like Phillips Thompson, Marks provides a forceful reminder of the significance of this moment of the Knights of Labor in the prehistory of Canadian radical and socialist thought.

What happened in the early years of the new century had also happened in the 1880s, but with one notable difference. In the decade of Knights of Labor upsurge Ontario's workers had few organic, committed, *bona fide* working-class leaders to guide them along the paths of labor reform. What the Knights of Labor took from the past, then, was *not* the personnel of previous struggles, an intellectual contingent capable of enthusiastic endorsement of social reform. A few "brainworkers," to be sure, did gravitate to the Order in the 1880s after considerable experience in previous decades, men like Phillips Thompson and A. W. Wright, although the latter's presence was, at best, a mixed blessing. And there were trade unionists like O'Donoghue, Jury, March, and Vale who could look back to the 1870s, but such men had been but mere apprentices in labor's reform effort (which was itself in its infancy in these years) in that early, and confusing, period; they grew to prominence in the 1880s, and they grew *with* the Knights of Labor.[111] The Order did, however, draw upon the past in its effort to "spread the light." It built directly on a class experience, on residual traditions of collectivity, easily turned toward mutual aid and solidarity. Out of this class experience came the George Collises and Joseph Markses, the "Vincent's" and "Knights of the Brush," and the Marie Joussayes, men and women who would reconstruct a class culture, forging a movement culture that allowed laboring people the vision of an alternative way of life.

## Challenging the dominant culture

Whole segments of the dominant culture may well have been challenged, if not undermined, by the critique raised by labor reformers and the movement culture of the Knights of Labor. Established religion, for instance, suffered setbacks in this era, and there is evidence that in many communities the Knights of Labor usurped the traditional role of the church.[112] Hamilton's "Vox Populi" voiced what must have been a common critique of the city pastors and their houses of worship: "You love Jesus Christ, you love to preach about him and do his will, I too with my Bro. Knights love his doctrine, and strive to carry out his will, also to obey his command, love one another . . . it is not Christ I find fault with, but, the inconsistent doctrines taught in or favored by the Church."[113] "Unity" commented on "the growing indisposition of the working class to attend church," attributing it to "the fact that many of our places of worship have become simply Sunday Clubs or opera halls, intended to attract rich congregations." Such "luxurious temples of Mammon" attracted few working people; if a minister wanted a working-class congregation, "Unity" suggested a few words from the pulpit on "usury, land grabbing, and the oppression exercised by capital."[114] One "Well Wisher," writing to the *Palladium of Labor*, was an example of what appeared to be a virtual tidal wave of attack crashing against the wall of religious indifference:[115]

> I could tell you how for years I attended church regularly, but for want of that brotherly society and sympathy fell away, and how becoming a K. of L. my soul rekindled with that human love, with that desire to help my brother man, and it grieves me to say that when I go to church instead of having more fuel placed to that fire it becomes quenched and smothered by the cold and intensely refined religious atmosphere which pervades the churches, and I would fair cry out with thousands of my fellow churchmen, O for a warm, kindly, Christ-like Church, a common place where we could all meet on an equality, and be brothers in Christ in this world, even as we hope to be in the next.

Such a church, this writer knew, would address "questions concerning the welfare of the working classes . . . for in these questions rest to a large extent the growth and prosperity of that church whose foundation [lies] in the humble Nazarene, Jesus Christ himself a carpenter and a workingman."[116]

In Smiths Falls Unity LA 6722 responded to the death of a local worker, expressing its sympathy to the young man's family, commending them "to the care and guidance of the General Master Workman of Assemblies above, who, chasteneth those whom he loves, who comforts those who mourn, and at last unites those loved ones together in the General Assembly above where there is no more sorrow or parting." Language like this suggests that the Order easily assumed a religious role, perhaps displacing the church or, at the very least, fulfilling certain working-class spiritual needs while it rooted them firmly in the worldly context of a particular community.[117]

Other aspects of the dominant culture also seemed to undergo change, shifting ground with the rise of the Knights of Labor. Temperance, once a plank in industrial-capitalist work discipline, became a mark of working-class independence and manliness, a cause for all Knights of Labor to champion vocally and practically. Instead of reading dime novels or popular religious tracts, workingmen and women began to pick up works of social criticism: George McNeill's *The Labor Movement; the Problem of Today* was advertised in Kingston newspapers; books on socialism and labor reform were readily available in Knights of Labor Assembly halls; newspapers of the Canadian Order, centered in Toronto and Hamilton, easily found their way to smaller towns like Lindsay or Port Dalhousie; and the works of Henry George could be debated in places as seemingly removed from labor reform as Prescott.[118] The cumulative effect of these, and other, developments altered dramatically the nature of social relationships in hundreds of Ontario communities, and pushed workers toward a new understanding of their place in the larger social order.

This process of heightened awareness of class interests reveals itself even at the point of critical assault upon the Knights and their international leadership. Albert V. Cross of Hamilton's LA 2481 addressed Powderly and the General Executive Board in 1887 on the question of Canadian autonomy, hoping that his communication would be "received in the same spirit that prompts us sending it," urging reform of the Order before "the majority of our people become monopolists anarchists or both and our members divided on questions of nationality and other prejudices proscribed by the Order":

> When we entered the Order we were taught that in home of labor there would be no distinctions of Country, Creed & Color because all were of the Earth and with equal rights to Earth, when we understood this great truth that all men are brothers we rejoiced, and we solomly resolved that we would do all in our power to strengthen the bonds of unity between the workers of the world and we are still steadfast to our principles and it is in this spirit we would draw your attention to these things.[119]

The promise of class unity that echoed in Cross's ears as he penned his lines of discontent was attractive to many other Ontario Knights of Labor. Indeed, for the Irish and for women, the Knights represented a concerted effort to challenge past cultural divisions and exclusionist practices. In attempting to overcome the residual experiences of a culture that denied a place to working women and pitted Irishman against Irishman, the Order raised the banner of class solidarity.

Throughout the history of nineteenth-century Canada Orange and Green stood as signposts attracting many workingmen to hostile and mutually exclusive camps. There are indications that this long-standing rift was on the verge of healing as early as the 1850s, and by the 1880s its impact had definitely subsided.[120] The Knights of Labor attempted to bury this "bloody shirt" forever during labor's upheaval, and all the evidence points toward a measure of success. Sectarian attachments wilted as the Order reconciled workers whose previous relationships had been rooted in adversity.[121] When St. Catharines members of the Emerald Beneficial Association marched with Merritton's True Blue Band in 1885, Hamilton's *Palladium of Labor* applauded this effort on the part of Orange and Green to bury the proverbial hatchet. Both the role of the Knights of Labor in overcoming this obstacle to labor unity, as well as the value of putting aside sectarian differences, were stressed: "we hail with delight this new departure, for just as long as capital can by hook or by crook, keep the masses separated, just so long is capital master of the situation but not a moment longer. Sectarian bigotry is now the only weapon that capital has to wield, and . . . the Knights of Labor is rendering it more and more harmless every day." "Take a leaf from the capitalist's book," urged the workingman's paper, "and never quarrel about religion." Such shifts in working-class practice, enriched by the Order's own assessment of change, mark the 1880s as a period of significant development for Ontario's workers.[122]

## The Irish

So pronounced was the change in this area that the fact of Irishness, which had long divided Protestant and Catholic, became a unifying factor, and was utilized to sustain the Knights of Labor and the movement culture of opposition. The institutional expression of this historical process was the Irish National Land League, a body that effectively wedded the North American Irish masses to the reform tradition. Upon the particular oppression of Ireland was constructed a passionate critique of privilege, power, and authority willingly embraced by the predominantly working-class Irish of North America.[123] As Powderly noted, this swelling of Irish nationalism fed directly into the Knights of Labor. "When the public, or Land League, meeting would be over," he recalled, a "secret meeting of the Knights of Labor would follow."[124]

The Canadian dimensions of this relationship between the Irish and the Order remain obscure, in part because discussion of Irish nationalism has concentrated on the pre-1870 history of Fenianism and the episodic and abortive raids of 1866.[125] But physical force nationalism had a platform in Toronto as late as 1877 and the city housed front organizations such as Hibernian No. 16, Emerald Beneficial Association, which certainly harbored Fenians. This "shadowy political underworld of the Irish in Canada in the 1870s and 1880s" has only been explored recently and no attention has been paid to the convergence of nationalist and labor-reform thought.[126] After 1879, however, when Devoy, Davitt, and Parnell created a New Departure uniting parliamentary, agrarian, and physical force organizations in order to achieve a just and permanent system of land tenure in Ireland and political autonomy for the country, the nationalist and labor-reform movements coalesced.[127] Parnell set the stage for this significant development in late 1879, his North American tour giving rise to a widespread network of Irish National Land League local branches. In Ontario the League was most active in Toronto, but Hamilton was also a center of organization and Irish and labor links were visible across the province.

Toronto's Irish Land League first surfaced in the early 1880s, drawing to its ranks such notable labor reformers as Daniel O'Donoghue, Phillips Thompson, A. W. Wright, and the English-born secularist Alf Jury. In the course of the next few years the Toronto League would prove a nursery of radical critics, spawning men like Bryan Lynch, active in the labor campaigns of 1886–7, and providing long-standing Irish nationalists like John McCormick with a vehicle to carry them toward an endorsement of independent labor politics. McCormick had written for Patrick Boyle's Fenian paper, the *Irish Canadian*, in the early 1870s, and by the opening years of the 1880s was an uncompromising advocate of the working class and author of the pamphlet *The Conditions of Labour and Modern Civilization*. More radical than most workers, McCormick nevertheless captured the drift of Irish nationalism into a class-based opposition to oppression and exploitation. With the enthusiastic reception afforded Henry George's views on land nationalization in the 1880s, buttressed by George's Toronto and Hamilton lectures in 1883 and 1887, the Irish land question and the labor-reform cause seemed as one. Phillips Thompson traveled to Ireland to investigate social conditions there, reporting back to his readers in the pages of the *Globe;* he also journeyed to Montreal when Parnell spoke on behalf of the Montreal Land League. With the rise of the Knights of Labor and the consequent organization of unskilled workers, the Irish Catholic working class found an independent voice for the first time. As Eric Foner has argued in the case of the American Land Leagues, the Knights of Labor quietly intersected with the more radical strains of Irish nationalism, providing "a social ethic that challenged the individualism of the middle class and the cautious social reformism" of the established political culture and the church.[128]

This process was visible wherever the Knights of Labor were strong, and in Ontario cities like London and St. Catharines Land Leagues emerged in the 1880s and endorsements of Home Rule for Ireland were backed up with cash donations for the struggle in the old country.[129] Gordon Bishop, a Gananoque steelworker, noted in his recollections that the Knights of Labor were led "principally by members of the Irish race who fled the slavery of peonage in their own land and who hated as fiercely the economic slavery of the New World." When Justin McCarthy spoke in Brockville's Opera House on the Land question and Home Rule for Ireland, residents from Bishop's Gananoque made the trek along the St. Lawrence to hear the lecture.

Terrence O'Toole traveled from Galt to Toronto to pay tribute to Michael Davitt, where he joined 4,000 others in honoring "this simple, honest, and fearless exponent of the 'eternal truths of justice.'"[130] Upon the formation of a Land League in Hamilton, prominent English Knight of Labor Ed Williams was quickly enlisted in the cause. He claimed that "the goodwill of every honest man was with the people of Erin in the struggle for their alienated rights and privileges." Campaigning for Hamilton Racey in 1886, George Collis claimed that 99 percent of the workingmen favored Home Rule. Before the 1887 Minneapolis General Assembly, Collis spoke at the ceremonies attending the reception given to Michael Davitt, "The Irish Patriot":

> In supporting these resolutions I ask no pardon as a representative of the country which was spoken of as being invaded. We shall never fear any such an invasion again. I feel proud to call you my friend, and let me assure you that among the five millions in the country there are a large proportion whose hearts beat in sympathy with those who are fighting the cause of Ireland. When the representative of Ireland came to Canada there were English and Irish ready to stand on the platform. Although we may feel that some of Michael Davitt's actions are not just the thing, we know the Irish have an honest representative; and although there may be some differences of opinion he always comes out right side up. He is working with us toward the one great end, the emancipation of the world. I sincerely pray, as a representative of the English class, that it may not be long until the Irish nation will take its place among the nation's of the world. Their fight is our fight.[131]

Men like these – Protestant, Catholic, secularist – formed the backbone of the Irish nationalist/Knights of Labor alliance. In espousing the cause of Irish radicalism, religious concerns became secondary for the labor reformers. Thus O'Donoghue, who could defend the Irish "Rebellions" as productive of much good, wrote to Powderly concerning the GMW's choice of three Knights of Labor to serve on a parliamentary committee: "You are right in assuming that they are too sensible to quarrel over religious matters – they are Knights of Labor, and will not forget the fact."[132] (Extremely conscious of religious persecution and always ready to speak on behalf of his fellow-Catholic workers, O'Donoghue was well suited to advise Powderly during the course of the sensitive negotiations with the Catholic Church in the aftermath of Quebec Bishop Taschereau's pastoral letter condemning the Order. But the essential point is that this whole affair, so prominent in historical discussion of the Order, caused only a minor stir in Ontario.)[133] Indeed, when reactionary political, religious, and intellectual figures convened an "Empire in Danger" meeting in Toronto in 1886, striking out against the agitation for Irish Home Rule, they were courageously opposed by Phillips Thompson and others. "Anti-Bigot" wrote to the *Palladium of Labor* to condemn such efforts to take "a lick at the papists," characterizing the meeting's attack on Irish self-government as "tyrannical and indefensible." Writing as neither an Irishman nor a Catholic, "Anti-Bigot" claimed to be simply one:

> Whose soul has learned to scorn
> Bigots alike in Rome or England born
> Who loath the venom whence so'er it springs,
> From Popes or Lawyers, Pastry Cooks or Kings.[134]

Under the impact of the Knights of Labor, then, sectarian concerns appeared to wither in the Ontario working-class world of the 1880s. The major ethnic cleavage within the English-speaking working-class would not disappear, of course, but a gap had been bridged and a division materially reduced. Irishness, once a force tearing apart the class, had become a source buttressing a more general radical social critique premised on an understanding of the need for unity. This awareness also led the Knights of Labor to address the woman question, so long ignored in the history of nineteenth-century labor reform.

## "Best men in the Order"

The introduction of women into the mass struggles and organizational upsurge of the 1880s, for instance, began to overcome decades of complacency. As we have seen in the cases of Toronto and Hamilton, the Knights of Labor drew women into the ranks with a wide range of theoretical considerations and practical activities. While the Order as a whole failed to get to the root of sex discrimination, inhibited as it was by the consensual norms of Victorian morality, it nevertheless raised the woman question within the Ontario labor movement for the first time. In doing so it heightened working-class awareness and moved toward solutions to the problems faced by women in general, and women workers in particular. To be sure, the Knights of Labor acted out of chivalrous intent, and did not abandon age-old conceptions of hearth and home, domesticity, and place. But they could turn this all to new purpose, and strike out at forces they felt to be undermining all that was good and proper in such traditions. In examining the fragmentary historical evidence of the Knights of Labor's relationship to women workers in Ontario we are struck, once more, with the Order's contribution as a force pushing constantly for alternatives, edging a culture toward an emergent sense of opposition and the need for unity and a class perspective. If the Order remained inhibited by the cultural norms of a society that circumscribed woman's role and established the usual proper sphere, it also ran headlong into those same norms in its attempts to build a movement encompassing all workers, male as well as female. Historians intent upon coming to grips with the Knights of Labor will have to confront the awkwardness of an experience that embraces many contradictions: at the same time that the secretary of a St. Louis tailors' Assembly confessed that contractors who were members of the Order were telling the parents of seamstresses that "no dissent girl belong to an assembly," shoe and garment workers throughout North America were in the midst of upheavals exhibiting militant mutuality bred of the unity of men and women operatives. While individual Knights might decry the despoliation of true womanhood in the factories and sweatshops of the 1880s, basing their arguments on the conventional wisdoms surrounding views of the female physique, the Ladies' Social Assembly of Olneyville, Rhode Island, established a socialistic day nursery in one of that milltown's largest churches. As the Order adhered to a romantic ideology that cherished gallantry and sentiment, women Knights like Leonora M. Barry departed from office wishing the new investigator of women's work success in "women's struggle for justice, equity and complete emancipation from political and industrial bondage." Finally, in an epoch not characterized by women's participation in the class struggle, events like the textile mill strikes in Cohoes (1882), Fall River (1884), Worcester (1884), and Louisville (1887), or the memorable Yonkers (1885) confrontation in the carpet-weaving industry, indicated that the Knights of Labor commitment to women's rights in the work place was not merely rhetorical.[135]

Hamilton's *Palladium of Labor* reflected the Order's refusal to ignore the plight of the woman worker at the same time that it echoed the confinements

Figure 11. Women delegates at the 1886 Richmond convention; Elizabeth Rogers, leader of the Chicago Knights, with child in center. *Source:* Powderly Papers, Catholic University, Washington, D.C.

of the age. It argued, on the one hand, that women came into the Order as the peers of men, equal to them and deserving of the same pay at the work place and the same recognition in the political and social sphere. There was apparently no position in the Knights of Labor a woman could not hold. On the other hand, however, this evaluation of equality ended up on the proverbial pedestal, buttressed by that predictable prop, the family, and the timeless innocence and preeminence of femininity: "Upon motherhood we base brotherhood, and in our family circle we pledge ourselves to defend the fair name and reputation of an innocent sister even with our lives. If there is any pre-eminence given either sex in our order, it is given to women."[136] Across the province the Knights defied convention by opening their Assembly halls to women workers at the same time that they extended this invitation to organize in a most traditional manner. When Canadian women were won to the cause it was seldom through the strike, the mass campaign, the boycott, or the demonstration. Rather, for the "fairer sex," the ticket into the Order was often stamped at the soirée, the hop, or the social. John Lawson of Toronto informed Powderly of a typical undertaking in 1889: "On Friday 12th we are giving an 'At Home' to the unorganized ladies here to try and persuade them to organize . . . We expect about 250 ladies present."[137] In a "Blunt Sermon for Young Ladies" the *Palladium of Labor* struck out, in its usual fashion, against the finery and pretense of the aristocracy of money and power, chastising the "ladies – caged birds of beautiful plumage, but sickly looks; pale pets of the parlor, who vegetate in unhealthy atmosphere, like the potato germinating in a dark cellar . . . pining and wasp-waisted, doll-dressed, consumption-mortgaged, music murdering, novel-devouring, daughters of fashion and idleness." Against this class, the paper held up the woman of virtue, the "real lady": "rosy cheeked and bright-eyed, who can darn a stocking and mend her own dress, who can command a regiment of pots and kettles, and be a lady when required." Such a woman, according to editor William H. Rowe, was "a girl that young men are in quest of for a wife." Similar (though seldom quite as offensive) statements appeared often enough in the early period of the *Palladium*'s life, when a "Women's Own Department" was featured regularly. This column was discontinued in October 1883, however, and these platitudes became increasingly rare. Yet even at this early date, alongside of Rowe's crude moralizing, Katie McVicar, writing under the pseudonym "the Canadian Girl," could pose the issue of central concern to working women in a more concrete manner: "organization is our only hope. Our employers are organized for the purpose of keeping the selling prices up and the manufacturing prices down, and we ought certainly to accept the assistance and invitation of our gentlemen Knights and organize; remain no longer strangers to each other, but combine and protect ourselves to some purpose."[138]

In later years McVicar's line of argument would be pursued by other, albeit often anonymous, writers. In an open letter to "working girls" an 1885 communication opened with the words: "Sister workers: The pleasant fiction about our being 'angels' and 'clinging ivy' is over. Angels don't wash, iron, bake, mend and darn hose. It would wear out their wings and temper." It closed on the forceful note that women workers must not look to the law, the employer, the church, or the "high-born sister women." Rather than trust in such allies, who were universally scornful, ignorant, or forgetful of women workers' actual conditions and needs, this reformer urged: "Sisters, by our dignity, co-operation, and organization, we must protect ourselves." Domestic servants and their problems were occasionally commented upon, and Hamilton's "M'Liss" communicated to the *Palladium* the particular indignities suffered by such "hired girls"; when teachers assembled in Toronto in the summer of 1886 to consider forming a Provincial Union they were endorsed heartily by the paper. Rowe's "Women's Own Department" commentary gradually gave way to a more sensitive appraisal. Where once the home had been extolled, and woman's place within it uncritically taken for granted, a subtle shift seemed to take place. A Montreal workingman wrote to suggest that "a thrifty, economical and thorough good housekeeper who can lay out to advantage [a] . . . fair day's wage, is just as essential to the well-being of the workingman as the fair day's wage itself." This, of course, stopped short of a critique of well-entrenched notions of woman's proper sphere, and the source can be read as an indication that subordination was still assumed. Yet in a context of pervasive, unquestioned male supremacy and patriarchy, the Knights of Labor struck many blows against the oppression of women. As the movement grew and more women became attached to the cause of reform, gains were made, gains in understanding that went part of the way toward lifting the restrictions of women's place:

Not with courtier's bended knee
  Bow ye to woman, deified;
Not with base falsehoods, flattery,
  Like Knights of old, but to deride,
But as she oft must toil for bread,
  Yet give her equal rights instead.

An equal place where she may toil,
  Equal reward for labor done –
And when proud Moloch would despoil,
  An equal crown for victory won,
As mother, sister, friend, and bride,
  Ye recognize her at man's side.

Only when industry shall be
  Released from Mammon's galling chains,
Can woman's true equality
  A real recognition gain.
Not man's dependent will she be,
  But his co-worker, equal free.

Arise! as waves upon the shore,
  United with dazzling crests!
Arise! as life forevermore
  Obeys the sun god's strong behests,
Ye Knights of Labor arise, unite,
  Your armament is truth and might.

In this Richmond, Virginia, woman's "Tribute to the K. of L." we see historical process in motion: as an alternative unfolded in which the woman question and the labor problem were addressed as part of a coherent whole, a critique of past and present emerged in which a hint of an understanding of the limitations of a specific context broke through the residue of past views of woman's character and place.[139]

At a London speech by the well-traveled and popular Knight, Richard Trevellick, members of the Order "raised their hands to heaven and pledged themselves that wherever women were employed, they would demand equal pay for equal work without regard to sex whatever." At another Knights of Labor meeting in the Forest City, Trevellick argued that, "Man must raise women up to his own status or capital would be used to bring man down to the present status of woman." An unidentified London woman revealed that the Knights did not necessarily stop and settle comfortably in this economistic niche, chastising those who would define women's rights in some narrow, limited way. The vehemence of her attack indicated that women also saw a role for themselves in the struggle for social equality:

> One would infer that "Anti-Woman's Suffrage" in Thursday's *Advertiser* is a lunatic when he does not believe a woman to be equal with man. The Knights of Labor, I believe, believe in what they preach, when they say woman is equal with man. I hope the K. of L. will see the day when women will get the same pay for doing the same work that a man does. I won't say much on behalf of the women now to "Anti-Woman's Suffrage" for fear it'll knock him out. I'd rather have his carcass for a dime museum – he'd make a fine curiosity.

Such an assault, penned in an era when universal male suffrage was not in practice, chipped away at the status quo at the very foundation of its perception of citizenship. While the Knights of Labor remained trapped within certain traditional confines, regarding women's votes in part as potential voices against a wide array of social impurities, their arguments often extended beyond the limitations inherent in such a view of women's suffrage as political housekeeping. In a number of Ontario communities it was the *act* of drawing women into the labor movement women who had before been isolated on the margins of trade union, political, and work place struggles – that was of lasting significance and ultimate worth. It was the Order's defense of "the right of women to be regarded in all matters of citizenship and all relations between the government and the people as the equal of men" that was paramount. This, according to Phillips Thompson, could "hardly be denied by any clear-sighted and consistent Labor Reformer." Henry George put the matter similarly when he argued that, "The women have a right to come into your organizations . . . The women are the best men we have."[140]

To comprehend fully how such labor reformers reacted to the woman question, and to understand how many women entered the ranks of the Knights of Labor and on what basis, we would have to move beyond such anecdotal and impressionistic evidence to more systematic studies of local situations and contexts. Lack of data limits such effort severely, and does not even permit reasonably accurate estimates of membership or the number of Ontario Assemblies that actually contained women. Nevertheless, as Table 8.1 reveals, the Order did make significant inroads in the organization of woman workers. (Prior to the coming of the Knights, Ontario women's participation in organized labor was virtually nonexistent. The first woman delegate to the TLC, for instance, was Mrs. Elizabeth Wright, representing

Table 8.1. *Locales where women were involved in the Knights of Labor*

| Place | LA | Name | Women's LA | LA with women as well as men | Women probably present | Membership |
|---|---|---|---|---|---|---|
| Hamilton | 3179 | Excelsior | X | | | 1884 (76); 1885 (26) cotton/shoe operatives |
| Toronto | 7629 | Hope | X | | | — |
| Toronto | 409 | Silver Fleece | X | | | tailoresses |
| Brantford | 3649 | Olive Branch | X | | | garment workers |
| Kingston | 10432 | Mayflower | X | | | tailoresses |
| Belleville | 4427 | | X | | | — |
| St. Thomas | 4650 | Grace Darling | X | | | 1886 (80) |
| Thorold | 8625 | Advance | X | | | — |
| London | 3502 | Confidence | X | | | 1884 (11); 1885 (25) |
| Stratford | 5542 | | X | | | — |
| Chatham | 5961 | Royal Oak | | X | | 1887 (400): mixed with 60 women in 1886; 10 women in 1887 |
| | 7150 | | | | | |
| Amherstburg | 10550 (10530?) | Victoria | | X | | — |
| London | 3558 | Beaver | | X | | 1885 (116) mixed |
| Hamilton | 3040 | Ontario | | X | | 1884 (145); 1885 (41) cotton/shoe operatives |
| Hespeler | 6058 | | | X | | 1886 (100) mixed |
| Toronto | 2163 | Morse | | X | | 1882 (125); 1883 (200) telegraph operatives |
| Stratford | 4378 | Green Mountain | | X | | — |
| Dundas | 5329 | | | X | | — |
| Merritton | 5933 | Maple Leaf | | | X | 1886 (500), cotton mill operatives |
| Cornwall | 6582 | | | | X | 1887 (180); 1886 (186) cotton mill operatives |
| | 6583 | | | | | |
| Toronto | 3491 | Unity | | | X | 1885 (39); 1887 (60) trunkmakers, |
| Toronto | 5743 | Hand-in-Hand | | | X | bookbinders |
| St. Catharines | 2573 | Advance | | | X | 1887 (42) tailoresses |

St. Thomas's Grace Darling Assembly in 1886.) Those work sectors that had undergone a significant degree of concentration – cotton mills, shoe factories, and the garment industry – were the realms most likely to provide fertile recruiting ground, while the more individual experience of domestics and clerks understandably proved a more difficult nut to crack with the appeal to collectivity. But even here we should emphasize that Table 8.1 illuminates only the tip of the organizational iceberg, which has long since melted into a range of working-class communities that have been lost from our view for almost a century. Where women joined the Order in specifically women's Assemblies, or where a record of female presence within an Assembly containing men and women exists, we can sometimes document the organization of women, and our educated guess is that women were involved in at least twenty-five LAs (10 percent). But there must have been countless others containing women that went unrecorded, and many a female operative, domestic, or clerk must have been lost in the general membership figures as simply one more dues-paying Knight of Labor. In Hamilton, for instance, there was said to be one woman's LA in 1886 and three LAs containing women workers as well as men, but we have been able to identify only one of the latter. Attempts to organize that stopped short of the actual founding of an Assembly may have produced gains that prove difficult to uncover or evaluate. Finally, as wives, mothers, sisters, and friends, women may well have helped to sustain Knights of Labor LAs, formally and informally, across the province.[141]

Many of the telegraph operative Locals of the early 1880s, prior to their defeat in August 1883, attracted women workers. Assemblies like those in Merritton and Cornwall probably contained many females, although we have little evidence to establish this. Women were an absolute majority of the work force in the cotton mills of these towns, and they followed the Knights of Labor into the streets in a series of late-nineteenth-century strikes that we will discuss in Chapter 9. Their presence, in Merritton at least, was alluded to by the general investigator of women's work and wages, Leonora M. Barry, who reported on a foray into Ontario in 1888. Barry, whose presence was often requested by various provincial DAs, visited Mikado Assembly of Waterloo in early January, and then traveled to Thorold and Merritton, where she held public and private meetings reporting on the general deterioration of wages and working conditions of female operatives in the cotton, knitting, and paper mills. Continuing to pursue women workers under the jurisdiction of DA 207, Barry noted that in St. Catharines women were employed at tailoring, dressmaking, millinery, domestic service, and in sales. Indeed, although the official proceedings of the Order reveal no indication of a woman's Assembly in St. Catharines, the *Welland Tribune* reported that "a ladies' assembly of the Knights of Labor" was organized in July 1886, noting that it was the first such LA in the Niagara District. (This may have been St. Catharines LA 2573.) Of the 1,000 women employed in the region, Barry estimated that approximately half of them were organized, and when the Order celebrated the civic holiday in St. Catharines in mid-August 1886, 300 "lady members" formed a part of the large procession.[142]

Beyond these limited indications and logical speculations surrounding women's involvement, we know, as well, that women could join the Order in strikingly different ways, playing forceful public roles or shielding themselves behind a notion of appropriate femininity: here context was all, in which the character of women's work, the strength of the working-class movement, perhaps even the role of middle-class reform women, exercised an impact. In Toronto, as we have seen, women entered into the industrial fray with vigor, but in Hamilton only Katie McVicar seemed capable of full-scale organizational activity. Rose Lemay of Amherstburg could fill the exalted position of DMW, corresponding with Powderly over the inner workings of the Order in the Windsor area, while in Kingston dispensation was granted to William Drennan of LA 9452 to preside over the women of LA 10432. Belleville's Marie Joussaye embraced the Order and endorsed its principles in lines of committed verse. Similarly, Picton's Elizabeth Johnson corresponded with the *Journal of United Labor*, defending class interests by attacking government's encroachments in usurping power over the mails. Like so many late-nineteenth-century labor reformers, Johnson's world-view was summed up in a self-composed poetry of rebellion:

> To do and dare in Freedom's cause
> While Tyranny o'er us reigns.[143]

Unlike Joussaye and Johnson, however, some women secured their place in the Knights of Labor through defiance of one sacred principle of Knighthood. John Brown wrote to Powderly of the details of the formation of London's first women's Assembly:

> On Nov 10th I organized a LA in this city consisting of 12 ladies. They were drawn from various parts of the city and were not acquainted with each other. Afterwards it transpired that one of them, an Englishwoman, was married to a negro, and this fact has so disgusted the other members, and prevented them from obtaining candidates for membership, that they *unanimously* declined to have anything more to do with the assembly while this one is connected with it. By my advice the M.W. and the R.S. of the assembly (both married women) waited on the lady in question and told her the position of affairs asking her if, for the sake of harmony, she would retire from the assembly. This she seemed unwilling to do, and afterwards called on me to ask my advice. All I could think of was to suggest the probability of getting her an Individual Membership card; this she was willing to accept.

> With regard to my own action in the affair I can see now that it would have been better had I ascertained, before founding the Assembly, if each one had been satisfied of the fitness of all the others but I had not at that time received the full organizers' supplies, nor did the instructions say anything on this point. I feel sure that should your ruling in this case be to the effect that the members of the assembly should rise above the boundary of color and treat all nations as equals, that these ladies will revolt, their detestation in this case being so strong that they will hardly be patient enough to allow the subject to be argued. It seems to me however that the offender (Elizabeth Waters) is now a member of the Order, and therefore must be provided for, that is, by being attached to some Local or the General Assembly.

Brown's tact no doubt solved the immediate problem, although the growth of an Assembly premised on such exclusion promised future difficulties. In 1884 London's ironically named "Confidence" Assembly reported a membership of eleven women, one less than the original dozen brought together to found the Local: the "offender," Elizabeth Waters, had her card, but the price had been sisterly exclusion from the bonds of unity. Such diverse and contradictory experiences remind us that the Knights of Labor struggled in many ways, with varying successes, to overcome the limitations of sex. These limitations were at one and the same time conditioned and sustained by consensual norms of women's proper sphere, traditional male attitudes, deeply held prejudices, economic imperatives in a capitalist society, and women's own restricted consciousness of their class and sexual oppression.[144]

In Knights of Labor centers like Belleville, Brantford, Stratford, Thorold, Hamilton, and Toronto, then, where "the ladies" joined the Order in Assemblies named "Hope" and "Advance," it was the possibility of women's emancipation forged in the 1880s that was on many women workers' lips. Attendance at musical and literary entertainments as "Goddesses of Liberty," or membership in an LA named "Excelsior"(perhaps one of the most popular of women's Assembly names in the United States, and expressive of elevated status), might be interpreted negatively today.[145] Yet, in the challenge of the 1880s such honorifics were less an indication of the passivity and ultimate virtue of femininity than they were articulations of dignity and worth felt to be the birthright of all individuals, including laboring women. To place toiling females so unambiguously within the general human condition was an advance of great magnitude over past practice, and played a not inconsiderable role in changing male workers' views of women and women workers' views of themselves. The possibility was far from realized, but it had reared its head; the Order had begun the process whereby the class and sex questions could be considered as one.

St. Thomas's women workers captured something of the meaning of that possibility when they named their LA after Grace Horsley Darling, an English plebeian heroine much in the public eye throughout the 1880s. Darling, the daughter of a lighthouse keeper on the Farne Islands, had been reared in a family setting that epitomized the character of the respectable working class. On 7 September 1838 a steamboat was wrecked off the island and most of the persons aboard were lost. Darling and his daughter, however, managed to save a few survivors who had found refuge on a rock, at great risk to their personal safety. As reports of this gallant exploit became widespread, an outburst of popular enthusiasm resulted: Grace and her father became national figures, subscriptions were taken up for them, and medals struck in commemoration of their act. Throughout it all Grace reacted with quiet dignity, and according to all accounts remained "a hardworking, sensible girl." She left her island occasionally, but saw nothing of the outside world that would have induced her to leave her home and marry. She died in 1842, at the age of 27, suffering from symptoms of consumption. For the working women of St. Thomas, Grace Darling's story was more than a tale of woman's proper sphere touched up with sentiment and propriety. Rather, it was an example of a woman of humble origin, given to self-sacrifice, who managed, even in the face of national exposure, to retain a sense of humility and of values that remained untarnished by the materialism and individualism of the times. As the women workers who took Grace Darling's name as theirs knew well, consensual norms can cut in many directions, and a possibility can look to the past to build a future. In that delicate balance, and in the ultimate potential of women's possibilities, resides the significance of a part of the 1880s, when the Knights of Labor provided the institutional and intellectual setting in which women first entered the Ontario labor movement.[146]

## A movement culture

The movement culture generated by the Knights of Labor thus provided Ontario's workers with their first explicit confrontation with the potential and possibility of a working-class unity that could change the world in which they lived. Manifesting itself in the initiation rites, the rhetoric and the public displays of the Order, the movement culture spawned a trenchant critique of society as it was then constituted. Whether we look toward the impassioned writing of labor's brainworkers, the diligent efforts of the Knights of Labor organizers, or the committed prose or poetry of countless forgotten men and women, we cannot help but see this accomplishment, and recognize how vitally it shifted the existing terms of class experience, drawing unskilled workers, women, and the Irish from the periphery into the center of the nineteenth-century labor movement. As Raymond Williams has argued, this process of wanting and actively struggling to convince others that a new human order is seriously possible is central to any attempt to create alternatives. It is part of a long history of resistance "where intention and consequence, desire and necessity, possibility and practice, have . . . bloodily interacted."[147] It was not so much Elizabeth Johnson, a Picton woman, who spoke in lines of verse dedicated to Walt Whitman, as it was the movement culture of which she was a part. "I dreamed in a dream I saw a city invincible to the attacks of the whole of the rest of the earth," wrote Whitman, and Johnson replied to this vision with one of her own, "a kingdom of human brotherhood . . . and democracy long prepared for":

> Through anxiety, struggle, failure, defeat, madness, despair –
> Slow as slow moving Time, sure as Eternity,
> Out, and on, in her last sweeping cycle,
> Life's slow-evolving wheel sweeps round again
> To her great crowning effort.[148]

In attempting to speed up the process that Johnson depicted innocently as the inevitable progression to Whitman's "City of Man," the Knights of Labor and the movement culture it had brought into being posed an alternative hegemony to the dominant hegemony of bourgeois rule.

The village of Gananoque, where 700–800 workers were said to have joined the ranks of the Order's LA 7508 by late 1887, revealed the force with which the movement culture struck the status quo. "Dark Knight" reported in November 1887 that, in spite of numerous improvements in the village, "an element, or a sentiment," had arisen "among the lower class of workmen." Known as the Knights of Labor, this body appeared "to be a dangerous faction, believing in neither syndicate nor Government monopolies," antagonistic to "landlordism and the degrading of the workmen." Such an order proved troublesome to "the better class of society . . . for if an election or anything of that kind should arise, there [was] no telling where those seven hundred would wander off to." For weeks debate raged in the local paper as various Knights of Labor challenged their critic, providing "Light for Dark Knight." Finally, on 3 December 1887, "L.C.S." stepped forward to enunciate the aims and objects of the Order in an articulate and lengthy statement on the movement. "The Order of the Knights of Labor is neither a church, temperance society, nor political party," he noted, "but has many of the good characteristics of all of these." Pressing against the seemingly inevitable debasement of the worker, the Knights of Labor were "engaged in solving the greatest problem of the age," urging all wage laborers to drink at the fountain of labor reform, rather than from the cesspool of "the capitalistic press," which consistently suppressed facts, failed to consider just causes, and aligned itself with "upper anarchy," money, and monopoly:

> Reforms emanate from the buffeted, stoned, crucified child of poverty, and members of the Order, do not forget, that the humblest Knight of Labor must do his part in the revolutions and overturning of bad old systems and practices . . . the Order is a school of education, with a very extended course, and every member should stand high in the grade. Educate yourself and you will be in a position to enlighten others.

That accomplished, working people had only to "obey the laws of knighthood, be loyal to self and manhood, defend the interest of the Order, and labor for the new era until it dawns upon the toilers of our country, until the weary men and women chained by the wage-system can see justice enthroned, and this, the land of the free."[149]

Like so many of his brothers and sisters who were building the movement culture out of the class experience, "L.C.S." was engaged in that quintessentially Knights of Labor activity, "spreading the light":

> 'Tis the foremost thing to do –
> Spread the Light!
> Till the world is made anew –
> Spread the Light!
> It is darkness that enslaves,
> Those who dwell in dens and caves,
> Knowledge strengthens – knowledge saves –
> Spread the Light![150]

It would be all too easy to attack the men and women involved in this forging of a culture, and take them to task for the imprecision of their language of reform, their lack of strategic, even tactical, direction, their eclecticism, both irritating and refreshing. A possibility, after all, is never easy to enunciate, and it is even more difficult to chart and guide into the future. Another facile approach would be to ignore such organic, working-class intellectuals, and bypass the villages, towns, and cities where they lived, write them out of the record of the past because they left their mark only in their initials or pen-name, and maintain "healthy," academic skepticism about the size and range of their constituency. Finally, it is equally possible to patronize these early labor radicals, "patting them on the head as 'in advance of their time.'" But, as Christopher Hill has suggested in another context, that is merely a tired cliché, an excuse for the lazy historian.[151]

These seem to have been the approaches common among Canadian historians, who have sniffed at this culture of the 1880s hurriedly, like anxious dogs about to lift their legs around a tree trunk, bouncing off to more enticing quests after relieving themselves on this enigma of working-class self-activity, the Noble and Holy Order of the Knights of Labor.[152] Because the movement failed,[153] because the culture faded into retreat, the movement of cultural preemergence represented by the Knights of Labor has been quietly dismissed. But we cannot readily ignore the movement that penetrated small town and large industrial city in the Ontario of the 1880s and 1890s, drawing 5,000 to a demonstration in Ingersoll or 3,000 to a labor picnic in Gananoque, and produced women like Marie Joussaye and Elizabeth Johnson and men like Phillips Thompson and Joseph Marks.[154] We have seen few such events and personages in our history. The culture is not to be sniffed at, even if, to our thoroughly modernized nostrils, it carries an odd scent. It is therefore necessary to rescue that moment of the 1880s and 1890s, to realize that its insights, its *poetic* insights, were achievements of considerable stature. With the vision of a more humane society always before it, the culture forged by the Knights of Labor is worth knowing today. In the words of Phillips Thompson, member of Toronto's LA 7814, the Victor Hugo Assembly, that culture taught men and women to dream of "what might be." By doing their part "in spreading the light," argued Thompson, labor reformers were close to realizing the "beautiful ideal" of "universal democracy and co-operation." Far from a utopian fantasy, the promise of a better social and economic order was merely "a faint presentation of what might be – what cannot be at present solely because of the blindness, ignorance, and want of union among workingmen – but what I trust yet will be when the scales of error, of misleading education and of temporary self-interest have falled from their eyes – so they can see the Light."[155]

Such efforts did not go unopposed, as we have seen in the cases of Toronto and Hamilton and in our examination of the Order's influential place in late-nineteenth-century Ontario politics. In these locales and in the electoral campaigns of the 1880s the Order attempted to "spread the light," and met the predictable resistance of those "dark" forces that found its dream of a better world menacing. The movement culture met its greatest test, however, in the class conflicts that erupted in the shops, mills, and factories of industrializing Ontario. There, in the heat of battle, the Order had to prove its mettle.

# 9. The people's strike: Class conflict and the Knights of Labor

## A fundamental ambivalence

At the turn of the century Albert R. Carman published his fictional account of a young Christian, Ryerson Embury, whose faith was troubled by a series of social questions and problems, particularly those involving the working class. Carman undoubtedly drew upon the experience of the Knights of Labor. His characters were quick to adopt the vocabulary and panaceas of the labor reformer, and Carman's book revealed the early connection between the social gospel and "the labor problem." In the midst of a bitter confrontation between the town's major employers and their workers, the idealistic Ryerson Embury found himself involved in a discussion of the strike. A worker explained his commitment: "No, with me it is not a question of win or lose. It is justice I'm after. The masters shall not lie to us with impunity. It is more than that! The time is coming when they will give us our fair share of the earnings of the 'works' or neither we nor anyone else shall work." A striker's son added a pessimistic note, emphasizing how the conflict had shifted the terms of social relations in the town, and drew Ryerson and his friend Madden into the debate:

"I see no immediate prospect of an end to the strike, and even if it should end now, I could not go back to the office. Father – father put a mortgage on the place the other day to raise funds to put in the Union treasury." "What! and you don't say so!" came from the two boys. "Yes, you see," he went on, "the men did not get quite so much outside help as they expected, and it's been a pretty hard pinch for some of them. So there was talk of giving in, but father and a few of the men who have property said they'd rather sell all they have than yield through starvation."

"Well, but supposing your father gets his increased wages, it'll take a long time to make up for that, won't it?" asked Madden, wonderingly.

"He don't look at it that way," he said. "It's, it's a religion with him to stand by his brother working men. He looks at it as you do at patriotism. If you went into the army in time of war you wouldn't expect to get paid for the risk you ran. Well, that's his position in regard to the strike. He believes it's right. He thinks the men are being defrauded out of their just earnings, and he is making this fight to get them justice."

"But it is going to fail, isn't it," asked Ryerson, a little breathless at this new view of the case. . . . "Speaking privately, I think so – have thought so from the first . . . But what could the men do? They must strike, or go on in the same old way, getting less than their share."[1]

Did these sentiments find support among Canadian advocates of the Noble and Holy Order of the Knights of Labor? Or, rather, was such a dialogue a mere fictional misrepresentation, with little relationship to reality? To pose the question in these terms is to address the Order's relationship to class conflict in the late nineteenth century, to open a window that looks out over a battleground on which strikes and lockouts polarized countless Ontario communities. On the periphery of this scene lie the solutions and successes of the Order, the cooperative ventures, boycott campaigns, and the few notable victories, as well as the sad defeats and serious divisions, especially the problematic issue of labor unity, threatened by rare, but significant, instances of rivalries and resentments separating Knights of Labor and trade unionists. Hanging over the entire scenario, as well, was the rhetoric of class antagonism, which both stimulated conflict and grew stronger with each developing struggle.

Virtually every North American student of the Knights of Labor recognizes the uneasy tension that rippled through the Order's history: the leadership's consistent opposition to strikes seems to fit poorly with the membership gains of 1885–6, when the Knights rode a series of mass strikes – on the railroads, in the valleys of the Saginaw and Hocking, in the cotton mills of Augusta, Georgia, and the packinghouses of Chicago, and on the street railways of Toronto or New York – to national prominence.[2] As Alan Dawley argues in his study of Lynn shoemakers, far-off huffings and puffings seldom brought the House of Strikes down. To be sure, the Order nowhere endorsed strikes indiscriminately, and everywhere favored arbitration, a process that loosely denoted settling industrial disputes by negotiation between employer, employee representatives, and supposedly disinterested third parties. Arbitration was designed to be a cordial process, and was meant to be a fair-minded reconciliation, with little of the adversity characteristic of the proceedings of modern collective bargaining. It also reflected workers' faith in the community, which they felt would not deny them a well-deserved justice. As Herbert Gutman has noted, this faith was not just a naive belief in class harmony, for merchants, small industrialists, and politicians often did side with workers in the midst of conflicts, and lent them their support. But the attachment to arbitration also represented the limitations of Knights of Labor thought. As in the case of politics, where the dominant and successful tendency was to seek representation in the workings of the state – thereby assuring the working class of a vote – arbitration was premised on the assumption that the capitalists would deal fairly with their workers if they were simply informed of the facts. We have seen what happened in the political realm, and in the class struggles of the 1880s and 1890s the story would not be altogether different. Arbitration, then, emerged out of a knowledge of past defeats and within an economic context in which small-scale competitive capitalism was giving way to, but was not totally engulfed by, monopoly. It was an understandable policy for the Order to adopt, but it also surrendered much to what the *Palladium of Labor* referred to as "the monster (Capital)." This is evident when we look at how arbitration actually worked.

When an arbitration agreement had been struck, labor's representatives took the verdict back to their membership and tried to persuade the workers of the wisdom of accepting the negotiated conditions; management did likewise. Quite often this process produced satisfactory results, and conflicts were averted. But in many cases, especially in situations where hostile employers or their hirelings denied the right of any labor organization to intrude upon their managerial prerogatives, arbitration was little more than a wishful hope. This became especially clear in the 1880s and 1890s as the community basis of power wilted in the face of the emergence of a national bourgeoisie, reliant upon the force of the state and the troops and national guardsmen it could muster to crush dissident workers. In a series of violent confrontations, culminating in the Homestead and Pullman struggles of the early 1890s, and echoed in countless other communities in many less episodic clashes, the intricate relationship of class and community disintegrated, and the social basis and effectiveness of arbitration was correspondingly diminished. In many settings, then, when fundamental issues of the rights and liberties of wage workers were threatened, strikes were seen as inevitable and were thoroughly supported by LAs. Across North America strikes raised problems for the Knights of Labor *not* because Knights opposed strikes, but because they entered into them, and then attempted to sustain them without the support (moral or financial) of the General Executive Board. Quite simply, the flexibility and eclecticism of the Knights of Labor allowed the LAs the leeway to pursue the justice they desired in ways they saw fit. In many Ontario towns and cities this led the Knights of Labor into conflict with employers. As we have seen, in those major confrontations with clearly perceived class enemies – monopolists like the telegraphers' opponent, Jay Gould, or the notorious street railway magnate Frank Smith (whose status as a leading figure in Macdonald's Tory government and a member of the "liquor interest" only inflamed the Knights' antagonism) – leaders and rank-and-file could unite and fight. Arbitration, every labor advocate knew, could not salvage cordial class relations when such employers denied their workers elementary justice.

Against such enemies the problem was not that the Order refused to strike, but that it often lacked the resources and staying power to carry the battle through to the end. Its opponents, after all, were among the most formidable capitalists in late-nineteenth-century North America. But in a large number of confrontations, waged against lesser figures, arbitration was more often a problematic vehicle that surrendered as much as it won.[3]

The workers were not drawn into these battles unaware of their leadership's views on the folly of strikes. In the pages of the *Journal of United Labor*, T. V. Powderly constantly raged against the ill effects of strikes upon the Order. After 1886, when Haymarket exploded in the labor movement's face and the Wabash and May Day work stoppages revealed the tragic failure of the mass strike, Powderly and his colleagues in the hierarchy of the Knights of Labor assumed an increasingly hostile posture toward strikes of any kind. In March 1886 John Devlin, U.S. Consul in Windsor and one of Powderly's long-standing allies, expressed his support for the cautious, conservative policies of the Order's MW:

> I believe that all the old time members who worked with us before the Order was known to the world, and who know the broad and noble views of my old friend U. S. Stevens, will stand by you and instead of allowing you to make way for some other man who would be likely to make of our Order a *Striking machine* and bring it into contempt and defete the very object for which it was founded will insist that you stay where you are until labor shall be properly recognized the time has now arrived when the friends of labor now in our Order must use every effort to hold the Order down and keep its members from overreaching themselves.[4]

Such views guided Powderly's public statements during the upsurge of 1885–6. His antistrike pronouncements were well known in Ontario, broadcast across the province by the labor-reform press as well as daily newspapers of Tory and Grit persuasion, which seldom failed to record the details of factional infighting within the Order or of strikes that had resulted in violence, sabotage, or riotous tumult.[5]

Powderly's message was carried to Canadian towns and cities by labor spokesmen like Richard Trevellick, Frank Fogg, and T. B. McGuire, who often punctuated their lectures and meetings with pronouncements on the negative consequences of ill-advised strikes.[6] Similarly, Ontario workers and labor advocates like George Collis, D. J. O'Donoghue, A. W. Wright, and J. W. Osborne addressed gatherings of working people and stressed that strikes were, at best, a last resort.[7] In his 1884 report, DMW William J. Vale of Hamilton noted that the DA had averted one strike and settled two others during the course of that winter. Galt's J. L. Blain expressed a common view when he wrote to Powderly that he did "not believe in working from the outside but rather in removing the *causes* at the bottom of the system." As strikes were but a symptom of the disease in the social system, they were of only marginal significance, "useful in drawing attention to the matter." When "L.C.S." undertook to explain the purposes and character of the Knights of Labor to the readers of the *Gananoque Reporter* he claimed that the Order was "directly opposed to strikes," the day not being far off "when all labor difficulties will be adjusted by arbitration, the just method inaugurated by the Knights of Labor."[8]

These views, prominent among the Order's ranks, must be distinguished from the harsh condemnation of labor organization and militance emanating from many quarters in the mid-to-late-1880s. Employers were often the source of such tirades, but the clergy, too, played a significant role. Sam Small, an itinerant evangelist, spoke in Toronto in 1887, attacking forms of working-class resistance, and from the *Christian Guardian* came this assault: "It has been assumed that the labor organizations by the simple fact of organization had acquired the right to settle all labor questions without much regard for public opinion . . . Strikes were ordered where there was not the slightest grievance, simply to show the power of the organization . . . That an anti-monopoly organization should indulge in the worst practice of monopoly was strange indeed."[9] Such thinly veiled criticisms of the Knights of Labor drew no support from wage workers. However much the men and women affiliated with the Order expressed their distaste for strikes, which they knew often led to misery and deprivation, they were equally aware that the cause of strikes lay not with working people and their excessive demands, but with the injustices of the system under which they labored. Strikes were an evil, to be sure, but a necessary one which, once abandoned, spelled out an even more oppressive lot for those dependent upon wages for sustenance.

A correspondent from Cornwall emphasized the disastrous consequences of strikes, but he was quick to lay the blame, not at the feet of the workingman, but on the employer's head: "At present," he argued, "when a labor strike takes place, capitalists resort to one or the other of these means to meet the trouble, either to argue the strikers into terms or to crush them out. These weapons may answer for a time but they will not avail very long. Weary and hungry, men are not open to arguments against weariness and starvation." In closing, this commentator urged capitalists to "think of the workingman's weary limbs and sore feet when their own are on easy chairs and velvet lawns . . . think of the workingman's bare table when they are at their own and fulness abounds, and if there be a spark of human sympathy left in their souls they will open their hands a little wider to the weary toilers of earth, and they will thus save themselves from future disaster and us from the horrors of a reign of terror." More emphatic was "A Laborer's Warning," printed in Hamilton's *Palladium of Labor* in 1885:

> Let me call your attention to this fact: If the strike riots of 1877 were repeated to-day, they would end in revolution! Ever since 1877 the people have been reading, thinking and awakening from the sleep of ages . . . This whole land is overflowing with everything needed to make all the people comfortable and happy, and at the same time millions of idle men, women and children are compelled to work from twelve to fourteen hours per day for starvation wages. If they ask for shorter days or more wages, or join a trade union, they are discharged and blacklisted, – and if they strike for their rights and a disturbance follows, they are killed. At the same time capitalists are making money and declaring dividends on watered stock . . . Blind is the man whose eyes have not been opened by the late Wabash troubles, and wretched indeed must be the condition of the toiler whose only help in time of need must come from the enemies of the Knights of Labor! . . . the very existence of the toilers is at stake . . . Our success is in our united force and discipline. "Thrice armed is he who had his quarrel just."

This "Laborer" urged mass meetings of the Knights of Labor, and suggested that the Order issue a public proclamation guaranteeing the protection of all members, "by the whole Order, if necessary." In this way the ranks of the Knights of Labor would be dramatically expanded, and the power of the workers enhanced. He closed with a metaphorical warning, likening the workers' movement of the 1880s to the great Chicago fire. Had a little water been applied to the conflagration at the proper time, he argued, much destruction could have been avoided. Similarly, if workers were granted the justice they demanded, the fires of their hearts, "kindled and fanned by their oppressors," would not rage out of control, destroying everything before them. The practical consequences of a strike were summed up in the Order's official journal: "a successful strike, undertaken because of a real grievance, must necessarily benefit the workmen directly or indirectly interested. The same is true, to a less extent, of an unsuccessful one; for, the strike will leave a much deeper hole in the employer's pocket book, relatively as well as absolutely. The hard knocks of experience will teach him respect for the rights of those under him. It will teach the workingman that success can only be attained by organized effort."[10]

In Ontario the Knights of Labor revealed their support for the strike as a tactic of resistance in the persistent opposition to the way in which the capitalistic press depicted workers' struggles. Hamilton's *Palladium of Labor*, for instance, attacked the Toronto *Monetary Times*'s view of a strike among the builders' laborers. When the financial paper argued that the men had lost heavily in their efforts to secure a 2¢ wage increase, the labor paper replied indignantly: "Well, and did the employers lose nothing? Was all the loss from six weeks' stoppage of business on one side only? If not, why lay the stress on what the men lost? What is the moral you mean to draw, anyway? That men should never resist injustice because they may lose by it?" Chastising "those journals which are always preaching of the folly and wrongfulness of strikes," the *Palladium of Labor* concluded: "With a great many labourers it is not a question of gain or loss – simply of living. They have nothing but enough to purchase them a bare existence from day to day; can save nothing out of their scanty wages. This being the case, if they and their families are alive and well at the end of a strike, they have not lost anything, simply because they had nothing to lose." This labor-reform paper would have had little sympathy for novel suggestions and schemes prominently advocated in the pages of newspapers across Ontario. It would have scoffed at the *Ingersoll Chronicle & Canadian Dairyman*'s suggestion that the workingman construct a "strike box," placing it in a convenient corner of his house. When asked to contribute "towards maintaining a lot of idle strikers," the worker could take the required amount and deposit it in his box, and at the end of the year the money could be put to good use. The same course, suggested the weekly, might well be adopted in the assembly hall of the Knights of Labor. Like its predecessor, the *Palladium of Labor*, the *Labor Union* also expressed little faith in the reliability of the "capitalistic press" concerning strikes: "When strikes are a success such papers call them 'compromises,' and when they are compromises, they are called 'defeats.'"[11]

The expulsion of Tom Barry from the Knights of Labor in the fall of 1888 revealed that among certain Ontario workers such views were well established. Barry, a member of the General Executive Board, represented the radical element of the Knights of Labor. While Powderly washed his hands of the Haymarket affair, Barry defended Albert Parsons, dedicating himself to gaining the commutation of the death sentence levied upon the anarchist and Knight of Labor. Unlike his counterparts in the Order's national leadership Barry often endorsed strikes, and attempted to move the organization toward a more aggressive stance on questions of work place rights. But by September of 1888, Barry had been isolated – "I shall now go it alone," he lamented as his only ally on the General Executive Board deserted him – and was on the verge of being expelled from the Order by Powderly. At the November 1888 General Assembly Barry was quickly dispensed with. Only 24 of the 146 delegates voted against expulsion, with Toronto's DA 125 playing an important role in the anti-Barry proceedings. Although Canadian workers hardly flocked to Barry's cause, his militance drew some support. He wrote to his friend Joseph Labadie in April 1888 that his proposals for reforming the Order had drawn considerable enthusiasm from some workers in Toronto, where he had addressed an audience of Knights. LA 9848, in fact, protested against DA 125's unfavorable reaction to this speech, and Barry's subsequent expulsion. In the St. Catharines–Dundas–Hamilton region Barry had a good deal of support, having worked as an axemaker in the area in the mid-1870s, where he met and married Maggie Devaney, daughter of an Irish farmer. J. T. Carey informed Powderly that the Axe Makers' Assembly of the St. Catharines region harbored some pro-Barry elements, and that members of the Assembly had received letters from the expelled leader urging them to withdraw from the Order. When one of Barry's advocates, Anthony Nelson, could not induce his fellow workers to follow this advice he chastised them severely, claiming "they had not the Back Bone of *Cats.*" Despite this failure, claimed Carey, Nelson had allies and promised future trouble if he was not quickly silenced. Other axemakers also rallied to Barry, a former DMW of the craft's National Trade Assembly. When Barry founded a new Order, the Brotherhood of United Labor, two Amherstburg Assemblies rumored to have 700 members (an exaggeration) quickly affiliated. Barry's efforts were to bear no fruit, and he and his reformed Order lapsed into insignificance. But from surviving fragments of evidence it is clear that Barry, and his aggressive stance, was endorsed by some Canadian workers.[12]

One prominent Canadian Knight of Labor, D. J. O'Donoghue, was no friend of Tom Barry, and he expressed dislike for the radical views of the East Saginaw labor organizer. O'Donoghue's refusal to endorse radicalism, however, did not imply that he turned away from militant confrontation. Opposing Powderly's stand on strikes, he wrote to the GMW: "Disastrous though strikes have been in many instances, and productive of financial loss always, yet they were necessary and ultimately productive of good. During the last 100 years the 'Rebellions' in Ireland were disastrous and productive of untold punishment, yet they did ultimate good; the 'strike' of the thirteen colonies produced loss of life and misery but ultimate good resulted. What a sacrifice of life and property in the late American civil war that slavery might cease, and yet all your illustrative argument would apply as to each and every one of them." Years in the early Canadian labor movement had taught O'Donoghue this much, and many of his co-workers in the Knights of Labor must have held similar beliefs. To regard the Order as categorically opposed to strikes, then, would be a gross oversimplification. As our earlier discussions of Toronto and Hamilton have shown, the Knights of Labor often found themselves embroiled in confrontation. While the Order seemed incapable of shaking off its fundamental ambivalence toward strikes, and often vacillated at an inauspicious moment with fatal consequences, the history of the Knights of Labor is nevertheless intimately connected with strikes, lockouts, and other forms of class conflict.[13]

Indeed, as we have seen, the Knights of Labor blossomed in Canada in the midst of the telegraphers' strike of 1883. This dramatic conflict, like so many of the Order's strike efforts, would end in dismal failure.[14] But before the operatives had been routed, and before National Trade District No. 45, the Brotherhood of Telegraphers of the United States and Canada, withdrew from the Order in disgust, Ontario workers had learned of a new organization that dared to assault the very bastion of monopolistic privilege, Jay Gould and his Western Telegraph Company, which controlled the major Canadian company, the Great North Western. As strikers in such Ontario towns as Kingston, Brockville, Belleville, Brantford, Ottawa, Peterborough, Georgetown, London, and Thorold stood "solid" behind the strike, public sympathy gravitated quickly to the men and women struggling for substantial wage and hour demands. The strike seemed to promise potential liberation, Kingston's *British Whig* commenting that the business community could be freed "of the load it is now carrying with Mr. Gould, his watered stock and his intolerable monopoly."[15] A Primitive Methodist organ, the *Christian Journal*, while believing that "striking" was a "desperate resort, and to be depreciated both in the interests of employers and employees," took its stand in favor of the telegraphers. "When employees can scarcely get a respectable living," argued the religious journal, "as we know is the case with some of the telegraphers in Toronto, it must be galling to them to know that they are helping to amass wealth for such a man as Jay Gould, who has more money than a dozen men can spend." The greatest dangers of the age, concluded the *Christian Journal*, were "grasping monopolists and a bloated plutocracy." From Streetsville, "A.B." urged "every workingman and working woman in America to help sustain our brothers and sisters while fighting monopoly for their just rights."[16] Belleville's J. Irby Isles proposed a popular solution when he endorsed public ownership, his letter indicative of the deep distrust many citizens felt for the large corporate concerns of the 1880s:

> Why all this useless talk and writing about the telegraph strike? when all that has to be done is to remove the cause of it? It has been brought about in the same manner that the GTR and all other strikes are, by the grinding down and by pinching salaries of employees for the benefit of the pockets of a whole host of impudent millionaires, who form a ring and control all large concerns of this kind. The method of operation in the telegraph matter is quite simple; let the people do as they did some years ago in England, hand it all over to the government.

Even after the operatives had succumbed to "unlimited capital unscrupulously employed," it was not frustration and apathy that grew out of the defeat, but a sense of purpose and potential. "The Telegraphers' strike is over," declared the *Palladium of Labor*. "The People's strike is now in order."[17]

In the years to come the Knights of Labor would play a leading role in a series of these people's strikes, struggles that developed along three distinct lines. First, small groups of workers, usually skilled, struck to gain or preserve a measure of control over specific work place environments, most often small shops or individual factories. We have noted a number of such conflicts in our discussions of Hamilton and Toronto. Second, other small confrontations often developed involving relatively unskilled workers who affiliated with the Order to overcome the insecurity, long hours, poor conditions, and low pay that seemed to follow inevitably from their status as unorganized laborers. Within this category we find a number of efforts to secure shorter hours for overworked clerks and salesmen through local early-closing movements. Finally, the Knights of Labor led a number of mass strikes that were similar to the epic battle waged on the Toronto street railway in that they involved hundreds of workers and polarized entire communities. Although different, all these struggles brought to the forefront the movement culture's keenly developed sense of class and, especially in the case of strikes waged in modest-sized manufactories, often culminated in attempts to establish cooperative factories in which work could proceed upon Knightly principles. We will discuss such cooperative undertakings after working our way through the three types of Knights of Labor strikes and close with a discussion of the problematic relationship of the Order to the trade unions. As we have noted earlier, this contentious realm was raised to prominence in the midst of a few key strikes, lockouts, and boycotts that were at the center of the history of the Knights of Labor in Ontario.

## Skilled workers and control struggles

As we have already noted, craft workers' efforts to retain a degree of autonomy at the work place and protect mechanisms of control, often institutionalized in shop regulations and trade rules, were a persistent phenomenon throughout the 1880s. Knights of Labor newspapers reinforced this commitment to control with coverage of workers' efforts to preserve work place rights, and offered their constant support. Toronto's *Labor Advocate* issued its statement of purpose on the publication of its first issue in December 1890: "Realizing that the monopoly of land, capital, and the means of exchange and transportation is the cause of the poverty of the masses the *Labor Advocate* will keep steadfastly in view the need of abolishing monopoly in all its forms, and asserting the right of the workers to control for their own benefit all the opportunities and requisites for production." In an article in the same issue, the labor-reform journal advocated working-class control of typesetting machines, insuring workingmen of the "full advantage of the invention, not the employing capitalist." This late-nineteenth-century concern with control was essentially a prerogative of the skilled. It remained largely a craft issue, even within the Knights of Labor, although the Order occasionally extended its meaning to embrace the unskilled, the destitute, and the poor. "To eliminate poverty," declared the *Journal of United Labor*, "we must control the elements of industry." Hamilton's *Palladium of Labor* consistently praised working-class measures designed to retain control over the pace and character of work, and argued that "the creator must take precedence of the thing created. Capital must be made the tool, not the tyrant of Labor." "Enjolras" came to similar conclusions, seeing a solution to labor's problems in the simple maxim that those who created wealth should control it.[18]

As workingmen of the 1880s cultivated an appreciation of their own sense of worth and independence, their respectability and craft competency, they understood that all of it rested upon their *demeanor* at the work place: superior workmen never "toadied" to the foreman or boss, while the inferior man used "all his artifices and chicaneries to keep in his good graces." London's M. H. Alfred, by no means a radical social critic, thought this was the key to reasonable relations among workers and employers. If superior workers retained their sense of craft pride, and preserved their autonomy on the job, "there would be less strikes, less trouble, less misery, and more harmony existing today between master and man, and more members in the unions today." Alfred chose to cast his view of work place control in the language of harmony, emphasizing that stable social relations flowed directly out of the employer's willingness to accept the independence of his skilled workingmen. This was undoubtedly one path that was followed. But as the Knights of Labor grew in stature, a more aggressive posture was easily adopted, and there were many employers who wanted no part of their workers assuming anything approaching control of the work environment. Turbulence, rather than stability, then came to dominate workers' relations with employers. Toronto's "J.L." outlined this second path in a poem, "The Knights of Labor":

Monopoly must not control
The Labor Market heart and Soul
And seek to pay with meagre dole,
The Knights of Labor.

While enterprise we will respect
Our rights we never shall neglect,
All tyranny we must reject,
While Knights of Labor.[19]

Much of this history of the struggle for control, and the place of the Knights of Labor in it, remains obscure. Craft struggles for control must often have been aided by workers who belonged, not just to their appropriate union, but also to LAs of the Knights of Labor. Indeed, the Order thrived at precisely the moment when any number of skilled crafts were flexing their muscles in a general upsurge of the laboring people.

A series of molders' strikes and lockouts at the James Smart Manufacturing Company in Brockville in the early 1880s illustrates this point. Smart's "sand artists" struck in March 1879, April 1880, May 1881, June 1883, and January 1884. The third strike (the first two were victories for the union) involved a classic bone of contention in the battle over craft control: apprentice limitation. Notifying Robert Gill of their grievance with an "anonymous letter," the union molders protested the excessive use of young boys in the company's shops which was in violation of their organization's rules. The men felt this could only lead to the "turning out of bad workmen, who would work for small pay and turn out improper work." Before the molders could act against this grievance, however, they were called together and addressed by John Gill. The manager claimed he was "very sorry," but that "he was compelled to announce that in the future they would not be dictated to by any body of men, but would be pleased to treat with everyone individually." He then read the roll of molders, asking each to renounce their union. Those who would not accept such terms could "pick up their kit and go." Gill declined the men's request to have a meeting, and to a man the union molders refused to submit and were discharged. An outraged employee claimed that "it is not the Union Molders that are on strike, but our Employers." He continued, explaining that those out of work intended to remain firm in opposing such tyranny: "we will not be forced to bow the supplicant knee to wealth, and earn by unprofitable toil a life so void of solace to confirm the very claims that bind us to our doom." Their object, claimed the molder, was not "to gain opulence," but rather to secure the right to "live and to labor and to be free men in our intents." By the end of May, after approximately two weeks, the men returned to work on their terms. The Knights of Labor played no role in this conflict, as they had not arrived in the city. But the molders' next strike, a six-week battle in 1883, flared at precisely the moment that the Order experienced rapid growth.[20]

The Knights of Labor had entered Brockville in August 1882, and Archer Baker of Odgensburg, New York, had laid a firm organizational foundation by November of that year.[21] When Smart's molders struck in June and July of 1883, again reasserting their commitment to control by demanding adjustments in the shop book's price scale, the Order was in the midst of an impressive organizational drive; in early July over 100 Knights were initiated, including 63 in one evening. Many of these were molders, affiliated with the

Franklin Assembly (2311), which met every Tuesday evening. When another molders' strike/lockout erupted in January 1884, the Order was well established, boasting a membership of 430 in the fall of 1883.[22] This protracted, seven-month conflict lasted well into the summer months. Again, the Gill brothers came directly to the heart of the matter. "The question at issue is simply one of control!" they asserted vehemently. They contended that the "present difficulty has nothing whatever to do with wages," but that the "indirect losses sustained by [them] owing to the control of the union [were] such that there would be no inducements for the company to continue operations." The union men saw things differently. They knew that the Gill brothers deeply resented their limited forms of control as institutionalized in the trade rules and regulations. For such men it was indeed difficult to walk through their establishment with pride, looking their men in the face, knowing "that they were [their] masters, that they decide who shall work and who shall be discharged." Rather than rebel, the Gill brothers should acknowledge the difficulty they must have in watching their men labor to produce all that they possessed. This difference in perspective kept the parties divided. The Gill brothers, bested many times by the Iron Molders' International Union, were determined to resist to the end in 1884. By late July the molders had returned to work, their union crushed, their vestiges of craft control vanquished.[23]

In the midst of this struggle, Brockville's Knights of Labor drew close to the Molders' Union. Indeed, as the conflict raged, the fortunes of the Iron Molders' International Union No. 197 and Franklin Assembly of the Knights of Labor became intricately entwined. LA 2311 sent Samuel Miller of the Molders' Union to the Philadelphia General Assembly of 1884, instructing him to urge the convention delegates to select Brockville as the site of the 1885 meeting. As the molders and the Gill brothers reached an impasse in the early summer of 1884, John S. McClelland, Secretary of the General Executive Board of the Knights of Labor, arrived in Brockville to address a special meeting of Franklin Assembly, and was greeted by a large audience. LA 2311 eventually received $500 from the Order's Assistance Fund, money that went, in part, to the beleaguered molders. It was hardly sufficient to carry the molders through to victory, but every dollar probably meant much to the union men, and demonstrated the commitment of the Knights of Labor to the principles of working-class independence and work place autonomy.[24]

In Oshawa events followed a similar course. Largely through the efforts of James R. Brown, the Order was established in the town with the organization of Etna Assembly (2355) on 12 August 1882. Brown's history in Oshawa labor circles reached back to the struggle for the nine-hour day in 1872 when, under the pseudonym "Heather Jock," he had written a series of letters to the Toronto *Ontario Workman* and the *Oshawa Reformer.* In this correspondence Brown emerged as a radical spokesman, attacking employers and battling the conciliatory attitude of the leadership of the Oshawa Nine Hours League, a group Brown thought guilty of "selling out" the interests of ordinary workingmen. When Michael Quigley, an Irish laborer, contested a municipal election in 1872, Brown was encouraged by the 170 votes the worker received. "It may seem a small matter to record," he noted, "but to those who know how the workingmen in the Oshawa Cabinet Factory and Joseph Hall Works are in general importuned at elections, the fact that so many of the men in those establishments voted for one of their own number, gives us reason to hope that they will do better next time." The Oshawa labor advocate was still professing such views in the 1880s, and Brown had developed into a thoughtful and articulate working-class leader. With the rise of Oshawa's Knights of Labor, Brown came under concerted attack. Eventually he was threatened by "some of the bosses," who attempted to secure his discharge for advocating a revision of "the law of value." Brown proposed that labor be the measure of all value, thereby rendering "rings" and "corners" impossible, setting up labor as "king," preparing the way "for industrial co-operation on an equitable basis." Such a proposition, Brown claimed, would "revolutionize the world, that is what the K. of L. desire." But the employers reacted with rancor, arguing that such a plan would destroy the manufacturers, and Brown, a crony of D. J. O'Donoghue, finally left his work in Oshawa to become a factory inspector for the Ontario government. The LA Brown had helped to found, 2355, was a mixed Assembly, 300 strong, although its core was undoubtedly composed of laborers and molders employed in the city's various iron works. Indeed, when Etna Assembly lapsed in July 1884, it was followed by the reorganization of LA 2355, as well as the emergence of a second trade Assembly, the Iron Moulders' LA 4279. As in Brockville, the molders and the Knights of Labor had made common cause.[25]

In October 1883 the laborers at the Malleable Iron Works struck work in protest against a wage reduction that cut their daily rate from $1.25 to $1.125. The president of the company, John Cowan, a staunch advocate of the National Policy and tariff protection for his own concern, rejected the men's claims that they could not provide for their families on the reduced wage, and argued that "they lived too high." When the laborers, who were members of the Knights of Labor, had the audacity to hold a meeting to state their grievances before the public, they were attacked in the local press as "the scum," "hard of cheek," and "glib of tongue." Their offer to submit the dispute to arbitration rejected, the laborers walked out, and as a consequence over sixty molders were thrown out of work. What seemed to be a mundane dispute over wages, however, quickly drifted into a confrontation over the right of the Iron Molders' International Union No. 136 to exist. Apparently the Malleable Iron Works had also cut molders' wages, and began shipping their work to the United States; in a hostile and uncompromising statement they warned they had no intention of employing union men, "and that unless they returned to work before the 1st of January at the terms offered by the Company the shop [would] be permanently closed against them." As one subscriber to the *Palladium of Labor* made clear, the union men were not simply innocent bystanders in the whole affair, passively resigned to being locked out in the midst of a laborers' dispute that had little significance for them, nor had they returned to work as the Hamilton journal had mistakenly reported. On the contrary, "the molders have not returned to work, nor are they likely to except by terms offered by the Company . . . The molders are certainly on strike."[26]

The company eventually prevailed and by mid-December the laborers affiliated with the Knights of Labor had returned to work reluctantly. Unfavorable press coverage, the depressed state of trade, and the existence of numbers of men willing to "scab" broke the men's resistance. James Brown, chairman of the striking laborers' Executive Committee of LA 2355, noted that "From the state of things at present, it would have broke Jay Gould with his seventy-three millions of stolen money to have kept labourers and immigrants away from here." The molders, however, took no action. Their union was defeated, and perhaps they understood that this spelled the end of any remnant of craft pride; rather than submit to the indignities of an open shop they simply drifted away or found employment in other businesses. The Knights of Labor had proved ineffectual in their efforts to protect the basic work place interests of their membership.[27]

But as future events would confirm, the Order's failure did not necessarily dampen all enthusiasm for the labor-reform cause, or dull the appreciation of the need to maintain control mechanisms. In Oshawa's Iron Molders' Union No. 136 there was a staunch group of labor advocates that remained true to the Knights of Labor and led the battle to establish and preserve the craft's essential control over the work process. At the helm of this contingent stood Lewis Allchin, "of English parentage and birth, Canadian citizen, though a resident for two years under the Stars & Stripes." Allchin had joined the Iron Molders' Union in 1878, and had been a charter member of LA 2355. In October 1884 he wrote to Powderly soliciting his advice regarding a profit-sharing plan he and others were trying to negotiate with their employer at the Oshawa Stove Company. His own commitment to the cooperative agreement was rooted in his years of experience in the class struggle: "I have always strictly obeyed the Laws & Regulations of the IMIU not only in the letter but in the spirit. I have been ostracised twice and had to leave town for fighting the Unions battles, I have been in one strike and one Lock-out, and never accepted one cent from the Union, as I prefer to get along without it as long as I am able. I never allowed myself the run in arrears, and I never was on the road without my card, although that was some times nearly all I had in my pocket." The molder also noted the union commitment to craft control, claiming that "we have affected every Reform obtained in the Shop, one for instance, piece workers used to work almost all noonhour, and not later than last spring we managed to institute a rigid observance of noonhour, we also limited the wages to $2.50 per day." These measures, of course, might draw the ire of "kickers" and "hoggish workmen" whose attachments were to their own individual betterment rather than the collective security of the molders as a particular group, and this may well have explained some of the resistance Allchin and others faced. As the leading figures in Oshawa's Molders' Union, serving as the officers of the local body, Allchin and his allies were angered by the opposition to the profit-sharing plan that developed in IMIU No. 136. "For myself," said Allchin, "I rather enjoy fighting the employers, but when it is common street talk that the men for whom we fought will drive us and our families out of town, it rouses my Saxon bulldog stubbornness, and I say if they *can* drive me out they are welcome to do so." But Allchin also recognized that *his* defeat spelled victory for the capitalists, who were "waiting patiently for the crisis." "I candidly think," concluded Allchin, "that if they force us out of the Union they will be breaking the back-bone of the grand old IMIU No. 136, and rendering themselves an easy prey to certain unscrupulous employers." Allchin was nevertheless quietly defeated, and temporarily suspended from the union.[28]

This setback did not terminate his activities in the interests of labor reform, however, and in 1887 he served as a delegate to the third session of the TLC. He played an active role (along with J. R. Brown) in the molders' strike at the Malleable Iron Works in early 1886, when the union, supported by LA 4279, again fought "in defence of its existence as an organization." Certainly Allchin continued to adhere to the principles of the Knights of Labor, of craft control, and of labor reform, popularizing them in the Molders' Union. Numerous letters from other Oshawa molders appeared in the trade's *International Journal*, suggesting the continuity and persistence of such forces, beliefs, and practices. Allchin adopted the pen name "Sand Artist" and also wrote a series of articles outlining the history of the IMIU. In many of these articles he linked the union and the Knights of Labor, presenting them as antagonists of the consolidating capitalist order. "The object, in brief," he claimed, "is *the complete emancipation of labor,* and the inauguration of a higher and nobler industrial system than this of the present, under which one human being is dependent upon another for the means of living." Denying at the outset later historians' views of the Knights, he emphasized that the Order was not a backward-looking body: "We cannot turn back if we would; we cannot return to a primitive system of working, however much we might desire it." Trusts and syndicates he viewed as an "inevitable phase" of "an excessive and pernicious competitive system," but they would not be "the *finale* of the whole question." They "contained within themselves the germs of their own dissolution," because "selfishness and greed were but foundations of sand to build upon." He would not predict the future, but he hazarded one final conclusion: "That no system which does not recognize the right of labor to a first and just share of its products, which refuses each and every toiler a voice in the business transactions of the enterprise, that does not establish a just and relative measure or standard of value for all services rendered, labor performed, products manufactured, and commodities exchanged, will ever be a just or permanent one." Given the movement culture's capacity to generate ideas like these and leaders like Allchin, it is no surprise to find him and his molder brother Knights involved in violent confrontation with employers.[29]

Indeed, they fought in approximately twenty-five strikes and lockouts in Ontario between 1880 and 1893, often drawing the Knights of Labor into conflict as well. The case of the employees of Sylvester Brothers in Lindsay, told by their employer that "labor organizations may go to Hades," was typical. On 1 March 1886 the bosses introduced "an unjust and tyrannical document" by which the workers were to bind themselves to the firm for a period of six months promising, on forfeit of $50, not to belong to any Knights of Labor or trade union body. As many of the employees were affiliated with the Order and with the Molders' Union they "refused to sign away their freedom" and "were accordingly discharged." All peaceful means of settling the dispute were exhausted and a boycott was organized against the castings and implements sold by the firm.[30]

In Kingston, too, ironworkers and Knights of Labor formed a sort of alliance and early found themselves in conflict situations. The *Brockville Recorder* claimed in the first week of April 1886 that "a branch of the Knights of Labor will be started in Kingston by the employees of the different foundries in that city within the next two weeks." Three weeks later it noted that blacksmiths at the locomotive works, the cotton mill employees, and Stevenson and Company's piano varnishers had all struck for higher wages, as had the Kingston and Pembroke railway employees. The paper concluded its meager reportage of these events with a cryptic comment: "Kingston recently organized a Knights of Labor Assembly." This was probably Frontenac Assembly, described as "composed exclusively of iron-workers, iron-workers' assistants and laborers employed in and around the foundries and shops."[31]

A year later, in May 1887, there was a strike at the Victoria foundry by a united group of molders, fitters, silver-platers, and laborers affiliated with the Knights of Labor and the Molders' Union. One hundred men marched out in a body, "for the wages paid in the west." But the strike did not turn exclusively on the rates of pay. Angered by the refusal of the owners (Cunningham and Chown) to allow the molders to work on day rates, one striker claimed that "the men want to be placed on day work at about two dollars a day." But if that request was not granted, the molders demanded a union shop, in which the scale of wages would be set by the shop committee. Protests were also raised against apprentices working by the piece before their four-year training stints were completed. Cunningham and Chown seemed uninterested in settling the dispute, and the ironworkers' grievance committee received no satisfaction. The men then decided to stay away from the shop, and told the bosses to approach them when they were ready to reopen negotiations. The employers merely reiterated their refusal to countenance any infringement on their authority. Cunningham traveled to Toronto and Hamilton to attend a stove manufacturers' meeting, where he undoubtedly received much advice from anti-union founders, while Chown rested in Kingston, studying trade journals in the hope of unearthing the secret of undermining strikes and defusing workers' militancy. The men, meanwhile, enjoyed a holiday, and two of the strikers set off for England.

What was at stake in the conflict, clearly, was the workers' right to organized status, and the threat that posed to Chown's and Cunningham's authority. The unity of the strikers seemed particularly irksome, Cunningham noting upon his return from Toronto that he had been in the business thirty years, but that this was the first "general strike" he had ever encountered. Chown, however, issued the most telling statement early in the strike when he refused to have any dealings with an appointed committee of three Knights of Labor who visited his office to discuss the strike. "We refused to engage in any conversation in the matter," he explained. "We do not know the Knights of Labor in this matter, and further we do not know that our men are members of that organization." In a blunt conclusion the owner expressed his inability to recognize that his men had affiliated with the Order: "In connection with the strike we are willing to discuss the matter with our men, but we do not want to know the Knights of Labor on the subject." With their heads, ostrichlike, buried in the sand, the employers continued their obstinate stand for ten days until, on 23 May 1887, they agreed to a reluctant compromise with their men. In the midst of this confrontation at the Victoria foundry cotton mill employees struck to recover a 10 percent wage reduction instituted two years earlier and molders, boilermakers, blacksmiths, and helpers stopped work at the Kingston Locomotive Works. Both strikes were probably orchestrated by the pioneer Kingston LA, 9452, known as Limestone, which embraced about 300 workers from all callings. Upon the granting of certain concessions, both disputes were settled. The Knights of Labor had arrived in the city of Kingston with something of a bang, and previously settled social relations had quickly been disrupted.[32]

Nearby, in Gananoque, the Knights of Labor also experienced a marked period of expansion in the years 1886–8. Paralleling this growth were strikes/lockouts at the Cowan and Britton Company, the woolen mills, and two confrontations at Skinner and Company's hame factory. (A hame was one of the two wooden or metal projections that formed a part of or were attached to the collar of a draft horse and to which the traces were fashioned.) The origins and outcome of the first two of these strikes are obscure, but it is likely that the Knights of Labor, who organized a number of LAs in the town in the late 1880s, were involved. Here, again, these conflicts may well have turned on workers' efforts to retain some measure of control over their working lives. (At the woolen mills, for instance, women weavers struck against their employer's tampering with the time clocks.) Certainly that was the case at the Skinner works, where the Knights of Labor took a stand against an obstinate employer that would result in serious divisions and disagreements within LA 10185.

The Order entered Gananoque in the spring of 1886, and quickly initiated a large membership in four Assemblies, three of which later amalgamated. By the end of 1887 the local newspaper claimed 800 had been drawn into the ranks. Employers in the vicinity were never all that tolerant of the Order's encroachments upon their terrain and at the Carriage Works George Toner, an MW active in local politics and a blacksmith, was rumored to have been dismissed.[33] But it would be Skinner's factory that would be the battleground upon which the Order waged war against antagonistic employers. The first confrontation developed in March 1886 as thirty-six hame-makers enrolled in the Knights of Labor struck work. The men left work when Skinner refused to fire an employee named Mallory, who would not join the Knights of Labor. The strikers also claimed that Mallory, who was an engineer, was a poor workman, and safety in the factory was compromised by his presence. Toner argued that the strike would continue until a person suitable to the Order was engaged to take charge of the factory's boiler and engine. A competent engineer was finally hired to tend to the boiler and the strike, which was supported financially by the Knights of Labor, terminated in a peaceable settlement.[34]

Prior to the second strike, in February 1888, Skinner's men had been idle for two to three weeks. After returning to work full-time, however, a foreman in charge of the polishing department was away from work for most of a week, and Skinner claimed that as a consequence work fell behind schedule. He hired a young man named Burridge to assist in the works; apparently he tended the troublesome boiler. The factory must have been thoroughly organized by the Knights of Labor, for Henry Woods, an employee of the shop and an official of the Knights of Labor, notified Skinner that if Burridge, who was not a member of the Order, were not discharged the men would walk out at noon. This effort to enforce the closed shop met with stiff rebuttal from the employer, who promptly informed all his workers (about forty in number) that they were no longer needed, and locked his doors at noon. He added insult to injury by promising to close the shop for a month. Toner again headed the strikers' negotiating effort, demanding that all the men on the lower flat be taken back to work, and that the man attending the boiler – probably Burridge – be discharged. But Skinner won the day easily, and within two weeks the factory was taking on new orders, working on a limited basis. Some of the men returned, while others remained out, but new workers quietly found their way into the discharged hands' jobs. Skinner regretted losing such experienced men, many of whom had been with him for some time, but he did not see how he could "have done anything differently and at the same time retained control" of his business. He let it be known that there would never again be work for three leaders of the Knights of Labor, who had figured prominently in the lockout.

The failure of Gananoque's Knights of Labor to emerge victorious out of their conflict with Skinner tells us something about the strategic weaknesses of the Order's local militants, as well as the work place ecology of the Skinner factory. To begin with, the effort to enforce the closed shop was carried through with little or no planning, and the two LAs, 7508 and 10185 (to which most of the Skinner men apparently belonged), were not even consulted. One contingent of workers even claimed that the matter had "not been taken up by or under the auspices of the Knights of Labor." This lack of a clearly defined strategy cost the Skinner men dearly, for it meant that many of those locked out harbored little resentment or grievance. In effect, the movement to resist Burridge and confront the employer had been waged by the highly skilled workers of the upper flat of the factory. Among those who remained out to the end were James McLennan, silver-plater and formerly foreman of the department; his brother John, a general hand; M. J. McDonald, shaper; T. Harrison, nickle-plater, A. Cummings, turner; Wesley Snider, molder; James Willis, brass finisher; George Cotnam, silver-plater; and D. Walker, blacksmith. Aside from one unskilled laborer, drawn by the ties of kinship, the second Skinner revolt, like the first, was sustained by the highly skilled hame-makers. Opposition (or indifference), however, developed among the men of the lower flat, many of whom probably possessed little, if any, skills, and it was claimed that this took in fully two-thirds of the employees (hence Toner's insistence that these men be taken back). Given this state of affairs it must have come as no surprise to the Skinner militants to see their fellow Knight of Labor workers return to the factory. After the debacle, members of LA 7508 and 10185 complained to Powderly of the illegality of the strike (it not having been sanctioned by the general Executive Board). H. S. Johnson, MW of LA 10185, officially ordered the locked-out Knights back to work, and as a consequence was brought before the Local court, tried, and expelled. Twenty-four Knights of Labor petitioned Powderly to investigate this "troublesome matter," contending that Johnson's trial had been "more of the nature of a Persecution than a Prosecution." Powderly never answered these pleas from the small Ontario town on the St. Lawrence River.

The Order in Gananoque foundered on the shoals of a conflict waged to protect the basic work place rights and interests of its members; after 1888 little record of the town's Knights of Labor survives. Meetings were held to keep up the charter, but "interest in the cause had died out." One member of the Order, however, had learned his lessons well. He clipped an article from Toronto's *Labor Record* on the cruelty of Pennsylvania's mine owners and sent it to the local newspaper. Eight months after the Skinner strike, he may have reflected back upon that event when he commented: "'Forewarned is sometimes forearmed,' so I ask you many readers, especially those of the K. of L., to keep posted and prepared to defend themselves from the onward march of the intolerant and tyrannical of the capitalistic oppressors."[35]

Harbor Assembly (LA 2513, of Port Dalhousie) faced a similar crisis in May 1889. James W. Linch, MW of the LA, confided to Powderly that some trouble had divided the carpenters and caulkers of LA 2513. A delinquent member of the Order worked among other members in the shipyard, and one day one of the Knights of Labor in good standing asked him when he planned to pay up his dues and assessments. The worker replied that he had not yet made up his mind as to whether he would pay or not. When he met with his employer, the carpenter was told "to keep his money in his pocket and he would be that much ahead." Emboldened by the proprietor's advice, the man returned to work and defied the Knights of Labor to refuse to work with him. When the carpenters and caulkers in the yard indicated their displeasure to their supervisor, also a fellow Knight, the owner dismissed the lot, "the Boss as well as the men." Three of the discharged workers later went back to work; the DMW endorsed their action, telling them that they could return to the yard as there was nothing in the Constitution that said they had to boycott the job site. Linch felt there was no excuse for such behavior, however, for all the men had work elsewhere, which they could have secured readily. Now that these men had returned, they were trying to get others to go back "whether they belong to the Knights of Labor or not." Eight of the Order's members remained firm in their opposition, and found work at other places. The question, in the minds of these workers, was whether the yard was a fair place for a Knight to work, and if the DMW had given the brothers wise counsel in advising them to terminate the boycott. But whatever Powderly's advice, the damage had been done, and the Order's Port Dalhousie stand for the closed shop had been undermined.[36]

Knights of Labor struggles to secure their members a measure of control over their lives at the work place were not always written in such pages of defeat. Indeed, the Order's victories in this realm may be obscured by the resulting lack of conflict. Where employers acquiesced to demands for shop rules, regulations, and committees, where apprentice limitation and restriction of output were routinely practiced, and where workers decided questions of hiring, firing, and the length of the working day, the historian is liable to see only peace and quiet. But this must not be mistaken for passivity, for often the foundation of such social harmony was a well-entrenched attachment to workers' autonomy, and recognized domains of mutual labor-capital rights.

In the Beamsville stone quarries, for instance, LA 8570 had a long history, starting with its organization in 1886 and lasting through years of depression until 1896. Only briefly, in April 1887, as far as can be determined, did resentments flair, as the stonecutters of the Assembly refused to accept the piece-rate system, "the stone being such that we cannot make wages on [it]." A few months later the difficulty had been settled, with the Beamsville correspondent reporting daily wage rates in the area to the *Journal of United Labor*. At the Amherstburg stone quarries of Mr. Ession, fourteen Knights of Labor stonecutters responded to the dismissal of their foreman and his replacement with a non-union man with a brief strike. Richard Summerville, MW of a Windsor LA settled the affair, but nearly half the workers left town in protest. Molders at the Smiths Falls Frost and Wood Company's agricultural implements works attempted to organize but were consistently thwarted by their antiunion employer. Their major period of success, however brief, came in the years 1886–8, when they affiliated with the Knights of Labor, "trying to educate ourselves on the all-important subject of labour." As their LA (6772) faltered in 1888 any remaining forms of work place control were probably displaced with the establishment of a set of factory rules by the firm's owners.[37]

Perhaps the most forceful indication of the Order's role in maintaining forms of job control for its members emerged in the midst of a minor confrontation at Cedardale, south of Oshawa. LA 9678 complained that a member had been discharged for being a Knight of Labor. When T. B. Barry traveled to St. Catharines to interview the head of the firm, the employer argued that he had not wronged his men. All of his employees at both his St. Catharines and Cedardale concerns (probably agricultural implements works) were members of the Order and he bore them no ill will. He allowed a shop committee to choose all new employees, and he thought it only natural that the men would choose fellow Knights. Moreover, the employer claimed that he had helped the Knights of Labor previously by spending his own money to recruit strikers from another plant to his works. He defended the firing of the Recording Secretary of LA 9678, a man named Barton, saying the workman was incompetent. Barry distrusted the employer's account, and suggested that Barton, who had worked at the Cedardale works for several years, had been fired for trying to recruit a worker for a job in Quebec. But this militant had no desire to upset the favorable balance of power in the Cedardale shop, or to tip the advantage to the employer by precipitating a strike over the issue. So he advised the LA to aid Barton until he could land another job, and urged the displaced worker to exercise more discretion in the future.[38]

When control became an issue, then, it generally involved workers who possessed at least a modicum of skill; when conflicts resulted from efforts to retain a measure of this control they were generally small affairs, led by the skilled. If relatively unskilled workers affiliated with the Order went on strike, they, too, might be involved in a struggle for control, but it was more likely that they were taking the preliminary step of attempting to secure an organization (a prerequisite in any prolonged effort to realize even the most limited forms of workers' control), or addressing a specific grievance, most often one concerned with the hours of labor or the rate of pay. These strikes ranged in size from minor affairs affecting only a few workers, to massive, almost general, strikes, involving hundreds of workers in towns or areas that had come to be dominated by a single industry. These mass strikes were most prominent in the mill towns of eastern and western Ontario, where the Knights of Labor attained considerable stature in the late 1880s and early 1890s.

## Laborers and others

Brockville's Knights of Labor, for instance, became embroiled in a number of strikes involving unskilled and/or unorganized workers. The most troublesome work site appeared to be on the lumber docks, where George Shields and other bosses seemed determined to resist any efforts to undermine their positions of authority. During the last week of July 1883 four men in the employ of Shields – John Sheridan, Tom Sheridan, Matthew Derenzy, and Robert Murphy (all members of Franklin Assembly 2311) – were dismissed for handling cargo in a rough and unsatisfactory manner. Shields agreed to take the men back if they were willing to "obey orders," but this seemingly reasonable request was refused. The dock workers appeared to have organized a local laborers' union, for there was some fear that the strike would be respected by the coal gang on the docks, which was known to sympathize with the discharged men. Shields conferred with Captain John Young and John Larocque, president and treasurer of the body, and both agreed that as they had a contract with Shields they would honor their commitment and the coal would be unloaded. But the workers on the lumber docks were resolute in their stand against the victimization of their fellow workers, and twenty of them quit Shields' employ. Their action was endorsed by the Knights of Labor, which must have included almost all the members of the dockers' local union (Young and Larocque, for instance, were prominent in LA 2311). By early August Shields had emerged the winner, having secured sufficient numbers of "scabs" to handle any loading that needed to be done. Some of the striking Knights returned to work in the face of this defeat. The next year Shields took no chances, and forced all those who applied for work on the CPR wharves to sign a contract for the entire season, in which a set wage scale was established and a small sum of each week's pay was held back until the end of the season. If a laborer did not complete the season he forfeited the amount. Applauded as an "excellent scheme" by the press, Shields' plan was simply to eliminate any resistance he might encounter; no Knights of Labor, it was well known in the town, need come to him for a job.[39] Four years later the Knights of Labor involved themselves in a similar dispute at the O. & L.C. freight warehouse, where laborers struck work when a man was discharged for responding impudently to a boss's demands. Three carloads of men were quickly imported and the strike was no doubt easily crushed. Finally, the Brockville Order may have played a minor role in a brief confrontation involving forty to fifty men building a CPR spur line in early June 1884, and in the fall of 1883 Captain Young and the Knights of Labor helped to settle a dispute between Italian navvies installing sewers for the town's Water Works Commission and a contractor who had failed to secure funds to pay the immigrant workers.[40]

Across the province minor skirmishes like these must have occurred regularly. Quickly defeated, they might draw only the most cursory comment in the local press. Thus, in May 1888, the *Brockville Recorder* noted that, "Knights of Labor in the employ of the Rathbun Company at Kingston who struck for higher wages have given in and returned to work." Often strikes may have facilitated organization. A conflict in a Merritton cotton mill in 1887, for instance, may have drawn workers to the Order, and followed on the heels of a number of work stoppages led by the Knights of Labor in 1886. Five years later, John T. Boucock, Recording Secretary of Maple Leaf LA 5933, wrote to Powderly asking him whether the Order could demand that a "dropped member" be dismissed from the mill where he worked, "where all are K. of L. members." Another strike erupted at Merritton in 1889 and the mill remained totally organized as late as 1892. None of these cotton workers' struggles, which generally turned on the issue of wages, represented a major victory, but in an industry known for its exploitation and antiunionism Maple Leaf Assembly's 500 workers were more successful than most. Their achievement may well have been one of the factors that led Canadian Coloured Cottons to shut down the plant after a merger in 1892. But in many small towns where the Order consolidated conflicts important in the history of the Knights of Labor have been buried in obscurity.[41]

A Chatham lockout of late December 1886 makes the point. Evidence has survived on this confrontation only because the Judge Advocate of LA 5961 took up his pen to inform the *Canada Labor Courier* of the difficulty. The origins of the dispute lay in the Order's effort to induce the council to have the town bell rung at five o'clock on Saturdays, thereby establishing, in effect, a universal early-closing hour. This tactic was quite common in the 1880s and was rooted in much earlier times. In Belleville, well before Confederation, Catholic workmen had paid their church to toll the bell at certain hours, before and after which no labor was allowed. Bell ringing thus stood as a symbolic reminder of the organic community of producers, linked in mutual agreement about the appropriate hours of labor. The London Trades and Labor Council petitioned the mayor in the spring of 1886 to have the town bell rung at seven o'clock and again at five o'clock, setting the limits of the working day. The mayor complied, for a brief few days, but pressure was exerted, and the bell no longer tolled. Terence O'Toole reported from Galt that workingmen in that town had carried out a similar "little reform" in October 1886: "The town bell is rung every night now at seven o'clock, and all are expected to close at that hour." Despite this successful venture, however, O'Toole did not expect the practice to last, for it did not strike deeply at the root of the problem. As far as workingmen in Galt were concerned, "everything is rotten in Denmark, and these things such as keeping stores open till late hours are but excrescences of that rottenness." What had worked in the 1830s and 1840s was thus opposed or grossly inadequate in the 1880s, and any notion of the harmonious organic community of the preindustrial period clearly out of place in the new conditions of the late nineteenth century.[42]

Chatham's LAs 5961 and 7150 ran into immediate difficulties in their effort to shorten the hours of Saturday labor. A committee from the Royal Oak and Maple Leaf Assemblies decided to support their request to the council by visiting local employers who were in the habit of working until six o'clock. They first called upon the firm of Thomas H. Taylor & Company, who operated flour and woolen mills. The proprietors declined the request, adding that they would never consider the proposition unless Messrs. Campbell, Stevens, and Company would institute the reform in their flour mill. When the latter agreed to the Order's suggestion that the Saturday hours of labor be reduced to nine, Taylor & Company still balked. They offered to give their hands an extra hour on Monday morning, but the Knights of Labor deemed this inadequate. As a consequence the Order agreed to allow its members to use their own judgment "as to whether [they] would use Thos. H. Taylor's flour, and also whether [they] would patronize grocers who would buy their flour." The millers reacted with vigor, and "set themselves to work to break up the K. of L." Taylor & Company led the way in the formation of a United Employers' Association, which issued an ultimatum to the Order to lift the boycott immediately. When the Knights of Labor refused to take any notice of this threat, the employers initiated a lockout of all workers belonging to the Order. Forty-eight Knights promptly found themselves without work. Many members felt that the act was a transparent effort to discredit the Order's political efforts to secure representation in the upcoming federal election, depicting the Knights of Labor as a "dangerous element, . . . demoralizing the trade of the country and in conflict with all enterprises." A settlement was effected to the Order's satisfaction early in January 1887, and pledges were publicly given by some employers. But these were violated, and a rupture once more forced upon the Knights of Labor, who were "determined to stand by their rights and compel their refractory opponents" to abide by their conditions. The outcome of the Chatham fight remains unknown, but the employers' willingness to turn their workmen out on Christmas eve, and the Judge Advocate's urgency in reporting the situation to the St. Thomas labor paper on Christmas day indicate just how strained labor-capital relations could become when the Knights of Labor enlisted themselves in the cause of working people.[43]

The Chatham LA's commitment to shortening the hours of labor was but part of a more general, provincewide effort. Beyond the well-known, but unsuccessful, agitation to secure the eight-hour day in 1886, Ontario's Knights of Labor played a marginal role in a scheme to establish Time Leagues in a number of Canadian cities. These leagues, dedicated to reducing the hours of labor to eight per day, promised a solution to unemployment and "the labour problem."[44] More widespread, and probably more effective, was the Order's involvement in the early-closing movement, which drew many clerks, salesmen, and other blackcoated or white-collar workers into the Knights of Labor. Stratford's dry goods clerks' petitions to secure the early closing of stores on Saturday evening were supported by the Knights of Labor, as they were in Hamilton and London. In the latter city, the summer months of 1886 witnessed a campaign led by the Women's Christian Temperance Union to induce the city merchants to close their stores by seven o'clock on Saturday evenings. The Knights of Labor, struggling to secure the nine-hour day on all work commissioned by the city, offered an early hand of support to this movement. In May 1886, John Gayton urged the store clerks of London to form an LA of the Knights of Labor, and "help us to help you." "Whether you work by the piece or the day," he reminded them, "reducing the hours increases the pay." This argument was reiterated in mid-July when an "Organized Mechanic" wrote to the *London Advertiser* in reply to a clerk's earlier communication:

> I have a better scheme to offer than An Employee whom I am led to believe by the tone of his letter is a clerk in one of our stores. I would suggest that all the clerks of the city organize themselves into an Assembly of the Knights of Labor. They can do this without much difficulty if some of the energetic ones among them only undertake it. They will have the united strength of over 4000 people to assist them. These 4000 men have the controlling power over say about 8000 women and children. If you will organize yourselves you can get support of these 12000 people to assist you in closing early on Saturday nights. If you do not do this you may keep on working Saturday night.[45]

When an Eastern DA of the Knights of Labor convened in June 1888, delegates from Kingston, Smiths Falls, and Cornwall determined to agitate for the enforcement of an early-closing act. Among St. Catharines' Knights of Labor, the notion that stores were kept open late for the benefit of the working class had been "pulverized," the Order in that city "urging members and friends to do their shopping before six o'clock, and pledging to patronize only the stores that close at the prescribed time." An April 1886 early-closing drive by the St. Thomas clerks' mercantile association resulted in the formation of a new LA. The Headlight (4069) and Fidelis (4929) Assemblies led the way in supporting the commercial workers' efforts to secure "an extra hour which they can utilize either in social intercourse or mental culture."[46]

The early-closing movement took its most interesting turn in Ottawa. Many clerks were attracted to the Knights of Labor during the last six months of 1891, and they joined LA 2806, composed entirely of commercial workers. After securing a bylaw instituting the six o'clock closing time, however, they stopped coming to meetings. George Kilt, an ingenious if rather Machiavellian local figure in the Order (it should come as no surprise to learn that he was a friend and ally of A. W. Wright), informed Powderly that when he took the chair of LA 2806 there were but six or seven members in good standing. "After taking charge," Kilt told Powderly, "I inaugurated a system of agitation on the outside that threatened the by-law, and then worked the clerks up to enthusiasm at open meetings, etc. by telling them that unless they joined the assembly and made it a power they would assuredly lose the benefits of the six o'clock movement." The wily MW reported that the subterfuge had worked wonders, and the LA was growing steadily again. He fully expected that it would have a membership of 200 before long.[47]

These small battles waged by the Knights of Labor, from the unsuccessful struggles on Brockville's docks to the industrial and commercial efforts to reduce the hours of labor, were indicative of the diversity and range of the Knights of Labor presence. The force of the Order, however, was more dramatically revealed in large mill strikes, which assumed the character of mass struggles. Typical of such confrontations were strikes in Cornwall, Gravenhurst, and Ottawa.

## The mass strike

Cornwall's Stormont Cotton Mills had been flooded with orders throughout 1886, its spinners, weavers, and other operatives forced to work full time on Saturdays and overtime much of the week, "the machinery rattling away till a late hour every night." In the midst of this economic boom its employees expressed some discontent. "An Operative" urged the mill to pay its workers every two weeks, instead of monthly, so that they could avoid the entanglements of credit and purchase their goods for 10–15 percent less, while a young girl engaged in the mill complained that she had drawn only $4 for two months' pay. Given these conditions the *Freeholder* predicted that the Knights of Labor "would take pretty well in Cornwall." In fact, in March 1886 the Order entered the town and held secret weekly meetings in East Cornwall, a French-Canadian district located near the cotton mills. These clandestine gatherings gave rise to the formation of LAs 6582 and 6583, the first composed entirely of spinners and weavers employed in the Stormont and Canada Company mills, the latter a mixed Assembly.[48]

The mill workers first tested their employer in the summer of 1887. Eighteen men engaged as raw cotton yarn dyers demanded that the hours of labor be reduced from ten to nine, and the Stormont mill manager proceeded to lock them out. All the discharged men were members of the Knights of Labor, and the Order supported them financially with $400 in assistance.[49] This relatively minor affair prefaced a more awesome confrontation that started during the first few days of February 1888. Wage reductions at both the Canada Company and Stormont mills precipitated strikes involving from 1,300 to 1,500 employees. The work force was approximately half French-speaking and half English-speaking, and included men, women, and children. (In 1881 Cornwall's three cotton factories – one was a relatively small firm – employed 133 men, 227 women, 186 boys, and 190 girls. Their yearly wages totaled $179,800, and $456,000 worth of material was used to produce a product valued at $883,000. By 1886 the work force had expanded considerably, and production no doubt jumped accordingly.) At the Canada Cotton Company the reduction was said to be on the order of 28 to 33 percent. The secretary of the Stormont mill, Archie Gault, argued that the reduction was simply an equalization of wages, some of the weavers' rates being brought into line with their lower-paid co-workers. This assessment may explain a slight breach of solidarity that occurred at the beginning of the strike, as seventy-eight weavers returned to work at the Stormont mills in spite of the declaration of a strike. Perhaps their wages had not, in effect, been cut. But these workers were quickly brought back into the fold by the ringleaders of the strike, undoubtedly prominent members of the Knights of Labor. No such divisions appeared at the Canada Company, where support for the strike seemed strong. Eventually, after approximately two weeks of negotiations, settlements were reached at both mills. Promising to pay the highest wages for mill workers in Canada, the companies induced their workers to return to the shopfloor. Wages would still be cut, but if a moderate 10 percent reduction did not set the wage rate higher than other Canadian mills, the older rate would be reinstituted. The Stormont workers returned on their own accord, while at the Canada Cotton Company the settlement was reached by arbitration.

This ended the difficulty at the Stormont mills, although a boss-carder complained of his female operatives' lack of work discipline and respect for authority; the women said he called them "bitches." But at the Canada Company a second strike resulted, a large proportion of the workers feeling that the company had circumvented the agreement on wages. It took a month for the disagreements to be ironed out and production to be resumed; when it was all settled, over $25,000 in wages had been lost owing to the strikes. Old antagonisms died hard, however, and there was some feeling among the operatives that the employers were prejudiced against members of the Knights of Labor. One leading figure in the Cornwall Order, John J. Bickley, had been fired from his position as overseer in a small spinning mill owned by Joseph Moyes. "I was given to understand," he testified in 1888, "that I was dismissed because I was a Knight of Labor, and because I took an active part in labor matters . . . that I would be 'black-listed' all over Canada."[50] In March 1889 the Knights of Labor again encountered difficulties at the Stormont mills and a five-week strike involving 600 operatives took place. The conflict developed when the weavers protested that the cuts woven were being made longer without a corresponding increase in pay for the extra work. A settlement was effected by a committee of workers and the manager, the latter agreeing to make the cuts a certain length according to the nature of the cloth.[51]

Along Muskoka Bay, in and around Gravenhurst, twelve shingle and lumber mills employed approximately 300–400 men. Work was seasonal, and seldom did an employee obtain more than eight months of paid labor. Up until 1887 the men worked an eleven-hour day and were paid, ostensibly, every month, although more often than not the companies did not actually settle with their workers until six or seven weeks had passed. Two weeks pay was quite commonly held back by the mill owners and, because of various subterfuges and the high cost of extensive reliance on credit, men to whom $80 or $90 was owed (wages seldom exceeded $1.25 a day) were rumored to have been offered $2–3. Under these appalling conditions the men decided to hold a series of meetings and finally approached the bosses to request weekly payment of wages and a two-hour reduction in the hours of labor, which they felt only their due as the Ontario Factory Act had established ten hours a day's work. They belonged to no organization. The bosses promptly refused their demands, which led to a spontaneous and thorough stoppage of work. A compromise was reached that for the remainder of the season the hours of labor would be set at ten-and-a-half per day, with the ten-hour system to be introduced in the spring of 1888. The matter of weekly pay was quietly forgotten. Out of this general uprising was born LA 10669, affiliated with DA 236, and centered in Lindsay and Uxbridge.

After the hard winter of 1887–8, the millmen were literally destitute, "glad to get any thing with which to earn food for their children." Seizing this opportunity, the employers passed a series of resolutions to the effect that the working day was to remain at ten-and-a-half hours, and that wages would be paid monthly. A provincewide agreement was apparently entered into by the Muskoka, Georgian Bay, and Ottawa River lumber barons, each mill owner agreeing not to reduce the hours of labor upon pain of forfeiting a deposited bond. The workers, almost all of whom were enrolled in LA 10669, naturally resented this violation of their previous agreement, and sought the counsel of DMW R. R. Elliot. He cautioned against a strike and urged them to strengthen their ranks and build up their treasury in anticipation of a coming contest. By June the Knights of Labor had secured 300 of the 375 workers in the area and appointed a committee to meet with the bosses. Insults were their reward, and after a series of frustrating interviews with individual employers the LA again petitioned the DA for advice. Elliot traveled to Gravenhurst to look into the situation and found things just as the men had described them. Even the mill owners were prepared to admit, casually, that the men's demands were justified, but they would give no ground. Questioning merchants, Elliot found that the monthly payment system was reducing the real value of the workers' earnings by as much as 35 percent, so exorbitant was the cost of credit. And this despite the mill owners' acknowledgement that they received their money every month from the lumber buyers. "Imagine a man working ten hours and a half a day and supporting a family on 75¢ a day for eight months' work in the year," the astounded Elliot wrote to Powderly. When the Knights of Labor official met with the bosses he found them determined not "to move one iota." There was no way out of the impasse, Elliot judged, and he reluctantly advised the Executive Committee of the DA to endorse strike action.

The strike began on 3 July 1888, after a committee of the workers again met individually with each proprietor to try to avoid conflict. For two weeks the strikers held out, bolstered by much public sympathy, and Elliot begged Powderly for immediate aid. The men also requested that Brother Barry be sent to the town to endeavor to bring about a settlement, the East Saginaw organizer's reputation apparently having drifted north along the shoreline of Lake Huron. After about a week two of the mills acceded to the Assembly's demands, but the remainder assumed a stance of determined opposition, threatening to "starve the dogs out." By 16 July one firm had reopened its doors, blowing its whistles at 6.30 a.m., and attracting a few workers who were not Knights of Labor. By September the "general strike in all the mills" had reached its conclusion, and the men were back at work. Some resentment was expressed by members of LA 10669, who felt that the District Executive Board should have issued a general appeal for assistance before the strike was entered into, insuring support for the strikers. Details on the settlement of the strike are lacking, but the implication of the resentment against the Order is that the men were forced back to work on the companies' terms. From Toronto, D. J. O'Donoghue claimed that a member of the General Executive Board, Brother Aylsworth, ended the strike. "He 'settled' the strike quickly enough, but at the same time he only aggravated the difficulty," reported O'Donoghue. "Acting on his advice each striker acted for himself and returned to work when he thought fit." Such a state of affairs produced immediate discontent.

William Sloan (Recording Secretary of LA 10669), for instance, was victimized in the aftermath of the conflict, a contracting foreman having tampered with the engineer's machine while he was away at the DA in Lindsay testifying in the proceedings held to determine the constitutionality of the Executive Board's actions and advice during the strike. Upon his return to Gravenhurst, Sloan found that the man had again interfered with his engine, "without giving me any intimation of it." Angered by this incursion upon his work prerogatives, the engineer confronted the foreman, who told him that the machine had not been giving satisfaction under his management. The Knight of Labor resented this attempt to "injure [his] reputation as a mechanic," and "high words" ensued. Sloan was then discharged, despite his questioning of the foreman's "right or authority to do so." He was thus stranded without work, and the time of year made it impossible to secure another position. "Will the Order assist me to show this man (who only discharges me because I will not agree with him as to the setting of the eccentric valve of the engine) that he can't leave a man helpless in this way?" Sloan asked Powderly. Ironically enough, Sloan, probably discharged for his prominence in the Order, had been the very voice of dissent (along with his brother Archy) criticizing the DA for its "hasty" granting of permission to strike. Locked out of work, Sloan must have felt as if he was being kicked when he was down as his LA refused to back him up in his criticism of the DA's Executive Board. Gravenhurst's 1888 mill strike was over and so, too, was the brief history of LA 10669. Nothing was heard from it after 1888.[52]

In the Chaudière region of the Ottawa-Hull area, another mill workers' strike erupted in September 1891. This conflict has drawn much comment, being perhaps the largest strike in Canadian history up to that time, and only a bare outline of the events will be provided here.[53] As in Muskoka, the Ottawa Valley was ruled by a closely knit group of entrepreneurs, men who had made fortunes and consolidated power on the basis of sawn lumber and lumber by-products. French-Canadian workers would figure prominently in the strike, as they had in the troubles at Cornwall. Their involvement, as well, would catapult the Catholic Church into opposition to the mill workers' militancy. Nine firms would be involved in the 1891 strike, and they were headed by some of Canada's most distinguished capitalists, notably John Rodulphus Booth, Erskine Henry Bronson, and Ezra Butler Eddy. The fortunes of these men had accumulated while their workers eked out a bare existence. In 1890 the mill hands' wages ranged from $7 to $9.50 per sixty-hour week (probably based on an eleven- to twelve-hour day, with reduced time on Saturday). This wage rate, as the *Annual Report* of the Ontario Bureau of Industries noted in 1889, did not even allow the yardmen to meet the annual cost of living, and produced a yearly deficit of $10.13. Although the Knights of Labor had entered the Ottawa region early, a telegraphers' Assembly (2334) having been organized in 1882 and the clerks' LA 2806 in 1883, the Order was not strong in the city. D. J. O'Donoghue visited his old residence in February 1886 to try to stir up interest in the Order, but his trip produced little in the way of organizational growth. Attempts were made to enroll the mill hands in the Knights of Labor as early as 1888, but the largely transient, unskilled, seasonal work force proved a difficult nut to crack. By the end of 1890 a number of LAs had been formed in Ottawa and Hull, but the Chaudière workers still resisted organization. On the eve of the great strike, for instance, less than a dozen of the 300 men employed at the Perley and Pattee Company were members of the Knights of Labor.[54]

The Chaudière conflict had its origins in the harsh winter of 1891, which delayed the opening of the saw mills. When work finally began late in the spring, the workers were informed that depressed conditions in the trade forced the owners to reduce wages by 50¢ a week, but that to compensate for this cut the ten-hour day would be introduced. The lumbermen seemed to accept this course of events as inevitable, but grew angry as the employers openly violated their own promise, running their establishments eleven and twelve hours daily. In May the workers sought the assistance of the Knights of Labor, requesting organizational aid and financial help if they struck work. The Order informed them that they must give six-months' notice before a strike could be sanctioned. As the mills would be closed within that time period, the Knights of Labor spokesman urged them to stay on the job, suggesting that little could be gained by trying to win concessions during the present season. Reluctantly, the workers followed this advice, and labored under the disputed conditions for the remainder of the summer. Their resentments festered, however, and as the community seemed united behind them they must have cultivated a keen sense of grievance. *United Canada*, an Irish

Roman Catholic weekly, referred to the destitution dominating life in the lumbermen's shantytowns and condemned the situation in the mills as "white slavery."

On Saturday, 12 September 1891, a handful of outside workers at the Perley and Pattee mill (were these, perhaps, those affiliated with the Knights of Labor?) decided that they had had enough, and asked their foreman to reinstate the wage rates of the previous season. Denied this request, they organized a Sunday meeting, and determined to strike if they could not receive satisfaction on Monday morning. Once again they were rebuffed, and as a result stopped work and encouraged others to join them. They were successful in stopping outside work at the mill, and an angry foreman responded by locking the inside workers out. An owner, G. B. Pattee, explained to the men that the wage reduction was general among all the mill owners, and that he could not break from established policy. Upon hearing this his workers proceeded to each of the mills in the area urging employees to drop what they were doing and join them. At the end of their trek, the lumbermen gathered outside Booth's mill to hear an address by Napoléon Fauteux, a popular, capable, and recognized leader thrown up from the ranks. Listening to him were 350 men from Perley and Pattee, 800 from Booth's, 300 more from the Buell, Orr, and Hurdman establishment, and 500 employees of the Bronson and Western Company, as well as many more from smaller mills, shipping yards, and docks adjacent to the lumber works. Although some of the employers would later claim that the strike was led by "walking agitators" and that it was "ordered by the Knights of Labor," the walkouts were, in effect, spontaneous demonstrations of a long-standing sense of grievance. The men's willingness to confront the owners at such an inopportune moment testified to their strong commitment to their cause.

The Knights of Labor quickly stepped into this organizational void, and assumed leadership of the strike. *Le Spectateur*, a Hull newspaper edited by Napoléon Pagé, became the strikers' voice, and over 2,000 mill workers were said to be enrolling in LAs 2966 (Chaudière) and 2676 (Canadienne), both of which contributed funds to the out-of-work lumbermen. Over the course of the next few weeks the millmen continued to reiterate their demand for a restoration of the wage cut; as well, they held out for the ten-hour day. Some firms agreed to these conditions, and the strikers returned to work. But the larger concerns remained firm in their denial of the strikers' demands, and Perley and Pattee, Bronson and Weston, and Booth were said to be offering board and $1.50 a day to strikebreakers from outside the area. As community support stiffened, massive meetings of 3,000 to 10,000 people demonstrated the widespread sympathy enlisted on behalf of the men. Skirmishes were common at many mills as the strikers confronted those who defied their order to cease work. When a few higher-paid saw-filers at Bronson's tried to return to work strikers intervened, threatening to tar and feather them if they again broke ranks. Ottawa's police force and the militia were secured in defense of the mill owners' property, drawing condemnation from across the country. In ritualistic derision some strikers gathered in Hull to mock the militia, parading with blackened faces and hoisting sticks on their shoulders in imitation of military movements. To thwart attempts to discredit the strikers as advocates of mob rule and destruction, Fauteux and James William Patterson, a printer with ties to the Knights of Labor, and prominent in working-class circles where he presided over the Ottawa Trades and Labor Council, posted squads of workers around the city, advising them to protect property from injury. The Knights of Labor expended $1,500 in aid of the strikers, and played an important role in coordinating the elaborate relief system established to cater to the strikers' needs. Supported by donations from local unions, merchants, and businessmen, as well as smaller contributions from sympathizers in Ontario and Quebec, two stores were set up to provide the men and their families with the necessities of life. (From far-off Toronto Powderly offered the strikers his sympathy, but denied that they were members of his Order, meaning that he could not plead their case before the General Executive Board.)

In spite of this disciplined response, the superior force and strength of the large companies eventually prevailed. By the end of September an impasse had been reached, and the strike leaders were urging all who could to seek work elsewhere; 600 workers took this advice and left the area. The structure of relief work collapsed at the end of the first week of October, and by 12 October 1891 all of the struck mills had resumed operations, and the strikers drifted back to work. Less than half the original lumbermen remained, however, and the mill owners had been forced to restore the wage cut, although they adamantly refused to institutionalize the ten-hour day. At Bronson's the resumption of work was a short one. Upon receiving their first pay on 14 October the men learned of their new job conditions. They received the 1890 wage rates, but the hours had not been significantly reduced, the company instead allowing them an hour for lunch. Two hundred workers promptly struck again, but it was a futile act. By the end of the month they were all back on their jobs. Victory did not rest securely with either camp: the men were frustrated in their attempts to secure the shorter working day; the employers were forced to grant the wage increase and other minor concessions. While the companies claimed their losses were nominal, LA 2966 argued that it would be "within the mark to estimate the employers' total loss at

$350,000." The 2,400 strikers had forfeited between $75,000 and $150,000 in wages. But their faith in the Knights of Labor had not been lessened. In March 1892, perhaps in anticipation of another battle, they organized DA 6, where J. W. Patterson headed an impressive contingent of 2,000 mill hands and general workmen. This body continued the demands of 1891, George Kilt informing Powderly in 1894 that the millmen still pursued their "reasonable request for a *ten-hour* day." It would finally be granted in 1895.[55]

The Ottawa Valley lumbering frontier would remain fertile ground for Knights of Labor activity well into the twentieth century. In a September-October 1906 battle at the James Maclaren pulp and paper mill in Buckingham, Quebec, men known as Knights of Labor (supposedly allied with the Building Laborers' International Protective Union of America) called a strike. Considerable ill feeling developed and the mills were closed down, the owners refusing to recognize the legitimacy of a union. Strikebreakers were imported from Ottawa and the militia were called in to keep the peace. An armed contingent of strikers confronted Alexander and Albert Maclaren, a large body of "scabs," and some hired constables. One union leader and an innocent bystander were killed. A coroner's jury found the Maclarens, four members of the police, and several unionists guilty of criminal responsibility in the deaths. The strike was eventually defeated, the owners acquitted of all charges, and the Knights of Labor banished from the region.[56]

## Cooperation

As all this makes abundantly clear, the Order's involvement in strikes seldom led to startling successes. It was for this reason, primarily, that the leaders seemed so firmly set against strikes, and opted for other solutions to the labor problem. Cooperation was one such panacea, and formed an essential part of the Knights of Labor reform ideology. It fit well, also, with workers' desires to preserve control over their working lives. The Order's official journal urged each LA to have its cooperative "missionary," one who would crusade zealously for the cause: "Labor reform has hitherto been but a voice in the wilderness, 'prepare ye the way,' but the time has come, when, if pioneers, self-devoted, self-controlled, and intelligent enough can be found, a path can be cleared and blazed so that the multitude can go therein. Where are the pioneers? Let us preach the exodus." Among such Canadian pioneers were William J. Vale, the Hamilton printer and prominent Knight elected to the international Co-operative Board, Phillips Thompson, who often lectured to Knights of Labor Assemblies in small towns like Peterborough, advising members to take up the principles of cooperation, Edward Allen, of the

Dundas LA 5329, Toronto's Alf Jury, a leading figure in the Toronto Central Co-operative Store, and John Sadler and George Evans, Recording Secretaries of LA 3305 in London, who pleaded with all true Knights to support the Order's cooperative coal mine to break the power of unscrupulous rings and dealers' associations throughout the province.[57] These advocates were bolstered in their efforts by the Order's constant defense of cooperation, and endless reminders of the pertinent literature on the subject that could, with profit, be sold to the rank-and-file.[58] Across Ontario the Order's commitment to the cooperative commonwealth was well known and reported in the pages of local newspapers.[59] This widespread publicity bore fruit and many cooperative stores and ventures thrived in the 1880s, supported by workingmen who knew something of the Knights of Labor and its principles even if they did not belong to an LA. Gananoque supported a cooperative society, London and Toronto cooperative stores, and a cooperative cigar factory about to be formed in Belleville in 1889 drew support from Kingston, Napanee, Prescott, and many other eastern Ontario towns.[60]

As we have seen in earlier chapters, the cooperative spirit thrived in the strongholds of Toronto and Hamilton, where many trades, especially the bakers, seemed addicted to cooperation. When trade proved dull, or in the midst of a strike/lockout where an employer refused to deal with the Knights of Labor, the cooperative alternative was often posed as the ultimate solution.[61] The ambitious effort to establish an alternative local transportation system in the midst of the Toronto street railway strike was undoubtedly the most dramatic such undertaking, but there were countless other less grandiose attempts. As Kingston molders and fitters struck at the Chown and Cunningham Victoria foundry in 1887, for instance, the local newspaper posed the question: "if the Knights start a cooperative foundry in opposition to the Victoria what will be the result?" Chown obviously thought very little of the idea, claiming that if the Order did follow such a path of resistance "the firm would sell out the plant at a reasonable rate." Indeed, strikes often proved the birthpangs of cooperative undertakings. Members of London's International Typographical Union struck at the *Free Press* in late May 1884 in an attempt to restore a wage cut. A demonstration of 2,000 was held to support the strike, and the city's leading Knight of Labor, John R. Brown, was one of many addressing the throng. The printers issued their own paper, in which notice was served on "them who defy the organized labor of London, who dare to arraign its leaders as malefactors in the press of this city, that persistent, relentless war on them is the only course which the outraged thousands, of whom they have vainly endeavored to browbeat, propose to pursue until they strike their colors and accede to the demand for union wages to *union men*." Promising to follow this paper, appropriately named

*Union*, with a cooperative paper published in the interests of labor, the *Evening News*, the men eventually induced the proprietor Blackburn to settle with them. Two years later London's LA 3305 asked the General Executive Board to endorse a notice to be circulated requesting support for a number of LAs seeking to establish a cooperative press.[62]

More dramatic was the outcome of the 1888 Gananoque strike at Skinner and Company. The dismissed hame-makers traveled to Merrickville, where they established a cooperative factory. Aided by a $1,000 town bonus, tax exemption for ten years, and free rent for twelve months, fourteen skilled workmen immediately left their native village to take up residence in their new home on the Rideau Canal. Promised financial support by their LAs, the men looked forward to establishing themselves in Merrickville, where thirty tenement houses were to be built for them. "Our embryo attempts at utilizing our experience for ourselves as well as a one man concern," suggested "M.H.C.," "need not know or look for anything else but success." Months later the men were said to be "succeeding as well as they had reason to expect." Their former employer confessed that the new business would "hurt" him, and predicted a drop in sales if the new shop received many orders. Well over a year later the Gananoque reporter for the Ontario Bureau of Industries noted that "the most marked effect of organization upon labor matters was seen in the material and moral support given to a co-operative industry, which was the outcome of a lock-out which happened two years ago." The correspondent noted that three Assemblies of the Knights of Labor provided the aid that enabled the twenty men involved to survive until they began to get returns for their work. "They have now a fine factory," he closed, "and are doing a safe and profitable business."[63]

Most Knights of Labor cooperative ventures were not the success stories of the Merrickville hame factory, even for limited periods of time, nor did they all emerge out of strikes and lockouts. But their presence may well have bred hostility on the part of employers, and they certainly cultivated the Order's sense of working-class independence and autonomy. Much of the recalcitrance of the employers of Chatham may be partially explained by the Order's establishment of a cooperative biscuit and confectionery manufactory. It started production in the fall of 1886 and was located in an old malt house on the banks of the Thames River. The concern was heavily subsidized by the town and supported by Knights of Labor across the country, who took out shares valued at $10 each. When it failed in June 1887, its goods had barely been introduced to the consuming public. It can hardly be accidental that its history coincided with the fierce offensive against the town's Knights of Labor.[64]

Similar cooperative undertakings were established in Stratford, where twenty to thirty members worked producing the "Little Knight" cigar, and in Woodstock, where a match factory was run on "strict Knight of Labor principles." The Woodstock cooperative had secured the services of W. H. Williams, reputed to be one of the most competent match makers in Canada, and urged all members of the Order to do their duty and buy the new factory's products. "Cooperation is the fundamental principle of our Order," concluded a report from the Woodstock Co-operative Manufacturing Association, "and in patronizing these matches, which will bear the K. of L. label, you are only doing your duty." In Norwich LA 5430 purchased a knitting factory, capitalized at $3,000 with six hundred shares of stock worth $5 each. The mainstays of the Norwich effort seemed to be a prosperous local member of the Order and John L. Moore, who managed the mill. Moore had, during the course of 1887, owned a grocery store, sold it, engaged in farming, purchased the grocery store once more, and managed the Knights of Labor factory. He supervised a group of local housewives who operated the hand-driven machinery to produce stockings. After a brief period the factory was closed down, and the machinery sold to the people of the town.[65]

Failure in such cases was not the most important aspect of the cooperative impulse. Such self-sustaining ventures had tangible and symbolic significance, and stood as testimonies to the capacities of common working people, reminding all of the potential of self-management. As George Collis raged against the wage system before a gathering of Knights of Labor in Brantford, he reminded them that workers should never be treated as "slaves." He pointed to the Knights of Labor tobacco factory in Paris, run by N. P. Benning, as an example of how the system could be turned to the workers' benefit. Even as they went under, cooperative efforts were seldom in vain, and many enterprises must have lapsed because of "mistakes" of generosity. James Brown, Master Workman of LA 2491, wrote to Powderly in 1884 explaining the demise of the Order's Brantford cooperative store. "On account of many of our members being out of work," he related, "we have carried them on until we have become embarrassed being unable to make collections we are able to meet our liabilities but the shareholders will lose their investments." In the midst of this difficulty, however, Brown could still see the bright side of things, and continued: "Our funds are about exhausted. We have a good many Sick Brothers to see after but taking all things into consideration the order is doing well. Our membership is holding good. I am about organizing another assembly here. Factory and sewing girls assembly. I think it will be a success."[66] The center of Ontario Knights of Labor support for cooperation was undoubtedly Petrolia, where the presence of the oil refineries seemed to flaunt the excesses of monopoly before the eyes of the membership. The Recording Secretary of Reliable Assembly (4570) informed the *Journal of United Labor* in 1887 that three attempts at cooperation had been made – an oil refinery, a flax manufactory, and a general store – although none had proved successful. The Petrolia commitment to cooperation, like so many other local efforts, had been persistent, but it had also been frustrating.[67]

## Craft versus class

Equally frustrating, at times, was the Order's attempt to preserve good relations with trade unionists in order to fulfill their desire for unity and general cooperation among all workers. We have already touched on this question in earlier chapters on Hamilton and Toronto, as well as in our discussion of strikes in this section, but it bears repeating that the Knights of Labor often entered into alliances with international craft unions, and the two organizations functioned as cordial partners. Both the successes and the failures of this unity often emerged most forcefully in the midst of conflict situations.

R. H. Hessel recalled that when the Knights of Labor supported strikes in London they simply called for assistance and then divided the take among the applicants. Because the London Order waged few, if any, struggles on its own, most of the recipients were probably trade unionists, some of whom probably had no connection with the Knights of Labor. LA 3305 petitioned Powderly in 1885 for permission to boycott the London stove manufacturing firm McClary & Company. Hugh McLean informed the GMW that the firm had been placed on unfair lists in Toronto, Hamilton, and Kingston, where Knights of Labor Assemblies were apparently boycotting it. Two years previously the molders had struck and lost, and the McClary firm had been nonunion since then. Union molders and Knights of Labor eventually came to work in the shop, but when an outside molders' LA had circulated petitions condemning McClary as an unfair employer all of these men had been discharged. Those Knights of Labor who had been dismissed, as well as the union molders, were strongly in favor of retaliation and argued that LA 3305 should "come out openly as K. of L. and Boycott them."[68] Knights of Labor leaders often came to the aid of craft workers who had been weakened by persistent employer assaults, as they did in a significant Ontario Rolling Mills Hamilton strike of January 1885. And many, many times, from one corner of the province to another, the Order offered material support and passed resolutions in favor of striking craft workers.[69]

Indeed, it was possible for an LA to function *precisely* in the same fashion as a craft union, even to the extent of raising initiation fees to keep out unwanted members. Kingston's LA 741, composed of mechanics connected with the building trades, asked Powderly if it would be acceptable to raise the fees for masons, bricklayers, and plasterers from $5 to $15 (they had already raised it from $2 to $5 without permission). They reasoned that as all of the tradesmen in the city now belonged to the LA, this would be an appropriate way to avoid "over-stocking the labor market for the time and shortening the work for our citizens." Powderly seemed to agree and granted their request.[70] Railroad workers in St. Thomas who affiliated with the Order almost always belonged to their craft brotherhoods, while woodworkers in that city, enrolled in LA 4435, expressed an almost craftlike exclusiveness in their concern with jurisdiction.[71] Welland members of the Order – stonecutters, trainmen, and quarry workers – protested when the DA levied an assessment to pay the expenses of delegates selected to travel to the 1886 Richmond General Assembly. "We think a cigar dealer and a printer don't know our wants," argued the discontented Knights.[72] In all these cases, whether the Order was involved in acts of solidarity or exclusion, there was little separating the practice of the Knights of Labor and the trade unionists. Prominent Knights seldom publicized the exclusionary side of this process, but they did often argue that the cause of the unions and the Knights of Labor was identical.[73]

Occasionally, however, Knights and unionists came to blows. Printers were often at the center of the controversy, as we have seen earlier in the cases of Toronto and Hamilton. While the Order was quick to sanction a boycott of the St. Catharines *News* in 1886 for using the same type on its evening editions that Buffalo newspapers employed in the morning, thus violating an essential rule of the International Typographical Union, Knights of Labor papers were often guilty of the same practice. "Brant" reported that an effort was being made in his city to clean up the printing trade, where the *Expositor* and the *Telegram* were "addicted to the use of boilerplate." These papers pleaded their case by noting that the St. Thomas *Labor Courier* was guilty of the same offense, and it was a workingman's journal. This produced nothing but jeers from organized labor in Brantford, however, for the *Courier*, a Knights of Labor organ, was judged to have been a weakling at birth, "heralded forth in the midst of a Dead Sea of the stalest kind of plate matter, and has continued so almost ever since." The irony was that "Brant" sent this communication, so full of contempt, to the *Palladium of Labor*. Less than a year later the editor of the Hamilton-based labor-reform journal would be charged with similar violations of trade standards.[74]

Even in St. Catharines, where printer–Knight of Labor unity had seemed strong in the spring of 1886, trouble eventually developed. John S. McClelland, whom we have met before, was a former member of the General Executive Board and a leading figure in the telegraphers' brotherhood during the 1883 strike. In 1888 he returned to his native St. Catharines to take over a local paper, the *Evening Star*. He enrolled in LA 5933, where his overbearing character and penchant for intrigue wrought much damage. During 1888 the local branch of the typographical union established a wage scale that was endorsed by the Executive Board of DA 207. One of the local newspapers (presumably the *News*, which had suffered at the hands of the 1886 boycott) paid the union rate, but the *Star* declined. A strike resulted, and three printers affiliated with the Order and the international union continued to work at the "scab" paper. The MW of LA 2056 ordered these men to honor the strike, and when they refused the offenders were tried and expelled. As editor of the struck paper, McClelland was scorned by many fellow Knights and did all in his power to undermine the legitimacy of the strike, abusing the members of LA 2056 through the *Star*'s columns. This led to much discussion in the St. Catharines region, and many workers boycotted the Order, disenchanted with a body that provided refuge for men like McClelland and failed to stand firm in the interests of labor solidarity.[75]

But it was in the cigarmaking trade where relations between Knights and unionists really took a turn for the worse. The Home Club affair that erupted in Hamilton in 1886 had its echoes around the province. There were murmurs of difficulty in the trade in Windsor, St. Catharines, and Belleville.[76] Toronto was affected and in Brantford the cigarmakers had abandoned the Knights of Labor by 1887. During a strike in August of that year the Brantford trade unions passed a resolution "to support the cigarmakers in their strike by using none but the C.M.I. union blue label cigars," indicating that the white label of the Order was no longer held in much esteem. Behind all these obscure difficulties lay the antagonism that had emerged in the mid-1880s between the Progressive Cigarmakers and the International Union. The former affiliated with the Knights of Labor, affixing the white label to their products, while the latter remained with the longer-established blue label. As the International urged a boycott of all cigars not bearing the blue label, Powderly reminded the union cigarmakers that it was the Order that had "fanned the flames of once-dead unionism" and he pleaded with the International Union not to attack the Knights of Labor: "Men may fade and pass away, isolated labor societies may struggle and die, but that which was intended to bar out sectional strife and bind all workers together must live on. So hands off, gentlemen, fight your enemies, and not your friends." It was the kind of bombastic proclamation Powderly was well suited to deliver, but it did little to heal the rifts in labor's ranks. It certainly had no impact in

London, where the summer months of 1886 saw Knights of Labor and union cigarmakers pitted against one another.[77]

London's cigarmakers had much to complain of, the city being notorious for its foul shops, unfair masters, and poor working conditions. Boys and girls abounded in the trade, and after being apprenticed for three to four years to learn a skill, boys entitled to a man's pay were quietly discharged, left "sponging upon their parents, looking out for a chance and falling into bad habits, or taking the road as tramps." One stogiemaker lamented the "Consequences of Monopoly." He waxed sarcastically on the cordial relations between masters and men in London. While strikes were common everywhere else, he noted that in the Forest City things were always settled amicably. Only last week, he confessed, an employer had asked his workers to return after dinner to do night work. This proprietor's feeling was that "hunger was the best sauce," and that the boys needed the work. But he judged wrongly, for the hands determined that they could not make much if they worked twenty-four hours a day, so small were the wages. They refused his kind offer and for their impertinence were unceremoniously fired. Relations between the cigarmakers and the employers worsened in the aftermath of these public critiques and in mid-July, after the cigarmakers participated in a large labor demonstration, two manufacturers locked out all the union men in their employ. The conflict turned on the hours of labor, the union rules stipulating that no member could work more than eight hours per day and the employers demanding nine hours of service. Like so many strikes/lockouts in the trade, this one drifted into an impasse.

By early September the cigarmakers had a new grievance, it having come to their attention that John A. Rose & Company were "palming off upon their customers and the public generally . . . certain inferior brands of cigars as Rose's K. of L." Rose, whose testimony before the Royal Commission on the Relations of Labor and Capital revealed the depths of his antipathy for Lodge No. 19 of the Cigar Makers' Union, refused to allow union men in his shop. This seemed characteristic of the employers in the city, as only 38 of 275 hands working in the tobacco industry were laboring in union establishments. As the union launched an assault upon Rose and his comanufacturers, they ran headlong into the Knights of Labor, whose white label adorned many of the cigars produced in the city. By November Hugh McLean, RS of LA 3305, was telegramming Powderly to ask if cigarmakers could belong to both the Knights of Labor and their union. "Answer at once," he closed, "as there is trouble here." Labor solidarity in the cigarmaking trade in London had foundered, just as it had in many other North American cities.[78]

## "To fight for your rights"

The pathway to justice, then, was strewn with many a roadblock, and the Order's involvement in strikes, lockouts, cooperative retaliation, early-closing movements, and trade union–Knight of Labor controversies revealed the multitude of problems confronting those attempting to lead the class to victories, however minor, via the people's strike. But for all the frustrations, all the defeats, all the bitterness, and all the divisions, the people's strike was both a persistent phenomenon and a valuable experience. It taught men and women that a stand could be taken – *for* independence and autonomy at the work place, *for* recognition and organized status, *for* the rights of labor, and *against* injustice. At the forefront were nearly always the skilled, who drew on craft traditions to take a stand for the class as a whole. These skilled workers embraced the unskilled and the unorganized, and called for better working lives for all. Even in the mass strikes of relatively unskilled workers at the Cornwall cotton mills or the Gravenhurst shingle and lumber mills, it was the dyers who first served notice of the Knights of Labor's willingness to strike, or an engineer like William Sloan who played a pivotal role. The Chaudière strikers quickly turned to East Elgin's Knight of Labor representative, Andy Ingram, a railway worker from St. Thomas's LA 4069, or the Ottawa printer, J. W. Patterson. Cooperation, if it were to succeed on any level, generally required the enlistment of some workers with craft knowledge and experience. And in the many smaller struggles to secure some measure of control over the working environment, epitomized at the Gananoque Skinner factory, skilled workers always seemed to take an active part. Like the fictional workers who drew Ryerson Embury's admiration, such advocates and practitioners of the people's strike regarded the strike as much more than a mere, economistic event. Skinner's hame-makers, for instance, would have agreed readily with the *Palladium of Labor*'s editorial attack on the Kingston *Whig*'s depreciation of strikes:

> Strikes may not "pay" directly, and yet may have an indirectly beneficial effect upon the condition of Labor. War does not often pay, and yet the knowledge that a nation is prepared to resist aggression frequently deters others from attacking it. So with strikes. Even an unsuccessful strike teaches employers to respect Labor, and makes them consider the consequences before provoking another conflict. The mere knowledge that workmen are organized and ready to make a prolonged fight often prevents the capitalist from reducing wages. The difference in the condition of organized and unorganized labor is a sufficient proof that strikes, or at least a readiness to strike, rather than submit to injustice – benefit the working class.[79]

It was men like the hame-makers, and sentiments like these, that helped to make an Order premised on the depreciation of the strike into a striking machine in countless Ontario communities. The skilled workers who stood at the center of this process had dared to struggle, even though they seldom tasted the fruits of a win.

However much the Knights of Labor ideal shied away from the strike, then, the reality was far different. Across Ontario workers associated with the Order were, like their counterparts in trade unions, drawn into the strike from a number of different directions, struggling to maintain limited forms of control, affirm the right to organize, or alleviate a specific grievance. To be sure, Knights and unionists did find themselves in opposing corners on occasion, but on the whole these were rare instances of confrontation and, aside from the cigarmaking trade and in Toronto during the years of the Order's decline, there were actually few blemishes on the Knights of Labor's historical relations with Ontario's craft workers. Outside of DA 125, where an entrenched, politically committed, and cautious leadership prevailed, the Order would function as all organized labor had to function. For an attachment to arbitration and a desire to avoid conflict meant little in the face of an employer who could not countenance any infringement upon his prerogatives: strikes were as much necessities forced upon workers as they were conscious choices. The weakness of an international body unable to control effectively its LAs but unwilling to support them fully in the midst of conflict then emerged. While victories were few, and most certainly concentrated in the pre-1887 years of greatest strength, the Knights of Labor made significant inroads into work sectors previously untouched by labor militance, and went a long way toward the creation of a labor movement that moved beyond privileged interests. On Toronto's street railway the Order launched one of the first mass struggles in Canada, a strike that predated organization on North American streetcars and that stood as a harbinger of labor relations in this transportation field in the years from 1893 to 1906. Metal trades workers throughout Ontario first demonstrated the effectiveness of a labor unity that transcended craft lines, linking skilled and unskilled, in a series of work stoppages led by Knights of Labor that ranged in size and significance from the successful Toronto Massey strike of 1886 to the defeat at the Oshawa Malleable Iron Works in 1883. And while the Knights of Labor retreated in central Ontario, the northern and eastern sections of the province surged ahead. In lumber and in cotton the late 1880s and early 1890s witnessed mass strikes of previously unorganized workers that would have seemed an impossibility before the coming of the Order and that would not occur again for many years, if not decades. The movement culture had registered its impact in the willingness of the class to fight oppression and injustice. Even if the choice was only to resist and be smashed, Ontario's Knights of Labor obviously preferred this to silence and acquiescence.

A semiliterate man from the small town of Alvinston, Ontario, wrote to Powderly at the high-point of the Knights of Labor presence in 1886, and conveyed some sense of this process. Having lived to see the efforts being made to "Shield the labouring man/From the . . . tironizin cruelty of monopolies and Rich Men," Howard Rickard requested information about the procedures and possibilities of "organising the Nigts of Labour" in his area. In passing he advised the GMW that the Order should proceed "cautiously and with all due respect to a well organize bodie of opponents" to oppose wrongs against the working class so that "beter days [could] be brought around." But he recognized the difficulties involved, and commented, "You have no small task before you." With his eyes riveted on the much-publicized confrontation with the railroads in the American Southwest, he closed militantly: "To look after and in speaking of the strikes of the Labouring of those railroads now unsetled as yet I regret that their should been any necesity to resort to fier arms as that nearly always results bad. But it is necessary sometimes to fight for your rights."[80] A worker brought to this elementary but vital class stance by the presence of the Knights of Labor in the Ontario of the 1880s, Rickard stood as a reminder of what the Order had accomplished and of why that evocation of tradition and innovation, chivalry, struggle, and solidarity, remained so important to North American labor in the years to come.

# Part IV. Conclusion

A man must have time for serious individual thought, for imagination – for dreaming even – or the race of man will inevitably worsen.

William Morris, artist and Socialist (1884)

"There are rifts and rifts," wrote Pisarev of the rift between dreams and reality. "My dream may run ahead of the natural march of events or may fly off at a tangent in a direction in which no natural march of events will ever proceed. In the first case my dream will not cause any harm: it may even support and augment the energy of the working men . . . There is nothing in such dreams that would distort or paralyse labour-power. On the contrary, if man were completely deprived of the ability to dream in this way, if he could not from time to time run ahead and mentally conceive, in an entire and completed picture, the product to which his hands are only just beginning to lend shape, then I cannot at all imagine what stimulus there would be to induce men to undertake and complete extensive and strenuous work in the sphere of art, science, and practical endeavour . . . The rift between dreams and reality causes no harm if only the person dreaming believes seriously in his dream, if he attentively observes life, compares his observations with his castles in the air, and if, generally speaking, he works conscientiously for the achievement of his fantasies. If there is some connection between dreams and life then all is well."

Of this kind of dreaming there is unfortunately too little in our movement. And the people most responsible for this are those who boast of their sober views, their "closeness" to the "concrete," the representatives of legal criticism and of illegal "tail-ism."

V. I. Lenin, Bolshevik (1905)

It was incredible, the proof in practice of what one knows in theory: the power and strength of the masses when they take to the streets. All one's doubts are suddenly stripped away, doubts about how the working class and masses are to be organized . . . Suddenly you feel their creative power; you can't imagine how rapidly the masses are capable of organizing themselves. The forms they invent go far beyond anything you've dreamt of, read in books. What was needed now was to seize this initiative, channel it, give it shape.

Narcisco Julian, Communist railwayman on Spanish Civil War

Thus, albeit in some new as well as some continuing forms, a socialist cultural revolution has still to be rooted in potential majorities which can, by their own organization and activity, become effective majorities. The principle of cultural revolution offers an outline of ways in which there can be both effective association and new forms of negotiation beyond specific associations. In this assertion of possibility, against all the learned habits of resignation and scepticism, it is already a definition of practical hope . . . We can agree that it will be long, hard, contentious and untidy – its criterion of success, for as far as we can see, being a possible majority of successes over its many failures . . . While many of its forms will be extensive and pervasive there will be certain decisive confrontations, with very powerful opposing forces, which will all too sharply remind us that we are attempting cultural *revolution* and not some unimpeded process of social growth. But what will get us through such confrontations, and in some important cases into them, is not only association and organization; it will be also what we can call . . . the "material force of the idea": the production and the practice of possibility.

Raymond Williams, Marxist critic, 1980

The sight of many people coming together out of their own volition encourages in deferential human beings a sense of their own worth. Democratic forms encourage people to feel like democrats, and, after a pause, to consider the heavy implications, to act like democrats that is, to overcome their deference and propose an initiative or suggest an idea. Beyond "alienation" lies a world of individual self-respect and collective self-confidence that can only be engendered within genuinely functioning mass institutions of politics. In a modern description these are E. P. Thompson's "unsteepled places" in which democratic social relations can be made plausible and teachable as part of the culture of the societies of the future.

Lawrence Goodwyn, historian of Populism, 1980

# 10. Accomplishment and failure

By the early- to mid-1890s the Knights of Labor in Ontario had spent themselves as a social and political force. To be sure, in certain regions the Order retained some power, especially in the Ottawa area, where DA 6 emerged and grew as lumbermill workers flocked to the Knights during and after the Chaudière strike of 1891. Across the province stalwart Assemblies hung on through grim days of decline, even mounting a recruiting drive for new members in the period 1898–1902. This persistence, and the long-standing commitment of powerful labor spokesmen like D. J. O'Donoghue, actually lent the Order the appearance of strength. The illusion was perpetrated in the halls of the TLC. At the 1893 convention of the Congress, for instance, forty of the seventy delegates were Knights of Labor, and the Order continued to play a significant role in shaping policy in this period. The post-1895 years, however, were quite another story, and witnessed the persistent decline of influence and importance of the Knights of Labor. International craft unionism and the AFL carried the day in 1902 at the Berlin convention of the TLC, and the Knights, along with other organizations unconnected to the craft unions, were banished from the ranks of "officially" organized labor. In a fight for survival these bodies formed the National Trades and Labor Congress, dedicated to unite all labor organizations in Canada in national unions and LAs while excluding international affiliates. Apparently unconcerned with this kind of inconsistency (for they themselves were, of course, affiliated to an international body), the Knights of Labor eked out six feeble years in the National Congress, when the last remnant of internationalism was exorcised. In 1908 the Canadian Federation of Labor was born, and replaced the National Congress. It promptly expelled the weak survivors of the Knights of Labor.[1]

The opening years of the twentieth century thus saw the final institutional demise of the Knights of Labor in Canada. In the United States the Order held on until the 1930s, but only as a mere shadow of its former self.[2] For seventy years historians have been preoccupied with this failure. Here, in conclusion, we want to analyze the movement's North American decline, while retaining an awareness of its significant achievements. In their inability to transform society, the Knights of Labor were severely constrained by the ideological, political, and social inhibitions inherent in the late-nineteenth-century structural and economic context in which they came to prominence. These constraints and this context, so often ignored in past attempts to locate the Order historically by placing it within an anachronistic utopian or reform wing of North American labor, provide the basis of an evaluation of the accomplishments and failures of the Knights of Labor.

Over the course of the nineteenth century the North American working class experienced two decades of profound transformation and dissolution. Both the 1850s and the 1890s were vital turning points that displayed striking similarities, including the prominence of major depressions that shifted the character of productive relations and forced working-class activists to retreat in the face of the harsh realities of the business cycle. It was in the period between these two points of crisis that the late-nineteenth-century North American labor movement came of age.

Industrial capitalism took the final unhesitating steps toward establishing its economic supremacy in North America in the 1850s, ushering in a late-nineteenth-century period of ruthless competition among entrepreneurs. In these years as well, the labor market was transformed, as waves of immigrants inundated North American shores, famine-stricken Irish finding their way to port cities in Canada and the United States and German '48ers establishing themselves in a number of American industrial cities. Such economic and demographic change conditioned a virulent nativism that may well have helped to undercut the early beginnings of working-class organization and solidarity, a process of disintegration facilitated by the onslaught of economic crisis in 1857.[3]

The 1890s, set against this earlier background of the 1850s, appears remarkably similar. A new stage of capitalist development appeared in the increasingly close connections of finance and industrial capital, which stimulated a series of vitally important mergers and pushed the economy toward monopoly and oligopoly. While this merger movement had attained some maturity in the United States by the 1890s, it appeared but tentatively in Canada, with significant consolidations in the textile industry, agricultural machinery production, and in the faint beginnings of the steel industry. American branch plants, especially those in nascent industries such as rubber, chemicals, and electrical products, began to invade Canadian territory, where they were quick to reap the benefits of markets, materials, and labor. As this shift in the character of capitalism proceeded, it was strengthened by new supplies of labor, as immigration from eastern and southern Europe restructured the internal composition of the North American labor force in the years from 1880 to 1910. Bolstered by the acquisition of plentiful supplies of unskilled labor and consolidated through the Depression's impact on the small shop and the family firm, the North American political economy entered the twentieth century in its monopoly phase. Once more, this process of transformation was accompanied by a nativist reaction, centered in the American Protective Association in the United States and its Canadian counterpart, the Protestant Protective Association.[4] The climate of anti-Catholicism in Canada was lent further force by a series of French–English disputes, beginning with the Jesuits Estates Act and culminating in the Manitoba Schools Question in the 1890s. In this period of ethnocentrism the workers' movement suffered tangible setbacks. By the end of the 1890s jingoism was also prominent in both countries, as America's popular war with Spain and Canada's patriotic response to the Boer War undercut class solidarities and emphasized national aspirations. Although not all workers were enthralled with such militaristic adventures around the world, and while a number of working-class recruits to the cause of imperialism were undoubtedly attracted by economic need and the soldier's stipend, these campaigns nevertheless enjoyed considerable support, especially among British immigrant and native American and Canadian workers.[5]

Equally significant developments in the political sphere paralleled these vast changes in the economy and society of late-nineteenth-century North America. Between 1860 and 1890 the national prominence of the state was emerging, overshadowing previously dominant concerns of particular regions and specific locales. In the United States, the state developed as a vital force in the aftermath of the Civil War, as the victory of the Republicans and the forging of national parties in the throes of conflict ushered in a new age. Similarly, north of the border, the Canadian state was forged in 1867, with the 1870s and 1880s as the first decades of national party activity in the newly created Dominion.

These large structural changes of the late nineteenth century are vital to an understanding of both the accomplishment and failure of the Noble and Holy Order of the Knights of Labor. The 1880s represented the culmination of an age of competitive capitalism and localism, and the Knights of Labor developed out of this context and embodied a working-class challenge that had been building strength for three decades. A series of perceptive studies, many of them as yet unpublished, demonstrate conclusively that in the United States the Knights of Labor were able to unite a working class long fragmented, bridging the divisions between workers that had been the historical legacy of the 1850s and drawing them out of the cross-class alliances that had developed during the contest against slavery. In the resulting "moral universality" of the Gilded Age labor movement, as David Montgomery has suggested, the Knights of Labor represented a "crusade" to "impose economic order" on a ruthlessly individualistic capitalism; a large part of the attraction of this orientation lay in its repudiation of the acquisitive egotism which that system spawned and acclaimed. This movement culture of alternative peaked, however, at precisely that moment, the 1880s, when the experience – economic, social, cultural, political – that had ushered it into being was on the brink of transformation.

The Knights of Labor that emerged in the context of an anarchic, laissez-faire capitalism, and shook its fist at monopoly, political corruption, and the drift toward centralized control of everyday life, thus found itself facing new conditions and staunch opposition as employers united to oppose its members and the omniscient state began an open intervention in the social relations of productive life. While the state's role in suppressing the insurrectionary railroad strikes of 1877 must have appeared as something of an aberration, worker militants came to see government repression as the norm by the 1890s, in the aftermath of Haymarket, Homestead, and Pullman. An eclectic radical critique, capable of uniting the working class around the perceived threat of an economic and political oligarchy tyrannizing labor saw its worst fears confirmed in the 1880s and 1890s. This new situation was further complicated by immigration and a severe depression, both of which weakened the bonds of unity. As the crisis deepened, the whole process of forging a collective response had to be begun anew. What had been adequate in the 1870s and early 1880s was now seen to be inadequate, and as a consequence the "moral universality" that the Knights of Labor had done so much to create began to disintegrate, and the fragmentation and consequent searching for solutions to labor's dilemmas were renewed in the late 1880s and 1890s.[6]

Splits between socialists and Knights, eclectic radicals and unionists, Home Clubbers and others ensued, as business unionism, revolutionary syndicalism, DeLeonite socialism, and ethnic politics vied for the allegiance of North American workers. While the depression of the 1890s, the nationalization of politics, the increasing prominence of ethnic allegiances, and the crisis of leadership unfolding in the upper echelons of the Knights of Labor all played a part in insuring the ultimate defeat of the Noble and Holy Order, the demise of the Knights and the victory of the AFL was anything but a settled issue in the 1880s. Major leaders, later identified with the rise of the AFL and the ideological primacy of craft unionism within the American labor movement, were themselves uncertain in these years of turmoil in the 1880s. P. J. McGuire of the Carpenters' Union, for instance, was known to advocate the liquidation of the trade unions into the Knights of Labor well past the crisis of 1886; yet he is often seen as the ideological ancestor of "Big

Bill" Hutcheson. Other labor leaders of the 1880s – Gompers, Thomas Morgan, Joseph Buchanan, Jo Labadie, and Frank Foster – were riding the wave of class militancy and consensus without a forceful sense of organizational direction or ideological clarity. All had been shaped in a radical milieu that contained Marxist, Lasallean, Anarchist, Greenback, Georgite, Freethinking, and Irish Nationalist influences.

Canada's labor leadership was more subdued ideologically, perhaps because economic lag meant that capital's consolidation had not proceeded as far in Canada and the state was therefore not compelled to utilize repression to the same extent. Also the demographic structure of the Canadian working class – predominantly English-speaking outside of Quebec – did not give rise to immigrant radicalism. There were few Marxist or anarchist influences in the debates of the 1880s in Ontario: it was Gladstonian liberalism, Irish nationalism, and Tory paternalism that more often than not formed the backdrop against which working-class militants argued out their differing perspectives on labor activism. But the situation was also complicated by attachments to the single tax, currency reform, Bellamyite nationalism, and other reform panaceas associated with Canada's particular variant of the producer ideology. Those who want to adopt the perspective of Gerald Grob and his predecessors and argue that business unionism in Canada was inevitable, will have difficulty explaining how the so-called father of the Canadian labor movement, Irish Dan O'Donoghue, defended and supported the Knights of Labor until its last twentieth-century days.

In short, while hindsight may facilitate North American historians' efforts to sift through the labor controversies of the 1880s, sorting out various positions and structuring them into supposedly coherent philosophical orientations, the participants themselves – Canadian and American – were far from intellectually sure-footed. In the late 1880s and 1890s they were propelled in a number of different directions, especially in the United States, where a more advanced economy and a radical and vibrant working-class immigrant community gave rise to more precise strategies for labor in the age of monopoly capital. The Canadian labor movement retreated into an effort to survive the hard years of the 1890s downturn, and reemerged in the economic upswing and craft union boom of the 1898–1904 years.[7]

The structural transformations of the late nineteenth century, and the attempt to come to grips with them ideologically and organizationally, thus underlay the demise of the Order across North America. Working themselves out unevenly, and in part colored by local conditions and developments, these transformations and responses wrote *finis* to the eclectic radicalism and movement culture of the 1880s. In Ontario this long death march had, as we have seen, started in the late 1880s and by the 1890s it had taken forceful and fateful strides. Commenting on a "general decrease . . . in the strength of the Knights of Labor," the 1889 report of the Ontario Bureau of Industries concluded that "It is doubtful if the Order has held its own in any city or town in the province, while in several places the local assemblies have either succumbed or are in a moribund condition."[8] In this context of precipitous decline it was easy for some of the Order's activists, and easier still for many outsiders and historians, to misread the record of achievement.

Politically, the independent and semi-independent campaigns of 1883–7 – where labor entered local politics for the first time and conceived of a national lobbying effort aimed at legislative action that would be realized in 1888 – came to be read as little more than chapters in the partisan intrigues of Grit and Tory. The exuberance of a Samuel Peddle, Edward Williams, or Alfred Jury, the municipal victories of the Gananoque blacksmith George Toner or the Hamilton carter Thomas Brick were forgotten as such men faded, and the Wrights and O'Donoghues remained, locked into an embrace with the dominant political culture. O'Donoghue, of course, sealed his pact with the Grits early in his career, and by the mid-1890s was no longer making any pretense to impartiality or independence, although his concern for working people was never in question.[9] In 1908 as notable an authority as T. V. Powderly could wish one of Canadian labor's old guards well in his bid to secure electoral victory for the Conservative Party. It was thirty years since they "first met on the field of industrial strife," the former GMW reminded A. W. Wright, "and not a day of all those years has dawned on you with your back to the enemy of the people." (This, indeed, may well have been Old Alec's most telling accomplishment, for he was never one to leave himself unprotected.) Powderly remembered, above all else, Wright's connections: "Twenty years ago, 1888, Sir John Macdonald told me that no man in the Dominion had his confidence to such an extent as you; that when he wished for advice on industrial matters and the truth as to the merits of any controversy, he always consulted you." A more cynical observer, Toronto radical D. S. Macorquodale memorialized Wright in his poem, "A Reformer of the Old School":

> "No more shall death the tyrant labour rob;
> Let the sweat-shop horror cease!"
> Thus spoke he once to a frenzied mob,
> But he's taken a job with a purse-proud snob,
> And he taketh his fee in peace.[10]

All of this, as we have argued, was certainly part of the Order's history, and a large part of its end. But it was far from the whole story. The Order's political efforts must also be seen as the culmination of a process beginning in the transformation of the 1850s, a context that will serve to shift our concerns away from the opportunism of certain figures at the center of the Order's history toward an understanding of the limitations that circumscribed the movement's political efforts. Central Canadian workers entered into an economic-political alliance with manufacturers and far-seeing mercantile elements in the 1850s and 1860s, a common front based on a view of the Canadian nation as one dominated by producers. This producer commonwealth came to be associated with the pragmatic economic nationalism of Macdonald's Conservative Party. Committed to high tariffs, railroad building, industrial growth, and westward expansion, Tory policy promised employment for workers caught in an age of insecurities. This politico-economic alliance consolidated in the 1860s and 1870s, but began to crumble in the post-1879 years: regional and farmer interests began to see that the nationalist promise was a hollow one, which brought difficulty as well as development. For the working class, as well, the 1880s was a decade of realization as cross-class unity broke down in the face of working-class grievance, and stimulated a movement away from the party of Macdonald toward the Reform (Liberal-Grit) Party of Edward Blake and Oliver Mowat or the more autonomous stand of independent political activity. By 1886–7 the elaborately constructed Tory producer alliance was in disarray and, although economic nationalism won a penultimate victory that year, its demise in the 1890s was clearly prefigured. In the 1880s, then, the Ontario working class entered politics in a significant way, breaking from past behavior; whether its continued presence would surface in a pluralistic *modus vivendi* with either of the major parties or through independent labor politics would in future depend on local circumstance and the general class configuration of the day. The Order's accomplishment throughout the 1880s was thus considerable, for it extracted concessions from the state and introduced Ontario workers to the possibilities of independent labor politics.

The Knights of Labor failure to revamp politically the social order of Ontario in the 1880s, however, was obvious, and at the level of national politics the labor-reform effort to mount an autonomous working-class challenge foundered on the shoals of partyism. This raises the question of the apparent incapacity of the working class to address frontally the role of the state. There is no doubt that the Liberal and Conservative parties that ruled provincially and federally mediated the conflicts of the 1880s through concession (labor bureaus, factory legislation, royal commissions), just as it is equally clear that the established political culture attempted to integrate workers into its ranks. The labor-reform challenge was, in part, deflected in the 1880s, particularly after the defeats of 1886–7.

Once again, this is a part of the story, but one that misses essential aspects of the Order's experience. What such an unambiguous overview understates is the local thrust of much Knights of Labor activity, and the structural context of late-nineteenth-century Canadian politics that lent this approach its logic and coherence. Across the United States, for instance, at least 180 local campaigns were waged by Knights of Labor activists who brought political issues into the Central Labor Unions or took to the hustings in labor political associations that bore names like the United Labor Party, Union Labor, Knights of Labor, Workingmen, or Independent. As in Ontario, where similar tickets attracted workers, the dominant experience within which labor reformers emerged in the 1870s and 1880s had actually been conditioned, not by national politics, but by local political power and needs.

The state, but recently arrived, was actually obscured throughout the 1880s by its essential unfamiliarity. Even when successful in incorporating labor in an early national policy that promised to speak for a wide amalgam of class interests, the state was often perceived through eyes that focused, not on the state as an emerging institutional force, but rather on local individuals who embodied a distant, mystical state in particular community settings and neighborhoods, championed state policies as their own, and promised specific benefits to their constituencies. In this personalized context, as Leon Fink has argued in the case of the United States, the Knights of Labor forged an alternative that looked neither to the state itself nor to its traditional, individualistic, locally rooted representatives, but to self-organized society. William Sylvis articulated this working-class orientation as early as 1865, writing: "It is not what is done for people, but what people do for themselves, that acts upon their character and condition." The state, viewed from such a perspective, was simply a mediator in a conflict between democracy and its enemies. Moreover, the historical experience within which labor reformers operated had been one in which that conflict was waged concretely at the local level. Local politics were the neutral ground upon which contending forces battled for political direction.

When Ontario's Knights concentrated their political efforts locally, and achieved significant concessions, victories, and gains, they were therefore functioning within a universe of possibilities that was eminently sensible. This was especially the case in Ontario's towns and cities where most of the decisions that directly influenced the conditions of daily life lay within the purview of the municipal government. Local improvements, taxes, and corporation jobs, to name only the most obvious, provided a material incentive for the predominant local vision of North American workers. But just as they mounted their seemingly spontaneous and localized political campaigns (that contained, of course, a regional if not national logic), a new political age was in the process of formation, an age in which the presence of national political concerns would supersede local ones. Like their critique of monopoly, the Knights of Labor's political efforts fell short of a mark that demanded a new strategic direction, one in which there was a conception of the state as a powerful and indeed autonomous force buttressing the status quo. Lacking such an orientation, the Order's members moved back into the party fold as the local upsurges of 1886–7 subsided, and the cause of labor reform went into its tailspin. By the twentieth century the role of the state in capitalist society and the issues to be confronted if society was to be transformed would be clearer to ex-Knights of Labor. But in the quickening pace of events over the course of the late nineteenth century precise strategies toward the state and national politics were weakly developed, often nonexistent. The political activities and accomplishments of the Knights of Labor were thus simultaneously a significant victory and a notable defeat. They have been ill served by an analytic framework that posits an idealist critique of labor's national political failures only to denigrate the local achievements attained in the 1880s.[11]

Similarly, in the case of the social and cultural significance of the Knights of Labor, eventual failure all too often conditioned facile comment. Thus, in 1889, the report came from Owen Sound that "there used to be an assembly of the Knights of Labor, but it has been defunct for over a year. It never did anything worth speaking of." In Owen Sound, where LA 6631 had a brief and uneventful life, and where no other labor organization existed, this might appear to be an accurate, if somewhat dour, assessment. But halfway across the continent, in Calgary, a group of workers had met in 1886 to form a mixed Assembly of the Knights of Labor, LA 9787. The organizers hailed from Winnipeg and from Owen Sound where the Order supposedly "never did anything worth speaking of." Owen Sound had in fact nurtured an anonymous labor-reform advocate who transported his principles to the Canadian West, helped to keep the *Journal of United Labor* informed of wage rates in the territories, and may have been involved in the effort to organize other Assemblies in Donald and Canmore.[12] Failure proved a poor guide to accomplishment.

Even looking at the 1890s, when the working class was definitely in retreat, points to the significant impact of the Knights of Labor – an impact, moreover, that reveals itself in rather strange quarters. For the 1890s, unlike the 1880s' labor upsurge, was a period of farmers' revolt centered in the Patrons of Industry.[13] Within this agrarian upheaval flourished the same kinds of rhetoric and analysis used by the Order throughout the 1880s. This should not surprise us, for the Patrons contained an active contingent of former Knights – Phillips Thompson, George Wrigley, A. W. Wright, and others – who sought to create a farmer–labor alliance capable of reforming society from top to bottom. These "brainworkers" continued the old attacks, their dreams of what might be expressing their negative assessments of the anarchy of industrial–capitalist evolution, the evils and corruption of partyism, or the inequities of a social system controlled by the drones.

"We want no imitation New York or second Chicago here, with their millionaires and their brutalized millions, their heartless, flaunting ostentation and their hideous poverty, their octopus corporations and their slavish, degraded denizens of the slums," thundered Phillips Thompson. "The ideal of the future which regards only accumulated wealth, extent of bricks and mortar and millions of population without a thought or care of the social welfare or comfort of the people," he continued, "is an unworthy and degrading one which will not command itself to the sound intelligence and broad humanity of the people." In the midst of Patron victories at the polls, Thompson and others stressed the lurking danger of partyism and the rule of capitalism. In all this, lessons from the days of labor's upsurge were far from forgotten:

> The present is essentially an age of organization. A small well-trained army can easily rout an undisciplined mob of ten times its numbers. Want of efficient organization; lack of strict discipline; laxity in the admission and retention of unworthy members and traitors in disguise, has been the cause of the overthrow of many promising independent political movements in the past. The Labor movement in politics in particular has, so far, in Canada been a failure for no other cause but this. Men who were Labor Reformers for 364 days in the year and Grits or Tories on election day were admitted freely to its councils and suffered no loss of influence from the fact of having openly opposed Labor nominees on the platform and at the polls.[14]

Attempting to win the farmers to the platform of a declining urban labor-reform group centered in the TLC, the radical free-lance wing of Patronism attacked state-aided immigration and resurrected the once-familiar battle cries of North American workers. "Class legislation?" queried the *Brotherhood Era*, "Never! Equal rights for all? Always!"[15] Indeed, the Knights of Labor had done more than a little, as we have earlier noted in passing, to prepare the way for the easy acceptance of this labor-reform language among farmers. "Vidette," for instance, had written from Lindsay in December 1886 that in Port Perry, Uxbridge, Midland, and Peterborough LAs were "all in a thriving condition" and "many of [the] best farmers [were] joining the ranks." The enthusiastic correspondent thought this spoke well "for the great future in store for us." A. W. Wright's *Canadian Labor Reformer*, similarly, supported "bringing the farmers in," urging that the Knights of Labor ally with Grangers (predecessors of the Patrons) or organize distinct farmers' LAs.[16]

Long after the Order had withered and effectively died, and the *Labor Reformer* had ceased to address Ontario workers, the ubiquitous A. W. Wright was still on the scene. Patronism, like patriotism, provided this scoundrel with one last nineteenth-century refuge before he rushed, unashamed, into the arms of the Tory machine that he had clandestinely courted for so many years. And yet even here, in this last stand, his contribution was not without benefit, for his radical critique of many aspects of society and economy fell on receptive ears, and must have deepened the farmers' understanding of the crisis of the 1890s. His "Spokeshave" articles on currency reform, for instance, hammered away at his own long-standing concern with the problems of the "producing classes," who suffered at the hands of the usurers, the exploiters, and the monopolists, enemies Ontario's farmers could readily identify and rally against:

> For the Drones will eat the honey,
> While the bees, the hive within,
> Through the winter starve and shiver,
> For the wealth that they have made.
> And the answer will be Never
> To the prayer that Toil has prayed.[17]

At his exhortatory best, Wright still wrote as the committed reformer:

> I don't want to assume that all farmers and workingmen realize that there exists a present pressing necessity for the wealth producers to organize . . . and I don't suppose it would be reasonable to expect that there are no longer people who, though they see that though the many who produce nothing have much, yet content themselves with supposing that all this happens in the natural order of things, and is the inevitable result of the working out of some economic laws which we have neither the time to investigate, the intelligence to understand, nor the wit to remedy. But though I realize that there are backbones that cannot be stiffened by any process, and men whom no appeal nor argument can rouse to manhood, yet I believe that these moral weaklings and human jelly-fish are only a minority, and a small one; and so I hope that the great mass of Canadian workingmen and farmers can be roused to assert their rights to the full enjoyment of the whole results of their labor.

And under the title, "Fealty to Principles More Desirable than Present Victories," Wright could argue for independence, attacking the evils of partyism and opportunism: "Let us stand prepared to strike at every wrong that helps the idle to appropriate the wealth the toilers produce, careless whether our striking may bring us votes or drive them away, and we cannot fail to win the only success worth the effort of true men."[18] But in private Wright was challenging former St. Thomas Knight of Labor editor George Wrigley, now publishing the *Farmers' Sun*, claiming that the Patrons were "hitting too pointedly at the [Conservative] Government." His exit from the Patron camp was not long in coming, and in March 1896 Wright was chastized and dismissed by the *Farmers' Sun*. Labeled a "deserter" from the ranks of Patronism, Wright's falling from grace had been occasioned by his return "to his old love," the Conservative Party. The farmers' movement's only regret was that it could not know "for a few weeks or months what kind of plum 'Spokeshave' [would] find in his little tin cup." But this mattered little to those who had seen a perfect illustration of one of "Spokeshave's" favorite ditties:

> To place and power all public spirit tends,
> In place and power all public spirit ends.[19]

With Wright's departure from the Patron camp, the farmers' cause had lost an able, if self-interested, voice. Other ex-Knights were soon to follow, not because they abandoned reform to feather their own political nests, but because they were moving toward that more twentieth-century camp, socialism. Phillips Thompson and George W. Wrigley were two such brainworkers whose trajectory from Knights of Labor to farmers' advocates to unflinching socialists revealed much about the late-nineteenth-century radical milieu and its contribution to the making of the Canadian left.[20] As Goldwin Smith ousted Wrigley from the editorial chair of the *Farmers' Sun*, classical economic liberalism replaced a radical social critique aimed at building a farmer–labor alliance in opposition to partyism, corruption, monopoly, and inequality. One Patron leader noted sardonically after the newspaper purchase that perhaps Smith's parents should have named him "Golden." Only one year later, George Wrigley's former lodge wrote to condemn the new *Sun*, advising the Smith management that they no longer regarded the paper as the "organ of the Patrons."

These developments contributed greatly to the decline of Patronism, and were in large part a reminder of just how important Knights of Labor intellectuals and reform thought had been in the farmers' agitation of the 1890s. As the Patrons of Industry collapsed in 1896, the "producing classes" demonstrated, in a negative way, that they would not be duped. Although they knew no way forward, they seemed to be saying that the new Patronism of Goldwin Smith was not for them. Wright had warned Wrigley of just this problem in 1895, although his words were penned in an attempt to move the Patron electoral strategy away from the Grits toward the Tories. "If the conservative farmers and workingmen come to look upon us as disfigured allies of their old time opponents," he wrote, "and if the reformers shall regard us as so many steps of a ladder by which they hope to pluck fruit hitherto beyond their reach, what chance will we have of winning converts from either side to the undying principles of the movement? From such sowing what harvest can we expect, except one of distrust, perhaps of contempt." And, indeed, the Patrons were to reap as they had sown.[21]

Outside the circles of the Patrons, as well, elements of the Knights of Labor hung on to carry forward the movement of opposition. Some of these, to be sure, were men drawn from the same mold as A. W. Wright. J. G. Kilt, editor of Ottawa's *Capital Siftings*, and an associate of Wright and Powderly (with an eye, like them, for the main chance), could still issue devastating assaults on the idle rich and the social chaos and decay for which they were responsible:

> What hope is there for a society with such extremes of wealth and poverty as our civilization shows? At the bottom rotting, corroding want and squalor; at the top, enervating luxury, reckless extravagance, useless, purposeless lives. At one extreme the inability to get work from which to live, at the other a contempt for work as degrading; a contempt for the workers as the lower classes. A very kingdom of topsy-turvy down. A state of moral as well as social anarchy. False standards everywhere. Pinchbeck, tinsel, stucco-never-ending sham. What hope of such a society except that it is susceptible of fundamental reform or radical change. Apart from its fastidious division of people into ranks and classes, apart from the consideration that it is multiplying a vast army of unemployed with which it does not know what to do, consider how fruitful it is of meanness, of over-reaching, of envy, jealousy, and all uncharitableness. How can it be anything else? A society which in its industrial constitution is at war with honor, honesty, and justice, is not likely to beget generosity. It inevitably generates the vices, not the virtues, the baser not the nobler qualities of the soul.[22]

Sentiments like these, despite the virtual eclipse of the Ontario Knights by 1895, remained behind, and pockets of reform-minded workers followed up the decline of the Order with the formation of industrial brotherhoods, workingmen's political associations, and radical clubs. In Kingston, the collapse of the LAs was followed quickly by the formation of a workingmen's political party. This body, organized in October 1889, was said to have a "growing membership whose object it is to secure justice by a more direct representation in our legislative assemblies." London's workers in Wards 3 and 4, led by former Knights of Labor activists R. H. Hessel and Joseph Marks, created a Workingmen's Legislative Club. Speaking in support of the platform of the Ward 4 club, Marks launched "an attack on the capitalists and political parties," condemning the practice of worshipping at "the altar of Capital." Marks, of course, would later popularize similar sentiments throughout central Ontario in the pages of his paper, the *Industrial Banner*, which began publication in 1892.[23]

When a Canadian socialist movement began to emerge in the 1890s, first with the arrival of the American Socialist Labor Party (SLP) and later with the evolution of the Canadian Socialist League, former Knights were central to the experience. In Montreal Knights of Labor leaders Kerrigan and Darlington led the new Local of the SLP. In Ottawa "Karl Marx, Junior" contributed a "Socialist Labor Party" column to George Kilt's *Capital Siftings*. Meanwhile Kilt himself argued:

> Capitalism is the power by which labor is robbed of the greater portion of its earnings. Labor will only be reconciled to this process as long as they are kept in ignorance of their rights and powers. And the greater the proportion of their products they succeed in wresting from Capital, the more they will want until they get the whole. Then capitalism will be abolished, as it ought to be, and capital, the creation and tool of labor, will be under the control of labor.

Slightly later, in Toronto and elsewhere in Ontario, former Knights of Labor such as George Wrigley and Phillips Thompson would champion the Canadian Socialist League. After the defeat of the Patrons they built this new organization in an attempt to unite the fragmented reform forces of the 1890s, and then proceeded to help lead it into the Socialist Party of Canada in 1903.

The Knights of Labor legacy extended to the work place as well. The commitment to organize all workers remained present in workers' memories but also stamped itself upon organizations such as the United Mine Workers, the Western Federation of Miners, the American Railway Union, and later the Industrial Workers of the World and the One Big Union. This was also evident in ongoing attempts to organize women, especially in the garment trades where "K. of L." (as well as William Lyon Mackenzie King) was exposing Toronto sweatshop conditions in the mid-1890s.[24]

It is difficult, then, to dismiss cavalierly the Order, even as it passed out of view. In terms of numbers alone, as we have already seen, the Order had a remarkable impact. Not only did the 1880s witness the highest percentage of the Ontario labor force organized until the CIO period, but the Knights of Labor also had a larger membership in industrial cities such as Toronto and Hamilton than that most pervasive of all Ontario fraternal societies, the Orange Order.[25] Exercising an important and continuous presence in the world of the late-nineteenth-century producing classes, the personages, practices, and principles of the Knights of Labor stood as something of a stored, or accumulated, energy that was easily and productively channeled into political, social, and cultural activities. Our own ignorance of this process reflects, not the actual historical process, but rather a failure of imagination and diligent research, although it is now becoming clear that the great divide separating the Knights unequivocally from later developments contains as many problematic dimensions as hard and fast answers. Buried in the 1890s, the corpse of labor reform did not rest unappreciated in its coffin; sons and daughters returned to the cemetery to whisper a few words over the tombstone, or place a bouquet at the foot of the grave. If the visits grew less frequent and then stopped altogether, even if the next generation remained unaware of the lineage, the Order lived, in a sense, because the dream of what might be, however flawed, contradictory, and problematic, had accomplished much that could not be eradicated. It had raised, often for the first time and at the highest level, banners that the working-class and radical movements would carry well into the twentieth century, if not to this day.[26]

The dream, as well, had been shaped in the context of a central moment in the experience of Ontario workers. If one can ever speak of the making of the Canadian working class, a class always severely limited by the regional, linguistic, and cultural barriers inhibiting its restricted forms of solidarity, it should be at this moment of the 1880s, during this moment of labor upsurge and radical thought, during this moment of the Knights of Labor. It was a moment of tremendous potential in which class seemed to override, for the first, perhaps only, time, the sectional, sexual, and ethnic divisions so prominent in the history of Canadian labor. At least that is the way it looked in Ontario, where industrial capitalism had penetrated to the core in these years of labor's first sustained opposition, when the province's workers seemed united as never before, and certainly as they never would be later. There were differences and divisions, to be sure, as there always must and will be, but there was also possibility, and a movement to push it forward: in the shop, political arena, or neighborhood gathering-spot, one senses that working men and women glimpsed and debated alternatives in which they created, out of their past and present realities and achievements, a new, if unrealized, conception of behavior and human nature. Awkwardness and uncertainty were part of this process, but on the whole the tenor of the times was part of a stubborn attempt to resist; this was, after all, a central strand in the emergence of what some might pompously proclaim a more "mature" socialist agenda. Perhaps it was all nothing more than threatened self-interest, but in the end this mattered little, and need not condemn the moment as reactionary, retrospective, or nostalgic. It is difficult to imagine any radical social criticism that is not conceived in response to threats, in a defensive posture, especially in capitalist societies, where repeated rationalizations, improvements, and innovations have, occasionally, been less than welcome, and far from beneficial to the majority of mankind.[27]

The Knights of Labor, so often attacked for looking backward, saw ahead to this conclusion and decided not to stand still while the onward march of capital engulfed them, sweeping them aside as it rolled on to victory after victory. Marshaling skilled and unskilled, male and female, the Order fought back – in politics, on the job, in the press, through education – attaining some of their more modest aims, suffering many losses, effecting countless compromises. When it was all over, the whole context had changed. We refer to change, of course, outside of or beyond any notion of victory. For in the end, the Knights of Labor were no success: their politics ended with a handshake with the state; their unity ended with faction, rift, and sectional division; their work place struggles ended in defeat, and then lapsed into an acquiescent silence. Ultimately, in this ever-worsening plot, their history ended in nothing. But history is not quite written backward. What, we have asked, about the beginnings? Should not every story start there? And those beginnings were impressive.[28]

The identification of the Knights of Labor with the organization of the entire working class was the Order's unique and indisputable achievement, and can perhaps best be seen in a Providence, Rhode Island, oration by T. V. Powderly. Published as a pamphlet, this speech provides unusual insight into the "moral universality" that the Knights attempted to cultivate throughout the 1880s, and that gained a foothold in the North American labor movement by 1886. Drawing on lessons learned by skilled workers in the 1860s and 1870s, Powderly outlined what he regarded as the essential task facing all labor reformers:

> The machinist goes to his home, the moulder to his, the carpenter to his; all go to the trades unions on their way; each one is so thoroughly selfish as to never look beyond the limits of his organization; none ask whether any other men had rights. We said to ourselves this is ignorance on the part of workingmen's trade unions; it is a crime and strong steps must be taken to remove this cause. Something must be done to bring these people together, so that they may know that a blow struck at labor in one place affects those in another; that the evil is felt everywhere men live, from the rising to the setting of the sun.

Not satisfied with overcoming class segmentation based on skill and on craft identity, Powderly turned his attention to other factors dividing American workers, and addressed the questions of ethnicity and religion. After mocking those who allowed such forces to split them apart, Powderly concluded: "Say what we will, do what we will, the line of battle lies between but two forces in this world of ours, and that line of battle is the wage system." Turning finally to another excluded sector, women workers, Powderly proclaimed: "We demand that when a woman performs the same labor as a man that she shall have the same pay." Women, Powderly closed, in a rhetorical flourish that had obviously become common during labor's upsurge of the 1880s, were the best men in the Order.[29]

This speech, atypical only in its publication, affirmed the accomplishment of the Knights of Labor. Powderly, a skilled machinist, spoke as one with North American workers of the 1880s. The whole history of the Order indicates that skilled workers in this period were affirming their values, their needs, and their conceptions of justice and morality in opposition to the perceived ruthlessness and illegitimacy of the new industrial men of power. Unlike virtually every previous chapter in the history of North American workers' rebellion, moreover, the Knights of Labor stamped these pages of the 1880s with concern for those whose status in the working-class community ill-suited them to wear the badge of respectability, a consensual cultural norm that the Order recast to express class antagonisms. The Knights of Labor – virtually always led by the skilled elements – fundamentally rejected exclusion and offered their ideals and their strengths as a force protecting and speaking for all those "below" them. As Leon Fink has argued, masses of workers who had never experienced the fruits of full citizenship joined the skilled, leadership sector of the Order, forging an alliance of the "privileged" working class and a younger, thoroughly proletarianized group, composed of male and female factory operatives and laborers. The racial and foreign-speaking immigrant component of this common front that Fink then goes on to stress was not to be found in Canada, largely because mass eastern and southern European immigration did not transform the structural makeup of the Canadian working class until after 1902, and blacks were never actually present in the work force in great numbers. But the accomplishments were nevertheless of a similar sort, as our discussion of the Order's role in organizing women and linking labor reform to the cause of the Irish suggests.[30]

This is not to deny the Knights' ultimate failure. They did not remake the world in their image. Their dreams were not realized. There were factions and divisions as we have shown, unscrupulous elements and problems with centralized authority, as the whole controversy over Canadian autonomy revealed. There were, as well, ruptures (most prominent after 1886) between Knights and unionists. Internal problems arose which, in conjunction with external factors (employer opposition and economic downturn), undoubtedly led to decline. But the Order's failure was also intimately related to the timing of the moment of upsurge. Peaking in the 1880s when North America was consolidating industrially and politically, the Knights of Labor articulated an eclectic radicalism that was rooted in the limitations of the late-nineteenth-century experience. As the first expression of the social, cultural, and political emergence of a class bred in the confines of the period 1860–90, the movement reached out to embrace all, and in its essential eclecticism, tried to be all things to all reform-minded people. This was just what we might expect a newly arrived class culture to do: it had little past that could tell it how to oppose the monopolistic drift in the economic sector, a drift discernible but not yet consolidated in the 1880s; it had little past that could direct it toward an appreciation of the importance of the state and the nationalization of political life that was emerging out of the breakdown of localism in the aftermath of Radical Reconstruction in the United States or the National Policy in Canada.

Given this context of uncertainty the Knights of Labor experience was characterized by programmatic ambivalence: these were years when the labor movement lacked knowledge of where and how to cut corners and present a disciplined front, as well as a conception of when it was appropriate to reach out for more and "up the ante." All this took place, for the most part, beyond the reach of the national leadership, which seldom exercised a forceful control over the Order's development. To argue in this way is to oppose vehemently the conventional wisdom that the Order was inept, confused, and utopian, and its failure inevitable, while the pragmatic policies of the more conservative AFL insured success. That was not the case. It is to suggest that a movement caught between two crises of dissolution and change (the 1850s and 1890s), a movement facing a situation that is on the brink of alteration (politically, economically, and demographically), will face difficult decisions. Such a movement, building upon a culture only recently arrived, and in the process of being transformed by the presence of the movement itself, will necessarily contain many diverse currents. Not yet fully consolidated, the movement will grope as much as it will march forcefully, and in the process there will appear many parasites, many internal factional intrigues, and many, many disappointments. These difficulties and disappointments were barely recognized in the heady days of the Order's expansion prior to 1886, but in the years of decline (which they themselves helped to bring about) they came increasingly to the forefront. Workers who had joined the movement saw their hopes shattered and their dream disintegrate; they went elsewhere, but in the interval the class and the culture, as well as the society, had experienced change, especially with the arrival of many new immigrants and the growth in effective power wielded by employers drawn together in national, even international, associations. Drawn to the Order by widely diverging principles (but class principles nevertheless), men and women were capable of leaving the movement when it seemed incapable of satisfying their needs and addressing grievances that began to appear in a clear focus for the first time. Nevertheless, no matter how briefly, the Knights of Labor experience did pose tangible possibilities and real alternatives, raising the banner of working-class solidarity. In North American working-class history there have been other such moments – 1919, the late 1930s, 1943–6 – and in each, for a short time, workers have opposed the existing status quo. The upsurge of the 1880s represented the first of these moments of challenge.[31]

It was the promise of overcoming barriers to working-class unity, then, and of the possibilities that beckoned, that made the Knights of Labor and its dream of what might be so significant in the history of Ontario's working class. "What Might Be" could never be realized, however, unless the world's workers were organized and educated. As Phillips Thompson outlined the "beautiful ideals" this state of affairs could bring about, he anticipated future historians, and their curt dismissals. "By this time, no doubt," he noted, "the readers who have followed me so far are ready to exclaim, 'utopian!' 'visionary!' 'Altogether wild and impracticable.'"[32] But Thompson did not agree, and he saw the way forward in continued agitation, persistent organization, and education. All of this, coupled with sacrifice, would breed the self-reliance that would win the day for "universal democracy and co-operation," routing the monopolies, ending wars, smashing privilege. At least half a century later one worker saw a need to return to this kind of unity and brotherhood, and he looked backward to the Knights of Labor to sustain his argument:

> Now the crux of the writers' belief in the weakness of the present United Steelworkers organization lies in the fact that the members realize little or no obligation to the organization. Perhaps it is because the organization has had to be pushed so rapidly in order to circumvent employer anti-union tactics that the members just sign a union card and wait for results. We suppose half the membership in some locals have never taken the spoken pledge. The writer believes that the old way under the Knights and the Amalgamated was the best way. This, modeled on the Oddfellows' ritual but acceptable to Catholic and Protestant, had the secret password and ritual. It was a solemn affair to join the union in bygone days and the members did not forget their obligation easily. It was a common occurrence for two hundred members to attend an ordinary meeting in Gananoque out of a membership of six hundred. Where do we get such a membership now except perhaps at contract time, and not even then in many cases . . . Now we have new members signed at the factory or mill and never mentioned or seen at the union meetings. We must have something to counteract all the social activities, movies, etc., that retard membership attendance and education at union meetings. Oh sure, we may say, the members get their money's worth and the union gets the dues, but we cannot build a really secure organization until we have explored all avenues to build the sense of unity and brotherhood and keep it alive in

our United Steelworkers. This was not lacking in the writer's recollection of the old Amalgamated.[33]

This statement underlines both the failure and the accomplishment of the Noble and Holy Order of the Knights of Labor in Ontario. In its stress on "secure organization" and focus on the Steelworkers as a self-contained body, it speaks of failure, for the Knights would never have expressed their concerns in language that smacked, however innocently, of exclusion. The decline of the Order, and the emergence of other, less altruistic, class organizations lay behind this aspect of this workers' statement. But in the awkward efforts to put his finger on the social and cultural needs of the class, Gordon Bishop groped toward the "bygone days" when the Knights of Labor had dreamed of "what might be" and taken significant steps toward the realization of their "utopian" vision. That capacity to dream, and those first uncertain steps forward deserve to be remembered. The possibilities they revealed would remain on the agenda for years to come.

At least that is the way we see it, and that is why we have written this book. We have quoted many voices in these pages and will end with yet another quote:

Our vote will change nothing. And yet, in another sense, it may change everything. For we are saying that these values, and not those other values, are the ones which make this history meaningful to us, and that these are the values which we intend to enlarge and sustain in our own present. If we succeed, then we reach back into history and endow it with our own meanings . . . In the end we also will be dead, and our own lives will lie inert within the finished process, our intentions assimilated within a past event which we never intended. What we may hope is that the men and women of the future will reach back to us, will affirm and renew our meanings, and make our history intelligible within their own present tense. They alone will have the power to select from the many meanings offered by our quarrelling present, and to transmute some part of our process into their progress.[34]

All of that, we think, is part of what dreaming of what might be, or of seeing the light, is about. And that holds for both past and present.

# Appendix. Preamble and declaration of principles of the Knights of Labor[1]

The alarming development and aggression of aggregated wealth, which, unless checked, will inevitably lead to the pauperization and hopeless degradation of the toiling masses, renders it imperative, if we desire to enjoy the blessings of life, that a check should be placed upon its power and upon unjust accumulation, and a system adopted which will secure to the laborer the fruits of his toil; and as this much desired object can only be accomplished by the thorough unification of those who earn their bread by the sweat of their brow, we have formed the order of the Knights of Labor, with a view of securing the organization and direction, by co-operative effort, of the power of the industrial classes; and we submit to the world the object sought to be accomplished by our organization, calling on all who believe in securing "the greatest good to the greatest number," to aid and assist us.

1 To bring within the fold of organization every department of productive industry, making knowledge a standpoint for action, and industrial, moral worth, not wealth, the true standard of individual and national greatness.
2 To secure to the toilers a proper share of the wealth that they created; more of the leisure that rightfully belongs to them; more society advantages; more of the benefits, privileges and emoluments of the world; in a word, all those rights and privileges necessary to make them capable of enjoying, appreciating, defending and perpetuating the blessings of good government.
3 To arrive at the true condition of the producing masses in their educational, moral and financial condition, by demanding from the various governments the establishment of bureaus of labor statistics.
4 The establishment of co-operative institutions, productive and initiative.
5 The reserving – of public lands – the heritage of the people – for the actual settler. Not another acre for railroads or corporations.
6 The abrogation of laws that do not bear equally upon capital and labor; the removal of unjust technicalities, delays and discriminations in the administration of justice; and the adopting of measures providing for the health and safety of those engaged in mining, manufacturing and building pursuits.
7 The enactment of laws to compel chartered corporations to pay their employees weekly, in full, for labor performed the preceding week, in the lawful money of the country.
8 The enactment of laws giving mechanics and laborers the first lien on their work for their full wages.
9 The abolishment of the contract system on national, state and municipal roads or corporations.
10 The substitution of arbitration for strikes, whenever and wherever employers and employees are willing to meet on equitable grounds.

11 The prohibition of the employment of children in workshops, mines and factories, before attaining their fourteenth year.
12 To abolish the system of letting out by contract the labor of convicts in our prisons and reformatory institutions.
13 To secure for both sexes equal pay for equal work.
14 The reduction of the hours of labor to eight per day, so that the laborers may have more time for social enjoyment and intellectual improvement, and be able to reap the advantages conferred by the labor-saving machinery which their brains have created.
15 To prevail upon governments to establish a purely national circulating medium, issued directly to the people, without the intervention of any banking corporations, which money shall be a legal tender in payment of all debts, public and private.

# Notes

## Introduction

1 Edward and Eleanor Marx Aveling, *The Working-Class Movement in America* (London, 1888), pp. 9, 139, 142, 148, 152. For a detailed account of this tour see Yvonne Kapp, *Eleanor Marx*, II (New York, 1976), pp. 133–91.

2 For additional evidence on the Knights' impact in England see Henry Pelling, "The Knights of Labor in Britain, 1880–1901," *Economic History Review*, 2nd ser., 9 (1956), pp. 313–31. More important, however, is the intriguing link in Fred Reid, *Keir Hardie: The Making of a Socialist* (London, 1978). Reid emphasizes Hardie's conversion to socialism in 1886–7. He notes that Hardie's platform for his new Labour Party was entitled "The Sons of Labour," suggesting that Hardie was directly influenced by the Knights of Labor. See Reid, *Hardie*, pp. 193–5.

3 Friedrich Engels, "Preface to the American edition of 1887" in *The Condition of the Working-Class in England*, W. O. Henderson and W. H. Chaloner, transl. and eds., (Oxford, 1958) pp. 353, 354, 356–7. For more critical, private views see Engels to Laura LaFargue, 24 November 1886 in Engels and Lafargue, *Correspondence*, I (Moscow, 1959), pp. 395–9, and Engels to Sorge, 29 November 1886, and Engels to Florence Kelley, 28 December 1886, in Marx, Engels, *Selected Correspondence* (Moscow, 1965), pp. 395–9. Engels himself later toured the United States and Canada with the Avelings in 1888 but avoided any public appearances. See Gustav Mayer, *Friedrich Engels, A Biography* (London, 1936), pp. 271–2, and Kapp, *Eleanor Marx*, II, pp. 277–8.

4 See Saul Alinsky, *John L. Lewis* (New York, 1949), p. 15; Melvyn Dubofsky and Warren Van Tine, *John L. Lewis: A Biography* (Chicago, 1976), p. 12.

5 Thomas R. Brooks, *Clint: A Biography of a Labor Intellectual – Clinton S. Golden* (New York, 1978), pp. ix, 17–18.

6 *Citizen and Country*, 4 May 1900.

7 Melvyn Dubofsky, "The Origins of Western Working Class Radicalism, 1890–1905," in Peter N. Stearns and Daniel J. Walkowitz, eds., *Workers in the Industrial Revolution: Recent Studies of Labor in the United States and Europe* (New Brunswick, N.J., 1974), p. 383.

8 David J. Bercuson, *Fools and Wise Men: The Rise and Fall of the One Big Union* (Toronto, 1978), p. 120.

9 Irving Bernstein, *The Lean Years: A History of the American Worker, 1920–1933* (Baltimore, 1960), p. 34.

10 Richard T. Ely, *The Labor Movement in America* (New York, 1905 [1886]), pp. 75–88.

11 For example, see Carroll D. Wright, "An Historical Sketch of the Knights of Labor," *Quarterly Journal of Economics*, 1 (January, 1887), pp. 137–68, quotation p. 168; M. A. Vilard, "Les Chevaliers du Travail," *Academie de Nîmes*, 7th ser., 10 (1888), pp. 267–287; Friedrich A. Sorge, *Labor Movement in the United States* (Westport, Ct., 1977 [1891–5]), ed. Philip S. Foner and Brewster Chamberlin, esp. pp. 247–62; and E. Levasseur, *The American Workman* (Baltimore, 1900), esp. pp. 181–97.

12 For a sampling of a vast literature on progressive labor reform see James Leiby, *Carroll Wright and Labor Reform* (Madison, 1960); Richard Ely, *Ground Under Our Feet: An Autobiography* (New York, 1938); John R. Commons, *Myself* (Madison, 1963). The critical literature includes Benjamin G. Rader, *The Academic Mind and Reform: The Influence of Richard T. Ely* (Lexington, 1966); Lafayette G. Harter, Jr., *John R. Commons* (Corvallis, Ore., 1962). On professionalization see Thomas L. Haskell, *The Emergence of Professional Social Science* (Urbana, 1977) and Burton Bledstein, *The Culture of Professionalism* (New York, 1976). An excellent thesis pursuing both themes is Bari Jane Watkins, "The Professors and the Unions: American Academic Social Theory and Labor Reform, 1883–1915," Ph.D. thesis, Yale University, 1976.

13 John R. Commons, et al., *A Documentary History of American Industrial Society*, IX (Cleveland, 1909–11), pp. 49–51.

14 Robert F. Hoxie, *Trade Unionism in the United States* (Chicago, 1917), p. 89, emphasis ours.

15 William Kirk, *National Labor Federations in the United States* (Baltimore, 1906).

16 Hoxie, *Trade Unionism*, p. 93.

17 Ibid., pp. 94–5, 98, 104.

18 John R. Commons and associates, *History of Labor in the United States*, II (New York, 1926 [1918]), pp. 195–540, and Selig Perlman, *A Theory of the Labor Movement* (New York, 1949 [1928]), pp. 192, 201–2.

19 Commons, *History of Labor*, II, pp. 350–4, 373–4, 396–7.

20 Lloyd Ulman, *The Rise of the National Trade Union* (Cambridge, Mass., 1955), pp. 349, 371–7.

21 Gerald Grob, *Workers and Utopia: A Study of Ideological Conflict in the American Labor Movement* (Chicago, 1961), pp. ix-x, 3, and esp. pp. 34–59, 187–9.

22 Norman J. Ware, *Labor in Modern Industrial Society* (New York, 1968 [1935]), p. 258.

23 Norman J. Ware, *The Labor Movement in the United States 1860–1895. A Study in Democracy* (New York, 1929), pp. xii-xviii.

24 Ibid., pp. xii, 350–70, and Leon R. Fink, "The Uses of Political Power: Towards a Theory of the Labor Movement in the Era of the Knights of Labor," Paper presented to the Knights of Labor Centennial Symposium, Chicago, 17–19 May 1979; Fink, "Workingmen's Democracy: The Knights of Labor in Local Politics, 1886–1896," Ph.D. thesis, University of Rochester, 1977.

25 See for example, Harry J. Carman, "Terence Vincent Powderly – An Appraisal," *Journal of Economic History*, I (1941), pp. 83–7; Terence V. Powderly, *The Path I Trod* (New York, 1940); and Henry David, *The History of the Haymarket Affair* (New York, 1936).

26 Edward T. James, "American Labor and Political Action 1865–1896: The Knights of Labor and its Predecessors," Ph.D. thesis, Harvard, 1954. James recently published an article based on this work, "T. V. Powderly, A Political Profile," *Pennsylvania Magazine of Biography and History*, 99 (1975), pp. 443–59.

27 Philip S. Foner, *History of the Labor Movement in the United States*, I and II (New York, 1947 and 1955).

28 For a sampling of Gutman see his *Work, Culture and Society in Industrializing America* (New York, 1976); for Montgomery see his *Beyond Equality: Labor and the Radical Republicans, 1867–1872* (New York, 1967) and *Workers' Control in America* (New York, 1979). Among the recently published community studies are: Alan Dawley, *Class and Community: The Industrial Revolution in Lynn* (Cambridge, Mass., 1976); Daniel J. Walkowitz, *Worker City, Company Town: Iron and Cotton Worker Protest in Troy and Cohoes, New York, 1855–84* (Urbana, 1978); and John T. Cumbler, *Working-Class Community in Industrial America: Work, Leisure, and Struggle*

*in Two Industrial Cities, 1880–1930* (Westport, Ct., 1979). It should be noted, however, that each of these depicts the Knights less fully than one would want. This is partially due to periodization, which in Walkowitz and Dawley leaves the Knights at the very end or slightly after their major period of interest; in Cumbler's case the Order appears at the beginning, with later developments covered in more detail. Recent essays by David Montgomery have placed the Knights of Labor at the center of a movement culture that spread across America, going well beyond the community to embrace the working class as a whole. See, for instance, David Montgomery, "Labor and the Republic in Industrial America: 1860–1920," *Le Mouvement Social*, 111 (avril-juin 1980), pp. 201–15; "To Study the People: The American Working Class," *Labor History*, 21 (Fall 1980), 485–512; "Labor in the Industrial Era," in Richard B. Morris, ed., *The U.S. Department of Labor History of the Industrial Worker* (Washington, 1976), pp. 104–28.

29 J. I. Cooper, "The Canadian General Election of 1887," M. A. thesis, University of Western Ontario, 1933.

30 Fred Landon, "The Knights of Labor: Predecessors of the C.I.O," *Quarterly Review of Commerce*, 1 (Autumn 1937), pp. 133–9.

31 Fred Landon, "The Canadian Scene, 1880–1890," *Canadian Historical Association Annual Report* (1942), pp. 5–18.

32 Douglas R. Kennedy, *The Knights of Labor in Canada* (London, 1956).

33 Robert W. Cox, "The Quebec Provincial General Election of 1886," M.A. thesis, McGill, 1948.

34 V. O. Chan, "Canadian Knights of Labor with Special Reference to the 1880s," M.A. thesis, McGill, 1949, esp. pp. 74, 204–5.

35 Harold Logan, *Trade Unions in Canada* (Toronto, 1948).

36 Frank Watt, "The National Policy, the Workingman, and Proletarian Ideas in Victorian Canada," *Canadian Historical Review*, 40 (1959), pp. 1–26.

37 Bernard Ostry, "Conservatives, Liberals, and Labour in the 1880s," *Canadian Journal of Economics and Political Science*, 27 (1961), pp. 141–61.

38 E. Z. Massicotte, "Les Chevaliers du Travail," *Bulletin des Recherches Historiques*, 40 (1934); Alfred Charpentier, "Le mouvement politique ouvrier de Montréal, 1883–1929," *Relations Industrielles*, 10 (1955), pp. 74–93; Jacques Martin, "Les Chevaliers du Travail et le Syndicalisme international à Montréal," M.A. thesis, University of Montreal, 1965.

39 Fernand Harvey, *Révolution Industrielle et Travailleurs* (Montreal, 1978) and "Les Chevaliers du Travail, les États-Unis et la Société Québécoise, 1882–1902," in F. Harvey, ed., *Le Mouvement Ouvrier au Québec* (Montreal, 1980), pp. 69–130.

40 Jacques Rouillard, *Les Syndicats Nationaux au Québec de 1900 á 1930* (Quebec, 1979).

41 Bryan D. Palmer, *A Culture in Conflict: Skilled Workers and Industrial Capitalism in Hamilton, Ontario, 1860–1914* (Montreal, 1979), and Gregory S. Kealey, *Toronto Workers Respond to Industrial Capitalism, 1867–1893* (Toronto, 1980).

42 Here we have drawn upon Raymond Williams, "Base and Superstructure in Marxist Cultural Theory," *New Left Review*, 82 (November-December 1973), pp. 1–16, and his *Marxism and Literature* (London, 1976).

43 Lawrence Goodwyn, *Democratic Promise: The Populist Movement in America* (New York, 1976). For the distinction between class struggle and class conflict, and its analytic importance, see Raymond Williams, *Politics & Letters: Interviews with New Left Review* (London, 1979), pp. 135–6.

44 Joseph R. Buchanan, *The Story of a Labor Agitator* (Westport, Ct., 1970 [1903]), p. viii.

45 H. V. Nelles, *The Politics of Development: Forests, Mines & Hydro Electric Power in Ontario, 1849–1941* (Toronto, 1974), pp. 48–107.

46 Thompson cited in Chan, "Canadian Knights of Labor," p. 152; *Journal of Com-*

*merce*, 7 September 1888, cited in Michael Bliss, *A Living Profit: Studies in the Social History of Canadian Business, 1883–1911* (Toronto, 1974), p. 120.

47 See Greg Kealey, ed., *Canada Investigates Industrialism: The Royal Commission on the Relations of Labor and Capital 1889* (Toronto, 1973), esp. pp. ix–xxvii; Fernand Harvey, *Révolution industrielle et Travailleurs.*

48 R. J. K. [Richard Kerrigan], "The Dynamic Year of 1886," *One Big Union Monthly*, 23 September 1927, courtesy of Allen Seager.

49 Bliss, *A Living Profit*, esp. p. 37.

50 On early-closing movements led by Knights of Labor in these places see *London Advertiser*, 17 May–18 September 1886; *Palladium of Labor*, 19 June 1886, 26 June 1886, 2 October 1886, 16 October 1886; *St. Thomas Times*, 24 April–22 May 1886; *Ottawa Citizen*, 17 July–2 December 1891; Ontario Bureau of Industries, *Annual Report*, 1887, p. 46, 1889, p. 28; J. G. Kilt to T. V. Powderly, 24 May 1893, Ottawa, Powderly Papers, Catholic University of America, Washington, D.C. Hereafter PP.

51 See W. J. C. Cherwinski, "Honoré Joseph Jaxon, Agitator, Disturber, producer of plans to make men think and Chronic Objector . . . ," *Canadian Historical Review*, 46 (June 1965), pp. 123–33; George F. G. Stanley, *The Birth of Western Canada: A History of the Riel Rebellions* (Toronto, 1961), pp. 298–306, 317, 323–4, 378; W. H. Riley to Powderly, 30 March 1886, W. H. Jackson to Powderly, 25 August 1886, PP.

52 See, for instance, *Palladium of Labor*, 3 October 1885, 11 July 1885; Russell G. Hann, "Brainworkers and the Knights of Labor: E. E. Sheppard, Phillips Thompson, and the Toronto *News*, 1883–1887," in G. S. Kealey and Peter Warrian, eds., *Essays in Canadian Working Class History* (Toronto, 1976), p. 45; Adolphe Ouimet, *La vérité sur la question Métisse au Nord-Ouest* (Montreal, 1889), pp. 371–4, trans. and cited in Stanley Ryerson, *French Canada* (Toronto, 1943), p. 77, and apparently published in *Irish World*, 21 November 1885; Joseph A. O'Donoghue to Powderly, n.d., East Portland, Ore., PP.

53 The distinction between empiricsm and an empirical idiom is outlined in E. P. Thompson, "The Peculiarities of the English," *Socialist Register, 1965* (London, 1965) pp. 336–7; idem, "The Poverty of Theory: or an Orrery of Errors," in *The Poverty of Theory & Other Essays* (London, 1978), esp. pp. 193–6, although the whole essay is itself a polemic against the assault on "empiricism."

54 Note the discussion in Raymond Williams, *Culture and Society, 1780–1950* (Harmondsworth, 1961); E. P. Thompson, "Romanticism, Utopianism, and Moralism: The Case of William Morris," *New Left Review*, 99 (September-October 1976), pp. 83–111.

55 Marx, "Eighteenth Brumaire" in Karl Marx, Frederick Engels, *Collected Works*, XI (New York, 1979), pp. 103–4.

## 1. The working class and industrial capitalist development

1 V. I. Lenin, *The Development of Capitalism in Russia* (Moscow, 1964), pp. 595, 599.

2 The literature on the staples thesis is now voluminous. But see Donald Creighton, *Harold Adams Innis* (Toronto, 1957); Robin F. Neill, *A New Theory of Value: The Canadian Economics of H. A. Innis* (Toronto, 1976); the special Innis issue of the *Journal of Canadian Studies*, 12 (Winter 1977); and Carl Berger, *The Writing of Canadian History* (Toronto, 1976), pp. 85–111, 187–207, which also contains some commentary on Mackintosh. Works exemplifying the left-nationalist approach include Daniel Drache, "Rediscovering Canadian Political Economy," *Journal of Canadian Studies*, 11 (1976), pp. 3–18; Ian Parker, "Innis, Marx and Canadian Political Econ-

omy," *Queen's Quarterly*, 84 (1977), pp. 545–63; R. T. Naylor, "The Rise and Fall of the Third Commercial Empire of the St. Lawrence," in Gary Teeple, ed., *Capitalism and the National Question in Canada* (Toronto, 1972), pp. 1–41; R. T. Naylor, *The History of Canadian Business*, 2 vols. (Toronto, 1975); Glen S. Williams, "The Political Economy of Canadian Manufactured Exports: The Problem, Its Origin, and the Development of Trade and Commerce, 1885–1920," Ph.D. thesis, York University, 1978. This interpretation, denigrating the force of nineteenth-century industrial capitalism through stress on the hegemony of commercial capital and the persistence of colonial relations vis-à-vis Britain and the United States is criticized in L. R. MacDonald, "Merchants Against Industry: An Idea and Its Origins," *Candian Historical Review*, 56 (1975), pp. 263–81 and in Bill Moore, "Staples and the Capitalist Mode of Production: A Study of Mining in Canada, 1845–1920," M.A. thesis, McMasters University, 1978, but it continues to permeate much recent writing. See, for instance, Wallace Clement, *Continental Corporate Power: Economic Linkages between Canada and the United States* (Toronto, 1977); Joseph Smucker, *Industrialization in Canada* (Scarborough, 1980).

3 Gustavus Myers, *A History of Canadian Wealth* (Toronto, 1972); H. C. Pentland, "The Development of a Capitalistic Labour Market in Canada," *Canadian Journal of Economics and Political Science*, 25 (1959), pp. 450–61; Pentland, "Labour and the Development of Industrial Capitalism in Canada," Ph.D. thesis, University of Toronto, 1960; Stanley B. Ryerson, *Unequal Union: Roots of Crisis in the Canadas 1815–1873* (Toronto, 1973); Gordon W. Bertram, "Historical Statistics on Growth and Structure of Manufacturing in Canada, 1870–1957," in J. Henripin and A. Asinakoupulos, eds., *C.P.S.A. Conference on Statistics, 1962 and 1963* (Toronto, 1964), pp. 93–146; Bryan D. Palmer, *A Culture in Conflict: Skilled Workers and Industrial Capitalism in Hamilton, Ontario, 1860–1914* (Montreal, 1979), pp. 3–31; Gregory S. Kealey, *Toronto Workers Respond to Industrial Capitalism 1867–1892* (Toronto, 1980), pp. 1–34.

4 *People's Journal*, cited in Steven Langdon, *The Emergence of the Canadian Working Class Movement* (Toronto, 1975), p. 3; *Journal of the Board of Arts and Manufacturers for Upper Canada*, 7 (1867), p. 220.

5 Bertram, "Historical Statistics," pp. 93–146; Warren Bland, "The Location of Manufacturing in Southern Ontario in 1881," *Ontario Geography*, 8 (1974), pp.8–39; T. W. Acheson, "The Social Origins of the Canadian Industrial Elite, 1880–1885," in David S. Macmillan, ed., *Canadian Business History: Selected Studies 1497–1971* (Toronto, 1972), p. 144; Peter Warrian, "The Challenge of the One Big Union Movement in Canada, 1919–1921," M.A. thesis, University of Waterloo, 1971, p. 11.

6 H. Beaumont Small, *The Products and Manufactures of the New Dominion* (Ottawa, 1868), pp. 136, 152.

7 William Wycliffe Johnson, *Sketches of the Late Depression* (Montreal, 1882), preface and passim.

8 See, for instance, Terry Copp, *The Anatomy of Poverty: The Condition of the Working Class in Montreal, 1897–1929* (Toronto, 1974); Michael J. Piva, *The Condition of the Working Class in Toronto – 1900–1921* (Ottawa, 1979); David Millar, "Study of Real Wages: The Construction, Use and Accuracy Check of a Constant-Dollar Plotter," unpublished research paper, 1980.

9 Jacques Ferland, "The Problem of Change in the Rate of Surplus Value Studied Through the Evolution of the 'Social Cost of Labour' in Canada, 1870–1910," M.A. thesis, McGill University, forthcoming 1981. Cf., Martin Nicolaus, "Foreword," in Karl Marx, *Grundrisse: Foundations of the Critique of Political Economy (Rough Draft)* (Hammondsworth, 1973), p. 48 (and text, p. 287): "The immediate

inverse identity of profits and wages holds only in the short run, and only if the intensity of exploitation (for example speed of production) is held constant. Over the somewhat longer term, specifically during the upward phase of the economic cycle, however, both wages and profits may show an absolute increase at the same time; and during such periods the worker may either take the risk of accumulating a small fund of savings for the next crisis, or may broaden the sphere of his consumption to take a small part in higher, even cultural satisfactions, . . . [for instance] agitation for his own interests, newspaper subscriptions, attending lectures, educating his children, developing his taste etc., constituting the workers only share of civilization which distinguishes him from the slave." Regardless of whether the high social cost of labor was a product of organization, or whether organization was a fruit of economic prosperity, Nicolaus correctly pointed to the notes in the *Grundrisse* as providing an important theoretical foundation for the discussion of the relevance of labor unions and movements (49). Our reading of the 1880s in North America suggests strongly that it was in this period of economic upsurge that labor did indeed take agitational steps of great importance. For a valuable discussion of Marx's theory of wages relevant to our brief comments on the social cost of labor see Roman Rosdolsky, *The Making of Marx's Capital* (London, 1977), pp. 282–313.

10 Bertram, "Historical Statistics," p. 133. On the importance of this period of price deflation in the United States see Harold G. Vatter, *The Drive to Industrial Maturity: The U.S. Economy, 1860–1914* (Westport, Ct., 1975); and on the twentieth century, Harry Braverman, *Labor and Monopoly Capital: The Degradation of Work in the Twentieth Century* (New York, 1974).

11 Acheson, "Social Origins of Elite," p. 162.

12 Jacob Spelt, *Urban Development in South-Central Ontario* (Toronto, 1972), pp. 101–86; Edward J. Chambers and Gordon Bertram, "Urbanization and Manufacturing in Central Canada, 1870–1890," in Sylvia Ostry and T. K. Rymes, eds., *C.P.S.A. Conference on Statistics, 1966* (Toronto, 1966), pp. 225–55; Bland, "Location of Manufacturing," pp. 8–39. See the important statement in Raphael Samuel, "The Workshop of the World: Steam Power and Hand Technology in Mid-Victorian Britain," *History Workshop Journal*, 3 (Spring 1977), pp. 6–72.

13 Spelt, *Urban Development*, pp. 124–7; James M. Gilmour, *Spatial Evolution of Manufacturing: Southern Ontario, 1851–1891* (Toronto, 1972), pp. 168–81; W. G. Phillips, *The Agricultural Implement Industry in Canada* (Toronto, 1956), pp. 38–53; Merrill Dennison, *Harvest Triumphant* (Toronto, 1948), p. 93; Robert Ozanne, *A Century of Labour-Management Relations at McCormick and International Harvester* (Madison, 1967).

14 David F. Walker, "The Energy Sources of Manufacturing Industry in Southern Ontario, 1871–1921," *Ontario Geography*, 6 (1971), pp. 56–66.

15 The following paragraphs, unless otherwise noted, are based upon the works of Chambers and Bertram, Bland, Spelt, and Gilmour, cited above, as well as census data. On Hamilton see also Palmer, *A Culture in Conflict*, pp. 3–31; and on Toronto, Kealey, *Workers Respond*, pp. 1–34. Insight can also be gleaned from H.A. Innis and A. R. M. Lower, eds., *Select Documents in Canadian Economic History, 1783–1885* (Toronto, 1933), pp. 588–616.

16 Note V. I. Lenin, *The Development of Capitalism in Russia* (Moscow, 1964), p. 551.

17 G. P. deT. Glazebrook, *A History of Transportation in Canada*, II (Toronto, 1964), pp. 91–118; Kenneth Lloyd Clark, "Social Relations and Urban Change in a Late Nineteenth-Century Southwestern Ontario Railroad City: St. Thomas, 1868–1890," M.A. thesis, York University, 1976. For Stratford see *Journal of the International Association of Machinists* (December 1890 and May 1893); W. Stafford John-

ston and Hugh H. M. Johnston, *History of Perth County to 1967* (Stratford, 1967), pp. 223–51.

18 Morris Wolfe, "A Short History of the Carling Breweries, Ltd. 1840–1930," unpublished paper, University of Western Ontario Archives.

19 Richard A. Trumper, "The History of E. Leonard & Sons, Boilermakers and Ironfounders, London, Ontario," M.A. thesis, University of Western Ontario, 1937; Benjamin S. Scott, "The Economic and Industrial History of the City of London, Canada from the Building of the First Railway, 1855 to the Present, 1930," M.A. thesis, University of Western Ontario, 1930, pp. 56–65, 169–70; Carrol J. Grimwood, "The Cigar Manufacturing Industry in London, Ontario," M.A. thesis, University of Western Ontario, 1934, p. 3; and on brewing and tobacco generally, see Innis and Lower, eds., *Select Documents*, pp. 605, 607, 614–15.

20 Innis and Lower, eds., *Select Documents*, pp. 594–6; James Young, *Reminiscences of the Early History of Galt* (Toronto, 1880), p. 232; "A History of the Bell Piano and Organ Company, 1864–1928," unpublished paper, University of Western Ontario Archives. On Brantford see C. M. Johnston, *Brant County* (Toronto, 1967); on Berlin see W. V. Uttley, *A History of Kitchener, Ontario* (Waterloo, 1937); on Guelph see Leo A. Johnson, *History of Guelph, 1827–1927* (Guelph, 1977), pp. 203–18; C. Acton Burrows, *The Annals of the Town of Guelph* (Guelph, 1877).

21 John N. Jackson, *St. Catharines, Ontario: Its Early Years* (Belleville, 1976), esp. chs. 10, 11, and 14, and Edwin Tweed, "The Evolution of St. Catharines, Ontario," M.A. thesis, McMaster University, 1960.

22 William Gillard and Thomas Tooke, *The Niagara Escarpment* (Toronto, 1975), p. 108; Innis and Lower, eds., *Select Documents*, pp. 595, 610–11.

23 George R. Osborne, *Midland and the Pioneers* (Midland, 1939).

24 Ruth McKenzie, *Leeds and Grenville: Their First 200 Years* (Toronto, 1967).

25 Leo Johnson, *History of the County of Ontario, 1615–1875* (Whitby, 1973), pp. 250–2; T. E. Kaiser, *Historic Sketches of Oshawa* (Oshawa, 1921), pp. 160–7; "The Canadian Locomotive Company Limited: History of the Works at Kingston," *Queen's Quarterly*, 10 (April 1903), pp. 455–65; Innis and Lower, eds., *Select Documents*, pp. 594–5; information on Smiths Falls courtesy Peter DeLottinville.

26 *Report of the Select Committee on the Causes of the Present Depression of the Manufacturing, Mining, Commercial, Shipping, Lumber and Fishing Interests* (Ottawa, 1876), pp. 142–8; Kealey, *Canada Investigates Industrialism*, pp. 179–92.

27 This and the following paragraphs touch on themes developed more fully in Bryan D. Palmer, "Class and Culture in Nineteenth-Century Canada: Cleavage, Antagonism and Struggle," unpublished ms., 1980.

28 Note the important discussion in Gerald M. Sider, "The ties that bind: culture and agriculture, property and propriety in the Newfoundland village Fishery," *Social History*, 5 (1980), pp. 1–39.

29 See Paul Campbell Appleton, "The Sunshine and the Shade: Labour Activism in Central Canada, 1850–1860," M.A. thesis, University of Calgary, 1974.

30 See Eugene A. Forsey, *The Canadian Labour Movement, 1812–1910* (Ottawa, 1974), pp. 4–7; *Labour Gazette*, 3 (July 1902-June 1903), pp. 606–7.

31 Palmer, *A Culture in Conflict*, esp. pp. 71–96; Kealey, *Workers Respond*.

32 David Montgomery, *Workers' Control in America: Studies in the history of work, technology and labor struggles* (New York, 1979), p. 176.

33 Palmer, *A Culture in Conflict*, pp. 35–70; Kealey, *Workers Respond*, pp. 98–123; Forsey, *Canadian Labour Movement*, p. 7.

34 Palmer, *A Culture in Conflict*, pp. 125–51; Kealey, *Workers Respond*, pp. 124–53.

35 Forsey, *Canadian Labour Movement*, p. 7; *Labour Gazette*, 3 (1903), pp. 606–7.

36 On the IMIU see C. B. Williams, "Canadian-American Trade Union Relations: A

Case Study of the Development of Bi-National Unionism," Ph.D. thesis, Cornell, 1964; Palmer, *A Culture in Conflict;* Kealey, *Workers Respond.* For the molders' important place in Smiths Falls, an eastern Ontario center, see *Rideau Record*, 30 May, 6 June, 22 June, 4 July 1889.

37 Our use of the word "moment" here and throughout the book is intentional. Marx, like Hegel, employed the term "moment" to refer to an element or factor in a general system. But he also added the senses both of "period of time" and of "force of a moving mass," thus conveying much of what we want to express in our formulation of the significance of the Knights of Labor and the particular context of North American society in the 1880s. See Martin Nicolaus, "Foreword," in Marx, *Grundrisse*, p. 29. These brief comments should indicate that the term "moment" is not the property of any particular tendency within Marxism, but rather a part of a long-standing Marxist vocabulary, employed by such diverse writers as Althusser, Sartre, and E. P. Thompson. As Dona Torr defined it in an editorial comment in the Marx–Engels *Selected Correspondence*, "moment" signifies an "element in the dialectical process of becoming." (See E. P. Thompson, *The Poverty of Theory & Other Essays* [London, 1978], p. 307.)

## 2. "Warp, woof, and web"

1 Terence V. Powderly, *The Path I Trod: The Autobiography of Terence V. Powderly* (New York, 1940), pp. 3–4 and 102. See also Powderly, *Thirty Years of Labor* (Columbus, 1889). On Powderly's career see Vincent Joseph Falzone, "Terence V. Powderly: Mayor and Labor Leader, 1849–1893," Ph.D. thesis, University of Maryland, 1970; and Samuel Walker, "Terence V. Powderly, Labor Mayor: Workingmen's Politics in Scranton, Pennsylvania, 1870–1884," Ph.D. thesis, Ohio State University, 1973.

2 The best Canadian overview of the Order is Eugene Forsey, *History of the Canadian Labour Movement to 1902* (Toronto, forthcoming). Cf., Douglas Kennedy, *The Knights of Labor in Canada* (London, Ont., 1956); and Victor O. Chan, "The Canadian Knights of Labor, with Special Reference to the 1880s," M.A. thesis, McGill University, 1949. For the Knights of Quebec, see Fernand Harvey, "Les Chevaliers du Travail, les Etats-Unis et la Société Québecoise (1882–1902)," in Harvey, ed., *Aspects Historiques du mouvement Ouvrier au Québec* (Montreal, 1973), pp. 33–118; Jacques Martin, "Les Chevaliers du travail et le syndicalism international à Montréal," M.A. thesis, University of Montreal, 1965. For the Knights in Manitoba see David Spector, "Winnipeg's First Labour Unions," *Manitoba Pageant*, 21 (1976), pp. 13–14 and his "The Knights of Labor in Winnipeg, 1883–1891," unpublished paper, October 1975. For British Columbia see Paul Phillips, *No Power Greater: A Century of Labour in British Columbia* (Vancouver, 1967). For U.S. data see Jonathan Garlock, "A Structural Analysis of the Knights of Labor," Ph.D. thesis, University of Rochester, 1974. The best discussion of the Order's structure is still William C. Birdsall, "The Problem of Structure in the Knights of Labor," *Industrial and Labor Relations Review*, 6 (1952–1953), pp. 532–46.

3 All organizational data throughout are based on our own calculations. We should note at the outset, however, a debt of gratitude to two pieces of pioneering research on the Knights that were of inestimable value to us. Eugene Forsey's massive compilation of materials on organized labor in Canada before 1902 includes much material on the Knights and a helpful attempt at a Local-by-Local reconstruction. See Forsey, *History of the Canadian Labour Movement*. Jonathan Garlock's *Knights of Labor Data Bank* (Ann Arbor, Michigan, 1973) and "A Structural Analysis of the Knights of Labor," have been of considerable help. For a description of

the Data Bank see Jonathan Garlock, "The Knights of Labor Data Bank," *Historical Methods Newsletter*, 6 (1973), pp. 149–60. Our corrections to the Data Bank material will be incorporated into the computer file at Ann Arbor. These corrections are based on the labor and local press of Ontario, on the Ontario Bureau of Industry reports, on various trade union minutes and proceedings, and on the Powderly Papers. The population data are from the 1881 census unless otherwise stipulated.

4 Knights of Labor, Register of Organizers, November 1886-October 1889, PP.

5 *Brockville Recorder*, 21, 23 August 1882.

6 In addition to its Ontario success DA 45 also spread into Quebec (Montreal, Quebec, Rivière du Loup, Sherbrooke), New Brunswick (St. John, Campbelltown, Moncton), and Nova Scotia (Halifax, Sydney). Here, too, it represented the earliest Knights' successes and, in the case of the Maritimes, virtually the only organizational gains, with the exception of the late 1890s efforts in the Cape Breton coalfields, which resulted in the short-lived Glace Bay DA 35.

7 *Annual Report of the Bureau of Industries for the Province of Ontario, 1886* (Toronto, 1887), p. 244. For the telegraphers' strike see Eugene Forsey, "The Telegraphers' Strike of 1883," *Transactions of the Royal Society of Canada*, 4th ser., 9 (1971), pp. 245–59.

8 Ontario, Bureau of Industry, *Report*, 1886, p. 246.

9 For a further discussion of mixed and trade Locals, see Garlock, "A Structural Analysis," pp. 40, 55–6 and 113–43.

10 On the American leadership's reactions to the 1885–6 upsurge, mass initiatives, and the ban on organizing, see Gerald Grob, *Workers and Utopia: A Study of Ideological Conflict in the American Labor Movement, 1865–1900* (Chicago, 1969), pp. 64–70; Norman Ware, *The Labor Movement in the United States, 1865–1900: A Study in Democracy* (New York, 1964), pp. 140–54; Michael J. Cassity, "Modernization and Social Crisis: The Knights of Labor and a Midwest Community, 1885–1886," *Journal of American History*, 66 (June 1979), pp. 41–61.

11 Stratford *Beacon*, 9, 16 October 1885.

12 L. J. Dillard to T. V. Powderly, December 1885, PP.

13 F. D. Phillips to Powderly, 1 March 1886, PP.

14 Stratford *Beacon*, 18 December 1885.

15 *Palladium of Labor*, 29 May 1886.

16 Ontario, Bureau of Industry, *Report*, 1887; *Report*, 1888.

17 *Statistics as Collected by Headlight Assembly, No. 4069, K. of L.* (St. Thomas, 1885); Warren Cron Miller, ed., *Vignettes of Early St. Thomas: An Anthology of the Life and Times of Its First Century* (St. Thomas, 1967), p. 152.

18 W. J. Shaw to Powderly, 28 November 1888, PP.

19 R. F. Trevellick to Powderly, 18 October 1884, PP.

20 See Shelton Stromquist, "The Knights of Labor and Organized Railroad Men," unpublished paper presented to the Knights of Labor Centennial Symposium, Newberry Library, Chicago, 17–19 May 1979; and Cassity, "Modernization and Social Crisis," pp. 41–61.

21 Ontario Bureau of Industry, *Reports*, 1886–9.

22 Joseph T. Marks to Powderly, 12 May 1890, PP.

23 W. J. Shaw to Powderly, 5 March 1888, PP.

24 A. W. Wright to Powderly, 4 September 1888, PP.

25 Shaw to Powderly, 28 November 1888, PP.

26 Joseph T. Marks to Powderly, 12 May 1890, PP.

27 Obediah Light to J. W. Hayes, 22 January 1890 and 9 October 1893, PP.

28 Michael J. Kelly to Powderly, 4 October 1886, PP.

29 Knights of Labor, General Assembly, *Proceedings*, 1887, Motion 120. For newspa-

per accounts of the Order in Welland see Fern A. Sayles, *Welland Workers Make History* (Welland, 1963), pp. 100–1.

30 O'Donoghue to Powderly, 3 November 1889, PP; Ontario Bureau of Industry, *Report*, 1889.

31 W. Hogan to Powderly, 6 October 1888, PP.

32 Ontario, Bureau of Industry, *Report*, 1887.

33 Gananoque *Recorder*, 14 January, 17 March 1888; *Rideau Record*, 12 January 1888.

34 Ontario, Bureau of Industry, *Report*, 1888.

35 Arthur Fields to J. W. Hayes, 11 February, 22 June, 8, 17 July 1891, 20 October 1892, 26 February, 29 March 1895, 17 January, 5 February 1896, 11, 16 January 1897, Hayes Papers, Catholic University, Washington, D.C. Henceforth HP.

36 J. S. Legge to A. W. Wright, 6 June 1893, PP.

37 *Capital Siftings* (Ottawa), 17 November 1894.

38 *Labour Gazette*, 1900–1907.

39 Knights of Labor, General Assembly, *Proceedings*, 1898.

40 *Labour Gazette*, 1901–1910.

41 See Robert H. Babcock, *Gompers in Canada: A Study in American Continentalism Before the First World War* (Toronto, 1974), pp. 85–97.

## 3. Toronto and the organization of all workers

1 George McNeill, *The Labor Movement* (New York, 1887), p. 403.

2 Note the discussions in Herbert G. Gutman, *Work, Culture and Society in Industrializing America: Essays in American Working-Class and Social History* (New York, 1976); "The Workers' Search for Power: Labor in the Gilded Age," in H. Wayne Morgan, ed., *The Gilded Age: A Reappraisal* (Syracuse, N.Y., 1963), pp. 38–68.

3 *The Wage Worker*, 22 March 1883.

4 On the Telegraphers see DA 45 circulars of 27 December 1882 and 20 May 1883 and Telegraphers' Code Book of 20 October 1882, PP.

5 Organizational data is drawn from the Toronto press, from Eugene Forsey's unpublished manuscript history of Canadian labor to 1902, and from Jonathan Garlock, "The Knights of Labor Data Bank," *Historical Methods Newsletter*, VI (September, 1973), pp. 149–60 and his "A Structural Analysis of the Knights of Labor," Ph.D. thesis, University of Rochester, 1974.

6 As quoted in William Kirk, *National Labor Federations in the United States* (Baltimore, 1906), p. 19.

7 As quoted in Douglas R. Kennedy, *The Knights of Labor in Canada* (London, Ont., 1956), p. 18.

8 *Globe*, 14 October 1884.

9 *New York Sun*, 29 March 1886, as cited in Richard T. Ely, *The Labor Movement in America* (New York, 1886), p. 78, note 1.

10 For a discussion of the 1882 Shoe strike see Gregory S. Kealey, *Toronto Workers Respond to Industrial Capitalism, 1867–1892* (Toronto, 1980), pp. 50–1. The quote is from *Trade Union Advocate*, 4 May 1882.

11 On Thompson see Russell Hann, "Brainworkers and the Knights of Labor: E. E. Sheppard, Phillips Thompson, and the Toronto *News*, 1883–1887," in Gregory S. Kealey and Peter Warrian, eds., *Essays in Canadian Working-Class History* (Toronto, 1976), pp. 35–57. O'Donoghue is the subject of popular treatment in Doris French, *Faith, Sweat, and Politics: The Early Trade Union Years in Canada* (Toronto, 1962); John O'Donoghue, "Daniel John O'Donoghue: Father of the Canadian Labour Movement," *Canadian Catholic Historical Association Annual Report*, 10 (1942–1943), pp. 87–96.

12 Charles March to T. V. Powderly, 7 October 1888, PP.
13 On Wright, see Chapters 5, 6, and 7.
14 D. J. O'Donoghue to Powderly, 12 February 1884, PP.
15 Powderly to O'Donoghue, 17 February 1884, PP.
16 Harry E. Griffiths to Powderly, 14 July 1884, PP. For more on the printers' strike see Kealey, *Toronto Workers*, ch. 6.
17 O'Donoghue to Powderly, 24 September 1883, PP. O'Donoghue's relationship with Powderly is illustrated by the sheer bulk of their correspondence – over 130 letters in the 1880s.
18 Griffiths to Powderly, 14 July 1884, PP.
19 *Palladium of Labor*, 14 November 1885.
20 Ibid., 28 November 1885.
21 O'Donoghue to Powderly, 9 December 1885 and 15 February 1886, PP.
22 Ontario, Bureau of Industry, *Report*, 1886, pp. 246–7
23 Knights of Labor, General Assembly, *Proceedings*, 1886–8.
24 O'Donoghue to Powderly, 9 December 1885, PP.
25 *Palladium of Labor*, 3 July 1886; *Cigar Makers Journal*, July and August 1886. The quote is from ibid., September 1886.
26 See, for example, George McNeill, *The Labor Movement*, p. 428.
27 *World*, 8 July 1885 and 14 October 1886.
28 Kealey, *Toronto Workers Respond*, ch. 3.
29 *Trade Union Advocate*, 1 February 1883.
30 *Globe*, 28 November 1885.
31 Jean Scott, "The Conditions of Female Labour in Ontario," *Toronto University Studies in Political Science*, I (1892), p. 27.
32 See G. S. Kealey, "Katie McVicar," *Dictionary of Canadian Biography*, XI, forthcoming, and Knights of Labor, General Assembly, *Decisions of the General Master Workman* (Philadelphia, 1890), p. 43.
33 *Canadian Labor Reformer*, 12 February 1887; *Globe*, 11 February 1889.
34 *Globe*, 21 March 1887.
35 *Canadian Labor Reformer*, 2 April 1887.
36 *Globe*, 21 April 1887.
37 For further information on this very important Knights' leader see Eleanor Flexner, "Leonora Barry," *Notable American Women*, I (Cambridge, Mass., 1971), pp. 101–102. For a useful general discussion see Susan Levine, "'The Best Men in the Order:' Women in the Knights of Labor," Canadian Historical Association, unpublished paper, 1978.
38 *Globe*, 13–15 April 1888; *Proceedings*, 1888, Report of General Investigator, pp. 6–7.
39 *Globe*, 15 April 1889; *Journal of United Labor*, May 1889.
40 *Journal of United Labor*, 9 May 1889.
41 Ibid.
42 *Globe*, 1 May 1889.
43 L. W. Lainson to Powderly, 5 April 1889, PP.
44 *News*, 4 October 1886.
45 For a full discussion of the role of ritual in the Order, see Chapter 8.
46 Roger Mullen to Powderly, 27 January 1883; Powderly to Roger Mullen, 2 February 1883, PP.
47 *World*, 15 April 1886.
48 *Trade Union Advocate*, 25 February 1883.
49 *Trade Union Advocate*, 4 May 1882; *The Wage Worker*, 15 March 1883.
50 *Palladium of Labor*, 15 May 1886; on the merger see *Globe*, 15 July 1887; on the new *Canadian Labor Reformer*, see *Typographical Journal*, 15 November 1889.

51 See *Palladium of Labor*, 16 August 1884. For a fine analysis of *The News* and its relationship to the labor movement see R. G. Hann, "Brainworkers and the Knights of Labor: E. E. Sheppard, Phillips Thompson, and the Toronto *News*, 1883–1887," in Kealey and Warrian, *Essays in Canadian Working Class History*, pp. 35–57.
52 O'Donoghue to Powderly, 17 November 1885, PP.
53 O'Donoghue to Powderly, 9 December 1885, PP.
54 O'Donoghue to Powderly, 13 March 1886, PP.
55 Knights of Labor, *Decisions of the GMW*, p. 42.
56 *World*, 15 April 1886.
57 *Palladium of Labor*, 5 December 1885.
58 O'Donoghue to Powderly, 24 May 1885, 28 March 1888, 31 August 1888, PP. See also *Palladium of Labor*, 6 December 1884, for appointment of William Bews of Hamilton to collect labor statistics.
59 Thompson, *Politics of Labor* (New York, 1887). This volume has been reprinted recently by the University of Toronto Press. The "introduction" to the reprint, however, should be used with considerable caution. See R. G. Hann's review, "An Early Canadian Labour Theorist," *Bulletin of the Committee on Canadian Labour History*, 4 (Autumn 1977), pp. 38–43. For a further discussion of Thompson's contribution see Chapter 8.
60 For complete Toronto strike data see G. S. Kealey, *Toronto Workers*, pp. 319–22.
61 Forsey, "Telegraphers' Strike," and Chapter 4.
62 On the nature of the struggle over control see David Montgomery, "Workers' Control of Machine Production in the Nineteenth Century," *Labor History*, 17 (Fall 1976), pp. 485–508; Gregory S. Kealey, "The 'Honest Workingman' and Workers' Control: The Experience of Toronto Skilled Workers, 1860–1892," *Labour/Le Travailleur*, 1 (1976), pp. 32–68; Craig Heron and Bryan D. Palmer, "Through the Prism of the Strike: Industrial Conflict in South-Central Ontario, 1901–1914," *Canadian Historical Review*, 58 (December 1977), pp. 423–58; Palmer, *A Culture in Conflict: Skilled Workers and Industrial Capitalism in Hamilton, Ontario, 1860–1914* (Montreal, 1979).
63 *Globe*, 10 February, 7 May 1886, 3, 8, 13 April 1886; *News*, 10 February 1886.
64 For gilders see *News*, 4, 8 May 1886; for plumbers see *Globe*, 29 May, 1, 2, 9 June 1886.
65 *Globe*, 23, 24, 25, 28, 31 March, 2 April 1887, 28 August 1889.
66 *World*, 17 April 1886; *Globe*, 19 April 1886.
67 *Globe*, 1 June 1887.
68 *Globe*, 18 November 1885; *World*, 19 November 1885.
69 *Globe*, 19, 24, 31 March, 10, 13, 20 April 1886. For an extended discussion of labor relations in baking see Ian McKay, "Capital and Labour in the Halifax Baking and Confectionary Industry during the last half of the Nineteenth Century," *Labour/Le Travailleur*, 3 (1978), pp. 63–108.
70 *Telegram*, 16 July 1887.
71 *Globe*, 27, 29, 31 May, 3, 4, 5, June 1889.
72 For a general history of the Massey Co., which tends to ignore labor relations, see Merrill Dennison, *Harvest Triumphant* (Toronto, 1949).
73 For descriptions and reports on these various groups see *The Triphammer*, February 1885–February 1886 in Massey Archives, Toronto.
74 Robert Ozanne, *A Century of Labor-Management Relations at McCormick and International Harvester* (Madison, 1967), esp. ch. 1.
75 *Palladium of Labor*, 27 October 1883.
76 Sam McNab to Powderly, 4 November 1884; Powderly to Sam McNab, 18 November 1884, PP.

77 Details of strike from *Globe*, 9–16 February 1886; *World*, 9–12 February 1886; *News*, 8–12 February 1886; *Telegram*, 8–13 February 1886.
78 *Triphammer* estimate which is higher than the daily papers' counts.
79 O'Donoghue to Powderly, 8 February 1886, PP.
80 *News*, 11 February 1886.
81 O'Donoghue to Powderly, 14 February 1886, PP.
82 *Triphammer*, February 1886.
83 *Globe*, 11 March 1886. For later chapters in the history of industrial relations at Massey's see Bruce Scott, "'A Place in the Sun': The Industrial Council at Massey-Harris, 1919–1929," *Labour*, 1 (1976), pp. 158–92.
84 *Canadian Labor Reformer*, 13 November 1886 and "Organization of Company, 1887," clippings file, Vol. 1, Massey Archives.
85 *Palladium of Labor*, 7 November 1885. There had been previous abortive discussions of unionization. In June 1881 the men had tried to create a benefit society, claiming they had no grievances with the company. This appeared to be a cover for an attempt to organize for at the end of the month they submitted a petition against new work rules and threatened to strike. Unfortunately there is no indication of how this conflict was resolved. One year later, however, an anonymous street railway employee wrote a letter condemning the extremely low wages paid by the company and drawing the public's attention to its high profits. Again a strike was threatened. *Globe*, 15, 22 June 1881, 19 April 1882.
86 *World*, 8 November 1885.
87 O'Donoghue to Powderly, 8, 15, 23, 24 November and 9 December 1885, PP. Also *Canadian Labor Reformer*, 14 May 1886. A published version of O'Donoghue's account is in Ontario, Bureau of Industry, *Report*, 1886, pp. 246–7.
88 O'Donoghue to Powderly, 9 December 1885, PP.
89 Kealey, ed., *Canada Investigates Industrialism* (Toronto, 1973), pp. 103–9, and *Rules and Regulations for Drivers and Conductors of the Toronto Street Railway Company* (Toronto, 1880), Baldwin Room, Metropolitan Toronto Central Library.
90 See Toronto press, 10–15 March 1886 for details. Of the various accounts of the street car strike, by far the best is David Frank, "Trouble in Toronto: The Street Railway Lockout and Strike, 1886," unpublished paper, University of Toronto, 1972. A more recent description is Desmond Morton, *Mayor Howland: The Citizens' Candidate* (Toronto, 1973), pp. 43–56.
91 *News*, 10 March 1886.
92 Ibid., 11 March 1886.
93 *Telegram*, 12 March 1886.
94 *News*, 11 March 1886.
95 Montreal *Star*, 11 March 1886, cited in V. O. Chan, "The Canadian Knights of Labor with Special Reference to the 1880s," M.A. thesis, McGill University, 1949.
96 *News*, 10 March 1886.
97 Ibid., 11 March 1886, and Morton, *Mayor Howland*, p. 48.
98 *News*, 12 March 1886.
99 Ibid., 12, 13 March 1886; *World*, 13 March 1886.
100 Frank, "Trouble in Toronto," p. 48.
101 For the attitude to street railways see Bryan Palmer, "'Give us the Road and we will run it': The Social and Cultural Matrix of an Emerging Labour Movement," in Kealey and Warrian, *Essays in Canadian Working Class History*, pp. 106–24. For the carters see *News*, 11, 12, 15, 16 February 1886.
102 O'Donoghue to Powderly, 13 March 1886, PP.
103 *Globe*, 14 April 1886.
104 *World*, 20 April 1886.

105 Ibid.
106 *Globe*, 10 May 1886; *Canadian Labor Reformer*, 15 May 1886. For details of strike see Toronto press May–June 1886.
107 *World*, 10 May 1886.
108 *News*, 10 May 1886.
109 For an excellent analysis of the origins of the boycott in the United States see Michael Gordon, "Irish Immigrant Culture and the Labor Boycott in New York City, 1880–1886," *Labor History*, 16 (1975), pp. 184–229. For Toronto printers see Kealey, "The Honest Workingman," *Labour/Le Travailleur*, 1 (1976), pp. 32–68.
110 *World*, 10 May 1886.
111 *News*, 12 May 1886.
112 *World*, 14, 21 May 1886.
113 *News*, 12 May 1886.
114 For examples of arrests and convictions see *News*, 11, 12, 13, 14, 20, 21, 28 May, 3 June 1886; *World*, 12, 13, 14, 15, 17, 18, 19, 21, 31 May 1886.
115 *News*, 12 May 1886.
116 *World*, 14 May 1886.
117 *News*, 11 May 1886.
118 *World*, 14 May 1886.
119 *News*, 19 May 1886.
120 *World*, 19 June 1886.
121 Ibid., 21 May 1886.
122 Ibid., 22 May 1886.
123 Ibid., 6 July 1886. See also *World*, 24, 26, 30 June 1886; *News*, 18, 22, 23, 24, 26, 29 June, 3, 10 July 1886; and *Telegram*, 18, 21, 22, 23, 24 June, 3, 5 July 1886.
124 It should be added that public support for the takeover and real consideration of public ownership in 1891 was undoubtedly due at least partially to these strikes. For details on the public ownership fight see Christopher Armstrong and H. V. Nelles, *The Revenge of the Methodist Bicycle Company: Sunday Streetcars and Municipal Reform in Toronto, 1888–1897* (Toronto, 1977), and Kealey, *Toronto Workers Respond*, ch. 14.
125 *Journal of United Labor*, 13 November 1890.
126 *Globe*, 6 May 1891. The new company organized a company union in 1894 in response to another attempt at unionization. Only in 1899 did the workers finally reorganize as a Local of the Amalgamated Association of Street Railway Employees. In 1902 they fought a virulent struggle with the company, which saw the reoccurrence of the crowd actions of 1886 in Toronto's streets. This time Mayor Oliver Howland (W. H.'s brother) had no compunction about calling up the militia "in aid of civil power." See David Frank, "Life and Work in Toronto, 1900–1914," unpublished manuscript, University of Toronto, 1972, pp. 50–7.
127 This is based on information in Toronto city directories in the 1887–90 period.
128 Ontario, Bureau of Industry, *Report*, 1886, p. 247.
129 *Proceedings*, 1887, General Executive Board Doc. 130, pp. 1286–7. See also *Canadian Labor Reformer*, 12 March and 19 March 1887 and *Globe*, 10 March 1887.
130 *Proceedings*, 1887, General Executive Board, Doc. 131. See also O'Donoghue to Powderly, 29 April 1887, PP. A caution should be added here that we are only discussing the Order's leadership. Local militants, as we have seen, were far less hesitant to engage in forms of direct action.
131 *Globe*, 10, 11 May, 1887; *Telegram*, 7, 14, 21, 28 May, 5 June 1887.
132 *Globe*, 1 June 1887.
133 *World*, 26 February 1887.
134 *Globe*, 1 June, 19 August 1887. See also *London Advertiser*, 19 August 1887.

135 *Cornwall Standard*, 15 March 1889, clipping in A. W. Wright Papers, Public Archives of Canada.
136 *Journal of United Labor*, 18 October 1888. On Barry, see Richard Oestreicher, "The Knights of Labor in Michigan: Sources of Growth and Decline," M.A. thesis, Michigan State University, 1973.
137 For carpenters see *The Carpenter*, July, August, October 1887. There was even tension among the carpenters within the Order. Document 1253 on the 1887 GA *Proceedings* was a request by LA 8235 (Toronto carpenters) to have the DA force carpenters who were members of mixed LAs to join carpenters' trade Assemblies. They gave as their reason the fact that trade Assemblies worked only nine hours while members in the mixed Assemblies were working ten. The General Executive Board refused permission to force the members to join craft Assemblies but did rule that members of mixed Assemblies had to abide by craft rules.
138 For shoemakers see *Globe*, 15 February 1890. The shoemakers' attempt to make the Order strong on the shop floor is clear in the *By-Laws of LA 2211* (Toronto, 1887). These rules included shop committees that had to report at every LA meeting. These committees, however, could not take action without LA and DA sanction.
139 E. Cannon to Powderly, 12 September 1887, PP.
140 Ibid., 19 September 1887.
141 General Assembly, *Proceedings*, 1887, p. 1287.
142 *Canadian Labor Reformer*, 20 August 1886, 4 September 1886. See also Sam McNab to Powderly, 3 September 1886, PP.
143 J. W. Commeford to Powderly, 21 January 1887, PP
144 O'Donoghue to Powderly, 4 January 1886, PP.
145 Ibid., 24 January, 14 February 1886, PP.
146 Ibid., 29 March 1886, PP.
147 Michael O'Halloran to Powderly, 20 October 1888, PP.
148 O'Donoghue to Powderly, 7 October 1889, PP.
149 O'Donoghue to Powderly, 23 August 1890, PP.
150 *Labor Advocate*, 1 May, 2 October 1891.
151 O'Donoghue to Powderly, 10 April 1891, PP; *Journal of United Machinists*, July 1892.
152 "The Hope of the Workers," PP, 1892.
153 *Proceedings*, 1894, General Executive Board Report.
154 For examples, see Bernard Feeny to Powderly, 1, 23 December 1893; Wright to Powderly, 4 June 1894; Powderly to Wright, 18 April 1894; O'Donoghue to John W. Hayes, 7 July 1894, Hayes Papers, Catholic University, Washington, D.C. Henceforth HP.
155 Isaac H. Sanderson to John W. Hayes, 12 May 1908, HP.
156 Sanderson to Hayes, 19 October 1908, HP.
157 Sanderson to Hayes, 22 September 1908, HP.
158 *The Wage Worker*, 22 March 1883.
159 As late as 1902, when Knights reflected on their own history, they proudly asserted their attempt to organize all workers as their greatest contribution: "A Knight of Labor is more than a mere Trade Unionist working for some single trade. He works for the good of all. Machinery will some day teach the Trade Unionist by sad experience that his only salvation lies in the K. of L. form of organization. The locomotive engineer, the 'aristocrat of labor,' will be replaced by the ordinary motorman, the printer by the machine, the cigarmaker by the machine cigar, the glass worker by the laborer, and so on." See Knights of Labor, DA 47 *Twenty Year History of . . .* (Cleveland, 1902), p. 75.
160 Boston *Labor Leader*, 5 February 1887, as cited in Leon Fink, "Class Conflict in

the Gilded Age: The Figure and the Phantom," *Radical History Review*, 3 (1975), pp. 56–74. See also Fink's excellent "The Knights of Labor and the Transformation of American Political Culture," Canadian Historical Association, unpublished paper, 1978.

161 O'Donoghue to Powderly, 23 August 1890. PP.

## 4. Hamilton and the Home Club

1 "Recollections of John Peebles, Mayor of Hamilton, 1930–1933," 7 February 1946, Hamilton Collection, Hamilton Public Library.

2 *Hamilton Spectator*, 26 August, 16 October 1885, 21 January 1888; *Report of the Commission on the Relations of Labor and Capital in Canada*, "Ontario Evidence," II (Ottawa, 1889), pp. 861–5; "Register of the Knights of Labor Organizers," PP. Peebles was praised as "an affable young man," his wares advertised in *Palladium of Labor*, 5 September 1885. Peebles was listed as a shoemaker in the Royal Commission Report, but this must have been an error. City directories identify him as a laborer (1883–4) and a watchmaker, jeweller, and optician (1885–90).

3 *Palladium of Labor*, 18 August 1883.

4 On the beginning of the Order in Canada, with reference to the first Hamilton Assembly see Douglas R. Kennedy, *The Knights of Labor in Canada* (London, 1956), p. 35; Victor Oscar Chan, "Canadian Knights of Labor with special reference to the 1880's," M.A. thesis, McGill University, 1949, pp. 1–45; D. J. O'Donoghue, "The Labor Movement in Canada," in George E. McNeill, ed., *The Labor Movement: The Problem of Today* (New York, 1892), p. 594; H. A. Logan, *Trade Unions in Canada* (Toronto, 1946), p. 50; Martin Robin, *Radical Politics and Canadian Labour* (Kingston, 1968), p. 20; "Hamilton Early Stronghold in Organized Labour Cause," *Hamilton Spectator*, 15 July 1946. None of these sources dates the establishment of LA 1852, and it is likely that they all rely upon O'Donoghue's account, or reprints of it. Our dating follows Fred A. Fenton to T. V. Powderly, 7 December 1882, PP. Eugene Forsey, "The Canadian Labour Movement, 1812–1902," Canadian Historical Association *Booklet #27* (1974), p. 7, notes that the Order was present in Hamilton as early as 1875 on a secret basis. On the secret Assembly cf., Jonathan Garlock, *Knights of Labor Data Bank* (Ann Arbor, 1978); Philip S. Foner, *History of the Labor Movement in the United States from Colonial Times to the Founding of the American Federation of Labor*, I (New York, 1947), pp. 509–10; *Journal of United Labor*, 15 May 1880.

5 *Record of the Proceedings of the Seventh Regular Session of the General Assembly of the Knights of Labor, Cincinnati, 1883*, pp. 528, 545, 549.

6 *Record of the Proceedings of the Eighth Regular Session of the General Assembly of the Knights of Labor, Philadelphia, 1884*, p. 796. Cf., *Palladium of Labor*, 11 August 1883, 8 September 1883.

7 *National Labor Tribune*, 23 May 1885. On the impact of the depression in Hamilton see the correspondence in *The Craftsman*, 18 October 1884, 25 October 1884, 1 November 1884, 22 November 1884, 13 December 1884, 20 December 1884, 10 January 1885, 17 January 1885, 7 February 1885; *John Swinton's Paper*, 28 September 1884, 19 October 1884, 22 February 1885. Cf., *Palladium of Labor*, 20 September 1884, 1 November 1884, 8 November 1884; Bernard Ostry, "Conservatives, Liberals, and Labour in the 1880s," *Canadian Journal of Economics and Political Science*, 27 (May 1961), p. 143.

8 *Record of the Proceedings of the Ninth Regular Session of the General Assembly of the Knights of Labor, Hamilton, 1885*, pp. 173, 192.

9 *Record of the Proceedings of the General Assembly of the Knights of Labor, Eleventh Regular Session, Minneapolis, 1887*, p. 1847.

10 *Proceedings of the General Assembly of the Knights of Labor of America, 12th Regular Session, Indianapolis, 1888*, "Report of the Secretary," p. 2. This source chronicles Canadian decline generally, although only DA 138 (St. Thomas) appears to have rivaled Hamilton in terms of the severity of the demise.

11 *Labour Gazette*, 1 (1901–2), pp. 560–1.

12 On the eclectic appeal of the Knights see Gregory S. Kealey, *Toronto Workers Respond to Industrial Capitalism, 1867–1892* (Toronto, 1980), pp. 175–215; Leon Fink, "Workingmen's Democracy: The Knights of Labor in Local Politics, 1886–1896," Ph.D. thesis, University of Rochester, 1977. The widespread appeal of the Knights forms an important component of an early, but still valuable discussion. See Norman J. Ware, *The Labor Movement in the United States, 1860–1890: A Study in Democracy* (New York, 1964), esp. pp. xi–xviii.

13 On the nature of nineteenth-century workers' control, obviously not a revolutionary phenomenon, see Gregory S. Kealey, "The 'Honest Workingman' and Workers' Control: The Experience of Toronto Skilled Workers, 1860–1892," *Labour/Le Travailleur*, 1 (1976), pp. 32–68; Bryan D. Palmer, *A Culture in Conflict: Skilled Workers and Industrial Capitalism in Hamilton Ontario, 1860–1914* (Montreal, 1979); Craig Heron and Bryan D. Palmer, "Through the Prism of the Strike: Industrial Conflict in South-Central Ontario, 1901–1914," *Canadian Historical Review*, 58 (December, 1977), pp. 423–58. On the relationship of the Knights of Labor to the practices of workers' control see the discussion in the pioneering American treatment, David Montgomery, "Workers' Control of Machine Production in the Nineteenth Century," *Labor History*, 17 (Fall 1976), pp. 498–501; and the explicit statement in *Official Handbook of the Rhode Island District Assembly 99, Knights of Labor, and Protective Association* (Providence, 1894), pp. 40–1. The quotes are from *Palladium of Labor*, 1 May 1886; *Labor Union*, 27 January 1883; *Proceedings, General Assembly, 1887*, pp. 1875–6.

14 *Canadian Labor Reformer*, 31 July 1886; *Hamilton Spectator*, 12 July 1887, 13 August 1887.

15 *Hamilton Spectator*, 19 April 1886.

16 Ibid., 22 April 1886, 29 April 1886, 3 May 1886, 11 May 1886, 13 May 1886; *Canadian Labor Reformer*, 15 May 1886.

17 *Proceedings of the Third Session of the Trades & Labor Congress of Canada, Hamilton, 1887* (Toronto, 1887), p. 11.

18 On the Gardner strike see *Palladium of Labor*, 8 November 1884; E. S. Gilbert to T. V. Powderly, 31 October 1884; Powderly to F. M. Wilson, 29 October 1884; Wilson to Powderly, 5 November 1884; Gilbert to Powderly, 5 November 1884; Gilbert to Powderly, 8 November 1884, PP; and Chapter 5.

19 *Labor Advocate*, 23 January 1891.

20 *Palladium of Labor*, 18 July 1885.

21 On the Hamilton struggle for the eight-hour day see *Palladium of Labor*, 14 March 1885, 4 April 1885, 18 April 1885, 12 December 1885, 20 March 1886, 27 March 1886, 1 May 1886, 15 May 1886; *Hamilton Spectator*, 22 March, 1886, 8 April 1886, 12 April 1886.

22 *Hamilton Spectator*, 22 March 1886.

23 Ibid., 8 April 1886.

24 *Journal of United Labor*, 16 May 1889.

25 This forms an integral component of the discussion of the Knights in Ware, *The Labor Movement in the United States*, esp. p. xviii; Philip S. Foner, *History of the Labor Movement in the United States*, II (New York, 1955), pp. 55–74; Charles Lip-

ton, *The Trade Union Movement of Canada, 1827–1959* (Montreal, 1968), pp. 71–2, makes the point for Canada.

26 Powderly, *The Path I Trod*, p. 42.

27 Cf., Foner, *History of the Labor Movement*, II, p. 55.

28 *Journal of United Labor*, 25 December 1890, Cf., *Palladium of Labor*, 3 October 1885; *Proceedings, General Assembly, 1886*, pp. 38–9.

29 *Canadian Labor Reformer*, 26 June 1886. On the first stirrings of women's organization in Hamilton see Fred A. Fenton to Powderly, 7 December 1882, PP. The following draws upon Gregory S. Kealey, "McVicar, Katie, Shoeworker and union leader," forthcoming, *Dictionary of Canadian Biography*, XI.

30 *Palladium of Labor*, 6 October 1883, 13 October 1883, 8 September 1883, 10 November 1883. It is possible that McVicar penned a series of letters signed "Sewing Girl" that appeared in *Hamilton Spectator*, 28 March 1882, 20 March 1882, 31 March 1882, 1 April 1882, 3 April 1882, 5 April 1882.

31 *Palladium of Labor*, 3 November 1883.

32 Powderly to Miss Annie Gillespie, 29 January 1887; Powderly to Miss Maggie Wilkes, 30 August 1887; Powderly to Miss Margaret Wilkes, 27 December 1887; Powderly to Lydia Salisbury, 3 December 1888, PP.

33 Given the apparent absence of any woman willing to serve as directress of LA 3179, it is possible that McVicar was "the lady member of LA 3040," referred to in *Canadian Labor Reformer*, 15 May 1886, as responsible for the growth of the Order in Dundas.

34 *Hamilton Spectator*, 17 September 1888.

35 *Palladium of Labor*, 20 March 1886. Cf., H. Francis Perry, "The Workingman's Alienation from the Church," *American Journal of Sociology* (4 March 1899), p. 626.

36 *Palladium of Labor*, 29 August 1885. Cf., ibid., 7 November 1885.

37 Ibid., 12 September 1885.

38 Cf., the account of Powderly's speech in the city in *Hamilton Spectator*, 30 November 1882; and an account of a delegate's speech at the 1885 General Assembly held in Hamilton, in *Palladium of Labor*, 17 October 1885. Finally, note the number of labor sermons preached by ministers sympathetic to the Knights' cause, chronicled in *Hamilton Spectator*, 25 October 1883; *Palladium of Labor*, 20 March 1886, 27 March 1886; *Journal of United Labor*, 28 May 1887.

39 *Palladium of Labor*, 28 November 1885.

40 *Trade Union Advocate*, 15 June 1882.

41 *Hamilton Spectator*, 13 October 1885; *Palladium of Labor*, 17 October 1885. On Foster see Ware, *Labor Movement in the United States*, pp. 115, 177, 181, 250, 254, 267, and passim.

42 *Palladium of Labor*, 3 November 1883.

43 On the importance of this, the first international strike, see Forsey, "The Telegraphers' Strike," pp. 245–60.

44 *Hamilton Spectator*, 19 July 1883. Cf., Powderly, *The Path I Trod*, pp. 101–13.

45 *Hamilton Spectator*, 19 July 1883; Forsey, "The Telegraphers' Strike," pp. 257–8.

46 *Hamilton Spectator*, 20 July 1883. On street railway struggles, strikingly similar in terms of the tactics and the language of opposition to a monopolistic service, see David Frank, "Trouble in Toronto: The Street Railway Lockout and Strike of 1886," unpublished manuscript, University of Toronto, 1970; Bryan D. Palmer, "'Give us the road and we will run it': The Social and Cultural Matrix of an Emerging Labour Movement," in Kealey and Warrain, eds., *Essays in Canadian Working Class History*, pp. 106–24; and Palmer, *A Culture in Conflict*, pp. 209–16.

47 *Hamilton Spectator*, 23 July 1883, 26 July 1883.

48 Ibid., 23 July 1883; *Palladium of Labor*, 11 August 1883.

49 *Hamilton Spectator*, 26 July 1883.
50 Ibid., 19 July 1883.
51 Ibid., 10 August 1883, 15 August 1883, 18 August 1883, 21 August 1883.
52 Ibid., 10 September 1883, 17 September 1883; Forsey, "The Telegraphers' Strike," p. 259.
53 See Ware, *The Labor Movement in the United States*, pp. 117–54.
54 *Palladium of Labor*, 18 August 1883. Cf., "Enjolras" in ibid., 19 April 1884.
55 On blacklisting of Hamilton's Brotherhood see *Hamilton Spectator*, 21 August 1883.
56 Ibid., 14 February 1884.
57 Ibid., 16 February 1884, 21 February 1884; *Palladium of Labor*, 15 February 1884, 23 February 1884.
58 *Hamilton Spectator*, 21 February 1884.
59 Ibid., 16 February 1884.
60 Ibid., 18 February 1884, 21 February 1884, 22 February 1884. The radicalization of shoeworkers, occasioned by the presence of women in the struggle, is outlined in Montgomery, "Workers' Control of Machine Production," p. 500; G. S. Kealey, "Artisans Respond to Industrialism: Shoemakers, Shoe Factories, and the Knights of St. Crispin in Toronto," Canadian Historical Association, *Historical Papers* (1973), pp. 145–6; Augusta E. Galster, *The Labor Movement in the Shoe Industry, with Special Reference to Philadelphia* (New York, 1924), pp. 55–7.
61 *Hamilton Spectator*, 16 February 1884.
62 *Palladium of Labor*, 23 February 1884; *Hamilton Spectator*, 21 February 1884.
63 *Hamilton Spectator*, 8 March 1884.
64 Ibid., 10 March 1884, 12 March 1884.
65 See Palmer, *A Culture in Conflict*, pp. 71–96. The Order also involved itself in a series of smaller strikes waged by workers (often unaffiliated with the Knights of Labor) attempting to secure some limited forms of control. See *Toronto World*, 12 January 1885, 19 January 1885, on a strike at the Ontario Rolling Mills, and *Hamilton Spectator*, 10 February 1887, 11 February 1887, 18 February 1887, on a dispute involving Knights of Labor boot and shoe workers at the Orr, Harvey & Company, where workers walked off the job protesting the dismissal of one of their number.
66 For a general introduction to the importance of the anti-Chinese agitations see McNeill, ed., *The Labor Movement*, pp. 429–54; Grob, *Workers and Utopia*, pp. 57–8; Isabella Black, "American Labor and Chinese Immigration," *Past & Present*, 25 (July, 1963), pp. 59–76; Ted Brush, "Chinese Labor in North Jersey, 1870–1895," *North Jersey Highlander*, 9 (1973), pp. 13–21; Alexander Saxton, *The Indispensable Enemy: Labor and the Anti-Chinese Movement in California* (Berkeley, 1971), pp. 179–234; Arthur G. Doughty and Adam Shortt, *Canada and Its Provinces*, XXI (Toronto, 1914), p. 259.
67 Some of "Ah Sin's" letters can be found in *Labor Union*, 17 March 1883; *Palladium of Labor*, 12 April 1884, 24 May 1884, 20 September 1884. Cf., "Hung Wah's" letter in *Labor Union*, 24 March 1883; and the discussions in *Palladium of Labor*, 12 April 1884, 31 May 1884, 16 August 1884, 13 June 1885, 20 June 1885.
68 *Palladium of Labor*, 12 April 1884.
69 Efforts to go beyond the racist contours of the exclusion argument can be found in *The National*, 29 January 1874; *Palladium of Labor*, 6 September 1884; and in Robert Coulter's speech before the CLU, recorded in *Hamilton Spectator*, 26 March 1885.
70 Accounts of Hamilton's anti-Chinese demonstration, the efforts to prepare for it, and its impact, can be found in *Palladium of Labor*, 27 September 1884, 4 October

1884; *Hamilton Spectator*, 2 October 1884, 3 October 1884; *The Craftsman*, 7 October 1884, 1 November 1884. On Sheppard and Thompson see Hann, "Brainworkers and the Knights of Labor," pp. 33–57.

71 *Hamilton Spectator*, 3 October 1884.

72 *The Craftsman*, 1 November 1884.

73 Note the interesting comments in Arthur Mann, "Gompers and the Irony of Racism," *Antioch Review*, 13 (Spring 1953), pp. 203–14.

74 On the Knights' endorsement of temperance see *Journal of United Labor*, 24 September 1887, 19 September 1889; Griffiths, "Protestant Attitudes in 1886," pp. 146–7; *Report of the Proceedings of the General Assembly, 1885*, p. 20; Ware, *Labor Movement in the United States*, pp. 89, 107, 223–7, 365.

75 See Powderly, *Thirty Years of Labor, 1859–1889* (Columbus, Ohio, 1889), pp. 580–626; David Montgomery, *Beyond Equality: Labor and the Radical Republicans, 1862–1872* (New York, 1967), pp. 171, 187–97, 202–6, and passim, on some prominent Knights and their temperance views; Samuel Walker, "Terence V. Powderly, the Knights of Labor and the Temperance Issue," *Societas*, 5 (Autumn 1975), pp. 279–94.

76 *The Temperance Journal and New Brunswick Reporter*, 11 August 1888.

77 *Palladium of Labor*, 10 October 1885. Cf., *Labor Union*, 13 January 1883; *Hamilton Spectator*, 24 August 1882, 30 November 1883.

78 See accounts of speeches in *Palladium of Labor*, 15 December 1883, 5 September 1885; *Hamilton Spectator*, 27 June 1883, 5 December 1885, 10 December 1883, 13 October 1885. Cf., the account of another lecture, by the well-known Knight, Victor Drury, in ibid., 22 April 1886.

79 On "Enjolras" and temperance see *Palladium of Labor*, 12 January 1884.

80 Ibid., 21 June 1884. Cf., *Labor Union*, 17 February 1883, on a wife's support for temperance.

81 *Palladium of Labor*, 31 May 1884.

82 *Canadian Labor Reformer*, 19 June 1886.

83 W. W. Buchanan, Dominion Secretary, Royal Templars of Temperance, to Powderly, 10 May 1886, PP. For accounts of this temperance gathering see *Hamilton Spectator*, 9 August 1886, 10 August 1886; *Palladium of Labor*, 24 July 1886, 31 July 1886. Powderly's presence at an annual temperance camp was again solicited in 1890. See Royal Templar Book and Publishing House to Powderly, 29 April 1890, PP.

84 *Palladium of Labor*, 8 August 1885.

85 Ibid., 7 August 1886.

86 On the temperance movement's endorsement of Racey see *Palladium of Labor*, 7 December 1886; *Evening Palladium*, 13 December 1886.

87 See, for instance, *Minute Book, Hamilton Trades and Labor Council, 1910–1914*, Hamilton Collection, Hamilton Public Library, p. 34.

88 *Palladium of Labor*, 16 May 1885.

89 Ibid.

90 Ibid., 2 May 1885.

91 Ibid., 11 August 1883, 2 August 1884, 9 August 1884; *Hamilton Spectator*, 4 August 1884.

92 *Hamilton Spectator*, 4 August 1884.

93 R. McDougall to Powderly, 6 January 1883, PP.

94 Powderly to McDougall, 26 January 1883; D. B. Skelley to Powderly, 15 December 1884, PP.

95 Charles Smith to Powderly, 3 March 1884, PP.

96 Fred A. Jones to Powderly, 11 August 1884, PP.
97 E. S. Gilbert to Powderly, 20 October 1884, PP.
98 Powderly to Gilbert, 20 October 1884, PP.
99 On the 1883 strike see *Labor Union*, 24 March 1883; *Hamilton Spectator*, 6 April 1883–1 June 1883.
100 *Hamilton Spectator*, 14 April 1885.
101 On the evolution of the dispute of 1885–1886 see *Palladium of Labor*, 2 April 1885–2 May 1885, *Cigar Makers' Official Journal*, October 1885; *The Craftsman*, 28 April 1885, 16 May 1885, 11 July 1885, 15 August 1885; *John Swinton's Paper*, 19 April 1885, 7 June 1885; *Hamilton Spectator*, 17 April 1885–29 July 1885; *London Advertiser*, 20 May 1885, 10 June 1885, 23 September 1885, 19 November 1885. On the Progressive Cigar Makers' Union see Ware, *Labor Movement in the United States*, pp. 262–79; Howard M. Gitelman, "Attempts to Unify the American Labor Movement, 1865–1900," Ph.D. thesis, University of Wisconsin, 1960, pp. 352–8, 379–84; *Progress: The Official Organ of the Cigarmakers' Progressive Union of America*, 20 September 1882, 28 September 1883, 21 August 1885; William Kirk, "The Knights of Labor and the American Federation of Labor," in Jacob H. Hollander and George E. Barnett, eds., *Studies in American Trade Unionism* (New York, 1907), pp. 363–5. On the Hamilton Local of the Progressive Union see *Hamilton Spectator*, 9 July 1886; *Palladium of Labor*, 17 July 1886.
102 See *Palladium of Labor*, 19 September 1885, 27 March 1886.
103 Ibid., 12 April 1885.
104 Ibid. The International Typographical Union would later consider striking the *Palladium of Labor*. See *St. Thomas Times*, 3 May 1887.
105 Ibid., 12 December 1885; *London Advertiser*, 19 November 1885.
106 Will. J. Vale to Powderly, 8 March 1886, PP.
107 *Hamilton Spectator*, 24 June 1886; *Canadian Labor Reformer*, 15 May 1886, 21 August 1886.
108 Ibid., 30 June 1886; *Palladium of Labor*, 3 July 1886; *Cigar Makers' Official Journal*, July 1886.
109 *Palladium of Labor*, 10 July 1886. On Cigarmakers' Union and Knights of Labor unity cf., Dennis East, "Union Labels and Boycotts: Co-operation of the Knights of Labor and the Cigar Makers' International Union, 1885–1886," *Labor History*, 16 (Spring 1975), pp. 266–71; Cigar Makers' Union No. 130, Saginaw, Michigan, *Minute Book*, pp. 20–1, 36–7, 88, Archives of Labor History and Urban Affairs, Wayne State University, Detroit, Michigan.
110 *Palladium of Labor*, 17 July 1886, 14 August 1886.
111 Ibid., 31 July 1886.
112 See *Cigar Makers' Official Journal*, August 1886; *The Craftsman*, 3 July 1886; *Palladium of Labor*, 17 July 1886, 31 July 1886, 14 August 1886, 21 August 1886, 4 September 1886, 25 September 1886; *Hamilton Spectator*, 12 August 1886. Cf., *Canadian Labor Reformer*, 21 August 1886. The *Cigar Makers' Official Journal* carried a note in German, English, and Bohemian stating that "The Hamilton *Palladium of Labor* deserves the hearty support of every cigarmaker in Canada. In a recent trouble it has taken a bold stand against the intrigues of the notorious Home Club." William H. Rowe, editor of the *Palladium*, took the appropriate bows, and replied with "modesty" that any labor reformer would have done the same for a group of workers "harassed and hounded to death by a series of combinations." See *Palladium of Labor*, 28 August 1886. But the Hamilton paper's relentless assault on the Home Clubbers did not go uncriticized in Canadian labor circles. Toronto's *Canadian Labor Reformer*, 18 September 1886, claimed that the Hamil-

ton paper no longer officially represented DA 61, and noted that it had been censured by another Ontario DA "for the unmanly and unfair course it has seen fit to pursue."

113 *Palladium of Labor*, 6 November 1886; *Brantford Expositer*, 5 November 1886; *Brantford Courier*, 2 November 1886, 30 November 1886; *Hamilton Spectator*, 31 August 1886; *John Swinton's Paper*, 5 September 1886.

114 *Proceedings of the Second Session of the Canadian Trades & Labor Congress, 1886* (Toronto, 1886), p. 40.

115 Powderly to James Henigan, 3 September 1886, PP.

116 *Hamilton Spectator*, 29 September 1887; *Record of the Proceedings of the General Assembly of the Knights of Labor, 1888*, p. 49, Documents 417 and 697; *Record of the Proceedings of the General Assembly of the Knights of Labor, 1889*, p. 16, Document 132.

117 *The Craftsman*, 2 October 1886.

118 *Hamilton Spectator*, 25 August 1888.

119 James Dore to Powderly, 1 October 1886; George Collis to Powderly, 1 October 1886, PP.

120 George Collis to Powderly, 9 September 1886, PP.

121 See *Hamilton Spectator*, 28 January 1887, 8 February 1887, 9 February 1887, 14 February 1887, 17 February 1887. This period saw increasing concern with trade jurisdictions, and even a retreat on the part of some Knights of Labor on the question of women's involvement in the Order. See Henry McStravick (Recording Secretary LA 8915) to Powderly, 30 October 1886; Clifton R. Waterman (Recording Secretary LA 1852) to Powderly, 19 January 1887; and William Berry (Recording Secretary LA 2132) to Powderly, 22 May 1888, PP. The last letter appealed to Powderly to overrule the decision of the MW of LA 3179 denying the legality of women members of LAs 2132 and 3179 voting with their male counterparts in the shoemaking and shoefitting trades in the election of a delegate.

122 *Hamilton Spectator*, 9 March 1887.

123 Ibid., 2 November 1887.

124 Martin O'Driscoll to Powderly, 31 July 1888, PP.

125 *Journal of United Labor*, 3 December 1887.

126 *Proceedings, General Assembly, 1887*, pp. 1729–30. Cf., James Henigan to Powderly, 21 August 1887, PP.

127 George Collis to Powderly, 4 February 1888, and 20 February 1888; Powderly to George Collis, 14 February 1888; Thomas Towers to Powderly, no date (February 1888?), PP. It is perhaps worth noting that DA 138 was created in the midst of the Home Club Affair. See *St. Thomas Times*, 3 July 1886, 14 July 1886, and Chapter 7 below.

128 *Palladium of Labor*, 21 August 1886.

129 See Ware, *Labor Movement in the United States*, pp. 111, 290, which also identifies D. R. Gibson as a member of the Home Club. On speeches of Mullen and Drury see *Palladium of Labor*, 24 April 1886, 1 May 1886, 17 October 1885; *Hamilton Spectator*, 21 April 1886, 22 April 1886, 26 April 1886.

130 *Palladium of Labor*, 2 April 1886.

131 Ibid., 17 October 1884. On Horan see *Toronto News*, 5 August 1884; Ware, *The Labor Movement*, pp. 94, 104–11.

132 *Labor Advocate*, 23 January 1891.

133 *Hamilton Spectator*, 16 January 1882.

134 George Collis to Powderly, 23 November 1884, PP; *Labor News*, 12 April 1814; *Palladium of Labor*, 12 September 1885.

135 Collis to Powderly, 23 November 1884, PP.

136 Gibson to Powderly, 3 July 1886, PP.

137 *Palladium of Labor*, 4 December 1886; *Hamilton Spectator*, 28 July 1887, 2 November 1887; *Proceedings, General Assembly, 1887*, p. 1831.
138 Note Gitelman, "Attempts to Unify the American Labor Movement," pp. 520–2.
139 See Melvyn Dubofsky, *Industrialism and the American Worker, 1865–1920* (New York, 1975), pp. 59–60.
140 *Hamilton Spectator*, 12 March 1889, 8 October 1889.
141 Henry McStravick to Powderly, 25 February 1890; Powderly to McStravick, 3 March 1890; Powderly to the Order Everywhere, 3 March 1890, PP.
142 J.N.P. to Powderly, 12 May 1891, HP.
143 E. S. Gilbert to John W. Hayes, 24 February 1892; Gilbert to Hayes, 9 June 1892, HP.
144 Edward Little to John W. Hayes, 4 October 1897, HP.
145 Gilbert to Hayes, 9 June 1892, HP.

## 5. The underside of the Knights of Labor

1 *Palladium of Labor*, 17 July 1886, 11 August 1883; *St. Thomas Times*, 12 May 1886.
2 See Norman J. Ware, *The Labor Movement in the United States, 1860–1890: A Study in Democracy* (New York, 1964), pp. 117–54, 299–319; Paul Buhle, "The Knights of Labor in Rhode Island," *Radical History Review*, 17 (Spring 1978), pp. 39–74; T. V. Powderly, *The Path I Trod: The Autobiography of Terence V. Powderly* (New York, 1940), pp. 101–39; Douglas R. Kennedy, *The Knights of Labor in Canada* (London, Ont., 1956), pp. 57–76; Victor Oscar Chan, "Canadian Knights of Labor with Special Reference to the 1880s," M.A. thesis, McGill University, 1949, pp. 46–110.
3 See, for instance, Wayne Roberts, "The Problem of Independent Labour Politics," unpublished manuscript, University of Toronto, 1977 which touches on the political experience of the 1880s and 1890s; Howard M. Gitelman, "Attempts to Unify the American Labor Movement, 1865–1900," Ph.D. thesis, University of Wisconsin, 1960, p. 382; and Thomas R. Hines, *The Anarchists Conspiracy; or the Blight of 3770, A True History of the Experience of Daniel Hines as a Knight of Labor* (Boston, 1887). Cf., the fictional account by John Rolf, *Great Dream from Heaven* (New York, 1974).
4 We know little of the underclass in general and more studies are needed. See Richard Cobb, *The Police and the People: French Popular Protest, 1789–1820* (London, 1972); Cobb, "L'Affaire Perken: A Double Murder on the Franco-Dutch Border, 1809," in Cobb, *A Sense of Place* (London, 1975), pp. 49–76; Louis Chevalier, *Laboring Classes and Dangerous Classes in Paris During the First Half of the Nineteenth Century* (New York, 1973); Charles Van Onselen, "'The Regiment of the Hills': South Africa's Lumpenproletarian Army, 1890–1920," *Past & Present*, 80 (August 1978), pp. 91–128.
5 *Journal of United Labor*, September 1883, February 1884, 10 May 1884.
6 Ibid., April 1884, 10 November 1884, 10 January 1885, 25 February 1885, 10 May 1885, 21 May 1885, 10 September 1885, 25 September 1885, 25 November 1885; *Journal of the Knights of Labor*, 1 November 1894, 4 June 1896; *Ottawa Citizen*, 6 May 1890; W. E. Smith to John W. Hayes, 28 March 1889, HP. Herbert Nicholson to Powderly, 3 December 1884; J. W. O'Brien to Powderly, 22 December 1883; J. T. Carey to Powderly, 13 December 1888; D. H. Smith to Powderly, 12 August 1887, PP.
7 Martin Daly to Terence V. Powderly, 18 December 1887, PP. On the courts and expulsions see Jonathan Garlock, "The Knights of Labor Courts: A 19th Century

American Experiment with Popular Justice," paper presented to the Knights of Labor Centennial Conference, Newberry Library, Chicago, 17–19 May 1979. This paper (p. 34) notes the expulsion of one Martin Daly, a laborer, for being "a professional deadbeat." On the importance of courts and the Knights' judicial procedures in Canada see, for example, J. T. Carey to Powderly, 21 June 1888; D. B. Skelly to Powderly, 24 October 1884, PP.

8 Thomas J. O'Neil to Powderly, 30 May 1887; O'Neil to Powderly, 12 September 1887; Powderly to O'Neil, 16 June 1887; Powderly to George Tomlinson, 2 June 1888; Powderly to D. H. Smith, 20 August 1887; Powderly to W. S. Smith, 29 May 1884; Robert H. Ward to Powderly, 21 June 1888; Thomas Chittle to Powderly, 24 April 1884, PP.

9 John W. Gardner to Powderly, 24 April 1884, PP.

10 John Dickson to Powderly, 24 April 1886, PP.

11 Arthur E. Peters to Powderly, 21 February 1886; Powderly to Peters, 10 March 1886, PP.

12 Powderly to Peters, 23 December 1885; Powderly to Peters, 18 February 1886, PP.

13 J. T. Carey to Powderly, 14 September 1888, PP.

14 *Canada Labor Courier* (St. Thomas), 13 January 1887.

15 *Palladium of Labor*, 4 October 1884, 12 October 1884; *Hamilton Spectator*, 2 October 1884; Brown to Powderly, 3 December 1884; Brown to Powderly, n.d. (1884?), PP.

16 *Journal of United Labor*, 25 September 1885, 25 November 1885.

17 Thomas McGeachie to Powderly, 11 July 1887; J. T. Carey to Powderly, 14 September 1888, 24 October 1888, 17 April 1889, 19 February 1889, PP. J. W. Hayes to Frank Brown, 6 June 1893, HP.

18 W. R. James to Powderly, 23 December 1888, PP. Cf., *Palladium of Labor*, 25 August 1883, 21 February 1885; *Ottawa Citizen*, 13 November 1891; J. T. Carey to Powderly, 30 April 1888; M. H. Hiltz to Powderly, 24 November 1888; D. H. Smith to Powderly, 23 March 1887; William Cunliffe to Powderly, 17 July 1888, PP; *Record of the Proceedings of the General Assembly of the Knights of Labor, 1888*, Document 901 (St. Catharines).

19 Thomas J. O'Neil to Powderly, 15 January 1889; Nickle to Powderly, 17 January 1886; John Whetford to Powderly, 23 May 1885; R. McDougall to Powderly, 6 January 1883; C. Hayward to Powderly, 26 May 1886: R. R. Elliot to Powderly, 18 June 1888; George Collis to Powderly, 22 April 1884; Thomas E. Kilroy to Powderly, 25 June 1887; D. M. Munro to Powderly, 3 February 1886; RS LA 3449 to Powderly, 27 February 1886, PP.

20 These paragraphs drew upon "Introduction," Scrapbook 5, and Scrapbook 7 ("On the Money Question, 1878–1880"), Alexander W. Wright Papers, Public Archives of Canada, MG 29 A15 (henceforth WP); H. Charlesworth, *A Cyclopedia of Canadian Biography* (Toronto, 1919); Gregory S. Kealey, *Toronto Workers Respond to Industrial Capitalism, 1867–1892* (Toronto, 1980); Bryan D. Palmer, *A Culture in Conflict: Skilled Workers and Industrial Capitalism in Hamilton, Ontario, 1860–1914* (Montreal, 1979), pp. 97–122; Roberts, "The Problem of Independent Labour Politics"; Russell Hann, "Brainworkers and the Knights of Labor: E. E. Sheppard, Phillips Thompson, and the Toronto *News*, 1883–1887," in Gregory S. Kealey and Peter Warrian, eds., *Essays in Canadian Working-Class History* (Toronto, 1976), pp. 35–57; Bernard Ostry, "Conservatives, Liberals, and Labour in the 1880s," *Canadian Journal of Economics and Political Science*, 27 (May 1961), pp. 141–61; *Journal of United Labor*, 20 September 1888, 16 August 1888; *Belleville Intelligencer*, 24 April 1882.

21 R. J. Kerrigan, "The History of the Trades and Labor Congress of Canada," *OBU Bulletin*, 23 September–3 December 1925, in Labour Department Files, Volume 1065, Public Archives of Canada (courtesy David Frank); Kerrigan to John W. Hayes, 30 December 1894, HP.

22 The above paragraphs draw upon clippings in Scrapbook 4, Section 3, "Addresses and Editorials on behalf of the Knights of Labor in the Year 1889," WP. On other Wright lectures see *Journal of United Labor*, 30 August 1888, 11 October 1888; and on Wright's attack on another Knight of Labor, suspected of misappropriation of funds, see H. J. Skeffington to Powderly, 9 June 1889, PP.

23 See O'Neil to Powderly, 15 January 1889; J. A. Macleod to Powderly, n.d. (January 1891?); John Devlin to Powderly, 11 January 1889, PP; Adolph Glaeser to Powderly, 21 January 1889, PP; *Journal of United Labor*, 21 March 1889; George S. Warren to A. W. Wright, 20 February 1893, HP.

24 Wright to Macdonald, 11 December 1879; Wright to Macdonald, 10 May 1882; Wright to Macdonald, 29 June 1882; Wright to Macdonald, 21 August 1882; Wright to Macdonald, 2 October 1882; Wright to Macdonald, 28 December 1884; Wright to Macdonald, 4 August 1884; Wright to Macdonald, 21 August 1885; Wright to Macdonald, 6 October 1885; Wright to Macdonald, 30 October 1885, Macdonald Papers, Public Archives of Canada, MG 26A. Hereafter MP.

25 Wright to Macdonald, 17 March 1884; J. Ferguson to Macdonald, 30 April 1884, MP. Steven Langdon, *The Emergence of the Canadian Working Class Movement* (Toronto, 1975), pp. 25, 31; David Hugh Russell, "The Ontario Press and the Pacific Scandal of 1873," M.A. thesis, Queen's University, 1970, pp. 15–22; Kealey, *Toronto Workers*, pp. 138–9. On Ferguson, the Knights of Labor, and Macdonald cf., Ferguson to Macdonald, 18 September 1886; John A. Thompson (Master Workman) to Dr. John Ferguson, 13 September 1886, MP.

26 Carey to Powderly, 14 September 1888, PP.

27 See, for instance, Wright to Powderly, 25 September 1889; Wright to Powderly, 20 December 1891, PP; Wright to John W. Hayes, 20 February 1890, Letterbook I; Wright to Powderly, 6 May 1890, Letterbook I; Wright to Tracey and Russell, 18 April 1890, Letterbook I; Wright to Hayes, 8 May 1890, Letterbook I; Wright to Powderly, 3 March 1893, Letterbook I, WP. On Wright's work load see Wright to J. S. Edsall, 10 May 1890, Letterbook I; Wright to Patrick Murphy, 22 March 1892, Letterbook I; Wright to Powderly, 29 December 1893, Letterbook II, WP.

28 Wright to Thompson, 9 March 1890, Letterbook I; Wright to John Lewis Childs, 3 May 1891, Letterbook I; Wright to Powderly, 20 April 1892, Letterbook I; Wright to Powderly, 13 March 1892, Letterbook I; Wright to R. H. Agnew, 21 September 1891, Letterbook I; Wright to Robert Glocking, 9 July 1890, Letterbook I; Wright to Dower, 29 June 1892, Letterbook I; Wright to Glocking, 21 February 1894, Letterbook III; Wright to Glocking 12 March 1894, Letterbook II, WP; Wright to Powderly, 11 June 1889; Wright to Powderly, 14 March 1889; Wright to Tom O'Reilly, 27 December 1891; Wright to Powderly, 31 March 1889, PP.

29 A sample of "Spokeshave" articles are found in *Journal of United Labor*, 23 August 1888, 16 August 1888, 20 September 1888, 19 September 1889, 17 January 1889, 22 August 1889; *Journal of the Knights of Labor*, 30 October 1890, 6 November 1890, 22 October 1891, 1 January 1891, 15 January 1891, 5 February 1891, 22 September 1892.

30 Wright to Powderly, 14 August 1892; Wright to Powderly, 30 July 1893, PP.

31 See Wright to Wiman, 24 April 1891, Letterbook I; Wright to Powderly, 10 September 1893, Letterbook II; Wright to Powderly, 18 October 1893, Letterbook II; Wright to H. G. Gray, 28 February 1893, 12 October 1893, Letterbook II; Wright

to Devlin, 15 February 1894, Letterbook III; Wright to H. S. Pingree, 24 March 1894, Letterbook III, WP; Wright to Powderly, 7 January 1893; Wright to Powderly, 14 February 1893; Wright to Powderly, 24 April 1893; Wright to Powderly, 18 April 1893; Powderly to Wright, 22 April 1893, PP; Ware, *The Labor Movement in the United States*, pp. 374–5; Powderly, *The Path I Trod*, p. 306.

32 Wright to Debs, 23 January 1893, Letterbook II; Wright to Devlin, 28 February 1893, Letterbook I; Wright to Devlin, 1 March 1893, Letterbook I; Wright to W. R. Meredith, 1 March 1893, Letterbook I; Wright to Bell, 1 March 1893, Letterbook I; Wright to Debs, 24 April 1893, Letterbook II; Wright to George W. McCaddin (Master Workman, DA 49, New York), 30 May 1893, 2 June 1893, Letterbook IV: Wright to A. J. Zoller (DA 197, Jersey City), 17 July 1893, Letterbook II, WP; Wright to Powderly, 30 December 1892, PP.

33 Wright to Powderly, 8 February 1890; Wright to Powderly, 4 September 1892, PP. Cf., Wright to Powderly, 12 May 1890, PP, on a grocery store "scheme," linked to the Tennessee-based Farmers' Mutual Benefit Organization; Powderly, *The Path I Trod*, p. 366; Wright to Powderly, 30 December 1892, PP. An early Wright "scheme" culminating in a lawsuit is outlined in *World* (Toronto), 14 May 1885.

34 Wright to Powderly, 17 January 1894, Letterbook III; Wright to Lorimer, 17 January 1894, Letterbook III;. Wright to Lorimer, 31 January 1894, Letterbook III; Wright to Devlin, 21 January 1894, Letterbook III; Wright to Powderly, 31 March 1894, Letterbook III; Wright to Devlin, 10 April 1894, Letterbook III; Scrapbook 5, Clippings from *Union Printer and American Craftsman*, 1897, WP.

35 Wright to Powderly, 9 January 1895, Letterbook III; Wright to Charles E. Tuthill, 14 January 1895, Letterbook III; Wright to George B. Lane, 30 January 1895, Letterbook III; Wright to De Saville, 4 October 1894, Letterbook III, Wright to Jack (*Hamilton Spectator*), 4 October 1894, Letterbook III; Wright to DeSaville, 5 October 1894, Letterbook III; Wright to Orville Reed, 12 December 1894, Letterbook III; Wright to De Saville, 12 December 1894, Letterbook III; Wright to De Saville, 18 December 1894, Letterbook III, WP.

36 Wright to Kribs, 26 January 1895, Letterbook III; Wright to J. W. Lynn, 1 February 1895, Letterbook III; Wright to Tuthill, 22 February 1895, Letterbook III, WP.

37 Wright to Devlin, 4 December 1893, Letterbook II, WP.

38 Wright to S. W. Coombes, 29 September 1894, Letterbook III, WP. On Wright's own feelings, conditioned by his wife's illness cf., O'Reilly to Powderly, 7 October 1893, PP. Another Knight of Labor expressed similar sentiments to Wright in George S. Warren to Wright (Montreal), 20 February 1893, PP.

39 *Robertson & Cook's Toronto City Directory for 1871–1872* (Toronto, 1871), p. 89; *Fisher & Taylor's Toronto City Directory for the Year 1874* (Toronto, 1874), p. 281; Enoch P. Morgan to Macdonald, 24 February 1885, MP. See the satirical attack on Beaty in the *Grip*, 13 December 1873, cited in Roberts, "The Problem of Independent Labour Politics." On Morgan's presence in Toronto in 1873 cf., *Palladium of Labor*, 26 April 1884, quoting *Toronto Sun*, 10 April 1873, and *Toronto Leader*, n.d.

40 The above paragraphs draw upon Morgan to Powderly, 5 November 1884; J. M. Brady to W. H. Rowe, 22 August 1884; 26 August 1884, PP; *Cleveland Plain Dealer*, 26 May 1877, 22August 1877; *Cleveland Daily Herald*, 26 May 1877; *Palladium of Labor*, 23 May 1885.

41 *Palladium of Labor*, 26 April 1884. As the advertisement was placed by Morgan himself its authenticity is suspect, although other verifiable statements did prove accurate.

42 Morgan to Powderly, 5 November 1884, PP; *Howe's Camden City and County Directory, 1883–1884* (Philadelphia, 1883); *Howe's Camden City and County Directory, 1884* (Philadelphia, 1884). Morgan and Harvey also apparently published the *Jersey Free Press*, "an advertising sheet for which they obtained the patronage of advertisers by the most notorious and boldfaced lying." See *Palladium of Labor*, 8 November 1884.

43 A. J. Milliette to W. H. Rowe, 4 August 1884, 12 August 1884; Joseph Mattack to Rowe, 13 August 1884, PP.

44 Morgan to Powderly, 5 November 1884; George Collis to Powderly, 10 December 1884, PP. On the financial troubles of the paper see *Palladium of Labor*, 1 March 1884; "Recollections of John Peebles, Mayor of Hamilton, 1930–1933," 7 February 1946, Hamilton Collection, Hamilton Public Library. On Morgan's early activities and the establishment of the Co-operative Store see *Palladium of Labor*, 26 April 1884, 7 June 1884, 5 July 1884. Rowe announced the journal's termination of Morgan's and Harvey's services in the *Palladium of Labor*, 2 August 1884. Cf., ibid., 6 September 1884, 4 October 1884, 18 October 1884, 1 November 1884; *Hamilton Spectator*, 2 October 1884. The Co-operative Association's rules are found in "Rules of District Assembly 61 Knights of Labor, 1884," Public Archives of Canada.

45 E. P. Morgan and Falconer L. Harvey, *Hamilton and Its Industries: Being a Historical and Descriptive Sketch of the City and Its Public and Private Institutions, Manufacturing and Industrial Interests, Public Citizens, Etc.* (Hamilton, 1884). The venture may have been quite profitable: the publishers claimed there was a demand for 3,000 more copies than were printed in the first edition.

46 Morgan to Powderly, 5 November 1884; Powderly to Smith, 7 October 1884; Powderly to Morgan, 16 November 1884, PP. Cf., *Palladium of Labor*, 12 October 1884.

47 *Record of the Proceedings of the Eighth Regular Session of the General Assembly of the Knights of Labor, Philadelphia, 1884* (Philadelphia, 1884), pp. 563–5; Morgan to Powderly, 5 November 1884; Powderly to Morgan, 16 November 1884; Powderly to Collis, n.d. (November–December 1884); Powderly to E. S. Gilbert, 23 December 1884, PP.

48 Collis, Chairman, Publishing Committee, Hamilton, to Officers of the Court of LA 2225, 28 August 1884, PP.

49 Collis to Powderly, 1 December 1884; 27 December 1884 (containing undated *Hamilton Spectator* clipping on Morgan's arrest); A. J. Welch, Judge Advocate, LA 2225, to D. B. Skelly, 13 December 1884; Welch to Powderly, 18 December 1884; Powderly to E. S. Gilbert, 23 December 1884, PP; *Palladium of Labor*, 27 December 1884.

50 Gilbert to Powderly, 8 November 1884, PP.

51 See *Palladium of Labor*, 23 August 1884; *Journal of United Labor*, 10 November 1884; Gilbert to Powderly, 8 November 1884; Herman Klinger to Powderly, 3 November 1884; Committee Appointed by LA 2225 in Klinger Case to Powderly, 15 November 1884; Powderly to Fred Aldridge, 19 November 1884, PP.

52 D. B. Skelly to Powderly, 15 December 1884, PP. This source, written by a member of LA 2225, seeks to discredit the act of DA 61, and defends LA 2132. For a different view see Collis to Powderly, 23 November 1884, PP.

53 Collis to Powderly, 23 November 1884, PP.

54 Skelly to Powderly, 15 December 1884, PP. On Skelly's long-standing efforts to exploit the Tory patronage system see Miscellaneous Papers (1872–3), D. B. Skelly to John A. Macdonald, 1872; John A. Macdonald to Ferguson, 5 March

1872; Skelly to Ferguson, 12 April 1872; Skelly to Macdonald, 6 June 1879, MP. Skelly thus corresponded with the same Ferguson that Wright had referred to in his 1884 letter to Macdonald.

55 A. J. Welch, Judge Advocate, LA 2225, to Skelly, 13 December 1884; Welch to Powderly, 18 December 1884, PP.

56 W. H. Bews to Powderly, 14 January 1885; Powderly to Fred Aldridge, 16 January 1885, PP; *Palladium of Labor*, 12 October 1884.

57 Morgan to Powderly, 5 November 1884, PP, establishes the Ailes–Morgan relationship.

58 On the Co-operative Store dispute see *Palladium of Labor*, 21 February 1885, 28 February 1885, 7 March 1885; *Hamilton Spectator*, 24 February 1885; *Toronto World*, 20 February 1885; D. J. O'Donoghue to Powderly, 18 March 1885, PP.

59 *Journal of United Labor*, 21 February 1885.

60 *Palladium of Labor*, 21 February 1885.

61 E. P. Morgan to Macdonald, 24 February 1885, MP. Morgan had enlisted the aid of one Charles Smith of the Hamilton Conservative Association, not to be confused with his enemy of the same name. This Smith was probably the printer mentioned in the *Palladium of Labor*, 26 April 1884, and may have had a bone to pick with the editor of the *Palladium*, W. H. Rowe. As we have seen in Chapter 4, Rowe's relations with Hamilton printers were anything but cordial.

62 *Journal of United Labor*, 25 February 1885.

63 Ibid., 10 May 1885. On McLaren's role at Ailes' trial see *Hamilton Spectator*, 24 February 1885.

64 *Palladium of Labor*, 21 March 1885.

65 See Ware, *Labor Movement in the United States*, pp. 103–16, on other splits from the Order, often more principled; *Palladium of Labor*, 27 October 1883. The birth of the UBUL and continued attacks on Morgan are outlined in ibid., 25 April 1885, 30 May 1885, 23 May 1885. On T. B. Barry's American effort to organize a radical split from the Knights of Labor, under the name of the Brotherhood of United Labor (similar in name, but not in purpose, to the Hamilton venture) see Richard J. Oestreicher, "The Limits of Labor Radicalism: Tom Barry and the Knights of Labor," paper presented to the Knights of Labor Centennial Conference, Newberry Library, Chicago, 17–19 May 1979.

66 *Palladium of Labor*, 20 June 1885.

67 *Hamilton Spectator*, 23 April 1885, 4 May 1885; *Palladium of Labor*, 11 April 1885, 18 April 1885, 25 April 1885, 16 May 1885.

68 *Palladium of Labor*, 29 August 1885.

69 Ibid., 19 September 1885.

70 Ibid., 22 May 1886.

71 Ibid., 11 April 1885.

72 "Complementary Banquet to Mr. Phillips Thompson, Albert Hall, Toronto," 17 January 1882, Correspondence File, 1907–1923, Phillips Thompson Papers, Public Archives of Canada, MG 29 D 71.

73 *Palladium of Labor*, 11 April 1885.

74 Ibid., Cf., Rowe's note in the *Craftsman*, 21 February 1885.

75 *Palladium of Labor*, 11 April 1885, 22 August 1885, 22 May 1886. Cf., Thomas Brick's letter disassociating himself from the paper, and other commentary, in ibid., 4 April 1885, 16 May 1885, 1 August 1885. On the Home Rule episode, filtered to Powderly by O'Donoghue, who sought to discredit DA 61 to Toronto's (and his) advantage, see D. J. O'Donoghue to Powderly, 10 August 1885, 19 August 1885; Powderly to O'Donoghue, 14 August 1885, PP. The issue of Canadian autonomy will be considered in detail in Chapter 7 on politicians and the Knights

of Labor, and probably engendered some rivalries among different Canadian DAs. Note D. J. O'Donoghue to Powderly (Toronto), 19 October 1885, PP: "The malignity of that fellow *Collis* of Hamilton, in aspersing my character, in doubting my sincerity, has cost me more than passing pain. The wretch!"

76 *Hamilton Spectator*, 23 April 1885; *Palladium of Labor*, 23 May 1885.

77 *Palladium of Labor*, 18 April 1885, 25 April 1885, 2 May 1885, 16 May 1885, 30 May 1885, 6 June 1885, 25 July 1885, 19 September 1885; *Hamilton Spectator*, 18 April 1885; *The Craftsman*, 3 October 1885. Skelly had, earlier in the spring, sought the city position of coal weigher. Described as "a noted button-hole politician," he was forced to withdraw his application. See *Palladium of Labor*, 28 March 1885, 1 April 1885.

78 See *Record of the Proceedings of the General Assembly, Knights of Labor, 1883* (Philadelphia, 1883), pp. 394, 485–6; *Proceedings, General Assembly, 1884*, p. 790; *Proceedings, General Assembly, 1885*, p. 174; *Journal of United Labor*, August 1883, 31 March 1884; *Hamilton Spectator*, 24 February 1885; Collis to Powderly, 23 November 1884; Bews to Powderly, 14 January 1885; Powderly to Smith, 7 October 1884, PP.

79 Cobb, *A Sense of Place*, pp. 3–4.

80 See J. G. Kilt to Powderly, 15 April 1894; Powderly to Kilt, 16 April 1894, PP; Gray to Hayes, 13 February 1894, 15 February 1894; Hayes to Gray, 21 February 1894; Gray, "For the Journal of the Knights of Labor," sent to Hayes, n.d. (February 1894?), HP.

81 *Toronto Mail*, 7 December 1888; William Keys, ed., *Capital and Labor; Containing the Views of Eminent Men of the United States and Canada on the Labor Question, Social Reform and Other Economic Subjects, Illustrated* (Montreal, 1904); *Journal of the Knights of Labor*, 30 April 1896, January 1901, July 1901, February 1902.

82 Fields to Hayes, 5 February 1896, HP.

83 See the sophisticated discussion of bureaucracy in Peter Friedlander, *The Emergence of a UAW Local, 1936–1939: A Study in Class and Culture* (Pittsburgh, 1975), esp. pp. 93–7. Note the general discussion in Warren Van Tine, *The Making of the Labor Bureaucrat, 1870–1920* (Amherst, Mass., 1973).

84 *National Labor Tribune*, 1 August 1885; *Palladium of Labor*, 21 February 1885; T. W. Brosnan quoted in John P. McGauhey Papers, Minnesota Historical Society.

## 6. The Order in politics

1 *Labor Union*, 17 March 1883; Henry Grace to Powderly, 16 December 1884, PP.

2 Macdonald to Sir Charles Tupper, 21 June 1886, in Sir Joseph Pope, ed., *The Correspondence of Sir John Macdonald* (Toronto, 1921), p. 382; Allchin to Powderly, 20 October 1884, PP.

3 George Havens to Powderly, 4 January 1883, PP. Gregory S. Kealey, *Toronto Workers Respond to Industrialism, 1867–1892* (Toronto, 1980), pp. 216–36. See also *The Carpenter*, 2 (November 1882), 3 (January 1883).

4 Morris to Macdonald, 15 January 1883, MP.

5 See Martin Robin, *Radical Politics and Canadian Labour, 1880–1930* (Kingston, 1968), pp. 86, 91, 115, 123–5; "Labor Owes Much to Fighting Quality of Allan Studholme," in *The Hamilton and District Trades and Labor Council, 60th Anniversary, Diamond Jubilee, 1888–1948* (Hamilton, 1948), p. 13; *Industrial Banner*, June 1908, December 1906, January 1907.

6 "Recollections of John Peebles, Mayor of Hamilton, 1930–1933," 7 February 1946, Hamilton Collection, Hamilton Public Library; *Palladium of Labor*, 3 No-

vember 1883, 27 October 1883, 24 November 1883, 31 May 1884; *Hamilton Spectator*, 21 June 1884; William Bews to Powderly, 28 December 1882, PP.

7 *Palladium of Labor*, 22 August 1885, 19 September 1884.

8 Ibid., 20 October 1883, 3 November 1883, 7 June 1884.

9 Biographical details are from *Labor Union*, 3 February 1883. For Macdonald see Joyce M. Bellamy and John Saville, *Dictionary of Labour Biography*, I (London, 1974).

10 See *Labor Union*, 3 February 1883, 17 February 1883, 24 February 1883; *Palladium of Labor*, 8 December 1883, 12 April 1884; *Hamilton Spectator*, 1 February 1883; on Witton see Bryan D. Palmer, *A Culture in Conflict: Skilled Workers and Industrial Capitalism in Hamilton, Ontario, 1860–1914* (Montreal, 1979), pp. 145–9.

11 Gibson to Powderly, 7 February 1883; Powderly to Gibson, 9 February 1883, PP.

12 *Labor Union*, 3 February 1883, 10 February 1883, 17 February 1883; *Hamilton Spectator*, 12 February 1883.

13 The results were:

| | | % | |
|---|---|---|---|
| Gibson | 2,077 | 39.8 | |
| Martin | 1,922 | 36.8 | |
| Williams | 1,222 | 23.4 | |
| Total | 5,221 | 100.0 | |
| Eligible voters | | | 8,345 |
| Turnout | | | 62.5% |

All election results in this chapter are from Sessional Papers – provincial and federal. See Michael Doucet, "Working Class Housing in a Small Nineteenth Century Canadian City: Hamilton, Ontario, 1852–1881," in Kealey and Warrian, eds., *Essays in Canadian Working Class History* (Toronto, 1976), pp. 83–105.

14 *Labor Union*, 3 March 1883. Cf., *Hamilton Spectator*, 28 February 1883; and the letter from Oshawa's John A. Brown in *Palladium of Labor*, 8 December 1883.

15 *Trade Union Advocate*, 1 February 1883.

16 Ibid., 11 January 1883.

17 Ibid., 11, 18, 25 January 1883.

18 Ibid., 25 January, 8 February 1883. See also TTLC, *Minutes*, 19 January, 2 February 1883 and *Globe*, 5, 9 February 1883.

19 *Trade Union Advocate*, 8 February 1883; *Globe*, 5 February 1883; Gregory S. Kealey, "Alfred Oakley," *Dictionary of Canadian Biography*, XI (Toronto, forthcoming).

20 *Globe*, 8 February 1883, 15 February 1883.

21 For more detail see Kealey, *Toronto Workers*. On the Sons of England see John S. King, *An Account of the Origin and Early History of the Sons of England Benevolent Society* (Toronto, 1891).

22 Full results were:

| Toronto East | | % | Toronto West | | % |
|---|---|---|---|---|---|
| Morris | 2,135 | 47.9 | Clarke | 2,634 | 52 |
| Leys | 2,011 | 45.2 | Carter | 2,427 | 48 |
| Heakes | 308 | 6.9 | | | |
| Total | 4,454 | 100.0 | Total | 5,061 | 100.0 |
| Eligible voters | | 8,909 | | | 11,453 |
| Turnout | | 50% | | | 48.5% |

23 *Trade Union Advocate*, 1 March 1883; *The Wage Worker*, 14 March 1883.
24 Small to Macdonald, 10 April 1883, MP.
25 *Palladium of Labor*, 25 August 1883.
26 Ibid., 28 September 1883.
27 Ibid., 17 November, 13, 20 October 1883.
28 Ibid., 24 November 1883.
29 Ibid., December 1883–January 1884, especially 5, 12 January 1884; *Journal of United Labor*, 10 April 1884; George N. Havens to Powderly, 4 January 1883, PP.
30 Ibid., 31 May 1884.
31 *Journal of United Labor*, 10 April 1884.
32 D. B. Skelly to Powderly, 15 December 1884, PP.
33 *Palladium of Labor*, 5 December 1884.
34 Ibid., 28 November, 5 December 1885, 15 May 1886; *Report of the Royal Commission on the Relations of Labor and Capital in Canada*, *"Ontario Evidence,"* II (Ottawa, 1889), p. 818. On Brick's Corktown background see J. G. O'Neill, "Chronicles of Corktown," *Wentworth Bygones*, 5 (1963), pp. 29–39.
35 *Palladium of Labor*, 9 May, 4 July 1885, 1 May 1886.
36 This account draws upon Kealey, *Toronto Workers*, pp. 83–97, 216–36. Cf., TTLC, *Minutes*, 18 April 1884, 2 May 1884, 16 May 1884; *Globe*, 21 July 1884; H. E. Griffiths to Powderly, 14 July 1884, PP. No doubt the carpenters' opposition was partially predicated on the hostility their international leader P. J. McGuire projected. McGuire had been an early socialist member of the Order but was expelled in the "Cuno Affair" of 1881–2, as Norman Ware argued, "after he kept up a running fight within and without the Order." See Norman J. Ware, *The Labor Movement in the United States, 1860–1890: A Study in Democracy* (New York, 1964), pp. 103–9.
37 *Globe*, 14 October 1884.
38 Boultbee to Macdonald, 12 September 1884; Boultbee to Macdonald, 29, 30 December 1884, MP.
39 Macpherson to Macdonald, 27 December 1884, MP; *World*, 20 December 1884, 3 January 1885; *London Advertiser*, 20 December 1884.
40 *Globe*, 22 December 1884; Boultbee to Macdonald, 6 January 1885, MP.
41 *World*, 9 October, 7 December 1885.
42 TTLC, *Minutes*, 4, 14, 18, 29 December 1885.
43 *Globe*, 10 December 1885; TTLC, *Minutes*, 14 December 1885; *World*, 15 December 1885.
44 *News*, 4 January 1886. The only Locals that failed to do so were shoemakers' Pioneer LA 2211 and harnessmakers Queen City LA 2782. The *Palladium of Labor* had endorsed Howland on 5 December 1885.
45 *World*, 5 January 1886.
46 See the rather cynical Desmond Morton, *Mayor Howland* (Toronto, 1973). Here Morton confuses to some degree the correct working-class tactics for contemporary Toronto labor in urban politics with the 1880s case. On the Order and temperance see D. J. O'Donoghue to Powderly, 16 March 1885, PP; *Globe*, 14 October 1884; *Mail* 9, 10 April 1894; *Globe*, 10 April 1894; *World*, 10 April 1894.
47 *News*, 5 January 1886.
48 *World*, 5 January 1886; *News*, 5 January 1886, 6 January 1886, 9 January 1886; O'Donoghue to Powderly, 7 January 1886, PP.
49 *World*, 1 January 1885, 13, 16 March 1886; TTLC, *Minutes*, 19 March 1886; Piper to Macdonald, 2, 3 February 1886, MP. For additional discussion see Kealey, *Toronto Workers*, pp. 83–97, 216–36.
50 O'Donoghue to Powderly, 29 March 1886, PP. Tory printers tried to mount op-

position to this settlement within the TTU but were outvoted. They had argued that Cameron had not consulted with them about the composition of the arbitration board. As the *World* explained, "Some of the malcontents saw the cloven hoof of politics sticking out of the award." See *World*, 12 April 1886.

51 "A Knight of Labor," Woodstock, to Macdonald, 1 February 1885, MP.

52 A. B. Ingram to Macdonald, 14 January 1886, MP.

53 Samuel Beal to Macdonald, 4 December 1886, MP.

54 For invitation see H. J. Guppy to Macdonald, 21 September 1886, MP; for speech and procession see Sir John A. Macdonald, *Speech to the Workingmen's Liberal Conservative Association of Ottawa and La Cercle Lafontaine* (Ottawa, 1886); *World*, 9 October 1886. On the question of factory acts and constitutional jurisdiction see Eugene Forsey, "A Note on the Dominion Factory Bills of the 1880s," *Canadian Journal of Economics and Political Science*, 13 (1947), pp. 580–3. For favourable labor comment on Mowat's action see *Canada Labor Courier*, as quoted in *London Advertiser*, 13 October 1886. For background, see also *Globe*, 16 September 1886.

55 See John Thompson to Macdonald, 3 July 1886, MP, recommending master carpenter Michael Walsh of Halifax ("although a master carpenter and to that – an employer, he is not by any means a capitalist") and Thompson to Macdonald, 2 September 1886, MP, regarding terms.

56 For studies of the Commission see Greg Kealey, ed., *Canada Investigates Industrialism* (Toronto, 1973), ix–xxvii; and Fernand Harvey, *Révolution industrielle et travailleurs: Une enquête sur les rapports entre le capital et le travail au Québec à la fin du 19e siècle* (Montreal, 1978). See also Susan Trofimenkoff, "One Hundred and Two Muffled Voices: Canada's Industrial Women in the 1880s," *Atlantis*, 3 (1977), pp. 67–82.

57 For statistical evidence on this point see Harvey, *Révolution industrielle*, pp. 50–2. If we reconstruct Harvey's table (p. 61) using simpler class categories, we discover that of the approximately 150 royal commissioners considered between 1867 and 1966, there were only eight workers.

58 Bunting to Macdonald, 10 September 1886, MP.

59 H. E. Clarke to Macdonald, 21 September 1886, MP; Macdonald to H. E. Clarke, 30 September 1886, Clarke Papers, Public Archives of Canada (PAC).

60 Macdonald to Clarke, 18 October 1886, 21 October 1886, 7 December 1886, Clarke Papers; *Canadian Labor Reformer*, 9 October 1886; and Clarke to Macdonald, 19 October 1886; Alfred Boultbee to Macdonald, 25 October 1886; F. A. Barwick to Macdonald, 25 October 1886; Alexander Morris to Macdonald, 26 October 1886; E. F. Clarke to Macdonald, 29 November 1886; H. E. Clarke to Macdonald, 1 December 1886, MP.

61 *Canadian Labor Reformer*, 9 October, 6 November 1886, 11 December 1886; *Canada Labor Courier*, 30 December 1886; *Palladium of Labor*, 11 December 1886. For Knights, see *World*, 11 December 1886. For TTLC, see *Minutes*, 18 December 1886; *Globe*, 18 December 1886; and *World*, 18 December 1886.

62 Hamilton General Labor Union to Macdonald, 12 January 1886, MP; *Palladium*, 11 December 1886. For McLean, see John Carling to Macdonald, 1, 28 July 1887. For Ottawa, see the quite extraordinary set of correspondence surrounding the demands of the Workingmen's Liberal Conservative Association: Guppy to Carling, 7 December 1886; Teague to Macdonald, 21 July 1887; Urias Carson to Macdonald, 9 September 1887; P. Robillard to Macdonald, 10 September 1887; Guppy et al. to Macdonald, 13 September 1887; Stewart and Teague to Macdonald, 21 September 1887; Perly to Macdonald, 22 September 1887; Teague to Macdonald, 24 September 1887; and La Cercle Lafontaine to Macdonald, 3 November 1887. All are in MP.

63 For a discussion of the Mowat government and labor, see Margaret Evans, "Oliver Mowat and Ontario: A Study in Political Success," Ph.D. thesis, University of Toronto, 1967, esp. ch. 3. Somewhat uncritical, Evans argues that Mowat was motivated by "genuine sympathy for the labouring man." (p. 82). See also the even more eulogistic reports on Ontario labor legislation prepared by D. J. O'Donoghue for the Bureau of Industry, especially in the *Annual Report* for 1889, pp. 70–7.

64 For biographical information see *Canadian Parliamentary Companion* (1887); J. K. Johnson, ed., *Canadian Directory of Parliament* (Ottawa, 1968), p. 286; and "An Old Campaigner Speaks: Electioneering Harder in Old Days But Opponents Held More Respect for One Another, Declares 'Andy' Ingram," undated clipping, *St. Thomas Times-Journal*, c. 1932.

65 A. B. Ingram to Powderly, 15 January 1886; Powderly to Ingram, 20 January 1886, PP.

66 *St. Thomas Daily Times*, 16 February 1886, 16 July 1886.

67 Ibid., 16 July 1886, 23 July 1886; *Canada Labor Courier*, 29 July 1886; A. B. Ingram to Powderly, 26 July 1886, PP.

68 *News*, 20, 24 July 1886; *Palladium of Labor*, 24 July 1886, 14 August 1886, 21 August 1886; *St. Thomas Daily Times*, 25 July 1886, 3 August 1886, 25 August 1886; *Canadian Labor Reformer*, 18 September 1886.

69 The above account draws upon Barbara A. McKenna, "The Decline of the Liberal Party in Elgin County," unpublished paper presented to the Canadian Historical Association, London meetings, 1978; *St. Thomas Daily Times*, November–December 1886; *Canada Labor Courier*, 30 December 1886; Warren Cron Miller, ed., *Vignettes of Early St. Thomas: An Anthology of the Life and Times of Its First Century* (St. Thomas, 1967), p. 152.

70 For material on Garson see William Garson to T. V. Powderly, 21 March 1884 and 22 October 1885, PP. On the election see Ontario, *Sessional Papers*, No. 13, 1887, pp. 45–6. The selected votes were:

| | Garson | Towers | Eligible voters | % turnout |
|---|---|---|---|---|
| Merritton | 177 | 109 | 418 | 66 |
| Beamsville | 99 | 47 | 211 | 69 |
| St. Catharines | 861 | 749 | 2804 | 57 |

The turnout in the entire riding was 63%. Cf. *Welland Tribune*, 31 December 1886; *Ottawa Citizen* 13 December 1886.

71 See *London Advertiser*, 13 December 1886; *Ottawa Citizen*, 15 December 1886; *Sarnia Observer*, 10 September 1886, 7 January 1887; *Palladium of Labor*, 18 December 1886; *Canada Labor Courier*, 13 January 1887; *Canadian Labor Reformer*, 4, 18 December 1886; *Globe*, 8 December 1886; *News*, 22 December 1886; *Toronto World*, 2 December 1886. Wright's Liberal counterpart, and strongest opponent, D. J. O'Donoghue, drew a similar attack earlier in the year as he collected his government salary and traveled across the province in the interests of the Order. See *Ottawa Citizen*, 2 March 1886. The official returns show that Wright won only two urban polls in Sarnia (of seven) and none elsewhere. Ontario, *Sessional Papers*, No. 13, 1887, pp. 41–2. In western Ontario Wright was denounced as a "political economist . . . posing as the candidate of the labour interest." See *London Advertiser*, 21 December 1886.

72 For the general contours of the London working class in this period, see Bryan Palmer, "'Give us the road and we will run it:' The Social and Cultural Matrix of an Emerging Labour Movement," in Kealey and Warrian, eds., *Essays in Canadian Working Class History* (Toronto, 1976), pp. 106–24. See also R. H. Hessel, "The

Labour Movement in London," *Western Ontario Historical Notes*, 21 (1965), and W. L. Davis, "A History of the Early Labour Movement in London, Ontario," M.A. thesis, University of Western Ontario, 1930. This brief outline draws upon *London Advertiser*, 5 January, 4 June, 8 September, 6, 13 October, 5 November, 16 December 1886; *Palladium of Labor*, 6 November 1886. Scarrow would go down to defeat in the first week of the new year, losing by 900 votes (2296 to 1369). See *London Advertiser*, 6 January 1887.

73 *Palladium of Labor*, 27 November 1886; *Labor Union*, 17 March 1883; *London Advertiser*, 20 November 1886; *Ottawa Citizen*, 10 December 1886.

74 *London Advertiser*, 24 November 1886, 9 December 1886, 10 December 1886. On temperance support in the city see *Iron Molders' International Journal*, 31 July 1886; *London Advertiser*, 10 July 1886. On Peddle and the Women's Christian Temperance Union see *London Advertiser*, 13 December 1886, 17 December 1886.

75 *London Advertiser*, 9 December 1886, 11 December 1886, 16 December 1886; *Palladium of Labor*, 27 November 1886, 11 December 1886; Hewit to Powderly, 13 December 1886, PP.

76 *London Advertiser*, 9 December 1886, 7 December 1886. Note letters and reports in ibid., 16 December–18 December 1886. Cf., *Palladium of Labor*, 27 November 1886.

77 *London Advertiser*, 22 December 1886.

78 *Canada Labor Courier*, 30 December 1886; *London Advertiser*, 29–30 December 1886, 7 January 1887, 11 January 1887.

79 See *Palladium of Labor*, 5 June, 19 June, 3 July 1886, especially the satirical column "Hubbub Hall" by the astute political observer "Picket."

80 W. W. Buchanan to Powderly, 3 May 1886, PP; *Palladium of Labor*, 4, 7, 11 December 1886; *Evening Palladium*, 18 December 1886. Considerable debate raged in Hamilton labor-reform circles over the tactics to be employed in the forthcoming provincial and federal campaigns. Ironically enough, Racey had been one of those who argued that they should run a candidate only in the federal election. But others carried the day, including John Peebles who defended involvement in both contests. Alluding to the votes cast for Ed Williams in 1883, Peebles claimed that "the old 1200 vote will be on hand." Those who, like James Henigan, suggested that the labor reformers should stay out of the provincial campaign because of the late date and because the Grit candidate, Gibson, was too popular with the workers, lost the day. See *Hamilton Spectator*, 12, 16, 26, 27 November, 24 December 1886; *London Advertiser*, 25 November 1886. In 1888 Racey left Hamilton to serve in the China mission. See Bryan D. Palmer, *A Culture in Conflict: Skilled Workers and Industrial Capitalism in Hamilton, Ontario, 1860–1914* (Montreal, 1979), p. 172.

81 *News*, 27 November 1886. Burns was also active in temperance and friendly-society circles and had grown to maturity in Hamilton. See the sketches in *Hamilton Spectator*, 26 November 1886, 9 December 1886.

82 *Palladium of Labor*, 4 December 1886; Freed to Powderly, 2 December 1886, PP. The attack on Burns must have seemed wholly justified to the labor-reform group, for the Tory molder had himself served on the independent labor supporters' committee to prepare a platform for the coming electoral struggles. See *Hamilton Spectator*, 20 November 1886.

83 *London Free Press*, 26 November 1886, as cited by Peter Dembski, "William Ralph Meredith: Leader of the Conservative Opposition in Ontario, 1878–1894," Ph.D. thesis, University of Guelph, 1977, p. 388.

84 *Palladium of Labor*, 4 December 1886; *Hamilton Spectator*, 27 November 1886.

85 *Palladium of Labor*, 7 December 1886.

86 *News*, 14 December 1886; *Hamilton Spectator*, 27 November 1886, 29 November

1886. The Palace Roller-rink meeting was the culmination of much political work. See *Hamilton Spectator*, 20 November 1886, 4 December 1886, 7 December 1886, 8 December 1886, 14 December 1886; *Evening Palladium*, 18 December 1886.

87 *Evening Palladium*, 18 December 1886; *Hamilton Spectator*, 22 December 1886. The official returns were:

| | | % |
|---|---|---|
| J. M. Gibson | 3,068 | 44.5 |
| J. Burns | 2,633 | 38.2 |
| J. H. Racey | 1,188 | 17.2 |
| Total | 6,889 | 99.9 |
| Eligible voters | 10,969 | |
| Turnout | 62.8% | |

88 *News*, 19 February 1886.

89 Wright to Macdonald, 9 June 1886, MP.

90 TLC, *Proceedings*, 1886, pp. 4, 12, 20–4.

91 Morris to Macdonald, 26 October 1886; R. A. Barwick to Macdonald, 25 October 1886, MP.

92 *News*, 26 November 1886; *World*, 17, 26 November 1886.

93 *News*, 1 November 1886, 13 November 1886; TTLC, *Minutes*, 5 November 1886; *Telegram*, 6 November 1886; *World*, 13 November 1886.

94 *News*, 15, 20, 24, 25 November 1886; *World*, 20, 24, 25 November 1886; *Globe*, 20 November 1886; *Mail*, 20 November 1886; *London Advertiser*, 22, 26 November 1886; TTLC, *Minutes*, 19 November 1886; *Palladium of Labor*, 27 November 1886; *Canadian Labor Reformer*, 27 November 1886. On McCormack and Royal Commission see McCormack to Macdonald, 21 September 1886, MP.

95 For convention accounts see *World*, *News*, *Globe*, 1 December 1886; and *Canadian Labor Reformer*, 4 December 1886.

96 *World*, 1 December 1886, 17 December 1886, citing the *Canadian Baptist; Palladium of Labor*, 13 December 1884.

97 *World*, 1 December 1886.

98 *News*, 2 December 1886; TTLC, *Minutes*, 3 December 1886; *Mail*, 9 December 1886.

99 *World*, 3 December 1886.

100 *World*, *News*, 7 December 1886.

101 *World*, 7, 11, 14, 16, 18 December 1886; *Mail*, 9 December 1886; *Globe*, 16, 18 December 1886; *News*, 8, 14, 16 December 1886; TTLC, *Minutes*, 18 December 1886.

102 *News*, *World*, *Globe*, 20 December 1886, 25 December 1886.

103 This paragraph is based on a scrutiny of the results:

| | | % |
|---|---|---|
| E. F. Clarke | 7,032 | 47.1 |
| H. E. Clarke | 6,883 | 46.1 |
| John Leys | 5,380 | 36.0 |
| Charles March | 4,055 | 27.2 |
| John Roney | 3,408 | 22.9 |
| No. of votes | 26,758 | |
| Actual no. voters | 14,916 | |
| Eligible voters | 33,296 | |
| Turnout | 44.8% | |

104 The ward returns allow a closer examination of voting patterns:

| | E. F. Clarke | H. E. Clarke | Leys | March | Roney | Actual no. voters |
|---|---|---|---|---|---|---|
| St. Andrew's | 678 | 651 | 476 | 529 | 458 | 1535 |
| St. David's | 1,026 | 993 | 635 | 425 | 335 | 1882 |
| St. James' | 655 | 647 | 713 | 288 | 200 | 1333 |
| St. John's | 795 | 764 | 504 | 412 | 359 | 1588 |
| St. Patrick's | 1,152 | 1,118 | 747 | 671 | 617 | 2387 |
| St. George | 357 | 342 | 356 | 225 | 143 | 836 |
| St. Lawrence | 456 | 448 | 433 | 305 | 195 | 1037 |
| St. Paul | 312 | 309 | 289 | 165 | 140 | 679 |
| St. Thomas | 491 | 489 | 507 | 203 | 127 | 1127 |
| St. Stephen's | 650 | 660 | 371 | 510 | 544 | 1457 |
| Parkdale | 169 | 176 | 157 | 102 | 105 | 407 |
| St. Matthew's | 205 | 205 | 130 | 133 | 120 | 445 |
| St. Mark's | 86 | 81 | 62 | 87 | 65 | 203 |
| Total | 7,032 | 6,883 | 5,380 | 4,055 | 3,408 | 14,916 |

For results and comment, *cf.*, *News*, *World*, and *Globe*, 29, 30 December 1886; and *Canadian Labor Reformer*, 1, 8 January 1887.

105 See *News*, 29, 30, 31 December 1886, 3, 4, 5, January 1887; *Mail*, *World*, 4, 5, January 1887.

106 *World*, 20 January 1887; *Mail*, 24 January 1887.

107 See, for instance, O'Keefe to Macdonald, 9 February 1887, MP; O'Donoghue to Powderly, 10 November 1886, PP; *Canadian Labor Reformer*, 29 January 1887; *Daily Standard*, 27 January 1887; *News*, 10 November 1886; 2, 3 February 1887; *World*, 5, 10 February 1887; Edward Blake, *Speeches in the Dominion Election Campaign of 1887* (Toronto, 1887), esp. pp. 329–75.

108 TTLC, *Minutes*, 21 January 1887; *World*, 19 February 1887; *News*, 2, 8, 11 February 1887; *World*, 8 February 1887; and *Globe*, 8, 11 February.

109 On Sheppard see Russell Hann, "Brainworkers and the Knights of Labor: E. E. Sheppard, Phillips Thompson, and the Toronto *News*, 1883–1887," in Kealey and Warrian, eds., *Essays in Canadian Working Class History* (Toronto, 1976), pp. 35–57; *News*, 16 February 1887.

110 *News*, 9, 16, 18 February 1887; *Canadian Labor Reformer*, 12 February 1887.

111 West Toronto returns:

| | | % |
|---|---|---|
| F. C. Denison | 3,895 | 53.2 |
| E. E. Sheppard | 3,428 | 46.8 |
| Total votes | 7,323 | |
| Total eligible | 13,781 | |
| Turnout | 52.4% | |

East Toronto returns:

| | | % |
|---|---|---|
| Alfred Jury | 1,603 | 34.7 |
| E. A. Macdonald | 164 | 3.5 |
| John Small | 2,858 | 61.8 |
| Total votes | 4,625 | |
| Total eligible | 9,925 | |
| Turnout | 46.6% | |

Macdonald ran as an independent without the backing of either major party. For comparative data see Kealey, *Toronto Workers*, Appendix IV, pp. 330–6.

112 *World*, 26 February 1887; *News*, 23 February 1887; *Canadian Labor Reformer*, 26 February 1887.

113 Palmer, *A Culture in Conflict*, pp. 80, 148, 299; *News*, 5 February 1887; *Hamilton Spectator*, 7 January 1887–24 February 1887.

114 The results were:

| | | % |
|---|---|---|
| Brown (Cons.) | 3,574 | 52.2 |
| McKay (Cons.) | 3,471 | 51.2 |
| Walters (Lab.) | 3,410 | 48.8 |
| Burns (Ref.) | 3,408 | 48.8 |
| Total votes | 13,863 | |
| Voters | 6,978[a] | |
| Eligible | 9,526 | |
| Turnout | 75.4% | |

[a] Only approximate because some voters may have cast only one vote. Quotations from Brick and others are from *Hamilton Spectator*, 24 February 1887. On Studholme see Palmer, *A Culture in Conflict*, pp. 168, 182, 211, 327–31.

115 *Evening Palladium*, 18 December 1886; O'Donoghue to Powderly, 7 April 1887, PP.

116 *News*, 24 February 1887.

117 The above draws upon *Brantford Courier*, 4 January 1886, 15 April 1886, 28 December 1886; *Brantford Expositor*, 16 April 1886, 20 August 1886, 24 September 1886, 17, 31 December 1886, 7 January 1887, 4 February 1887; *Palladium of Labor*, 17, 31 July 1886, 14 August 1886, 6 November 1886; *Iron Molders' International Journal*, 31 January 1890.

118 *Expositor*, 4 February 1887; *Welland Tribune*, 19 February 1887.

119 *Palladium of Labor*, 23, 30 October 1886; Victor Lauriston, *Romantic Kent: The Story of a County* (Chatham, 1952), pp. 586–91; *Canada Labour Courier*, 13 Jan. 1887.

120 Sullivan to Powderly, 1 February 1887, PP; *Brockville Recorder*, 4 January 1888. Our thanks to Peter DeLottinville for the information on the cotton mill.

121 *Brockville Recorder*, 16 December 1887; *Gananoque Reporter*, 13 December 1887, 9 June 1888, 5, 12 January 1889; Gordon Bishop, "A Brief History of Trade Unions in Gananoque," and "Recollections of the Amalgamated," n.p., n.d. (These pamphlets were published by the United Steelworkers of America, Kingston Sub-District Office, c. the late 1940s.)

122 *Brockville Recorder*, 2 June 1887, 24 December 1887, 10 January 1888; *British Whig* (Kingston), 9 June 1887; *Gananoque Reporter*, 2 November 1888. For the capital city see *Ottawa Citizen*, 3, 16, 27 May, 3, 8, 30 July, 7 October, 21, 26 November, 18 December 1890. On similar events in Hull see *Citizen*, 13, 17, 21, 27 January 1891, where the Order ran a candidate unsuccessfully in the mayoralty race. "Hullite" claimed that the defeat was a consequence of coercion and a reduced voters' list, arguing that "those who now ridicule the efforts of the labor party in Hull speak of something they know nothing about." The Patterson denunciation is outlined in *Citizen*, 27 February, 2–9 March 1891. Patterson was prominent in the local typographers' union, chaired Knights of Labor meetings, and was a president and vice-president of the Ottawa TLC; he was active in organizing for Labor Day in 1890 and had presented a petition attacking immigration aid to the legislature. On the persistent political presence of the Ottawa Order, often linked to Mowat's Reform party and its local advocate, timber baron E. H. Bronson, see Robert Peter Gillis, "E. H. Bronson and Corporate Capitalism: A Study in Canadian Business Thought and Action, 1880–1910," M.A. thesis, Queen's University, 1975, pp. 69–137; *Free Lance*, 21 April 1894; 15 December 1894; O'Donoghue to H. E. Bronson, 11 May 1896; O'Donoghue to Sir Oliver Mowat, 13 April 1896, Bronson Family Papers, PAC, MG 28 III 26.

123 *Capital Siftings* (Ottawa), 5 May 1894, 3 November 1894.

124 Bernard Ostry, "Conservatives, Liberals and Labour in the 1880s." *Canadian*

*Journal of Economics and Political Science*, 27 (1961), pp. 141–61; Martin Robin, "The Working Class and the Transition to Capitalist Democracy in Canada," *Dalhousie Review*, 47 (1967), pp. 326–43.

125 *Palladium of Labor*, 28 August 1886. Powderly as cited in William Kirk, *National Labor Federations in the United States* (Baltimore, 1906), p. 70.

126 *Palladium of Labor*, 3 July 1886.

## 7. "Politicians in the Order"

1 *Labor Record*, 14 May 1886; Powderly to Carey, 1 May 1889; Carey to Powderly, 19 February 1889, 17 April 1889; George Goodwin to Powderly, 20 November 1888, PP.

2 See Gregory S. Kealey, *Toronto Workers Respond to Industrial Capitalism 1867–1892* (Toronto, 1980), esp. pp. 238–9; O'Donoghue to Powderly, 24 January 1886, 29 March 1886, PP.

3 See *Canadian Labor Reformer*, 26 February, 5, 12, 26 March, 2 April 1887; *Brockville Recorder*, 19, 21 February 1887; Kealey, *Toronto Workers*, pp. 254–6.

4 *Canada Labor Courier*, 10 February 1887; *St. Thomas Times*, 29 January, 9 February, 22 March, 28 June 1887.

5 C. B. Williams, "Canadian-American Trade Union Relations: A Case Study on the Development of Bi-National Unionism," Ph.D. thesis, Cornell University, 1964.

6 See Henry Pelling, "The Knights of Labor in Britain, 1880–1901," *Economic History*, 9 (1956), pp. 313–31; Ronald Bean, "A Note on the Knights of Labor in Liverpool, 1889–90," *Labor History*, 13 (1972), pp. 68–78; and H. Roth, "American Influences on the New Zealand Labor Movement," *Historical Studies*, 9 (1961), pp. 413–20.

7 The only trade dispute involving Canadian and American Knights that we have uncovered involved sailors associated with the Great Lakes National Trade Assembly. Those affiliated with St. Catharines-based DA 207 were often embroiled in conflict with American-based freshwater sailors. Membership cards issued by Carey in 1886 were apparently not being honored in Toledo, Ohio, and other U.S. ports. As a consequence a number of protests were lodged with Powderly. "Surely a knight is a knight the world over," argued the Recording Secretary of LA 2573, Port Dalhousie, "and if our members are not what are the necessary qualifications to go on board of a vessel." While superficially a nationalist quarrel, the conflict actually turned on factional in-fighting within the Trade Assembly, where Carey was leading an opposition movement against Chicago's Richard Powers. See Carey to Powderly, 31 December 1887, 14 March 1888, 22 March 1888; F. J. Quinn to Powderly, 29 November 1886, PP; General Assembly *Proceedings*, 1888, Document 136.

8 Committee to Powderly, 19 and 25 December 1882; and W. H. Bews to Powderly, 4 January 1883; General Assembly *Proceedings*, 1884, p. 728.

9 E. P. Morgan to Sir John A. Macdonald, 24 February 1885, MP.

10 W. J. Vale to Powderly, 30 July 1885, PP.

11 D. J. O'Donoghue to Powderly, 10 August 1885, PP.

12 Powderly to O'Donoghue, 14 August 1885, PP.

13 O'Donoghue to Powderly, 18 August 1885, PP.

14 *St. Thomas Times*, 21, 22 January 1887.

15 O'Donoghue to Powderly, 7 April 1887, PP.

16 O'Donoghue to Powderly, 29 April 1887, PP.

17 *St. Thomas Times*, 21 July 1887.

18 Albert E. Cross to Powderly, 9 June 1887, PP.
19 T. V. Powderly to the Order throughout the Dominion of Canada, 29 August 1887, *Official Circular* No. 17, PP.
20 James Henigan to Powderly, 21 August 1887, PP.
21 *London Free Press*, 19 August 1887.
22 E. Cannon to Powderly, 12 September 1887, PP.
23 W. L. Taylor to Powderly, 21 September 1887, PP.
24 *Journal of United Labor*, 3 September 1887.
25 General Assembly, *Proceedings*, 1887, Document 240, pp. 1729–30.
26 Ibid., Document 241, p. 1730. See also *St. Thomas Times*, 4 October 1887.
27 O'Donoghue to Powderly, 3 October 1887, PP.
28 *Journal of United Labor*, 15, 29 October 1887.
29 General Assembly, *Proceedings*, 1887, p. 1537.
30 O'Donoghue to Powderly, 9 November 1887, PP.
31 Powderly to O'Donoghue, 23 November 1887, 9 December 1887; O'Donoghue to Powderly, 29 November 1887, PP.
32 Powderly to O'Donoghue, 23 November 1887; O'Donoghue to Powderly, 29 November 1887; J. T. Carey to Powderly, 14 December 1887, PP.
33 W. J. Shaw to Powderly, 24 January 1888, 5 March 1888; Powderly to Shaw, 27 January 1888, PP.
34 A. W. Wright to Powderly, 3 February 1888, PP.
35 Thomas Towers to Powderly, 21 February 1888; J. T. Carey to Powderly, 4 February 1888; George Collis to Powderly, 4 February 1888, PP.
36 Powderly to Collis, 14 February 1888; Collis to Powderly, 20 February 1888, PP.
37 J. F. Redmond to Powderly, 19 January 1888, PP.
38 J. T. Carey to Powderly, 30 April 1888; O'Donoghue to Powderly, 31 March 1888, PP.
39 O'Donoghue to Powderly, 25 May 1888; Powderly to O'Donoghue, 2 June 1888; A. F. Jury to Powderly, 28 May 1888; Powderly to Jury, 12 June 1888; and Jury to Powderly, 6 July 1888, PP.
40 Powderly to Jury, 9 July 1888, PP. For the details of legislation in this period see Kealey, *Toronto Workers*, pp. 262–3.
41 Wright to Powderly, 11 July 1888, 4 August 1888; Powderly to Wright, 25 July 1888, PP. A. T. Lepine was named lecturer for Quebec. See Powderly to Lepine, 27 August 1888 and Lepine to Powderly, 31 August 1888, PP. Lepine had been recommended by Montreal DA 114, by Quebec Factory Inspector Louis Guyon, and by Knights' leader Urbain Lafontaine among others. See Guyon to Powderly, 17 August 1888 and Lafontaine to Powderly, 17 August 1888, PP. For biographical detail on Lepine, see *Journal of United Labor*, 11 October 1888.
42 O'Donoghue to Powderly, 9 August 1888, PP. See also J. T. Carey to Powderly, 14 September 1888; Michael O'Harroran to Powderly, 20 October 1888; O'Donoghue to Powderly, 12 November 1888, PP.
43 General Assembly, *Proceedings*, 1888. The Canadian delegates were Benoit (Montreal), Devlin, (Windsor), Elliot (Uxbridge), James (St. Catharines), Parks (Windsor), Toner (Gananoque), Towers (Hamilton), and Wright (Toronto). Wright and Devlin, as we have seen earlier in Chapter 4, were allies, and undoubtedly active in bringing into being the new legislative committee. See Wright to Powderly, 2 December 1888, PP.
44 O'Donoghue to Powderly, 28 November 1888; Robert Glockling to Powderly, 28 November 1888; Carey to Powderly, 13 December 1888, PP. Much later O'Donoghue and Jury wrote the following version in a letter to Powderly, 28 February 1890, PP: "Previous to the 1888 session of the GA, DA 125 passed a resolu-

tion recommending the reappointment of the old 'Canadian Legislative committee,' but the recommendation never, so far as we ever learned, reached its destination and when this man [Wright], who was our delegate to that session of the GA, was questioned about the matter, he said he had not received the resolution referred to, that even if he had he wouldn't have complied with the request . . . on the ground that Bro. Redmond had refused to support the labour candidate in Montreal East. One of Bro. Redmond's colleagues being present, promptly questioned the truthfulness of this charge . . . [proved to be false] . . . At the next meeting of DA 125, after his return from the session of the GA, Mr. Wright . . . once more denied receiving any such instruction but said that even if he had he would resign rather than recommend the reappointment of the committee, for the reason that while at Ottawa he [Wright] had been informed by a member of the Government that everything that Bro. Jury brought before the House was concocted in Room No. 6 which is the conversation room of the Liberal Party in the House of Commons, & that on that account he would not recommend the reappointment of the Canadian Parliamentary Committee . . . He undertook to condemn Bro. Jury before the DA on the strength of *what he knew to be a lie on* the part of the man who, he alleged, told him that every measure Bro. Jury had pressed upon the House had been concocted in Room No. 6, or that it was a lie concocted by himself."

45 Glockling to Powderly, 14 December 1888; Powderly to John Hayes, 30 December 1888, PP.

46 Carey to Powderly, 17 April 1889; O'Donoghue to Powderly, 7 May 1889, 3 August 1889, PP. The first letter provided the quotation of the title to this chapter. For the labor legislation of the 1870s and a fuller discussion of the Wallace Act and its implications see Kealey, *Toronto Workers*, pp. 124–53, 267.

47 J. W. Lainson to Powderly, 6, 8, November 1889; E. Little to Powderly, 9 December 1889. See also similar resolutions from LA 10829 (Levis) and 10061 (Quebec City) in LA 10829 to Powderly, 8 November 1889 and LA 10061 to Powderly, 12 November 1889, PP. The Quebec letters often linked Elliot to the by now publicly repudiated Knights of Labor lecturer, A. T. Lepine, about whom more later.

48 Wright to Powderly, 20 January 1890; Elliot to Hayes, 25 March 1890, PP. For details of Elliot's activities that session see: Powderly to Elliot, 9 March 1890; Elliot to Powderly, 25 March 1890; Elliot to Powderly, 20 April 1890; Elliot to Powderly, 24 April 1890; Powderly to Elliot, 28 April 1890, PP.

49 Jury to Powderly, 16, 19 November 1889, PP. All indications are that Powderly embraced the Tory connection. See Powderly to Wright, 7 May 1908, PP, indicating a long-standing party attachment.

50 Powderly to Lepine, 20 April 1889; Lepine to Powderly, 30 April 1889; Powderly to Lepine, 14 May 1889; Powderly to Hayes, 19 April 1889; Powderly to The Order, 31 July 1889, PP.

51 The breakdown in the Report of 31 July 1889 was:

| | $ | | $ |
|---|---|---|---|
| Salary | 504.00 | Postage | 3.33 |
| RR Fares | 232.65 | Conveyances | 17.10 |
| Hotel | 371.35 | Telegraphs | 9.88 |
| Baggage | 1.00 | Unexpended Balance | 30.69 |

This actually totals $1,170 not the reported $1,100. See also O'Donoghue to Powderly, 28 October 1889, PP.

52 Wright to Powderly, 3 November 1889, PP. See also Powderly to Glockling, 7 November 1889; Powderly to Gilmour, 7 November 1889; Wright to Powderly,

3 November 1889; Glockling to Powderly, 25 November 1889, PP. In a letter to Wright (7 November 1889) Powderly predicted that "the growlers will not like what they've received" and explained further that while "not poetical by any means . . . I wrote these words without hesitation, and after reading them, hanged if I don't believe every word of them, and that is more than I can say of everything I've written this year"[!]

53 Charles Miller to Hayes, 29 November 1889, PP.

54 LA 2305 to Powderly, 4 January 1890, PP.

55 The key document is O'Donoghue and Jury to Powderly, 18 December 1889. Cf., O'Donoghue to Powderly, 25 January 1889, 13 February 1889, 26 October 1889, 28 October 1889, 14 February 1890; Powderly to James Gilmour, 17 March 1890, 20 March 1890, 25 July 1890; Gilmour to Powderly, 28 February 1890, 20 March 1890, 27 March 1890, 24 June 1891. Wright drew some Canadian support, J. A. MacLeod of Ottawa's Capital Assembly 5222 writing to Powderly in 1891 endorsing Wright and attacking the "Toronto ring" that sought to subordinate all issues to party politics. See MacLeod to Powderly, n.d. (January 1891?). All letters in PP.

56 David A. Carey to Powderly, 6 April 1891; Powderly to William Glockling, 7 April 1891, PP.

57 Canadian General Assembly delegates to Powderly, 21 November 1890; LA 10061 to Powderly, 16 December 1890; O'Donoghue to Powderly, 1 April 1890; Powderly to O'Donoghue, 6 April 1891; O'Donoghue to Powderly, 10 April and 6 May 1891; W. Glockling to Powderly, 6 April 1891, 12 April 1891; Powderly to Glockling, 7 April 1891, 23 April 1891; J. H. Gilmour to Powderly, 24 June 1891, PP.

58 Wright to Powderly, 25 September 1890, PP; Kealey, *Toronto Workers*, pp. 272–3.

59 Hayes to Powderly, 14 September 1891, 17 September 1891; Powderly to Emma, 28 September 1891, PP.

60 See Norman Ware, *The Labor Movement in the United States, 1860–1890: A Study in Democracy* (New York, 1964), pp. 103–16, 155–242. On Toronto and Barry see *Journal of United Labor*, 18 October 1888; Richard J. Oestreicher, "The Knights of Labor in Michigan: Sources of Growth and Decline," M.A. thesis, Michigan State University, 1973 and his "The Limits of Labor Radicalism: Tom Barry and the Knights of Labor," unpublished paper, Knights of Labor Centennial Symposium, Newberry Library, Chicago, May 1979.

61 For these denunciations and many, many more see O'Reilly to Powderly, 3 October 1890, 5 November 1890, 7 November 1891, 21 January 1892, 10 May 1892, 9 August 1892, 25 August 1893, 4 September 1893, 18 October 1893, 24 October 1893, and 11 December 1893, PP.

62 The following draws on the fleeting descriptions in the standard accounts and Vincent Joseph Falzone, "Terence V. Powderly: Mayor and Labor Leader, 1849–1893," Ph.D. thesis, University of Maryland, 1971, pp. 336–44.

63 Hayes to Powderly, 23 February 1893, 4 March 1893; Powderly to Wright, 10 January 1893; Powderly to T. B. McGuire, 11 March 1893; Wright to Powderly, 5 December 1892, PP.

64 Powderly to Wright, 18 February 1893, 11 March 1893; Powderly to Hayes, 19 February 1893; Hayes to Powderly, 26 February 1893; Samuel Jacobson to Powderly, 7 March 1893, 15 March 1893; Powderly to Jacobson, 10 March 1893; Wright to Powderly, 12 March 1893, 19 March 1893, PP.

65 Powderly to Jacobson, 20 March 1893; Jacobson to Powderly, 21 March 1893; Powderly to Jacobson, 22 March 1893; James A. Wright to Powderly, 23 March 1893 [?]; and Jacobson to Powderly, 24 March 1893, PP.

66 Case of NTA 231 against A. W. Wright: Hearing before the General Executive

Board, 25 March 1893; Wright to Hayes, 30 March 1893; Wright to Powderly, 31 March 1893; Powderly to Cavanaugh, 5 April 1893; Powderly to Wright, 2 April 1893; Jacobson to Powderly, 4 April 1893, PP. On Powderly's disillusionment see Powderly to O'Reilly, 29 August 1893, 11 September 1893, PP.

67 Hayes to Powderly, 4, 18, March 1893, 10 April 1893; Powderly to Hayes, 11 April 1893, 10 May 1893. Among others: O'Reilly to Powderly, 15 May 1893; Powderly to Wright, 16 May 1893, 19 May 1893; Powderly to Mary Stephens, 26 May 1893; Mary Stephens to Powderly, 31 May 1893; Carey Taylor to Powderly, 10 June 1893; and Wright to the General Executive Board, 13 June 1893, PP.

68 Powderly to Wright, 14 June 1893, 3 July 1893; Powderly to O'Reilly, 13 June 1893, 21 June 1893, 27 June 1893; Powderly to O'Keefe, 19 June 1893, PP.

69 Hayes to the General Executive Board, 9 July 1893; Hayes to Powderly, 10 July 1893, PP.

70 Powderly to Wright, 13 June 1893; Powderly to O'Reilly, 11, 18, 20 July 1893; O'Reilly to Powderly, 20, 22, 27, 29 July 1893, PP.

71 Powderly to O'Reilly, 9 July 1893; Cavanaugh to Powderly, 7 August 1893; Powderly to Cavanaugh, 10 August 1893, PP.

72 Note Powderly to Wright, 30 August 1893, 14, 17, 22 October 1893; Powderly to O'Reilly, 22 August 1893, 1 November 1893; Devlin to Powderly, 24 August 1893, 22 September 1893; Powderly to Emma, 20 September 1893; O'Reilly to Powderly, 13, 16, 19, 29 October 1893; Cavanaugh to Powderly, 17 October 1893; Powderly to Cavanaugh, 20 October 1893; Gray to Powderly, 15 October 1893; Powderly to Gray, 15 October 1893; Wright to Powderly, 18, 22, 24 October 1893; Wright to Gray, ? October 1893, PP.

73 Gerald N. Grob, *Workers and Utopia: A Study of Ideological Conflict in the American Labor Movement, 1865–1900* (Chicago, 1961), pp. 132–3; L. Glen Seretan, *Daniel DeLeon: The Odyssey of an American Marxist* (Cambridge, 1979), pp. 141–53.

74 A. W. Wright, "Manifesto," in PP, c. mid-December 1893; Wright, *Report of . . . Delegate from DA 125 to the Philadelphia Session of the General Assembly, Knights of Labor* (Toronto, 1894). Cf., T. V. Powderly, "Statement of . . . to the Order of the Knights of Labor," Scranton, 31 May 1894, PP; and James R. Sovereign, "A Letter to Powderly," 11 August 1894, in Samuels Papers, State Historical Society of Wisconsin.

75 Joseph R. Buchanan, *The Story of a Labor Agitator* (New York, 1903), p. 439. See also John R. Commons, et al., *History of Labor in the US*, II (New York, 1926), p. 486. For orchestration of Powderly forces for this meeting see: Wright to Powderly, 3 April 1894, PP; Wright to Bob [Simpson?], 12 March 1894; Wright to Glockling, 13 April 1894; Wright to Beales, 16 April 1894; Wright to Glockling, 23 April 1894; and Wright to J. G. Kilt, 24 April 1894, WP.

76 Buchanan to Powderly, n.d. (c. 7 December 1893) includes printed circular "Rally, Labor, Rally!" for 15 December release, PP.

77 Powderly to Wright, 7 February 1894; Powderly to Devlin, 11 February 1894; Powderly to Cavanaugh, 24 May 1894, 27 February 1895 (the former also being sent to O'Reilly, Devlin, Feeny, Quinn, Charles Martin, Lawlor, and Wright); Powderly to O'Reilly, 3 August 1894, 11 February 1895; Powderly to Buchanan, 27 February 1895; Powderly to McBridge, 8 February 1895, PP; Ware, *Labor Movement*, p. 116.

78 Bernard Feeny to Powderly, 1 December 1893; Wright to Powderly, 15 December 1893, PP.

79 Powderly to Wright, 26 February 1894; Powderly to Feeny, 27 February 1894, PP.

80 Powderly to Wright, 4 April 1894, 18 April 1894, PP. See also *Mail*, 9, 10 April 1894; *Globe*, 10 April 1894; *World*, 10 April 1894.
81 Wright to Powderly, 4 June 1894, PP; O'Donoghue to Hayes, 7 July 1894, HP.
82 Richard J. Kerrigan, "The Dynamic Year of 1886," *One Big Union Bulletin*, 23 September 1927 (courtesy Allen Seager).
83 As quoted in Ware, *Labor Movement*, pp. 375–6.
84 One Big Union, Leaflet No. 2, "The Knights of Labor, the American Federation of Labor and the One Big Union," Winnipeg, n.d., c. 1920, Kenny Papers, University of Toronto.

## 8. "Spread the Light!"

1 See Ronald Fraser, *Blood of Spain: An Oral History of The Spanish Civil War* (New York, 1979), esp. pp. 291–2; Lenin, *Collected Works*, 33 (Moscow, n.d.), pp. 278–88. Note the decisive statement in Raymond Williams, "Beyond Actually Existing Socialism," *New Left Review*, 120 (March–April 1980), pp. 3–19.
2 Edward and Eleanor Marx Aveling, *The Working Class Movement in America* (London, 1888), p. 18.
3 The notion of a movement culture is developed in Lawrence Goodwyn, *Democratic Promise: The Populist Movement in America* (New York, 1976), a rich treatment of the American agrarian counterparts of the Knights of Labor. Cf., Goodwyn, "The Cooperative Commonwealth and Other Abstractions: In Search of A Democratic Premise," *Marxist Perspectives*, 10 (Summer 1980), pp. 8–43.
4 Henri Lefebvre, *Everyday Life in the Modern World* (New York, 1968), p. 14. The essential theoretical formulations concerning culture are drawn from Raymond Williams, *Marxism and Literature* (Oxford, 1977), pp. 11–20, 121–8; Williams, "Base and Superstructure in Marxist Cultural Theory," *New Left Review*, 82 (November–December 1973), pp. 3–16.
5 *Ordine Nuovo*, 12 July 1919 (transl. Stephen Hellman).
6 Williams, *Marxism and Literature*, pp. 108–14, 126–7.
7 *Brockville Recorder*, 17 November 1883. Information on Miller provided by Dale Chisamore.
8 George E. McNeill, *Unfrequented Paths: Songs of Nature, Labor, and Men* (Boston, 1903), pp. 111–12.
9 See E. P. Thompson, *William Morris: Romantic to Revolutionary* (New York, 1977); Thompson, "Romanticism, Moralism and Utopianism: the Case of William Morris," *New Left Review*, 99 (September–October 1976), esp. pp. 108–9.
10 W. Peter Ward, *White Canada Forever: Popular Attitudes and Public Policy towards Orientals in British Columbia* (Montreal, 1978), p. 44.
11 See, for instance, E. B. Irving to T. V. Powderly, 16 November 1885, 1 December 1885, PP. Both letters, from the Recording Secretary of LA 4069, end with the following sign:

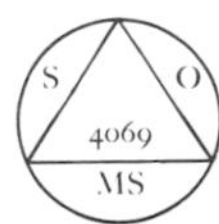


Cf., T. V. Powderly, *The Path I Trod: The Autobiography of Terence V. Powderly* (New York, 1940), pp. 431–3.
12 "General Assembly, Noble and Holy Order, Knights of Labor of North America, Charter of the Knights of Hope Assembly, Port Hope, Ontario," 20 November 1882, Public Archives of Canada, MG 28 I 54.

13 "The Great Seal of Knighthood" and "Secret Circular: Explanation of the Signs and Symbols of the Order," PP. Cf., Eugene Forsey and Lloyd Aitkinson, "Report #1: Brantford," in Canadian Labor Congress Files, Volume 249, File Folder 15, Public Archives of Canada, MG 28 I 103.
14 *Palladium of Labor*, 5 June 1886.
15 *Adelphon Kruptos*, n.p., n.d., 2, in State Historical Society of Wisconsin; Powderly, *Path I Trod*, p. 436. Cf., George Simmel, "The Sociology of Secret Societies," *American Journal of Sociology*, 11 (January 1906), pp. 441–98.
16 Note the comments in E. P. Thompson, "Folklore, Anthropology, and Social History," *Indian Historical Review*, 3 (January, 1978), pp. 247–66; Thompson, "Eighteenth Century English Society: class struggle without class?" *Social History*, 3 (May 1978), esp. pp. 154–5; William Reddy, "The Textile Trade and the Language of the Crowd at Rouen, 1752–1871," *Past & Present*, 74 (February 1977), esp. pp. 82–3, 87–8; John Brewer, *Party Ideology and Popular Politics at the Accession of George III* (London, 1976), pp. 163–200; Gerald M. Sider, "Christmas Mumming and the New Year in Outport Newfoundland," *Past & Present*, 71 (May, 1976), pp. 102–25; Cynthia M. Truant, "Solidarity and Symbolism among Journeymen Artisans: The Case of Companonnage," *Comparative Studies in Society and History*, 21 (April 1979), pp. 214–25.
17 There are some useful, but also some problematic, assertions in E. J. Hobsbawm, *Primitive Rebels: Studies in Archaic Forms of Social Movement in the 19th and 20th Centuries* (Manchester, 1959), pp. 152–4.
18 Gordon Bishop, "Recollections of the Amalgamated," United Steelworkers of America mimeograph, c. 1940s.
19 See Ezra Cook, ed., *Knights of Labor Illustrated*, *"Adelphon Kruptos." The Full Illustrated Ritual Including the "Unwritten Work" and an Historical Sketch of the Order* (Chicago, 1886). Cook also published numerous other secret society rituals, including those of the Freemasons, Oddfellows, and Knights of Templar. Earlier editions of the *Adelphon Kruptos*, one of which is cited above, never mentioned the Order, substituting asterisks for each reference to Knights or Knightly activities. Note the discussion in Julie Blodgett, "Fountain of Power: The Origins of the Knights of Labor in Philadelphia, 1869–1874," paper presented to the Knights of Labor Centennial Symposium, Newberry Library, Chicago, 17–19 May 1979. In 1881 the ritual was changed by the elimination of Scriptural passages, references to God, and the oath of secrecy, to placate the Roman Catholic Church. See Norman Ware, *The Labor Movement in the United States, 1860–1890: A Study in Democracy* (New York, 1964), pp. 26, 77; Henry Joseph Browne, *The Catholic Church and the Knights of Labor* (Washington, 1949).
20 On this background see Hobsbawm, *Primitive Rebels*, pp. 150–74; E. P. Thompson, *The Making of the English Working Class* (New York, 1963), pp. 421–2, 510; and esp. Carrol D. Wright, "An Historical Sketch of the Knights of Labor," *Quarterly Journal of Economics*, 1 (January 1887), pp. 142–3.
21 Cook, ed., *Knights Illustrated*, 37; Powderly, *Path I Trod*, pp. 434–5. In each LA there were a number of officials, ranging from the MW to the Unknown Knight, responsible for examining initiates. See *By-Laws of Pioneer Assembly No. 2211 of Toronto, Ontario, Founded September 1882* (Toronto, 1887), p. 3.
22 Cook, ed., *Knights Illustrated*, pp. 28–9; *Adelphon Kruptos*, pp. 16–17.
23 Cook, ed., *Knights Illustrated*, pp. 32–7.
24 As an introduction see Gregory S. Kealey, "The Orange Order in Toronto: Religious Riot and the Working Class," and Bryan D. Palmer, "'Give us the road and we will run it': The Social and Cultural Matrix of an Emerging Labour Movement," in Kealey and Warrian, eds., *Essays in Canadian Working Class History* (To-

ronto, 1976), pp. 13–34 and 106–24; Palmer, *A Culture in Conflict: Skilled Workers and Industrial Capitalism in Hamilton, Ontario, 1860–1914* (Montreal, 1979), pp. 35–70. Note Michael J. Cassity, "Modernization and Social Crisis: The Knights of Labor and a Midwest Community, 1885–1886," *Journal of American History*, 66 (June 1979), p. 49.

25 George W. Goodwin to Powderly, 20 November 1888, PP.

26 *Palladium of Labor*, 13 October 1883, 29 May 1886; O'Donoghue to Powderly, 29 November 1883, PP.

27 *London Advertiser*, 17 April 1886; Shaw to Powderly, 3 March 1888, PP.

28 James R. Brown to Powderly, 1883, PP; *Palladium of Labor*, 23 August 1884; *Welland Tribune*, 16 July 1886.

29 *Journal of United Labor*, 25 May 1884; *Brockville Recorder*, 23 January 1886; *Brantford Expositor*, 12 March 1886; *Brantford Courier*, 2 November 1886; A. Barlett (Recording Secretary LA 9216) to Powderly, 26 December 1887; D. H. Smith to Powderly, 12 August 1887; Edward Baer to Powderly, 7 February 1887; George J. Lamont to Powderly, 14 December 1885; J. R. Brown to Powderly, 29 September 1882, PP. Note, too, the discussions of ritual's importance in Toronto and Hamilton, Chapters 3 and 4 above.

30 *Palladium of Labor*, 28 February 1885; *Hamilton Spectator*, 23 February 1885; A. E. Fields to John W. Hayes, 26 February 1895, HP.

31 *Journal of United Labor*, November 1882.

32 On the Order's appreciation of its own history, symbolized in the seal, see Powderly, *Path I Trod*, pp. 438–43.

33 *Palladium of Labor*, 17 October 1885.

34 See Doris French, *Faith, Sweat, and Politics: The Early Trade Union Years in Canada* (Toronto, 1962), p. 9.

35 On these papers see Robert Peter Gillis, "E. H. Bronson and Corporate Capitalism: A Study in Canadian Business Thought and Action, 1880–1910," M.A. thesis, Queen's University, 1975, pp. 75–6, 88–9; *Palladium of Labor*, 21 June 1884; *Brockville Recorder*, Souvenir Edition, 1906, cited in "Ontario Towns and Cities," Folder 14, Volume 249, Canadian Labour Congress Files, Public Archives of Canada, MG 28 I 103. See also, Douglas R. Kennedy, *The Knights of Labor in Canada* (London, 1956), pp. 45–7; G. Weston Wrigley, "Socialism in Canada," *International Socialist Review*, 1 (1 May 1901), p. 686. Cf., *Journal of United Labor*, 3 December 1887; *Palladium of Labor*, 5 July 1884.

36 Early statements include Bernard Ostry, "Conservatives, Liberals and Labour in the 1880s," *Canadian Journal of Economics and Political Science*, 29 (May, 1961), pp. 141–61; Frank W. Watt, "The National Policy, the workingman, and Proletarian Ideas in Victorian Canada," *Canadian Historical Review*, 40 (1959), pp. 1–26.

37 *Ontario Workman*, 27 March 1873.

38 *Palladium of Labor*, 15 August 1885.

39 *Trade Union Advocate*, 20 July 1882.

40 *Palladium of Labor*, 15 December 1883.

41 *Official Programme and Souvenir of the Labor Day Demonstration Held at Dundurn Park, Hamilton, Ontario, 1897, 6 September, Held Under the Auspices of the Trades and Labor Council* (Hamilton, 1897), pp. 3–5.

42 See, for instance, Bryan D. Palmer, "Discordant Music: Charivaris and Whitecapping in Nineteenth-Century North America," *Labour/Le Travailleur*, 3 (1978), p. 37.

43 See Palmer, *A Culture in Conflict*; Gregory S. Kealey, *Toronto Workers Respond to Industrial Capitalism, 1867–1892* (Toronto, 1980); and the essays in Kealey and Warrian, eds., *Essays*, pp. 13–34, 35–57, 83–105, 106–124, 125–42.

44 *Thorold Post*, 30 July 1886, 6 August 1886, 17 December 1886, 7 January 1887, 21 January 1887, 28 January 1887, 11 February 1887, 25 February 1887.

45 See, for instance, *Gananoque Reporter*, 27 November 1887, 31 December 1887; *Ottawa Citizen*, 2 January 1890, 11 August 1890; *Ingersoll Chronicle and Canadian Dairyman*, 13 November 1884; *Brockville Recorder*, 27 November 1883; *Labor Leaf*, 17 February 1886.

46 *Sarnia Observer*, 5 December 1884.

47 *London Advertiser*, 5 March 1886, 24 April 1886, 27 April 1886, 15 May 1886, 15 July 1886.

48 *Palladium of Labor*, 2 May 1885, 27 June 1885, 3 October 1885, 10 October 1885, 4 April 1885, 24 April 1886; *Journal of United Labor*, 25 March 1885.

49 *Palladium of Labor* (Toronto edition), 24 April 1886.

50 See *Palladium of Labor*, 11 August 1883, 18 August 1883; *Hamilton Spectator*, 31 July 1883, 4 August 1883; Keith W. Ross (Oshawa and District Labor Council) to Eugene Forsey, 1 June 1964, in "International Molders and Allied Workers," Volume 248, CLC Files, PAC; Toronto Trades and Labor Council Minutes, 1881–1893, 15 June 1883, Volume 2, 190, Public Archives of Canada, MG 28 I 44. On the Oshawa molders see Nancy Stunden, "Oshawa Knights of Labor Demonstration Medal," in *Newsletter of the Committee on Canadian Labour History*, 4 (1974), p. 1.

51 *Belleville Intelligencer*, 19 August 1884; *Journal of United Labor*, 25 April 1886; *Labor Record*, 14 May 1886. On Joussaye's Toronto efforts see *Globe*, 10 January 1893, 19 January 1893; Wayne Roberts, *'Honest Womanhood': Feminism, Femininity, and Class Consciousness Among Toronto Working Women, 1893–1914* (Toronto, 1977). These poems, along with many others, appear in slightly different versions in Joussaye, *Songs That Quinte Sang* (Belleville, 1895). There were other women poets in Belleville. See Marianne Farningham, "The Lower Orders," *Belleville Intelligencer*, 19 March 1887. The organization of the 1884 demonstration is outlined in *Intelligencer*, 26 July 1884, 29 July 1884, 30 July 1884, 5 August 1884, 14 August 1884.

52 *Sarnia Observer*, 10 September 1886; *London Advertiser*, 26 June 1885; *Palladium of Labor*, 5 July 1884; *Labor Leaf*, 7 October 1885; *Brockville Recorder*, 16 January 1887.

53 On the Order and internationalism see, for instance, *Palladium of Labor*, 17 January 1885; *Report of the Royal Commission on the Relations of Labor and Capital in Canada*, "Ontario Evidence," II (Ottawa, 1889), p. 874; Powderly to O'Donoghue, 14 August 1885; W. H. Springer to Powderly, 31 August 1886, PP; John David Bell, "The Social and Political Thought of the Labor Advocate," M.A. thesis, Queen's University, 1975, p. 13.

54 O'Neil to Powderly, 12 September 1887, PP. O'Neil probably referred to the Napanee-area farmers' financial fiascos with cooperation under the Patrons of Husbandry or Dominion Grange. Grangers in Napanee, then a great barley port, built a stone grain elevator with a capacity of 100,000 bushels in 1880, only to have it collapse as soon as it was filled. W. N. Harris, a leading figure in the Grange's Wholesale Supply Company, originally promoted this effort with a cooperative store in Napanee. The undertaking had failed by 1889, Harris was dismissed, and a series of lawsuits followed. See Robert Leslie Jones, *History of Agriculture in Ontario, 1613–1880* (Toronto, 1946), p. 346; Louis Aubrey Wood, *A History of Farmers' Movements in Canada: The Origins and Development of Agrarian Protest, 1872–1924* (Toronto, 1924), esp. pp. 77–9.

55 Johnson to Powderly, 31 May 1887, PP.

56 *Palladium of Labor*, 21 August 1886. Cf., William Hogan to Powderly, 6 August 1886, PP.

57 *Canadian Labor Reformer*, 18 September 1886; *John Swinton's Paper*, 19 September 1886.
58 *London Advertiser*, 9 July 1886, 10 July 1886; Palmer, "Give us the road," in Kealey and Warrian, eds., *Essays*, p. 117; *Brantford Expositor*, 16 July 1886.
59 *London Advertiser*, 17 July 1886, 14 August 1886, 20 August 1886; *Canadian Labor Reformer*, 21 August 1886; *Palladium of Labor*, 7 August 1886, 21 August 1886, 17 July 1886, 23 October 1886; *Brantford Expositor*, 6 August 1886; *St. Thomas Times*, 16 July 1886, 30 July 1886, 14 August 1886; *Welland Tribune*, 19 August 1887.
60 *Ingersoll Chronicle and Canadian Dairyman*, 9 June 1887, 16 June 1887, 25 June 1887, 7 July 1887; *St. Thomas Times*, 2 July 1887; *London Free Press*, 2 July 1887.
61 *Palladium of Labor*, 4 July 1885.
62 *Ottawa Citizen*, 16 July 1890, 2 September 1890, 3 September 1890; *Le Spectateur*, 5 September 1892; E. McKenna, "Unorganized Labour Versus Management: The Strike at the Chaudière Lumber Mills, 1891," *Histoire Sociale/Social History*, 5 (November, 1973), pp. 186–211; Eugene Forsey, "History of Canadian Trade Unionism," unpublished manuscript, Reel M-2214, ch. 7, Public Archives of Canada; *Journal of United Labor*, 26 September 1890.
63 *Gananoque Reporter*, 29 October 1887. On Smiths Falls-Perth Knights of Labor participation in a trades' procession see *Rideau Record*, 26 May 1887.
64 *Canadian Labor Reformer*, 21 August 1886; *Palladium of Labor*, 8 August 1885, 5 September 1885, 12 September 1885, 7 August 1886, 21 August 1886; Palmer, *A Culture in Conflict*, p. 55; W. G. Cook to Powderly, 14 July 1887, PP.
65 See *British Whig*, 22 May 1888, 25 May 1888; *Brockville Recorder*, 4 September 1883, 5 September 1883, 25 July 1884, 16 June 1887; *Gananoque Reporter*, 23 July 1887.
66 *Gananoque Reporter*, 9 July 1887, 23 July 1887, 30 July 1887, 6 August 1887, 18 August 1887, 25 August 1887.
67 "Memorial Service of the Knights of Labor," PP.
68 *Palladium of Labor*, 15 November 1884.
69 See *British Whig*, 8 July 1887; *Brockville Recorder*, 3 December 1883; *Cornwall Freeholder*, 18 March 1887; *Journal of United Labor*, 2 May 1886, 25 September 1886; *Sarnia Observer*, 5 December 1884; *Palladium of Labor*, 23 August 1884, 18 July 1885, 8 May 1886, 10 July 1886; J. R. Brown to Powderly, 10 April 1883, PP.
70 *Canadian Labor Reformer*, 25 September 1886. On generosity and the class culture, see *Ottawa Daily Citizen*, 9 July 1891. Harry Lindley, a compositor on the *Tribune*, described printers: "Charitable? I should say they are. They are charitable to a fault. They will give their last dime to a brother in distress." Cf., *Brotherhood Era*, 16 October 1895; C. Hayward to Powderly, 26 May 1886, PP. Cf., on funerals, *Cornwall Freeholder*, 18 March 1887; Victor Oscar Chan, "The Knights of Labor in Canada," M.A. thesis, McGill University, 1948, p. 7.
71 *Brockville Recorder*, 12 June 1883, 13 June 1883, 14 June 1883; Daniel J. Walkowitz, *Worker City, Company Town: Iron and Cotton-Worker Protest in Troy and Cohoes, New York, 1855–1884* (Urbana, Ill., 1978), pp. 211, 213, 239–40; Bryan D. Palmer, "An Epitaph for William Hutcheson," *Labour/Le Travailleur*, 4 (1979), pp. 261–7.
72 Note the comments in Russell Hann, "Brainworkers and the Knights of Labor: E. E. Sheppard, Phillips Thompson, and the Toronto *News*, 1883–1887," in Kealey and Warrian, eds., *Essays*, p. 57; Goodwyn, *Democratic Promise*, pp. 540–3.
73 *Palladium of Labor*, 5 September 1885.
74 O'Neil to Powderly, 13 January 1889, PP.
75 *Statistics as Collected by Headlight Assembly No. 4069, K. of L., for Its Exclusive Use* (St. Thomas, 1885), p. 3. Cf., Shelton Stromquist, "The Knights of Labor and Orga-

nized Railroad Men," paper presented to the Knights of Labor Centennial Symposium, Newberry Library, Chicago, 17–19 May 1979, p. 18, quoting Trevellick to Powderly, 18 October 1885, PP. Interest in statistics was also expressed in Belleville. See Thomas Sullivan to Powderly, 1 February 1887, Belleville, PP.

76 *Labor Union*, 13 January 1883. In Toronto, the *Canadian Labor Reformer*, 15 May 1886, campaigned under the motto, "We demand all the reform that justice can ask for, And all the reform that justice can give."

77 *Journal of Commerce*, 13 March 1891, cited in Michael Bliss, *A Living Profit: Studies in the Social History of Canadian Business* (Toronto, 1974), p. 78.

78 *Annual Report, Ontario Bureau of Industries* (Toronto, 1888), Part IV, p. 18; *Palladium of Labor*, 21 February 1885; *St. Thomas Times*, 21 April 1886; *Journal of United Labor*, 27 August 1887. Trevellick is quoted in *National Labor Tribune*, 1 August 1885. Note, too, *Journal of United Labor*, March 1883, quoted in Leon R. Fink, "Workingmen's Democracy: The Knights of Labor in Local Politics, 1886–1896," Ph.D. thesis, University of Rochester, 1977, p. 399; Andrew Roy, *A History of the Coal Mines of the United States* (Westport, Ct., 1970), p. 262. On radical education in general see Richard Johnson, "'Really useful knowledge': radical education and working-class culture, 1790–1848," in John Clarke, Chas Chritcher, and Richard Johnson, eds., *Working Class Culture: Studies in History and Theory* (London, 1979), esp. pp. 84–8, 91–100.

79 "Recollections of John Peebles, Mayor of Hamilton, 1930–33," 7 February 1946, Hamilton Collection, Hamilton Public Library; Wrigley, "Socialism," p. 686. Note, too, the valuable discussion of reform editors and the language of Populism in Goodwyn, *Democratic Promise*, pp. 351–86. Cf., Bell, "Social and Political Thought of the *Labor Advocate*," esp. pp. 150–9. Rowe and Wrigley have been discussed in previous chapters. On Wrigley and Ingram see *Canada Labor Courier*, 10 February 1887; *St. Thomas Times*, 29 July 1886, 25 August 1886, 25 August 1887; *Canadian Labor Reformer*, 2 October 1886; and the discussion on the Order and politics in Chapter 6 above.

80 *Palladium of Labor*, 5 January 1884.

81 Watt, "The Workingman and Proletarian Ideas," p. 21. Cf., Martin Robin, *Radical Politics and Canadian Labor, 1880–1930* (Kingston, 1968), pp. 22–8; Bell, "Social and Political Thought of the *Labor Advocate*," pp. 1–29; Ramsay Cook, "Henry George and the Poverty of Canadian Progress," Canadian Historical Association, *Historical Papers* (1977), pp. 143–56.

82 Albert R. Carman, *The Preparation of Ryerson Embury* (Toronto, 1900), pp. 179–80. Cf., Agnes Maule Machar, *Roland Graeme: Knight* (Toronto, 1892); Mary Vipond, "Blessed are the peacemakers: the labour question in Canadian social gospel fiction," *Journal of Canadian Studies*, 10 (August, 1975), pp. 32–43. A Kingston lawyer named Machar (perhaps a relative) attempted to attend the International Labor Convention as a delegate of the Knights of Labor, and was described by A. W. Wright as a "thoroughgoing friend of the Labor cause." See Wright to Powderly, 11 June 1889, PP.

83 See Hann, "Brainworkers and the Knights of Labor," pp. 35–57; Kennedy, *Knights of Labor in Canada*, p. 45. Note the testimony of Kingston's R. Meek, a member of the Knights of Labor, in Greg Kealey, ed., *Canada Investigates Industrialism: The Royal Commission on the Relations of Labor and Capital, 1889* (Toronto, 1973), pp. 172–5; and the discussion of "intellectual prostitutes" in *Labor Advocate*, 28 August 1891.

84 T. Phillips Thompson, *The Future Government of Canada; being Arguments in Favor of a British American Republic* (St. Catharines, 1864).

85 On Thompson see Jay Atherton, "An Introduction," in Thompson, *The Politics of*

*Labor* (Toronto, 1975), pp. vii–xxiv. Atherton's assessment of Thompson, treating him as a precursor of the welfare state, understates his importance in the evolution of Canadian working-class thought, and distorts Thompson's eventual socialist commitment. Fortunately other work, most notably that of Russell Hann, is currently underway, promising to establish Thompson as a figure of central importance. Preliminary statements of Hann's work, upon which we draw heavily below, include, "Brainworkers and the Knights of Labor," pp. 35–57; and "An Early Canadian Labour Theorist," *Bulletin of the Committee on Canadian Labour History*, 4 (Autumn 1977), pp. 38–43. Cf., Bell, "Social and Political Thought of the *Labor Advocate;*" Frank William Watt, "Radicalism in English Canadian Literature Since Confederation," Ph.D. thesis, University of Toronto, 1957, pp. 117–21; Ramsay Cook, "The Professor and the Prophet of Unrest," *Transactions of the Royal Society of Canada*, 4th ser., 13 (1975), pp. 228–50; Palmer, *A Culture in Conflict*, pp. 116–20; Kealey, *Toronto Workers*, pp. 278–90.

86 See, for instance, *Palladium of Labor*, 5 January 1884, 20 September 1884, 22 August 1885, 29 August 1885.

87 See *Ingersoll Chronicle and Canadian Dairyman*, 25 February 1886, 4 March 1886; *Stratford Beacon*, 18 December 1885, 16 April 1887; *Palladium of Labor*, 21 August 1886.

88 *Palladium of Labor*, 23 May 1885, 11 August 1883, 15 December 1883, 22 December 1883, 5 September 1885, 27 March 1886, 17 April 1886; *Labor Union*, 13 January 1883, 20 January 1883, 10 February 1883, 3 March 1883; *London Advertiser*, 10 October 1884, 17 February 1885, 16 May 1885, 19 February 1886, 17 March 1886, 12 July 1886; *Belleville Intelligencer*, 16 October 1884, 17 October 1884, 18 October 1884; *Brockville Recorder*, 21 August 1882, 22 August 1882, 23 August 1882, 2 March 1889; *Prescott Messenger*, 15 November 1889; *Rideau Record*, 1 March 1888; *Ingersoll Chronicle and Canadian Dairyman*, 2 October 1884, 16 October 1884; *British Whig*, 13 March 1888, 21 March 1888; *St. Thomas Times*, 16 March 1886, 20 April 1886, 21 April 1886, 5 July 1886; *Henry George in Canada* (London, England, 1884).

89 Blain to Powderly, 10 April 1886, PP. Cf., William Chalmers to Powderly, 2 March 1886; A. H. Derke to Powderly, 18 November 1885; R. M. Wood to Powderly, 9 October 1884; M. F. Baker to Powderly, 8 December 1889; W. Arnold to Powderly, 25 February 1886, PP. *Journal of United Labor*, 30 August 1888, 11 October 1888, 20 March 1890; *Cornwall Freeholder*, 1 July 1887. A small town like Ingersoll could play a significant organizational role in the expansion of the Order in Canada. The MW of Ingersoll's LA, for instance, founded the first Assembly in the nearby, and much larger, city of London. Ingersoll's Knights of Labor boasted of a membership of 375 early in the 1880s. See *London Advertiser*, 4 March 1884, 18 March 1884.

90 Walter A. Ratcliffe, *Morning Songs in the Night* (Toronto, 1897), esp. pp. v–vii, 62, 67; *Citizen and Country*, 11 March 1899; Ratcliffe, *Laurier and Victory* (Toronto, 1896), a collection of verse originally appearing in the *Globe*.

91 *Palladium of Labor*, 24 January 1885, 7 November 1885; *Labor Union*, 10 February 1883, 24 February 1883, 10 March 1883.

92 See Russell G. Hann, "Introduction," in Daphne Read, ed., *The Great War and Canadian Society: An Oral History* (Toronto, 1978), pp. 9–38; David Frank and Donald Macgillivray, "Introduction," in Dawn Fraser, *Echoes From Labor's War: Industrial Cape Breton in the 1920s* (Toronto, 1978), pp. 9–28; and two unpublished papers by Debi Wells, "'Unknown Scribes of Unknown Worth': The Working Class at the Turn of the Century in Canadian Poetry and Novels of Social Criticism," Carleton University, March 1979; and "The Shadow of the

Workingman," Carleton University, May 1979. The quote is from *Ontario, Bureau of Industry, Annual Report*, 1892, Part VI, p. 18.

93 *Canadian Labor Reformer*, 22 May 1886.

94 *Palladium of Labor*, 27 June 1885, 17 August 1885, 26 September 1885.

95 Ibid., 17 July 1886, 31 July 1886, 14 August 1886; *Brantford Expositor*, 20 August 1886.

96 *Palladium of Labor*, 21 August 1886, 18 September 1886.

97 Ibid., 23 February 1884.

98 *Labor Union*, 27 January 1883.

99 *Palladium of Labor*, 15 May 1886.

100 *Journal of United Labor*, 25 March 1886. Cf., London's "Omnia Vincit Labor" in *London Advertiser*, 13 October 1886.

101 *Stratford Beacon*, 16 October 1885.

102 See *Palladium of Labor*, 4 September 1886, 16 October 1886, 30 October 1886, 6 November 1886, 13 November 1886, 27 November 1886, 11 December 1886, 18 December 1886.

103 Ibid., 19 September 1885.

104 *Journal of United Labor*, 28 May 1887. Such foreign-language Assemblies were rare in Ontario, although German-American socialist LAs were quite common in the United States. See Paul Buhle, "Knights and Socialists," unpublished paper presented to the Knights of Labor Centennial Symposium, Newberry Library, Chicago, 17–19 May 1979.

105 See Robin, *Radical Politics*, pp. 30, 87, 124–5, 135, 219–20, 224, 229, 234–42, 246; Palmer, *A Culture in Conflict*, pp. 227–31.

106 *Journal of United Labor*, 25 February 1888.

107 Marks to Powderly, 12 May 1890, London, PP. On "Nationalist Clubs" in western Ontario in the 1880s and 1890s see Wrigley, "Socialism," p. 686. Decline is recorded in *Proceedings of the General Assembly of the Knights of Labor in America, 1888, Indianapolis, Indiana* (Philadelphia, 1889), p. 2. On Marks cf., *Labor Advocate*, 30 January 1891, 29 May 1891.

108 W. L. Davis, "A History of the Early Labour Movement in London, Ontario," M.A. thesis, University of Western Ontario, 1947, p. 28; Wrigley, "Socialism," p. 686.

109 See *Labor Advocate*, 29 May 1891, 10 July 1891; Robin, *Radical Politics*, p. 30; Jacqueline Flint Cahan, "A Survey of Political Activities in the Ontario Labour Movement, 1850–1935," M.A. thesis, University of Toronto, 1946, pp. 10–14.

110 See *Hamilton Spectator*, 27 February 1897, 15 January 1898, 29 January 1898; *Proceedings of the Eleventh Annual Session of the Trades and Labor Congress, London, 1895* (Ottawa, 1895), p. 4; *Industrial Banner*, May 1903, June 1903, September 1903, May 1905, February 1906, June 1907, June 1909.

111 On the strengths and weaknesses of the 1870s see Bernard Ostry, "Conservatives, Liberals, and Labour in the 1870s," *Canadian Historical Review*, 41 (1960), pp. 93–104; John H. Battye, "The 'Nine Hour Pioneers': Genesis of the Canadian Labour Movement," *Labour/Le Travailleur*, 4 (1979), pp. 25–56; Steven Langdon, *The Emergence of the Canadian Working-Class Movement* (Toronto, 1975); Gregory S. Kealey, *Toronto Workers Respond*, pp. 124–71; Palmer, *A Culture in Conflict*, pp. 125–52; Debi Wells, "Workingman's Representative: Daniel O'Donoghue; the 1870s," unpublished manuscript, Carleton University, April 1979.

112 Unidentified and undated clipping regarding sermons in Woodstock, London, and Stratford in Joseph T. Marks to Powderly, 12 May 1890, PP; *Ingersoll Chronicle and Canadian Dairyman*, 3 June 1886, 27 May 1886; *Stratford Beacon*, 16 April 1886; *Palladium of Labor*, 5 June 1886, 20 March 1886, 27 March 1886, 7 No-

vember 1885; *Hamilton Spectator*, 25 October 1883; *Journal of United Labor*, 28 May 1884; *London Advertiser*, 5 January 1884, 31 March 1886.

113 *Palladium of Labor*, 12 December 1885.

114 Ibid., 8 September 1883.

115 See the comments in the poems, "Why Don't the Working Man Go to Church," and "The Workingman," *Ottawa Daily Citizen*, 26 May 1876, 22 September 1891; Machar, *Roland Graeme;* Albert Carman, *Ryerson Embury;* Alan Sullivan, *The Inner Door* (Toronto, 1917), pp. 206–7; *Globe*, 6 February 1892; *Palladium of Labor*, 28 September 1883, 17 November 1883, 12 September 1885, 14 March 1885, 31 October 1885, 20 March 1886, 24 April 1886, 3 July 1886, H. Francis Perry, "The Workingman's Alienation from the Church," *American Journal of Sociology*, 4 (March, 1899), p. 626.

116 *Palladium of Labor*, 28 November 1885. Cf., *Cornwall Freeholder*, 1 July 1887; *Labor Union*, 10 March 1883, 13 January 1883, 20 January 1883, 27 January 1883, 3 February 1883, 17 March 1883, 24 March 1883; *Palladium of Labor*, 31 October 1885, 17 April 1886, 13 November 1886, 28 February 1885, 14 March 1885, 24 April 1886; *Labor Advocate*, 5 December 1890, 6 February 1891, 3 July 1891, for a wide range of criticisms of the church, often linking true religion to the cause of the Knights of Labor.

117 *Rideau Record*, 14 July 1887.

118 On temperance see *Gananoque Reporter*, 13 August 1887; *Canadian Labor Reformer*, 19 June 1886, 10 July 1886, 17 July 1886, 28 August 1886, 19 November 1886; *Journal of United Labor*, 24 September 1887; *Labor Union*, 13 January 1883; *Palladium of Labor*, 11 August 1883, 1 December 1883, 12 January 1884, 31 May 1884, 7 August 1886, 27 November 1886, 7 December 1886; *London Advertiser*, 4 June 1886; *Belleville Intelligencer*, 26 September 1883, 9 February 1884, 18 October 1884, 10 March 1887; David Brundage, "The Producing Classes and the Saloon: Denver in the 1880s," paper presented to the Knights of Labor Centennial Symposium, Newberry Library, Chicago, 17–19 May 1979; Samuel Walker, "Terence V. Powderly, The Knights of Labor, and the Temperance Issue," *Societas*, 5 (Autumn 1975), pp. 279–94. For working-class readers see *British Whig*, 15 June 1887; *Palladium of Labor*, 17 October 1885, 24 October 1885; *Labor Union*, 27 January 1883; *London Advertiser*, 20 October 1886, 22 October 1886; *Prescott Journal*, 27 March 1890, 10 April 1890, 17 April 1890, 1 May 1890, 15 May 1890.

119 Cross to GMW and the General Executive Board, 9 June 1887, PP.

120 See Paul Campbell Appleton, "The Sunshine and the Shade: Labour Activism in Central Canada, 1850–1860," M.A. thesis, University of Calgary, 1974; Gregory S. Kealey, "The Orange Order in Toronto: Religious Riot and the Working Class," in Kealey and Warrian, eds., *Essays*, pp. 13–24; Palmer, *A Culture in Conflict*, pp. 43–6.

121 See *Palladium of Labor*, 12 October 1884, 18 July 1885, 15 August 1885, 27 March 1886, 27 November 1886.

122 Ibid., 15 August 1885.

123 See Eric Foner, "Class, Ethnicity, and Radicalism in the Gilded Age: The Land League and Irish America," *Marxist Perspectives*, 1 (Summer 1978), pp. 6–55. Cf., David Montgomery, *Beyond Equality: Labor and the Radical Republicans, 1862–1872* (New York, 1967), esp. pp. 127–34; Walkowitz, *Worker City, Company Town*, pp. 160–75; Oscar Handlin, *Boston's Immigrants* (New York, 1968); James D. Young, *The Rousing of the Scottish Working Class* (London, 1979), pp. 145–55.

124 Powderly, *Path I Trod*, p. 179. Cf., John W. Bennett, "The Knights of Labor and the Clan-Na-Gael," paper presented to the Knights of Labor Centennial Conference, Newberry Library, Chicago, 17–19 May 1979.

125 See Hereward Senior, *The Fenians and Canada* (Toronto, 1978).
126 Note the intriguing discussion in D. C. Lyne and Peter M. Toner, "Fenianism in Canada, 1874–1884," *Studia Hibernica*, 12 (1972), pp. 27–76.
127 See, for instance, James Hunter, "The Gaelic Connection: The Highlands, Ireland and nationalism, 1873–1922," *The Scottish Historical Review*, 54 (1975), pp. 178–80.
128 Kealey, *Toronto Workers Respond*, pp. 274–7; Foner, "Class, Ethnicity and Radicalism," p. 46.
129 *London Advertiser*, 21 February 1885, 10, 11, 14 November 1885, 8 December 1885, 6 February 1886.
130 Gordon Bishop, "Recollections of the Amalgamated;" *Palladium of Labor*, 27 November 1886; *Brockville Recorder*, 13 November 1886.
131 *Palladium of Labor*, 10 October 1885, 27 March 1886, 7 December 1886; General Assembly, *Proceedings*, 1887, p. 1841.
132 See O'Donoghue to Powderly, January 1887, PP.
133 O'Donoghue to Powderly, 12 December 1887; O'Donoghue to Barry, 11 January 1887, PP; *Ottawa Citizen*, 6 February 1886. On the Taschereau condemnation see Henry Joseph Brown, *The Catholic Church and the Knights of Labor* (Washington, 1949); Chan, "Canadian Knights of Labor," pp. 100–203; Kennedy, *Knights of Labor in Canada*, pp. 77–98. One Ontario note of distress regarding the Catholic Church's antagonism was sounded in London. See Hugh A. McLean to Powderly, 26 February 1886, PP.
134 *Globe*, 9 March 1886; *Palladium of Labor*, 27 March 1886.
135 See David Montgomery, *Workers' Control in America* (New York, 1979), p. 21; *Palladium of Labor*, 3 November 1883, 4 October 1884; Paul Buhle, "The Knights of Labor in Rhode Island," *Radical History Review*, 18 (Spring 1978), p. 58; Susan Levine, "Women in the Knights of Labor," paper presented at Third Berkshire Conference on Women's History, Bryn Mawr, Pennsylvania, June 1976; "'The Best Men in the Order': Women in the Knights of Labor," paper presented to the Knights of Labor Centennial Conference, Newberry Library, Chicago, 17–19 May 1979; Philip S. Foner, *Women and the American Labor Movement: From Colonial Times to the Eve of World War I* (New York, 1979), p. 206; Nancy Dye, "Louisville Woolen Mills Operatives and the Knights of Labor," paper presented to the Knights of Labor Centennial Conference, Newberry Library, Chicago, 17–19 May 1979.
136 *Palladium of Labor*, 19 June 1886.
137 John Lawson to Powderly, 5 April 1889, PP.
138 *Palladium of Labor*, 29 September 1883.
139 Ibid., 12 September 1885, 13 December 1884, 24 July 1886, 25 April 1885, 2 October 1886; and on the problems inherent in organizing women employed as domestics, teachers, seamstresses, etc., see Roberts, *'Honest Womanhood.'*
140 *Brantford Expositor*, 16 July 1866; *London Advertiser*, 30 October 1886, 17 February 1885. Both the strengths and weaknesses of the Order's position are revealed in Phillips Thompson, "Woman's Rights," *Palladium of Labor*, 20 March 1886. Cf., *Journal of United Labor*, 10 October 1884, 25 September 1885, 8 January 1887, 15 January 1887. If the Knights failed to go to the root of women's oppression, however, it needs to be stressed that no other sector confronted the issue so squarely. See, for instance, Wayne Roberts, "'Rocking the Cradle for the World': The New Woman and Maternal Feminism, Toronto, 1877–1914," in Linda Kealey, ed., *A Not Unreasonable Claim* (Toronto, 1979), pp. 15–46. George is quoted in *Palladium of Labor*, 9 August 1884.
141 Ontario, Bureau of Industry, *Annual Report*, 1887, p. 44; and 1886.
142 Fred A. Fenton to Powderly, 7 December 1882, PP; General Assembly, *Proceed-*

*ings*, 1889, p. 3; General Assembly *Proceedings*, 1888, pp. 3–4; *Welland Tribune*, 16 July 1886, 19 August 1887.

143 Rose LeMay to Powderly, 26 September 1888; Powderly to LeMay, 13 October 1888; Powderly to Thomas Melone, 22 August 1888, PP; *Journal of United Labor*, 3 March 1892. Picton's Elizabeth Johnson would appear frequently in Phillips Thompson's *Labor Advocate*, and she would be one of only four correspondents and supporters Thompson thanked as the journal failed. See *Labor Advocate*, 29 May, 17 April, 15 May, 10 July, 7 August, 14 August, 18 September, 25 September, 2 October 1891. The lines of verse conclude a poem on "The Fourmies Massacre," *Labor Advocate*, 29 May 1891.

144 John R. Brown to Powderly, 3 December 1884, PP.

145 See *London Advertiser*, 29 October 1886; *Journal of United Labor*, 25 September 1885.

146 On Darling, see *Dictionary of National Biography* (Britain), XIV, p. 57.

147 Williams, "Beyond Actually Existing Socialism," pp. 3–4.

148 *Canadian Magazine*, 4 (1894–5), p. 587.

149 *Gananoque Reporter*, 5 November 1887, 12 November 1887, 19 November 1887, 26 November 1887, 3 December 1887.

150 *Palladium of Labor*, 24 November 1883, 4 October 1884.

151 Christopher Hill, *The World Turned Upside Down: Radical Ideas During the English Revolution* (New York, 1972), p. 310.

152 See Robin, *Radical Politics*, p. 28; Ostry, "Conservatives, Liberals, and Labour in the 1880s," p. 161. Even Goodwyn, the most sensitive U.S. critic of the Populists' movement culture, denies a similar culture to American workers and the Knights of Labor. But Goodwyn appears to define the failure of American workers to forge such a culture solely in terms of political success, arguing that "a working-class culture of economic and political consciousness essential to the maintenance of an insurgent posture in the presence of the continuing cultural influences of the corporate state" had not developed. (*Democratic Promise*, p. 308.) Such an orientation, which ignores noninsurgent electoral struggles, and deifies "politics," seems to strain the historical record. Note here the discussions in Leon R. Fink, "Workingmen's Democracy: The Knights of Labor in Local Politics, 1886–1896," Ph.D. thesis, University of Rochester, 1977; Fink, "The Uses of Political Power: Towards a Theory of the Labor Movement in the Era of the Knights of Labor," paper presented to the Knights of Labor Centennial Symposium, Newberry Library, Chicago, 17–19 May 1979; Fink, "Class Conflict in the Gilded Age: The Figure and the Phantom," *Radical History Review*, 3 (1975), pp. 56–74. An explicit critique of Goodwyn's failure to address the strengths of a late-nineteenth-century working-class movement culture is found in David Montgomery, "On Goodwyn's Populists," *Marxist Perspectives*, 1 (Spring 1978), pp. 166–73.

153 "Failure is much commoner than success, at any period, though it has seldom been accorded even a small corner in the work of historians; it is also more endearing, and much more human." Richard Cobb, *Death in Paris, 1795–1801* (New York, 1978), p. 102.

154 There are those who will suggest that the figures are grossly exaggerated, but we doubt it. Estimates often appeared in local papers, sources with little to gain from inflating the size of a Knights of Labor crowd. On other occasions crowds were actually counted to the person, as in London in 1886, when someone counted 4,019 workers on parade, or in Toronto in 1886 when the labor press recorded the numbers of workers marching in each trade grouping or LA. See Palmer, "Give us the road," p. 117; *Canadian Labor Reformer*, 18 September 1886.

155 *Palladium of Labor*, 26 December 1885.

## 9. The people's strike

1 Albert R. Carman, *The Preparation of Ryerson Embury* (Toronto, 1900), esp. pp. 127–8, 130–2. Cf., Mary Vipond, "Blessed are the peacemakers: the labour question in Canadian social gospel fiction," *Journal of Canadian Studies*, 10 (August, 1975), pp. 32–43; Ramsay Cook, "Henry George and the Poverty of Canadian Progress," Canadian Historical Association, *Historical Papers* (1977), pp. 142–58; Gene Howard Homel, "Fading Beams of the Nineteenth Century: Radicalism and Early Socialism in Canada's 1890s," *Labour/Le Travailleur*, 5 (Spring 1980) 7–31.

2 See Norman J. Ware, *The Labor Movement in the United States, 1860–1890: A Study in Democracy* (New York, 1964), pp. 117–54; Gerald M. Grob, *Workers and Utopia: A Study of Ideological Conflict in the American Labor Movement, 1865–1900* (Chicago, 1969), esp. pp. 37, 148–9. Numerous papers presented at the Knights of Labor Centennial Symposium, Newberry Library, Chicago, 17–19 May 1979, addressed this theme. Among them: Richard J. Oestreicher, "The Limits of Labor Radicalism: Tom Barry and the Knights of Labor;" Steven J. Ross, "Strikes, Knights, and Political Fights: The May Day Strikes, The Knights of Labor, and the Rise of the United Labor Party in Nineteenth-Century Cincinnati;" Jeremy Brecher, "The Knights of Labor and Strikes, 1885–86." Cf. despite the interpretive deficiencies, Michael J. Cassity, "Modernization and Social Crisis: The Knights of Labor and a Midwest Community, 1885–86," *Journal of American History*, 65 (June 1979), pp. 41–61. For Canada see Douglas R. Kennedy, *The Knights of Labor in Canada* (London, 1956), pp. 57–76.

3 The above paragraphs draw upon Alan Dawley, *Class and Community: The Industrial Revolution in Lynn* (Cambridge, 1976), pp. 190–1; Herbert G. Gutman, *Work, Culture, and Society in Industrializing America* (New York, 1976). But note, for the disintegration of the class-community relationship, David Montgomery, "Herbert Gutman's Nineteenth-Century America," *Labor History*, 19 (Summer 1978), pp. 419–29; John T. Cumbler, "Labor, Capital and Community: The Struggle for Power," *Labor History*, 15 (Summer 1974), pp. 395–416. The *Palladium of Labor* quote is from 15 August 1885.

4 Devlin to Powderly, 23 March 1886, PP.

5 See, for instance, *Ingersoll Chronicle and Canadian Dairyman*, 24 June 1886; *Ottawa Citizen*, 13 October 1885, 8 March 1886, 9 March 1886, 20 March 1886, 3 April 1886; *Thorold Post*, 12 March 1886, 2 April 1886; *Prescott Messenger*, 7 May 1886, 3 August 1886, 17 August 1894; *Cornwall Freeholder*, 12 February 1886, 16 April 1886; *Perth Expositor*, 15 April 1886; *London Advertiser*, 5 April 1886, 16 April 1886; *Palladium of Labor*, 2 April 1886, 10 April 1886; *Labor Union*, 13 January 1883; T. V. Powderly, *The Path I Trod: The Autobiography of Terence V. Powderly* (New York, 1940), pp. 104–5; *Record of the Proceedings of the General Assembly Held at Hamilton, Ontario, October 5–13, 1885*, p. 20; *Proceedings, GA, Cleveland*, 19 February 1886.

6 *Palladium of Labor*, 8 December 1883; *Journal of United Labor*, 22 October 1888; *London Advertiser*, 19 February 1886.

7 *Palladium of Labor*, 23 May 1885; *Stratford Beacon*, 16 October 1885; *Ottawa Citizen*, 6 February 1886, 20 August 1887; *Gananoque Reporter*, 16 March 1889.

8 *Journal of United Labor*, April 1884; Blain to Powderly, 10 April 1886, PP; *Canadian Labor Reformer*, 15 May 1886; *Gananoque Reporter*, 3 December 1887.

9 *London Advertiser*, 22 September 1887, and *The Christian Guardian*, 18 May 1887, quoted in Kennedy, *Knights of Labor in Canada*, pp. 110–11. Cf., *London Advertiser*, 3 March 1886; *Palladium of Labor*, 17 July 1886, for other typical anti-Knights of Labor statements.

10 *Cornwall Freeholder*, 15 July 1887; *Palladium of Labor*, 31 October, 1885; *Journal of United Labor*, 2 April 1887.

11 *Palladium of Labor*, 8 August 1885; *Ingersoll Chronicle and Canadian Dairyman*, 8 July 1886; *Labor Union*, 27 January 1883.

12 This overly brief discussion of Barry draws upon Ware, *Labor Movement;* and especially Oestreicher, "The Limits of Labor Radicalism." Cf., *Journal of United Labor*, 18 October 1888; *Proceedings, GA, Indianapolis, 1888*, Document 541; Carey to Powderly, 19 February 1889, St. Catharines, PP.

13 See O'Donoghue to Barry, 11 January 1887; O'Donoghue to Powderly, n.d. (January 1887?), PP. Such a negative perspective on strikes draws heavily upon Grob's *Workers and Utopia*, an intellectual history that avoided any substantive discussion of local situations or rank-and-file sentiments. It is therefore a poor guide to the Order's actual relationship to class conflict.

14 Note the discussion of the strike in Eugene Forsey, "The Telegraphers' Strike of 1883," *Transactions of the Royal Society of Canada*, 4th ser., 10 (1971), pp. 245–59.

15 *Whig*, 4 August 1883; *Brockville Recorder*, 25 August 1883; *Palladium of Labor*, 18 August 1883; *Belleville Intelligencer*, 30 July 1883, 31 July 1883, 6 August 1883, 7 August 1883; *Brantford Expositor*, 20 July 1883, 27 July 1883; *Ottawa Citizen*, 20 July 1883, 25 July 1883, 1 August 1883, 20 August 1883.

16 *Christian Journal* and "A.B." quoted in *Palladium of Labor*, 11 August 1883.

17 *Belleville Intelligencer*, 8 August 1883; *Palladium of Labor*, 25 August 1883. On public ownership, cf., *Palladium of Labor*, 18 August 1883; *Toronto Daily Mail*, 26 July 1883; Forsey, "Strike," p. 258.

18 *Labor Advocate*, 5 December 1890; *Journal of United Labor*, 10 September 1884; *Palladium of Labor*, 19 January 1884, 19 June 1884. Cf., Bryan D. Palmer, *A Culture in Conflict: Skilled Workers and Industrial Capitalism in Hamilton, Ontario, 1860–1914* (Montreal, 1979), pp. 71–96; Dennis M. Zembala, "Glassworkers and the Knights of Labor: Technology, Labor and the Roots of Modernism," paper presented to the Knights of Labor Centennial Symposium, Newberry Library, Chicago, 17–19 May 1979; Gregory S. Kealey, *Toronto Workers Respond to Industrial Capitalism, 1867–1892* (Toronto, 1980), pp. 37–97. In 1886 the *Boston Evening Transcript* claimed that the Knights of Labor were so strong that they held "almost absolute control in the workrooms of every important factory." See Cumbler, "Labor, Capital, Community," p. 402.

19 *London Advertiser*, 7 October 1886; *Palladium of Labor*, 1 May 1886.

20 *Brockville Recorder*, 14, 16, 30 May 1881.

21 Ibid., 17, 21, 23 August 1882, 3 November 1882.

22 Ibid., 20 June 1883, 5, 24 July 1883. Dale Chisamore has compiled a list of 36 members of LA 2311 (1882–1886) in conjunction with his Queen's University M.A. thesis research on Mechanics' Institutes in eastern Ontario. Many of the members were union molders, probably employed at Smart's. We are grateful to Mr. Chisamore for sharing his research with us. Cf., *Proceedings, GA, Cincinnati, 1883*, p. 164; *Brockville Recorder*, 17 November 1883.

23 The strike is described in detail in Dale Chisamore, et al., *Brockville: A Social History* (Brockville, 1975), pp. 85–91. Cf., *Brockville Recorder*, 15 January 1884, 10, 11 March 1884.

24 *Brockville Recorder*, 28 August 1884; *Proceedings, GA, Philadelphia, 1884*, pp. 43, 642.

25 On Brown and the early organization of the Knights of Labor in Oshawa, see Brown to Powderly, 29 September 1882, 16 January 1882, 10 April 1883, 1 October 1886, PP; *Brockville Recorder*, 27 September 1887; *Gananoque Reporter*, 1 October 1887. On Brown's involvement in the 1872 struggle, see Leo A. Johnson, *History of the County of Ontario, 1615–1873* (Whitby, Ontario, 1973), pp. 336, 373. Note also

Eugene Forsey to Keith W. Ross, Secretary-Treasurer, Oshawa District Labour Council, 12 July 1966, Canadian Labour Congress Files, MG 28 I 103, Volume 248, Public Archives of Canada; Jonathan Garlock and N. C. Builder, "Knights of Labor Data Bank," Inter-University Consortium for Political Research, Ann Arbor, Michigan, 1973.

26 *Palladium of Labor*, 20, 27 October 1883, 17 November 1883, 1, 8 December 1883.

27 See Brown's letter in ibid., 15 December 1883.

28 Allchin to Powderly, 20 October 1884, 25 October, 1884, PP.

29 *Proceedings of the Third Session of the Trades and Labor Congress, Hamilton, 1887* (Toronto, 1887), pp. 26–8; Toronto Trades and Labour Council, *Minutes*, Volume 4, 58 (5 February 1886), 62 (19 February 1886), 64–5 (23 February 1886); *Toronto News*, 23 February 1886, 6, 15 March 1886. See *Iron Molders' International Journal*, January 1884, April 1884, August 1885, October 1885, December 1885, January 1886, July 1886, September 1886, October 1886, January–March 1887, October 1887, November 1887, September 1888–October 1889, 31 January 1891.

30 *Labor Record* (Toronto), 14 May 1886; Iron Molders' International Union Local 191, *Minutes*, 1886, Gainey Collection, Trent University, Peterborough.

31 *Brockville Recorder*, 2 April 1886, 22 April 1886. Cf., *London Advertiser*, 23 April 1886; Ontario, Bureau of Industry, *Annual Report*, 1887, p. 44, and 1888, p. 17.

32 Details of the strikes are found in *British Daily Whig*, 13, 14, 16, 18, 19, 23 May 1887, 14 June 1887, 8, 12, 13, 23 July 1887; Ontario, Bureau of Industry, *Annual Report*, 1887, p. 42; *Gananoque Reporter*, 21 May 1887; Greg Kealey, ed., *Canada Investigates Industrialism: The Royal Commission on the Relations of Labor and Capital, 1889* (Toronto, 1973), pp. 176–9. Cf., A. E. Shields to John W. Hayes, 20 October 1892, HP, for a comment on an ironworker's autonomy.

33 *Brockville Recorder*, 15 May 1886; *Gananoque Reporter*, 19 November 1887, 3 December 1887.

34 See *Gananoque Reporter*, 26 March 1887; *Brockville Recorder*, 26 March 1887; *Annual Report, Bureau of Industries, 1887*, pp. 42–4.

35 Details on the Order in Gananoque, with special reference to the second conflict at Skinner's. are found in *Gananoque Reporter*, 25, 26 February 1888, 3, 10 March 1888, 13 October 1888; *Brockville Recorder*, 27 February 1888, 7, 10 March 1888; Gordon Bishop, "A Brief History of Trade Unions in Gananoque, Ontario," unpublished typescript; Garlock and Builder, "Knights of Labor Data Bank;" David H. Brown, RS, LA 10185, to Powderly, 22 October 1888 (?); H.S. Johnson, MW, LA 10185, to Powderly, 22 October 1888, PP; Ontario, Bureau of Industry, *Annual Report*, 1888, p. 17; Ontario, Bureau of Industry, *Annual Report*, 1889, p. 24.

36 Linch to Powderly, 11 May 1889, PP.

37 *Journal of United Labor*, 23 April 1887, 10 September 1887; *St. Thomas Times*, 1 August 1887; *Journal of United Labor*, 10 August 1887; Garlock and Builder, "Knights of Labor Data Bank;" Frost and Wood Company, *Factory Rules* (Smiths Falls, n.d.); Eugene Forsey, *History of Canadian Trade Unionism*, forthcoming, 1982, Chapter 7, Public Archives of Canada, Reel M-2214.

38 *Proceedings, GA, Minneapolis, 1887*, p. 1427; Forsey to Ross, 12 July 1866, CLC Files, PAC. On the Cedar Dale shop see Johnson, *Ontario County*, pp. 328–9. Cf., the successful stand taken by shoemakers at Hamilton's MacPherson & Company, where members of the Order twisted the company's arm to submit to the shop committee demands, outlined in Palmer, *A Culture in Conflict*, pp. 85–6.

39 *Brockville Recorder*, 30 July 1883, 31 July 1883, 3 August 1883, 17 April 1884; *Proceedings, GA, Philadelphia, 1884*, p. 642.

40 *Brockville Recorder*, 3 September 1888, 23 November 1883, 28 November 1883.

The CPR conflict was probably exacerbated by the political economy of railroad construction. Brockville had "bonussed" the line in the amount of $10,000 and many workers must have resented such a subsidy. Information courtesy of Dale Chisamore.

41 Ibid., 8 May 1888; *Stratford Beacon*, 3 May 1887; Boucock to Powderly, 27 July 1892, PP; Peter DeLottinville, "The St. Croix Manufacturing Company and its Influence on the St. Croix Community, 1880–1892," M.A. thesis, Dalhousie University, 1979; Ontario, Bureau of Industry, *Annual Report*, 1886, 1889, p. 22, 1890. Cf., Sara Jeanette Duncan, *Selected Journalism* (Ottawa, 1978), p. 12.

42 Susanna Moodie, *Life in the Clearings* (Toronto, 1959), p. 8; *London Advertiser*, 21 May 1886, 4 June 1886; *Palladium of Labor*, 16 October 1886.

43 *Canada Labor Courier*, 30 December 1886, 13 January 1887. The Bureau of Industries, *Report*, 1887, p. 46, reported from Chatham: "The United Business Men's Association . . . is still in existence and in about the same standing – about 40 members. Its councils are secret, and it is used as a sort of protective association for the benefit of its members only. It has no political significance but is very adverse to the Knights of Labor." With the passing of the Knights of Labor, the Chatham employers' association disbanded. See Ontario, Bureau of Industry, *Annual Report*, 1889, p. 28.

44 *St. Thomas Times*, 15 November 1887; *Journal of United Labor*, 16 May 1889.

45 *Palladium of Labor*, 26 June 1886; *London Advertiser*, 17 May 1886, 14, 16, 20, 28 July 1886, 8 September 1886.

46 *British Daily Whig*, 8 June 1888. On the beginnings of early closing agitation in Cornwall see *Cornwall Freeholder*, 29 April 1887, 15 July 1887, 22 July 1887. On Gananoque see *Gananoque Reporter*, 6 August 1887. On St. Catharines and St. Thomas see *Palladium of Labor*, 19 June 1886, 2 October 1886, *St. Thomas Times*, 24 April 1886, 1, 5, 7, 8, 20, 22 May 1886.

47 *Ottawa Citizen*, 17 July 1891, 21 July 1891, 12 September 1891, 2 December 1891; Kilt to Powderly, 24 May 1893, PP.

48 *Cornwall Freeholder*, 22 January 1886, 19 March 1886, 26 March 1886, 23 April 1886; Garlock and Builder, "Knights of Labor Data Bank."

49 *Brockville Recorder*, 12 July 1887; Ontario, Bureau of Industry, *Annual Report*, 1887, pp. 42–3.

50 The above draws upon *Gananoque Reporter*, 4 February 1888, 11 February 1888, 18 February 1888; Ontario, Bureau of Industry, *Annual Report*, 1888, p. 15; Kealey, ed., *Canada Investigates Industrialism*, pp. 179–92; Forsey, *History of Canadian Trade Unionism*, ch. 7; *Census of Canada, 1880–81*, III (Ottawa, 1883), p. 485.

51 *Gananoque Reporter*, 16 March 1889; Ontario, Bureau of Industry, *Annual Report*, 1889, p. 22.

52 The above paragraphs draw upon the following: R. R. Elliot to Powderly, 12 July 1888 (telegram and letter), 19 July 1888; William Hogan to Powderly, 21 September 1888, 5 November 1888 (letter and enclosure); Archy Sloan to Powderly, 16 July 1888; William Sloan to Powderly, 3 September 1888; T. V. Powderly to Sloan, 10 September 1888, PP; *Journal of United Labor*, 12 July 1888 (letter from William Sloan); Garlock and Builder, "Knights of Labor Data Bank." The importance of the lumber and shingle mills in the Muskoka region as a whole is revealed in *Census of Canada, 1880–81*, III, p. 378. Over 800 adults and 64 children worked in the 74 mills. Their total yearly wages hovered around the $200,000 mark, and they produced products valued in the neighborhood of $775,000. Cf., O'Donoghue to Powderly, 9 August 1888, PP; *Globe*, 25 July 1888, 10 August 1888.

53 The following relies upon Edward McKenna, "Unorganized Labour Versus Man-

agement: The Strike at the Chaudière Lumber Mills, 1891," *Histoire Sociale/Social History*, 5 (November 1972), pp. 186–211; Forsey, *History of Canadian Trade Unionism*, ch. 7; Robert Peter Gillis, "E. H. Bronson and Corporate Capitalism: A Study in Canadian Business Thought and Action, 1880–1910," M.A. thesis, Queen's University, 1975, esp. pp. 72–81; Ontario, Bureau of Industry, *Annual Report*, 1892, pp. 38, 40, 42, 45; as well as a reading of the Ottawa newspapers, the *Citizen* and the *Journal*, for the months of September and October 1891.

54 See Garlock and Builder, "Knights of Labor Data Bank;" *Journal of United Labor*, 20 August 1887; *Ottawa Citizen*, 6 February 1886, 13 March 1886, 20 August 1887, 7 December 1888, 16 June 1890, 16 August 1890, 9 September 1890, 2 December 1890; *Le Spectateur*, 15 September 1891.

55 Bryan D. Palmer, "Discordant Music: Charivaris and Whitecapping in Nineteenth-Century North America," *Labor/Le Travailleur*, 3 (1978), p. 37; Ontario, Bureau of Industry, *Annual Report*, 1892, p. 45; Kilt to Powderly, 28 October 1894; A. W. Wright to General Executive Board (Philadelphia), 23 August 1893, PP; J. W. Clarke to E. H. Bronson, 27 May 1895, Bronson Papers, PAC.

56 W. E. Greening, *The Ottawa* (Toronto, 1961), pp. 150–2; James W. Thompson and J. A. Bryant, *Lumbering on the Rivière du Livre* (Ottawa, 1973), p. 81. Our thanks to Gerald Tulchinsky for bringing these sources to our attention. Cf., Pierre Louis Lapointe, *Buckingham, 1906* (Hull, 1973).

57 *Journal of United Labor*, 10 May 1884, 25 November 1884, 4 June 1887; *Labor Advocate*, 6 February 1891; *Canadian Labor Reformer*, 4 December 1886; Evans to Powderly, 25 August 1885, PP. On opposition to coal dealers in Kingston see *Proceedings, GA, Indianapolis, 1888*, Document 990, and in Brockville see Chisamore, et al., *Brockville*, p. 95.

58 See *Canadian Labor Reformer*, 21 August 1886, 15 January 1886; *Journal of United Labor*, 10 October 1884, 25 February 1886, 7 April 1888, 13 September 1888; *Palladium of Labor*, 23 February 1884.

59 *London Advertiser*, 17 March 1886; *Brockville Recorder*, 13 August 1888, 30 December 1887; *St. Thomas Times*, 16 November 1886.

60 *Gananoque Reporter*, 6 April 1889, 11 May 1889, 1 June 1889, 7 September 1889; *London Advertiser*, 27 January 1883, 27 August 1884, 1 January 1885; *Toronto World*, 30 December 1884; *Palladium of Labor*, 23 February 1884, 24 May 1884, 13 November 1886.

61 *Labor Union*, 3 February 1883; *Palladium of Labor*, 1 March 1884, 20 June 1885; *Journal of United Labor*, 25 October 1885; Palmer, *A Culture in Conflict*, pp. 93–4. A sketch of the Order's cooperative activities is provided in Forsey, *History of Canadian Trade Unionism*, ch. 7; Kennedy, *Knights of Labor in Canada*, pp. 42–5, where efforts of Quebec and British Columbia Knights of Labor are also described.

62 *British Daily Whig*, 18 May 1887; *Palladium of Labor*, 31 May 1884, 7 June 1884, 14 June 1884, 21 June 1884; *Proceedings, GA, Richmond, 1886*, pp. 129, 133; Kennedy, *Knights of Labor in Canada*, p. 43. London's LA 3305 supported cooperation enthusiastically, contributing to the Order's coal mine and urging other Assemblies to do likewise, breaking down the power of the coal rings and striking a blow for working-class self-sufficiency. See *Journal of United Labor*, 25 November 1885.

63 On the Merrickville venture, see *Gananoque Reporter*, 10 March 1888; *Brockville Recorder*, 13 August 1888; Ontario, Bureau of Industry, *Annual Report*, 1889, p. 28.

64 On the Chatham biscuit factory, see *Palladium of Labor*, 11 September 1886; *Monetary Times*, n.d., quoted in *Brantford Expositor*, 17 June 1887; *Canada Labor Courier*, 13 January 1887, 30 December 1886; Victor Lauriston, *Romantic Kent: The Story of a County* (Chatham, 1952), p. 588, implies that the establishment of the cooperative

venture coincided with involvement in the political campaign of 1886–7, which the *Canada Labor Courier* hinted was at the root of the employers' antagonism to the Order. Lauriston also states that the cooperative undertaking was financed by workingmen in amounts of from $2 to $500, totaling $10,000. He also suggests some wrongdoing associated with the failure, writing that, "The publication of the stock book of this institution would make interesting reading." None of these assertions and implications are documented.

65 *Palladium of Labor*, 15 May 1886, 26 June 1886, 3 July 1886, 10 July 1886, 21 August 1886, 20 November 1886, 29 May 1886; *Brantford Expositor*, 26 November 1886; *London Advertiser*, 26 May 1887, cited in Kennedy, *The Knights of Labor in Canada*, p. 43.

66 *Brantford Courier*, 30 November 1886; Brown to Powderly, 2 February 1884, PP.

67 *Palladium of Labor*, 21 August 1886, 20 November 1886; *Journal of United Labor*, 7 May 1887; F. D. Phillips to Powderly, 1 March 1886; William H. Lloyd to Powderly, 7 August 1886, PP.

68 R. H. Hessel, "The Labor Movement in London: Some Personal Recollections," unpublished manuscript, Regional Collection, University of Western Ontario; McLean to Powderly, 26 December 1885, PP.

69 *London Advertiser*, 13 January 1885; *Palladium of Labor*, 17 January 1885; Palmer, *A Culture in Conflict*, pp. 83–5; *Report of the Royal Commission on the Relations of Labor and Capital in Canada* (Ottawa, 1889), "Ontario Evidence," II, pp. 790–1. Note a typical case, an Ottawa tailors' strike in 1891. See *Ottawa Citizen*, 16–28 April 1891.

70 Joseph Wilae to Powderly, 17 May 1888; Powderly to Wilae, 23 May 1888, PP.

71 See N. J. White, RS, LA 4435, to Powderly, 27 March 1886; E. B. Irving, Recording Secretary, LA 4069, to Powderly, 1 December 1885, 30 April 1886; Richard Trevellick to Powderly, 18 March 1885, PP. Cf., Shelton Stomquist, "The Knights of Labor and Organized Railroad Men," paper presented to the Knights of Labor Centennial Symposium, Newberry Library, Chicago, 17–19 May 1979.

72 David Jones to Powderly, 30 August 1886, PP.

73 See *Labor Leaf*, 23 February 1889; *Labor Advocate*, 19 January 1891, 11 September 1891.

74 See *London Advertiser*, 30 April 1886; *Ottawa Citizen*, 3 May 1886, 11 April 1890; *Palladium of Labor*, 15 May 1886, 20 November 1886; *Canadian Labor Reformer*, 7 May 1887.

75 J. T. Carey to Powderly, 14 September 1888; W. R. James to Powderly, 23 December 1888; John S. McClelland to Powderly, 16 August 1888, PP.

76 Thomas E. Kilroy, LA 3281, to Powderly, 25 June 1887; Charles F. Duycott, Recording Secretary, LA 2900, to Powderly, 20 September 1887, PP; *Proceedings, GA Minneapolis, 1887*, p. 1283.

77 See *Brantford Expositor*, 16 August 1887, 19 March 1886; *Journal of United Labor*, 25 February 1886.

78 The above draws upon *London Advertiser*, 14, 28 May 1886, 13, 22 September 1886; Kealey, ed., *Canada Investigates Industrialism*, pp. 132–43; McLean to Powderly, 3 November 1886, PP. The developing antagonisms between Knights and union cigarmakers turned on many issues. An attack on child labor seemed to be the union's main thrust, and many members of the Order supported their stand; some Knights, however, realized the difficulties an all-out attack would pose for them, because most tobacco workers affiliated with the Order worked in "foul" shops where the labor force was primarily adolescent. Finally, the Knights in London were deeply committed to temperance, and had endorsed the Scott Act, thus

advocating the closing of many taverns. Union cigarworkers opposed this policy, arguing that it cut into their trade, as many cigars were sold in these places, often smoked along with or in lieu of a beer as part of the plebeian custom of "treating."

79 *Palladium of Labor*, 17 May 1884.

80 Howard Rickard to Powderly, 12 April 1886, PP.

## 10. Accomplishment and failure

1 On this history, in which Quebec is more significant than Ontario, see Douglas R. Kennedy, *The Knights of Labor in Canada* (London, 1956), pp. 99–120; Charles Lipton, *The Trade Union Movement in Canada, 1827–1959* (Montreal, 1968), pp. 131–52; H. A. Logan, *Trade Unions In Canada* (Toronto, 1948), pp. 370–1; Jacques Rouillard, *Les Syndicats Nationaux Aux Québec de 1900 à 1930* (Quebec, 1979), pp. 13–135.

2 For a visit to Knights of Labor headquarters in the early 1930s see Fred Landon, "The Knights of Labor: Predecessors of the CIO," *Quarterly Review of Commerce* (Autumn 1937), pp. 5–18.

3 For U.S. evidence see Bruce Laurie, *Working People of Philadelphia, 1800–1850* (Philadelphia, 1980); Milton Cantor, "Introduction," *American Workingclass Culture: Explorations in American Labor and Social History* (Westport, Connecticut, 1979); Steven Ross, "Workers on the Edge: Work, Leisure, and Politics in Industrializing Cincinnati, 1830–1890," Ph.D. dissertation, Princeton University, 1980; Susan Hirsch, *Roots of the American Working Class: the Industrialization of Crafts in Newark, 1800–1860* (Philadelphia, 1978). Canadian early working-class activity is documented in Paul C. Appleton, "The Sunshine and the Shade: Labour Activism in Central Canada, 1850–1860," M.A. thesis, University of Calgary, 1974, while the nativist response to the famine-stricken Irish is revealed in the growth of the Orange Lodge in the 1850s and the Clear Grit reaction to Catholic "state churchism" and "priestism." See Cecil J. Houston and William J. Smyth, *The Sash Canada Wore: A Historical Geography of the Orange Order in Canada* (Toronto, 1980); J.M.S. Careless, *Brown of the Globe: The Voice of Upper Canada, 1818–1859* (Toronto, 1959).

4 On the American Protective Association (APA) see Donald C. Kinzer, *An Episode in Anti-Catholicism: The American Protective Association* (Seattle, 1964). The APA's disruptive impact on the labor movement is discussed in John Higham, *Strangers in the Land: Patterns of American Nativism, 1860–1925* (New York, 1963), pp. 81–2; Mike Davis, "Why the U.S. Working Class is Different," *New Left Review*, 123 (1980), p. 34; Richard Oestreicher, "Solidarity and Fragmentation: Working People and Class Consciousness in Detroit, 1877–1895," Ph.D. dissertation, Michigan State University, 1979. Debs and Populist leader Ignatius Donnelly claimed that the APA was an instrument of the railway magnates, employed to crush unionism, and Powderly was often held up to APA derision, caricatured as the expression of a Catholic labor leadership determined to undermine American institutions through the encouragement of strikes and boycotts. On the Protestant Protective Association in Canada, see James T. Watt, "Anti-Catholicism in Ontario Politics: The Role of the Protestant Protective Association in the 1894 Election," *Ontario History*, 59 (1967), pp. 57–67; "Anti-Catholic Nativism in Canada: The Protestant Protective Association," *Canadian Historical Review*, 48 (1967), pp. 45–58.

5 On the Jesuits Estates Act, see Roy Dalton, *The Jesuits' Estates Question, 1760–1888: A Study of the Background for the Agitation of 1889* (Toronto, 1968); J. R. Miller, "The Jesuits Estate Act Crisis," *Journal of Canadian Studies*, 9 (August 1974), pp. 36–50. On the Manitoba Schools Question, see Paul Crunican, *Priests and Politics: Mani-*

*toba Schools and the Election of 1896* (Toronto, 1976). Jingoism deserves further study but note David Montgomery, "Labor and the Republic in Industrial America: 1860–1920," *Le mouvement social*, 111 (avril–juin 1980), p. 210; Carman Miller, "A Preliminary Analysis of the Socio-economic Composition of Canada's South African War Contingents," *Histoire Sociale/Social History*, 8 (November 1975), pp. 219–37.

6 See Ross, "Workers on the Edge," p. 596; Oestreicher, "Solidarity and Fragmentation," p. 193; Susan Levine, "Their Own Sphere: Women's Work, the Knights of Labor, and the Transformation of the Carpet Trade, 1870–1890," Ph.D. dissertation, City University of New York, 1979; David Bensman, "Artisan Culture, Business Union: American Hat Finishers in the Nineteenth Century," Ph.D. dissertation, Columbia University, 1977; Michael Gordon, "Studies in Irish and Irish-American Thought and Behaviour in Gilded Age New York City," Ph.D. dissertation, University of Rochester, 1977; Clare Dahlberger Horner, "Producers' Cooperatives in the United States, 1865–1890," Ph.D. dissertation, University of Pittsburgh, 1978; Montgomery, "Labor and the Republic," p. 204; Davis, "Why the U.S. Working Class is Different," esp. pp. 26–30; Leon Fink, "Workingmen's Democracy: The Knights of Labor in Local Politics, 1886–1896," Ph.D. dissertation, University of Rochester, 1977.

7 David Lyon, "The World of P. J. McGuire: A Study of the American Labor Movement, 1870–1890," Ph.D. dissertation, University of Minnesota, 1972, p. 271; Ralph W. Scharnau, "Thomas J. Morgan and the Chicago Socialist Movement, 1876–1901," Ph.D. dissertation, University of Northern Illinois, 1969; Gene Marlatt, "Joseph Buchanan: Spokesman for Labor during the Populist and Progressive Eras," Ph.D. dissertation, University of Colorado, 1975; George Cotkin, "Working-Class Intellectuals and Evolutionary Thought in America, 1870–1915," Ph.D. dissertation, Ohio State University, 1978; Mari Jo Buhle, "Feminism and Socialism in the United States, 1820–1920," Ph.D. dissertation, University of Wisconsin, 1974; Stuart B. Kaufman, *Samuel Gompers and the Origins of the American Federation of Labor, 1848–1896* (Westport, Ct., 1973).

8 Ontario, Bureau of Industry, *Annual Report*, 1889, p. 23.

9 O'Donoghue to H. E. Bronson, 11 May 1896; O'Donoghue to Sir Oliver Mowat, 13 April 1896, Bronson Family Papers, PAC, MG 28 III 26.

10 Powderly to Wright, 7 May 1908 (Washington), PP. For poem see *Moon* (Toronto), 2, 36 (31 January 1903), p. 151. Our thanks to Russell Hann for this reference.

11 For sensitive discussions of the Order's political impact and its local strengths see Leon Fink, "Politics as Labor History: A Case Study of Labor Organization, Town Meeting, and Political Organization in Nineteenth Century New England," paper presented to New England Labor History Symposium, Smith College, 4–6 March 1979; Fink, "The Uses of Political Power: Towards a Theory of the Labor Movement in the Era of the Knights of Labor," Knights of Labor Centennial Conference paper, Newberry Library, Chicago, 17–19 May 1979. Sylvis is quoted in Montgomery, "Labor and the Republic," p. 206.

12 Ontario, Bureau of Industry, *Annual Report*, 1889, p. 25; Warren Caragata, *Alberta Labour: A Heritage Untold* (Toronto, 1979), pp. 10–11.

13 On the agrarian revolt in Ontario see Russell G. Hann, *Farmers Confront Industrialism* (Toronto, 1975); S.E.D. Shortt, "Social Change and Political Crisis in Rural Ontario: The Patrons of Industry, 1889–1896," in Donald Swainson, ed., *Oliver Mowat's Ontario* (Toronto, 1972), pp. 211–35; L. A. Wood, *A History of Farmers' Movements in Canada* (Toronto, 1924). A masterful U.S. treatment is Lawrence Goodwyn, *Democratic Promise: The Populist Moment in America* (New York 1976).

14 *Farmers' Sun*, 18 September 1895, 26 September 1894, 10 October 1894.

15 *Brotherhood Era*, 1 April 1896, 25 March 1896; *Farmers' Sun*, 3 October 1894, 28 April 1895. On the roots and meaning of the "equal rights" cry see Alan Dawley, *Class and Community: The Industrial Revolution in Lynn* (Cambridge, 1976).

16 *Palladium of Labor*, 4 December 1886; *Canadian Labour Reformer*, 19 June 1886.

17 For "Spokeshave's" contribution see, for example, *Farmers' Sun*, 12 December 1894, 21 November 1894, 7 November 1894, 12 September 1894, 24 October 1894; Scrapbook 7, "On the Money Question," A. W. Wright Papers, PAC, MG 29 A 15.

18 *Farmers' Sun*, 12 September 1894, 23 January 1895, 20 March 1896.

19 Wright to Wrigley, 10 March 1895, and n.d., Letterbook III, Wright Papers, PAC, pp. 300–3, 306–8; *Farmers' Sun*, 20 March 1896. In this period Wright was at work on his *Report Upon the Sweating System in Canada*, in *Sessional Papers*, XXIX (1896), No. 61. Note the reaction in *Brotherhood Era*, 18 March 1896; *Daily Mail and Empire*, 9 October 1897, both favorable. But in some circles Wright's appointment was denounced, and he was attacked as a "labor fakir." See *Ottawa Citizen*, 23 January 1896.

20 A point not sufficiently well developed in Norman Penner, *The Canadian Left: A Critical Analysis* (Scarborough, 1977). Cf., Bryan D. Palmer, *A Culture in Conflict: Skilled Workers and Industrial Capitalism in Hamilton, Ontario, 1860–1914* (Montreal, 1979), pp. 97–122; G. Weston Wrigley, "Socialism in Canada," *International Socialist Review*, 1 (May 1901), pp. 685–9; Gregory S. Kealey, *Toronto Workers Respond to Industrial Capitalism, 1867–1892* (Toronto, 1980), pp. 274–95.

21 W. D. Gregory "Autobiography," pp. 112–16, and Diary, 13 December 1896, in Gregory Papers, Queen's University Archives, Kingston, Canada; Wright to Wrigley, March 1895, Letterbook III, pp. 300–3, Wright Papers, PAC. These comments on Patronism are hardly sufficient, and the subject deserves far more study. We have drawn upon Hann, *Farmers Confront Industrialism*, esp. the brief suggestive comments in the preface, and find Goodwyn's work indicative of the potentially rich material yet to be explored. See Goodwyn, *Democratic Promise;* "The Co-operative Commonwealth and Other Abstractions: In Search of a Democratic Premise," *Marxist Perspectives*, 10 (1980), pp. 8–43; "Organizing Democracy: The Limits of Theory and Practice," *Democracy*, 1 (1981), pp. 25–40.

22 *Free Lance*, quoted in *Brotherhood Era*, 30 October 1895. On Kilt's early link to Wright see *Ottawa Citizen*, 7 December 1888.

23 W. L. Davis, "A History of the Early Labor Movement in London, Ontario," M.A. thesis, University of Western Ontario, 1947, pp. 23–8; Martin Robin, *Radical Politics and Canadian Labor, 1880–1930* (Kingston, 1968), p. 30; Jacqueline Flint Cahan, "A Survey of Political Activity in the Ontario Labor Movement, 1850–1935," M.A. thesis, University of Toronto, 1945, pp. 10–11; Gene Howard Homel, "Fading Beams of the Nineteenth Century: Radicalism and Early Socialism in Canada's 1890s," *Labour/Le Travailleur*, 5 (1980), pp. 7–31; Ontario, Bureau of Industry, *Annual Report*, 1889, p. 24; *Farmers' Sun*, 6 February 1894; R. H. Hessel, "The Labor Movement in London: Some Personal Recollections," unpublished manuscript, Regional Collection, University of Western Ontario.

24 *Capital Siftings* (Ottawa), 30 June 1894; 3 November 1894; Robin, *Radical Politics*, pp. 1–43. On the later period see Larry Peterson, "The One Big Union Movement in International Perspective: Revolutionary Industrial Unionism, 1900–1925," *Labour/Le Travailleur*, 7 (1981), 41–66. For women see "K. of L.," "Where Labor is Not Prayer," *Walsh's Magazine* (1895–1896), pp. 111–16, in Irving Abella and David Millar, eds., *The Canadian Worker in the Twentieth Century* (Toronto, 1978), pp. 153–8. Cf., G. Weston Wrigley, "Socialism in Canada," *International Socialist Review*, 1 (1 May 1901), p. 685.

25 There were 36 Orange lodges in Toronto in 1886 compared with some 50 LAs of the Knights of Labor. In terms of total numbers Knights' LAs generally appear to have been larger than the Orange lodges. For further evidence see Kealey, *Toronto Workers*, pp. 106–13. The Orange Order was never as powerful in Hamilton. See Palmer, *A Culture in Conflict*, pp. 43–6. Note the discussion of the Orange Order in Houston and Smyth, *The Sash Canada Wore*.

26 See, for instance, the argument in E. P. Thompson, "A Special Case," in *Writing by Candlelight* (London, 1980), pp. 65–76. Note as well, Marjorie Murphy, "Progress of the Poverty of Philosophy: Two Generations of Labor Reform Politics: Michael and Margaret Haley," paper presented to the Centennial Conference on the Knights of Labor, Newberry Library, Chicago, 17–19 May 1979; Gene Howard Homel, "James Simpson and the Origins of Canadian Social Democracy," Ph.D. dissertation, University of Toronto, 1978; F. W. Watt, "Radicalism in English Canadian Literature Since Confederation," Ph.D. dissertation, University of Toronto, 1957. Leading member of the revolutionary syndicalist Industrial Workers of the World, "Big Bill" Haywood learned his "first lessons" in unionism from an Irish Knight. See Haywood, *Autobiography* (New York 1969), pp. 30–1; Alan Dawley, *Class and Community: The Industrial Revolution in Lynn* (Cambridge, Mass., 1976), pp. 190, 290. Those who think our metaphor morbid and out of place should consult Terence O'Toole's letter in *Palladium of Labor*, 4 September 1886. Although interpretively problematic, see Landon, "The Knights of Labor: Predecessors of the CIO."

27 Here the comments in Leon Fink, "Class Conflict in the Gilded Age: The Figure and the Phantom," *Radical History Review*, 3 (Fall–Winter 1975), pp. 56–72; and E. P. Thompson, "A Nice Place to Visit," *New York Review of Books* (6 February 1975), pp. 33–7, are to the point.

28 This conception of history is thoroughly argued for in E. P. Thompson, "The Poverty of Theory; or an Orrery of Errors," in *The Poverty of Theory & Other Essays* (London, 1978).

29 T. V. Powderly, *Address . . . Delivered in Music Hall, Providence, R.I.* (Boston, 1886), esp. pp. 13–14, 19–20.

30 See *News*, 15 November 1886; Fink, "Workingmen's Democracy," esp. pp. 389–409. Ontario LAs undoubtedly contained immigrant workers, especially Germans, but nowhere outside of Berlin's Germania Assembly (9691) were they a significant or influential force. In the United States, however, as Fink has shown for Milwaukee, Poles and Germans often proved dominant ("Workingmen's Democracy," pp. 308–88). Moreover, Germans contributed greatly to socialist and anarchist circles within the American Order, especially in Detroit and Chicago. No such radical enclaves existed within Ontario. See Paul Buhle, "Knights and Socialists," and Alan Dawley, "Socialists, Anarchists, and the Knights," papers presented to the Knights of Labor Centennial Conference; Oestreicher, "Solidarity and Fragmentation"; and Montgomery, "Labor and the Republic," pp. 207–8. The question of race was of only slightly more significance. We have touched upon it in our discussions of Hamilton and Toronto where, aside from the blindspot of the Chinese workers (see Carlos Schwantes, "Race and Radicalism in the Pacific Northwest," paper presented to the Knights of Labor Centennial Conference), the Order did much to overcome racial barriers to class solidarity. Across the province isolated indications of racism within the Knights' membership did crop up: Windsor's white members of LA 3281 threatened to leave the Order in 1889, "on account of their coloured brethren which are largely in the majority." Richard Avery to Powderly, 22 October 1889, PP. Black Knight D. H. Smith, Financial Secretary of Amherstburg's LA 4139, complained of racist exclusion, arguing that "co-

lered people are kept out." Smith to Powderly, 8 August 1887, PP. Cf., the attack on "Nigger Reynolds" in D. M. Munn (?) to Powderly (St. Thomas), 3 February 1886, PP. Such isolated cases indicate that race may well have proven divisive in specific local settings. But nowhere in Ontario were black workers of the same importance as they were in Knights' strongholds like Richmond, Virginia. See Fink, "Irrespective of Party, Color, or Social Standing: The Knights of Labor and Opposition Politics in Richmond, Virginia," *Labor History*, 19 (1978), pp. 324–49; Peter Rachleff, "Black Richmond and the Knights of Labor," paper presented to the Knights of Labor Centennial Conference; Kenneth Kann, "The Knights of Labor and the Southern Black Worker," *Labor History*, 18 (1977), pp. 49–70. For a useful discussion of labor and the Irish, see Dorothy Suzanne Cross, "The Irish in Montreal, 1867–1896," M.A. thesis, McGill University, 1969, esp. pp. 255–6.

31 Other comments on the Order's decline worth considering are found in Fink, "The Uses of Political Power." A perspective similar to ours is found in Dawley, *Class and Community*.

32 Words well aimed at Gerald Grob, *Workers and Utopia: A Study of Ideological Conflict in the American Labor Movement, 1865–1900* (Chicago, 1969). A more recent and more sophisticated attempt to dissect the origins of failure is found in Michael J. Cassity, "Modernization and Social Crisis: The Knights of Labor and a Midwest Community, 1885–1886," *Journal of American History*, 66 (June 1979), pp. 41–61, where decline appears to flow out of the existence of contending factions based on associational, economic, and political goals or aspirations, complicated by a modernist-traditionalist divide that pitted workers adhering to a central authority against those who sought to maintain bases of community power. All of this may be attractive to those who need such pigeon-holes (and social scientists seem to need them often, for they provide a much sought after analytical clarity). We know these divisions to be nonsense; at least everything that happened in Ontario suggests they were. Political, economic, and fraternal impulses beat in all Knights of Labor breasts; to unravel them is to create an illusion for the sake of clarity. Phillips Thompson's quote is from *Palladium of Labor*, 26 December 1885.

33 Bishop, "Recollections of the Amalgamated," p. 5.

34 Thompson, *Poverty of Theory*, p. 234.

## Appendix

1 This is an abbreviated version of the preamble and principles that appeared in the Hamilton-based *Labor Union* in 1883. For the more extended later statements, essentially the same in content but with seven additional principles, see Douglas R. Kennedy, *The Knights of Labor in Canada* (London, Ont., 1956), pp. 14–17.

# Selected bibliography

This bibliography is intended as a guide for easy reference to the major published materials and theses used in this book. It does not contain manuscript material, newspapers, or works cited infrequently. It is organized in three sections: books, articles, and theses.

## Books


Abella, Irving, and David Millar, eds. *The Canadian Worker in the Twentieth Century*. Toronto, 1978

Alinsky, Saul. *John L. Lewis*. New York, 1949

Armstrong, Christopher, and H. V. Nelles. *The Revenge of the Methodist Bicycle Company: Sunday Streetcars and Municipal Reform in Toronto, 1888–1897*. Toronto, 1977

Aveling, Edward, and Eleanor Marx. *The Working-Class Movement in America*. London, 1888

Babcock, Robert H. *Gompers in Canada: A Study in American Continentalism Before the First World War*. Toronto, 1974

Bercuson, David Jay. *Fools and Wise Men: The Rise and Fall of the One Big Union*. Toronto, 1978

Berger, Carl. *The Writing of Canadian History*. Toronto, 1976

Bernstein, Irving. *The Lean Years: A History of the American Worker, 1920–1933*. Baltimore, 1960

Blake, Edward. *Speeches in the Dominion Election Campaign of 1887*. Toronto, 1887

Bledstein, Burton. *The Culture of Professionalism*. New York, 1976

Bliss, Michael. *A Living Profit: Studies in the Social History of Canadian Business, 1883–1911*. Toronto, 1974

Braverman, Harry. *Labor and Monopoly Capital: The Degradation of Work in the Twentieth Century*. New York, 1974

Brewer, John. *Party Ideology and Popular Politics at the Accession of George III*. London, 1976

Brooks, Thomas R. *Clint: A Biography of a Labor Intellectual: Clinton S. Golden*. New York, 1978

Brown, Henry Joseph. *The Catholic Church and the Knights of Labor*. Washington, 1949

Buchanan, Joseph R. *The Story of a Labor Agitator*. Westport, Ct., 1970 (1903)

Carman, Albert R. *The Preparation of Ryerson Embury*. Toronto, 1900

Chevalier, Louis. *Labouring Classes and Dangerous Classes in Paris During the First Half of the Nineteenth Century*. New York, 1973

Chisamore, Dale, et al. *Brockville: A Social History*. Brockville, 1975

Clarke, John, Chas Critcher and Richard Johnson, eds. *Working Class Culture: Studies in History and Theory*. London, 1979

Clement, Wallace. *Continental Corporate Power: Economic Linkages between Canada and the United States*. Toronto, 1977

Cobb, Richard. *Death in Paris, 1795–1801*. New York, 1978

— *The Police and the People: French Popular Protest, 1789–1820*. London, 1972
— *A Sense of Place*. London, 1975
Commons, John R. *Myself*. Madison, 1963
Commons, John R., et al. *A Documentary History of American Industrial Society*. Cleveland, 1909–11
— *History of Labor in the United States*. New York, 1926 (1918)
Cook, Ezra A., ed. *Knights of Labor Illustrated*. Chicago, 1886
Copp, Terry. *The Anatomy of Poverty: The Condition of the Working Class in Montreal, 1897–1929*. Toronto, 1974
Cumbler, John T. *Working-Class Community in Industrial America: Work, Leisure, and Struggle in Two Industrial Cities, 1880–1930*. Westport, Ct., 1979
David, Henry. *The History of the Haymarket Affair*. New York, 1936
Dawley, Alan. *Class and Community: The Industrial Revolution in Lynn*. Cambridge, Mass., 1976
Dubofsky, Melvyn. *Industrialism and the American Worker, 1865–1920*. New York, 1975
Dubofsky, Melvyn, and Warren Van Tine. *John L. Lewis: A Biography*. Chicago, 1976
Duncan, Sara Jeanette. *Selected Journalism*. Ottawa, 1978
Ely, Richard. *Ground Under Our Feet: An Autobiography*. New York, 1938
— *The Labor Movement in America*. New York, 1905 (1886)
Engels, Friedrich. *The Condition of the Working-Class in England*, W. O. Henderson and W. H. Chaloner, eds. Oxford, 1958
Engels, Friedrich, and Paul and Laura LaFargue. *Correspondence*. Moscow, 1959
Foner, Philip S. *History of the Labor Movement in the United States*. New York, 1947, 1955
— *Organized Labor and the Black Worker, 1619–1973*. New York, 1974
— *Women and the American Labor Movement: From Colonial Times to the Eve of World War I*. New York, 1979
Forsey, Eugene A. *The Canadian Labour Movement, 1812–1910*. Ottawa, 1974
— *Trade Unions in Canada, 1812–1902*. Toronto, 1982
Fraser, Dawn. *Echoes from Labor's War*. Toronto, 1978
Fraser, Ronald. *Blood of Spain: An Oral History of the Spanish Civil War*. New York, 1979
French, Doris. *Faith, Sweat and Politics: The Early Trade Union Years in Canada*. Toronto, 1962
Friedlander, Peter. *The Emergence of a UAW Local, 1936–1939: A Study in Class and Culture*. Pittsburgh, 1975
Galster, Augusta E. *The Labor Movement in the Shoe Industry, with Special Reference to Philadelphia*. New York, 1924
Garlock, Jonathan, and Nick Builder. *Knights of Labor Data Bank*. Ann Arbor, 1973
Gilmour, James M. *Spatial Evolution of Manufacturing: Southern Ontario, 1851–1891*. Toronto, 1972
Goodwyn, Lawrence. *Democratic Promise: The Populist Movement in America*. New York, 1976
Grob, Gerald N. *Workers and Utopia: A Study of Ideological Conflict in the American Labor Movement, 1865–1900*. Chicago, 1961
Gutman, Herbert G. *Work, Culture, and Society in Industrializing America*. New York, 1976
Hann, Russell G. *Farmers Confront Industrialism*. Toronto, 1975
Harter, Lafayette G., Jr. *John R. Commons*. Corvallis, Ore., 1962
Harvey, Fernand. *Revolution Industrielle et Travailleurs*. Montreal, 1978
Haskell, Thomas L. *The Emergence of Professional Social Science*. Urbana, 1977
Haywood, William. *Autobiography*. New York, 1965

Hill, Christopher. *The World Turned Upside Down: Radical Ideas During the English Revolution.* New York, 1972
Hines, Thomas R. *The Anarchists' Conspiracy; or the Blight of 3770, A True History of the Experience of Daniel Hines as a Knight of Labor.* Boston, 1887
Hobsbawm, E. J. *Primitive Rebels: Studies in Archaic Forms of Social Movement in the 19th and 20th Centuries.* Manchester, 1959
Hollander, Jacob H., and George E. Barnett, eds. *Studies in American Trade Unionism.* New York, 1907
Houston, Cecil J., and William J. Smyth. *The Sash Canada Wore: A Historical Geography of the Orange Order of Canada.* Toronto, 1980
Hoxie, Robert F. *Trade Unionism in the United States.* Chicago, 1917
Johnson, Leo. *History of the County of Ontario, 1615–1873.* Whitby, 1973
Jones, Robert Leslie. *History of Agriculture in Ontario, 1613–1880.* Toronto, 1946
Joussaye, Marie. *Songs that Quinte Sang.* Belleville, 1895
Kapp, Yvonne. *Eleanor Marx*, 2 vols. New York, 1976
Kealey, Gregory S. *Toronto Workers Respond to Industrial Capitalism, 1867–1892.* Toronto, 1980
Kealey, Gregory S., ed. *Canada Investigates Industrialism.* Toronto, 1973
Kealey, Gregory S., and Peter Warrian, eds. *Essays in Canadian Working Class History.* Toronto, 1976
Kealey, Linda, ed. *A Not Unreasonable Claim.* Toronto, 1979
Kennedy, Douglas R. *The Knights of Labor in Canada.* London, Ont., 1956
Keys, William, ed. *Capital and Labor; Containing the Views of Eminent Men of the United States and Canada on the Labor Question, Social Reform, and Other Economic Subjects.* Montreal, 1904
King, John S. *An Account of the Origin and Early History of the Sons of England Benevolent Society.* Toronto, 1891
Kinzer, Donald L. *An Episode in Anti-Catholicism: The American Protective Association.* Seattle, 1964
Kirk, William. *National Labor Federations in the United States.* Baltimore, 1906
Kleppner, Paul. *The Cross of Culture: A Social Analysis of Midwestern Politics, 1850–1900.* New York, 1970
*Labor: Its Rights and Wrongs.* Washington, 1886
Langdon, Steven. *The Emergence of the Canadian Working Class Movement.* Toronto, 1975
Lefebvre, Henri. *Everyday Life in the Modern World.* New York, 1968
Leiby, James. *Carroll Wright and Labor Reform.* Madison, 1960
Lenin, V. I. *The Development of Capitalism in Russia.* Moscow, 1964
Levasseur, E. *The American Workman.* Baltimore, 1900
Lipton, Charles. *The Trade Union Movement of Canada, 1822–1959.* Montreal, 1968
Logan, Harold. *Trade Unions in Canada.* Toronto, 1948
Macdonald, Sir John A. *Speech to the Workingmen's Liberal Conservative Union and La Cercle LaFontaine.* Ottawa, 1886
Machar, Agnes Maule. *Roland Graeme: Knight.* Toronto, 1892
Macmillan, David S., ed. *Canadian Business History Selected Studies 1497–1971.* Toronto, 1972
McNeill, George. *The Labor Movement.* New York, 1887
— *Unfrequented Paths: Songs of Nature, Labor, and Men.* Boston, 1903
Marx, Karl. *Grundrisse: Foundations of the Critique of Political Economy.* Harmondsworth, 1973
Marx, Karl, and Friedrich Engels. *Collected Works.* New York, 1979
— *Selected Correspondence.* Moscow, 1965

Mayer, Gustav. *Friedrich Engels: A Biography.* London, 1936
Montgomery, David. *Beyond Equality: Labor and the Radical Republicans, 1867–1872.* New York, 1967
— *Workers' Control in America.* New York, 1979
Morgan, H. Wayne, ed. *The Gilded Age: A Reappraisal.* Syracuse, 1963
Morton, Desmond. *Mayor Howland: The Citizens' Candidate.* Toronto, 1973
Myers, Gustavus. *A History of Canadian Wealth.* Toronto, 1972 (1914)
Naylor, Tom. *The History of Canadian Business,* 2 vols. Toronto, 1975
Nelles, H. V. *The Politics of Development: Forests, Mines and Hydro Electric Power in Ontario, 1849–1941.* Toronto, 1974
Ozanne, Robert. *A Century of Labour-Management Relations at McCormick and International Harvester.* Madison, 1967
Palmer, Bryan D. *A Culture in Conflict: Skilled Workers and Industrial Capitalism in Hamilton, Ontario, 1860–1914.* Montreal, 1979
Penner, Norman. *The Canadian Left: A Critical Analysis.* Scarborough, 1977
Perlman, Selig. *A Theory of the Labor Movement.* New York, 1949 (1928)
Phillips, Paul. *No Power Greater: A Century of Labour in British Columbia.* Vancouver, 1967
Piva, Michael J. *The Condition of the Working Class in Toronto, 1900–1921.* Ottawa, 1979
Pope, Sir Joseph, ed. *The Correspondence of Sir John A. Macdonald.* Toronto, 1921
Powderly, T. V. *Address . . . delivered in Music Hall, Providence, R.I.* Boston, 1886
— *Thirty Years of Labor.* Columbus, 1889
— *The Path I Trod.* New York, 1940
Rader, Benjamin G. *The Academic Mind and Reform: The Influence of Richard T. Ely.* Lexington, 1966
Read, Daphne, ed. *The Great War in Canadian Society.* Toronto, 1978
Reid, Fred. *Keir Hardie: The Making of a Socialist.* London, 1978
Roberts, Wayne. *'Honest Womanhood': Feminism, Femininity, and Class Consciousness among Toronto Working Women, 1893–1914.* Toronto, 1977
Robin, Martin. *Radical Politics and Canadian Labour, 1880–1930.* Kingston, 1968
Rosdolsky, Roman. *The Making of Marx's Capital.* London, 1977
Rouillard, Jacques. *Les Syndicats Nationaux au Québec de 1900 à 1930.* Quebec, 1979
Roy, Andrew. *A History of the Coal Mines of the United States.* Westport, Ct., 1970
Ryerson, Stanley B. *Unequal Union: Roots of Crisis in the Canadas, 1815–1873.* Toronto, 1973
Saxton, Alexander. *The Indispensable Enemy: Labor and the Anti-Chinese Movement in California.* Berkeley, 1971
Sayles, Fern A. *Welland Workers Make History.* Welland, 1963
Senior, Hereward. *The Fenians and Canada.* Toronto, 1978
Seretan, Glen. *Daniel DeLeon: The Odyssey of an American Marxist.* Cambridge, Mass., 1979
Smucker, Joseph. *Industrialization in Canada.* Scarborough, 1980
Sorge, Friedrich. *The Labor Movement in the United States,* ed. Philip S. Foner and Brewster Chamberlin. Westport, Ct., 1977 (1891–1895)
Spelt, Jacob. *Urban Development in South-Central Ontario.* Toronto, 1972
Stanley, G. F. G. *The Birth of Western Canada: A History of the Riel Rebellions.* Toronto, 1961
Swainson, Donald, ed. *Oliver Mowat's Ontario.* Toronto, 1972
Thompson, E. P. *The Making of the English Working Class.* New York, 1963
— *William Morris: Romantic to Revolutionary.* New York, 1977
— *The Poverty of Theory and Other Essays.* London, 1978
— *Writing by Candlelight.* London, 1980

Thompson, Phillips. *The Future Government of Canada; being Arguments in Favor of a British American Republic*. St. Catharines, 1864
— *The Politics of Labor*. New York, 1887
Ulman, Lloyd. *The Rise of the National Trade Union*. Cambridge, Mass., 1955
Van Tine, Warren. *The Making of the Labor Bureaucrat: Union Leadership in the United States, 1870–1920*. Amherst, 1973
Vatter, Harold G. *The Drive to Industrial Maturity: The US Economy 1860–1914*. Westport, Ct., 1975
Walkowitz, Daniel J. *Worker City, Company Town: Iron and Cotton Worker Protest in Troy and Cohoes, New York, 1855–1884*. Urbana, 1978
Ward, W. Peter. *White Canada Forever: Popular Attitudes and Public Policy towards Orientals in British Columbia*. Montreal, 1978
Ware, Norman J. *The Labor Movement in the United States, 1860–1895: A Study in Democracy*. New York, 1929
— *Labor in Modern Industrial Society*. New York, 1968 (1935)
Williams, Raymond. *Culture and Society, 1780–1950*. Harmondsworth, 1961
— *Marxism and Literature*. London, 1976
Wood, Louis Aubrey. *A History of Farmers' Movements in Canada*. Toronto, 1975 (1924)
Wright, A. W. *Report of . . . Delegate from DA125 to the Philadelphia Session of the General Assembly, Knights of Labor*. Toronto, 1894
Young, James D. *The Rousing of the Scottish Working Class*. London, 1979

## Articles

Battye, John. "'The Nine Hour Pioneers': Genesis of the Canadian Labour Movement." *Labour/Le Travailleur*, 4 (1979), 25–56
Bean, Ronald. "A Note on the Knights of Labor in Liverpool, 1889–1890." *Labor History*, 13 (1972), 68–78
Birdsall, William C. "The Problem of Structure in the Knights of Labor." *Industrial and Labor Relations Review*, 6 (1952–3), 532–46
Black, Isabella. "American Labor and Chinese Immigration." *Past & Present*, 25 (1963), 59–76
Bloch, Herman D. "Terence V. Powderly and Disguised Discrimination." *American Journal of Economics and Sociology*, 33 (1974), 154–60
Buhle, Paul. "The Knights of Labor in Rhode Island." *Radical History Review*, 17 (1978), 39–74
Carman, Harry J. "Terence Vincent Powderly – An Appraisal." *Journal of Economic History*, 1 (1941), 83–7
Cassity, Michael J. "Modernization and Social Crisis: The Knights of Labor and a Midwest Community, 1885–1886." *Journal of American History*, 66 (1979), 41–61
Charpentier, Alfred. "Le Mouvement politique ouvrier de Montréal, 1883–1929." *Relations Industrielles*, 10 (1955), 74–93
Cherwinski, W. J. C. "Honoré Joseph Jaxon, Agitator, Disturber, Producer of Plans to Make Men Think and Chronic Objector." *Canadian Historical Review*, 46 (1965), 123–33
Cook, Ramsay. "Henry George and the Poverty of Canadian Progress." *Historical Papers* (1977), 143–56
— "The Professor and the Prophet of Unrest." *Transactions of the Royal Society of Canada*, 4th ser., 13 (1975), 228–50
Cumbler, John T. "Labor, Capital and Community: The Struggle for Power." *Labor History*, 15 (1974), 395–416

Davis, Mike. "Why the U.S. Working Class is Different." *New Left Review*, 123 (1980), 3–44

Dubofsky, Melvyn R. "The Origins of Western Working-Class Radicalism, 1890–1905." *Labor History*, 7 (1966), 131–54

East, Dennis. "Union Labels and Boycotts: Co-operation of the Knights of Labor and the Cigar Makers International Union, 1885–1886." *Labor History*, 16 (1975), 266–71

Fink, Leon. "Class Conflict in the Gilded Age: The Figure and the Phantom." *Radical History Review*, 3 (1975), 56–72

— "'Irrespective of Party, Color, or Social Standing': The Knights of Labor and Opposition Politics in Richmond, Virginia." *Labor History*, 19 (1978), 325–49

Foner, Eric. "Class, Ethnicity, and Radicalism in the Gilded Age: The Land League and Irish America." *Marxist Perspectives*, 1 (1978), 6–55

Forsey, Eugene. "A Note on the Dominion Factory Bills of the 1880s." *Canadian Journal of Economics and Political Science*, 13 (1947), 580–3

— "The Telegraphers' Strike of 1883." *Transactions of the Royal Society of Canada*, 4th ser., 9 (1971), 245–59

Garlock, Jonathon. "Knights of Labor Data Bank." *Historical Methods Newsletter*, 6 (1973), 149–60

Goodwyn, Lawrence. "The Co-operative Commonwealth and other Abstractions: In Search of a Democratic Premise." *Marxist Perspectives*, 10 (1980), 8–43

— "Organizing Democracy: The Limits of Theory and Practice." *Democracy*, 1 (1981), 25–40

Gordon, Michael. "Irish Immigrant Culture and the Labor Boycott in New York City, 1880–1886." *Labor History*, 16 (1975), 184–229

Griffiths, Carl Warren. "Some Protestant Attitudes on the Labor Question in 1886." *Church History*, 11 (1942), 138–48

Harvey, Fernand. "Les Chevaliers du Travail, les États-Unis et la Société Québécoise, 1882–1902," in Harvey, ed., *Le Mouvement Ouvrier au Québec*. Montreal, 1980

Heron, Craig, and Bryan Palmer. "Through the Prism of the Strike: Industrial Conflict in South-central Ontario, 1901–1914." *Canadian Historical Review*, 58 (1977), 423–58

Hessel, R. H. "The Labour Movement in London." *Western Ontario Historical Nuggets*, 21 (1965), 49–50

Homel, Gene. "Fading Beams of the Nineteenth Century: Radicalism and Early Socialism in Canada's 1890s." *Labour/Le Travailleur*, 5 (1980), 7–31

Hunter, James. "The Gaelic Connection: The Highlands, Ireland and Nationalism, 1873–1922." *Scottish Historical Review*, 54 (1975), 178–204

James, Edward T. "T. V. Powderly: A Political Profile." *Pennsylvania Magazine of Biography and History*, 99 (1975), 443–59

Kann, Kenneth. "The Knights of Labor and the Southern Black Worker." *Labor History*, 18 (1977), 49–70

Kealey, Gregory S. "Artisans Respond to Industrialism: Shoemakers, Shoe Factories, and the Knights of St. Crispin in Toronto." *Historical Papers* (1973), 137–57

— "The 'Honest Workingman' and Workers' Control: The Experience of Toronto Skilled Workers, 1860–1892." *Labour/Le Travailleur*, 1 (1976), 32–68

— "Alfred Oakley." *Dictionary of Canadian Biography*, XI. Toronto, 1982

— "Katie McVicar." *Dictionary of Canadian Biography*, XI. Toronto, 1982

Landon, Fred. "The Knights of Labor: Predecessors of the CIO." *Quarterly Review of Commerce*, 4 (Autumn 1937). 133–9

Lyne, D. C., and Peter M. Toner. "Fenianism in Canada, 1874–1884." *Studia Hibernica*, 12 (1972), 27–76

MacDonald, L. R. "Merchants Against Industry: An Idea and Its Origins." *Canadian Historical Review*, 56 (1975), 263–81

McKay, Ian. "Capital and Labour in the Halifax Baking and Confectionary Industry during the last half of the Nineteenth Century." *Labour/Le Travailleur*, 3 (1978), 63–108

McKenna, E. "Unorganized Labour Versus Management: The Strike at the Chaudière Lumber Mills, 1891." *Histoire Sociale/Social History*, 5 (1973), 186–211

McLaurin, Melton A. "The Racial Policies of the Knights of Labor and the Organization of Southern Black Workers." *Labor History*, 17 (1976), 568–85

Mann, Arthur. "Gompers and the Irony of Racism." *Antioch Review*, 13 (1953), 203–14

Massicotte, E. Z. "Les Chevaliers du Travail." *Bulletin de Recherches Historiques*, 40 (1934), 452–3

Montgomery, David. "Gutman's Nineteenth-Century America." *Labor History*, 19 (1978), 416–29

— "On Goodwyn's Populists." *Marxist Perspectives*, 1 (1978), 166–73

— "Labor and the Republic in Industrial America: 1860–1920." *Le Mouvement Social*, 111 (1980), 201–15

O'Donoghue, John. "Daniel John O'Donoghue: Father of the Canadian Labour Movement." *Canadian Catholic Historical Association Annual Report*, 10 (1942–1943), 87–96

Ostry, Bernard. "Conservatives, Liberals, and Labour in the 1880s." *Canadian Journal of Economics and Political Science*, 27 (1961), 141–61

Palmer, Bryan D. "Discordant Music: Charivaris and Whitecapping in Nineteenth-Century North America." *Labour/Le Travailleur*, 3 (1978), 5–62

Pelling, Henry. "The Knights of Labor in Britain, 1880–1901." *Economic History Review*, 2nd ser., 9 (1956), 313–31

Pentland, H. C. "The Development of a Capitalist Labour Market in Canada." *Canadian Journal of Economics and Political Science*, 25 (1959), 450–61

Perry, H. Francis. "The Workingman's Alienation from the Church." *American Journal of Sociology*, 4 (1899), 621–9

Peterson, Larry. "The One Big Union in International Perspective: Revolutionary Industrial Unionism, 1900–1925." *Labour/Le Travailleur*, 7 (1981), 41–66

Reddy, William. "The Textile Trade and the Language of the Crowd at Rouen, 1752–1871." *Past & Present*, 74 (1977), 62–89

Robin, Martin. "The Working Class and the Transition to a Capitalist Democracy in Canada." *Dalhousie Review*, 47 (1967), 326–43

Roth, H. "American Influences on the New Zealand Labor Movement." *Historical Studies*, 9 (1961), 413–20

Samuel, Raphael. "The Workshop of the World: Steam Power and Hand Technology in Mid-Victorian Britain." *History Workshop Journal*, 3 (1977), 6–72

Scott, Bruce. "'A Place in the Sun': The Industrial Council at Massey-Harris, 1919–1929." *Labour/Le Travailleur*, 1 (1976), 158–92

Scott, Jean. "The Conditions of Female Labour in Ontario." *Toronto University Studies in Political Science*, 1 (1892), 84–113

Sider, Gerald M. "Christmas Mumming and the New Year in Outport Newfoundland." *Past & Present*, 71 (1976), 102–25

— "The Ties that Bind: Culture and Agriculture, Property and Propriety in the Newfoundland village fishery." *Social History*, 5 (1980), 1–39

Simmel, George. "The Sociology of Secret Societies." *American Journal of Sociology*, 11 (1906), 441–98

Spector, David. "Winnipeg's First Labour Unions." *Manitoba Pageant*, 21 (1976), 13–14

Thompson, E. P. "A Nice Place to Visit." *New York Review of Books* (6 February 1975), 33–7

— "Romanticism, Utopianism and Moralism: The Case of William Morris." *New Left Review*, 99 (1976), 83–111

— "Eighteenth Century English Society: class struggle without class?" *Social History*, 3 (1978), 1

— "Folklore, Anthropology, and Social History." *Indian Historical Review*, 3 (1978), 247–66

Trofimenkoff, Susan. "One Hundred and Two Muffled Voices: Canada's Industrial Women in the 1880s." *Atlantis*, 3 (1977), 67–82

Truant, Cynthia M. "Solidarity and Symbolism among Journeymen Artisans: The Case of Companonnage." *Comparative Studies in Society and History*, 21 (1979), 214–25

Van Onselen, Charles. "'The Regiment of the Hills': South Africa's Lumpenproletarian Army, 1890–1920." *Past & Present*, 80 (1978), 91–128

Vilard, M. A. "Les Chevaliers du Travail." *Academie de Nimes*, 7th ser., 10 (1888), 267–87

Vipond, Mary. "Blessed are the peacemakers: the Labour question in Canadian Social Gospel fiction." *Journal of Canadian Studies*, 10 (1975), 32–43

Walker, Samuel. "Terence V. Powderly, the Knights of Labor and the Temperance Issue." *Societas*, 5 (1975), 279–94

Watt, Frank. "The National Policy, the Workingman, and Proletarian Ideas in Victorian Canada." *Canadian Historical Review*, 40 (1959), 1–26

Watt, James T. "Anti-Catholicism in Ontario Politics: The Role of the Protestant Protective Association in the 1894 Election." *Ontario History*, 59 (1967), 57–67

— "Anti-Catholic Nativism in Canada: The Protestant Protective Association." *Canadian Historical Review*, 48 (1967), 45–58

Williams, Raymond. "Base and Superstructure in Marxist Cultural Theory." *New Left Review*, 82 (1973), 1–16

—"Beyond Actually Existing Socialism." *New Left Review*, 120 (1980), 3–19

Wright, Carroll D. "An Historical Sketch of the Knights of Labor." *Quarterly Journal of Economics*, 1 (January 1887), 137–68

Wrigley, G. Weston. "Socialism in Canada." *International Socialist Review*, 1 (1901), 685–9

## Theses

Appleton, Paul Campbell. "The Sunshine and the Shade: Labour Activism in Central Canada, 1850–1860." M.A. thesis, University of Calgary, 1974

Bell, John David. "The Social and Political Thought of the *Labor Advocate*." M.A. thesis, Queen's University, 1975

Bennett, John William. "Iron Workers in Woods Run and Johnstown: The Union Era, 1865–1895." Ph.D. thesis, University of Pittsburgh, 1977

Bensman, David Harlan. "Artisan Culture, Business Union: American Hat Finishers in the Nineteenth Century." Ph.D. thesis, Columbia University, 1977

Buhle, Mari Jo. "Feminism and Socialism in the United States, 1820–1920." Ph.D. thesis, University of Wisconsin, 1974

Cahan, Jacqueline Flint. "A Survey of Political Activity in the Ontario Labour Movement, 1850–1935." M.A. thesis, University of Toronto, 1945

Chan, V. O. "The Knights of Labor with Special Reference to the 1880s." M.A. thesis, McGill University, 1948

Clark, Kenneth Lloyd. "Social Relations and Urban Change in a Late Nineteenth Century Southwestern Ontario Railroad City: St. Thomas, 1868–1890." M.A. thesis, York University, 1976

Cooper, J. I. "The Canadian General Election of 1887." M.A. thesis, University of Western Ontario, 1933

Cotkin, George Bernard. "Working-class Intellectuals and Evolutionary Thought in America, 1870–1915." Ph.D. thesis, Ohio State University, 1978

Cox, Robert. "The Quebec Provincial Election of 1886." M.A. thesis, McGill University, 1948

Davis, W. L. "A History of the Early Labor Movement in London, Ontario." M.A. thesis, University of Western Ontario, 1947

DeLottinville, Peter. "The St. Croix Manufacturing Company and its Influence on the St. Croix Community, 1880–1892." M.A. thesis, Dalhousie University, 1979

Dembski, Peter. "William Ralph Meredith: Leader of the Conservative Opposition in Ontario, 1878–1894." Ph.D. thesis, University of Guelph, 1977

Evans, Margaret. "Oliver Mowat and Ontario: A Study in Political Success." Ph.D. thesis, University of Toronto, 1967

Falzone, Vincent J. "Terence V. Powderly: Mayor and Labor Leader, 1849–1893." Ph.D. thesis, University of Maryland, 1970

Fink, Leon. "Workingmen's Democracy: The Knights of Labor in Local Politics, 1886–1896." Ph.D. thesis, University of Rochester, 1977

Garlock, Jonathon. "A Structural Analysis of the Knights of Labor." Ph.D. thesis, University of Rochester, 1974

Gillis, Peter. "E. H. Bronson and Corporate Capitalism: A Study in Canadian Business Thought, 1880–1910." M.A. thesis, Queen's University, 1975

Gitelman, Howard M. "Attempts to Unify the American Labor Movement, 1865–1900." Ph.D. thesis, University of Wisconsin, 1960

Glazer, Sidney. "Labor and Agrarian Movements in Michigan, 1876–1896." Ph.D. thesis, University of Michigan, 1932

Gordon, Michael Allen. "Studies in Irish and Irish-American Thought and Behaviour in Gilded Age New York City." Ph.D. thesis, University of Rochester, 1977

Homel, Gene Howard. "James Simpson and the Origins of Canadian Social Democracy." Ph.D. thesis, University of Toronto, 1978

Horner, Clare Dahlberg. "Producers' Co-operatives in the United States, 1865–1890." Ph.D. thesis, University of Pittsburgh, 1978

Hough, Leslie S. "The Turbulent Spirit: Violence and Coaction Among Cleveland Workers, 1877–1899." Ph.D. thesis, University of Virginia, 1977

James, Edward T. "American Labor and Political Action, 1865–1896: The Knights of Labor and its Predecessors." Ph.D. thesis, Harvard University, 1954

Kessler, Sidney H. "The Negro and the Knights of Labor." M.A. thesis, Columbia University, 1950

Lawrence, John Alan. "Behind the Palaces: The Working Class and the Labor Movement in San Francisco, 1877–1901." Ph.D. thesis, University of California at Berkeley, 1979

Levine, Susan Beth. "Their Own Sphere: Women's Work, the Knights of Labor, and the Transformation of the Carpet Trade, 1870–1890." Ph.D. thesis, City University of New York, 1979

Licht, Walter Martin. "Nineteenth Century American Railroad Men: A Study in the Nature and Organization of Work." Ph.D. thesis, Princeton University, 1977

Lyon, David Nicholas. "The World of P. J. McGuire: A Study of the American Labor Movement, 1870–1890." Ph.D. thesis, University of Minnesota, 1972

Marlatt, Gene Ronald. "Joseph R. Buchanan: Spokesman for Labor During the Populist and Progressive Eras." Ph.D. thesis, University of Colorado, 1975

Martin, Jacques. "Les Chevaliers du Travail et le Syndicalisme international à Montréal." M.A. thesis, University of Montreal, 1965

Moore, Bill. "Staples and the Capitalist Mode of Production: A Study of Mining in Canada, 1845–1920." M.A. thesis, McMaster University, 1978

Oestreicher, Richard J. "The Knights of Labor in Michigan: Sources of Growth and Decline." M.A. thesis, Michigan State University, 1973

— "Solidarity and Fragmentation: Working People and Class Consciousness in Detroit, 1877–1895." Ph.D. thesis, Michigan State University, 1979

Pentland, H. C. "Labour and the Development of Industrial Capitalism in Canada." Ph.D. thesis, University of Toronto, 1960

Ross, Steven Joseph. "Workers on the Edge: Work, Leisure, and Politics in Industrializing Cincinnati, 1830–1890." Ph.D. thesis, Princeton University, 1980

Russell, David Hugh. "The Ontario Press and the Pacific Scandal of 1873." M.A. thesis, Queen's University, 1970

Scharnau, Ralph W. "Thomas J. Morgan and the Chicago Socialist Movement, 1876–1901." Ph.D. thesis, University of Northern Illinois, 1969

Scrontas, Charles Andrew. "Two Decades of Organized Labor and Labor Politics in Maine, 1880–1900." Ph.D. thesis, University of Maine, 1968

Stortz, Thomas Gerald John. "John Joseph Lynch, Archbishop of Toronto: A Biographical Study of Religions, Political and Social Commitment." Ph.D. thesis, University of Guelph, 1980

Walker, Samuel. "Terence V. Powderly, Labor Mayor: Workingmen's Politics in Scranton, Pennsylvania, 1870–1884." Ph.D. thesis, Ohio State University, 1973

Warrian, Peter. "The Challenge of the One Big Union Movement in Canada, 1919–1921." M.A. thesis, University of Waterloo, 1971

Watkins, Bari Jane. "The Professors and the Unions: American Academic Social Theory and Labor Reform, 1883–1915." Ph.D. thesis, Yale University, 1976

Watt, Frank W. "Radicalism in English Canadian Literature since Confederation." Ph.D. thesis, University of Toronto, 1957

Watt, James T. "The Protestant Protective Association in Ontario: A Study in Anti-Catholic Nativism." M.A. thesis, McMaster University, 1965

Williams, C. B. "Canadian-American Trade Union Relations: A Case Study in the Development of Bi-National Unionism." Ph.D. thesis, Cornell University, 1964

Williams, Glen S. "The Political Economy of Canadian Manufactured Exports: The Problem, its Origin, and the Development of Trade and Commerce, 1885–1920." Ph.D. thesis, York University, 1978

# Index